D1195616

THE RUSSIANS AND AUSTRALIA

Known for his pioneering work on Russia's early exploits in Australia and the Pacific, historian Glynn Barratt again breaks new ground in presenting the first comprehensive study of Russian naval, social, mercantile, and scientific enterprise in New South Wales between 1807 and 1835.

Through Tsar Peter the Great's Dutch contacts, Russia was early aware of the existence of "New Holland" and a number of unsuccessful attempts were made to reach what is now Australia. Following a description of these efforts, Barratt focuses on the seventeen visits that Russian ships made to Australian ports on voyages from the Baltic carrying supplies of the settlements in Kamchatka and Alaska.

As a result of the goodwill generated by the Anglo-Russian alliance against Napoleonic France, relations between the British colonists and the Russian seamen were extremely cordial. While visiting Australia, Russian naval officers pursued a range of scientific activities, including botany, zoology, ethnography, and mineralogy, and collected specimens and artefacts. They also studied the British penal system and filled journals with detailed observations.

Available in Russian archives and museums and examined there by Barratt, the journals and collections which until now have largely remained unexplored by historians reveal the high level of skill and education of these early visitors to Australia. The author's notes on the archival sources as well as his detailed bibliography and references will be invaluable information for others studying this period of Russian history and represent a significant contribution to the field of Slavic studies.

The first volume of a series entitled *Russia and the South Pacific, 1696–1840*, this book is particularly timely in view of Russian expansion in the southwest Pacific since 1978, for it corrects the common misconception that Russia is a newcomer to the Pacific Basin.

GLYNN BARRATT is professor of Russian at Carleton University and the author of many books in Russia's naval and diplomatic history, among them *Russia in Pacific Waters, 1715–1825* (1981) and *Russian Shadows on the British Northwest Coast of North America* (1983).

University of British Columbia Press

PACIFIC MARITIME STUDIES SERIES

*Volume 1 of Russia and
the South Pacific,
1696–1840*

THE

RUSSIANS

AND

AUSTRALIA

Glynn Barratt

UNIVERSITY OF BRITISH COLUMBIA PRESS
Vancouver 1988

This book has been published with the help of a grant from the
Social Science Federation of Canada, using funds provided by the
Social Sciences and Humanities Research Council of Canada.

Canadian Cataloguing in Publication Data
    Barratt, Glynn.
       The Russians and Australia

    (University of British Columbia Press Pacific maritime
studies; 5)
    (Russia and the South Pacific, 1696–1840; V.1)
    Bibliography: p.
    Includes index.
    ISBN 0-7748-0291-X

    1. Australia – Relations – Soviet Union – History –
19th century. 2. Soviet Union – Relations – Australia –
History – 19th century. 3. Scientific expeditions –
Australia – History – 19th century. 4. Soviet Union –
History, Naval. I. Title. II. Series. III. Series: Barratt, Glynn.
Russia and the South Pacific, 1696–1840; v. 1.
DU113.5S65B37 1988   994.02   C88-091148-4

International Standard Book Number 0-7748-0291-X

Printed in Canada

Plate 4 is reproduced by courtesy of the National Gallery of New
Zealand; plates 5, 12 & 28 by courtesy of the National Library of
Australia, Canberra; plate 11 is reproduced by permission of the
National Maritime Museum, London; plate 13 by permission of
the Mitchell Library, Library of New South Wales; and plates
14–15 & 20–22 by permission of the State Russian Museum,
Leningrad. The author is responsible for plates 26, 29, & 30.

Contents

ILLUSTRATIONS

Preface and Acknowledgements

This book concerns the origins and early development of Russian interest and dealings in Australia (New Holland). More specifically, it focuses on Russian naval, social, mercantile, and scientific enterprise in New South Wales; the matter of Australian responses *to* that enterprise is also touched upon. I have chosen not to dwell on those responses (which evolved into a strident Russophobia in 1831–33) for two main reasons—first, this volume is the first part of a comprehensive survey of the Russians' social, maritime, and scientific dealings in the South Pacific Ocean, and therefore the emphasis must reasonably fall upon the Russians' own approaches and responses to Australia, not vice versa; second, Australasian Russophobia is a significant and interesting subject in itself and well deserves separate treatment. I am hopeful that my own New Zealand-oriented overview of 1981 (see Bibliography) will soon be balanced by a Sydney or a Melbourne counterpart.

Surprisingly, not one writer, either Soviet or Western, has deliberately focused on the history of Russian maritime or scientific dealings in Australia, or on an early Russian study *of* Australia. It is as though, by some conspiracy of silence and omission, both Western and Soviet scholarship have predetermined that the educated reader should be conscious of the *North* Pacific areas of Russian naval interest—Hawaii, California, the Northwest Coast, the Carolines so lovingly surveyed by Kotzebue and by Lütke—and of Bellingshausen's triumphs on the fringes of Antarctica (1819–21), rather than aware of Australia as seen within the context of Pacific/Russian history.

The North Pacific seaborne fur trade has its annalists (Berkh and Khlebnikov, Polonskii, Okun' and Makarova, Golder and Gibson); yet those writers pay no heed to the prolonged and crucial visits paid to Sydney by the Russian-American Company ships *Neva* (1807), *Suvorov* (1814), *Riurik* (1822), and *Elena* (1825). There are students of specific expeditions to the North and South Pacific in the early 1800s (Nevskii, Komissarov, Sgibnev); of expeditions planned during the eighteenth century that would, if realized, have brought the Russians to the fringes of Australia (Grenader and Sokolov); and of the Anglo-Russian maritime entente of the Napoleonic period. Yet none of these has added anything to Verity Fitzhardinge's lonely, pioneering article of 1965, "Russian Ships in Australian Waters, 1807–1835"; nor, in the case of antecedent works, does any adumbrate it. Certainly, Australian and Soviet archival fonds are far apart. But, as I indicate below in an extended "Note on Soviet Archival Sources and Research Relating to the Early Russian Presence in Australia" (pp. 230–51), Soviet archives hold a wealth of nineteenth-century material directly bearing on the subject of this book and it is generally accessible to the accredited and patient Western visitor. As for the difficulty of collating Soviet, Australian, and other source materials, it has been practically removed by modern air travel and interloan. My work in Soviet and Western archives has, I hope, deepened knowledge based on published literature, on the history of science, and on Australian and Russian naval history. I may observe that in the case of certain main Soviet archives, it has always been my custom to seek access to such manuscript materials as have been published or, at least, described by Soviet historians. Because most documents are kept with other papers in a single *delo* (file), it is a policy that has enabled me at times to wander slightly from the "academic tour." One need hardly add that matters, and in consequence procedures, are quite different in Tallin and in Tartu (Estonian SSR).

Had I not myself lived for some years in the South Pacific, I would not have taken more than passing interest in Russian dealings there almost two centuries ago. To be a Slavist or historian with Russian interests in modern Sydney is, however, to be conscious of Australian myopia and rooted animosity where Russia is concerned. Throughout Australia, there are residual folk memories of the repeated "Russian scares" of the later nineteenth century. Old guns mounted on cracking concrete platforms are reminders of those times and are symbolic of continuing Australian concerns. By contrast, few Australians recall that in the early 1800s the relations between colonists and Russians were extremely cordial. Still fewer know or care that there were educated Russians at Port Jackson (Sydney) by the time of Captain Bligh, late of the *Bounty,* or that scientists and government officials in St. Petersburg had shown an interest in New South Wales since the mid-1770s. Is it surprising that Australians, like North Americans who for professional or other reasons might have troubled to inform themselves of the reality, are ignorant of the existence of enormous geological and zoological collections from colonial Australia in Leningrad? Of hundreds of unpublished aquarelles by Russian travellers; of hundreds of unpublished journals, all predating 1840; of important ethnographical collections; of immense herbaria? Possibly not. But in this writer's view, it is both sad and unacceptable that an entire period of Anglo-Russian amity, during the course of which hundreds of Russian naval officers and men were well received in New South Wales and Tasmania, should thus be shut out of the national memory. To follow friendly patterns, it is helpful to recall them.

Russian visits to Australia were not quite commonplace events during the early 1800s. But a dozen by the time of Governor Sir Thomas Brisbane (1825) sufficed not only to accustom his officials to the Russian flag and anthem, but also to in duce the Russian Naval Ministry and the directors of the Russian-American (fur trading) Company to view Port Jackson as a routine port of call. And there were reasons why a vessel from the Baltic with a cargo for Kamchatka or the North Pacific settlements should pause at Sydney. Anglo-Russian understanding and alliance in the struggle with Napoleonic France had lasted twenty years and resulted in a fund of public memories on which—at least as late as 1829—a Russian captain in the colony could draw. There were victuals and water to be had, almost for certain; and the harbour was both spacious and secure. If the Russians needed meat, fruit, and a respite from their 20,000-mile marathon around the world, their British hosts welcomed a modicum of trade and sociability, variety, and European news. The Russian visits passed pleasantly, therefore, within a context of residual goodwill and economic common sense. Far more importantly for us, the Russian visitors, who were in general well-educated, cultivated men as befitted representatives of the elite branch of their navy, a Pacific "special service" with the promise of advancement and distinction for the few, extracted maximum advantage from the doors that the British opened as they came. They danced at balls, indeed, and dined, and made the tourist trip to Windsor, Parramatta, and the Emu Plain; but they also botanized, and collected animals, and filled journals, and examined the Cammeraigal tribe along the North Shore of Port Jackson, and determined the longitude of Kirribilli Point (across from Sydney's sailing, white Opera House).

This book offers a survey both of eighteenth-century and later Russian scientific interest in *Novaia Gollandiia* (New Holland)—with especial emphasis on botany, ethnography, and cartography—and of the early naval visits to the continent itself. The undertakings of the Russians and their passengers while in Australia are treated under three main headings: social, naval, scientific. And the visits themselves are viewed in the context of the pattern of the Russian Navy's North Pacific-oriented venture as a whole. If I stress non-naval science undertaken by the Russians in Australia, it is because neither Soviet nor Western specialists (Vucinich, Vorob'ev, Pasetskii, Heidemaa) give it more than fleeting glances. If I emphasize the fact that Russian sources, left by trained, objective men, may be of value to the student of colonial Australia itself, it is because the very fact that they exist is, now as before, all too commonly ignored throughout the West.

I am grateful to the staffs of many libraries and archives for assistance, and to many individuals for their constructive criticisms of the first draft of this survey. The archives and manuscript repositories include the Central State Archives of Ancient Acts and of the Navy of the USSR (TsGADA and TsGAVMF), each with its dependent library; the Central State Historical Archive in Leningrad (TsGIAL); the Archive of the Foreign Policy of Russia (AVPR); the Archive of the Geographical Society of the USSR (AGO); the Central State Historical Archive of the Estonian SSR (TsGIAE) in Tartu; the Estonian State Museum of

History in Tallin; the Lenin Public Library, Moscow; the Public Record Office, London, the Bancroft Library, Berkeley, California; the United States National Archives (National Archives and Records Service), Washington, DC; and the Mitchell Library and State Library of New South Wales in Sydney, Australia.

Among the Soviet scholars to whom I am indebted for help and advice, and who showed me personal kindness, are Eve Peets and Sirje Annist of Eesti NSV Riikliik Ajaloomuuseum, Tallin; Dr. Y. Kakh, Director of the Institute of History at the Estonian Academy of Sciences; Captain I. Solov'ev of TsGAVMF; Irina Grigor'eva, Head of the International Exchanges Division of the Saltykov-Shchedrin Public Library, Leningrad; Dr. Rudolf Its, Director of the Peter-the-Great Museum, Institute of Ethnography and Anthropology of the Academy of Sciences of the USSR, Leningrad, and his able colleagues there, Dr. Nikolai A. Butinov and Tamara K. Shafranovskaia, of that Institute's Australia and Oceania Division; Dr. A. S. Gur'ianov, of the Main Library, Kazan' State University, Kazan'; Dr. V. M. Rastiapin, of the State Historical Museum on Red Square, Moscow; and two members of the erudite and charming Staniukovich family, of literary and naval antecedents, Tat'iana Vladimirovna and her daughter Mar'ia, both of Leningrad and MAE.

I also express my thanks, for assistance of many kinds, to Dr. Anders Sandström, of the Statens Sjöhistoriska Museum in Stockholm; Professor Richard A. Pierce, of Queen's University, Kingston, Canada; Mr. A. W. H. Pearsall, of the National Maritime Museum, Greenwich; Christopher Lloyd, R.N. (Ret.) and Captain Stephen W. Roskill, R.N. (Ret.); Dr. Terence Armstrong, of the Scott Polar Institute, Cambridge; Mr. E. Häkli, Chief of Research Library, Helsinki University, Finland; Dr. George Lewinson, of London; and Mrs. Ruth Dudgeon, of Alexandria, Virginia. Gratitude is also due to Dr. Marvin Falk, Curator of Rare Books at the Elmer E. Rasmuson Library, University of Alaska at Fairbanks, Alaska. To these must be added Australian names: Mr. H. Vaughan Evans and Dr. Hazel King, of the Royal Australian Historical Society, Sydney; Professor Brian H. Fletcher, of the University of Sydney; the late Verity Fitzhardinge, of Queanbeyan; Mr. D. J. Cross, of the Archives Office of New South Wales; Mrs. Mary McRae, of the State Library and Archive of Tasmania; Professor Boris Christa, of the University of Queensland; Gavan Daws and Susan Margarey, of the Australian National University, Canberra, ACT. Among numerous natural scientists who have shown patience with my ignorance of their specialties and guided my steps when necessary, I wish to mention Dr. Stephen Davies, Director of the Royal Australian Ornithologists' Union and Mr. R. Cowling, Chairman of the Union Research Committee.

Finally, I am grateful to the Social Sciences and Humanities Research Council of Canada, for research grants; to Carleton University, Ottawa, for research and travel assistance over a six-year period; and to my friends in Leningrad for help and hospitality beyond the call of academic duty.

Preliminary Notes

Occasionally, Russian and Australian primary sources differ over dates. With few exceptions, such discrepancies result from the use of different calendars in nineteenth-century Australia and Russia. Russians employed the (Old Style) Julian calendar, introduced by Julius Caesar, until 1917. In British colonies, Pope Gregory XIII's (New Style) calendar had been in use since its adoption by the government at home (1752). By 1800 the Gregorian calendar, in use at Sydney, was twelve days ahead of the Julian, which Russians used whether in Russia or at sea and on the far side of the globe. Further adjustments are often necessitated by the seaborne reckoning of dates from noon to noon: Russian and British ships' logs were maintained thus until relatively modern times.

A modified form of the Library of Congress system for the transliteration of the Russian alphabet has been used here. Thus: Andrei, Fedor, Lisianskii. However, recognized anglicized forms are used for proper names, e.g., Alexander I, cossack, Moscow. Rouble values are expressed in silver. Certain measurements of length and weight are left, in translated passages, in original forms, e.g., *arshin* and *pood*. These units of weight, length, and value will be found in the text:

Arshin	Linear measure: 28 inches.
Kopek	One-hundredth of a rouble; 0.5 US cents in 1820.
Desiatin	2.70 acres.
Piastre	Spanish dollar; approx. US$1 in 1820.
Pood	Weight measure: 36.11 pounds avoirdupois.
Sazhen'	Linear measure: 7 feet or 2.13 metres.
Verst	0.66 English miles.
Vershok	1.75 inches.
Toise	Linear measure (French): 6.395 feet.

The following terms may also be unfamiliar to some readers:

Baidarka	Aleut craft of skins stretched over a frame.
Delo	File or dossier.
Fond	Archival sub-collection, fund.
Opis'	Inventory.

Prikazchik   Clerk or factor.

Promyshlennik   Hunter-trader in Russian-American Company domains and elsewhere.

Razriad   Class or category.

Russian Vessels in Australia, 1807–35

	VESSEL	TONNAGE	COMMANDER	PORT OF CALL	ARRIVAL	DEPARTURE
1	Company ship *Neva*	370	Lt. L. A. Hagemeister	Sydney	15.6.1807	1.7.1807
2	Company ship *Suvorov*	335	Lt. M. P. Lazarev	Sydney	25.8.1815	15.9.1815
3	Navy sloop *Blagonamerennyi*	305	Capt.-Lt. G. Shishmarev	Sydney	28.22.1820	26.3.1820
4	Navy sloop *Otkrytie*	900	Capt.-Lt. M. Vasil'ev	Sydney	2.3.1820	26.3.1820
5	Navy sloop *Vostok*	900	Capt. F. Bellingshausen	Sydney	11.4.1820	20.5.1820
6	Navy sloop *Mirnyi*	530	Lt. M. P. Lazarev	Sydney	15.4.1820	20.5.1820
7	Navy sloop *Vostok* (repeat)	900	Capt. F. Bellingshausen	Sydney	21.9.1820	12.11.1820
8	Navy sloop *Mirnyi* (repeat)	530	Lt. M. P. Lazarev	Sydney	22.9.1820	12.11.1820
9	Navy sloop *Apollon*	900	Lt. S. P. Khrushchev	Sydney	7.6.1822	25.6.1822
10	Company brig *Riurik*	180	Navigator E. Klochkov	Sydney	27.7.1822	16.8.1822
11	Navy frigate *Kreiser*	1100	Capt. M. P. Lazarev	Hobart	30.5.1823	21.6.1823
12	Navy sloop *Ladoga*	530	Capt.-Lt. A. Lazarev	Hobart	30.5.1823	21.6.1823
13	Company ship *Elena*	400	Lt. P. E. Chistiakov	Sydney	4.4.1825	24.5.1825
14	Company ship *Elena*	400	Lt. V. S. Khromchenko	Sydney	26.3.1829	30.4.1829
15	Navy sloop *Krotkii*	?	Capt-Lt. Hagemeister	Sydney	6.4.1829	1.5.1829
16	Navy transport *Amerika*	655	Capt-Lt. Khromchenko	Sydney	9.5.1832	10.6.1832
17	Navy transport *Amerika*	655	Capt-Lt. von Schants	Sydney	19.3.1835	16.4.1835

Sources: N. A. Ivashintsev, "Russkie krugosvetnye puteshestviia," *ZGDMM*, (1850): 163–90; P. Tikhmenev, *Historical Review of Formation of the Russian-American Company*, trans. D. Krenov (Seattle, 1939–40) 1: 407–11; James R. Gibson, *Imperial Russia in Frontier America* (New York, 1976), pp. 78–81.

"To the Commodore of the Russian Squadron,
Bound for Kamtschatka, Now Lying in the
Harbour of Port Jackson"

Hail! Chieftain, from the distant lands
That own the Czar's imperial reign;
With British hearts and British hands
We greet you welcome from the main:
Then rest your weary keels awhile,
Enbosomed in Australia's isle.

Go, then, and speed the glorious day
Predicted for the Kamtschadale,
When, Commerce cheering every bay,
Religion gladdening every vale,
His bleak and barren land shall be
A land of light and liberty.

So shall the Russ and Briton vie
In friendly strife along the deep,
Where pagan isles unnumbered lie,
And the vast South Sea's billows sweep.

Sydney Gazette (30 April 1829)

1

BEGINNINGS, 1696–1796

RUSSIAN KNOWLEDGE OF AUSTRALIA: THE ORIGINS

Tsar Peter Alekseevich (Peter the Great) showed active interest in the remote Pacific fringes of his empire at intervals throughout his life. Both as
protector of the Russian China trade, which was not healthy in the early
1690s, and as student of geography, he was particularly conscious of the
problem of the "Strait of Anian," which was supposed by most geographers to separate the continents of Asia and America.[1] The modest
volume of all Russo-Chinese trade and the impediments placed in the way
of Russian merchants by the ever-xenophobic Chinese government suggested the importance of a navigable sea-route to the Orient—if one existed.[2] The discovery and exploitation of such a sea-route, Peter recognized, would have Imperial but also major scientific value.[3] Many times
during his life, in fact, he was exhorted by his own like-minded, forward-
looking subjects and especially by foreigners to send a major expedition
to the uttermost northeastern rim of Asia, where the strait might be expected to be found. Some of the projects and petitions handed to him on
that subject and, more generally, on the need for proper mapping of the
far northeastern limits of the empire, were purely scientific and dis-
passionate in nature.[4] The great German scientist Gottfried Wilhelm von
Leibnitz, for example, urged the tsar to undertake, at state expense, a major programme of magnetic observations from the Baltic to the North Pacific shores;[5] and as in Germany, so too in France there were savants who
argued eloquently for cartography and/or hydrography in what is now
known as Chukotka.[6] (Peter promised the *Académie* in Paris that the Russians would investigate the Strait of Anian, but he declined to let French
scientists participate in what was later to take shape as the First Bering

Expedition (1725–30).[7] Other projects and petitions that the tsar read were commercial in their emphases. Whether or not they stressed the trade and international implications of discovering the Strait of Anian, however, all these projects fully recognized the value of geography itself and made the tsar more conscious of it in Siberian and North Pacific contexts. Peter's interest in "all things that relate to seafaring"[8] being so deep, and such Siberian-Pacific exploration being indisputably a mission for the infant Russian Navy, he merely brought about the probable when in the last weeks of his life he signed the orders that sent Captain Vitus Bering to the far Northeast of Asia and beyond (1725).[9] By the same token, his awareness of the immense potential value of a navigable sea-route to the Orient, which would give the Russians an advantage over Western European trading companies in China and, conceivably, in Japan,[10] made it predictable that he would look for information about China and Japan, about the Strait of Anian, about Pacific trade and maritime conditions generally, from the people then best able to provide it—the Dutch. Dutch merchant vessels had been calling at Japan, where they enjoyed a trade monopoly at the expense of other foreign ships, and had been sailing the Pacific for the best part of a century.[11] No less important, from the standpoint of their function as suppliers of hard data to the Russian government, Dutch merchants had been active in the Moscow foreign quarter since the early 1600s, and a few had met the tsar during his stormy adolescence.[12]

In the course of his Grand Embassy to Western Europe (1697–98), Peter spent some time (August–September 1697) in the company of the geographer, historian, and scientist who, as the mayor of Amsterdam, was his official host, Nicolaes Witsen (1641–1717).[13] Since returning to the Netherlands with the Dutch embassy which he had joined at Moscow long before (1664), Witsen had acted as "an unofficial minister for Muscovite affairs" at Amsterdam.[14] For thirty years he had maintained personal, business, and political relations with the Muscovites. His study, *Noord en Oost Tartarye...* of 1692 was an authoritative work, based upon Dutch and Russian primary materials, on the remote Northeast of Asia and Japan. Peter was thoroughly familiar with it, as with its author, having made good use of Witsen as his main Amsterdam agent for the purchasing of vessels and for other naval business in the 1690s.[15] Witsen's own Muscovite informants, too, were known to Peter: for example, Andrei Vinius, career diplomat and in the 1690s the effective head of the *Sibirskii Prikaz,* that is Siberian Department, of the government in Moscow.[16] Reaching Amsterdam in 1697, Peter recognized and treated Witsen as a friend.[17]

It was the tsar's object, however, to reverse the flow of geographical and scientific information, not to add to what the Dutch already knew about the far Northeast of Asia thanks to Vinius. It was to gain technical knowledge and politically or scientifically important information, not to spread it, that his Embassy had come. Accordingly, during the course of conversations with his erudite and well-read host, Peter referred directly to the matters of the Strait of Anian and Dutch discoveries in "Tartary." Witsen himself, as Peter knew, had made a study of Dutch seaborne exploration on the far side of the globe, paying particular attention to the 1643–45 maritime venture led by Maerten Gerritszoon Vries, and had more recently used Vries's cartographic data in a new map of Japan.[18] At the time of Peter's visit, he was working on a fresh draft of his 1687 map (printed in 1690) of the far Northeast of Asia.[19] Necessarily perhaps, under the circumstances, he presented his exalted guest from Russia with a copy of his new map of Japan, with the remark that Russian seamen might in due course find it useful. Recognizing the validity of Dutch savants' contention (to which Witsen joined his voice) that Russian mariners would win great honour by discovering a seaway over Asia to the Orient, which English mariners had failed to do, Peter promised that their hopes would be fulfilled; and he sent orders to the Dutchman Andrei Vinius in Moscow that, if feasible, a cossack expedition from Iakutsk should be dispatched to find the Strait, which was, presumably, beyond the River Anadyr'.[20] To this extent, the exchange of information between Peter and the Dutch remained reciprocal, at least potentially. It is indisputable, however, that Peter gained far more and better geographical and other information from the Dutch (as from the British) than he gave.

While in Amsterdam, he gave orders for Dutch books and map collections to be purchased.[21] More were purchased or donated in the coming years. Others travelled to the infant Baltic city of St. Petersburg with Russians who had undergone practical training in the Netherlands. Among these acquisitions were Dutch maps based on the globes and maps of Joan Blaeu of 1645–49, which themselves embodied data from the voyages to "Southland" (or Australia) by Abel Janszoon Tasman and his pilot-major, Franchoijs Jacobszoon Visscher (1642–44).[22] These maps, dating from 1652–66, were far from being new when the Russian visitors acquired them; but Dutch cartography of "Southland" had advanced hardly at all since Blaeu's diligent associates saw the Tasman-Visscher journals, charts, and drawings in the Archive of the Netherlands East Indies Company.[23] It was, the Russians understood, on those same Tasman-Visscher logs and charts of 1643–44 that local craftsmen had essentially depended when, some six years later, they had set two detailed hemispheres into the floor of Amsterdam Town Hall, presenting data about "Southland" or New Holland.[24] As distinguished tourists, Peter and his party were of course shown the Town Hall, where the two hemispheres provided permanent and tantalizing evidence of Tasman's visits to a country on the far side of the world.[25] Through acquisition of Dutch maps of even fifty years before, in sum, the Grand Embassy of 1697 brought the Russians to the same level of knowledge as the Western Europeans where the mapping of New Holland was concerned.

The Russian Embassy accomplished more than this, however, by encouraging subsequent purchases of first-hand narratives of distant voyages. Another early acquisition—not surprisingly, in view of Peter's link with Witsen—was a copy of the second (1705) edition of the latter's *Noord en Oost Tartarye*.[26] The first volume of this new edition gave five drawings "illustrating" Tasman's voyages of 1642–43 and 1644, as well as references indicating some familiarity with Visscher's journals, then unpublished. It also, twenty years before the publication of Francois Valentijn's account of Tasman's 1642–43 voyage in the third part of his *Oud en Nieuw Oost-Indien* (1726), contained the following:

> The west part of Hollandia Nova, called by some the Southland, was first discovered by the Netherlanders in 1619, in longitude 133° E., and seen in longitude 195° in another year. . . . In the south, it was recorded—at great cost to the Netherlands East India Company—in latitude 43°30′ in the year 1644. . . . The northwestern part was first visited in 1678 by members of the Netherlands East India Company, and was found to be rich in very attractive rivers and bays; but the land itself was, to judge by its outward appearance, a wasteland and entirely wild. . . .
>
> The aborigines around this northwest part are pitch black, of medium height, not unlike the natives of Malabar; their hair is less curly than the kaffirs', and in the black of their eyes there is a gleam of red, from which one may easily enough infer their bloodthirsty and murderous nature. This has, in fact, been borne out by distressing experience: the loss of certain young men who were perfidiously killed and dragged into the bush and there eaten. These people walk around mother-naked without shame. . . . Their weapons consist of bamboo bows with small arrows, which have sharpened fishbone tips. . . . As for their morals and religion, one can only observe that they behave more like wild beasts than rational human beings. For they give birth to their young in the fields or on paths or wherever they chance to be at the critical time. . . .
>
> In Southern latitude 17°12′, Tasman met very bad, and barbarous, naked black Men, who had curly hair; having as weaponry, Arrow, Bow, Javelins and Spears, they came once with doubled weaponry

fifty in number, onto a beach, dividing into three groups, intending to attack the Hollanders. . . .

For drinking, one uses here large shells. Here one uses Canoes made of bark of Trees. There are here dangerous Coasts: there is little earth-fruit; the People use no Houses.[27]

This passage, specifically naming Tasman as the observer, was evidently based by Witsen on a journal of the 1644 voyage of *Limmen* (flagship), *Zeemeeuw,* and *Bracq.*[28] As such, it gave the Russians equal opportunity with other foreign readers to glimpse "Southland" through the eyes of the explorer. Witsen gives no reference to longitude in this terse section of his work, and so, regrettably, it is uncertain where the scene is set. In the opinion of the New Zealand student of the Tasman expeditions, Andrew Sharp, who argues solely on the basis of the primary materials, the Witsen reference is to a stretch of coastline on the west side of Cape York Peninsula (in about latitude 17°12′), or else round Roebuck Bay.[29] At all events, it is apparent that the Russians were presented with a snapshot of Australia's north coast and of a watchful, hostile people. It is interesting to observe that at the first moment of real contact with that country, the Russian reader was directed to that area of interest, ethnography, in which his countrymen were later to make major contributions on the spot (see Chapter Six). And from the first moment of contact, Russian knowledge of the country was an offshoot of a (logically) far more intense and stable curiosity about the fringes of the North Pacific Ocean. In these two respects, a pattern was established at the outset of the eighteenth century that marked the Russians' later dealings with Australia and the Australians.

Of other information about "Southland" or New Holland deriving from Dutch sources and in the Russian Admiralty College's possession by the early eighteenth century, mention should be made of M. Thevenot's map showing the "fifth part of the world." Published in his warmly received and widely read *Relations de divers Voyages curieux* (Paris, 1663; part 1), the map was annotated cryptically to the effect that it was based on data also used in the creation of the celebrated pavement at the Amsterdam Town Hall.[30]

Also available to members of the Admiralty College, as to other foreigners, was William Dampier's *New Voyage Round the World* (1697), of which no less than five editions had been printed in six years—besides a German version (1702).[31] Again, the image of Australia presented was an arid, uninviting one;[32] but then the Russians were in any case unable to accept such invitations to the far side of the globe, as they lacked the maritime resources for such an enterprise.[33] Even a plan to send two ships to Madagascar and Bengal, conceived and formally presented to the Admiralty College by Vice-Admiral G. Wilster of the Russian Navy in December 1723, was broken on the reefs of practicality.[34] For the time being, Russian interest in the remote countries that Dampier and Tasman had examined briefly could be only academic—a reality acknowledged formally at the establishment of the St. Petersburg Academy of Sciences (1726).

With the establishment of that Academy, the Admiralty College's responsibility for map collecting and cartography grew narrower. Henceforward, it concerned itself mainly with sea and coastal charts; and theoretically the compilation of new charts of foreign shores was also its affair.[35] In reality, the members of the new Academy were far more active than the members of the College in that area. A consequence of overlapping expectations was that maps and works relating to New Holland were, throughout the century, at the disposal of the Admiralty College and Academy alike, and often held in duplicate.[36]

Of non-Dutch maps showing New Holland, the best known in Russian academic circles by the late 1720s was the 1714 production of the eminent cartographer and *géographe du roi* Guillaume Delisle (1675–1726). He was granted a brief audience with Peter when the latter went to Paris (1717), and they discussed the better charting of the (now Russian-controlled) Caspian Sea. Delisle was a much respected figure in St. Petersburg, and the Delisles maintained professional and private links with Russia for the next three decades. Joseph-Nicolas and Louis, younger brothers of Guillaume, both pursued their careers there. Joseph-Nicolas, unhappily, lent his authority to errors made by Guillaume (who was by far the more reliable cartographer and scholar).[37] Thus mistakes or misconceptions where New Holland was concerned were perpetuated doggedly for decades in holdings of the Admiralty College and Academy of Sciences. For a distinctive feature of the French school of Pacific-cum-Australian cartography was, in the words of R. V. Tooley, "the insertion, greatly enlarged, of the discovery of Quiros. . . . And by joining up Australia, New Guinea, Terra de Quiros and Tasmania (Van Diemen's Land), one vast continent was formed."[38] Family pride and vanity induced Delisle to append his name to maplike but essentially imaginative reconstructions of remote parts of the globe and to defend his brother's errors to the hilt.[39]

Wholly dependent upon ageing foreign maps of the new southern continent and wanting ships and men fit to attempt a hydrographic expedition (or a speculative trading venture) on the far side of the globe, the Russian Navy had perforce to make great efforts to acquire, through agents, recent charts from foreign governments. And the Admiralty agents did their best to provide new maps, in London, Paris, and the Netherlands (but not in

Spain, whose government regarded the Pacific Ocean as a Spanish *mare clausum*.[41] Nor was the Admiralty College lacking senior hydrographers by the mid-century who, like Captain Aleksei I. Nagaev (1704–81), could see the value of such maps and would have welcomed, in a scientific spirit, many more of the Pacific and New Holland, among other distant regions—regardless of the Russian state's own lack of trading or strategic interests so far away.[42] At the Academy of Sciences, there was by 1758 a Geographical Department to whose functioning a major contribution had been made by the great poet-scientist, Mikhail V. Lomonosov (1711–65).[43] It too was actively collecting maps, in the first instance of the Russian Empire itself, but also of remoter lands.[44] At College and Academy alike, in short, there was a *will* to read whatever could be read about the North and even South Pacific Ocean. By misfortune, however, Russian institutional attempts to gather data on that ocean coincided with the rise of French cartography (1725–70), whose theorizing and imaginative tendency was most apparent in the context of New Holland.[45]

Guillaume Delisle, whose work was widely known in later Petrine Russia, had at least shown a due regard for fact, omitting from his maps what was unknown. In this he followed Nicolas Sanson (1600–67) and Alexis Jaillot (1632–1712), the great Parisian cartographers of the preceding generations. The same cannot be said of his brother Joseph-Nicolas (1688–1768), who passed some twenty years in Russia and was long de facto head of the St. Petersburg Imperial Observatory, or of the equally successful and respected Philippe Buache (1700–73). Abhorring a vacuum, such men filled gaps of Western European knowledge of the globe with theoretical conceptions, so producing the least trustworthy and most fantastic maps ever compiled for New Holland.[46] It was not the Russians' fault that the supposedly best representations of that region, by Jean Bellin (1753) and Didier Robert de Vaugondy (1752, 1766), rested on pure hypothesis where its entire eastern shoreline was concerned.

EFFECTS OF CAPTAIN JAMES COOK'S VOYAGES, 1771–74

As the Russo-Dutch connection had enabled Russia to remain fully abreast of an advance in Western European knowledge of New Holland in the early eighteenth century, so at the century's close Anglo-Russian naval links enabled the Russians to assess without delay the information brought to England from the three great expeditions led by Captain James Cook (1768–71, 1772–75, 1776–80). There had been British naval officers and shipwrights in the Baltic and in Russian pay since Tudor times,[47] and one result of the Anglo-Russian maritime *entente* was that the

Russian naval school (*kadetskii korpus*) was among the very few training establishments in Russia to teach English to its students. Consequently, there were youthful Russian officers willing and able to read Cook's and his subordinates' various *Voyages* and, incidentally, to make a forward leap in knowledge of New Holland and the Great South Sea at large.[48] Nor was this all that Russia gained from her traditional and mutually serviceable link with Britain (of which commerce formed one strand, exchange of personnel another),[49] where the rapid acquisition of new geographical and other data was concerned. For one thing, there were Russian Volunteers on secondment to the Royal Navy who were in London in the years when Cook's and other *Voyages* relating to the Great South Sea were being published.[50] For another, there were Englishmen and Scots in Russian service in the Baltic Fleet.[51] They too were ready channels for such news. To the extent that they held influential posts, even flag rank, and were the representatives and beneficiaries of the immense prestige the Royal Navy then enjoyed in Russia, men like Admirals Charles Knowles and Samuel K. Greig of Inverkeithing[52] could but sharpen Russian consciousness of British seaborne exploration. Knowles and Greig were both at Kronstadt in the mid-1770s, that is, precisely when the *Voyages* in question were appearing and the foundations of Cook's Russian reputation was being laid.[53]

Accounts of Cook's achievements in *Endeavour* and historic landings in New Holland were available to Russians, as to other nationalities, by 1771, in the form of the texts of James Magra and Cook himself as drafted (or rewritten) by the hired stylist Nicholas Hawkesworth.[54] To these was added Sydney Parkinson's in 1773. In 1772, world maps were published which, in broad terms, showed New Holland's eastern littoral correctly.[55] Even Didier Robert de Vaugondy (1723–86), prone though he was to fantasy, in 1773 gave bearings for that country as reported by Cook's expedition. Those imperial officials and well-educated naval officers who read of Cook's discoveries, however, had no thought during the seventies of drawing practical advantage from them. It was true that Russian squadrons had in 1769–70, with the assistance of a British government (and British officers) known to be willing to inflict a blow upon Turkey, won a major naval victory at Chesme Bay in Asia Minor and performed most creditably, in the latest of a long series of Russo-Turkish wars, in the Aegean Sea.[56] But that Russian vessels should investigate the South Pacific Ocean was in 1772 (as it had been forty years earlier, when Captain Nikolai F. Golovin and Rear-Admiral Charles Saunders had advanced the same proposal),[57] not within the Russian Navy's capability. So much is evident from what is known of the imperial response to a memorial of 1773 from the mathematician Leonhard Euler (1707–83) recommending that a squadron make its way from the Baltic to Petropavlovsk-in-Kamchatka by the South Pacific route.

By the mid-1770s, Russia and Spain had long been nervous about each other's hypothetical advances on the Northwest Coast of North America, to which both crowns laid guarded claim.[58] Each accordingly sent reconnoitring and charting expeditions to discover the positions of the other's forward bases on that coast.[59] Each felt its trade monopoly and sovereignty gravely threatened by the other on the empty, fur-rich shores of what is now southeast Alaska. "It is perfectly well known to our Court," wrote José de Galvez, *visitador* or viceroy of New Spain in January 1768, "that the Russians have now familiarized themselves with the Sea of Tartary. It would be neither impossible nor even very difficult for the Muscovites to establish a colony at the port of Monterey, in Alta California, and when least expected."[60] Other high officials of the king in other parts of the Pacific and in European capitals were equally alive to Russian menace from the North, though it had yet to show itself. The Spanish ambassador to Russia, Francisco Antonio, Conde de Lacy (1731–92), for example, was in 1772 almost obsessed with secret Russian enterprise on the Pacific shores of Asia and America.[61] In numerous despatches to Prime Minister José Grimaldi in Madrid, Conde de Lacy did his xenophobic best to paint that enterprise in the most sinister, foreboding light.[62] At first Madrid was not impressed. By the spring of 1773, Conde de Lacy recognized the futility of his attempt to scare Grimaldi into action by alarmist tracts. In a less frenetic vein, he sent his government far more convincing information. "The Russian empress," he reported on 10 May 1773, "having told the famous Euler, a professor at the Academy here, of discoveries made in America, the latter has presented her with a detailed memorial."[63] When peace had been concluded with the Porte, Euler urged,

> part of the Russian squadron from the [Greek] Archipelago should be sent round the Cape of Good Hope to Kamchatka, in whose ports it could refit after its long voyage and afterwards continue with conquests advantageous to the Russian Empire. According to Euler, that empire has more right to America than any other Power.

Conde de Lacy's despatch is of great interest in the Pacific naval context. There had certainly been earlier suggestions that a Russian squadron sail to Okhotsk or Petropavlovsk by a southern route; mention has been made of Golovin's and Saunders's scheme. There had quite possibly been similar proposals made in Catherine the Great's own reign. But none of these had sent ripples through St. Petersburg or chanceries abroad. Now, for the first time, such proposals caused disturbance outside Russia. It was well for Spain that Euler was unversed in naval matters, though indeed he had at one time been proposed as a lieutenant in the Russian Navy by the Dutchman Peter Sievers.[64] He had, however, kept up friendships with such former members of the First or Second Bering Expeditions as the German scientists Georg-Wilhelm Steller and Johann-Georg Gmelin,[65] and his private correspondence offers ample evidence of a deep interest in the persistent international search for northern passages to the Pacific. As it happened, he held incorrect, exaggerated notions of the Russians' long-range naval capabilities, which were perhaps to some extent the result of the recent victory at Chesme Bay. But Euler was correct in his perception of the meaning and importance that would necessarily attach to the arrival of a Russian naval force in the Pacific by a southern route. The moment had arrived, he rightly judged, to play that hand, before a European power made a serious new move into those areas which Catherine herself viewed as a Russian zone of influence, that is, the waters east of Kodiak or north of the Pribylov Islands. Cook, like Commodore John Byron, had been sent to the Pacific to augment the wealth and power of the British and had probably succeeded. Foreign vessels almost certainly would be in North Pacific waters in the search for any navigable passage over Asia or America into that ocean. And such factors made it virtually certain that the British, like the Spanish, would be troublingly active in the region of Kamchatka.[66] Euler's prophecies were fully realized in 1779, with the arrival in Kamchatka of Cook's vessels, *Resolution* and *Discovery*.

Logically, any foreign threat to Russian trade or other interests on the Pacific littoral should have been met by Russian ships based at the naval and administrative centre of Okhotsk. In fact, however, Okhotsk had been synonymous with carelessness and backwardness since Bering's time, and it lacked the human and material resources to do more than aid the cossack hunter-traders in their push through the Aleutians.[67] Maximally distant from St. Petersburg and long neglected by the Admiralty College, those few servants of the Navy who remained on active duty in the far Northeast and East at mid-century were by and large left to their own devices. State officialdom had judged that state investments in remote northeastern regions had, despite the known achievements of the Bering expeditions, all produced a poor return.[68] This damning attitude was all too faithfully reflected in the fact that, at the centre of the Navy's eastern presence, less than thirty craft were built in the fifty years from 1716 to 1766. Nor could many of the galiots that sailed to Kamchatka from Okhotsk throughout the century have safely ventured on a voyage to Japan or China, let alone more distant parts.[69] Enormous trading opportunities were being squandered by the mid-1760s for a want of European-standard vessels, seamen, charts, and pilots. Martin Sauer, German secretary to the Arctic and Pacific expedition of 1785–92 led by one of Cook's former subordinates, Mate Joseph Billings, left this cameo of the Okhotsk that he himself observed:

> The city of Ochotsk... is built on a neck of land five versts long and from 15 to 150 fathoms wide, its direction due east. It is chiefly composed of sand, shingles, and driftwood, the whole thrown up by the surf. The town occupies the space of about one verst in length, containing 132 miserable wooden houses, a church and belfry, several rotten storehouses.... The main channel of the Ochot is only navigable for small empty vessels... and a very violent surf constantly breaks over the bar and all along the shore. At the time of the equinoctial gales, the spray wets the houses of the town.[70]

Though no seaman, Sauer promptly recognized Petropavlovsk-in-Kamchatka's great superiority over Okhotsk, whose leaking galiots laden with trading knives and hatchets, rough tobacco, beads, and drunkards sometimes foundered in sight of the inhabitants.[71] Given Avacha Bay's deep, sheltered water, he reported rightly, it could easily accommodate six or eight warships "anchored head to stern."[72] But nothing could be done. Okhotsk was Russia's naval centre in the East and so remained till 1812. Though used occasionally by such charting and exploring expeditions as those led by Petr Krenitsyn and Mikhail Levashev (1769–70) and, as seen, by Joseph Billings, Petropavlovsk was an embryonic port in the time of Cook and Euler.[73] If Russians were to enter the Pacific from the south, even an ardent naval patriot like Mikhail Levashev was obliged to recognize upon returning to St. Petersburg in 1771, it would perforce be from the Baltic, not from Okhotsk or any other Eastern settlement.[74] Only at Kronstadt, Russia's major naval base near St. Petersburg, were there officers, vessels, and seamen of a quality to make it possible even to think of circumnavigating the globe.

> And the *thought* of the possibility and benefits of round-the-world communications with the eastern extremities of Russia arose long before the formation [in 1799] of the Russian-American Company.... In 1764, when Captain Krenitsyn and Lieutenant Levashev were being sent to describe the Aleutian Islands, it was the government's intention to dispatch two ships to Kamchatka from Kronstadt. But a Russo-Turkish war erupted and that enterprise was put off. And in 1781, the Vice-President of the Admiralty College, I. G. Chernyshev, had a ship constructed at his own expense in the Crown dockyard, had her laden with goods, and was fully intending to send her to

the Northwest Coast of North America. This expedition, too, failed
to proceed, apparently for technical reasons.[75]

For "technical reasons," we may read lack of official will, and—to a far
lesser extent—local experience of distant voyaging.

EFFECTS IN RUSSIA OF COOK'S LAST VOYAGE, 1778–85

By the time Cook reached Unalaska Island off the Northwest Coast of
North America with *Resolution* and *Discovery* in October 1778,
Catherine II had for fifteen years deliberately not supported an expanding
cossack enterprise in the Aleutians.[76] As a result, the Russians' maritime
and military weakness in an area so large and rich in peltry, or "soft
gold," was self-perpetuating. The empress was, as Levashev had found
to his chagrin in 1772,[77] simply unwilling to provoke either the Spanish or
the British by assertiveness in North Pacific waters that could lead to con-
frontation and retreat. In the years following 1772, government officials
in both St. Petersburg and Siberia showed ever deepening anxiety at
rumours of advances on the Northwest Coast planned in Madrid, New
Spain, or London.[78] And well they might, given the value and extent of
Russian fur-based interests and their country's weakness in those distant
islands. This official apprehension of continuing Spanish advances up the
coast of North America toward the Russian zone of influence was plain
enough even by 1774, when Catherine formally promised a hospitable
reception to the ships of friendly powers calling at Kamchatkan or
Aleutian settlements. It grew abruptly in June 1776, when information arrived from Spain that Juan Perez, who had been active in the latitude of
55°N two years previously, had been followed on his northern track by
other men of the Spanish Navy, Juan de la Bodega y Quadra and B. H. de
Heceta.[79] Cossack activities along the Northwest Coast, it was reported
from the embassy in Spain, had caused much worry in New Spain and
were moreover almost certain to accelerate the Spaniards' missionary
work and occupation of the littoral of Alta California due north of San
Diego.[80] In short, some unexpected intercourse with foreigners along the
coast, on the Aleutian Island chain, or even on Kamchatka was becoming
likelier.

News of the *Resolution*'s and *Discovery*'s appearance on the shores of
Unalaska, and of Cook's and his associates' activities and objects to the
north of the Aleutians, as reported by the hunter-trader Gerasim Izmailov
through Major Magnus H. von Behm (1727–1806), governor of Kamchatka,[81] caused the government concern despite the empress's ukase of

1774. News of their putting in at Petropavlovsk twice, in May and August 1779, and of more probings in an area claimed tacitly by Russia as reported by Vasilii I. Shmalev, an extremely xenophobic army officer then serving in Kamchatka,[82] led to action.

Shortly after Cook's sudden death at the Hawaiians' hands, the *Resolution* and *Discovery*, commanded now by Captains Clerke and Gore, made their way into Avacha Bay to water and provision.[83] It was time, once more, to seek the Northwest Passage home to England. Alarmed by the arrival of two unfamiliar and unexpected ships, the little garrison of Petropavlovsk—thirty soldiers and a sergeant—looked on as King and J. Webber, *Discovery*'s Swiss artist, crossed the ice sheet and proceeded up the shore. All guns were loaded. But the crisis quickly passed. As soon as King greeted the governor of the peninsula, Behm, who had just travelled up in haste from Bol'sheretsk, he understood that he was fortunate to have encountered him. Behm was a generous and widely read official, a Livonian by birth. On his instructions, Clerke was given all he needed to repair and victual his ships. As he departed, Clerke gave Behm a sealed packet, containing both his own latest reports and other documents by Cook, King, and astronomer William Bayly, to be forwarded to London overland with the assistance of imperial officialdom.[84] The governor proved worthy of the trust.[85] Nor was he any less obliging when the foreigners returned to Petropavlovsk and, at midday on 26 August, buried Clerke.[86] Again the British were assisted and most handsomely provisioned on his orders.

Clerke's sealed packet to the Admiralty Board in London was by no means the sole evidence of British movement in the North and South Pacific that was passed across Siberia, over the Urals, to St. Petersburg in 1779–80. Gratefully conscious of their debt to Behm (a debt that London later formally acknowledged and attempted vainly to discharge),[88] the British visitors of 1779 had given him a small collection of Pacific "curiosities," notably Tongan, Tahitian, and Hawaiian artefacts.[89] These too provoked discussion in St. Petersburg before being deposited in the *Kunstkammer* of the Academy of Sciences. They have remained in the Academy's good keeping to this day, and may be seen in the museum of the N. N. Miklukho-Maklai Institute of Anthropology in Leningrad.[90] Few though they were, these Polynesian artefacts served to increase official Russia's consciousness of the Pacific as a whole and of the South Sea in particular.

Behm, in the meantime, had reported Clerke's two visits in despatches to Irkutsk which were forwarded at once to A. A. Viazemskii, the procurator-general, who showed them to the empress. Other papers from Siberia represented the repeated British visit in a far more sinister, uncompromisingly aggressive vein.[91] As a result, orders were issued for more guns to be transported overland to Petropavlovsk. Catherine's own attitude toward Cook's final expedition and the prospect of more British naval probings from the South and mid-Pacific was subtly reported by Sir James Harris in a despatch from St. Petersburg dated 7 January 1780. "The Empress," wrote the British minister to Sandwich of the Admiralty Board, "feels the great utility which must result from such a voyage, & is anxious to promote its success—she express'd a very *earnest* desire of having Copys of such Charts as may tend to ascertain more precisely the extent & position of those remote Parts of her Empire."[92] The Russian government might well, as Harris knew, have wished for copies of "such Charts": it had too few that were reliable. And since the empress had no warships in the far Northeast or East, how was even the Aleutian Island chain to be regarded as a safe, integral portion of her empire? From sheer expediency, Catherine and Russian high officialdom concealed whatever doubts they entertained as to the purity of scientific motive in the Cook-Clerke expedition, but they at once took steps to learn all that they could about its movements and results. Perhaps the Russians had no choice but to await the publication of accounts of that same venture by the participants, taking note of all fragmentary accounts printed in Göttingen and Leyden news gazettes or in the *London Magazine* in the spring of 1780. (Significantly, copies of the issue of A. Friedrich Busching's *Wöchentliche Nachtrichten von neuen Landcharten* that offered glimpses of *Discovery*'s and *Resolution*'s movements in the Arctic and Sub-Arctic twelve months earlier were sent directly from Berlin via the Russian Baltic Provinces and Riga to the Admiralty College in St. Petersburg.)[93] But meanwhile, the state-sponsored translation into Russian of the English (1777) text of the *Adventure-Resolution* expedition (1772–75) could at least proceed at an accelerated pace.

Never, once having addressed their minds to it, would the affected high officials in the Admiralty College or Imperial Commerce Commission cease to welcome new attested information about physical conditions in the North Pacific basin or about the fur trade.[94] Incidentally, but surely, information about South Pacific islands and New Holland also came to the Russian government. Suddenly, thanks to Cook's success as an explorer and hydrographer, the Russian Court became receptive to accounts of *any* voyages into the North Pacific Ocean from the South; and Russian knowledge of New Holland, or, more accurately, of its rich southeastern fringe, began to grow. Russian government officials, naval officers, and readers thus became aware of New Holland in connection with sea otter skins and in the context of the international struggle to control the Northwest Coast, even before the vast potential of the Coast-to-Canton fur trade was fully recognized by the authorities in London and St. Petersburg. It was the pattern of the future, well reflected in the fact that when at last a Russian vessel paid a visit to New Holland, in 1807, she was on her way from Kronstadt to the Russian Northwest Coast (see Chapter Three).

With the aid of English merchants in Canton, John Gore of the *Discovery* had had no trouble in disposing of the mostly torn sea otter skins that he and other men had casually gathered on the Northwest Coast of North America for about £2,000.[95] Seamen had even fled the ship, taking a boat, in hopes of entering the Coast-to-Canton fur trade on their own account;[96] and their superiors themselves had freely entertained such notions. News of the great sums that Chinese merchants were prepared to pay even for torn skins from the Pacific rim caused a considerable stir in European Russia. Russo-Chinese trade in furs was conducted by convention and exclusively at the remote and inland border point of Kiakhta-Mai-mai-ch'eng.[97] The national interest could not fail to be affected by the patent inability of merchants based in Kamchatka or Okhotsk to send their peltry to Canton. Okhotsk was full of rotting and disintegrated vessels—poor examples of local shipwrights' art.[98] And that incompetence at sea which made the sending of supplies and men to the Aleutian settlements so perilous made it effectively impossible for Russia to compete with other nations in the Canton mart. As for Kiakhta and the inland China trade, it had been suddenly suspended by the Chinese government before and could again be simply halted. So it was, in May 1785, for seven years.[99]

Considerations like these induced several well-placed grandees with immediate or incidental Eastern and Pacific interests or ministerial responsibilities (among them Count Aleksandr R. Vorontsov of the Imperial Commerce Commission; P. P. Soimonov, private secretary to the empress; and Count A. A. Bezborodko)[100] to urge the Admiralty College to acquire all possible data about Cook's activities in the Pacific. For example, what Pacific charts relating to his final or preceding expeditions had been forwarded from the embassy in London in response to the imperial request of 11 December 1779? Had a translation of Cook's first or second *Voyages* been undertaken, and, if not, what French translations were available for use by other colleges?[101] It was at this juncture that news came of the first of many speculative voyages from Britain, New England, and Bengal to the localities that *Resolution* and *Discovery* had charted and described: that of James Hanna in the little brig *Sea Otter* (1785).[102] Vorontsov and Soimonov were profoundly troubled by it. Once again they urged the Admiralty College to address itself to the study of Cook's *Voyages*. The College did so, the more zealously as a result of news that reached St. Petersburg in time to underline the menace of *Sea Otter*'s enterprise. Comte J. F. de G. de la Pérouse had left for North Pacific waters with the French frigates *Boussole* and *Astrolabe* in August 1785.[103] It was officially, the embassy in Paris had reported, with the purest scientific motives that the count had sailed for the Northwest Coast of North America and Bering Strait.[104] In fact, however, both the French and Russian governments well recognized the economic and strategic implications of a French discovery of any Northwest Passage from Pacific to Atlantic tidal waters, and indeed of Frenchmen entering the North Pacific fur trade. Russian scrutiny of Cook's and his companions' published *Voyages* acquired fresh urgency in 1785–87.[105]

EARLY RUSSIAN AWARENESS OF VAN DIEMEN'S LAND

Among the works examined in the hope of countering the foreign threat to Russian interests in the Pacific was Cook's *Voyage to the South Pole and Around the World. . .* of 1777.[106] Perhaps it could not throw light on British dealings with the Aleuts and in countries claimed by Russia, but it could certainly illuminate the larger pattern of imperialist probing. Thus, in a North Pacific context as always, did the Admiralty College and the Academy of Sciences come to examine Captain Tobias Furneaux's observations on the shoreline of Van Diemen's Land as charted ten years previously from the *Adventure* (1773) and incorporated in Cook's *Voyage*.[107] Had the scientific Forsters, George and Johann Reinhold, been with Furneaux in *Adventure* and not with Cook in *Resolution,* Russian readers would unquestionably have been even more aware of the supposed southern extremity of *Novaia Gollandiia*. Both men published books upon their return to Europe. The son, George, did so in 1777 in defiance of official prohibition. He was in contact with the Admiralty College by the mid-1780s, but even before then the Russian government was well apprised of the fertility and temperate conditions that prevailed in Van Diemen's Land, thanks to the extant Dutch and British data.[109] In January 1777, *Resolution* and *Discovery* had spent five days in or around Adventure Bay, Cook and his officers duly recording all they saw.[110] To information on the place that had been printed in *Voyage to the South Pole,* Russian officers could add all that appeared in the several unauthorized accounts of Cook's last voyage which appeared in the space of eighteen months in 1781–82 (by Ellis, Rickman, and Zimmermann),[111] as well as those that came out in 1784 in London, in the government-financed, official *Voyage*. Thus did Cook's men of the second and, especially, the final expedition offer Russian high officialdom a cornucopia of information about an island as remote from Russian interests as any in the world: Van Diemen's Land. They represented it in highly favourable terms, drawing attention to safe anchorages, handy springs, and an abundance of good timber. The fair impression thus created long remained in the official Russian mind.

Two of the early unauthorized accounts of Cook's last venture, those by Lieutenant John Rickman and Coxswain Heinrich Zimmermann of *Discovery,* were widely read and well viewed in St. Petersburg in 1782–86. It is instructive to consider why those texts especially, rather than Surgeon William Ellis's of the same period (1782) or the official Cook-King narrative (1784), fixed Russian attitudes towards Van Diemen's Land. In brief, they were accessible thanks to adequate translations from the English, which the Russian gentry read but little, into German and French, or Russian in the case of Zimmermann.

Rickman's anonymous *Journal,* surreptitiously published by the London printer Newbery in April 1781,[112] was translated into German that same autumn and issued with an introduction by Johann Reinhold Forster. This fact commended itself to the St. Petersburg Academy, indeed to all learned society in Russia. Forster senior, who had spent eighteen busy but frustrating months in Catherine the Great's employ (1765–66) writing an unacceptably direct and critical report on German colonies then being founded on the Volga steppe,[113] was internationally known as a prolific and profound natural scientist.[114] His *Observations Made During a Voyage Round the World* (1777), that is, with Cook in *Resolution,* and more recent publications that related to his South Seas scientific efforts, were respected in St. Petersburg. He and his son George, who had lived with him in Russia when still a boy of twelve, had had professional and personal connections in that city for many years.[115] Ever enterprising, George came very close to realizing the political and academic capital they had gained by their connection with Cook when, in July 1787, he was asked to organize a large Pacific expedition for the Russian government.[116] As we shall see, that expedition—which would very probably have brought the Russians to New Holland in the reign of Catherine—was cancelled at the last moment, as war with Turkey loomed and pressure grew to keep all first-rate naval units nearer home. The publication in 1782–83 of no less than three French versions of the Rickman text (the French were genuine admirers of Cook) further promoted its success with Russian readers.[117]

Even Rickman's importance as a source of first-hand data on New Holland for the Russians pales by comparison with Heinrich Zimmermann's, however. The Russians could read Zimmermann's account of *Cook's Last Voyage Round the World* (*Poslednee puteshestvie okolo Sveta Kapitana Kuka*) in their own language by July 1786.[118] It was the first eye-witness text published in Russian, and it happened to go on sale at the very time when, in response to mounting international pressures on Kamchatka and the Northwest Coast, a Russian squadron was preparing to sail to defend the national interest: Captain Grigorii I. Mulovskii's expedition (see below).

Zimmermann, a restless, multitalented native of Speyer (Baden-Wurtemberg), was coxswain in *Discovery* from 1776 to 1780. According to the opening three sentences of his *Account of the Third Voyage of Captain Cook around the World. . . ,*[119] to give the work its English title, he had worked in early life as an apprentice saddler, a brazier, a bell founder, a swordmaker, a gilder, and a workman in a small sugar refinery. As coxswain, he was certainly not privy to Cook's hopes or aims at any given time during the voyage. In fact, his narrative is full of errors of the sort to be expected when a member of the lower deck, and a foreigner at that, tries to report things that he knows only imperfectly, perhaps by hearsay. Nonetheless, it is a valuable narrative, replete with colourful, objective cameos and sensible remarks, the whole presented in a lively style. In its first edition (Mannheim, 1781), it appeared as *Reise um die Welt mit Capitain Cook.* Zimmermann had kept a diary during his voyage, making entries in abbreviated German, and apparently ignored official orders from the Admiralty Board, relayed by Cook himself, to the effect that all such jottings be surrendered ("seal them up for our inspection")[120] at the expedition's end. At all events, the *Reise* rested unmistakably on some first-hand account: a strict chronology prevails, with repeated references to the date, weather, and ship's movement that inspire confidence. A second German edition appeared in Mannheim in 1782, then, in 1783, a French translation, *Dernier Voyage du Capitaine Cook. . . par Henry Zimmermann, témoin oculaire,* came out in Berne, Switzerland. The translator, E. Roland, was a follower of the encyclopaedists, with a taste for those religious-philosophical discussions so attractive to the French—and Russian—*monde* throughout the eighties. Still, the work was a translation, not a paraphrase. This French edition was itself translated tolerably accurately into Russian and appeared in the bookshops of St. Petersburg in time to satisfy another surge of public interest in Cook, provoked, in part, by La Pérouse.[122] The book sold well in Russian dress. A second printing followed in 1788, at the risk of Petr I. Bogdanovich (1756–1806), littérateur, linguist, and pedagogue.[123] Two supplements or extra parts were appended: "A Detailed Description of the Island of Otaheiti and Its Natives" (pp. 191–306) and "Concerning America In General" (pp. 307–411). Bogdanovich himself had, with a view to further boosting sales among educated readers whose awareness of Cook and the Pacific had been sharpened by his own efforts, composed this last piece—or, more accurately, filched it from *Academy Reports (Akademicheskie izvestiia)* for 1781.[124] Once more, Russians were offered information about New Holland in the context of fast-growing international competition for control of the resources of America's remote northwestern coasts.

Here, now, are extracts from the thousand-word "Van Diemen's Land passage" of the first Russian edition of the Zimmermann *Poslednee puteshestvie.* The passage played an early, crucial part in the formation of the Russian attitude toward, and picture of, Van Diemen's Land, its people, climate, harbours, and resources:

> On 26 January 1777, we reached the southern extremity of New Holland, known as Van Diemen's Land, dropping anchor in a secure harbour in latitude 42°30'S. and about 150°E. There being a number of springs and plenty of timber, everything was quickly made ready to stow a good supply of water and wood alike.
>
> Shortly afterwards, seven natives came down to the shore, where they played with the stoppers of our water-casks, eventually knocking the casks over and rolling them to and fro. They were peaceful and did not in the least hinder us in our work. . . . This same day, Captain Cook and some of his men pushed quite a distance inland and were lucky enough to bring about nine of these savages back to our ship. He gave them mirrors, white shirts, glass bead necklaces. . . gifts which produced so powerful an effect that the next day, of their own volition, 49 male and female savages appeared. Some were given gifts, in their turn; but like the others, they refused to come on board. They were of a dark brown hue, with short woolly hair. Both sexes went completely naked, the females carrying infants in a stretched skin on their back. . . . We observed no weapons of any kind and so took these people to be quiet and not dangerous. It was a matter of much wonder to Captain Cook that these savages should be so very unlike the wild and menacing ones on the New Holland coast.
>
> So far as we could judge in little time, these people ate mussels, oysters, fish, and all kinds of roots. There was no trace of fruit trees or agriculture or, indeed, of any huts to live in. They took bread from us, but cast it away at once. . . . We set sail for New Zealand on the fourth day.

Unwittingly, Zimmermann was directing the nature of the growth of Russian interest in South Sea Islands and New Holland by so dwelling on the aboriginal Tasmanians.[125] Taken together with the corresponding emphases in Rickman's text and, especially, in the official Cook-King *Voy-*

age,[126] his willingness to focus on the physical appearance, unwarlike attitude, and diet of the group at Adventure Harbour went some way towards
establishing a tendency among the Russians to regard ethnography[127] as the
fundamental natural component in all European study of New Holland.
This tendency reached fruition in the competent ethnography of Russian
officers and scientists in contact with the Cammeraigal and other groups
in the Port Jackson region in the early 1800s[128] and in steady but discrimi-
nating artefact collecting. It was enhanced and not diminished by
Roland's and others' Rousseauesque reflections on the primary accounts.
What, after all, was better calculated to improve Zimmermann's chances
of delivering the message that Tasmanians were kind and inoffensive than
couching it in the then fashionable medium (the *voyage pittoresque*) and
style (elegant à la Rousseau)? It is important to recall that to educated
Russians of the eighteenth century, French was *la langue de la politesse,*
the crucial prism through which European thought, culture, and science
were refracted into Russia. Cook's science and thought proved no exception.

COOK IN FRENCH AND RUSSIAN TRANSLATION, 1778–1805

It fell to a young aristocrat with naval interests and family connections,
Loggin Ivanovich Golenischev-Kutuzov (1769–1845) to translate
Cook's second (1777) and third *Voyages* (1784).[129] Through his efforts,
Russian officers and others with inadequate command of French or German learned, in the period of the Napoleonic Wars (1793–1815), a good
deal of what they knew about New Holland. That being so, Kutuzov's
youth merits attention: he was sixteen when he started work on a translation which, through no fault of his own, would not be published till
eleven years later.[130] Service duties, transfers, even departmental politics
reduced the time and energy he could devote, without assistants, to the
project. (He was not alone in that predicament—or in precocity as a translator. Ivan Iakovlevich Novikov, whose *Beauties of Australia, the Fifth
Part of the Earth*... appeared in 1805,[131] had published a translation of a
treatise on commercial practices by the encyclopaedist F. Veron de Forbonnais [1722–1800] at the age of twelve.)[132]
    Kutuzov was the second son of Admiral Ivan Logginovich
(1729–1802), head of the Admiralty College in the reign of Paul I
(1796–99). From his adroit and able father, he inherited both maritime
and literary interests. As recreation and a respite from his duties as director of the central school for future naval officers, *Morskoi Kadetskii
Korpus,* Ivan Logginovich had written sentimental letters à la Fenelon

and made translations from Voltaire (*Zadig,* 1765).[133] Regrettably perhaps, but not surprisingly, in view of later-eighteenth-century conventions where translation was concerned, the father's attitude toward that pastime was passed on to the son: neither thought literal precision in translating foreign texts a worthy altar for the sacrifice of elegance.[134]

Kutuzov did not choose to work from Cook's own text of 1777 when, at government request, he brought *Puteshestvie v Iuzhnoi polovine zemnago shara* (*Voyage in the Southern Hemisphere*) to the notice of his countrymen.[135] Instead, he turned to *Voyage dans l'hémisphère australe et autour du monde fait... en 1772, 1773, 1774 et 1775..., dans lequel on a inséré la relation du capitaine Furneaux... traduit de l'Anglois par M. Suard* (Paris, Hôtel de Thou, 1778). The effort by the fiery and energetic Jean-Baptiste-Antoine Suard (1733–1817) had certain merits, for example, the inclusion of fine maps by Hodges on the basis of the Cook-Furneaux hydrography in southern waters[136] and, moreover, of the elder Forster's *Observations.* Nonetheless, it was essentially a free rendition of the 1777 London text. As he had ten years earlier in his translation of the *Voyage of John Byron,* and again within the past few months in an attempt on William Robertson's *Histoire de l'Amérique,* a work soon to enjoy as huge a popular success in Russia as in France,[137] Suard had striven for fluidity of style. Accuracy was desirable, but secondary in importance on the Paris market.[138] The decision to translate at second hand was not a happy one; nor, having settled on the French text, was Kutuzov able to complete his work and see it quickly through the press. The first part of his six-part *Puteshestvie v Iuzhnoi polovine* went on sale in St. Petersburg in May 1796. It was an elegant quarto edition,[139] but it came too late to benefit from Zimmermann and was itself a commentary on the diligence of other, French translators and their general acceptance by the Russian reading public. A. F. J. de Fréville (1749–1832) in 1772, Suard in 1778, Jean-Nicolas Demeunier (1751–1814) in 1785: each, in his turn, had made the news of Cook's discoveries accessible to an extensive Russian audience.[140] Demeunier especially was known in Russia: barely fifteen months after the publication of the English text of the historical geographer William Coxe's general *Account of the Russian Discoveries Between Asia and America* (1780), a book prepared in Russia with the knowledge and assistance of the government and which the empress was anxious to examine, he had rushed his version (*Nouvelles Découvertes...*) into print. If there was any distant region in which foreigners' activities concerned the Russian Court in the last quarter of the eighteenth century and the first years of the nineteenth, it was that between America and Asia north of 51 degrees of latitude. Belated though they were, Kutuzov's elegant Russian translations—first of La Pérouse's

Voyage in the South and North Pacific Ocean (1800), then of Cook's last *Voyage* (1805)—were assured a warm reception in St. Petersburg.[141]

Kutuzov's rendering of La Pérouse's narrative (*Puteshestvie La Peruza v Iuzhnom i Severnom Tikhom okeane*), which was based on the Paris edition of 1798, reminded Russians of the British colony of New South Wales, where the Frenchman had been civilly received in 1788.[142] La Pérouse had left a description of his visit to Port Jackson, the approving tone and factual content of which were well reflected in Kutuzov's Russian version.[143] The Russian translation of Cook's last *Voyage,* though, by echoing the Zimmermann and other earlier descriptions of *Discovery*'s and *Resolution*'s January 1777 visit to Van Diemen's Land,[144] did most to fix New Holland's physical existence and conceivable future utility in Russian minds. Again the Russians were reminded of Cook's interest in native peoples,[145] of the natural resources of Van Diemen's Land, and of the safe and adequately charted anchorages in a land controlled by Great Britain, Russia's major ally in the struggle with Napoleonic France. All those attitudes, in short, which had been reinforced by Zimmermann and Forster in the eighties were now deeply etched into the consciousness of naval scientific circles in St. Petersburg. Such were the legacies of Cook, Furneaux, and Zimmermann.

To summarize, the value of Kutuzov's Russian versions of Cook's *Voyages* was lessened by the choice of basic text, by the work of French translators of the same period, and, less markedly, by their belated publication. Nonetheless, his versions did spread knowledge of discoveries in the Pacific, of New Holland, and of Cook among a broader Russian readership. Like the multilingual accounts of recent voyages performed by La Pérouse and Captain George Vancouver, in the absence of accounts by other visitors to Cook's New Holland such as Malaspina and Bruni d'Entrecasteaux,[146] they also spread some knowledge and awareness of New Holland among Russian naval officers and high officials conscious of the commerce and economic promise of the East.

Because the narratives of Cook and his subordinates were accessible to the whole fleet by 1805, his star stood still higher in the naval firmament, rather than declining.[147] Not until 1823–26 did the most brilliant of younger Russian officers cease to revere the name of Cook; nor, later, did such influential admirals as Ivan F. Kruzenshtern (1770–1846) and Faddei F. Bellingshausen (1779–1852) cease to think of Cook's professional descendants, George Vancouver and Matthew Flinders, with a measure of the same profound respect.[148] There were indeed arch-patriotic officers, notably Makar' I. Ratmánov and Vasilii M. Golovnin, who were prepared in the early 1800s to disparage Cook's supposedly humane treatment of natives in the North and South Pacific[149] and to question his alleged infallibility as a hydrographer.[150] Their criticisms did not harm Cook's reputation, which, in Russia as in France, had always rested on his obvious success as the commander of a seaborne expedition. For the educated Russian of the era, it was practically impossible to think of New South Wales (*Novyi Iuzhnyi Valis*) or Van Diemen's Land and not think of "the immortal Cook."[151]

The popular successes of Demeunier's, Suard's, and Golenishchev-Kutuzov's versions of Cook's *Voyages* both strengthened and were strengthened by two other kinds of literature in the last years of the century, both of which further spread Cook's posthumous celebrity in Russia: the biography and the compendium of voyages. In a society and age so friendly toward travel literature as a whole,[152] it could not hurt if a biographer aimed at a double readership by taking Cook as his hero. Such reasoning led Timofei Ivanovich Mozhaiskii, a talented but impecunious young linguist and acquaintance of the Petr I. Bogdanovich who had brought out Zimmermann's Russian-language *Poslednee puteshestvie* in 1786,[153] to set to work on a translation of the latest life of Cook.

Mozhaiskii was, like Kutuzov, happier translating from a French than from an English text. Bogdanovich himself had largely subsidized the publication in 1786 of his friend's Russian translation of *Les Nuits Champêtres* (in Russian, *Sel'skie nochi*) of the sentimentalist French poet Jean Charles Thibault de Laveaux (1749–1827)[154] and had received a fair return on the investment. The best-known *Life of Captain Cook*, indeed the only comprehensive one as yet available, was by Andrew Kippis (1725–95), nonconformist scholar and divine.[155] Kippis's work was published in London in July 1788 and was translated into French by an efficient journeyman soon to be widely known to Russians for his *Histoire de Catherine II* (1800) and for his French version of Martin Sauer's *Voyage* (1802): Jean-Henri Castéra (1749–1838). Recognizing opportunity when it confronted him, Mozhaiskii worked hard at a Russian version of Castéra's narrative. His *Circumstantial and Authentic Description of the Life and All the Voyages of the Most Famous English Seafarer Captain Cook* (*Podrobnoe i Dostovernoe opisanie Zhizni i vsekh Puteshestvii...kapitana Kuka*) was published by the St. Petersburg house of B. L. Gek in 1790. All steps were taken to enhance its sales prospects: the inclusion of a frontispiece engraving of the famous Cook, and, for good measure, of a poem, "The Morai," by Miss E. Maria Williams. Sales exceeded expectations.

Of the several collections of sea voyages published in Russian in the ten-year period from 1786 to 1796 which likewise served to keep Cook before a steadily expanding Russian readership, suffice it to mention two of the most popular: by Antoine François Prévost d'Exiles (1697–1763),

as edited and modified by Jean-François de La Harpe (1739–1803) and
well translated by Mikhail Ivanovich Verevkin (1732–95);[158] and by
Joachim Heinrich Campe (1746–1818), as translated by at least two unknown hands.

It was essentially to raise funds that the writer, journalist, and publicist
La Harpe, who was in worsening financial straits in 1779–80, edited,
substantially reorganized, and added fresh material to Prévost d'Exiles's
Histoire des Voyages of 1745–70. The abbé had himself seen seventeen
sections or volumes through the Paris press before he died. La Harpe
added material of major interest to recent readers—for example, on the
voyages of Cook—and, somewhat shamelessly, brought out his *Histoire
Générale des Voyages de M. l'Abbé Prévost, abrégé et redigé sur un
Nouveau Plan* (Paris, 1780–86; 21 vols.). Volumes 16 to 21 dealt with
voyages of circumnavigation and polar probes. The work was well received in Russian academic circles and, beginning in 1782, was steadily
translated by the dramatist and pedagogue Mikhail I. Verevkin as it came
into the bookshops of St. Petersburg and Moscow.[159] In Russian dress, La
Harpe's bold reconstruction of Prévost's work became *Istoriia o
stranstviiakh voobshche po vsem kraiam zemnago kruga...* (*A History of
Travels Generally to All Regions of the Terrestrial Sphere...*).[160] It was
published by the free thinker and mason, Nikolai I. Novikov, and enjoyed
wide popularity. Verevkin presented Cook's exploits in Volume 21
(1787), and for it Novikov borrowed four illustrations from La Harpe's
French edition, notably engravings from original drawings by Charles N.
Cochin. The net effect was very handsome.

Campe, for his part, relied on Hawkesworth's account of the discoveries of Commodore John Byron and Captains Wallis, Carteret, and
Cook,[161] that is, on far more recent data than La Harpe's, in his *Sammlung
interessanter... Reisebeschreibung für die Jugend* (1786–90; 8 vols. in
4). Parts 3 and 4 of a four-part Russian translation of Campe's *Sammlung,*
entitled *Sobranie liubopytnykh... puteshestvii* (St. P., Ridiger i
Klaudius, 1795–98), offered two different versions of the first thirteen
chapters of Cook's and Hawkesworth's account of the voyage of the
Endeavour in 1768–71. The version in Part 4, published in St.
Petersburg in 1798 and headed "A Description of the Voyage Round the
Globe Performed by the English Ship's Captain Cook and by the *Savants*
Banks and Solander," presented the first thirty-four chapters of the Cook-
Hawkesworth *Voyage* and ran to 550 pages.[162] Axiomatically, it included
that section of Hawkesworth's text based upon Cook's journal of 19 April
to 23 August 1770. Russians were thus able to follow Cook again from
Point Hicks (modern Cape Everard, Victoria) right up the east coast of
Australia to Cape York and Endeavour Strait in modern Queensland.

2

TRANSLATING PROJECTS
INTO ACTION, 1783–1803

COOK'S SUBORDINATES IN RUSSIAN NAVAL SERVICE, 1783–90

Cook's final expedition (1776–80) had immense significance for the development and shaping of the Russian naval presence in the North and South Pacific in the early 1800s. The appearance of the British, first on Unalaska Island and then in Petropavlovsk harbour, served as a powerful reminder of the economic value and potential of Kamchatka and the North Pacific islands.[1] Later, men who had served under Cook but were thwarted in their hopes of swift advancement in a shrunken Royal Navy, entered Russia's naval service (1783–87). Some drew Catherine's attention to the far Northeast and East and to the wonderful potential of the oceanic otter trade, which they themselves had started almost casually at Canton.[2] One at least, Lieutenant James Trevenen (1760–90), late of *Resolution*, played a large part in evolving Russian plans to send a squadron from the Baltic to the fur-rich North Pacific, with revictualling calls in southern ports.[3] Trevenen's "North Pacific Project" adumbrated that Pacific plan adopted when at last, in 1803, the Russian government did send two vessels, the *Nadezhda* and *Neva,* from Kronstadt roads to the Pacific. Once again, Cook's was a crucial role in the development of Russian intellectual and, later, physical connections with New Holland (as, in deference to Tasman and traditional cartography, the Russians called Australia until the later 1830s).

As we have seen, even in 1779, some of the men aboard *Discovery* and *Resolution* at Canton were thinking of entering the North Pacific fur trade on their own account. Others, more practical and less impetuous than those who simply stole a longboat,[4] were already scheming how to gain official British, or American, or even Russian backing for such an enterprise. On their return to England, these imaginative individuals were led, mainly by economic pressure and the threat of unemployment, to develop and attempt to sell their North Pacific plans. Two members of Cook's final expedition in particular, Trevenen and John Ledyard (1751–89), the Connecticut marine who, while on Unalaska Island, had established the first contact between Russian and American in the Pacific,[5] clung to memories of the enormous profits made in China, where a single otter skin bought for a hatchet could be sold for sixty dollars.[6] In due course, both men went to Russia, where a third former subordinate of Cook, Able Seaman Joseph Billings, had for three years (1783–86) been flourishing as an imported, newly minted officer and even lately as commander of a naval expedition to the Arctic and Pacific.[7] Typically, however, Captain Billings had refrained from writing projects on the basis of his knowledge of the Coast-to-Canton trade; unlike Trevenen, he was not a writing man.

Much is obscure about the relatively humble early life and work of Billings. His biography has yet to be attempted. After his return from the Pacific with *Discovery,* he vanishes from Admiralty records, reappearing two years later as the first mate of a British merchantman (1782–83). On reaching Russia at the age of twenty-five, he was accepted in the Baltic Fleet as midshipman. Shortly thereafter he was given his lieutenancy. Even the social disadvantages of modest origins, which would assuredly have hindered his professional advancement in his native land, were thus removed in Russian sight.

The Russian Admiralty College was impressed by his assertion that in early life he had been "Cook's companion" and the "astronomer's assistant" of *Discovery* and, by extension, that he had considerable knowledge of conditions in the North Pacific Ocean.[8] Economic and political developments in the remote Northeast and East and news of La Pérouse's venture made the College and the empress still more conscious of the possible usefulness of the experience that Billings and other Englishmen had had in the Pacific.[9] What was more logical than to employ a man like Billings in the region of Kamchatka? Thus, because he had "already been there," he was given, at twenty-eight years of age, overall command of the most costly and extensive expedition to be sent across Siberia to the Pacific shores since Bering's time. Simply by holding such an influential post, Billings reminded his political superiors of Cook's Pacific movements, predisposing Catherine to approve Trevenen's application for a post in Russian service. Such, essentially, is the significance of Billings's Arctic and Pacific expedition of 1785–94 from the standpoint of the Russians' growing consciousness of *South* Pacific landfalls. It was Trevenen who brought the prospect of a Russian naval move into the South Pacific Ocean, with attendant possibilities of visits to South Africa, Port Jackson, and Hawaii, to the notice of his own and Billings's ultimate superior: the empress. In itself, Billings's protracted "geographical and astronomical"[10] investigation of the far Northeast and East, and of the cold waters beyond, marked an important step in that long process whereby members of the Admiralty College were staking out a claim in the Pacific for the Navy.[11] And in this sense, too, he contributed toward the origins of Russian naval visits to Port Jackson: no such visits, after all, could occur until the Navy had established its legal claim to represent the national interest in the Pacific.[12]

For Trevenen as for Billings, the decision to serve Catherine brought both professional advancement and an early death. Ledyard, alas for his extraordinary commercial schemes, was not allowed by the imperial authorities to walk in peace across Siberia towards Virginia or to attach himself to Billings on his way to Bering Strait.[13] Nevertheless, the ex-marine had time enough, while in St. Petersburg, to offer useful information about natural resources and conditions on the Northwest Coast and in Canton to the imperial authorities—represented by the German-Russian scientist Peter Simon Pallas (1741–1811)[14]—and, more generally, to provoke awareness of the Pacific in both naval and academic circles.[15] In England at the end of Cook's last venture (October 1780), Ledyard had managed to remain outside the war then being waged against his countrymen by British troops and warships.[16] On returning to New England in 1782, he had immediately set about composing his own *Journal of Captain Cook's Last Voyage*. Having properly surrendered his own notebook to the Admiralty Board three years before, he saw no option but to plagiarize the newly published but anonymous Rickman account.[17] His effort was presented to the public in June 1783 and was an instantaneous success. Ledyard, however, was not destined to succeed in realizing his commercial schemes in Russia. Notwithstanding the good offices of Pallas, who considered him a curious and interesting man, the would-be intercontinental traveller's known link with Cook worked, paradoxically and unlike those of Billings and Trevenen, to his disadvantage.[18]

Like many other officers in 1784, Trevenen found himself on half-pay and depressed about his prospects in the Royal Navy. Accustomed to excitement and variety, he set off for the Continent with John King, late of the *Discovery*. The continent, however, quickly palled. Again in England, he examined his position. Unsuccessful at the Admiralty Board, he thought of venturing what capital he had in a commercial undertaking on the Northwest Coast or in New Holland. On 16 November 1786 he wrote:

> I am now in London. . . . You may have heard of our projected settlement at Botany Bay in New Holland. That was one reason for my

coming. . . but I was too late. Commercial schemes are carrying on here with great Spirit, and among others the fine furs we discovered on the Coast of America are carried thence to China and exchanged with great profit. If I do not get employed in government, I shall most likely engage in that trade—indeed I am in some measure already, but difficulties are to be got over which concern charters and monopolies.[19]

Regrettably, these "difficulties" could not be "got over," nor was anything forthcoming from the Admiralty. It was at this sorry juncture, writes his fellow Cornishman and first biographer, Charles Vinicombe Penrose (a man with Russian service contacts of his own),[20] that the lieutenant's "ardent mind embraced the World as his country, and he formed a Plan."[21] The plan was offered to the minister plenipotentiary for Russia in Great Britain, Semen R. Vorontsov (1744–1832).

From Trevenen's point of view, there could have been no better Russian representative; nor could the timing of his letter to the minister, who was the brother of the president of the Imperial Commerce Commission, have been happier. Vorontsov, a lifelong Anglophile, was aware of Anglo-Russian naval contacts and had powerful connections of his own in British Admiralty circles.[22] As was proper in his post, he had been following developments both in the international search for the elusive northern passage to the Orient and in the North Pacific fur trade. Only recently, he knew, a trusted agent of Siberian fur trading interests named Fedor I. Shemelin had presented formal plans to send a European vessel to Kamchatka, the Northwest Coast, and China. The vessel was to carry bulk provisions for the settlements of Petropavlovsk and Okhotsk, taking whatever route her captain might consider the most economical. She should be Russian-built and manned, if possible, but otherwise an Anglo-Russian venture might be contemplated.[23] Vorontsov had also learned of Captain Hanna's trading coup. Within six weeks of *his* arrival on the Coast from India, the English captain had obtained five hundred otter skins in prime condition. He had sold them for some 20,000 piastres.[24] Now the hunt for the sea otter was proceeding in a region to which Russia had a claim. An edict had been issued on the matter on 22 December 1786, which Vorontsov had read through only days before Trevenen's letter reached him. Peltry, poaching, and the North Pacific fur trade were in consequence still on his mind. In recent weeks, more British vessels were reported to have traded with the Aleuts and the Tlingit Indians, whom Russians called Kolosh, exchanging guns, powder, and ironware for skins. The expedition led by Comte de La Pérouse was one more factor in a troublesome equation. Who could better guard the Russian North

Pacific interest than the ex-servant of the British navy? Given Catherine's new stance towards the British and Bostonian fur poachers,[25] the Trevenen plan to send three vessels from the Baltic Sea to deal with them seemed promising. A year before, the empress had been wary when confronted by the distant possibility of conflict with the British, French, or Spanish in the North Pacific area. Her latest edict was assertive.[26]

Trevenen's "North Pacific Project" had been drafted with a view to catching Vorontsov's and, later, Catherine's attention. It was basically commercial in its objects, but it lent itself to other, more warlike ends. Being adaptable, it answered the needs of the new policy, expressed as follows by the edict of 22 December 1786: "To Russia must belong the American coast from latitude 55°21′N. extending northward... all the islands situated near the mainland and... extending westward in a chain, as well as... the Kurile Islands of Japan."[27] Vorontsov speedily forwarded the Project, with his own stamp of approval, to his mistress. She responded favourably. "Lieutenant Trevenen," she declared through Vorontsov, "may rest assured that by quitting the English service he shall not only lose nothing, but shall find it *much* to his advantage."[28] Trevenen sailed from Harwich in the Helvoetsluys packet on 2 June 1787. In his luggage went the North Pacific Project, of which extracts follow:

Feb. 1787

NORTH PACIFIC PROJECT

The plan has for its immediate objects: 1) the augmenting the consequence of Kamchatka and its value to Russia by increasing its commerce to America for furs. 2) A consequence of the first, the increase of trade with China. The accomplishment of these will open the prospect for others, secondary indeed, but no less important and by no means chimerical: 1. The opening a trade with Japan... ; 2. The creating an excellent nursery for Russian seamen by means of navigation which will make them acquainted with the varieties of climate and manoeuvre. 3. The augmenting the Imperial revenue....

We will begin with the first article. In order to carry this prospect into execution with effect, it will be necessary to equip three stout ships in Europe and send them round Cape Horn to Kamchatka. These vessels must be loaded with those articles which are best adapted to commerce with the inhabitants of America and which are not to be procured in Kamchatka.... It will be proper to embark on the ships a more than ordinary proportion of armourers, smiths, and shipwrights. The ships, which ought to sail from Europe in the month of September, will touch at some Spanish or Portuguese part of South

America, and after having doubled Cape Horn will proceed to some of the Islands in the South Sea. . . . They will employ the summer in collecting furs the whole length of the Coast. . . .

The second object, viz., the augmenting of trade from Kamchatka to China, naturally follows from the first; for it appears to us beyond a doubt that the consumption of China will be equal to any quantity of furs that America can supply. . . . We have reason to believe that it will be very possible to open communications with ports nearer to Pekin. To this effect, we propose that two out of the three ships shall quit the coast of America early enough to be able to arrive at Kamchatka, disembark the artisans and all provisions for that colony, and be ready to depart by the beginning of September, leaving the third ship on the Coast of America employed in collecting furs. These ships will return by way of China and the Cape of Good Hope and will bring home to Russia the productions of the East. . . .

We have already remarked the advantage that must result to the seamen in regard to practical manoeuvre. Russia will be supplied with all the produce of the East Indies in her own ships, it will afford a considerable exportation of her own manufacture, and create an equally considerable nursery of seamen. . . . And it will become as necessary as advantageous to Russia to keep always a respectable force at Kamchatka. . . .

Some little islands of little consequence may remain undiscovered within the immense extent of the South Seas. . . . The Empress of Russia will have the glory of putting the finishing stroke to the so much celebrated discoveries of the maritime nations, and of rendering the geography of the globe perfect. . . . Of the three ships that go out from Europe, one ought to be of 500 tons, the others of 300 tons each.[29]

Trevenen's project was prophetic and in many ways prefigured that adopted by the Russian government in 1802–3, when the *Nadezhda* and *Neva* were readied for their voyage. As he urged, those vessels watered and provisioned in a port of South America (Brazil) before proceeding round the Horn to fertile "Islands in the South Sea" (the Marquesas and Hawaiian archipelagoes). They carried trading articles of the variety envisaged by Trevenen, and their officers strove to begin a trade with Japanese as well as Chinese merchants. Finally, their voyage did indeed result in minor geographical discoveries and did indeed serve as a "nursery for seamen."[30] "Being very willing to employ this officer," the empress wrote to Vorontsov, "I leave you to forward the affair. . . There is nothing to prevent such an expedition as he is proposing."[31]

Making haste, Trevenen suffered great delays en route from Holland to the Russian Baltic Provinces. He fractured his leg and lay immobile in a tavern in Livonia for fifty days, racked both by fever and by panic lest a golden chance of earning fame be lost. Not till September did he reach St. Petersburg, in shaky health; and on the road he heard things to depress his spirits.[32] On 9 September, the empress had at last issued a counter-proclamation to the Ottoman Porte's declaration of hostilities five weeks earlier. It thus became unlikely that a first-rate naval unit, which could serve against the Turks, would be released to sail slowly[33] round the globe. Still more depressing was the news that for some weeks four Navy vessels had been fitting out at Kronstadt for a passage to the North Pacific Ocean, if they had not sailed already, thus conceivably avoiding an imperial embargo that could now be expected. One Grigorii Ivanovich Mulovskii was to lead, or would have led, that four-ship squadron.

Trevenen had not named Port Jackson in his project as the likeliest of resting and revictualling stations for a North Pacific-bound or, for that matter, a returning Russian squadron. Nor had Billings when, in late July 1786, he had suggested to the Admiralty College that the cumbersome and complex expedition he was leading should return by sea to Kronstadt from Kamchatka once its work in the remote Northeast of Asia had been done. ("Will orders not be issued... to return around the Cape of Good Hope and straight to Kronstadt port, with a view to diffusing knowledge and the naval arts? This apart, all the objects and rarities collected could be delivered intact with more convenience and smaller risk."[34] Even so, just by bringing such proposals to the government's attention, Billings and Trevenen set the stage for the eventual despatching of a squadron round the world.

THE PROPOSED MULOVSKII EXPEDITION

Captain Grigorii Ivanovich Mulovskii's squadron consisted of two larger vessels, *Kolmogór* (600 tons) and *Solovki* (530), and two smaller ones, the *Sokol* and the *Turukhtan* (both about 450 tons).[35] It had been commissioned in the White Sea ten months previously, ostensibly for purposes of commerce and discovery in North Pacific waters. In reality, as could at once have been deduced from their acknowledged destination and the nature of the vessels' reconfiguring, Mulovskii and his men were to comprise an armed deterrent in an area to which the Russian Crown laid claim and which it now perceived to be threatened by the British, the New Englanders, and—since the call of the *Boussole* and *Astrolabe* at L'tua Bay—even the French.[36]

Catherine's private secretary, Pavel Soimonov, had no doubt that La
Pérouse's venture was, like Cook's, basically an imperialist probing for
such wealth as could be found at Russia's far Northeastern doorstep—or
indeed within her house.[37] Had not the British effectively slipped through
a wealthy Russian province, undetected till for reasons of necessity they
had arrived at Petropavlovsk? Reacting to an escalating problem in the
East, Soimonov sent a memoir headed "Notes on Trade and Hunting in
the Eastern Ocean" to both Count A. R. Vorontsov, head of the Commerce College, and Count Ivan G. Chernyshev, now director at the Admiralty College.[38] Both officials liked its message: that the influence of
foreigners was swiftly growing in Canton and would most probably result
in the decline of Kiakhta-Mai-mai-ch'eng as an important fur-mart; that
the British had commercial and imperial designs on "certain Russian
forts and islands"; and that common sense dictated the despatching of
armed vessels from the Baltic to the North Pacific Ocean. Thus originated
the ukase of 22 December 1786, which included these directions for the
Admiralty College: "The College... shall send forthwith two ships
armed like those employed by Captain Cook and by other mariners on
discovery, together with two small armed sloops. The latter shall be Navy
craft or not, as the College may think best."[39]

The College acted quickly under pressure. A committee was established to determine, among other things, routes for the vessels. Peter
Pallas wrote a scientific programme for Mulovskii and his officers to follow in the North and South Pacific. And a formal invitation to accompany
the coming expedition in a senior capacity and to assist in planning it was
sent to George Forster in Vilno, where he now held a chair of botany.[40]
The ships themselves, meanwhile, were prepared for "ocean cruising":
wooden strips coated with pitch were affixed below the waterline, masts
were strengthened and rigging altered.[41]

That Mulovskii's enterprise was to be different from all preceding ones
in the Pacific was apparent from the relatively minor role that the Academy of Sciences was playing in its complex preparation. To be sure,
Pallas attended certain meetings. His opinions, however, did not domi-
nate proceedings as Delisle's had at the time of Bering's Second Expedition[42] or as Lomonosov's had during the 1760s. If Mulovskii's expedition
had departed, as it very nearly did, its members would no doubt have undertaken useful scientific work. Yet the very fact that Forster did not join
it is significant in retrospect: it was an accurate reflection of the venture's
proper purpose, which, being naval and strategic, had little need of German learning.[43]

One must add in defence of George Forster and especially his father
Johann Reinhold, however, that they understood that the imperial author-

ities were counting less on George's undoubted academic competence or organizing skills than on his long experience of seaborne science. Both well recognized the length and huge discomfort of a voyage from the Baltic to Kamchatka and the Coast, the elder Forster writing grimly on that subject:

> I am really afraid that under the command of a Russian, who seldom leaves his natural ferocity. . . you may not suffer much on this expedition, perhaps be destroyed by the hardships, frettings, Scurvy. . . & other miseries. . . with the worst of Seamen, bad accommodations, wretched Barbers instead of Surgeons, indifferent, ignorant, overbearing Officers; in a Sea where they are utter strangers.[44]

The "Sea" in question was, of course, the Great South Sea. By 25 August 1787, when Johann Reinhold sent these sombre lines from Halle, he and George had both read newspaper reports in which the musings of the Admiralty College-Senate "routes committee" were unmistakably reflected.[45] That joint committee, which had been at work since March, had come to grips with the inevitable problem of a long, unhealthy passage through the South Sea and the tropics.[46] Inexperienced in tropical conditions, Russian bureaucrats persisted through the eighteenth century in viewing them as almost fatal to their countrymen and in exaggerating the dangers attendant on all voyaging south of the line.[47]

The routes committee recommended that Mulovskii's squadron make for South America by the established, well-known route employed by foreign merchantmen, but not attempt to round Cape Horn. Instead, it recommended that it head east, around South Africa, and thence around New Holland or through the Sunda Strait, as conditions might suggest.[48] In either case, an element of greater safety under steady and assisting winds would have been purchased at the cost of quicker passage. Rest and victualling calls would, by extension, be essential. The squadron would anticipate a safe and useful stop at the Hawaiian (Sandwich) Islands, then divide into two units. Two vessels would proceed with an investigation of the Kurile Islands, of the River Amur's estuary, and of Sakhalin (Sagalinanga-gata). Meanwhile, commanded by Mulovskii, the other two would make for Nootka Sound. Sailing from there to the latitude where, in July 1741, Bering's second-in-command, Captain-Lieutenant Aleksei I. Chirikov had first sighted the mainland of America,[49] Mulovskii would "possess himself of that whole coast" in Russia's name. He would deposit iron crests marked with the year and the Russian state insignia at certain places, indicating sovereignty, and would "level and destroy" any such "Signs of other Powers" as he chanced on.[50] The whole coastline of the continent northward from 55° would be annexed with proper ceremony.[51]

Notwithstanding Catherine's belated cancellation of Mulovskii's venture,[54] the instructions issued to him are replete with points of interest. First, they remind us of the growing strength and meaning of the Anglo-Russian naval link. The Admiralty College was very willing to draw lessons from the British where long ocean voyages and practice on the high seas were concerned. What could be borrowed to advantage should be borrowed or adapted: maps, equipment, even "stoves for the distilling of sea water into pure."[53] Second, they give early evidence that an essential difficulty in all efforts to maintain a naval squadron in the East was understood: that, lacking dockyards in the far Northeast, the Russian government must keep on sending ships around the world at great expense. The moral was straightforward. Either adequate facilities for the construction and repair of naval vessels of some size must be acquired, or the Crown must bear the burden of maintaining its authority and dignity so far away. As Soimonov justly emphasized, "equipping three or four frigates in *those* waters is quite as costly as equipping a whole fleet in Europe; and furthermore no little time would be needed for such an undertaking."[54] But, of course, whether or not the Russian Navy had appropriate facilities in the remote Northeast, it would continue to be crucial to have friendly ports of call along the routes to Petropavlovsk-in-Kamchatka. And Mulovskii's orders, lastly, indicate to what extent Russian awareness of New Holland was expanding in the late 1780s. No longer, as it seriously weighed the pros and cons of a Russian company and possibly a valuable cargo clawing round a storm-racked, menacing Cape Horn, had Count Chernyshev's College only academic interest in New South Wales and Hawaii. After all, by declining to take the westward route to the Pacific, Catherine's navy was effectively committed to a policy of taking full advantage of the British colonies and Dutch possessions in the East and the Pacific. In the circumstances, Russian visits to New Holland might be seen as almost inevitable.

TREVENEN, MULOVSKII, KRUZENSHTERN

The plans of Trevenen, Mulovskii, and Forster to bring the Russian flag into the Great South Sea promptly collapsed with the eruption of hostilities on two fronts: with the Porte in the South and with the Swedes in the Baltic. As was usual in Russo-Turkish wars, it was supposed that full control of the Black Sea would bring immediate strategic gains to the controlling side. Among the fifteen Russian ships ordered to hasten to the eastern Mediterranean with this in view was *Rodislav*, Trevenen's frigate.[55] As was frequently Trevenen's lot, however, his position was abruptly altered by political developments abroad. The Swedish declaration of war led to an action between warships within days, and both Trevenen and Mulovskii saw much gunfire over the next two years. In July 1790, Trevenen received a thigh wound that proved fatal.[56] Mulovskii too was dead within the year.

Before they died the two men met several times. Mulovskii's ship, the *Mstislav*, was on station with the *Rodislav* in 1789. It was accordingly predictable that even midshipmen would meet on some occasions. Trevenen had at least one pleasant meeting with a Baltic German midshipman, named Kruzenshtern, serving in the *Mstislav*. The latter was to realize large portions of his own and Mulovskii's thwarted North Pacific plans, bringing the Russians one step closer to Port Jackson. In Lieutenant Kruzenshtern, indeed, the North Pacific outlooks and ambitions of Trevenen and the prosperous Kamchatka-based fur traders were surprisingly and happily combined and reconciled.[57] Kruzenshtern was the embodiment of the connection between Anglo-Russian maritime entente and Russian mercantile-imperial ambition in the North Pacific basin. It was natural that in the South Pacific context he should also be the link between the age of Cook and Billings and an age of Russian visits to Port Jackson.

Born at Haggud (Gongund) in Estonia (in Russian, Estliandiia), Johann-Anton von Kruzenshtern (in Russian, Ivan Fedorovich) came of a noble Baltic family of distant German origin.[58] It was the custom for the younger sons of Baltic German families long settled in Estonia to join the Navy or, more commonly, the Guards.[59] Haggud lay relatively close to Reval, modern-day Tallin, which was then a major Russian naval base. Kruzenshtern entered the Naval Cadet Corps in his fifteenth year and shone in every class. At the outbreak of the Russo-Swedish war, he was placed aboard the *Mstislav*. Thus, in May 1788, was forged the first link in a chain of circumstances and events that was to bind him to the North Pacific enterprise for thirty years. It is certain that Mulovskii spoke to Kruzenshtern and others in his ship of the aborted Pacific expedition that he was to have commanded and of happenings along the Northwest Coast of North America.[60] Kruzenshtern was with Mulovskii when he died. Also aboard the *Mstislav* at the time, to reinforce Pacific consciousness, was a Lieutenant Iakov Bering, Vitus Bering's lineal descendant.[61] And the commander of the squadron was Rear-Admiral Vasilii Ia. Chichagov (1726–1809), once the leader of a naval expedition (1765) to the ice northwest of Spitzbergen en route, in theory, to the Pacific.[62] There were patterns of example and suggestion round the youthful Kruzenshtern, and his awareness of the Pacific, thus enhanced on Baltic duty, grew even keener when, in 1794, he went to England as a Russian Volunteer. Such secondment to the Royal Navy was a mark of high professional promise. Kruzenshtern, who was expected to remain abroad three years, was placed aboard HMS *Thetis* (thirty-eight guns). His travelling companion and friend, Lieutenant Iurii F. Lisianskii (1773–1839), an intelligent and bluff Ukrainian,[63] was appointed to the ship *L'Oiseau*.[64] Both sailed for North America with Rear-Admiral George Murray, whose brother was commanding *Thetis*, on 17 May 1794.[65]

The Russians had professional and personal connections, for the next several years, with a dozen British officers with Russian interests and some experience of Eastern waters; and by virtue of their duties on secondment, they spent time in many British ports and colonies (Bermuda, Antigua, Barbados, Guiana, Nova Scotia), whose administrative practices and commerce they examined.[66] They recalled that Russia too had island-colonies. They sought extension of their leave, which was granted, though without pay. From the West, they turned their thoughts to the East Indies. Kruzenshtern returned to England with Lisianskii and Trevenen's academically inclined brother-in-law, Charles Vinicombe Penrose, after an absence of some thirty months.[67] Wasting no time, he sought assistance from S. R. Vorontsov, now full ambassador in London, in developing a plan that he had nurtured: to proceed to the East Indies and, if possible, to China; to consider how the British were effectively controlling sections of the China trade with the assistance of their navy; and to see what countermeasures might be taken to increase the Russians' economic and strategic influence in the Far East.

> For several years past [wrote Kruzenshtern a few years later], the confined state of the active trade of Russia had occupied my thoughts. During the time that I was serving with the English Navy in the revolutionary war of 1793–99, my attention was particularly excited by the importance of the English trade with the East Indies and China. It appeared to me by no means impossible for Russia to participate in the trade by sea with China and the Indies. The chief obstruction... was the want of people capable of commanding merchant ships.... I determined upon going myself to India.[68]

Captain Charles Boyles of *Raisonnable,* then at Spithead, was instructed to give passage to Cape Colony, South Africa, to three young Russians: Kruzenshtern, Lisianskii, and Baskakov. From the Cape, seized from the Dutch by British forces only eighteen months before, the Russian passengers were to proceed, when next a navy vessel could assist them, to

Bengal. The Russians left for Africa on 21 March 1797.[69]

At first, on Baltic duty, the Russians' links with officers who had experience of Eastern waters had been few in number and coincidental. As they served with distinction in British warships on the North Atlantic station,[70] the factor of coincidence decreased, for there were numerous such officers around them and they came to seek their company. Now, at the Cape, they were alert to sights and incidents that underlined the huge significance and value of the "English trade with the East Indies" and of British naval dominance in the Pacific. As it happened, there were several high-ranking officers at Cape Town or at the Navy's base of Simonstown when Kruzenshtern, Lisianskii, and Baskakov visited, who had not only first-hand knowledge of the China trade and commerce at Canton, but also genuine pro-Russian sympathies. Lisianskii in particular, who was detained in southern Africa a year (1797–98) by a bout of yellow fever first contracted on the Caribbean island of Antigua,[71] was the beneficiary of their experience. No British officer could fail to recognize the value of the friendship between Russia and Great Britain in the struggle with Napoleonic France. Nor could Lisianskii's own personal service in that struggle be dismissed. Taken together, these immediate and general considerations weighed immensely in Lisianskii's and the other Russians' favour at the Cape and also later in Bengal. It was as though, through wartime service and the Russian government's hostility towards the new and revolutionary France, the young lieutenants had obtained a cousin's right to at least a degree of genuinely useful information. What they sought, it bears repeating, did not bear upon Cape Colony itself.[72] It was the East and the Pacific that concerned them.

Having nothing to detain him but an obligation to the British Board of Admiralty, Kruzenshtern soon took his leave of Simonstown aboard *L'Oiseau*. In modern terms, he worked his passage to Madras and thence, aboard another vessel, to Calcutta. Being indigent (his government had ceased to pay him) and obliged to keep the favour of the British who could give him onward passage, he then served as officer aboard a frigate cruising in the Bay of Bengal for fourteen weeks.[73] In Calcutta he made useful contacts with the representatives of leading merchant houses such as Daniel and Thomas Beale and the associates of J. H. Cox and David Reid,[74] and with a fellow Baltic German, Karl von Torckler, who had traded at Kamchatka and along the Northwest Coast of North America some four years previously in a chartered merchantman, *La Flavia*.[75] Torckler had much to say about the North Pacific fur trade from which Russia was excluded still; the Reids about the Bengal Fur Society. Such information and such knowledge of the "country trade" as Kruzenshtern now gained, at the expense of his own health, proved very useful six years later at Canton, when he arrived there with *Nadezhda* and *Neva*.[76] It was on China, indeed, that all his thoughts were focused now; nor, when he reached it after many months of illness and frustration in Malacca, did it disappoint him.

LISIANSKII IN THE SOUTH AND LOOKING SOUTHWARD, 1797–1800

Kruzenshtern having departed for Madras aboard *L'Oiseau*, Lisianskii had no option but to make the close acquaintance of the British naval officers then stationed at the Cape. But duty quickly proved a pleasure. Both the officer commanding the efficient squadron then at Simonstown, Vice-Admiral Sir Thomas Pringle, and his second-in-command, Commodore John J. Blankett, were hospitable and courteous. Pringle had but lately served with Admiral Lord Duncan and Vice-Admiral M. I. Makarov in the Anglo-Russian joint blockade of the Dutch coast, which, more than any other naval operation of the nineties, had impressed the fact of Anglo-Russian amity on Paris.[77] In the course of that successful operation in the North Sea, he had met and liked several Russians. Few knew more than Pringle did about the movements and commerce of the Dutch in the East Indies. Having first settled Lisianskii into the frigate *Sceptre* (Captain Edwards), he did nothing to repress the Russian's keenness to learn anything he could about those Indies and the trade that centred on them.[78] As for Blankett, he had even stronger personal and service links with Russia. As a midshipman in Canada in 1759, his curiosity had been aroused about the possible existence of a navigable Arctic passage to the Orient.[79] Also disturbed by thoughts of Russian hegemony in the far Northeast of Asia and perhaps along the Northwest Coast of North America, he had in 1763 made an officially acknowledged working visit to St. Petersburg, collecting data on the cossacks' ventures off Kamchatka and activities on the Aleutian Islands. His report had stressed the maritime potential and resources of Kamchatka. In the future national interest, he argued, Cabinet should cultivate the Russians' friendship.[80] (After all, might it not serve to squeeze both French and Spanish influence out of the North Pacific basin?) Blankett too was well disposed towards a Russian Volunteer. As a former captain of the *Thetis,* in which Kruzenshtern had also served, and as a visitor to China,[81] he could hold their interest. Even the Governor himself, Earl Macartney (1737–1806), whose tenure at the Cape practically coincided with Lisianskii's sojourn there, made no effort to conceal his own fond memories of Russia. As a youthful diplomat with good political connections, he had spent three years (1764–67) negotiating a commercial treaty in St. Petersburg. (More recently, in 1793–94, he had been envoy to the Emperor of China and, like Blankett, he had come to recognize the vast potential of the China trade and Britain's stake in Eastern waters.)[82]

When his duties on the *Sceptre* would allow, Lisianskii, taking full advantage of his situation, went inland to take a look at the plantations of the long-entrenched Dutch colonists, to ponder their treatment of the Hottentots (the half-caste children of the slave women, Khoi, were everywhere apparent), and to botanize. Later, when his health was stronger, he made longer journeys to the veld, collecting herbaria and studying the Africans he met. In Table Bay and on the seashore, he collected shells.[83] He was a man of many interests, possessed of genuinely scientific instincts. Necessarily, his thoughts turned to the southernness of Cape Town, of which Khoi, local flora, Boer speech, and even the night sky served as regular reminders. A cruise to the remote Atlantic colony and naval base of St. Helena in 1798 increased his consciousness of Britain's need for distant outposts: it, too, he soon understood, assisted Britain to develop and increase her trade *far* to the east. As he put it in a letter to his brother Ananii, "Africa itself, and especially its southern tip, are entirely necessary for those sailing to the east of it."[84]

Lisianskii finally left Cape Colony in *Sceptre*, reaching Madras on 7 November 1798. From Madras he went on to Bombay. Three months in India sufficed to make him realize that he was anxious to press on, southward and eastward. In Bengal, he had learned something of Lieutenant Matthew Flinders's survey work in the *Norfolk*, then proceeding on the coast of New South Wales north of Sydney. Flinders's earlier successes in the eight-foot-long *Tom Thumb* had reached Madras some time before. In recent weeks, it had been said that London was intending to dispatch another, more impressive scientific and surveying expedition to New Holland.[85] Such plans caught the imagination of Lisianskii in March 1799. He had already looked at British island colonies in the West Indies, and he welcomed any chance to see another in the South Pacific Ocean. He was quite familiar with Captain George Vancouver's recent *Voyage of Discovery* (London, 1798), with its description of Van Diemen's Land and first-rate maps; and it was obvious that there was work still to be done around New Holland by professional hydrographers with energy, like Flinders and himself. For all these reasons, he was tempted by the thought of joining Flinders if permission could be gained to do so. But Lisianskii went no further east that season. As he put it in a still unpublished diary, held at the Central Naval Museum (TsVMM) in Leningrad:

I had only just started to fit myself out for a voyage to New Holland, in a small frigate that had instructions to survey those parts. . . . I feared, however, the authorities might not be pleased with my going. . . and so did not proceed.

He was shortly after ordered to return to active duty in the Baltic.[86] Loyal but frustrated, he took passage on a homeward-bound Indiaman, the *Royalist,* bringing his plans to visit China and New Holland back to Europe for a final eighteen months of incubation.[87] At Kronstadt in 1800, he was given command of a new frigate. He was twenty-eight years old.

CIRCUMNAVIGATION PLANS: LIEUTENANT KRUZENSHTERN
IN CHINA, 1798–99

Kruzenshtern, meanwhile, had arrived in, studied, and departed from Canton, seat of the new and fast-expanding Coast-to-Canton seaborne fur trade. Everything he had been told about that trade by Daniel and Thomas Beale and their agents in Bengal he quickly verified at first-hand in Canton.[88] During his stay, several vessels came directly from the North-west Coast laden with otter skins. Among these vessels was the *Caroline,* ex-*Dragon* (Captain Lay),[89] a little sloop-rigged craft of barely fifty tons.

> She had been fitted out in Macao. The whole voyage did not occupy above five months, and the cargo, which consisted entirely of furs, was sold for 60,000 piastres. . . . It appeared to me that the advantages would be infinitely greater if the Russians were to bring their goods to Canton direct from the Islands or the American Coast. During my voyage from China [in the Indiaman *Bombay Castle*], I drew up a memoir with the intention of handing it over to M. von Soimonoff, at that time minister of commerce. . . . I proposed that two ships should be sent from Cronstadt to the Aleutic islands and to America, with every kind of material necessary for the construction and outfit of vessels; and that they should likewise be provided with skilful shipwrights, workmen of all kinds, a teacher in navigation, as well as charts, books, nautical and astronomical instruments. The money obtained from the sale of furs in Canton should be appropriated to the purchase of Chinese wares, which could be sent to Russia in ships fitted out in the Eastern Sea.[90]

Thus, in the introduction to his *Voyage Round the World . . .* , printed in Russian at the government's expense (1809–13) and soon translated into

English (1814) and a half-dozen other languages,[91] did a phlegmatic Kruzenshtern describe the genesis of Russian circumnavigation, one result of which was a predictable series of Russian naval visits to Australia starting in 1807. Kruzenshtern was a particularly self-controlled and balanced officer, and he wrote with studied objectivity, the more so in a state-financed, official narrative and record like the *Voyage*. His deliberately paced, cool prose does not reflect, but rather hides, the tension and excitement he experienced while in Canton. For that, we must perforce look to his private correspondence, which, regrettably, remains largely unpublished to this day. (It has been carefully preserved and organized by the authorities of TsGIAE, the Central State Historical Archive of the Estonian SSR, Tartu, Estonia.)[92] In fact, the Canton sojourn was a time of new horizons, new and unexpected friendships in the European merchant colony,[93] deep impressions, and continual surprises. On the one hand, Kruzenshtern was coming to appreciate the fact that if the Russians did not move beyond the confines of the rigid Kiakhta system fairly soon, the British and American free-traders, now so active in the seaborne peltry trade, would undermine and end that inland trade.[94] On the other hand, he was fast coming to terms with the immense naval and economic implications of a Russian seaborne answer to the challenge of the English-speaking nations on the Coast and in Canton.

Even before coming to China, Kruzenshtern had learned of the persistent lack of solid vessels and efficient seamen at Okhotsk to bring sea otter skins from the Aleutians straight to the great peltry mart on the Whampoa River. At Okhotsk, indeed, there were so many rotting cossack traders' vessels that a commandant, Captain Minitskii, would be speaking of "a regular museum" of the shipwright's art.[95] Often, two years would elapse between the sending of supplies and foodstuffs from Irkutsk to the Pacific outposts and the day that they arrived at Kodiak, commonly spoiled by a drenching.[96] It was obvious to Kruzenshtern that Russian shipping, overcoming all such obstacles, must enter Chinese ports in competition with the British and Americans.[97] Thus did political and mercantile considerations lead directly to reflections of a purely naval sort. What Russian ships should sail to Canton, at whose expense, and by what route? As the Soviet naval historian Vladimir Nevskii rightly emphasized in 1951 in introducing "the first voyage of Russians round the world" to a new Soviet audience, the second part of Kruzenshtern's memoir of 1799 was wholly given over to "a demonstration of the need to improve the Russian Navy," by means of long voyages, till it reached the level of the best foreign fleets. "Russia should catch up with foreign navies, the British in particular, in the science of such voyaging. And to this end, Kruzenshtern proposed that not only youths of noble birth but youths of every other condition also be admitted to the Naval Cadet Corps.''[98]

As his comrade Lisianskii had benefitted in South Africa and in Bengal from Anglo-Russian amity, so in Canton did Kruzenshtern. Among those British residents who offered him the benefit of their experience of life and trade in China were Sir George Staunton (1781–1856), who had accompanied Macartney's embassy in 1793; James Drummond, then chief factor of the East India Company; and principals of Beale, Shank, and Magniac and Company (whence sprang the celebrated company of Jardine, Matheson and Company).[99] To be aware of the international commerce of the town and of the scope, value, and rapidly evolving trading patterns of the ships in the Whampoa was itself, however, to receive an education. Kruzenshtern was a perceptive officer. He took an interest in the mechanics of the seaborne China trade and, by extension, in the routes taken, both to and from Canton, by foreign merchantmen. Under these circumstances, it was inevitable that he would be reminded periodically of the British colony established twelve years earlier in New South Wales.

> One would not, certainly, assert that this Australian enterprise concerned the China trade immediately. . . . It was to disencumber British prisons full to overflowing that. . . the first convoy had left Portsmouth in May 1787 and reached Botany Bay the following January, putting off a party of 717 convicts. Still, a certain connection with China had been established very soon. . . . In 1794, merely six years after the foundation of the little colony on the eastern coast of New South Wales, Captain Butler of the Honourable Company Ship *Walpole* had passed round Australia and Tasmania on his passage from the Cape to Canton. And this link had also taken a more concrete and, above all, more profitable form: instead of returning empty, transports that had deposited their cargoes of convicts at Botany Bay had begun to call at Canton, taking on tea for London. This movement had started as early as 1788, with visits by three such vessels.[100]

As Louis Dermigny, the eminent French annalist of European commerce at Canton, proceeds to emphasize, these early and direct connections between New South Wales and Canton were affected only slightly by official Chinese efforts to cut them. Faced with an order (1796) that no foreign ship might enter the Whampoa if she brought no saleable (and therefore dutiable) cargo, London agents of the Company merely placed a little lead, always in short supply in China, in the holds of transports carrying fresh convicts to the colony. Thus, access to Canton was guaranteed at slight expense, and very serviceable contact with the colony and with Batavia and other parts was maintained to the advantage of Company and government alike.[101] To Kruzenshtern, who knew a good deal about New Holland from the published works of Forster, Cook, and Zimmermann, the very fact that British traders could export Chinese black tea to New South Wales was a striking demonstration of the value of a European colony per se. When, he reflected, would the day come when the North Pacific colonies of Russia could assist her economy in such a way, importing goods at something close to international market price? When would the Russians cope with the New Englanders in the Pacific, as the British could, by making *use* of distant colonies, acknowledging their value to the state and recognizing their political and mercantile importance?[102] With regard to the New Englanders who had become so enterprising in the seaborne China trade during the 1790s, they had been practically declawed as a trade menace by the fact that Britain had such far-flung colonies. Kruzenshtern develops this thought in Volume 2 of his *Voyage Round the World* (Chapter Eleven: "An Account of China"). One hardly need belabour the significance of such allusions to New Holland as the following, as indications of that colony's reality to Kruzenshtern and other forward-looking Russian naval officers by 1800:

> In 1789 the Americans sent fifteen ships there [to Canton], and their commerce has increased in the same proportion as that of other nations, with the exception of the English, has declined. The English trade cannot, however, as was at first feared, receive any injury... all the Chinese goods shipped on board of English vessels being consumed either in England... or in their extensive colonies in the East and West Indies, in America, and New Holland.[103]

Kruzenshtern returned to England in 1799 with an East India Company convoy of more than twenty vessels, several of whose captains had visited New Holland. His thoughts, however, were directed not to the remote Southwest Pacific but to Kronstadt and St. Petersburg, where the case for Russian circumnavigation must be made. Anxious to waste no time, he forwarded a copy of his memoir from London to the minister of commerce, Count I. Soimonov. The response was coldly formal. Kruzenshtern's Pacific projects were immediately shelved. Even attempts to interest the leading speculative merchants of St. Petersburg and Moscow came to nothing.[104] Hurt and bitter, he thought briefly of retiring to an estate, even of teaching at the grammar school in Reval, in his beloved

Estonia. He hesitated, and a small delay sufficed: Tsar Paul was murdered, and with the accession to the throne of Alexander I, a new and (temporarily) more liberal era began.

THE KRUZENSHTERN-LISIANSKII EXPEDITION, 1803–6

It was Kruzenshtern's fortune to deal, in 1801, with a new naval minister, Admiral Nikolai S. Mordvinov (1754–1845), whose experiences as a Russian Volunteer with the Royal Navy on the North Atlantic station (1771–74), lifelong interest in commerce, broadly liberal political persuasions, and awareness of the Pacific he himself completely shared.[105] Mordvinov, who immediately recognized the value and potential of the memoir as "rearranged" by Kruzenshtern early in 1802, gave it his blessing and presented it for comment to Count Nikolai P. Rumiántsev, the Chancellor and minister of commerce.[106] He too signalled his support. Rumiántsev's interest, almost essential though it was for an imperial involvement in the enterprise that was envisaged, made it virtually certain that the naval and commercial aspects of that enterprise would be confused and interwoven.[107] And, in that respect, it bore directly on the nature of the coming naval visits to Australia.

For Rumiántsev, as perforce for the monopolistic Russian-American (*Rossiisko-Amerikanskaia*) fur trading Company which had been formed in 1799 from two earlier rivals for control of the resources of the Kurile and Aleutian Island chains,[108] an expedition to the North Pacific settlements for which the Company had lately (and officially) become responsible, must be essentially commercial. Very probably, its officers would be seconded from the Navy. They, however, must regard the Navy's function in the settlements and China from an altogether mercantile perspective. In the early 1800s, as in Captain Billings's and Levashev's day, in short, strife between mercantile and naval service interests in the Pacific was inherent in the representatives of those same interests.[109] As if to guarantee continuation of these strains, it was agreed that any seaborne expedition round the globe should be financed not by the Crown alone, but jointly by the state and by the new Russian-American Company Board.[110] Open collision between Company and Navy interests in the Pacific was perhaps still quite remote when, on 7 August 1802, Mordvinov offered Kruzenshtern command of his Pacific venture.[111] Such collision became imminent when, in the spring of 1803, Rumiántsev personally made it known to Kruzenshtern that the most powerful official of the Company, who happened also to be friendly with the emperor, would be accompanying him aboard his ship to the Pacific. The official was the procurator general and "Correspondent" of the Company, Nikolai Petrovich Rezanov (1764–1807). Rezanov was the virtual director of the Company in whose employ the naval officers would be, though by a complex and original arrangement, they remained in naval service for the purposes of pay and seniority.[112] It was an augury of coming complications. Count Rumiántsev meanwhile was doing what he could to bring about collaboration between agents of the Company and of the ministry of commerce: what the Admiralty College could contribute to the venture was a bonus, in his view. "The shaky colonies of the Russian American Company," Rumiántsev noted with the Company's own chairman, Mikhail Buldakov, "could be given a sound *economic* foundation; the fur trade to China, long monopolized by Russians, might be salvaged."[113] In these overlapping, even mutually contradictory and clashing antecedents of a Navy-managed circumnavigation of the globe, that is, the Kruzenshtern-Lisianskii expedition, lay the origins of that distinctly twofold nature of ensuing Russian visits to Australia. Of the eleven Russian ships that called at Sydney up to 1825, suffice it to note in this regard, four were the Company's and on commercial business (the *Neva, Suvorov, Riurik,* and *Elena*), and seven were Navy ships on naval business—if the term may be extended to political and scientific missions.

Kruzenshtern offered Lisianskii the position of second-in-command of the whole venture and command of the smaller of the two ships to be sent because he knew him to be loyal and, above all, competent.[114] So too with other officers, he looked for steadiness of temper and a first-rate service record.[115] Meanwhile, because there were no vessels suitable for such an enterprise in Russian ports or yards, two English ships were purchased and internally adapted for Pacific voyaging. Drawing an order on the Russian government for more than £20,000, Lisianskii personally bought *Leander,* built in London in the spring of 1800 as a 425-ton sloop, and the *Thames,* fresh off the slipway and a vessel of 371 tons. *Thames* was thus only a trifle heavier than Cook's *Endeavour* of 368 tons, though without the reinforcement and the massive, blunt construction of the Whitby collier, and it appears that the Russians kept Cook's preference of ship size well in mind when forming theirs.[116] Though the purchase price and cost of alteration were considerable, both ships served the Company at least as well as was predicted by Lisianskii and far better than the Company's own naval critics would allow.[117] The two ships were renamed *Nadezhda (Hope)* and *Neva* and left for Kronstadt late in April 1803. They entered Kronstadt roads on 28 May.[118]

For Vorontsov, who as ambassador in London had materially helped

Lisianskii from the first week of his grand ship-buying mission to the last, it was a happy circumstance that Russia's new Pacific enterprise should thus renew and strengthen Anglo-Russian maritime accord.[119] He took pleasure in discussing the political significance of that accord when in society. Nor, since the coming expedition was no secret but had more than once been touched on in the Hamburg and Copenhagen papers, did he hesitate—even before he knew Rezanov was to sail in *Nadezhda* to Japan as Russian envoy—to discuss the mission's aims with English friends. The Russian ships, he freely (and of course correctly) recognized, were to proceed in company to South America, double Cape Horn, and separate at the Hawaiian (Sandwich) Islands, then head north. As the Hamburg *Gazette* had put it:

> The Russian-American Company is much concerned for the expansion of its trade, which, in time, will be extremely useful to Russia; and is now busying itself with a great enterprise of moment not only for commerce but also for the honour of the Russian nation, viz.: it is equipping two ships that will take on foodstuffs, anchors, cordage, canvas, etc at Petersburg, and will then proceed to the Northwest Coast of America. . . there take on furs, and exchange them in China for local goods.[120]

But what of the return passage to Kronstadt from the China Sea? Neither the Company main office nor the naval officers in its employ, it seemed, could give much detail to foreign journalists. It was supposed that Captain Kruzenshtern ("a most skilful officer, long in the East Indies") would return by the Cape of Good Hope as he had before.[121]

Vorontsov, we know, had in September or October 1802 received a copy of a memorandum, dated 29 July, which the Board of the Russian-American Company had submitted to the tsar through Count Rumiántsev as the minister of commerce.[122] In this formal memorandum, the reasons for a seaborne expedition to the Northwest Coast and China were laid out. The second article contained the following suggestive comments:

> The Company may well open a profitable trade in furs at Canton; and by thus initiating trade with Japan and China, the Company trusts that it may soon get the upper hand of foreign nations. On the return passage from Canton, it expects to essay trade in the settlements of foreign East Indies companies—Calcutta, Bengal, Batavia, and other places besides—where, according to Mr. Kruzenshtern who has himself been there, all ports and peoples are quite ready to receive us in a friendly way.[123]

It was, in short, made plain to Vorontsov that Kruzenshtern might well look in at Dutch or British settlements en route to Cape Town from the East and that a good deal of flexibility remained in the whole venture. Vorontsov retained these broad considerations in his mind even in April 1803 when he was finally given full details of the political and diplomatic mission to Japan as represented by *Nadezhda*'s noble passenger, Rezanov.[124] As was proper, he expressed them in diplomatic form to the authorities in London. In itself, the very fact that major diplomatic objects had been added to the scientific, naval, and commercial aims of Kruzenshtern's forthcoming venture made it necessary that the British, Dutch, and Portuguese colonial authorities be notified; and first came notices for the respective central governments. Vorontsov gave formal notice of the coming expedition to Lord Hobart, secretary of state for the colonies, who wrote to Philip Gidley King in Sydney:

London, June 1803

Sir,

His Excellency Count Woronzow, Ambassador Extra-Ordinary and Minister Plenipotentiary of His Imperial Majesty the Emperor of Russia at the Court of St. James's, having notified His Majesty's government of an intended Expedition of two Russian Vessels on a Voyage of circumnavigation and discovery. . . I am to desire that in the event of the said Vessels arriving within the limits of your government, you do afford them every assistance, and that you do give directions to the Lieutenant-Governors of the Settlements under your Command, to shew them every mark of Hospitality and Friendship which the subjects of His Imperial Majesty are entitled to expect. The names of the Vessels are the *Neva* and *Nadegada,* commanded by Captains Krusenstiern and Liseanskoy.

I have, etc.,
Hobart[125]

THE EXPEDITION AS A PRECEDENT FOR LATER VOYAGES TO THE PACIFIC

Nadezhda and *Neva* did not, after all, call in at Sydney. Had they done so, they would scarcely have been preceded by Lord Hobart's warning note, which King received only on 15 May 1804. They did, however, set important precedents for later Russian expeditions, ten of which put in at Sydney before 1825; and certain promises formally made to Vorontsov were kept in full when, in June of 1807, the *Neva* herself entered Port

Jackson on her second voyage out to the Pacific settlements. "So began a
series of voyages between the Baltic and the Bering Seas. From 1803
through 1864, at least 65 such voyages were launched. . . or roughly one
every year. Thirteen proceeded eastward via the Cape of Good Hope."[126]
Three precedents established by the Kruzenshtern-Lisianskii expedition
which directly bore on later Russian visits to Port Jackson, among other
distant parts, were the employment of particularly able officers and
seamen on a socially prestigious undertaking; the emergence of overt
hostility between the Navy and the Company, as represented by the captain and the envoy; and the emphasis placed upon science. By his attitudes as much as by his actions, Kruzenshtern went far, in 1802–6, towards determining the nature of the coming Russian visits to Australia.

To turn, first, to the matter of particularly able personnel on duty in the
South and North Pacific in the early 1800s: Makar' Ivanovich Ratmanov,
whom Kruzenshtern took as his first lieutenant in the *Nadezhda,* had
commanded ships of war for fourteen years. Second Lieutenant Fedor
Romberg had achieved renown while with the frigate *Narva,*
Golovachev, third lieutenant, while at Kronstadt. Fourth Lieutenant
Levenshtern (von Loewenstern) had served with Nelson's less than certain friend and ally, Admiral F. Ushakov, in the Mediterranean Sea
(1799–1800).[127] All were specialists, devoted to the service. It was solely
on the basis of their records that such officers, and able seamen, mates,
and surgeons too, had gained a berth aboard *Nadezhda* or *Neva.* As for
the expedition's scientists, Wilhelm Gottfried Tilesius von Tilenau
(1769–1857), naturalist, Johann Caspar Hörner (1774–1834),
astronomer, and Dr. Karl Espenberg, doctor and friend of Kruzenshtern
from Reval days,[128] they formed a circle of distinction at the expedition's
core. In a humane, pragmatic spirit, Kruzenshtern saw that his people had
the very best available supplies. It was his object to establish an esprit de
corps by handsome pay, good food, high expectations. From the outset,
he proposed to place *his* officers and crews apart from others in less fa-
voured Russian vessels. Both the Company and Navy meant, indeed, that
the Pacific seaborne service should be special, with an enviable promise
of distinction and advancement for the few. With this view, they
countenanced the disproportionately large number of German-speaking
officers whom Kruzenshtern appointed to his ship.

It was predictable that Kruzenshtern should turn a favourable eye on
Baltic Germans like himself; and a degree of local pride was proper in a
scion of the German *Herrenvolk* based in Estonia. The community
wielded a political and social influence in Russia as a whole quite disproportionate to its size or its wealth.[129] Fourth and fifth lieutenants of

Nadezhda were Hermann Ludwig von Loewenstern and Fabian Gottlieb von Bellingshausen; the latter would later command an expedition to the South Pacific Ocean of his own. Loewenstern's counterpart aboard *Neva* was Vasilii N. Berg, or Berkh, future recorder of the Russian enterprise in the Aleutians and America.[130] Also with Kruzenshtern went two young sons of August von Kotzebue, German playwright and Russian civil counsellor: the family was now living in Reval. The youths, Otto and Moritz, were supported by the emperor himself.[131] Its German element, in short, gave to the Kruzenshtern-Lisianskii expedition a yet more prestigious aura than it would in any case have had—an aura stronger at the expedition's end, in 1806, than at its start. Both Alexander and his mother went to Kronstadt to congratulate Lisianskii and to stroll over *Neva*, the first ship home from the Pacific. They were highly entertained by what they saw. The Empress Dowager left golden snuff-boxes and watches for the officers, "ten ducats" for the seamen, and a "costly diamond ring" for the commander.[132] Regardless of the expedition's failure as a mercantile and diplomatic venture (it was only by pretending to be ill that Rezanov had set foot in Japan),[133] it was regarded as a triumph by government and Company alike. There were promotions, pensions, prizes, and awards for all connected with it. When *Neva* arrived in Sydney twelve months later, it seemed natural enough that her commander should be a Russian-speaking German. Thanks in essence to a pattern that was set in 1803–4, Australia would see only the cream of Russia's navy. The fact is important in relation to the value of those officers' reports on infant Sydney.

As the distinction of those Russian naval officers who paid a visit to the Sydney or Hobart of the early nineteenth century reflected the reality aboard *Nadezhda* and *Neva* in 1803–6, however, so too did a tension between servants of the Navy and the Company which now and then surfaced in Sydney. Kruzenshtern clashed publicly and dangerously with Rezanov on the Danish coast, at Teneriffe, at the Marquesas Islands.[134] There were strains between the captain of the Company-owned ship *Suvorov*, Mikhail Petrovich Lazarev, and an employee of the Company named Herman Molvo; and these strains, as will be seen, somewhat affected the *Suvorov*'s Sydney stay in 1814.

Lastly, the scientific-academic precedent established by the Kruzenshtern-Lisianskii expedition may be amplified in the Australian and South Pacific context. It was Kruzenshtern's particular achievement to have turned his multipurpose enterprise, which had originally not been scientific in its aim, into a venture of importance to the learned world.[135] Geology and mineralogy, astronomy and physics, botany, cartography, even ethnology (in deference to Cook) were systematically pursued by the savants and officers of the *Nadezhda* and *Neva*. Repeated reckonings of latitude and longitude; checkings of compasses and other instruments purchased in London; testings of the air and water temperature, headway, water content, air humidity; inspections of the insects, larger animals, and flora of the vessels' ports of call: all went on regularly, day by day, under the watchful eyes of Hörner and the German naturalists.

We are reminded by the strict routines imposed by Kruzenshtern that twenty, even thirty, years after Cook's death, the form and very emphases of his Pacific missions were seen as proper to such ventures. Cook had received no special orders to concern himself particularly or at length with "curiosities," as ethnographica continued to be termed, on setting out on any of his voyages. That paragraph of his instructions that related to such "natives" as he might encounter in Pacific waters was, indeed, extremely terse—and the same for all three major voyages. "You are likewise to observe the Genius, Temper, Disposition and Number of the Natives, if there be any, and endeavour by all proper means to cultivate a Friendship and Alliance with them, making them presents of such Trifles as they may value, inviting them to Traffick... taking Care however not to suffer yourself to be surprized by them."[136] No word here of the scientific value of the artefacts that native tribes might "traffick": the political was to take precedence over the strictly scientific where first contact was concerned. In the *Endeavour,* it was for several reasons that Cook had sailed: first, to gaze on Venus in Tahiti; second, to discover and survey the Southern Land if possible; and, third, to complete a grand botanical design. Nonetheless, both he and Banks had shown a lively and persistent interest in native artefacts, and in the languages, beliefs, and social customs of the distant peoples they encountered; and the pattern was repeated on the second and the final voyages. Officially, the emphasis fell first upon discovery and the attendant naval sciences (hydrography, marine astronomy), then on the twin natural sciences (zoology and botany). In fact, however, Cook and his people made as full and as close a study of the natives whom they met as time allowed,[137] and, sketching, brought an infant science forward. Note was taken of techniques and customs, diet and religious practice, dress and navigation.[138] The example was not lost on Kruzenshtern or even later when another Russian naval expedition, led by Captain Fabian G. Bellingshausen, entered South Pacific waters. Held intact by Russian officers too young to have known even Cook's junior subordinates who had transferred to Russian service, Cook's very spirit was to go with Bellingshausen to Port Jackson in a way that set at nought the intervening forty years.

To the extent that the first Russian seaborne venture in the East and Polynesia was a success, it was as a training voyage and, above all, as a scientific exercise. As Cook had recognized the value of ethnology, so in his turn, had Kruzenshtern. It was on 7 May 1804 that the *Nadezhda* entered Taio-hae Bay in Nukuhiva, in the Washington-Marquesas group, the first true meeting between Slav and Polynesian.[139] For eleven days, the Russians were in daily friendly contact with a South Pacific people. The event had been exercising Kruzenshtern, who understood that such a meeting called for careful management if all the errors that had clouded the relations between other Europeans and such peoples were to be avoided. For a guide, he turned to Cook. Kruzenshtern's orders to the people of *Nadezhda,* as she coasted up to Taio-hae Bay, patently rest upon Cook's. In themselves, as a reminder of the dangers facing European captains in the South Seas—petty theft, overfamiliarity, and lethal retribution by the gun—and as a touchstone for all subsequent official dealings between Russians and Pacific peoples (for example, between Bellingshausen's seamen and the Cammeraigal people of the North Shore of Port Jackson in 1820), Kruzenshtern's "Marquesan orders" bear quotation:

The principal object of our calling at the Marquesas Islands is to water and take on fresh provisions. Though we might well accomplish all this even without the consent and goodwill of the natives, risks to them and to ourselves prevent our having recourse to any such approach. And I am sure we Russians shall leave the shores of a tranquil people without leaving behind a bad name for ourselves. . . .

It will be entirely natural if, on our arrival, new articles provoke a desire in many to possess them; and you, for your part, would very gladly barter European goods, consisting mostly of trinkets, for the various curios of these people. But lack of caution here might have very undesirable results, as the islanders, anxious to get hold of objects of ours and obtaining them in plenty in exchange for things of small value to themselves, would no doubt end by wanting things we could not surrender—before they would satisfy even our legitimate needs. It is therefore prohibited for anyone to barter with natives aboard the ship. Only when we have furnished ourselves with all provisions necessary for the continuation of our voyage shall I give sufficient notice for every man to barter his own things for others, according to his means and inclination. To ensure the orderly purchasing of foodstuffs for officers and men alike, Lieutenant Romberg and Dr Espenberg are hereby appointed. Only through them are exchanges to be made. It is emphatically reaffirmed that no member of the lower deck will use a firearm, on deck or ashore, without particular orders to that effect from the officers.[140]

To a remarkable extent, judging by subsequent accounts of the Marquesan visit, Kruzenshtern succeeded in preserving Russian seamen from temptation and averting the misfortunes he had properly foreseen.[141] It is the Russians' just boast that not one drop of blood was spilled as a result of their visits to the South Pacific Ocean, not one European sickness introduced, not one society destroyed.[142] As for the ethnographic value of the Kruzenshtern-Lisianskii expedition, which visited many parts of Polynesia (Easter Island, Nukahiva, the Hawaiian Islands), it can hardly be exaggerated. Day by day, through peaceful barter, artefacts were gathered, drawn, and stowed aboard *Nadezhda*. Like another Sydney Parkinson, the expeditionary artist, Stepan I. Kurliandtsev, painted articles in use. Natural scientists Tilesius von Tilenau and Georg Heinrich Langsdorf laid the basis of the Russian contribution to Pacific botany, zoology, and, for good measure, musicology.[143] As to the factor always present at Port Jackson but conspicuously missing from the Taio-hae Bay the Russians visited, that is, the presence of another, ruling, European force (headed by Bligh, King, or Macquarie), suffice it to remark that while that presence plainly influenced the Russians' private dealings with the native group in question[144] (for example, by imposing certain sanctions on specific forms of barter), it resulted in no obvious divergence from the attitudes of 1804—other than that to be explained by Aboriginal aloofness or the length of Russian visits to their country. Cook and Kruzenshtern together thus set standards of behaviour for the Russians in Australia and the Pacific, and established scientific emphases that would be acknowledged throughout the nineteenth century. As they afterwards recognized, Kruzenshtern formed a crucial human link for Bellingshausen and Cadet Otto von Kotzebue (1787–1846), who was also in his ship, between the present and the time of Cook's great voyages.

3

THE FIRST RUSSIAN VISITS
TO PORT JACKSON, 1807–14

NEW PERSPECTIVES ON AUSTRALIA, 1802–5

Even as the Kruzenshtern-Lisianskii expedition was unfolding, Russian booksellers were offering their customers a fresh assortment of materials relating to Australia.[1] No longer satisfied with French or Russian paraphrasts' attempts on Cook's earlier voyages or with miscellanies including passages by Zimmermann, Forster, or Hawkesworth,[2] an expanding readership looked for more recent and more varied information about places seen by Cook. Moreover, this readership rewarded publishers of Russian-language books and periodicals: Nikolai M. Karamzin's new venture, *Vestnik Evropy*, or *The Messenger of Europe*, was but one of several to turn a profit while exerting social influence by introducing Russian readers to the latest literary, social, and political developments abroad.[3] To be sure, the educated Russian reader could still turn—for lengthy pieces on Australia, for instance—to the Viennese *Magazin von Merkwürdigen neuen Reisebeschreibungen*. There, he could find the classic narratives of infant New South Wales by the likes of White and Hunter.[4] And Demeunier, Suard, and other Frenchmen had not ceased to make their major contribution to the spread of Russian knowledge of Australia: not till the later 1830s would they vanish as a factor in that sense. Nevertheless, it is appropriate to stress the simultaneous and complementary development of two new trends at the beginning of the nineteenth century, where Russian knowledge and awareness of New South Wales was concerned: a growing tendency to look to Russian-language works and an increasing readiness to view Australia in either a commercial or a Polynesian context.

Russians had been predisposed from the beginning to see Cook's

Botany Bay in an exotic South Seas sense. They were not alone in this: so had the British, French, and Germans.[5] When the second Russian edition of Zimmermann's account of his experiences in *Discovery* appeared in 1788, P. Bogdanovich, its publisher, rightly supposed he would increase its sales by embellishing the text "with an appendix describing in detail the island of Otaheiti."[6] And when, eighteen months later, Timofei I. Mozhaiskii produced his Russian version of the Reverend Andrew Kippis's seminal *Life of Captain Cook,* it was likewise made fashionably striking and exotic, by "The Morai, a Poem by Miss Elena Maria Williams."[7] This was part of a broad European trend and, not surprisingly in view of Russian sensitivity to foreign cultural and literary fashion, it persisted through the first third of the century. It was the golden age, perhaps, of travelogues, replete with quasi-Rousseauesque description, local colour, and exotically remote locales. Why, in this framework, should not Aboriginals be viewed as natives of another (rather drier) South Sea island? Why should convicts, as a theme, not be exploited for their colour and entertainment value? So they were, respectively, in Semeon Zubkov's *Brief Historical Survey of Islands Discovered... in the Most Vast Ocean... Which is Called Polynesia, Australia, or South India by the Latest Geographers* (Kursk, 1804),[8] and in Prince Aleksei Petrovich Golitsyn's translation of George Barrington's *Voyage to Botany Bay, with a Description of the Country and the Customs, Mores, and Religion of its Native People* (St. P., 1803; reprinted, 1809).[9] Titular Councillor Zubkov's work, being provincially produced, perhaps had a restricted circulation in the capitals; but this most certainly was not the case with the adventures of the celebrated Irish pickpocket and publicist George Barrington, among whose many noble victims had been Prince Grigorii Orlov; who had been sentenced to hard labour in the Thames hulks (1777–79); had thwarted a conspiracy to seize the convict ship transporting him to Sydney; and who afterwards, a free man, had been paid superintendent of the convicts.[10] To consider the career of Prince Golitsyn (1754–1824), the intermediary in St. Petersburg of George Barrington and other convicts, is in itself to understand the huge success of his translation. Guards officer long stationed in the capital, competent linguist lacking the opportunity to live abroad, civil governor of a provincial city, Golitsyn needed vicarious adventure and, like many Russians, travelled in his fancy. So respectable a functionary, he had a taste for foreign rogues and scenes of banishment even before the Irish trickster crossed his path. Hence his translations of a play, *The English Orphan,* by a minor dramatist, C. H. Longueil (1775), and of a veritable reference book on infamous, unfortunate, and otherwise distinguished individuals by Louis M. Chaudon (1796).[11] As Barrington in Russian dress provoked a lasting Russian interest in the mechanics of transported convicts' life (one thinks of Bellingshausen's study of Macquarie's prison public works arrangements as they stood in 1820),[12] so early inclination to consider New South Wales as a part of Polynesia led to curious conflation of the Cooks who found Australia and had been killed by the Hawaiians. In the long poem *Ten' Kukova na Ostrove Ovgi-gi (The Shade of Cook on the Island of Ovgi-gi,* i.e., Hawaii) (St. P., 1805), for example, an assortment of unlikely chords was struck.

Such works were useless to the reader who, like Kruzenshtern, Lisianskii, and Rumiántsev, was interested in New South Wales as a marginal but growing element in the Pacific-Eastern trade based on Canton. Such readers, many of them serving naval officers or servants of the Russian-American Company, needed hard data on the youthful British colony and, more particularly, on its chief harbour, Port Jackson, and its economic life. If Russian ships were to participate in the Pacific-Eastern fur trade, after all (as the new Company proposed by 1802),[13] they might be calling at Port Jackson. Some, in short, were viewing Sydney with the strategist's and international trader's careful eye. It was for them, and not for lovers of exotica, that merchant's son Ivan Iakovlevich Novikov brought out, in 1805, *The Beauties of Australia, the Fifth Part of the Globe, Presented Historically, with the Addition of Brief Reports on the Customs, Mores, and Lifestyles of the Peoples Inhabiting It.*[14]

Novikov was a Muscovite, a graduate of the Commercial Institute that had been founded there in 1773 to train the merchants of the future. Among his previous translations were an extract from a guide to sciences, arts, trades, and commerce by the French writer François Veron de Forbonnais (Moscow, 1781) and *Letters From a Father to his Son Describing the Principal Duties of the Merchant Class and Necessary Knowledge for the Prosecution of a Profitable Trade* (Moscow, 1797).[15] More recently, in 1800, he had written *The Calculator without Pen and Pencil*—a thirty-page aid to ready reckoning for Russian merchants and their staffs, complete with tables. Like Mozhaiskii, translator of the Kippis *Life of Captain Cook* (1790), and like Mikhail Verevkin (1732–95), translator of the *Histoire générale des Voyages* by A. Prévost d'Exiles and J.-F. de La Harpe (1782–87),[16] Novikov was representative of the pragmatic, pedagogical, and non-aristocratic element in Russian literary life during the last years of the reign of Catherine. That such a man should publish on the beauties and potential of Australia was, in itself, a reflection of evolving Russian attitudes toward that place. Within ten years of the appearance of his book, another graduate of the Commercial Institute, like him connected with the Russian-American Company's plans for the Pacific settlements, would be in Sydney and assessing local needs and trade potential for himself.[17] Within two years (1807), another servant of the Company, Clerk Rodion Zakharov, would be weighing up the prospects of exporting Russian goods to New South Wales.[18] Such reflections were assisted by a copy of Loggin Golenishchev-Kutuzov's Russian version of Cook's *Voyage to the North Pacific Ocean*. Finally, in 1805, the future admiral had managed to complete his long-delayed Russian translation of the lengthy South Pacific portion of Cook's final narrative; and he had done it on the basis of the London text.[19] It was a fitting end to thirty years of preparation for a Russian naval visit to Australia and a Russian venture in Canton.

"NEVA" ARRIVES IN SYDNEY, 1807

Lisianskii's ship *Neva* was being readied for a second voyage out to the Pacific settlements within a month of her return to Kronstadt roads on 24 July 1806. It was apparent to the Company Main Office that essential foodstuffs and supplies could be delivered to those outposts twice as speedily by sea as overland across Siberia; and the directors did not want to waste one week.[20] *Neva* was hastily rerigged, recaulked, and laden while the Company looked to the Navy, as before, for likely officers and men.

Among the officers applying for command of the new mission was Lieutenant Ludwig Karl von Hagemeister (in Russian, Leontii Adrianovich Gagemeister, 1780–1833). As the name suggests, he was a Baltic German. As his record and his countrymen's success aboard *Nadezhda* and *Neva* made probable, his application was successful, making him the beneficiary, though not a protégé, of Kruzenshtern, between whose early life and service and his own there were arresting similarities.

Lieutenant Hagemeister was descended from an ancient Baltic family of distant German origin[21] which, like the Kruzenshterns, had looked to Russia for professional advancement and political security since Swedish hegemony in the Baltic States had ended in 1711.[22] Again like Kruzenshtern, he had done well at the Naval Cadet Corps before entering the Baltic Fleet and soon becoming midshipman (1795), distinguishing himself aboard a frigate and arriving as a Russian Volunteer in the fleet blockading Holland's River Texel under Admiral Lord Duncan.[23] On secondment to the Royal Navy, he too travelled widely, seeing action off the Caribbean island of Saint Lucia and in the western Mediterranean approaches.[24] He returned to Baltic service and promotion in August 1805, bringing a note of commendation to the Russian Admiralty in the hand of Admiral Lord Nelson.[25] The *Neva* returned to Kronstadt twelve months later. Stowed below, by mid-October 1806, were dry supplies and naval stores for Petropavlovsk-in-Kamchatka to the value of a hundred thousand roubles. As her captain, Hagemeister took his orders from the Company Main Office, not the Naval Ministry; nor was he left in any doubt that the objective of his voyage was essentially commercial.[26] Not for him the latitude that Kruzenshtern had been accorded to indulge in scientific exercises and research: this time, the Company directors named no naturalist or astronomer or artist to *Neva*, trimming the lower deck, moreover, by a half-dozen seamen.[27] Now, economy and profit were the aim. The Board accordingly insisted that an agent of the Company, Zakharov, make the voyage and protect its interests as other agents, F. Shemelin and N. Korobitsyn, had done in 1803–6. Once more, inherent contradictions between mercantile and naval aspirations in the North Pacific basin were embodied and, indeed, given a cameo existence in a solitary ship.[28]

Neva weighed from Kronstadt on 22 October 1806. Ice was already forming thinly round the coasts and would assuredly have locked Hagemeister in for winter had he waited any longer. It was late for any ship to sail with a view to rounding South America before the southern fall turned into southern winter.[29] But the Russians made poor time to Copenhagen, where additional supplies and heavy maritime equipment were surveyed, purchased, and stowed. Opposing winds then kept *Neva* ten days off Elsinore. Hagemeister now decided, with his deep natural caution, not to expose his precious cargo to the risk of an attack by sailing south, where a French cruiser might be lurking (France and Russia were at war), but to head north round the furthest tip of Scotland. He accordingly set sail for the Shetlands, so ensuring that *Neva* would not make any easy passage round Cape Horn before the start of the southern winter. He soon paid for the decision: it was getting on towards March before the Russians reached Bahia in Brazil. But here *Neva* was once again delayed while a cracked bowsprit was replaced and while the Company commissioner or clerk, Zakharov, did some business in the town. It was too late to try the stormy clockwise passage round Cape Horn into the South Pacific Ocean. Hagemeister therefore decided to take the other route, southeast and eastward. All was readied for the long and weary voyage to Australia. Because *Neva*'s easterly course influenced later Russian voyages from South America to Sydney, we may pause here to quote the dry account of it written in 1849 by the Russian chronicler of early circumnavigation, Rear-Admiral Nikolai A. Ivashintsev:

Lieutenant Hagemeister sailed from Bahia on February 26 1807 and held a course for the Cape of Good Hope. On March 13, he crossed the southern tropic in longitude 35°W.; and the meridian of Greenwich was crossed in latitude 39°30′S. Hagemeister continued along this latitude, eastward as far as longitude 68°30'E., then moved southeast. On May 21, in latitude 45°37'S. and longitude 137°E., he began to move north. The southeastern tip of Van Diemen's Land came into sight on May 26. On June 4, *Neva* arrived in Port Jackson. . . . On their passage from the Cape of Good Hope to Australia, the Russians had had mostly W. and NW. winds, at times extremely strong.[30]

Ivashintsev barely hints at the reality of such a passage for a company quite unaccustomed to the monstrous waves and brave west winds found in the "Roaring Forties." Here, to complement the list of dates and figures, is the more dramatic picture painted recently by Geoffrey Blainey:

> Sailors who had spent a life at sea in the Baltic and Mediterranean and North Sea did not appreciate the strength and staying power of the westerlies in the chill waters of the southern hemisphere. They had no idea of the speeds which a ship could sustain for days on end in the Roaring Forties, and no idea of the fierceness of the waves. . . . She was followed for weeks by long ridges of water running high and fast, the crests of the waves white with froth, or a clear brilliant green. . . . At times, a ship running in a gale under reefed foresail found herself in a hollow so deep that the wave running behind snatched away the wind and almost becalmed her; there was then a danger that the following wave would break right over her.[31]

Tidal waves excluded, these were very probably the greatest waves on earth. It was as well, given the storms *Neva* encountered in the South Indian Ocean, that her officers and seamen were efficient and her masts in proper order. As before, the Baltic element loomed large. Moritz Berg, the first lieutenant, was a future admiral, historian, and advocate in Kronstadt of the Russian Navy's North Pacific mission.[32] Karl Mordhorst was her surgeon, and among her youthful master's mates was one, Efim Klochkov, who was in due course to return to New South Wales as commander of his own vessel, the *Riurik* (1821). Despite his relatively humble origins, Klochkov rose to be captain and the officer responsible for instrument improvement at the Hydrographic Depot in St. Petersburg.[33] Second Lieutenant Aleksandr I. Kozlianinov, too, did very well in naval service before premature retirement. As for Lieutenant Hagemeister, who was later to return to the Pacific twice, with the *Suvorov* (1816–17) and the *Krotkii* (1828), he was afterwards the Governor of Russian North America.[34] In sum, the officers and seamen of *Neva* were of exceptional ability and fully capable of leaving factually accurate reports on what they found in New South Wales at the conclusion of their voyage. *Neva* entered Port Jackson on 14 June 1807. By the Russians' reckoning, it was 2 June; and in their logs and journals they continued to observe the Old Style (Julian) calendar.[35] Once ashore, however, Hagemeister had no choice but to acknowledge dates and times as these were specified at Sydney. There were many more adjustments to be made after the bruising three-month voyage from Bahia. Winter winds did not assist *Neva* over the last lap, from the entrance to Port Jackson to the low huddle of buildings by the Sydney waterfront. Too long deprived of fresh-killed meat and greenstuffs though they were (as Captain Bligh, the local Governor, informed Sir Joseph Banks in a long letter of 7 November 1807),[36] Hagemeister and his people had no choice but to be patient and accept local direction. As he afterwards reported to the directors of the Russian-American Company:

> The Port Jackson pilot was unable, because of the contrary wind, to bring us in to Neutral Bay until 4 p.m. From the entrance of the Bay to Sydney town is perhaps one Italian mile. Before dropping anchor, we saluted the fort with eleven guns, to which the fort replied in like manner. The local Governor, Mr. Bligh, was at the time engaged on an inspection of towns lying inland, the officer commanding in his absence being Major Johnston. Mr. Campbell, as head of the Naval Department here, showed us all possible courtesy.[37]

Thus casually are we introduced through Russian eyes to personalities so dominant in early records of colonial Australia: Governor William Bligh, late of the *Bounty*; Major George Johnston, Bligh's deposer in the course of what is called the Rum Rebellion of 1808; and the wealthy magistrate and merchant Robert Campbell (1769–1846), who, more flagrantly than any other man perhaps, had been illicitly importing rum into the colony. If there is anything attractive and potentially important in these early Russian narratives, it is precisely that their authors *see* such men as Bligh and Johnston independent of their now overfamiliar political and social framework. To be sure, the Russians' ignorance of local happenings and understandable unwillingness to look too closely into tensions and hostilities among their hosts severely limits the importance of those documents as aids to the study of political developments in Sydney. It is not, however, for such insights that we turn to Hagemeister and the officers and scientists who followed him. Rather, we look to Russian primary material for new perspectives on the early trade and commerce of

the colony, on European-Aboriginal collision, on administrative problems posed by settlers, and on the maritime dimension. In these respects,
the primary material is rich.

Sydney was accustomed to a cycle of unbroken isolation from the outside world followed by multi-ship invasion. Corresponding to that cycle
was another, grimmer pattern of extreme shortage of foodstuffs, sometimes verging upon famine, and of glut.[38] In 1807, as it happened, Europeans were not desperate for the arrival of provision ships from England.
Even so, the Russians quickly recognized the psychological and economic consequences of irregular supplies of wheat, given the local floods
and droughts and modest harvests at the best of times. As Hagemeister
put it:

> Prices here still largely depend on the shipment of various wares from
> England, and every article is excessively costly. A bushel of maize,
> for instance, may go for six shillings, and a bushel of wheat may
> fetch up to thirty shillings. . . . The land is certainly fertile; but still,
> for various reasons, there is often an extreme want of provisions. The
> present Governor will no doubt, by his sensible arrangements,
> quickly increase the colony's prosperity. One of its principal exports
> presently is seals, an enormous number of which are slaughtered in
> the bays.[39]

Hagemeister spent some time investigating, insofar as he was able as a
foreigner and guest, the further economic meaning and potential of this
overall colonial dependence on remote supplies of food and other goods.
Having lately visited Brazil, he was induced to make the following remarks:

> The price fetched by goods brought here depends entirely on the oc-
> casion. It would, for instance, be possible to sell Brazilian tobacco
> costing around 13 kopeks a pound in Brazil for six roubles a pound in
> Sydney, though generally the price does not rise above 40 kopeks. A
> 5% duty is paid to the local exchequer on imports, as well as certain
> other taxes, those on spirituous liquors being rather high. And it must
> be supposed that, in time, this country will produce an abundance of
> grain and everything else necessary for life. A healthy trade should

open up, in view of the small distance from these parts to China and
the East Indies and in view of local need.

Hagemeister saw no reason why the colony should not produce more
than enough food for itself. All that was needed was a further adaptation
to the local agricultural conditions and, above all, cheaper labour. Norfolk Island might be virtually emptied of its convicts and the latter given
"tickets" by the Governor, as many men in New South Wales had already, but the colony would still be short of workers on the land:

> Many of the exiles who had settled Norfolk Island have now moved
> here, and here they are allocated land. The reason for all this is the
> absence of a single anchorage or harbour on that island, which is ac-
> tually a very fertile one. So now there remains there only a small gar-
> rison to form a guard over the very worst convicts, whom it is consid-
> ered necessary to separate as far as possible from society.
>
>   Those deported to Sydney are either kept at work in a special build-
> ing, under strict guard and at the government's expense, or else, if
> their behaviour has been meritorious, given tickets that permit them
> to earn their keep through some trade. Such is the price commanded
> by labour that many of the deported have actually managed to amass
> a fair amount of capital in the course of ten years. One in particular is
> now worth £30,000 sterling or more.

All this, however, was of future relevance to any Company activity in
the Pacific. What had bearing on the present was the fact that, sealskins
apart, the infant colony did have exportable resources which the Company, whose ships would doubtless be continuing to sail around the
globe, might wish to carry back to Europe at a profit:

> Given a late departure from Russia, the route round New Holland,
> where westerly winds assist, is a highly advantageous one. Ships
> reach it from England in four or five months and there have even been
> instances of the voyage being completed in three and a half. Perhaps
> the Company might draw advantage from a speculative trade with
> this part of the world. All our own products fetch high prices here and
> from hence it would be possible to carry a timber known as she-oak,
> an excellent redwood used in furniture. Certain English vessels that
> had brought convicts out and returned by way of Canton, to pick up
> cargo for the English East India Company some three years ago, took
> hence a few planks of this particular wood. It was to be used to pack

tea in. On returning to London, those ships' owners sold the planks at a great profit.

As for Neutral Bay, it was an excellent, safe harbour. Better still, the British Governor was friendly towards Russian ships and officers on principle: such were his orders.

Neva's unheralded arrival in midwinter had, in fact, produced a flush of hospitality in Sydney. Foreign shipping was, by 1807, not the rarity that it had been. "At least 22 American ships bound for China called at Sydney on their way in the thirteen years 1795 to 1805; and... in the wake of Yankee ships bound for China came the Boston and Nantucket whalers."[40] As it happened, though, no vessel had arrived from Europe or New England for ten weeks when the *Neva* slipped in; and thanks to Hobart's warning letter to the elder King, her name was recognized and she was welcomed formally. Neither the Governor, nor Major Johnston, nor the visitors had heard of Tilsit or the temporary Russian understanding with Napoleon.

Major Johnston introduced the Russian officers to Bligh's de facto enemies and rivals for authority over the colony, the New South Wales Corps. To what extent was Hagemeister conscious of the struggle then unfolding between Bligh and an alliance of the rum-importing New South Wales Corps officers and that extremely well-connected sheep importer, Captain John Macarthur?[41] Circumstantial evidence suggests that he was well aware of it but looked away. At all events, we know he thought it proper to be courteous to Johnston and more polite to Bligh, while making preparations to be gone. Bligh soon returned to Sydney from his tour, was immediately visited by Hagemeister, and gave orders that *Neva* be given greenstuffs, bread, and meat. These supplies, however, were not gifts; and, comments Hagemeister, "truth to tell, I had not wanted to pick up fresh viands here, where meat cost two shillings a pound; but we were to leave in five days and I was determined not to lose time on this account." As was usual, the *Sydney Gazette* noted the coming of the European vessel, somewhat tardily on 21 June. The late, casual reference reflects the calm with which Bligh viewed the presence of the Russians. He briefly reported their arrival to the government in London on the last day of October: "She... received every supply wished for, and every respect and attention was shown to the Imperial Flag."[42] Bligh again mentioned *Neva* some eight days later in a letter to Sir Joseph Banks. The Russians, he observed, had been delighted to get meat on reaching Sydney.[43]

Quite apart from his instructions to be friendly to such visitors, Bligh was disposed to be hospitable to "Hagenmeister" (as he called him) and his men. He had had dealings with the Russians twice before, in rather pleasant circumstances. As the master of Cook's *Resolution,* he had been on Unalaska Island and encountered cossack hunters led by Gerasim Izmailov, who had been of use to the British company (October 1778).[44] More recently, in 1796, he had met officers of Rear-Admiral Makarov's North Sea squadron, then assisting Duncan in the weary task of blocking up the River Texel, and again at Camperdown. In recognition of Anglo-Russian friendship, Bligh gave a formal ball and supper for the Russians on 23 June. The *Gazette* had this to say about the evening and the Russians' presence generally:

> On Wednesday arrived His Imperial Majesty's ship *Neva,* Captain Hagamaester, on her passage to the island of Kagack on the North-West Shore of America, with stores for the use of the Russian settlement there. She sailed from Cronstadt the 2nd of November last. . . with the intention to go round Cape Horn, but being too late for the season, called here to wood and water. . . .
>
> On Thursday morning, His Excellency visited the Russian sloop-of-war; on which occasion the ship was manned and a salute fired. In the evening, a ball and supper were given at Government House to Captain Hagamaester and his officers; at which the Officers Civil and Military and other Gentlemen attended with their Ladies. At 11 were displayed a handsome firework. . . retired to the supper room. . . dancing till an early hour.[45]

Such classically bromidic and complacent pieces were, it seems, the true reflection of official attitudes towards the Russians. They were interesting, mildly exotic passers-by, bound for a chill Alaskan island of which nobody knew much; they would be gone within the week; and international politics combined with present inclination to oblige the colony to throw a ball for them. Bligh and the "Officers Civil and Military" would have been much surprised had they had sight of Hagemeister's and Zakharov's long reports on New South Wales and its commerce to the Company Main Office. Neither man wasted his time in Neutral Bay even, as happened from 25 to 30 June, if rain was heavy. Nor, perhaps, would Bligh and Johnston have been happy had they known how critically their Russian guests viewed certain aspects of their work. "The English," comments Hagemeister disapprovingly, "have yet to press more than sixty Italian miles from the coast hereabouts, though they do have settlements near the towns of Paramat and Gokosburi [i.e., Hawkesbury], situated sixteen and fifty miles hence. Hence, the interior of this vast island, which is shielded by mountains, remains entirely unknown." Again, "this settlement is still in its initial state, though a surprising amount has indeed been done already. . . and everything is excessively expensive."

Only two other vessels stood at anchor on the day Bligh visited *Neva*: the *Sydney Cove,* an English trader last from Rio de Janeiro, and the New England brig *Hannah and Sally,* Canton-bound, also from Rio.[46] Consequently, there was little to distract local attention from her gunfire and pennants. On the other hand, local skilled labour was so scarce that, for all his brave assertion that economic and time factors alike decided him not to repair *Neva*'s thin copper sheathing while at Sydney,[47] Hagemeister really had no option in the matter if he meant to reach the Northwest Coast in summer. Refreshed and well-provisioned, he waited out four days of rain and strong easterly winds before, at midday on 1 July, *Neva* could finally move out of Neutral Bay. She left Port Jackson only two days later, but arrived at the Russian-American Company's chief outpost on the Northwest Coast, Novo-Arkhangel'sk (Sitka), within ten weeks.[48] There she was unloaded before going on to Kodiak to winter.

Neva returned to Sitka in 1808, and early the next year Hagemeister was at Kauai and Oahu, ostensibly to pick up foodstuffs; in reality, it seems, to gauge the prospects of establishing a well-armed Russian farm on the Hawaiian Islands.[49] He recommended Molokai but suggested that no forcible or friendly action be begun until the genuine extent of British claims to the Hawaiian Islands had been ascertained. Then, probably, two Russian warships would suffice to take and hold whatever island was selected by the Company Main Office for its mid-Pacific colony.[50] At Russia's main Pacific settlement, Okhotsk, later in 1809, Hagemeister found instructions from St. Petersburg. He was to leave *Neva* in the Pacific and return with all his people overland. He did so, reaching St. Petersburg in March 1811. Like a second Kruzenshtern, he was rewarded with a medal, a promotion, and a pension—in his case, 600 roubles.[51] His report on New South Wales had preceded him by two full years. Even so, as he discovered, the directors had not yet found an opportunity to act on his suggestion that a Company-owned ship look in at Sydney.

In the first place, war conditions had dissuaded them from risking any valuable shipments of supplies for the Pacific settlements since 1807. French cruisers were known to be at large in the North Sea and would not hesitate to confiscate Company goods. Perforce, Company servants on the Northwest Coast itself were buying foodstuffs from New England trading captains, who at least had not stopped visiting that Coast because of European struggles.[52] In the second place, the Board was not convinced that profit margins on exotic wood from Sydney, for example, or Hawaii (sandalwood), justified changes in a long-range North Pacific trading pattern. Hagemeister had no time or inclination to dispute the point: by February 1812 he was established at Irkutsk, Eastern Siberia, and—in that geographically improbable location—working hard at his career.[53]

As it happened, the one Russian vessel since his own to have sailed for the North Pacific settlements from Kronstadt, the sloop *Diana* (fourteen guns; Lieutenant Vasilii M. Golovnin commanding), had come as close to putting in at New South Wales as was possible, given the Franco-Russian military pact of 1807.[54] Similarities between *Diana*'s and *Neva*'s courses from South America towards Australia in the southern winter, and between their captains' sanguine expectations of Port Jackson once the unavoidability of a protracted eastward voyage to the South Pacific Ocean had been recognized, both justify brief comments on the place of New South Wales in official and, particularly, unofficial Russian naval thinking in the first years of the nineteenth century. These are best offered in the context of *Diana*'s southern passages and Golovnin's early career.

Diana's voyage was, ostensibly, one of provisionment, surveying, and discovery in North Pacific waters. In reality, as was made plain to Golovnin, the Naval Ministry had one more end in view.[55] The further object was to demonstrate effective Russian hegemony over certain tracts of water between Asia and the Northwest Coast. In build, *Diana* was a storeship displacing some 300 tons. Nevertheless, she was regarded as a warship and she was, in fact, well armed.[56] Moreover, Golovnin took orders from the Naval Ministry, not from the Company. Like Hagemeister and Lisianskii, he was a particularly able officer who, as a Russian Volunteer (1802–6) with the Royal Navy, had been subject to British influence for years. Even earlier indeed, in adolescence, he had fallen under James Trevenen's influence, had mastered English, and had read Cook's and Vancouver's *Voyages* in the original.[57] When not in action under Collingwood or Nelson as a Volunteer, he had seen much convoy duty and had visited Jamaica.[58] Like his predecessors, he had studied the colonial administration of the Caribbean island where he chanced to spend the most time and had grown conscious of the functions of Great Britain's farflung colonies, dependencies, depots, and farms. Though certainly no ardent Anglophile, Golovnin was highly conscious of the reach of British maritime and economic power. As a patriotic pragmatist, moreover, he was ready to exploit Anglo-Russian amity. Thus, he arrived with the *Diana* first at Portsmouth, where he spent nine useful weeks securing instruments and naval stores, then, after a vain attempt to enter the Pacific round Cape Horn (mid-February 1808), at Cape Town.[59] Then, we know, he had been planning one more stop, to wood and water and provision in another "friendly port" east of South Africa, specifically in New South Wales.[60]

The political position on the Continent was tense when Golovnin set out from Kronstadt. It was not supposed, however, that events would move so rapidly as to would affect *Diana*'s mission. But the meaning of the Franco-Russian pact arranged at Tilsit had been obvious for weeks. The Russians were received kindly at Portsmouth; nor were difficulties made when, after two months, they sailed suddenly for South America, having no doubt received intelligence of a coming crisis. Orders followed, when the break between the Russian and the British Courts did come, for British squadrons to intercept *Diana*. London also cancelled papers lately issued to her captain, guaranteeing safe, unhindered passage through all regions where the British writ then ran. After a pause at Santa Catarina Island in Brazil, *Diana* headed round Cape Horn (12 February); but the weather was ferocious and the Russians fought for thirteen days to make a mile of headway westward. Finally, the elements prevailed. *Diana* entered Simon's Bay, South Africa, on 21 April. She was boarded by armed British sailors and her people were arrested and removed by jolly boat. The Russians were detained for thirteen months and would assuredly have languished longer had not Golovnin made a most brilliant escape during a storm on 16 May 1809.[61]

Of necessity, Golovnin reviewed his route. He had planned, on leaving Santa Catarina Island, to put in at Sydney. Now he decided to avoid the place for fear of meeting British warships, but conceded that a passage round the Horn was not a practical alternative. Such were the origins of the *Diana*'s non-stop voyage from South Africa to the New Hebrides (Vanuatu), where Golovnin called at Port Resolution, Tana, using Cook's old anchorage.[62] The Russians passed Van Diemen's Land, in latitude 40°S, on 17–18 June 1809. They remained 120 miles offshore as a precaution.[63] Strong northwesterlies speeded them on their way into the Tasman Sea (20 June). Golovnin was an accurate and shrewd observer, and it was unfortunate he could not have added a description of a faction-ridden Sydney to his pictures of Cape Colony, Kamchatka, and Japan.[64]

Like Hagemeister two years previously, Golovnin had thought of Sydney as a natural port of repair once he had settled on the eastward route. Russian naval consciousness of New South Wales had, in fact, become a function of the long British connection. And the Russian naval presence in Port Jackson, like Lisianskii's, Kruzenshtern's, and Hagemeister's volunteer service with the British, was an echo of political entente. Although a temporary break in that entente in 1807 had prevented Golovnin from seeing Sydney, *Diana*'s problems had not changed the basic pattern.

Golovnin's acceptance of the need to make the longer eastward passage, calling at least once at "friendly ports," strengthened *Neva*'s example and provided other Russians with a viable alternative to that established by *Nadezhda* in the spring of 1804, that is, a quicker but more risky passage round Cape Horn to the Marquesas.[65] Finally, it gave the strong sanction of custom to the route that Hagemeister had selected: both *Diana* and *Neva* kept, in the main, between 39° and 40°S, passing close to the French outcrops of New Amsterdam and St. Paul Islands, moving southeast with full, taut sails to a higher latitude (43° to 45°S) south of Australia itself.[66] Among the later Russian vessels to retrace this route across the South Indian Ocean (which was, incidentally, more southerly than that preferred by most supply-ships sent to Sydney by the British in the early 1800s) were *Suvorov* (1814), *Otkrytie* (1820), *Riurik* (1822), *Krotkii* (1829), and *Amerika* (1832).[67] Not only did the captain of the Company-owned ship *Suvorov* (Mikhail Petrovich Lazarev) regard Port Jackson as a natural and proper port of call en route from South America to the Pacific settlements, but he also knew the "Russian route" to get there. In his cabin he had copies of the logbooks of *Diana* and *Neva,* as well as many Russian, French, and British charts and printed narratives, to help him on his way.

PREPARATIONS FOR THE VOYAGE OF "SUVOROV"

For four years after the *Diana* passed deliberately out of sight of New South Wales, war made further Russian voyages to the Pacific settlements imprudent. Hard political realities were echoed by insurance costs for shipping. In St. Petersburg, alarm and jingoism alternated; in the Company Main Office deep inertia reigned after the *Grande Armée* traversed the River Niemen to invade the Russian provinces. Perforce, the Company's chief manager in the Pacific, Aleksandr A. Baranov, was again left in complete control of Company affairs on and about the Northwest Coast.[68]

Even the flowering of trade with the New Englanders, however, could not halt a steady shrinkage in the quantity of heavy naval stores and other goods at the disposal of Baranov and his people. It was possible indeed to send such stores, and even iron bars and cannon, overland across Siberia and ship them from Okhotsk when, for an hour, tide and weather would allow;[69] but it was inconvenient in the extreme and very costly.[70] Things went better for Baranov in these years of war in Europe and America than the directors of the Company had any right to hope. He handled the supply problems that war had brought with pragmatism, not regarding the American free-traders as his foes simply because their government was struggling with Britain, Russia's ally.[71] Even so, it was unfortunate from the perspective of the Company's own servants that the European struggle had detained both the *Diana* and *Neva* in the Pacific. *Neva* might otherwise have made another useful voyage of provisionment from Kronstadt to the ever-hungry North Pacific outposts. In despatches to the Company main office in St. Petersburg, Baranov urged that a supply-ship be despatched as soon as feasible to Novo-Arkhangel'sk.[72] That time arrived in June 1813. The *Grande Armée* had been destroyed. An armistice had been initialled by the Russians and the French. The Baltic Sea and its extensive southern shore were clear of enemies. Sensing the wind of change and conscious of a duty toward both their shareholders and agents in the settlements, the Board took action.

The *Suvorov,* which they chose to carry long-delayed supplies and to provide moral support for the Pacific outposts, was a handsome, French-built merchantman of 337 tons or slightly less. On the recommendation of Admiral Spafarev, they offered the command of her to Fleet-Lieutenant Mikhail P. Lazarev (1787–1849). Like Lisianskii, Hagemeister, Kruzenshtern, and Golovnin, he had seen action (at Riga and Danzig, 1812–13) and had served in British men-of-war. Like them, he nurtured patriotic hopes and aspirations which his travels and experience abroad had greatly widened. And like them, he understood and fundamentally deplored the Navy's secondary and subordinate position in the Company-controlled Pacific venture.[73] Still, he hastened to accept the offered post, coming to terms on length-of-contract, salary, subordinates, and other matters. From the first, he understood that the *Suvorov* would give passage to a trained Company clerk owing allegiance to the Board. In the event, the Company placed two men on his ship: the expected clerk, Fedor Krasil'nikov, and Mr. Hermann (in Russian, German) Molvo, supercargo.[74] From the first, there was the prospect of collision.

Lazarev was given liberty to choose his own subordinates and as his second-in-command, he chose Semeon Lieutenant Unkovskii (1789–184?). Here too, old patterns were repeated: Unkovskii had served in British warships (1803–6) and spoke English.[75] Pavel Povalo-Shveikovskii was *Suvorov*'s junior lieutenant; Maksim Samsonov, her navigator; Aleksei Rossiiskii and Joseph Desilvier, her master's mates. They formed a first-rate company. Ice was imminent and days were cold when, on 9 October, they left Kronstadt, reaching Karlskrona in Sweden six days later and for safety's sake joining a British merchant convoy. Lazarev reached Portsmouth in the first week of December.[76]

Intending to retrace *Nadezhda*'s 1804 route around Cape Horn, Lazarev tried to hasten the provisioning and purchasing of scientific instruments in London. Neither Molvo, however, nor another awkward passenger with Company credentials, Dr. Georg-Anton Schaeffer, a persuasive but erratic German surgeon whom the Board had lately hired,[77] would be hurried. *Suvorov* was ready to set sail in December when, as

Lazarev reported it, "a letter was received from Mr. Molvo, then in London."[78] The cargo would be supplemented and the ship would wait. The extra goods would be arriving soon. Weeks passed and naval tempers mounted. "Necessarily," writes Lazarev, "we changed the route proposed: instead of sailing west around Cape Horn, we would take the longer eastward passage, round Australia." The Russians left at last, in evil spirits, with a large West Indies convoy under cover of five Royal Navy vessels, reaching Rio de Janeiro on 5 May 1814.

Since their departure from the Baltic, allied troops had taken Paris, and the Russian emperor himself had strolled its boulevards, a courtly conqueror. The news reached Rio in May, and it consoled Lieutenant Lazarev for the delays he had been put to, yet again, by Hermann Molvo. No official documents make mention of hostility or tension between officers and Molvo or Krasil'nikov or Schaeffer on *Suvorov*'s outward voyage, but the characters of Lazarev and Molvo and events in New South Wales make it probable that much antipathy existed in the ship and that resentment smouldered even as *Suvorov* left Brazil. A lengthy voyage was not likely to extinguish it, and it was not until 12 August that the southwest of Van Diemen's Land at last came into view.[79]

THE ARRIVAL OF "SUVOROV" IN SYDNEY, AUGUST 1814

The arrival of *Suvorov* and her company in Sydney on 25 August was triumphant. They brought news of Bonaparte's first overthrow and the presence of a corps of Prussian infantry and Russian cavalry in Paris.[80] More than this, they brought the news in as reliable a form as any Englishman could wish: Lieutenant Lazarev brought letters for the Governor of New South Wales, now Lachlan Macquarie, from Strangford, the ambassador at Rio de Janeiro, which were based on despatches and reports direct from London. There are various descriptions by Russians and colonists alike of the spontaneous and joyful celebrations that *Surorov*'s news provoked in a community that wanted recent information about progress in the European war. All stress the genuine pro-Russian sentiment that rolled over Sydney for two days. Never again was Anglo-Russian friendship to be quite so fervid in Australia, although the memory of the *Suvorov* visit lingered to provoke fresh hospitality when other Russians came to Sydney in March 1820. Navigator Aleksei Rossiiskii's account of the first day in Sydney typifies Russian reports:

> Hardly had we managed to drop anchor before a roar of guns in all the forts proclaimed the joyful news, which we ourselves had brought, of

the capture of Paris. Everyone ran to find out the reason for the salvo, and there was much bustling and hurrying in the streets. Finally, after midday, the tidings were triumphantly announced in public—and *then* it was a sight to behold, with what rapture people met us, and with what esteem they welcomed every man going ashore! They dragged our seamen off to taverns, standing them drinks and repeating, "Russian—dobro! Russian—dobro! French—no good!" Towards evening, all the streets of the town were illuminated, lampions being put up in front of every house; and even in the poorest dwelling, three or four candles were placed in each window, or more candles, according to the inhabitants' means. And rockets went up in a number of places, while the residence of the Governor, Macquarie, was magnificently lit and there were fireworks outside. By this time, the populace was gathering in throngs on a square. From one corner there resounded a military band, from another, the sound of a choir, and overall one heard the discordant shouts of tipsy revellers. In short, the whole town seemed the happiest then in existence. Who among us could have guessed that we should be passing the time so joyfully on the very first days of our visit here?[81]

It was to "Harbour-Captain Piper," that is, John Piper (1773–1857), that the news of the defeat sustained by Bonaparte was first imparted as *Suvorov* made her way across Port Jackson. Piper had come out to "Bindle-Bank" (as Rossiiskii calls it), *Suvorov* having crossed the path of an outgoing craft "bound for Port Derwent in Van Diemen's Land" an hour earlier, at 10:00 AM.[82] Piper welcomed Lazarev, gave him "instructions as to how we should conduct ourselves throughout our sojourn here, and offered us his services." While he hastened to inform Macquarie of the Russians' news, *Suvorov* entered Neutral Bay:

We let go anchor at 2 p.m., about two miles from the town itself, saluting the forts with eleven guns; we soon received a 13-gun salvo in reply. From our anchorage, a hospital on a hill ashore bore S 16° W., the water being eight fathoms, mud bottom. But at 4 p.m., Mr. Piper returned from the shore to inform us, in the name of the Governor, that we might move closer to the town. Even though this was forbidden to foreign shipping, he said, we were permitted—out of respect for the Russian flag—to enjoy such privileges as Englishmen themselves enjoyed; and the Governor (through Mr. Piper) asked our pardon for not having responded to our salute speedily enough! He had been outside the town.[83]

Lieutenant Unkovskii, author of the above, perhaps overestimated Macquarie's eagerness to be obliging to his guests. Nevertheless, Macquarie made a series of such gestures on 25 and 26 August; and by midday on the second day, *Suvorov* stood at anchor in Sydney Cove. There, four hours later, Lazarev fired an extraordinary twenty-one-gun salvo, and the local fort replied at once. Lazarev, who with his officers had visited Macquarie first at 5:30 PM the day before ("Mr. Piper then recommending a Mr. Brooks to us as a person who would assume responsibility for helping us put the ship to rights),"[84] called on the Governor again. It was a very friendly meeting. Strangford's letters were, it seems, already being copied out, and Howe, the local printer, also known as Happy George, was to produce a special issue of the *Sydney Gazette* because the next regular number was not due till Saturday. The special issue was ready that same evening and began as follows:

> Intelligence of the highest and most important nature having been received yesterday by His Excellency the Governor by the Russian ship *General Suwarrow*, commanded by Captain Lazaroff, in a communication from Lord Strangford at Rio de Janeiro whence this ship sailed on the 4th of June last, His Excellency is happy in giving it the earliest and fullest publicity through the medium of a Gazette Extraordinary, and most cordially congratulates all His Majesty's subjects in this territory on the glorious series of victories which have attended His Majesty's arms, in conjunction with those of his magnanimous allies, the Sovereigns of Europe, and finally crowned them with complete success over the usurper of France, the common Enemy of Mankind.[85]

Details followed of the latest allied military moves, with an allusion to the fact that Alexander, Emperor of Russia, was in Paris with his troops. By way of a finale, there came patriotic comments on the end of the U.S.S. *Essex* under H.M.S. *Phoebe*'s guns. Throughout the earth, it was suggested, British arms had proved victorious—with slight assistance from the tsar. *Suvorov*'s company were quite fortuitously in a privileged position in Australia. For them, possible difficulties and restrictions melted easily away. They took advantage of the fact, leading a busy social life, pursuing scientific interests, investigating Sydney and the country to its west, and, since *Suvorov* was a Company-owned vessel, building diligently on the basis of the Hagemeister-Zakharov reports on local commerce.

Suvorov's officers were entertained repeatedly by Governor Macquarie and his family, by officers of the 46th Foot Regiment, by Captain Piper, and by other influential officials in the colony. As for the ordinary seamen—the *Suvorov* had a lower deck of twenty-six as well as seven Aleut hunters on their way back to their native seas—they spent little time ashore in Sydney proper, it would seem, after the early celebrations. The news of French defeat served as a passport for the Russians to the local British heart, but this was not the only factor that contributed towards the warmth with which the visitors were welcomed. There were also Anglo-Russian naval contacts of the past two generations, shared experiences outside Europe, and Macquarie's own experience of Russians in St. Petersburg. Lazarev had been sixteen when he had first arrived in England, and exposure at so early and impressionable an age had left its mark. As for Unkovskii, he had survived a shipwreck off the Dutch coast at the same age (1803), been taken in a British ship to Lincoln, served a year in *L'Egyptienne* (Captain the Honourable Charles Fleming), then— in Kruzenshtern's footsteps—gone to India. More recently he had spent twenty months in a French prison before serving with the Baltic Fleet once more. In 1812 he had returned to southern England with a squadron led by Admiral George Tate.[86] Lieutenant Povalo-Shveikovskii, too, had British contacts. As the purser of the large frigate *Orel* (1812–13), he was particularly suited to the service on secondment with the Company that the *Suvorov*'s mission called for. Like Rossiiskii, who was, however, not a naval graduate but a particularly able product of St. Petersburg's Commercial Institute,[87] Lieutenant Povalo-Shveikovskii took a penetrating interest in matters of supply, demand, and quota.

As these Russians had had their earlier relations with the British, so had Governor Macquarie had his amicable dealings with the Russians, more especially with Russian naval officers at home. In 1807, at the very time of Hagemeister's visit to Australia, he had been forced by the Napoleonic War's southern extension to return on leave from India by way of Persia, Astrakhan, and Moscow. He and his companions had cursed the inconvenience to which they had been put by xenophobic and suspicious bureaucrats. Hoping to travel somewhat faster by himself, Macquarie was arrested as a spy close to Moscow and detained three days while all his documents were checked.[88] By comparison, his sojourn in St. Petersburg when finally he reached it was delightful. Bitter memories receded and his spirits revived under the influence of courtesy and comfort. Then, on 11 September 1807, he was taken from the centre of the capital, which he considered "the finest and most regular built City in the world,"[89] by open boat down the Neva towards the naval base of Kronstadt, where H.M.S. *Calypso* was expecting him:

> At half past six o'clock, we passed through the fleet of Russian men-of-war, into the harbour of Cronstadt, and went on board the Guardship at the mound-head accompanied by Captain Booning [Bunin] of the Russian Navy. This gentleman received us in a most polite and friendly manner... and treated us with coffee. He then proposed to wait upon Admiral Hanekoff [Khanykov] at his house on shore, being both Admiral of the Port and Governor of the island and town of Cronstadt. We did so accordingly, and met with a most polite and friendly reception from Admiral Hanekoff, who was kind enough to order his own barge to be got ready immediately to carry us on board the *Calypso*.[90]

As Governor of New South Wales, Macquarie had instructions to be civil to his Russian visitors; but he was strongly predisposed to be hospitable. His example was immediately followed by his deputy at Sydney, Colonel Erskine of the 48th Foot Regiment, and by the "Civil Officers" with Broughton at their head. Unkovskii records a dinner given for *Suvorov*'s officers by Erskine's officers on 29 August. More than forty sat at table. Vintage wine, crystal, and music saw both visitors and hosts through the inevitable toasts to George IV and Alexander, given eloquently by Colonel Noelle.[91] Other such dinners followed, in the course of which friendships were made, as, for example, between New South Wales's ablest beef farmer, the younger George Johnston, and Unkovskii. Interestingly, Johnston was happy to be taken by the Russian as "an agent of the East India Company, here on commercial business." The two took several long walks out of the settlement, each pumping the other for the kind of information that he wanted. Johnston took an interest in Russian commerce in the East; his Russian visitor, in Sydney's prospects.[92] By and large, Unkovskii and his fellow officers were favourably struck by them, and by the town's appearance too:

> For the traveller who comes by sea, Sydney offers a sublime sight and most splendid picture, worthy of an artist. Its central part stands in a valley, but its fringes spread to both sides of that valley, over slopes and on to higher ground. Behind, windmills may be seen. These windmills first reveal themselves to the voyager at sea, but almost slip from view as one comes nearer. . . . The houses are, in general, of brick or stone The local stone is particularly suitable for building purposes, by virtue of its softness, and many of the houses

are three-storeyed and compare with the finest in England. The fair climate of the place contributes greatly to the well-being of this colony; and every inhabitant of Sydney has a tastefully cultivated garden by his house and enjoys all sorts of garden produce in abundance, in return for a small outlay of labour.[93]

As Unkovskii magnified Macquarie's gratitude to Alexander, so, one thinks, Johnston minimized the problems that had always blighted husbandry and horticulture in the infant colony. Still, it is useful to have pen-sketches of infant Sydney that are not of British origin, have colour and perspective, and show the familiar in strikingly new light. Here is another cameo:

> On the morning of the 31st [18th], Mr Johnston very kindly offered us mounts on which to ride into the country, and himself promised to keep us company. At 3 p.m., the horses were ready and Shveikovskii and I, accompanied by Mr Johnston, set off. We decided to visit the hamlet of Parramatta, some 16 miles from Sydney, and so took that road. This Parramatta road has actually been laid out with no bends. It is well cleared to a width of ten or twelve fathoms [21–26 metres]. Large but sparse timber, good for any building needs, stands on either side of the roadway. We arrived at the place in question at 4.30 p.m.
>
> Such is its delightful situation that Parramatta may be called an earthly paradise. It stands by a stream of the same name, which flows down into Sydney Cove. The houses are mostly small, but they are all built to a plan and with some taste. The hamlet is surrounded by flatlands, which are ever green. There is a residence for the Governor, a building for the education of orphans, and a female asylum— a particularly grand structure. We stopped at an inn, rather tired from our unaccustomed horse-ride. In fact, we were not intending to leave our rooms again that day and had already arranged to have a good supper, postponing curiosity till the morrow. But very soon afterwards a man came to us from Mr Marsden, pastor in this place and principal cleric of all the settlements in the Port Jackson area. So we called on the reverend father. Mr Johnston, who knew him well, recommended us to him and we were received with special politeness.
>
> Mr Marsden, a man of about 45, has a wife and eight daughters. He is head of a mission sent to the Society Islands to preach Christianity, and he told us that many of those islanders had already in fact been converted, divine service being held in the Tahitians' mother tongue. He himself was intending to set out, for the same basic pur-

pose, to New Zealand, in which connection two New Zealand kings and twelve of their relatives had been invited over. These New Zealanders were all in Mr Marsden's own house and apparently had the greatest confidence in him. Some of them spoke some English. . . . Shortly afterwards, some of them began to dance, demonstrating how they enter into battle and triumph after victory.[94]

Such vignettes reveal as much about the writer as the subject. It is evident, for instance, that Parramatta's growing "to a plan" is in its favour, and one rightly anticipates Unkovskii's dislike of Sydney's lack of rigid street-plan. But these passages do offer shards of information for the regional historian. It is of interest that Johnston was already in possession of a stable at his property west of the future site of Brisbane stills;[95] his celebrated father had returned to New South Wales from London barely fifteen months before, and the disruption of his personal affairs had been profound. Again, the glimpses of Macquarie's roadbuilding, the Reverend Samuel Marsden and his daughters, and Maori activities in early Parramatta are all welcome, though perhaps of modest value in themselves.[96] The sum of the significance and use of such vignettes, taken together, is invariably greater than the value of minute component parts.

MARITIME AND COMMERCIAL ASPECTS OF "SUVOROV'S" VISIT

Captain Lazarev gave orders for the masts and rigging to be thoroughly inspected. Meanwhile he himself attempted to find caulkers and other tradesmen needed to put the ship to rights. The considerable storms we had met during our voyage had somewhat damaged *Suvorov*'s deck and her sides too; and besides this, several sails were torn, while others had ceased to be serviceable.[97]

Like *Neva* before her, *Suvorov* reached Australia in need of general repairs. With only occasional exceptions, the Russian ships were fir or pine-built vessels and deteriorated rather rapidly in alternating warm and freezing waters. Most of those coming to Port Jackson needed spars and canvas, and from very early days Sydney provided all such stores and chandlery at a high price. Captain Piper had suggested Richard Brooks as a ship's chandler for *Suvorov* and as agent for the services of workmen.[98] Lazarev accepted the suggestion the more readily for gathering that Brooks had more than once visited Kronstadt in his own small trading vessel: in the 1790s, he had traded in the Baltic with indifferent success and had known St. Petersburg. Since his arrival in Australia, he had done better. For a price, he at once provided both the services of skilled men and the necessary stores. These local men and Russian seamen worked together on *Suvorov* for nine days (26 August to 3 September). While some worked on the caulking, others, skilled in carpentry, worked on new cross-trees. The cracked and stressed old cross-trees and the rigging had been landed at Benelong's Point on 25 and 26 August. "Four caulkers," wrote Unkovskii, "were sent from shore and these men started work on the right side. For the checking of chronometers we selected a place called Benevelong Point, and there we began making observations."

Work at this land base was largely directed by Aleksei Rossiiskii, who left the following picture:

My duty was to check the chronometers, and for that purpose I selected a spot, called Benelong's Point, which by its situation might be called romantic. On one side, seacliffs rose in ledges, washed by waves that broke and foamed over the rocks beneath; on the other side stretched flowery dales, shaded by sweet-smelling groves, whence came the most delightful birdsong. Once our morning observations were complete, we would sit on the soft grass in the shade of a bush, to keep the sun's rays off, and quietly enjoy the spectacle of such surroundings. A good part of the town of Sydney, the harbour, and ships standing therein, were all visible. And there were always many walkers. In fact, a number of Englishwomen came up to us out of curiosity and watched us work. We made their acquaintance and were happy that they did not overlook us on their visits. Benelong's Point was also a trysting place. How gaily we passed the time there! Our readings all made, we ran and sported till evening fell, when we were again obliged to occupy ourselves with tedious astronomical observations. When these too had all been made, we would return to the ship with the instruments.[99]

The checking of chronometers remained Rossiiskii's duty throughout *Suvorov*'s voyage, and he grew very proficient at it, "tedious" though possibly it was at times. Rossiiskii also maintained a log, kept careful daily notes, and "fully justified his appointment, by his conduct as by his familiarity with the navigator's duties."[100] Somewhat edited, his journal of 1813–16 appeared in a St. Petersburg general interest and literary periodical, *The Emulator of Enlightenment and Beneficence (Sorevnovatel' prosveshcheniia . . .*), in 1820.[101] Because *Suvorov*'s officers had not published accounts of their experiences in the Company's employ (the Naval Ministry would not publish a voyage undertaken under extra-naval auspices), Rossiiskii's alone gave Russian readers an idea of the 1814 visit to Australia. As was appropriate, given his post, he paid due attention in his narrative to the maritime and economic aspects of the visit. It is the charm of his account, however, that commercial and professional concerns are touched on lightly, in a thoroughly Australian (if not "romantic") context. As he goes about his task with the chronometers, for instance, five Aboriginals approach him, one a woman, and "examine the sextant, chronometer, and artificial horizon with astonishment." The woman sees her own reflection in the mercury and shouts. There is alarm, delight, insistence; and the Russian, taking off his wristwatch, fascinates the Aboriginals by pointing out its cogs and wheels, into which they thrust a twig. A nasty moment comes and goes; the natives laugh again and leave.[102]

Meanwhile, other parties from *Suvorov* had been reprovisioning, wooding on the North Shore with Macquarie's full consent, and slowly watering at Sydney's Tank Stream. Lazarev himself dealt with the matter of supplies. A quantity of foodstuffs had been soaked in a gale off Van Diemen's Land. As a result, all the remaining biscuits needed a rebaking. Of the beef stowed at Portsmouth or elsewhere, much proved inedible. Lazarev and Robert Campbell came to terms. Obliged to pay for victuals, the Russians did their best to limit spending in other areas. Upon arrival, they had been given port instructions, one of which banned the importing of "intoxicating liquor" into New South Wales. As a personal concession by Macquarie and in recognition of *Suvorov*'s news of victory, these regulations had been slightly bent. The visitors, it was agreed, were not to offer spirits to the natives (as in fact they later did); but every man could take ashore, for his consumption or especially for use in barter, one bottle of rum. As Captain Piper's records indicate, there was no shortage of the latter in *Suvorov*: on the day of her arrival in Port Jackson, she was carrying "two casks, 216 gallons" for a company of forty-two, including officers and others.[103] Lazarev accordingly allowed rum to be offered both for local artefacts and for essential services, notably laundering of clothes.[104] This led to later accusations by *Suvorov*'s supercargo, Hermann Molvo, that Lazarev had actually flouted printed orders while at Sydney. Lazarev successfully refuted the charge, when it was considered by a special naval court in July 1816.[105]

Suvorov was officially a merchant vessel. In reality she was a well-armed transport. The supplies she had for Sitka, which included eighteen hundred pounds of powder and much heavy ironware, could, as the Russians knew, have fetched a good price in Australia—if they had been for sale. Nor had Lazarev the least intention of pursuing the trading lines which Hagemeister and Zakharov had proposed. In this respect, *Suvorov*'s visit set a major precedent: for it could easily have marked the start of Anglo-Russian commerce in Australia. Instead, it put an end to solid prospects for such commerce, reinforcing the political and academic meaning of the Russian naval presence in Port Jackson and indeed the South Pacific. At the time of the *Suvorov* visit, the British Navigation Acts restricting, for example, Russian trade in British colonies, were practically being ignored. In the words of the maritime historian John Bach:

> Legally, Australian overseas trade was limited... to those ships which came out under government charter... and to the vessels of those Indian-based merchants who enjoyed the privilege of private trade with ports within the area of the East India Company's monopoly. In practice, however, those [restrictions] stemming from the Navigation Acts were often ignored and while the European War continued American neutral traders were able to find a welcome in both Sydney and Hobart. For a time, indeed, the colonists depended upon them for a wide range of commodities.[106]

Although in Company employ, *Suvorov*'s captain was by temperament averse to commerce; and in any case the Company directors had no interest in trade in New South Wales. So died the mercantile potential of the voyage, at least two participants of which, Unkovskii and Rossiiskii, took an informed and steady interest in international trade. In their 1814 journals, both touched often on the Sydney market of the day:

> East Indiamen come annually with rich cargoes and in fact during our stay at Sydney all kinds of East Indian goods, silk scarves, silken materials, linen and calico, muslin and cambric, were on sale there very cheap. By contrast, Russian products such as sailcloth, Flemish linen, heavy canvas, hemp rope, and iron, were expensive—glassware particularly so. During our stay, a dozen ordinary tumblers sold for 24 shillings. Manufactured articles and goods of every kind may be bought at Sydney, with the exception of rum, the importing of which is strictly banned. All disembarking men are searched for it. By special concession on the Governor's part, we ourselves were allowed to take ashore not more than one bottle per man, not for sale but for use in barter if occasion arose. . . . Trade in spirits is actually forbidden to private citizens. Spirits must be sold, if at all, to special contractors whose privilege it is to purchase them. In return for this privilege, the contractors are obliged to build hospitals for the government. The control of this trade was purchased for a period... to expire this present December [1814]. Thereafter, free trade in Euro-

pean manufactures will be permitted. Russian canvas and other Russian products are especially costly now; but it does appear that in time New Holland will become one of the wealthiest English colonies.[107]

Most of the money circulating is paper money issued by the Governor, who is bound to redeem it, if required, in silver or in promissory notes drawn on the English Government. Very few copper coins circulate, and almost no silver ones. Not long before our arrival, the English Government had actually sent out some 50,000 Spanish piastres (20,000 roubles), in the centres of which holes the size of a shilling had been cut. Around was stamped the inscription,"New South Wales," and on the obverse face, "Five Shillings." The part cut out of the middle circulated as fifteen pence; that message is stamped on one face, a crown on the other. This curious expedient was adopted to stop the exporting of silver coins from New Holland. The special coins are legal tender only in that country. One may indeed request permission to take a few coins away as curios and our captain, officers, and I myself all took a few. But we gave them all away on reaching New Albion and Peru. I gave my last one away to the Viceroy at Lima.[108]

All in all, the Russians give an accurate and interesting picture of the economic life of "postwar" Sydney. Inexpensive clothes, expensive glass and ironware, visiting New England whalers, and an ever-present market for the demon rum are all familiar enough from Peter Cunningham, Burford, and Lycett, among other chroniclers, but they are freshly and intelligently painted. Moored a few yards from *Suvorov* was the English trader *Broxborneburry,* almost certainly the source of much of the cheap cambric mentioned by Rossiiskii, as she had brought two massive trunks of the material from London.[109] Also anchored nearby in Sydney Cove were *Alligator* (Captain Savigny) and *Surry* (Captain Raine). Other vessels came and went:

We finished repairs aboard on [22 August] 3 September. The ship had been caulked and painted on the exterior, the rigging had been put to rights, and we had watered. That same afternoon a three-master came in from the sea; she was the Jefferson (Captain Barnes), in from New Zealand where she had been whaling. Captain Barnes told us he had killed seventeen whales during a fifteen-month voyage, of the sort called spermaceti. He had come only to rest, and meant soon to set out again to hunt whales.[110]

Like Macquarie and Captain Brooks, Barnes had had friendly dealings with the Russians. He had several times visted Arkhangel, in Russia's frozen North, and now, in Sydney, he did his best to entertain *Suvorov*'s officers. The *Broxborneburry* had brought convicts to Port Jackson and because of this was of some interest to Lazarev. Unkovskii, on the other hand, was more intrigued by the *Seretoptam* (as he called her):

> This vessel had been captured by the American frigate Essex but retaken by seven imprisoned English seamen who had been aboard. This uprising had occurred by the Marquesas Islands. The seven seamen in question, having taken the ship, had brought her into Port Jackson after seven weeks at sea.[111]

Besides restretching *Suvorov*'s standing and rigging and repairing her boats and sails, Lazarev's people had meanwhile finished work on a new topmast and cross-trees. Benelong's Point, on Sydney Cove's eastern shore, remained the Russian headquarters. There, in early September, Robert Campbell and others handed over to *Suvorov*'s acting purser, Povalo-Sheveikovskii, 136 *pood* or almost 5,000 pounds of timber, paint, biscuits, and other ship's supplies. There, the Russians poured fresh brine over the fresh-killed beef sold by George Johnston, Jr.[112] And there Lazarev drafted the letter to the Company Main Board that left Australia aboard an "English schooner bound for Isle de France" on 5 September[113]—one full week before *Suvorov* could make sail. "The ship," wrote Unkovskii heavily, "was ready to sail indeed; but here again we were detained by the business dealings of our supercargo and so could not depart Port Jackson till the 2/14 September."[114]

Lazarev had had his difficulties with Molvo both in England and in Rio de Janeiro. They were antagonists, potential if not actual, on reaching New South Wales. Tensions grew during the visit; and a crisis of authority developed when, at Novo-Arkhangel'sk, Chief Manager Baranov issued orders to *Suvorov*'s seamen that related to the handling of the ship. Eventually, the Chief Manager had fortress cannon trained on the *Suvorov,* whose commander, he asserted, was persisting in a conscious policy of non-cooperation with the Company's own servants. Leaving the awkward German surgeon, Georg-Anton Schaeffer, and a boy behind, Lazarev slipped away for Europe overnight. Enraged, Baranov sent a letter to the Company Main Board via Irkutsk, accusing Lazarev of a variety of moral and professional shortcomings.[115] Reaching Kronstadt in July 1816, Lazarev found himself confronted by a special court, convened to weigh the accusations made, first, by Baranov and, second, by Herr

Molvo. The latter's allegations against Lazarev concerned *Suvorov*'s stay at Sydney.

There were two principal charges. One revolved around the treatment of the Company clerk Krasil'nikov by Lazarev. Krasil'nikov, said Molvo, had been treated like a rating, gagged, and flogged aboard *Suvorov*. Lazarev replied that he had certainly instructed that the man be punished, having been insulted by him publicly. Krasil'nikov had drunk too heavily on numerous occasions. Molvo's second charge had international implications. While a guest in New South Wales, Lieutenant Lazarev had, in defiance of the printed regulations of that colony, of which he was aware, sold rum for cash and even promissory notes against the British government. This accusation also was refuted, but less happily; for in responding to the charge, Lazarev pointlessly raised other issues:

> Rum was at no time sold in Port Jackson. It is true that we exchanged rum for various curiosities, as payment for laundering services, etc. But we certainly did not use up two whole pipes for these purposes; at most, we used a third of a pipe. . . . If something of the sort did occur in Port Jackson (of which I knew nothing), then it most likely occurred by the agency of Mr Molvo who, without my prior knowledge or consent, did one night take a cask of rum into his own quarters. This could not have been completely consumed, so very possibly some was sold by him. . . . But I cannot believe that Mr Molvo would have had the Governor's permission to do that, inasmuch as the said Governor never allowed more than two or three gallons to be taken from *any* ship at any one time. . . .
>
> As to other goods referred to as sold by me, they had been entered to the accounts of *Suvorov*'s previous officers and were in the ship when I boarded her. . . I myself took some of them at cost price, not with a view to profit indeed (and all the goods that were sold went for not more than £100), but in order to oblige the vendors. In all events, transactions of this kind were not forbidden in Port Jackson, where everything except rum is freely sold.[116]

It is unclear whether or not Lazarev's property, allegedly worth less than £100, was sold in Port Jackson. Even so, it is apparent that *Suvorov*'s visit made an impact on the colony's economy. Five thousand pounds avoirdupois, or two and a quarter tons, of supplies were bought from local dealers. Russian goods worth hundreds of roubles were bartered on the Sydney waterfront. And spirits did in fact enter the colony from the *Suvorov*, almost certainly beyond the stipulated volume. So extensive was the Navy's influence over the Company by 1816 that Lazarev was soon acquitted of all charges. Still, the very nature of the Molvo accusations indicate that the official versions of events were almost certainly unbalanced and incomplete; and they remind us that, though crises or collision between servants of the Navy and the Company might have St. Petersburg and Sitka as their epicentres, even Sydney saw the ripplelike effect.[117]

Macquarie again gave a dinner for *Suvorov*'s officers (and for the dilatory Molvo) on 14 September and continued to make gestures of respect towards "the Russian Flag." On the 15th, as the Russians were about to leave the cove, he sent Lazarev a basket of preserves and local oranges and responded to *Suvorov*'s last salute with two more guns than were required. Anglo-Russian amity had reached high noon in New South Wales.

Suvorov's officers rightly supposed that other Russian vessels would be coming to Australia along the eastward route, and so left notes for their successors. Here is one:

> Having sighted Van Diemen's Land, one is ill-advised to pass through the Bass Strait. . . since the passage can be rather lengthy because of a powerful current and frequent calms. On weathering Van Diemen's Land, however, it is not advisable to stand too great a distance offshore, as the winds at New Holland mostly prevail from landward. The entrance to Port Jackson itself is, thanks to the uniformity of the entire coastline nearby, very difficult to make out. One must get into the parallel of the port and simply approach: the entrance will unfailingly be recognized by great descending cliffs on either side. . . and the great beacon.[118]

Together, *Suvorov* and *Neva* had marked the route to Sydney Cove for Russian shipping.

THE RUSSIANS, PORT JACKSON, AND HAWAII

Count Nikolai Petrovich Rumiántsev (1754–1826) had in 1802 been instrumental in the launching of the Kruzenshtern-Lisianskii expedition. As minister of foreign affairs and, since 1809, as Chancellor of Russia, he continued to regard it as his duty and his pleasure to support the Russian venture in the North Pacific basin and the quest for a navigable passage over Asia to the Orient.[119] A rich grandee, he had been vexed by the constraints which the Napoleonic Wars had placed on science and discovery in general. He was aware that the Russian Baltic Fleet was in decline and that morale was very low.[120] In view of these unhappy circumstances, Rumiántsev resolved to send his own small ship to the Pacific and the Arctic on a voyage of discovery symbolic of official recognition of the value of whatever Northeast Passage might exist. He turned to Captain Kruzenshtern for aid and, in May 1814, an order went to Erik Malm, shipwright of Abo, to construct a solid brig, the future *Riurik*. Command of the new scientific enterprise went to Lieutenant Otto Evstaf'evich Kotzebue (1787–1846), once a cadet in Kruzenshtern's *Nadezhda* (1803–6) and a young officer of academic bent;[121] and invitations were despatched to and accepted by savants of international reputation: the naturalists Johann-Friedrich Eschscholtz (1793–1831) and Adelbert von Chamisso (1781–1838).[122] The voyage of the small but well-equipped, manned, and supplied brig (which flew the Russian Navy's pennant by imperial consent), showed unmistakably that, with the final restoration of political stability to Europe, another era had begun for Europe's navies. More than this, it demonstrated that the principal non-diplomatic objects of the Kruzenshtern-Lisianskii mission—resupplying and supporting Russia's North Pacific settlements both physically and morally, and furthering commerce and discovery as well as science—would be energetically but also more selectively pursued in a new era.[123] Scientific emphases, in short, would not disrupt an underlying continuity of outlook among forward-looking servants of the Navy, merely rearrange the parts of a mosaic of intention. Overall, the picture had not changed. Thus, Kotzebue represented continuity and change alike in the Pacific naval context. Like his mentor Kruzenshtern, he was a native of Estonia, a pupil at the Domschule in Reval. Like Lisianskii, Hagemeister, Golovnin, and Lazarev, he had done well at the Cadet Corps, read voraciously, felt foreign influence. His reputation was that of an extremely able, scientifically disposed, and steady officer.[124] Albeit incidentally, he was about to play a role in bringing Sydney once again to the attention of the Russian naval ministry and wider reading public.

Kotzebue and his second-in-command and friend, Lieutenant Gleb Semenovich Shishmarev (1782–1835), sailed from Kronstadt on 12 August 1815.[125] Having rounded Cape Horn and made a call at Talcaguano on the bleak Chilean coast, they pressed on north towards Kamchatka. Six months later they were entering the Arctic gulf still known as Kotzebue Sound. They found no navigable passage home to Europe. From the port of San Francisco, on the first of two slow sweeps across the South Pacific Ocean, Kotzebue made his way to the Hawaiian archipelago. He and his men had been preceded there by Dr. Georg-Anton Schaeffer, whom

Lazarev had landed on the Russian Northwest Coast from the *Suvorov*—
and had gladly left behind; Dr. Schaeffer's "Hawaiian Adventure" had
been under way for fifteen months before the *Riurik* reached Oahu.[126]

Schaeffer had been sent down to the Islands by Chief Manager Baranov
as an agent to recover what was still recoverable from the cargo of a
Company-owned ship that had been wrecked and pillaged on the coast of
Kauai. He had embarked on an imperialist venture, drawing maximal advantage from the struggle for political and military power in the Islands
between Kings Kamehameha I and Kaumualii. Both had treated him with
kindness; both had granted him extensive tracts of land. Kamehameha,
however, had been angered by his putting up a fort at Honolulu, where
the Russian flag was flown. Schaeffer had withdrawn to Kauai, where his
ally, Kaumualii, welcomed him and tolerated the construction of block-
houses. Kamehameha's English-born adviser, the old seaman John
Young, and certain New England trader-settlers, became alarmed. The
Russian menace was apparent.[127]

When *Riurik* reached Oahu, six years had passed since Kamehameha
had addressed King George III and asked for evidence of friendship and
protection.[128] And it was four years since Honolulu had been visited by
Captain James Tucker, R.N., in H.M.S. *Cherub*. Well received by the
Hawaiians and concerned to limit Russian and American commercial and
political control alike, Tucker had written to the Admiralty Board on the
matter of presenting the reliably Anglophile Kamehameha with a vessel.
The Hawaiian king, he noted, would interpret the political significance of
such a friendly gesture in a way likely to benefit his ally, George III.
Tucker's despatch went to Lord Bathurst, who, in turn, wrote to Macquarie on 27 July 1815.[129] Macquarie was asked to have a "small Vessel,"
in size and rig like a contemporary "Cowes or Southampton Passage
Boat," built for the king in Sydney Dockyard. No "very great expense"
should be incurred, but work should start without delay. In the event,
work went ahead only too slowly, and the schooner *Prince Regent* was
not launched until April 1819. She was a craft of forty tons and mounted
six modest brass guns.[130]

Tucker's "Passage Boat" was thus conceived before the birth of Dr.
Schaeffer's adventure. It was not as a response to Schaeffer's actions that
Macquarie had had his orders to construct her.[131] Kotzebue, nonetheless,
was much impressed by the political significance of such a gift from such
a source, and of the building of a vessel for the king in New South Wales.
He also learned from a New Englander, James Wilcocks, that the Governor of New South Wales was in friendly, if not regular, communication
with Kamehameha and had written to him on his own account, as well as
having forwarded two letters from Lord Bathurst.[132] Wilcocks, it would

seem, wished Kotzebue to appreciate the implications of the fact that British shipwrights in Australia were building for the independent kingdom of Hawaii. He himself could not rejoice in any prospect of increasing Russian influence over the Islands. Kotzebue was, in any case, fully alive to implications of that kind:

> Mr Wilcocks further told me that a very fine ship was building at Port Jackson, by order of the English Government, for Tamaahmaah [Kamehameha]. From all this, it must be concluded that England has taken the Sandwich Islands under her particular protection—perhaps already, in silence, considers them her property, and will certainly take entire possession of them as soon as circumstances shall permit. [133]

As the true extent of Schaeffer's power had been consciously exaggerated in 1816–17 by New Englanders who wished to limit it, so, long before she even reached Hawaii, the schooner *Prince Regent*'s significance assumed exaggerated and unjustified proportions in the Russian mind. On their return to St. Petersburg in 1818, both Kotzebue and his erudite young naturalist Chamisso made full reports to Count Rumiántsev on their voyage. Both suggested that the building of the schooner in Port Jackson was an earnest of political intention. "Should any foreign Power," wrote Kotzebue, "conceive the foolish idea of taking possession of these Islands, the jealous vigilance of the Americans. . . and the secure protection of England, would not be wanting to frustrate the undertaking." [134] The imperial authorities misread the symbol that was King Kamehameha's "Passage Boat," but they were not wrong in recognizing that the stable and increasing British presence in Australia had implications for the South Pacific Ocean certainly, but also for potential European colonizing further north.

The publication of Kotzebue's *Voyage of Discovery* (*Puteshestvie v Iuzhnyi okean...*) in 1821 spread new awareness of Australia in educated Russian circles. Chamisso, for instance, three times touched on it, in strictly scientific contexts, in his learned contributions to that *Voyage*. Dr. Eschscholtz followed suit, using the butterfly *Sphynx pungens* from Port Jackson as his cue. [135] And, not surprisingly in view of *his* professional preoccupations with hydrography and the employment of efficient naval officers in peacetime, Kruzenshtern, who wrote the introduction to the book, took the occasion to make "various remarks" about the country that he always linked with Flinders:

> Almost every country takes advantage of the present happy season of peace and sends men of learning to remote countries. An English ex-

pedition is engaged in completing the labours of Flinders and finishing the survey of north-western New Holland. . . . It is not impossible but the question may be asked, what advantage can arise to Russia from such enquiries? It would not be easy to make a better or more suitable answer than by repeating what Barrow has said on the occasion of the English North Pole expedition: "With equal contempt we notice insinuations of the inutility of the measure. A philosopher should despise the narrow-minded notions entertained by those who, viewing the subject as merely one of profit and loss, are unable to form any other notion of its utility."[136]

In its generous allusions to both Parry and Phillip Parker King, to both the Arctic and Australia, to both the Anglo-Russian nexus and discovery, the passage serves to introduce the next great Russian expedition to the South: that linked with Bellingshausen's name.

4

THE 1820 VISITS:
BELLINGSHAUSEN AND VASIL'EV

THE DOUBLE POLAR EXPEDITION, 1819–21: ORIGINS AND INCEPTION

Riurik had been designed and built for scientific work and for discovery. *Suvorov* had been modified and reconfigured as a transport. Neither ship had heavy armament, yet both had unmistakable political significance in the Pacific. In the post-Napoleonic age, as in the time of *Resolution* and *Discovery*, "the aims of science and of empire were essentially one and the same."[1] Knowledge was power.

Kotzebue was the last Russian commander for some time to sail from the Baltic to the North Pacific settlements without provoking that suspicious interest in London that had always been expected of Madrid. For had he found the Arctic passage that he vainly sought, whatever scientific aims he might have had would have been more or less irrelevant. This was acknowledged by the British government in 1817.[2]

Profoundly though he scorned the Russian government and fleet, John Barrow, secretary to the Admiralty Board in London, was aroused by news of Kotzebue's venture. There were Russians, it appeared, on the Kurile and Aleutian Islands; on Oahu, Kauai, and Molokai in the Sandwich or Hawaiian Island chain; by San Francisco; and along the Northwest Coast. Even despatches from the Governor of New South Wales made allusion to the intermittent presence of the Russians in the Great South Sea, en route to settlements and bases in the North.[3] It was disturbing inasmuch as Russia patently enjoyed advantages over all other would-be finders and exploiters of whatever Northern Passage to the Orient and Indies might exist: control and knowledge of Alaska, ports and wintering facilities quite close at hand, and food supplies from California, the Hawaiian Islands, and Siberia.[4] The British government had no objection to the Russians calling in at New South Wales on their way to Petropavlovsk-in-Kamchatka and/or Novo-Arkhangel'sk. Perhaps it did object to Russian imperialist schemes on the Hawaiian Islands; but New Englanders were also active there, and there were certainly no plans in 1817–18 to establish British rule at Honolulu.[5] Possible control by Russia of a navigable Arctic passage to the North Pacific Ocean, on the other hand, was an intolerable prospect that demanded action. "It would," protested Barrow, "be mortifying if a naval power of but yesterday should complete a discovery in the nineteenth century which was so happily commenced by Englishmen in the sixteenth."[6] The Commons sympathized, conscious of damage that the Russians' domination of the North might deal to the British China trade, and a reward was duly offered for the finding of a navigable passage through the Arctic to the Orient.[7] The golden age of Arctic exploration had begun—an exploration that directly bore on the development of Russian scientific dealings in the South Pacific Ocean and Australia.

The time had come, it was agreed in May 1818, when news reached Kronstadt of the Franklin-Buchanan expedition with the *Trent* and *Dorothea* to the North and of the Ross and Parry ventures north and west through Baffin Bay, for Russia also to win laurels and political advantage, if not profit, from another major scientific effort overseas. What was needed was another, even grander undertaking on the lines of Kotzebue's, but supported by the state. Where should the Russian thrust be made? Not to persist where *Riurik* had done so well was hardly thinkable. Unlike the British, however, the Russians could not compensate for failure there by progress on the shores of South America, South Africa, or Asia. Thus originated the idea of a double expeditionary effort.[8] While one Russian squadron sought a navigable passage in the North linking Atlantic and Pacific tidal waters, another would proceed to the farthest South, where, since Captain Cook's return in 1775, no expedition had done any work whatever. In Antarctica, if anywhere, a Russian squadron might still complement the work performed by Cook. Ports in Brazil and New South Wales, now familiar to Russian vessels, could be used as much as necessary both as resting and revictualling stations and, more generally, as *points d'appui* to that distant southern venture. The Russian naval ministry resolved to send two vessels, a naval sloop and a reconfigured, sloop-rigged transport, to the Arctic, and an almost identical unit to the farthest South. The ships chosen and readied for this two-pronged polar venture, all of which were to pass weeks in New South Wales in 1820, were *Vostok* (*East*), *Otkrytie* (*Discovery*), *Mirnyi* (*Peaceable*), and *Blagonamerennyi* (*Well-Intentioned*).

Vostok and *Otkrytie* had been built in the River Okhta yard by the shipwright Stoke and were of the same class: 900 ton displacement, 39.5 metres in length, 10 metres in the beam, mounting 28 guns. They were launched in 1818. The transports, *Mirnyi* and *Blagonamerennyi,* (ex-*Svir*), were smaller craft at 530 tons each, 36.5 metres long and 9 in the beam, both mounting 20 guns. Both were reconfigured as sloops for the coming protracted voyages.[9]

This selection of craft of different types proved less than happy on the high seas and in high winds: necessarily, the transports were less speedy than the sloops. And, not surprisingly in view of the *Vostok*'s and *Mirnyi*'s work in the icy waters of Antarctica, their sails and pine construction needed serious attention when they reached Australia. In short, the vessels were not equal to their officers and seamen, all first-rate, and more importantly were barely equal to their tasks so far from home. Again, the Russians were to make good use of the repair facilities and chandlery of Sydney when, perforce, they visited.

For the Arctic venture, Captain-Lieutenant Mikhail Nikolaevich Vasil'ev (1770–1847) was appointed to the sloop *Otkrytie,* Lieutenant Gleb Semeonovich Shishmarev, late of *Riurik,* to the armed transport *Blagonamerennyi.*[10] As midshipman and young lieutenant, Vasil'ev had served against the French in the Mediterranean (1798–1801). Ten years later, in the Russo-Swedish war of 1809, he had seen action on the River Aa in gunboats. He remained on active service in the Baltic Sea until, in 1818, he was given his own frigate, *Pollux.* He was afterwards Vice-Admiral and General Intendant of the Fleet.[11] As for his second-in-command, Shishmarev, he too later reached flag rank and wielded influence at Kronstadt.[12] *Otkrytie* carried a complement of three lieutenants, Avinov, Zelenoi, and Boyle; a pair of midshipmen, Stogov and Gall; as well as a surgeon, Kovalev; a highly skilled astronomer, Pavel Tarkhanov; and an artist on secondment from St. Petersburg's Academy of Arts, Mr. Emel'ian Korneev.[13] Tarkhanov was afterwards astronomer in the St. Petersburg Observatory. Shishmarev's people, too, did well in their careers which, indeed, their polar service of 1819–21 much enhanced. Among those to leave accounts of their experiences with the *Blagonamerennyi* in Australia and the Pacific were Second Lieutenant Aleksei Petrovich Lazarev (1791–1844), the youngest of the three Lazarev brothers in the Navy,[14] all of whom came to Australia in 1814–24;[15] the captain's brilliant young nephew, Midshipman Nikolai D. Shishmarev; and Midshipman Karl Gellesem (or Hulsen).[16] Also aboard *Blagonamerennyi* in New South Wales were Lieutenant I. Ignat'ev;

Navigator Vladimir Petrov, who had followed his captain from the *Riurik*; Staff-Surgeon Grigorii A. Zaozerskii, amateur palaeontologist; and Father Mikhail Ivanov, chaplain to the squadron. The lower ranks aboard *Otkrytie* numbered 63, aboard *Blagonamerennyi*, 71. Together the two ships' companies numbered 156. Most of the hands were twenty-five years old or younger, and skilled in two different trades.[17] All were robust and literate.

Commander of the "First (Southern) Division" of the double expedition to the North and South Pacific was Captain-Lieutenant Fabian Gottlieb von Bellingshausen (in Russian, Faddei Faddeievich, 1779–1852), once a midshipman in Kruzenshtern's *Nadezhda* (1803–6). The scion of a noble German family long settled on the Isle of Oesel (modern-day Saaremaa), Estonia, he was an officer of academic temperament in Kruzenshtern's own mould. Since his return from the Pacific, he had won promotion twice and was well known for his meticulously thorough charting of the Black Sea coasts. It was a Southern Russian version of Cook's service on the shores of Newfoundland.[18] Mikhail P. Lazarev, late of *Suvorov*, was commander of the *Mirnyi*. Among *Vostok*'s distinguished company, as she headed out from Kronstadt in July 1819, were Captain-Lieutenant (later Admiral) Ivan Zavadovskii, the future Decembrist insurrectionary Konstantin Torson,[19] Kazan' astronomer Ivan Mikhailovich Simonov (1794–1855), and artist Pavel Nikolaevich Mikhailov (1780–1840).[20] Among the *Mirnyi*'s people who left valuable records of their doings in Australia and the Pacific basin from 1820 to 1821 were Midshipman Pavel Mikhailovich Novosil'skii and Surgeon Nikolai Galkin.[21] *Vostok* carried a lower deck of 105, *Mirnyi*, 65. Together, the two ships' companies numbered 189. With one or two exceptions (Torson, Lieutenant Arkadii Leskov), their officers developed the Pacific naval pattern of the early 1800s: subsequent promotion, acquisition of some influence used to sustain official consciousness of Russia's enterprise in the Pacific, social eminence.[22] No ordinary seaman was accepted in *Vostok* or *Mirnyi* "unless aged under thirty-five, extremely fit, more than capable of enduring hard work at sea, and possessed of a knowledge of at least one trade in addition to his own."[23] Numerous seamen, as well as Bellingshausen, Lazarev, Shishmarev, and the master of *Blagonamerennyi*, Petrov, were on their second voyages into the Great South Sea. For those aboard *Vostok* or *Mirnyi*, at least, that second voyage was to guarantee professional success, once the Pacific and Antarctic had been weathered. For the Arctic-bound contingent, things were different.

What Vasil'ev was asked to do was an impossibility, given the time and his equipment and facilities; but circumstantial factors made his

Arctic failure the more certain. Vasil'ev lacked Golovnin's or M. P. Lazarev's distinction as a hard sea officer; nor had he Kruzenshtern's or Bellingshausen's scientific gifts. *Otkrytie* and *Blagonamerennyi* were less well suited to their Arctic tasks than even Kotzebue's little *Riurik* had been, and quickly parted on arrival in the North. No Northwest Passage back to Europe was discovered through the pack ice and, despite some small achievements in the Bering Sea and, more especially, the Carolines,[24] the Northern probe was rightly viewed at its conclusion as a costly disappointment.[25] Recent Soviet encomia of the tenacity and seamanship displayed by both Vasil'ev and Shishmarev are unjustified within the broad context of Russian Arctic exploration and do not redeem the loss sustained by half-a-dozen sciences as a result of the more sober nineteenth-century assessment of their work.[26] From that assessment, after all, sprang the decision not to publish at the government's expense official records of the Northern expedition. To the consequent frustration of ethnologists from Sydney to Alaska, ethnographic information has been gathering dust in naval archives to this day;[27] and one or more portfolios of drawings by the artist in *Otkrytie,* Korneev, at least twenty-one of which we know to have depicted Aboriginals, birds, local scenes, and buildings in the Sydney-Windsor-Richmond area or in the Great Dividing Range, remain unseen beyond the reach of art historians.[28] What the *Otkrytie* had failed to do was largely left for *Blossom* and Frederick William Beechey to achieve.[29]

By contrast, Bellingshausen's expedition was a brilliant success. "It would," observes a recent student of Antarctic exploration, "be invidious to compare Cook and Bellingshausen. Cook has well been called incomparable; but no pioneer ever found a worthier disciple and successor."[30]

Both polar-bound squadrons, together with two other vessels bound for England only, sailed from Kronstadt on 17 July 1819. Both were splendidly provisioned. In their holds were a substantial quantity of goods to barter with Pacific Islanders for victuals and native artefacts, for once again ethnography was an important object.[31] The departure date was earlier than usual, for it was not to a familiar Pacific that the ships were headed. Both squadrons were under orders to make eastward passages into the South Pacific; both accordingly anticipated sojourns in Australia before proceeding to the farthest North and South, respectively, or, in the latter case, perhaps during the voyage. Governor Macquarie was informed of it.[32] *Vostok, Mirnyi, Otkrytie,* and *Blagonamerennyi* sailed in company from Portsmouth to the northeast coastline of Brazil and down to Rio de Janeiro (13–14 November).[33] From there, Bellingshausen and his people pressed due south, sighting South Georgia Island on 27 December and beginning an exhaustive clockwise sweep of the Antarctic seas that was to bring them, on 18 February 1820, into sight of the Antarctic continent.[34] Fold after fold of shining icecap stretched away to the horizon. The expedition pressed on east, remaining south of 60°S for a full quarter of a circuit of that line of southern latitude. Finally, when food and firewood were dangerously short, the expedition made its way towards Australia.[35] Conditions were appalling for *Vostok* and *Mirnyi*: for days on end, the sun did not appear. Still, the Russians held tenaciously and admirably to their scientific rounds, *Vostok* and *Mirnyi* making their independent ways towards Australia by planned different routes, so as to maximize the scientific usefulness. *Vostok* at last dropped anchor at Sydney on 11 April 1820; *Mirnyi* followed four days later. Both ships' companies were cheerful but exhausted.[36] Bellingshausen was surprised to learn that the Vasil'ev-Shishmarev North-bound squadron had departed only two weeks earlier (26 March), after a pleasant, month-long visit. He himself, however, quickly proved the beneficiary of that same visit, then the longest ever made by Russian seamen in Australia.[37]

"OTKRYTIE" AND "BLAGONAMERENNYI" IN NEW SOUTH WALES

While Bellingshausen and Lazarev were struggling around the fringes of a continent that they suspected to exist, perhaps concealed behind a fringe of mist and ice, Vasil'ev and Shishmarev were making their passage from Brazil into the "Roaring Forties," skirting Cape Town at a distance of twelve miles on 5 January 1820.[38] High winds helped them eastward for three weeks, rising occasionally to become alarming hazards, till Australia was sighted on 28 February after an eighty-three-day voyage. *Blagonamerennyi* was, surprisingly, ahead of *Otkrytie,* which had been damaged by a storm. Lieutenant Aleksei P. Lazarev, *Blagonamerennyi*'s second lieutenant, wrote perhaps the most circumstantial and readable account of his armed transport's visit to Australia.[39] Though more the courtier and man-about-town than his elder brothers Andrei and Mikhail (who was now on the edge of Antarctica in *Mirnyi*), Aleksei was like them a highly competent and well-adjusted naval officer. Spurning St. Petersburg's temptations,[40] he remained in active service until 1828, when he saw battle by the Dardanelles as captain-lieutenant and commander of his ship. His journal, edited for publication in 1830 but, to his great chagrin, never actually printed in his lifetime,[41] throws light on almost every aspect of the 1820 visits of *Otkrytie* and *Blagonamerennyi*. Here, for instance, is his picture of the armed transport's arrival and reception by the prosperous John Piper, "Harbour Captain":

> We were in the latitude of Port Jackson on 1 March and so supposed we should be entering it next morning; but the current bore us more than thirty miles south in less than 24 hours, and the wind also turned against us. In fact, we remained at sea another three days, finally entering the bay on 3 March and dropping anchor by Sydney. . . . Port Jackson must, though, be considered the most superb harbour ever created by Nature. . . . A revolving beacon erected on the south side of the entrance in 1816 is the most obvious landmark there, and judging by it one can hardly mistake the entrance. As a vessel enters Port Jackson, she is met by a pilot who comes four or five miles out. By the beacon there stands a telegraph post, to inform the town of the approach of any vessel, from north or south, and of her size. When the vessel is halfway between the entrance and the town, she is met by the Harbour Captain with instructions relating to all arriving shipping. . . . At length, we sighted Sydney proper in a narrow inlet, and there we let go anchor, right by Captain Piper's house. We moored so that gangplanks could be run out: we could plainly hear everything that was said in the Captain's dwelling! We were standing in six fathoms of water, mud bottom. Regulations required every vessel entering Sydney roadstead to pay £7, to promote the colony's prosperity, and we duly paid up. Regulations also stipulate that no person be taken aboard a ship without the Governor's permission, that the roadstead not be littered, and that crews be supervised whilst ashore. Next morning, the captain and all the officers of our sloop called on Major-General Macquarie, the Governor of New Holland. He received us most kindly and, on our explaining our saluting procedure, agreed to respond with an equal number of guns.[42]

Even before anchoring, the Russians had been following instructions from the Russian Naval Ministry and drawing maximal advantage from this visit from the strictly naval standpoint. Soundings were made and coastal currents measured at frequent intervals. As a result, an accurate chart of Port Jackson could be prepared on the basis of Russian data alone.[43] Always, Russian hydrography had a distinctly patriotic, nationalistic character.[44] These conscious scientific emphases, proper enough in such a naval expedition, were allowed free rein ashore. Almost at once, Macquarie was requested to allot a site as an observatory, forge, and small repair yard. Almost at once, a more original and delicate request was made, and granted, in the name and field of science: Fedor Shtein, natural scientist aboard *Blagonamerennyi,* hoped to pursue combined botanical and geological investigations in the hills due west of Sydney. In Lazarev's words: "With regard to the place for our observatory, Macquarie left the choice to Captain Shishmarev, who postponed the decision until the arrival of *Otkrytie.* But the naturalist was then and there given a ticket granting him free passage everywhere; and the English even wanted to provide him with horses and guides for a journey into the Blue Mountains."[45] Macquarie would perhaps have granted Dr. Shtein permission to go anywhere he pleased, even had someone other than Shishmarev asked him for it. Still, the Governor's particularly warm reaction to Shishmarev is apparent from surviving documents; and it was certainly a happy chance that led Shishmarev to become the Russians' spokesman at the outset. He was, in the words of the great German poet-naturalist Adelbert von Chamisso, who had sailed with him in the *Riurik* to Polynesia in 1815–17, "a man who spoke Russian only; with a face serenely beaming, like a full moon, agreeable to behold; a man who has not forgotten how to laugh."[46] Shishmarev was treated most hospitably by other prominent officials of the colony; nor did his ignorance of English—years of service in the Baltic Sea had not, for him, led to secondment with the Royal Navy[47]—seem to lessen the enjoyment he derived from meeting Phillip Parker King, Governor King's explorer son, to whom Macquarie introduced him.[48]

Understanding English better, Aleksei P. Lazarev and *Otkrytie's* second lieutenant, Pavel Zelenoi,[49] were more able and (in keeping with their orders) predisposed to draw Lieutenant King into informal conversation. ("The Governor acquainted us, whilst we were at his residence, with the English Lieutenant King who, some time before our arrival, had of course surveyed the entire coast of New Holland and Van Diemen's Land in a brig.")[50] What Lisianskii had in vain hoped to discuss with Matthew Flinders, Lazarev and the linguistically more able officers of the *Otkrytie* (Zelenoi and Roman Boyle) now discussed with his successor, King the younger.[51] Their instructions, after all, put no restriction on the *kinds* of scientific information they should gather while ashore in the Pacific. On the contrary: they, like Vasil'ev and Bellingshausen, were enjoined "to pass in silence over nothing new, useful, or curious" they saw, "this applying... in the broadest sense and to such matters as might widen any area of human knowledge."[52] Conscious that their duty and their curiosity happily coincided, many officers from the *Otkrytie* and *Blagonamerennyi* engaged in scientific work while in Australia. Some, like Lieutenant Aleksandr P. Avinov, occupied themselves with local charting and with draughtsmanship. Avinov, a hydrographer by training, was to end a brilliant career as full admiral and member of the Admiralty College.[53] Others served as regular assistants to astronomer Pavel Tarkhanov once the shore observatory had been established on the North Shore east of Kirribilli Point. Tarkhanov, "functionary of the ninth class and *ad'iunkt* at the Academy of Sciences,"[54] was not as versatile a scientist perhaps as was his counterpart aboard *Vostok*, Ivan Mikhailovich Simonov (1794–1855), afterwards *rektor* of Kazan' (now the Kazan' State) University.[55] But he was gifted as a practical astronomer and was afforded all facilities he needed by his British hosts.[56] Other officers again took opportunities, as they arose in early March, to pursue specialized interests and hobbies. Assisted by a group of seamen and despite the summer heat and flies, Staff-Surgeon Grigorii A. Zaozerskii of the *Blagonamerennyi* matched Shtein's investigative energy by digging holes along the North Shore. He was looking not for metals but for bones, and he was soon rewarded for his efforts by uncovering "two skeletons of animals no longer living in New Holland." These skeletons were duly stowed aboard the transport and eventually given to the care of the Academy of Sciences.[57] They were among the ethnographica and objects of natural history which, unassisted by Shtein's rock samples, filled forty-five large drawers or cases at the Navy's own museum in the period immediately following the Arctic expedition (1822–28).[58] Several cases, it is certain, housed Australian insects and birds, including one or more "blackbirds," small crested parrots, and friar birds. Lazarev was one of several young officers with interests in ornithology or entomology. "For friendship's sake," Lieutenant Phillip Parker King presented him "with a little collection of birds and insects from the country, which he had carefully gathered for himself."[59] This collection, at least, remained in private hands. Doubtless others also did so, notwithstanding all instructions that all objects of the sort from the Pacific should be handed to the Naval Ministry.[60]

THE RUSSIANS MOVE INLAND, MARCH 1820

Like those of *Suvorov* six years earlier, the officers of the *Otkrytie* and *Blagonamerennyi* were showered with hospitality in Sydney and adjacent settlements. Macquarie had them visit him at Government House on several occasions, and himself called on them twice in his official launch "flying the English jack," with Coxswain Cadman at the tiller.[61] Ever conscious of the realpolitik of Anglo-Russian harmony, the now ageing Governor made every effort to be friendlier to Russians than to Frenchmen. Captain Louis de Saulces de Freycinet of *Uranie* had not been

treated, on his 1819 visit to the colony, with the unstinting and unasked-
for generosity with which he now treated Vasil'ev. For Freycinet, proper
politeness had sufficed. Here is Lazarev:

> There was a large green meadow facing the Governor's residence,
> and over it, while we were there, ran a number of marsupials and
> cockatoos. English soldiers stood on guard by the house itself. Learn-
> ing my name, the Governor was much interested to hear about my
> brother, asked us to call on him as often as we might and told me how
> he himself had once travelled by post in Russia, living awhile in
> Astrakhan. In that same connection, he recalled the Russian word
> *podorozhnaia* [order for post-horses], which had remained indelibly
> in his memory because, he said, he had been asked for it at every
> single station. For a man of sixty, he was remarkably active and was
> liked by all. . . .
>   During our stay in Port Jackson, the senior officials and the mess
> of the officers whose regiment was stationed there, vied with each
> other in pressing us to call on them. Macquarie and his estimable
> wife, especially, received us as their own; and despite his advancing
> years, the general rode out with us to inspect building work on a local
> lighthouse.[62]

Lazarev was wrong to think Macquarie "liked by all," but, like his fellow officers, he did not look too closely into local controversies or dis-
putes. After ten days, the Russians had too many invitations to cope with
from colonial officialdom and so "began to go out as parties of captain
and not more than three or four others." These dinner engagements even
became "wearying," detaining the Russians from their duties by the
sloops "and especially from astronomical observation work."[63] Still,
these social occasions did extend their range of possibly informative acquaintances and bring them into contact with the naturalist, breeder, *bon
vivant,* and magistrate Sir John Jamison (1776–1844), knight of the future "Regentsville";[64] the wealthy merchant Robert Campbell
(1769–1846), who provided them "with everything required for the
coming voyage on";[65] and the commanding officer, 48th Foot Regiment,
Lieutenant-Colonel James Erskine.[66] Such men, in turn, inspired others to
be helpful to their Russian guests. Faint echoes of these contacts may be
caught in private papers and, of course, in Howe's *Sydney Gazette* for
March and April 1820.[67] Sir John Jamison's relations with the Russians,
or at least with those of scientific temper, were particularly cordial. In his
readiness to entertain them grandly, he presided for the last time at a din-

ner in his private Sydney house. Within the week, it was to open to the public as a rather grand hotel.[68]

Captain-Lieutenant Vasil'ev arranged that half his company and one or more lieutenants should at all times be on board or by *Otkrytie,* and Gleb Shishmarev did the same. Essential work thus went ahead regardless of the socializing front. Both vessels watered from the Tank Stream, with some inconvenience, and wood was cut along the North Shore as before. *Otkrytie*'s ship's carpenter, Nikolai Fedorov, worked on her spars; her sailmaker, Pavel Bank, mended canvas; caulkers caulked.[69] There was no idleness. Men not required on the ships went off "in rowing boats, to survey newly discovered spots and unknown shores [within Port Jackson]." Regular contact was maintained with the sloops by means of signals: numbers 1 to 100. Aboriginals, it was supposed, might take the chance to rob or otherwise assault outlying boats.[70] It was a busy scene, presided over by the colony's small guardship:

> This guardship, actually a brig, stood in the roadstead with us and fired a volley at sunset, again at 8.30 pm for the evening watch, and again at 6 am for the morning watch. Also standing with us were twelve English merchantmen and one French trading vessel. . . . It was little trouble to fell timber and bring it to the sloops from the nearby woods; but watering took quite some time and was attended by no small labour. . . . The climate is truly splendid, and there is timber in abundance as well as an abundance of animals and birds. But there is little water. In Sydney, it is obtained from a single creek, which by no means oversupplies the town; and for shipping, it must be brought in casks over several hundred fathoms, over rocks moreover, so that these casks soon enough get broken.[71]

Work, then, went ahead aboard the sloops and in Port Jackson for as long as there were Russians present. As the range of scientific interest had been extended since the 1814 visit, so had the range of Russian movements through the colony. Most if not all of the two ships' officers travelled at least to Parramatta. The majority pressed further north and west, from William Lawson's handsome house at Prospect Hill, Veteran Hall, into the Hawkesbury, visiting Windsor with Macquarie or some other escort.[72] They rode along the Turnpike Road built in 1813 to the South Creek at Windsor township.[73] Rain had begun to fall quite heavily since their arrival in Australia. As a result, the Russians could themselves see the beginnings of potential floods. The South Creek flowed impetuously under John Howe's bridge while, further north, the Hawkesbury itself surged ominously past its low and sloping banks.[74] For months, the Russians gathered, there had been no rain; but both the year before and 1817 had seen great flood disasters. Crops of maize and wheat, much livestock, even settlers' slab huts had all been swept away.[75] The Russians noted with approval such precautions as the local people took against recurrences of floods.[76] Since 1806 at least, boats had been tied up at the free settlers' houses for immediate escape or rescue work:

> Windsor is a little township on the Hawkesbury River, which flows from the Blue Mountains to empty into Broken Bay. Around March, there are sometimes very heavy rains in the area, making the river rise more than 70′ now and again. At that season, it acquires a very powerful current and may flood all the surrounding countryside by Windsor, bearing off grain, crops, cattle, anything it meets. According to the local people, the Hawkesbury may overflow with such speed that they cannot even drive their stock to safety or gather in grains. But then, the soil is exceedingly fertile after an inundation, wheat yielding fifty-fold, eighty-fold, even 120-fold. For this reason, those with land there do not elect to move away to another spot. It so happened that we ourselves saw a boat tied up by the window of a wealthy landowner's house, so that people could get away in the event of the river's overflowing its banks.[77]

The toll house that had opened in 1815, George Howe's more recent wharf, and other structures that the Russians saw in 1820 have since vanished.[78] But a few remain today, notably the inn called "The Macquarie Arms," St. Matthew's Anglican Church (being rebuilt to Francis Greenway's new design in 1820), and the red brick wall which once enclosed the Military Barracks.[79] In the main, the Russians thoroughly approved Macquarie's building urge. Their records of their visits to the Hawkesbury, as of their stays at Parramatta, throw an incidental light on that dimension of Macquarie's final years in Australia.

Parramatta was, again, the centre of official courtesy towards the Russians. Vasil'ev himself, in his official journal of the voyage, felt constrained to note that "Governor Macquarie, being predisposed to satisfy our curiosity completely, went himself with us to Parramatta and to Windsor."[80] In reality, Macquarie and his wife Elizabeth had other reasons for a stay at Parramatta in mid-March, and would have been there in the absence of any Russians.[81] Even so, it is apparent that "they strove to entertain. Trying to anticipate in all things," Elizabeth, who was Macquarie's second wife and second cousin to the Earl of Breadalbane, a noblewoman of determined energy, "even discovered in the course of conversation just which dishes best pleased Russians and at what hour they breakfast."[82] The strain of entertaining Russian gentry singlehanded proved too much: by 17 March she was unwell and forced to stay a few days more at Parramatta, where she missed at least a couple of the ten or fifteen dinners that were given for her guests.[83] While at Parramatta, Vasil'ev, Shishmarev, and their people saw the sights that Bellingshausen was to see later that year: the hospital, the barracks, the school for native children. Vasil'ev noted that the latter were obliged to tend vegetable plots and learn the rudiments of husbandry, as well as read aloud and sew.[84] Taking advantage of Macquarie's openness, he collected data for a paper which was published for the first time by the Soviet authorities in 1950, headed "Observations about New South Wales."[85] "Former participants of the 1819–21 Arctic expedition did not manage to publish their results, even subsequently... and yet, it has been established that almost all the officers in question kept a journal."[86] Vasil'ev's paper is replete with facts and figures and so overlaps Bellingshausen's report, "A Short Notice on the Colony of New South Wales."[87] Here are extracts that reflect Vasil'ev's Parramatta stay and Russian visits to the Hawkesbury:

> By 1820, there were already 31,571 persons in the country, if one includes the 7,000 settled in Van Diemen's Land. This last place is more highly praised than New Holland proper, as having a more moderate climate, soil no worse, and better behaved natives.... Towns are now being laid out to a plan... and this naturally entails immense outlays by the government: the inhabitants have not yet been assessed for any tax. In the present year, 1820, there are reckoned to be a total of 65,913 horned cattle, 247,497 sheep and rams, and 3,935 horses. It is to be regretted only that the inhabitants suffer somewhat from water shortage....
>
> Windsor stands by the Hawkesbury River, which receives the waters of four creeks from the Blue Mountains; and when there *are* heavy and protracted rains, these so overfill the river that... its water-level may be 60' or 80' higher than ordinarily. The river is sometimes in this condition for twelve days at a stretch, currents increasing to six knots.... Whilst we were there, in March, heavy rains did fall and it was anticipated that the river would flood.[88]

While inland, the Russians noted the variety of enterprise and local agriculture: here flax imported from New Zealand ten years earlier was growing adequately; there, Indian corn, barley, and wheat. Sheep were being raised for wool, which was exported from the colony in modest quantity, together with "the whale-oil obtained from the New Zealand coasts."[89] Vegetable gardens, too, were very numerous.

While at Parramatta, Vasil'ev and Shishmarev kept in daily contact with their ships by courier. Their thoughts remained, perforce, at Kirribilli ("Russian") Point. Their eyes, however, were at intervals directed to the range of hills due west, beyond the Emu Plain and the Nepean River. On 8 March, the Expeditionary Artist Emel'ian Mikhailovich Korneev (1778–183?) and the naturalist-surgeon Fedor Shtein had hiked into these hills.

RUSSIANS IN THE BLUE MOUNTAINS, MARCH 1820

Shtein had received a wide medical training but was nonetheless a mineralogist at heart. Even before his arrival in Australia, he had been hoping for permission to investigate the rocks of the Blue Mountains. Once a student, still a lifelong admirer of the German mineralogist and classifier Abraham Gottlob F. Werner, he supposed that the Blue Mountains were ancient and was anxious to confirm this by analysis and observation on the spot.[90] Shishmarev and Vasil'ev both raised the matter with Macquarie, who at once offered the necessary transport and the service of a guide. The foreign visitor could well get lost among the ridges and escarpments of those mountains, which, besides, had for a decade harboured runaways. These convicts, some with native wives or mistresses and families, were armed and dangerous to solitary travellers. A warning had been printed in the *Sydney Gazette* in 1817.[91]

As naturalist of the Russian expedition, Shtein was charged with botany and entomology, and not only geology, while in the mountains. As Chamisso had upcountry on Oahu Island three years earlier, Shtein was to travel with equipment to preserve and isolate the flowers, leaves, and seeds that he collected.[92] As he proved again in 1821, while investigating the Alaskan coast between Cape Derby and Cape Newenham by open boat with his associate Avinov, nine tough seamen, and a Creole,[93] he was versatile enough to meet such challenges—and fit enough to see them through.

Horses were provided on Macquarie's orders, stores prepared, and instructions sent to Lawson, whom the Governor had chosen to escort the visitors to Emu Plain. Now Commandant of Bathurst, in which area he had received the first land grant (1815) made to a settler and stockman,[94] Lawson happened to be visiting his property, Veteran Hall, barely ten miles from Parramatta, when Macquarie thought of him. That he was excellently qualified to take the Russians on their climb there was no doubt: few men had crossed the ranges or explored the Western Districts more persistently or frequently, had stock there longer, or done more to open up the Bathurst Plains to settlement.

Matters already augured well for Dr. Shtein on his forthcoming trip. It was at this juncture, however, that the only man more obviously suited to accompany him than Lawson, the botanist-explorer Allan Cunningham (1791–1839), offered his services without Macquarie's prompting. His offer proved a valuable one to Russian science.

Cunningham, son of a humble Scottish gardener, was recognized as a distinguished botanist even before he reached Australia. An emissary from the international circle of Kew Gardens, he and Charles M. Frazer (1788–1831), his compatriot and also a distinguished botanist whom other Russians were to meet in New South Wales,[95] had together lent a scientific lustre to John Oxley's probing party in 1817. Since then, he and Lieutenant King in the cutter *Mermaid* had made scientific and surveying voyages to Cape Voltaire and Cambridge Gulf—and so to Timor and around Australia in anticlockwise fashion—of enormous risk and daring. In the words of his recent biographer:

> Cunningham, pathetically weak, struggled ashore at every opportunity, and in these depressing weeks [in Admiralty Gulf]. . . collected over 400 specimens, 200 packets of seeds, and a number of bulbs. . . . The cutter anchored in Sydney Cove on 12 January 1820. . . . Cunningham was by now beginning to put down roots in the colony and, aware that Banks' support of him had been made very clear to the Governor, he was much more happy and secure. . . . Still rather debilitated by his illness and the hardships which followed it, he worked slowly at the routine of preparing spcimens and reports for Kew until March, when he felt strong enough to act as guide to the Russian naturalist Shtein and his artist-assistant.[96]

Like Macquarie, Cunningham had had connections with Russians and Russified Germans and was willing to repay his debts of kindness. While collecting plants in South America, where he had passed two years en route to Sydney, he had benefitted from assistance by the Russian consul-general at Rio de Janeiro, the Georg Heinrich Langsdorf whose appearance had in 1803 been looked for in Australia by Phillip Parker King, as well as other "Russian gentlemen." He resolved to help "Messrs. Shtein & Karneyeff" and if necessary, as he roundly noted to Sir Joseph Banks, to defray all the expenses of their trip out of his pocket—since the government's might once again prove empty.[97] Like Lawson, he was pretty well acquainted with the rugged, empty country north and west of Mounts Victoria and York, as they are called today; and having practically recovered from his illness and from a conflict with Macquarie that had shaken him, he was again in need of exercise. From the beginning, his relations with his Russian guests were excellent.

The latter called on him in Parramatta on 6 March, admired his extensive plant collection, including those just recently obtained during his voyage in the *Mermaid,* and explained they had been granted twelve days' leave for their "intended tour." Both men had the Governor's permission "to visit the western country beyond the Blue Mountains," as well as an accompanying "passport to pass through the mountains, agreeable to his General Order published in the *Gazette* on that head."

As Cunningham quickly perceived, Korneev was no mere assistant to the naturalist but was managing his own important work. He was, in fact, atypical of Russian expeditionary artists in the South Seas and Australia in one major respect: he was a nobleman by birth. Orphaned in youth and lacking wealthy relatives, he was entrusted to the care of the St. Petersburg Academy of Arts, his drawing talent being obvious; and there he stayed, a pensioner or boarder and, it seems, a favourite of the director.[98] Later, he inherited a minuscule estate in the Poltava Province: his official service record speaks, phlegmatically, of "5 serfs of the male sex."[99] But this did not remove the need to earn a livelihood, and "draughtsman 14th class Korneev" was relieved to be appointed, "by imperial command, to accompany General-of-Infantry Baron Sprengtporten across Russia, Siberia, and foreign parts, there to draw views and costumes of various peoples." This was Baron Göran Magnus Sprengtporten (1740–1819), noble Finnish conspirator who, by secretly aiding the Russian cause, had played a large role in the Russian annexation of his country (1808) and briefly served as Russian Governor.[100] Always, Korneev moved in lofty social circles. He did well in "foreign parts," caught the attention of a grand duke, and was given a gold watch and 3,500 roubles to defray engraving costs. He was seconded to the Navy from the ministry of mines for which, since 1817, he had been delicately drawing medals and medallions. In 1820, he was forty-two years old and at the height of his artistic powers.

Heavy rain fell on 7 and 8 March as Cunningham, Shtein, and Korneev were about to leave for Emu Plain; but time was pressing, so they headed out. "The timber," as Vasil'ev had seen a little west of Parramatta, grew in size "until at length, well inland, scrub has given way to tall, stout, branchy trees. Beautiful, sweet-smelling plants are scattered widely through the valleys and about the hills, and flocks of multicoloured parrots both enliven them and entertain the weary traveller."[101] The party followed G. Blaxland's route (1813) perhaps twelve miles west. Progress was slowed by river beds and swollen creeks:

Every remarkable stone in the bed of the [Nepean?] river at the ford was examined, and the quality of every rill of water ascertained by its sediment. . . . After making some examinations and experiments with chemical acids upon the water supplying this station [Emu], which was found to be much impregnated with irons, we proceeded on our journey to the westward.[102]

Shtein continued to test water acidically and to identify geologically the ores and sediments encountered for the next several days. His data, in "Mineralogical Remarks on New South Wales," were abstracted by Vasil'ev and submitted to the government, together with his own reports, in 1822.[103] They were of value in themselves, as they were highly accurate, and have their place within the history of science in Australia. Few mineralogists had preceded Shtein into the area. Described in his "Remarks" were, in Vasil'ev's own words:

(1) The soils and strata of the earth, clays, sands, etc., seen over the country in question. . . (2) The hills, elevations, and mountains of that country; (3) the various minerals observed, e.g., sandstones, slate, granite, feldspar, quartz, porphyry, syenite, ordinary and precious garnets, pyrites gold-bearing and otherwise, gypsum, gneiss, basalt, etc. Also found were traces of gold, silver, copper, iron ore, and lead.

The Blue Mountains, covered though they are from foot to summit by tall trees, must in Shtein's opinion be considered among the very oldest on earth. . . . Thus far, only a small portion of them is known, over an extent of 200–300 English miles. The Newcastle coal deposits are to be regarded as belonging to the same range. Those coal deposits consist of schists and clays and contain incalculable quantities of plant- and, especially, reed-imprints. According to Shtein, the Blue Mountains adjoin and are actually linked to the Asian ranges to the north, when viewed as part of the global system of ranges linked by islands lying between New Holland and Asia. . . .

No volcanic hills were observed anywhere. Shtein thinks, on the basis of comparisons between the mountains he saw and rock types and strata formations in other lands that yield precious stones, that New Holland and the adjacent islands will also be producing such stones, and that these will in time be found.[104]

Korneev's portfolios provided pictorial asides to Allan Cunningham's own terse description of the westward hike. "View of Prospect Hill, Property of the Commandant Lawson Ten English Miles Distant from

Parramatta''; "Ford Over the Nepan River at Emu Settlement, by the Foot of the Blue Mountains''; "Waterfall Known as Prince Regent's Falls'': such drawings could perhaps be made in haste and touched up later, but they were nonetheless sufficient to ensure that the travellers reached only "Regent's Glen'' by the first night. Shtein was in any case collecting plant and insect specimens when opportunity arose, measuring heights, gathering rocks:

> About 7 pm on the 9th March we arrived at the King's Table Land, where the steep perpendicular cliffs of the Regent's Glen so delighted Mr Karneyeff the painter that it was proposed we should encamp on its verge at night, to afford him an opportunity to make some sketches, particularly of a cascade or cataract originally discovered by Lt. Lawson.[105]

To the west of the Cumberland Plain, the geological formation with which Russians had hitherto been familiar, the scarp of the Blue Mountains rises brusquely from the bank of the Nepean River, on the bed of which Shtein easily found iron traces.[106] From afar, the plateau, topped with so-called Hawkesbury Sandstone, offers a comparatively flat and level skyline; but this is deeply dissected by rivers which have cut impressive canyons through it. Though the valleys are quite broad with gently sloping lower slopes, their upper slopes commonly culminate in "steep perpendicular cliffs" of the kind that charmed Korneev. By collating Cunningham's and Russian records of this 1820 trip, we see that Shtein, Korneev, and their escort had, like Blaxland, Lawson, W. C. Wentworth, and more recently Surveyor G. W. Evans, simply travelled up a ridge until they arrived on the great plateau.[107] "King's Table Land" was one small part of this plateau. The Russians had in fact followed the track, running due west from Emu Plain, that William Cox, prominent settler and magistrate in Windsor district, had laid while *Suvorov* was in Sydney in the spring of 1814.[108] This in turn suggests that Cunningham, aware that his guests had little time to spare, followed Evans's route yet further, and descended the scarp of the plateau beside Mount York.[109] Plainly, the party had traversed eucalypt forests with some undergrowth along the westward-tending ridge, crossed the plateau and Cox's River, and at least caught sight of the extensive Western Districts of today.[110] It is impossible to specify their route exactly. The portfolios left by Korneev and the Shtein report suggest a brief stop on the south edge of the area of the Jenolan Caves ("Shtein discovered a vast cave near the King's Table Land, hitherto unsuspected, and named it Lawson Cave after the commandant"),[111] and another pause above the Campbell River. Among

Korneev's sketches—lost today, regrettably—was one headed "Campbell Tableland in the Blue Mountains of New Holland." However that may be, it is apparent that the Russians found a limestone cave of huge proportions to the west of Mount Victoria, detected gold in one or more mountain creeks, collected insects large and small, and botanized. The party doubled back to reach Castlereagh on 12 March. The steady rain made them appreciate the wine, food, warmth, and conversation offered by the lonely Reverend Henry Fulton.[112] Undeterred by soggy ground and swollen creeks, they then pressed on to Windsor, putting up at a small inn, and so to Prospect Hill, Commandant Lawson's property. On the 16th, they returned to Parramatta.

Among the holdings of the Central State Historical Archive of the USSR (TsGIAL) in Leningrad are papers formerly held at the St. Petersburg Academy of Arts which throw light on the extent and nature of Korneev's work in New South Wales.[113] Besides his service record, there are detailed lists of two portfolios, of thirty-six and sixty-five drawings, respectively, and correspondence between the Academy's director and the Hydrographic Depot of the Navy on the question of the drawings' publication in a volume by Korneev himself, by Vasil'ev, or even by "Retired Major Karl von Gillesem in Riga," i.e., the ex-midshipman of *Blagonamerennyi*. In addition, there are papers indicating that Korneev, who had failed to extract 45,000 roubles from the Crown to defray the cost of printing 150 copies of a Voyage with engravings (1822–23) but had at least obtained a pension of 720 silver roubles, was in 1830 still a bachelor and in possession of at least seventy extra drawings made in 1819–21.[114] The descriptive lists are doubly important, as indications of Korneev's work in New South Wales and as clues for archive searches. The following items clearly derive from Korneev's 1820 visit. Titles precede numbers indicating, first, the portfolio (that of thirty-six sketches being taken as No. 1 and that of sixty-five as No. 2) and, second, the 1822 ordering.

"Campbell Tableland in the Blue Mountains of New Holland" (1:1)
"Crested Parrot from New Holland" (1:2)
"*Ornithorhynchus* from New Holland" (1:3)
"*Ornithorhynchus*" (1:4a)
"Blue Mountains Parakeet" (1:4b)
"Blackbirds of New Holland" (1:5)
"Sun-fish or Prickle-fish" (1:6:1)
"'Varieties of Diodon" (1:6:2–3)
"Medusa in New Holland" (1:6:4)
"Clothing and Weaponry of the Natives of New Holland" (1:7)

"*Alca arctica* or Marine Parrot" (1:8)
"Nocturnal Gathering of New Hollanders" (1:13a)
"Continuation of a New Hollanders' Dance" (1:13b)
"Levson's [i.e., Lawson's] Cave, Blue Mountains" (1:19)
"A View of Port Jackson in New Holland" (1:34)

"View of Prospect Hill, Property of Parramatta Commandant Levson
    [i.e., Lawson], 10 English Miles from Parramatta" (2:3a)
"Castlereagh Hamlet, 16 English Miles from Parramatta" (2:3b)
"Waterfall Known as Prince Regent's Falls" (2:4)
"Large Cascade in the Blue Mountains of New Holland, Known as
    Campbell Falls, 75 English Miles from Port Jackson" (2:7)
"Kangaroo Dance, at Night, Dance of the Natives of New Holland at
    Port Jackson" (2:16)
"Dress of the Natives of New Holland" (2:22)
"Ford Across the Nepan [Nepean] River at the Settlement of Emu at
    the Foot of the Blue Mountains" (2:24)
"Varieties of Ornament and Weaponry of the Natives in Port Jack-
    son" (2:28)
"Large New Holland Bunting" (2:43)
"Port Jackson" (2:62)
"The Indian Fig-tree in Port Jackson" (2:65)

How deeply New South Wales had impressed Korneev the observer is
apparent from the fact that fully one-quarter of the 101 drawings that he
submitted to the Naval Ministry were from Australia, where he had spent
one month out of the thirty-seven of his voyage. Like his counterpart
aboard *Vostok*, Pavel Mikhailov, he was fascinated by the flora, fauna,
Aboriginals, and scenery of New South Wales and determined to provide
his countrymen with an authentic record of them. Like his comrades
Lazarev and Gillesem, he struggled long but unsuccessfully, in 1822–30,
for permission and the necessary funds to print that record.[115] Gillesem at
least managed, in 1849, to publish more or less "improved" and polished
extracts from his journal from the *Blagonamerennyi* in a St. Petersburg
periodical.[116] Unhappily from the Australian perspective, these bore
mainly on the expedition's Arctic probing work, passing in silence over
Sydney and its hinterland. Again, the Soviet archival records tantalize: by
1830, it is certain, Gillesem had written a complete account, in German,
of his voyage round the world. The fourth chapter concerned Australia
and had this précis: "Friendly reception by Governor and inhabitants of
Sydney town—trip to Paramata [sic], Windsor, and towards the Blue

Mountains—notes on the banished convicts—the colonial regulations—Natives—animals and plants—departure from Port Jackson."[117]

Gillesem and Lazarev were both among the officers who helped make Cunningham feel comfortable aboard their sloop when, at Shishmarev's and Shtein's invitation and in recognition of his help, he was invited out to Sydney Cove. Cunningham himself records the pleasant hour spent in Shtein's book-laden quarters in the transport and the pleasure that he took there in examining Alexander von Humboldt's "most magnificent works on the botany of South America." Lazarev had spent some time already with Cunningham's old friend and comrade from the *Mermaid*, Phillip Parker King, and in his memoirs of his voyage speaks of Cunningham, ongoing exploration, and the need to make a full investigation of "the New South Wales ranges."

Otkrytie and *Blagonamerennyi* were ready to depart by 23 March. Both were packed with fresh and dried provisions for, as Gillesem observed, "we were now to sail no little time, moreover towards lands that offered no hope of such supplies or anything even remotely like them."[118] Only one more thing was wanted: an accommodating wind. The wind blew hard into the cove, bringing unpleasant, heavy rains. While the Russians waited patiently, the Governor came out "accompanied both by his family and by a number of officials and their ladies; and he spent some time aboard the sloops. A thirteen-gun salute was fired."[119] Finally, at dawn on the 26th, anchors were weighed and sails set. This time, *Otkrytie* saluted with a twenty-one gun volley, to which the Dawes Point battery responded with its long-bored eighteen-pounders.[120] The noise induced Macquarie to combine another brief inspection visit to the South Head light recently built to Francis Greenway's plan with one last courtesy to the departing Russians. "Passing the first cape to the right from Sydney town," writes Lazarev, "we sighted the Governor, standing there with an adjutant and several officers. All waved their hats, shouting 'Hurrah!' We replied, we and our companies at large."[121] For guests and hosts alike, it was the end of an uncomplicated interlude. It had been welcome to the Russians on the ground of need alone and had provided a diversion from administrative troubles for the Governor. The scene was set for Bellingshausen's visits.

"VOSTOK" AND "MIRNYI": ARRIVAL IN AUSTRALIA, APRIL 1820

Vostok's lookout sighted Van Diemen's Land (Cape Pedra Blanca) from his crow's-nest at approximately 2:15 PM on 6 April. It was cause for celebration.[122] Thoughts of rest and warmth were uppermost after a voyage of Antarctic exploration that had taken *Mirnyi* and *Vostok* more than a quarter of the way around the globe—south of the sixtieth degree of latitude. It had been an epic cruise, during the course of which both officers and men had lived in physical discomfort and considerable danger. *Otkrytie* and *Blagonamerennyi* indeed had needed various repairs on arrival in Port Jackson, and their companies had been relieved to step ashore. But Lazarev's and Bellingshausen's ships had far more need of what the colony could offer; and the same held for their men. For days on end, even the sun had not been sighted on the fringes of Antarctica. Firewood had grown so short that, aboard *Mirnyi,* the possibility of using wine- and water-casks for fuel had been discussed. And still "Port Jackson was distant 120° of longitude and 31° of latitude, that is to say, by the shortest possible route we should still have to travel 5,000 miles."[123] Never had Russian ships arrived at Sydney after such a gruelling or scientifically important voyage, or in such transparent need of a recuperation period.

And yet there had been nothing hurried or impromptu about Bellingshausen's and his company's approach to New South Wales. As he had ashore, so on his way that academically inclined and careful officer had executed his instructions to the letter. Day by day, there had been testings of the air and water temperature, wind and current measurements, astronomic observations, record keeping, even some zoology by Simonov, *Vostok*'s versatile scientist.[124] When at last *Vostok* and *Mirnyi* had headed for Australia, they had pursued different routes, lest some discovery or scientific opening be missed on the horizon. *Vostok* alone took constant barometric readings, made a running coastal survey, and—for good measure—investigated seabirds as she ran along the south shore of Van Diemen's Land towards Cape Howe and Gabo Island. Day by day, the cold and damp diminished. Wood and iron fittings sweated, after months in the Antarctic, and had to be constantly wiped. New South Wales was in sight by 8 April. Next day was Orthodox Easter:

> All dressed themselves in clean holiday clothes. . . . We said matins and all the prayers. The crew had Easter cakes for breakfast. . . . We sailed in sight of the high hills of New South Wales, and already imagined that we should be in Port Jackson by the next day and enjoy ourselves. . . but a foul wind from the north set in. On the 29th [10 April], we beat up in sight of shore, all the crew now enjoying the beautiful weather, joking, and amusing themselves. They. . . cleaned the sextants and cleaned the lenses of the telescopes so as to see objects on shore more clearly.[125]

Keen observers that they were, the Russians thus established the prevailing tone of their forthcoming visit to Australia while still at sea. More obviously even than the North-bound polar enterprise, the Bellingshausen-Lazarev Antarctic expedition was essentially a scientific one. This was apparent for as long as it remained in Australasia.[126]

Using the British atlas printed in 1814 on the basis of *Investigator* surveys (1798–1803), and, moreover, highly conscious of the shade of Matthew Flinders, Bellingshausen made his way along the coast from Pigeon House near the head of the Clyde River up to Jervis Bay, keeping some twenty miles offshore.[127] A dozen telescopes were trained on George's River, yellow sand and, just beyond, a small white house. Botany Bay was passed at 8:00 AM on the 11th, and within two hours, with a pilot aboard, *Vostok* was passing by the reef called Sow and Pigs. "The green shores of Port Jackson," more particularly modern-day Taylor's Bay, Rose Bay, and Athol Bay, were all "surrounded by forests and. . . beautiful valleys."[128] Harbour Captain Piper boarded her off modern Bradley's Head. Like Vasil'ev and unlike Freycinet, Bellingshausen was invited to proceed past Neutral Bay and anchor in the road facing the town. He did so, anchoring in seven fathoms at a spot whence Benelong's Point, three cables off, bore S 14°E. Boats were put down, and, with the amiable Piper, Bellingshausen went immediately to present himself to Governor Macquarie at his "little country house," that is, the residence. Macquarie was predictably hospitable. Fifteen-gun salutes were then exchanged.[129]

Now in the last months of his term as Governor, Macquarie had received sufficient foreigners, including Russians, to be able to anticipate requests, making allowance for the nature, port of origin, and cargo of a vessel. Bellingshausen was accordingly well served by the colonial authorities. There is indeed a certain smoothness and inevitable movement in the record of *Vostok*'s first days in port. A proper site for an observatory and workshops was proposed almost at once, at "Russian" (Kirribilli) Point, wood-felling privileges granted on the North Shore (modern-day Mosman), news exchanged. Supplies were bought from Robert Campbell and from other local merchants, also easily and speedily. The French, never well liked or fully trusted in the early New South Wales, had not been similarly welcomed by the populace at large; and certain shopkeepers had shown a rather pointed coolness, twelve months earlier, to Captain Freycinet's appointed representative, the would-be buyer of their goods. Macquarie had eventually ordered that the Commissary General himself should take French bills, which were drawn upon the government in Paris and which certain Sydney merchants would not touch.[130] For Bellingshausen's buyers there were no such local hurdles to be crossed: only a month before, Campbell and others had had com-

fortable and profitable dealings with Shishmarev. It was indeed while
Otkrytie remained by Sydney Cove that "just and gentlemanly" Campbell had officially announced the re-establishment of his commission
business. He had profited from and been encouraged by her presence.[131]
As for items in the *Sydney Gazette* drawing attention to Russia's strength
and forward policy across the Balkans and the Near East,[132] they were ignored as danger signals by Macquarie and the army officers at Sydney.
Necessarily, Macquarie recognized the military might and the political
ambitions of the Russian Crown: he had observed them personally. Nor
were Russian naval movements in the North and South Pacific Ocean un-
remarked by him. Neither his orders nor his personal persuasions, on the
other hand, induced Macquarie to consider Russian policies in other
quarters of the globe—for instance, Turkey, the Northwest Coast, or
China—to be relevant to Sydney and its future.

"VOSTOK" AND "MIRNYI" AT SYDNEY: NAVAL WORK AND SOCIAL CONTACTS

Bellingshausen and Lazarev, who had arrived on 15 April, had urgent
reasons for establishing their base ashore without delay. Signs of scurvy
had appeared on two of *Vostok*'s seamen and all of the sheep and pigs
aboard her, as well as one or two of *Mirnyi*'s people. While the men were
kept ashore and given lemon juice and pinol essence, bought expressly
for such cases from the London firm, Donkin and Hall, eight months before,[133] the stock were landed, penned, and fed sweet grass. They ate with
painful, blue, and swollen gums. As twice before in recent weeks, a
"Russian dockyard" was set up on "Russian" (Kirribilli) Point. Tents
were erected under Captain-Lieutenant Zavadovskii's eye: some for the
sick, others for officers, others again for stores and instruments, carpenters' gear, commissary records, canvas mending. All was movement.
While *Vostok*'s two smiths worked on her "portable ship's forge" and
sailmakers, headed by Migalkin, set to work on damaged canvas, Bellingshausen himself turned to the large question of health, hygiene, and
food. Without delay, he organized a "steam-tent" and an enormous, fes-
tive clothes-wash. It was Australia's first sauna:

> Water was boiled partly upon a stove built from our metal ballast and
> partly in another spot, by means of heated cannon-balls. When all
> was in readiness, the tent was closed and water was poured con-
> tinually onto it from the ship's fire-engine... lest steam escape
> through the cloth.[134]

Such procedures were of interest both to the British and, particularly, to the Aboriginals, who had already paid the Russians lengthy visits. Led by Boongaree, the "king from Broken Bay" to whom Macquarie had in 1815 given the chain and copper plate drawn by *Vostok*'s own artist, Pavel Nikolaevich Mikhailov (see Plate 21), these were members of the Cammeraigal tribe.[135] They understood a little English, but they sought no explanation of the Russians' odd behaviour. Empty casks and other moveables, meanwhile, had been taken off the ship to lighten her; and masts had been unstepped and gently lowered. Just above, Simonov's transit instrument stood firmly on its latest base, which was a massive lead-filled stove minus its chimney.

> It was necessary first to raise the ship, in order to repair the copper plates which had been torn by slight collisions with the ice, and to replace the copper nails torn from the sheathing. . . . Fifteen sailors with a quartermaster went to cut down timber to be used as firewood; and we started on the mending and setting up of rigging, which the frost and damp had made extremely taut, but which the warmth here in Port Jackson made so slack that it was necessary to reset it and, in large measure, to re-splice it.[136]

Next came caulking and repainting, while the ship's boats carried water from the Tank Stream. *Mirnyi*'s arrival at this point raised morale another notch. Almost at once, the "Russian dockyard" grew in area with extra tents, a second forge, sick-bay, and livestock pen. No Russian vessel in Australia had ever needed such attention to the hull and stem as did the *Mirnyi*. All the repairs called for by *Neva, Suvorov,* and *Otkrytie,* and extra ones, were unavoidable results of one collision and one slight brush with an iceberg in Antarctica. Her captain, Lazarev, recalled the incidents and Port Jackson as follows:

> We spent an entire month in Port Jackson, putting the sloops to rights and repairing parts damaged by ice. Lest you lightly dismiss the perils we had run amongst the icebergs, I will simply observe that we inserted a new section, 6'2'' long, into *Mirnyi*'s stem. . . . To do this, I was obliged to unlade her almost completely, to trim her by the stern, and to beach her on a sand-bar at high tide in a full moon. The task did not prove too small for 45 strong men. However, it was achieved, and two weeks later our topgallant yards were again raised.
> It was most fortunate that we had struck the ice head-on: a fraction to the starboard or port and we should certainly have been stove in,

and not a man would then have survived to tell our whereabouts. Aboard the *Vostok* too several sections of outer sheathing, which the ice had damaged severely, were replaced, besides which it proved necessary to add several new knees and stanchions, the old ones having been weakened by great and frequent storms. The same reason required all *Vostok*'s yards and her topmast to be reduced and her sails adjusted.[137]

As Bellingshausen adds, a major problem for the carpenters was that, so close to Sydney, there was precious little timber to be had that was not twisted. "Tall 'Red Gums' grew in the small valleys running back from each bay, while the ridges between carried more twisted and less attractive members of the eucalypt family. Scattered amongst the trees of both valleys and ridges were fir-like casuarinas."[138] Seamen had been felling timber on the North Shore for a quarter-century by 1820, and such cedar as had once flourished within an easy walk of Sydney had been taken long before. *Mirnyi*'s carpenters looked with disgust at *Casuarina torulosa* and *Eucalypta haemastoma* and *gummifera*, "their hearts twisted . . . the wood too hard and heavy to be joined to pine." Suitable timber was, however, found and brought down to the spot, very near modern Sydney Bridge, where *Mirnyi* lay. At ebb tide, the crushed and splintered section of her hull was taken out and replaced by cedar planks. Repairs continued on *Vostok*'s copper sheathing and cracked bowsprit stem for seven days. The stem was reinforced by heavy iron bands and sloping wooden knees.[139]

Zavadovskii, in the interim, had come to terms with Sydney merchants and was buying foodstuffs at local market prices. Food was plentiful. Free settlers were prospering inland despite the vagaries of drought and sudden flooding, and the colony had largely freed itself of trade restrictions.[140] Half-a-dozen firms imported goods from London and the East India Company's domains. Standing at anchor in Sydney Cove in April 1820 were a dozen merchantmen, besides the transport *Coromandel* (Captain Downey), which had lately brought out convicts, and King's diminutive *Mermaid*. The Russians took an interest in Downey and the transportation system,[141] and some pleasure in the company of other trading captains: William Spiers of the *Seaflower*, John Gordon of the *Acteon*, and Benjamin Orman of the ship *Haldane*.[142] Such pleasant intercourse, however, did not keep them from their basic naval tasks while in Port Jackson. No task was more essential than provisioning.

On leaving England in August 1819, *Vostok* and *Mirnyi* had been supplied with the very best and latest sea provisions by the firm Messrs. Donkin and Hall, which had pioneered tinned iron containers for such perishable products. "Mr. Donkin," Bellingshausen notes, had supplied not only "specially prepared fresh soups with vegetables and beef tea in tins," but also essence of spruce or "pinol essence," to be used on lengthy polar voyages.[143] Such tinned supplies and antiscorbutics had been tried out and approved by British officers; and Captain Parry, who had just left for the Arctic Ocean, had taken them along. At Teneriffe and Rio de Janeiro, Bellingshausen had again bought local foodstuffs, this time fresh-killed meat, wine, vegetables, and fruits; and so had Lazarev. such was the nature of the subsequent Antarctic cruise, nevertheless, that both *Vostok*'s and *Mirnyi*'s companies reached Sydney plainly suffering from the beginnings of vitamin deficiency.

Nothing that the colony could offer Russians on discovery, like Bellingshausen, or en route to Petropavlovsk-in-Kamchatka and/or Sitka, like his naval predecessors, was as vital as an adequate water supply (if nothing more) and an abundance of fresh viands and, particularly, vegetables and citrus fruit. To read the Russians' own accounts of Sydney visits, with their numerous allusions to the colony's expanding citrus groves, beef herds, and healthy kitchen gardens, is to see the central reason for the Russian naval presence in Australia. Too often, students of that presence, rightly concerned not to overlook the scientific and social elements of Russian visits, have deliberately underplayed the naval aspect.[144] In reality, *Vostok*'s and *Mirnyi*'s Sydney visits of 1820 were as fruitful in the maritime connection as they were both socially and scientifically. Thanks to the published narratives of Bellingshausen, Simonov, and (rather later) Midshipman Pavel Novosil'skii of the *Mirnyi*,[145] all three facets of those visits were far better known to Russians than were Lazarev's or Hagemeister's earlier Australian encounters—and considerably better known in Russia than abroad. Here, to illustrate the point, are brief remarks made by the same Frank Debenham who, as the editor of Bellingshausen's narrative of 1831, did more than any other European scholar in this century to bring the Bellingshausen voyage to the notice of the English-speaking world:

> Contemporary reports of what the British thought of the Russians are rather meagre, but. . . the contacts were in fact not very close, partly because the crews were kept very busy at refitting the ships, partly because they were somewhat isolated both by the language difficulty and by their land headquarters being on the northern, uninhabited shore of the harbour.[146]

Was it really possible that highly educated officers, some with a good command of English, who had been at sea for months and had been welcomed in a new and very interesting country by its Governor and whose under-officers and craftsmen were particularly competent, would be deterred from social contact by "the language difficulty" and a sense of isolation brought about by, say, two hundred yards of water? They were busy, certainly; and time was pressing. Even so, they and occasionally ordinary

Russian seamen too had social dealings with the Cammeraigal tribe and, far more frequently, with Englishmen and Scots of three main kinds: Governor's people, friends, relations, and supporters; other officers and prosperous free settlers who might or might not be admirers and supporters of the Governor; and merchants and their agents. With the convicts and their lower-ranking British guards, they had no dealings whatsoever out of courtesy and from a feeling of propriety. Among the individuals referred to once or more in Russian narratives, or whom the 1820 visitors are known to have encountered, were the following: Lawson, Piper, and King; James Erskine of the 48th Foot Regiment; Hector Macquarie, the Governor's equerry; Reverend Henry Fulton of Castlereagh and Windsor; George Johnston; Lieutenant Raines of the 46th Foot Regiment; D'Arcy Wentworth and Richard Brooks, magistrates at Sydney; Stephen Milton and William Cossar of Sydney Dockyard; Surveyor Hawkley; King's Commissioner John Thomas Bigge; Robert Campbell; Mrs. Shelley of the Parramatta School for Native Girls; and James Squire, brewer of Ryde. The list, though incomplete, is a suggestive one and does not point to "isolation" or reserve amidst an endless round of tasks and duties on the North Shore. Like his naval predecessors, Bellingshausen was as kindly and conspicuously feted as he wished. Macquarie's diary reflects the fact: "24 April. Entertained the Russian officers and a large party of Civil and Military Officers at dinner—39 persons sat down to table. . . "; "28 April. Commodore Bellingshausen, Capts. Lazaroff and Savadoffkie and 10 other officers belonging to the Russian ships came up from Sydney this morning, to spend a few days with us at Parramatta."[147] There are other indications that the Russians, of the lower deck as well as from the wardroom, were not quite as isolated on the North Shore as Debenham believed. On leaving Sydney for the second time at least, in mid-November, certain seamen had venereal disease.[148]

The Russians went to Parramatta in two groups, three in the Governor's own carriage, nine by cutter. Those who took the turnpike road were quite impressed by "signs of industry," by free settlers' houses, and by abundant local flora as they sped past "gentle hills" and "strong, sparse timber." Parramatta too impressed:

Its streets are wide and even and run at right angles to one another. The houses for the most part are of wood, clean, and having gardens or orchards running down to the street; which keeps the air in the town fresh, and gives to the place a pleasant rural appearance. A few of the inhabitants have already stone, instead of wooden, houses. We passed through the town to the Governor's. He. . . took us to the upper story, reserved for the use of guests. He assigned. . . a double room to our astronomer, Mr Simonov, and to our artist, Mr Mikhailov, observing that science and art should be closely allied. The other officers put up for the night at inns. We remained three days. . . .

After breakfast we went and spent some time in the town with the Governor's Adjutant, Lieutenant Macquarie. He showed us the hospital and the stone barracks which were almost ready for the military garrison; women are employed at the place in the day-time, where they spin and weave clothes for the convicts who are employed in public work for the Government. . . . From the women's factory we went to the school for the girls of the natives of New Holland. They are neatly dressed and are taught to read, write, draw and sew. On the completion of their education, they are free and can marry Europeans by mutual consent. . . . Farther on we came to the Parramatta River. . . passed a dam built to prevent the water mixing with the salt water during flood tides. . . then passed by a new building which had already been carried up as far as the roof, intended for female convicts sent out from Britain every year.[149]

From his Rose Hill base, which now forms part of King's School, Parramatta, Bellingshausen made those observations and enquiries that laid the basis for his three related essays on the colony of 1820: "Short Notes on the Colonies of New South Wales," "An Account of the Government of New South Wales," and "Van Diemen's Land." With both Elizabeth and Hector Macquarie close at hand, he lost no chance of making pleasant times instructive. He had orders to be busy when in places like Australia and to record all that he saw, so social visits and the sightseeing encouraged by Macquarie could be seen as service duties.[150] Unlike Lazarev in 1814 and Vasil'ev the month before, Bellingshausen was amenable to hospitality but, at the same time, quite prepared to recognize that there were tensions in the colony. He was, for instance, well aware of Marsden's efforts to make trouble for the Governor in London by suggesting that in openly permitting female convicts to betake themselves to Parramatta settlement when they had done their day's quota of work, he was in fact promoting evil and licentiousness.[151] Again, he recognized Macquarie's semi-failure to persuade the Aboriginals, whose free nomadic lifestyle reminded him of the Russian gypsies', to enrol their children in the new government schools. Nevertheless, Bellingshausen in general approved of Macquarie's policies and, unlike Bigge, who was considering them at precisely the same time, chose to present them in a favourable light. There are, in fact, arresting contrasts between Bigge's and Bellingshausen's assessments of the overall success of institutions like the native school and women's factory at Parramatta.[152] Bellingshausen had no local axe to grind, even evincing satisfaction in his fellow Europeans' new achievements in New Holland—a disarming trait and worthy of the vanished age of the Encyclopaedists, whose admirer he remained throughout his life. Macquarie, for his own part, took some pleasure in accompanying soberly perceptive Russian officers to such stone monuments as the "Macquarie Tower" (Greenway's South Head Light), the Sydney hospital, and Parramatta barracks. Only the Russians' weariness, after a seven-mile ride on horseback, and the pressure of the calendar, it seems, stopped him from taking the *Vostok*'s and *Mirnyi*'s officers to Windsor in the steps of their compatriots. Here is Bellingshausen on the new road to the Hawkesbury laid down by William Cox barely a year before,[153] that is, the modern Blacktown Road:

> This road is beautifully laid out and on a sloping hillside little houses and gardens and behind them green cornfields could be seen. The woods in the vicinity had been burned in order to prepare the ground for sowing. In the midst of this wild country, we met everywhere with evidences of the taste, intellect, and labour of Europeans. Flocks of white parrots continually flew across the road with shrill screams.[154]

Of the remainder of Bellingshausen's Parramatta stay, suffice it to note that he surveyed the flora of Elizabeth Macquarie's garden (wattles, citrus, European fruits); called on Lieutenant King "of Norfolk Island, educated in the globe's five continents"; admired native girls singing in Parramatta Church; and, with the Governor, walked out to gash-like gullies, "washed out by the rains."[155] It was a pleasant interlude.

Vostok and *Mirnyi* sailed from Sydney on 20 May. both were in excellent repair and well provisioned for a voyage of discovery in warmer climes. They passed four months about the Tuamotu or Low Archipelago east of Tahiti, at Tahiti itself, and in the Lau Archipelago of Fiji, making numerous discoveries and sorting cartographic fantasy from fact.[156] With some regret, the expedition made its way back to Port Jackson with the onset of southern spring, to be ready for another sweeping voyage to the South by mid-November. The two ships entered it again in the third week of September.

"VOSTOK" 'S AND "MIRNYI" 'S SECOND STAY AT SYDNEY, SEPTEMBER–
NOVEMBER 1820

Notwithstanding a note in the *Gazette* on the enormous size and growth of Russia's armies, Bellingshausen's reappearance proved a homecoming and party. And for Simonov the scientist and younger men like Pavel Novosil'skii, in particular, the lengthy second sojourn in Australia proved very happy:

> We entered to the joyous greetings of our Sydney acquaintances, and Captain Piper boarded us half-way across the bay: he had spotted *Vostok* from his cottage, which he had named in honour of his wife Eliza, and had come out in his gig without delay. . . . I crossed to that very same stretch of shoreline where our tents had stood before; and from that very day, our previous activities, labours, and pleasures were resumed. And this time, General Macquarie not only offered us entertainment and much hospitality, but also performed a considerable service for the expedition proper, by providing us with excellent dried timber and skilled craftsmen. . . . Our own people did smaller repairs ashore, near the tents where I had established myself with my astronomical instruments. Lieutenant Annenkov of *Mirnyi* was my neighbour.[157]

Macquarie had the dried cedar brought up from Bulli; but it did not reach the North Shore for three weeks and, predictably, the Russians' scholarly and social life proceeded at a high pitch ("invited out to dinner constantly. . . gatherings, parties, and dances. . . open-hearted hospitality detained us from our works.)"[158] Late in September, Bellingshausen launched himself into an all-embracing study of the colony. Buildings, administration, convict life, resources, native policy and commerce, customs, diet, husbandry, and other things were scrutinized with patience. Bellingshausen's "Short Notes on the Colonies of New South Wales," which appeared in his narrative *Repeated Explorations in the Southern Icy Ocean* (1831), marked the high point in Russian study of Australia up to that time. They were not only comprehensive, clearly written, and well balanced, but also incorporated data from the journals of half-a-dozen officers besides his own. The following brief passages, which give some notion of the essay's tone, reflect its author's special interests:

> When a convict vessel arrives at Port Jackson and the necessary arrangements for the housing of prisoners are complete, they are sent

ashore. The Governor personally superintends the disposal of the convicts and asks questions as to their conduct on the voyage, etc., then distributes them among the landowners, who are allowed to select workmen. In this case the landowners must give an undertaking that they will feed them and pay them £10 sterling per annum. . . . A few of the minor officials, such as clerks, overseers of the convicts, cattle-inspectors, also receive one, two, three or more convicts, who must work for them in return for food and a dollar a week. . . . Convicts going into service now receive a weekly ration of 10 lbs of flour and 7 lbs of beef or, instead of the latter, 4 lbs of pork. . . . In addition, each convict receives per month two gallons of wine, one ounce of lemon-juice, and the same amount of sifted sugar daily. The women are given tea. . . . The convicts employed on either public or Government works, work from sunrise to sunset; they have 2 1/2 hours for breakfast and dinner. But although they are engaged almost all day, work proceeds very slowly, for the overseers are convicts themselves and turn a blind eye to leisurely work.[159]

Here was a situation that the Russian naval officer could recognize. Order, constraint, humane but disciplined conditions, some abuse: all seemed familiar. And Bellingshausen does not hide his admiration of Macquarie's innovations, for example, Sydney's Savings Bank, a regular bank founded in 1817, and special currency: the Spanish dollar with a "dump" cut from the centre by the convict silversmith William Henshall.[160] As for the Governor's acceptance of the disadvantage at which deported Roman Catholics (including priests) still found themselves in New South Wales ("the established form of religion is Protestant, Catholic priests are not allowed to celebrate mass, and in consequence the Irishmen bring up their children themselves"), it seemed to Bellingshausen unavoidable and just. It was the soldier's lot to follow his instructions, not amend them. By the same token, the lack of seasoned troops to keep "full order" among "desperadoes" was a consequence of London's policies and not Macquarie's:

The Governor has a selected bodyguard consisting of one sergeant, one corporal, and ten soldiers of a light cavalry regiment. During our stay, the military force consisted of the 48th Regiment and one company of veterans brought out from England. . . . While we were at Port Jackson, there were altogether in Sydney, Parramatta, Liverpool, and the inland districts—19 officers, 33 sergeants, 27 corporals, 10 drummers, and 370 privates. In Newcastle there were 3 officers, 4 sergeants, 3 corporals, and 75 privates. The remainder were in Van Diemen's Land. One can readily understand that this small military force is quite inadequate.

Little information was withheld from Bellingshausen and his officers, and as a consequence his "Notes" were full of figures. As a recent writer comments, "Bellingshausen set out a whole page of statistics prepared by Macquarie himself in 1819. . . showing the numbers (men, women, and children), land under cultivation, ownership, and stock."[161] His data on Sydney market prices, for example, are of interest today ("100 lbs potatoes—7/-; goose—5/-; duck—3/-; bull in good condition—£7; sheep in good condition—£1"); but no less valuable are the personal opinions, interspersed among such data, which lend colour to the whole. "Notes on the Colonies" are no dry gazetteer.[162] On considering the flooding of the Hawkesbury, for instance, Bellingshausen is reminded of the stormy Kacha River in the Russian Crimea, likewise fickle, likewise generous with "fine, rich mud deposit which manures the soil." As for Aboriginals, they are born wanderers like the *tsygany* of the Southern Russian steppe. With certain minor reservations, Bellingshausen and his officers approved and liked what they could see of New South Wales. They foresaw a prosperous, if not quite certain, future for the place:

> The colony has not yet become self-supporting, except perhaps in the matter of wool—and that does not amount to much—and is compelled to pay for all imports in cash. . . . Imported spirits are disposed of generally throughout New South Wales, amounting to an annual total importation of 60,000 gallons. With the development of wheat-growing, permission will probably be given to distil alcoholic beverages, and then the £12,000 annually leaving the country. . . will remain. The beer and stout are fairly good. The dressing of the kangaroo and other furs is very serviceable and not expensive. . . and four miles farther inland the soil is excellent.[163]

Much naval and scientific work had been completed, in the interim, at "Russian Point" and Sydney. Of the scientific work, suffice it to note that Dr. Shtein's compiling of barometric data had been carried on, with help from "Mr Hawkley, land-surveyor," by Simonov and others, while Korneev's ethnography had been continued by *Vostok*'s artist Mikhailov and half-a-dozen officers.[164] Botany too had been well served (see Chapter Five). *Vostok*'s refit was complete by 11 November, and the next morning the "shore observatory with its establishment and many other things" were stowed aboard her. Last came healthy livestock: hens and sheep, forty-six pigs. As in April, there were memorable kindnesses and grand

"Royal salutes from Ships and Batteries" as Bellingshausen left Sydney forever.[165] Piper remained aboard *Vostok* until her mainsails were spread. "Loud hurrahs," we learn from Simonov, who liked him, "followed him towards Eliza Point, where his own little cannon saluted our flag."[166] "I have every reason," wrote Macquarie to his minister in London, "to believe they went away highly gratified with the attentions they were paid."[167]

Bellingshausen's double visit to Australia provided able men with ample opportunity to develop those activities that, in their time, men of *Suvorov* and *Neva* had all pursued. Colonial acceptance of the need to be obliging to the Russians was efficiently converted by the latter into scientific studies and enquiries of lasting worth. Good personal relations, crystallized in social functions, were the crucial catalyst in that conversion. In the next two chapters, something will be said of those five sciences—hydrography, zoology, botany, geology, and ethnography—to which the Russians made a solid contribution in Australia at the beginning of the nineteenth century. That contribution will be viewed in the context of the Russian naval visits of the eight-year period 1814–22.

5

NEW SCIENTIFIC EMPHASES:
THE VISITORS OF 1822

THE "APOLLON" IN SYDNEY, 1822

Early in January 1818, Chief Manager Baranov, founding father of an entity long known as Russian North America, was brusquely ousted from a post that he had held for many years much to the Company's advantage.[1] His immediate replacement by that naval officer, Captain-Lieutenant Hagemeister, who had visited Australia a decade earlier, marked the conclusion of a basically political campaign that had been waged by a handful of ambitious naval patriots against the Company's pretensions to control the Russian North Pacific outposts. These patriots, headed by Captain-Lieutenant V. M. Golovnin, had long insisted that the Navy, not the Company, should guard and foster Russian national interests in the Pacific. They resented the Pacific settlements' dependence on New Englanders for foodstuffs and deplored the spread of "poaching" by Americans in waters claimed by Russia off the Coast.[2] By 1820 Golovnin's political significance no longer corresponded with his rank; and, at his instance, the Company's new charter from the Crown, the first of which had just expired, fixed the limit of the Russian jurisdiction in the North Pacific basin at the 51st degree of latitude and not, as earlier, at 54° 40'. The stage was set for two imperial ukases of September 1821, confirming this assertion of authority and even banning foreign shipping from, effectively, a Russian offshore province.[3] By November, the decision had been taken to despatch two extra vessels from the Baltic to the settlements: a recent ban on trade with foreign subjects at the North Pacific outposts made it crucial to supply them, and without delay.

Early in 1821, there were fitted out at Kronstadt the *Apollon,* a 28-gun sloop, and the *Aiaks,* a brig, both to deliver a mixed cargo to

Kamchatka and Novo-Arkhangel'sk. On reaching the Pacific
colonies, the former was to perform cruising duty by the shores of
Russian America with a view to protecting Russian trade and halting
contraband.[4]

Command of *Apollon* went to an officer without experience of the Pacific, Captain Irinarkh Tulub'ev. Like *Otkrytie,* the *Apollon* was of about
nine hundred tons. Well equipped and manned, she mounted thirty-two
new guns. She was the nucleus at least of a Pacific squadron, but, since
further clear initiatives were needed if the rights so boldly claimed (but
now disputed by the British and Americans) were to be guarded, two
more warships shortly followed her from Kronstadt round the globe.
These were the *Kreiser,* a frigate, and the *Ladoga* (ex-*Mirnyi* of the Bellingshausen South Pacific enterprise). Both were to call at Hobart Town
within the year (see Chapter Seven). *Aiaks,* whose instructions were to
keep in company with *Apollon* to the Pacific, was entrusted to Lieutenant
Nikolai Filatov. If Tulub'ev lacked a first-hand knowledge of the East,
Filatov made amends for it: he was a veteran of Golovnin's two voyages
around the world, in the *Diana* (1807–9) and *Kamchatka* (1817–19),
and was Golovnin's own protégé. Also selected for the *Apollon* because
of admirable records with *Kamchatka* two years earlier were Midshipman
Lutkovskii, Master Nikiforov, Lieutenant F. Kutygin, and Surgeon A.
Novitskii.[5] Like *Kamchatka, Apollon* carried a large lower deck of 119
men, extremely competent lieutenants, and one brilliant outsider. This
was a young linguist named Akhilles Pavlovich Shabel'skii.[6] We are indebted to Shabel'skii for the only published record of the *Apollon's* Port
Jackson visit of 7–25 June 1822.

Driven north by early winter storms, the *Aiaks* grounded and was
seriously damaged on a sandbar off the Dutch coast. She was finally
abandoned and the *Apollon* went on alone, making for Portsmouth, which
for Russian vessels bound for the Pacific was effectively a routine call.
Here too there was a setback. The sloop had proved unstable in a high
wind, so her ballast was increased while English carpenters reduced her
spars. Six vital weeks were lost in England. Then, in January, calms
delayed her further. Unaccustomed to the hot, humid conditions that they
met at the Equator, *Apollon's* seamen and officers all suffered; and when
finally the sloop came into Rio de Janeiro, Tulub'ev was found to be con-
sumptive. Alternating torrid days and chilly nights hastened his end, for
his condition was already far advanced and proper medical facilities were
lacking in Brazil. He died in mid-Atlantic and command of *Apollon* fell to
Lieutenant Stepan Khrushchev.[7] No storms were met with in the South Indian Ocean, where they could well have been expected; nor did other
misadventures plague the voyage that had started so disastrously. Strong

westerly winds took *Apollon* towards Australia in a band between 42° and 44°S. Cape Pedra Blanca was passed, just out of sight it seems, on 25 May. *Apollon* entered Port Jackson on 7 June after a taxing twelve-week passage from Brazil.[8] Like many men on previous Russian ships, some of her seamen reached Australia with symptoms of disease, notably scurvy.

The scurvy was arrested by the climate and citrus fruit of Sydney-Parramatta; but later, on the Northwest Coast, the *Apollon* was once more struck by the effects of long-term vitamin deficiency—with most unfortunate results from the Australian perspective. Disease and weakness in the crew were only two of many failings in the mission. When the *Apollon* returned to Kronstadt in 1824, the logs and journals of her people were collected, read, and shelved. No serious attempt was made to publish them, or even a synopsis or single narrative based on them, at the government's expense. The former officers of *Apollon,* one thinks, were disinclined to press the matter, for by publishing they would be linking their careers yet more firmly to a failure and an unsuccessful North Pacific policy.[9] Then, on 14 December 1825, came the Decembrist insurrection in St. Petersburg. Among the many naval officers arrested and imprisoned in a dank, forbidding fortress for their membership in liberal and antiautocratic groups known as the Northern and Southern Societies was Mikhail K. Kiukhel'beker, late of *Apollon.*[10] Whatever chance Khrushchev might earlier have had of seeing any formal record of his doings in Australia in print thereby dissolved. By 1826, however, the one narrative that *is* in print, that by Shabel'skii, had found its way under the nets of censorship and auto-censorship into a leading periodical, *Severnyi arkhiv,*[11] and into hardcover as well, under the title *Voyage aux colonies russes de l'Amérique.*[12] That feat alone must give Shabel'skii some right to Australians' attention.

Like Pushkin the poet, whom he knew intimately, Akhilles Pavlovich Shabel'skii had received an education at the *lycée* of Tsarskoe Selo, outside the capital.[13] He passed a privileged and pleasant adolescence, finding time to master English, French, and Latin. He was planning a career in the ministry of foreign affairs when, in 1821, the chance arose to join the warship *Apollon* as extranumerary "interpreter." As Constantin Hotimsky has remarked, he proved "a keen and very accurate observer" of Sir Thomas Brisbane's colony,[14] as well as an efficient diplomat. A traveller by choice, he was in 1825 named Second Secretary at the Russian Mission in the United States;[15] and there, as in Sydney, he observed and drafted statements and interpreted for his superiors in service. In America as in Australia, he took an interest in prisons and relations between government and prisoners. He later published on the subject.[16] In itself, and as a record of evolving Russian scientific dealings in Australia, Shabel'skii's narrative is of especial interest.

The *Apollon,* it must be borne in mind, was on a naval and strategic mission quite devoid of scientific emphases. Tulub'ev's sailing orders made no reference to sciences outside the strictly naval context. Yet her visit to Australia was far from barren scientifically. Her officers, like those of 1820, had immediate entrée to Sydney's social life and scientific circle and they seized the chance to take up scientific interests or hobbies in a strange and foreign land, "where unusual phenomena attract the wanderer at every turn."[17] Dinners were given, by the Colonel of the 3rd Foot Regiment, William Stewart; by the Governor, Sir Thomas Brisbane; by the "knight of Regentville," John Jamison; and by other local men of wealth. As more than once in 1820, "Hyde Park rooms" were taken over with the Russian naval visitors in mind, and Sydney residents gave a subscription ball and supper for their guests. "Stepan Chroolstoff" and all his comrades, so we learn from the *Gazette,* "were quite enraptured at the splendid entertainment" they were given.[18] As before, prominent merchants sought or readily accepted Russian custom. Khrushchev himself produced a good impression on the colony as one whose "unaffected manners" were becoming in an officer and gentleman abroad.

As sightseers, the officers of *Apollon* retraced the steps of Bellingshausen's and Vasil'ev's lieutenants two years earlier. The fact enhances rather than diminishes the value of their evidence. As the Russian records of the Aboriginals' activities about Port Jackson gain significance from being written in all seasons of the year, so do data that relate, over a concentrated eight-year period (1814–22), to individuals, specific institutions, single buildings. Like a sharply focused film, the Russian narrative and illustrative evidence for Sydney as a whole shows evolution and rapid change. Macquarie's military barracks, for example, are quite different by 1822 from the imposing yet depressing block of 1820 as described by Bellingshausen. Now, according to Shabel'skii, they were spacious, "the most beautiful buildings in town," and were surrounded by a "gallery... in keeping with the local climate." By comparison, the small Anglican church seemed "insignificant": it was as well that, with the government's support, another church was being built. This was St. James's, Sydney. Other buildings caught Shabel'skii's eye:

> The prisoners' barracks, located close to the hospital building, provide little consolation in the lives of the most unwanted elements of the peoples of Great Britain, who are forced to live here under strict order. . . . But I was greatly surprised to see how well everything is kept in the surroundings in which they live: a pound of bread, a pound of meat, vegetables, a daily portion of tea—this is the lot of these felons. They are undoubtedly much happier in New Holland than they would have been in their native land.[19]

The Russians much approved of Francis Greenway's architecture, which they thought solid and regular, and of the grid-pattern of streets in infant towns. The Sydney streets were, by comparison, unsatisfactory. Numerous pickpockets and thieves, the Russians learned, had brought "unpleasant consequences" to the few small stage presentations that Macquarie had allowed despite the absence of a regular theatre. Even so, the Sydney populace regretted the situation and indeed, while *Apollon* remained at anchor, petitioned Brisbane for permission to establish a theatre. Shabel'skii sympathized. He also sympathized with Brisbane's open policy towards free settlers, whose immigration he encouraged. One last passage from Shabel'skii's narrative will illustrate the feeling, widely shared by Russian visitors to Sydney, that while Australia was likely to relieve the British government of criminals for many years to come, she was, far more importantly, going to grow into a prosperous and self-sufficient colony of fabulous extent:

> At this stage, flocks of merino sheep cover vast tracts of land in the County of Cumberland: Captain Macarthur has 10,000. . . . As the area of the land was not sufficient to provide for the influx of population, it was found necessary to extend the limits of the colony; and, as convicts formed the greater part of the settlers, it was decided to spread their settlement as widely as possible, thus ensuring that there can never be any serious danger of revolt. . . . It is now impossible to determine the limits of the English colonies on this great continent: they expand every year.[20]

An amateur astronomer of note, Sir Thomas Brisbane did his best to help the Russians at their land observatory, as in all other service-scientific matters.[21] *Apollon* remained at Sydney eighteen days. It was a relatively brief but busy visit. Dawes Point's battery responded to a thirteen-gun salute as she made sail on 25 June and coasted east. Like Bellingshausen, Khrushchev took many sightings on the shores of New South Wales both before and after entering Port Jackson. En route to Novo-Arkhangel'sk, he passed and carefully determined the position of Ball's Rock (31°48'S, 159°20'E).[22]

THE COMPANY BRIG "RIURIK" AT SYDNEY, 1822

The grounding and abandonment of *Aiaks* was a costly setback for the Russian-American Company Board; but it was followed by an absolute disaster, the abandonment of an American-built merchantman, *Elizaveta*, that had recently been purchased for a high price. All had augured well enough for the directors when, in 1821, *Aiaks* and *Apollon* had been preceded out of Kronstadt on the North Pacific run by other Company-owned vessels, *Riurik* and *Elizaveta*. Of the four ships, two soon ran into trouble.

Riurik was Kotzebue's little brig of 180 tons, re-rigged and modified internally for trading purposes.[24] She had a valuable cargo of supplies for the Pacific outposts (Atka, Novo-Arkhangel'sk) and was commanded by a veteran of Hagemeister's North Pacific voyages, Efim Aleksevich Klochkov (178?–1833). As well as half-a-dozen Aleuts being taken back to Atka, she had twenty-two seamen aboard and, with hydrography and Company requirements in mind, no fewer than three sound navigators.[25] One, Maksim Samsonov, had visited Australia with the *Suvorov*. Another, Vasilii Nabokov, reached the rank of Navy captain. The third, Ivan Iakovlevich Vasil'ev, was a geographer and amateur ethnographer of note.[26] As in Australia, so also in Alaska with immensely greater energy and over longer periods, he was to scrutinize the country and its natives with a scientific eye.[27]

Elizaveta's outward voyage was unfortunate from the beginning. Her commander, Kislakovskii, brought her limping to Brazil whence he accompanied Klochkov towards Cape Horn; but then a large leak in her hull threatened to sink her. She struggled into Simon's Bay, South Africa, with pumps always at work. She was examined, found to be half-rotten, and disposed of to the (frugal) highest bidder then in Cape Town.[28] Klochkov pressed on towards Australia alone on 3 June 1822. "Steering south to avoid the Agulhas Shoal, he then proceeded along the 42nd parallel . . . with those same W and NW winds which are almost always strong and almost always bring hail and thunderstorms in their wake."[29] Van Diemen's Land was sighted on 3/15 July. Also observed that day was what appeared to be "a stony outcrop in latitude 43°S, longitude 147°42′30′′E." It was unmarked on recent charts, notably Flinders', which Klochkov had brought along to ease his way, and it was therefore considered a discovery. On Kruzenshtern's great *Atlas of the South Sea* (1826), it was shown as "Riurik Shoal" and estimated at three hundred fathoms length.[30] The remainder of the passage to Port Jackson, which was sighted on 27 July, was accompanied by moderate but variable winds. The crew were healthy and the air was refreshing. Nonetheless, Klochkov continued to administer "tea with a little rum" to one and all, and kept his "hanging braziers below the deck" alight, as a precautionary measure.[31] Once in Port Jackson, the *Riurik* was becalmed and so continued under tow. She reached "the roadstead," where ten English merchant vessels stood at anchor, at approximately 8:00 PM. Eleven-gun salutes were saved till morning.

Riurik stood a mere twelve days by Sydney (27 July–8 August 1822),

revictualling, watering, and undergoing swift repairs. Klochkov was anxious not to lose more time, having already been delayed too many weeks
by the misfortunes of *Elizaveta*. Governor Brisbane did his civil best to
help and at his instances, the Naval Officer's Department also hastened
into action. Here are extracts from the 1822 Klochkov report to the directors of the Company in whose employ he was, regarding Sydney.[32] Like
Hagemeister's, they are here given for the first time in English:

16/28 July. I called on the Governor, Lieutenant-General Brisbane,
who offered me all the assistance I might possibly require. Shortly after, indeed, he sent greenstuffs over for our crew; and the local Intendant sent timber, of which we were much in want. Our people
were put to work at various tasks and we immediately began putting
the brig's rigging to rights. Other matters, too, were attended to: we
set our tent up on the nearest islet, and we carried out the instruments
and ship's chronometers, all to be checked. We were attempting to
waste as little time here as possible and to arrive at Novo-
Arkhangel'sk, for as is well known, the storms prevalent up there late
in the year and the shorter days do render navigation dangerous.

20 July/1 Aug. At the Governor's invitation, I went to take dinner
with him at the village of Paramada [sic], some forty versts distant
from the town of Sydney. Both this village and the town itself have
already been described, as have also the picturesque scenes surrounding them, in a number of voyages. Still, the large castle in which the
convicts are held when they have been brought out from England, the
Governor's Observatory, and the Botanical Gardens, are all particularly noteworthy.

27 July/8 August. At 10 AM, the Governor paid a visit to our brig in
his own ceremonial launch, with flag flying. The honour guard accompanying him consisted of twelve armed men. Having looked over
the whole vessel, taken breakfast, and wished us a prosperous onward voyage, he returned to shore. As he did so, we saluted him with
a 12-gun volley.

Terse though it is, Klochkov's report makes very clear that, again, a
Russian company without instructions to indulge in academic interests in
Sydney had surpassed the bounds of common sightseeing. Not only had
Sir Thomas Brisbane's new observatory been visited;[33] so also had the
flourishing and rather large Botanical Garden, then in Charles Frazer's
care. One may suppose that, since the officers of *Apollon* had called on

Frazer less than three weeks earlier, he knew what was most likely to amuse those of the *Riurik*.[34] Well laden with provisions, *Riurik* left Sydney for the North Pacific colonies amidst a flurry of benevolent and patriotic gestures.[35] The linkage between visits to Australia and subsequent professional success held good for her. Klochkov was not of lofty birth like Bellingshausen, and his talent was his fortune, yet he filled the post of Keeper of the (Hydrographic) Instruments within the Admiralty Office in St. Petersburg after retiring from the service of the Company in 1823 and reached the rank of Captain, Second Class, despite the lack of either family or private influence.[36]

RUSSIAN BOTANY IN NEW SOUTH WALES, 1814–22: A SURVEY

Trained observers, Russian officers carefully described the local scene, paying attention to that region of the kingdom of plants that most affected them professionally: trees. Although not botanists, indeed, such men could leave a serviceable record of the trees (still) to be found in the Sydney area, at a specific time. This interest was complemented, in the case of the visitors of 1820–22 who were participating in official, state-run scientific ventures, by a purely scientific impulse: to continue down the path that Banks and Solander had pointed out in 1771–80. "The primary task of Banks and Solander was natural-historical study."[37]

Twenty, even forty years after Cook's death, the emphases of his explorations were still seen as proper to such voyages. Among those emphases were certain scientific ones. Cook's people had collected plants and seeds: so too, in 1803–6, would Kruzenshtern's. The German naturalist Wilhelm-Gottlieb Tilesius von Tilenau (1769–1857) was accordingly appointed to *Nadezhda*.[38] Like Georg Heinrich Langsdorf (1774–1852), who also joined the ship as private secretary-doctor to the courtier N. P. Rezanov,[39] von Tilenau proved worthy of the call. At the Marquesas Islands (Nukuhiva) in particular, he gave a brilliant display of scientific versatility, making important zoological, botanical, and ethnographic contributions, among others, to South Pacific studies.[40] From the outset, thanks to Kruzenshtern, the Russian naval enterprise in the Pacific paid its dues to botany. It was to realize a grandiose botanical design as well as gaze at Venus on Tahiti, after all, that Cook had sailed in *Endeavour*. As Tilesius von Tilenau was invited to take passage in *Nadezhda,* so in 1819 were other German botanists encouraged to take passage in *Vostok* with Bellingshausen. Invitations went to Gustav Kunze (1793–1851), a specialist in microscopic analysis of fungi and bacteria, and Karl-Heinrich Mertens (1796–1830), whose study path had similarly taken him from medicine to botany.[41] The Russian Naval Ministry, in fact, recalled

Cook's voyages in terms of breadfruit, birds, and other "naturalia." *Discovery* and *Resolution* had the Forsters, father and son; Kruzenshtern had Langsdorff and Tilesius von Tilenau; and *Vostok* should not go wanting. By misfortune, neither Kunze nor Mertens could join the expedition, as arranged, at Copenhagen. The significance of I. M. Simonov's preoccupations with astronomy and anthropology increased accordingly.[42] Not even he, however, was devoid of the spirit of botanical enquiry; and, more importantly, the impulse towards botany was manifest in Russia's naval enterprise at large.[43] Among the ship's surgeons at Sydney with professional and therefore scientific interest in local plants and herbs, five may be mentioned: Iakov Berkh of *Vostok,* Nikolai Galkin of *Mirnyi,* Ivan Kovalev of *Otkrytie,* Grigorii Zaozerskii of *Blagonamerennyi,* and Anton Novitskii of *Apollon.*[44]

All Russian visitors from Hagemeister on noted the tall "red gums" (*Angophera lanceolata*) and fir-like casuarinas (*Casuarina torulosa* and *C. glauca*) that then grew along the valleys and ridges of the North Shore behind their anchorage. Hagemeister's interest, perhaps, was more commercial than scientific ("a timber known as 'she-oak,' an excellent redwood used in furniture"),[45] but it did draw his attention to the soil underneath. Aleksei Lazarev of *Suvorov* (1814) first reflected on arboreal results of soil differences—thin and poor at Sydney Cove, alluvial and tolerably rich at Parramatta. Benelong's Point was pleasant indeed, "its flowery dales shaded by sweet-smelling groves" of *Banksia*;[46] but on the Parramatta Road stood "large, sparse timber."[47] This was the eucalypt woodland through which Bellingshausen also passed, in 1820, on his way west to Rose Hill ("strong, sparse timber which a carriage could pass through everywhere"),[48] and over which the richer settlers were hunting kangaroo on horseback.[49] *Melaleuca* spp. mixed easily with casuarinas, cypress pines, and occasional shrubs, notably wattles, bottle brushes, and Waratahs (*Telopea speciosissima*) of the kind drawn by *Vostok*'s artist Mikhailov.[50]

Several Russians considered local timber in an ethnographic context. Ironbarks or ironwoods, for instance, led a man to scrutinize the oval shields of the Aboriginals he met,[51] "beefwood" on the natives' fragile craft. (For Bellingshausen's people, ironbark suggested hardwood to be used in the repair of a bowsprit.)[52]

Russian evidence suggests that European wood-cutting had practically destroyed the cedars of the Sydney area by 1820, but that other species were abundant still: "red mahogany," for instance, on the North Shore,[53] so-called tea trees, and smooth-barked apples also. "Blackboys" (*Xanthorrhoea* spp.) and wattles were in evidence at Sydney and attracted Mikhailov's attention.[54] The Russians understood that coastal scrub was a result of thin, crumbling sandstone and high, salt-laden winds, and turned instinctively towards those "low flowering shrubs" which, in the words of William Wentworth, "render that wild heath the most interesting part of the country for the botanist."[55] "At every step," wrote Simonov, "we encountered sublime *Banksia* of various sorts."[56] Well might he refer to *Banksia* as trees: as Shabel'skii found in 1822, "various kinds of gum-tree and Acacia" reached "gigantic proportions in Cumberland County."[57] Russian botanizing concentrated less on trees and coastal scrub than on the bright, sweet-scented shrubs and flowers that could grow only where salt-spray did not reach. It was associated chiefly with the names of Fedor Shtein, Bellingshausen, and Shabel'skii.

Shtein, the naturalist with *Otkrytie* and *Blagonamerennyi,* was by temperament a classifier; and restricted though his time was in Australia, he did his utmost to collect and so contribute to that international classifying effort still connected with the names of Michel Adanson (1727–1806) and Joseph Gaertner (1732–91). It was his great good fortune to win the sympathy and help of Allan Cunningham, King's Botanist, and to examine plants that Cunningham was at the time (March 1820) preparing to despatch to Kew Gardens.[58] Together with Korneev, Shtein ascended the Blue Mountains to King's Table Land. "One," reported Vasil'ev phlegmatically to his superiors, "discovered several new plants and certain minerals . . . and the other drew beautiful views."[59] Such words did not do credit to the pair. Korneev's portfolio was full, and "views" did not predominate in it. Shtein's new herbarium was stowed and found its way back to St. Petersburg in August 1822.[60] It was presented by the Naval Ministry to the Academy of Sciences' botanical garden by the small Fontanka River in St. Petersburg. The timing was most fortunate. Perhaps some plants had perished from exposure to the freezing Arctic air they had passed through in 1820–21 or from more recent accidents at sea;[61] but the survivors were guaranteed attention.

Thanks to the disgust felt by a grandee and personal acquaintance of Tsar Alexander I, Count Viktor P. Kochubei, on comparing that same garden with its counterparts abroad, a grand reorganizing effort had begun early in 1823.[62] Peter the Great's former "Apothecary's Garden," the botanical garden had been little better than a "field with a few small trees and grasses here and there and a wooden orangery much in disrepair" by the early 1800s.[63] And despite the sterling efforts of the Russian botanist T. A. Smelovskii to arrest the slide,[64] decline had not been halted. At the instances of Kochubei, Friedrich-Ernst (in Russian, Fedor Bogdanovich) von Fischer (1782–1854) was appointed first director of the new Imperial Botanical Garden. Money poured into the institution, which was soon being restored on modern principles.[65] It fell to Fischer, a distinguished botanist who had since 1806 been running Russia's foremost private garden, Gorenki, to take the plant and seed arrivals from Australia into his care.[66]

The *Otkrytie* collection, so to speak, was complemented and increased by the *Vostok* collection, also formally entrusted to that branch of the Academy to which the energetic Fischer had been posted while the ships had been at sea. And here we are fortunate in having published data. In its length and precision, Bellingshausen's list of plant specimens taken from Sydney to St. Petersburg not only points to a co-operative effort at Port Jackson by his officers, but also underlines the loss to science of all data in the other, Shtein collection. Bellingshausen's list appears in his essay "An Account of the Government of New South Wales," between brief factual sections on Port Jackson and the port and town of Sydney. It is introduced as follows:

> The shores of this bay are covered with all sorts of different flowers and trees. I kept some of each species, which have since been examined by the naturalists Eichenwald and Fischer. I append the names of these for lovers of Natural History.[67]

Such lists as Bellingshausen's have importance in the history of botany. Here, brief comments only will be made, a larger treatment of the Russian naval botanizing effort being properly reserved for other botanists and (in connection with transcription and transliteration problems, which are obvious) historians of science. The *Vostok* collection, then, contained at least one representative of twenty-five plant families in New South Wales. The largest sub-collection by far, in numbers of species, were the Proteaceae (13). Like other European visitors to Sydney, one infers, the Russians were particularly struck by those indigenous and most exotic plants. Also well represented were the Leguminosae (9), Compositae (6), and Myrtaceae (6). Bright flowers predominated; shrubs were rather few (*Kunzea* and *Bursaria* being conspicuously absent); and grasses were, it seems, not represented at all. Still, Bellingshausen and Vasil'ev together brought a major new Australian herbarium to Russia, just in time to be received in the new gardens of St. Petersburg (Botanicheskii Imperatorskii sad). The Russians made some effort to repay their Sydney hosts botanically, prefiguring those ethnographic and botanical exchanges that were later to develop between Melbourne and St. Petersburg in Ferdinand von Mueller's time. Fresh from Tahiti and the Lau Archipelago of Fiji, *Vostok* had numerous tropical plants to offer the Australians. Macquarie was given sugarcanes, sprouting coconuts, and ripe Tahitian "apples," while Harbour Captain Piper was presented with a clump of taro roots.[68]

Another aspect of the Russian contribution to Pacific botany in 1820 is the illustrative record. Both Emel'ian Korneev and Pavel Mikhailov drew flora of the Sydney area. No scene of Aboriginals, or waterfall, or harbour-front lacked plants, bushes, or trees. *Xanthorrhoea* spp. and *Leptospermum* spp. caught their eye especially and, like *Acacia,* they were incorporated into half-a-dozen drawings of considerable ethnographic value.[69] Not surprisingly, both men were drawn to the exotic and peculiar: they had not visited Australia before, were most unlikely to return, and had instructions (private taste apart) "to sketch all noteworthy places seen."[70] Few places in Australia were bare. Korneev went further, to produce a careful study of, as he called it, "the Indian fig tree of Port Jackson."[71] Mikhailov, attracted by the bottle brushes (*Callistemon* spp.) and the Waratahs (*Telopea*) that lent colour to the area (as Bellingshausen was attracted by "the masses of yellow downy Mimosa," that is, wattle),[72] placed the former in his study of the colonists' "Prince Regent Bird" or *Gymnorhina tibicen,* the latter on a sheet of his portfolio all by itself. It was reproduced by Shvede (1960) and by Debenham (1945).[73]

While in New South Wales, Russian officers were assisted by knowledgeable men: Cunningham, Frazer, Lawson, and Sir John Jamison (1776–1844). Breeder, naturalist, and effective magistrate, John Jamison took pleasure in the company of educated strangers. By coincidence, he had no sooner reached Port Jackson with the *Broxborneburry* (1814) than the Russians of *Suvorov* crossed his path. In 1820, he offered sumptuous and pleasant entertainment for new Russian visitors.[74] In 1822, he was obliging to Akhilles Shabel'skii, whose botanical enquiries commended him as an intelligent and sympathetic tourist. Jamison himself sent flora annually to Great Britain: since 1811 he had been an absent member of the Werner Natural History Society of Edinburgh, and his 1818 trip into the Warragamba country had been crowned by the botanical and zoological collections that were later to enrich the new Australian Museum.[75] While on his way to the Nepean River in mid-June 1822, Shabel'skii was struck by the varieties of non-coniferous *Acacia* that, it seemed, sprang up wherever trees had been reduced to stumps by axe or fire. He pulled out these new growths to see if their roots were connected with the stump. The cause of propagation was unclear.

> I discovered that they grew independently; but in the roots I sometimes found large whitish worms, which are considered a great delicacy by the natives of the land. When I enquired of Sir John Jamison the reasons for this strange natural phenomenon, he told me wild pigeons feeding on the seeds of the Acacia prefer to pick them up in open spaces near half-burnt stumps, and that these seeds, transmitted by pigeons and falling on fertile soil, shortly sprout into trees.[76]

Thus made aware of the peculiarities of local propagation, Shabel'skii looked again at the European wheat, Indian maize, citrus, and other fruiting plants then being grown in "sandy loam" between Richmond and Emu Plain. What new varieties of fruit or cereal might grow, or spread, or change once brought to New South Wales? Vines might well be introduced to Bathurst plains. Shabel'skii's curiosity took him to Frazer's and Cunningham's domain for a discussion of such matters and a look at artificial propagation and hybridization. Not the least of early Russian contributions to the history of science in Australia are cameos of men like Allan Cunningham and Charles Frazer at work. Here is Frazer, experimenting happily in Sydney's infant gardens:

It is not many years since these botanical gardens were established, but one is impressed to see that they are beautifully kept. Experiments are being carried out here in the propagation of exotic plants, many of which are brought from New Zealand, Van Diemen's Land, the Cape of Good Hope, and Brazil. I saw coconuts and bread[fruit] trees, but to produce them in quantity is practically impossible because of severe frosts; the same applies to coffee plants and sugarcane. The manna tree, which was brought here from the central parts of New Holland, has grown to three times its normal size within a period of one year and eight months. The milky sap flows down, hardens, and forms into manna. In charge of these gardens is Mr Frazer, a sincere and untiring botanist, who showed me the areas proposed for new botanical gardens. These lie in a wide open space through which flows a stream.[77]

Governor Brisbane cancelled his predecessor's fifteen-acre grant at Double Bay, to which Shabel'skii had been taken; but Frazer's Middle Garden[78] remains above Farm Cove, and sugarwoods (*Myoporum platycarpum*) still exude their sweet white sap there, to foreigners' approval.[79] Coffee, too, now prospers, under glass.

RUSSIAN ZOOLOGY IN NEW SOUTH WALES: A SURVEY

The three most competent zoologists on Russian ships in the Pacific in the early 1800s were Tilesius von Tilenau and Langsdorf, both of Kruzenshtern's *Nadezhda,* and Johann Friedrich Eschscholtz (1793–1831), who accompanied Kotzebue twice as naturalist, first with *Riurik* (1815–18) then with *Predpriiatie* (1823–26).[80] Polynesia's gain is Sydney's loss, since none of those three ships called there. In passing, one may note that Eschscholtz's important contributions to the botany and, more especially, zoology of Oceania remain unrecognized in Australasia and, indeed, the West.[81] Russia's contribution to the systematic study of the fauna of Australia was, on the other hand, rather modest. Nevertheless, the early Russian visitors to New South Wales did a great deal to broaden knowledge of Australian marsupials and birds in Northern Europe.

This familiarizing process had three stages: allusion to specific birds or animals in printed works, with passing reference to habitat or habits; illustrative record; and presentation of the fauna, stuffed or otherwise preserved if not alive, to Russian subjects and in due course to the European public (in the form of learned papers from St. Petersburg's Academy of Sciences or other institutions).[82] We begin, first, with the references to specific mammals, birds, fish, and insects of Australia that stud the narratives of Russian and other early European visitors to Sydney-Parramatta.

Few if any Russian texts relating to a sojourn in Australia are bare of such allusions. What may lend them modest scientific value are *associated data*, throwing light on, for example, diet, local distribution, even adaptations to encroaching human contact. For those birds and mammals and insects that the Russians saw were living under threat of human contact, whether in the Sydney area, or in the Hawkesbury, or west by Wentworth Falls. Here, to illustrate, is Bellingshausen on the "Windsor Road" due west of Parramatta in April 1820 (9:00 AM): "Flocks of white parrots continually flew across the road with shrill screams. . . . Red lories with variegated rose-coloured plumage, and the particularly fine Blue Mountain parrots, were perched in the trees in pairs or in flocks."[83]

Bellingshausen was no ornithologist; but other, local evidence allows us to detect here large groups of slender-billed cockatoos. Ground-feeders, they were doubtless swooping low on sprouting seeds or other foodstuffs on the fields by the road. They had, in short, made an efficient, swift adjustment to the fact of human presence. Other species, it is plain from other parts of Bellingshausen's narrative, were still holding their own by busy Kirribilli Point or modern Mosman in the early 1820s. Every day, *Vostok*'s lieutenants went shooting for the pot or in the interests of science, returning with game-bags "full of birds, chiefly red parrots, quails, and various kinds of swift flying birds, of which the largest were of a beautiful colour and known as 'king-fishers'."[84] Few *Dacelo* survive in these localities today. Among other bird species mentioned by the Russians as living in the Sydney area in 1814–22 were: Turdinae (subf. of Muscicapidae); Alcedinidae (sub. of Coraciiformes); Cracticidae; Meliphagidae (subfg. of Passeriformes); *Dacelo*; *Kakatoe*. Not unnaturally, the Russians also report on those mammals and birds in which the colonizing British had evinced a special interest. Lieutenant Aleksei P. Lazarev, for instance, notes the beginnings of Australia's first zoo on the lawn before Macquarie's residence above Farm Cove (1814):

> General Macquarie's house is constructed of soft stone and everything connected to it has been finished with that neatness proper to the English. Facing the house is a large green meadow, on which there run a good many marsupials and many cockatoos.[85]

Lazarev in 1814 and Simonov in 1820 describe the North Shore as being full of songbirds, practically all unknown to them.[86]

To turn, next, to the drawings of Korneev and Mikhailov of 1820: in the course of his Australian visit, Korneev appears to have drawn five birds, a kangaroo, a platypus, a fish, a bat, and two or more butterflies. Intrigued by the creature, he drew the platypus twice. The birds were: (1) "Crested parrot," that is, a tufted cockatoo; (2) "Blue Mountain parakeet"; (3) "Blackbirds of New Holland"; (4) "A Van Diemen's Goose"; and (5) "Ostrich of New Holland." The solitary fish was a "sun-fish or prickle-fish." Most of these terms being obsolete, such lists offer a happy hunting-ground to the historian of science.[87] Mikhailov, whose total output was less than half Korneev's over the period 1819–22, left a proportionately smaller group of fauna drawings from Australia. What he produced, however, was of the highest quality. Besides "two tropical fish" caught in Port Jackson, reproduced by both Debenham (1945) and Shvede (1960), we have from his brush "The Prince Regent Bird" and "The Abbot Bird."

Mikhailov's "Prince Regent Bird" is, in fact, an Australian magpie, known to ornithology as *Gymnorhina* (Family Cracticidae).[88] Its black and white markings, strong legs, and stout, slightly hooked bill are clearly shown. Mikhailov's specimen is the black-backed bell-magpie, *G. tibicen,* usually found in localities north of Sydney. The bird's carolling call-notes and modulated whistles attracted the Russians, who found it coping well with *Homo sapiens* in open woodlands and pastures near the town. As for the "Abbot Bird," it is a friarbird in light disguise: confusion of ecclesiastical terms may be forgiven in a foreigner. Known to Australians as leatherhead, this is a honeyeater (Genus *Meliphagidae*), an arboreal, mainly nectar- and fruit-eating bird. Of the thirty-eight known species, that depicted by Mikhailov is *M. philemon.* As the aquarelle suggests, the friarbird somewhat resembles the jackdaw but has a black and partly naked head and a horny protuberance on the bill. Again, the call attracted the attention of the visitor: a noisy chattering or, now and then, gurgling chorus. Friarbirds were prospering too, despite the colonists in

1820: to their native fruits, they could add various introduced varieties. The damage they were starting to inflict on certain orchards had not yet led to effective countermeasures by the humans who had thus enlarged their diet.[89] As Mikhailov suggests by his setting, *Meliphagidae philemon* lives and feeds mainly on blossoming shrubs and trees. It is a vital pollinator. As the birds and blooming shrubs of New South Wales were interdependent, one may comment in conclusion, so were birds and plants depicted and collected by the Russians. The largest element in Bellingshausen's plant and seed collection for St. Petersburg from Sydney, were Proteaceae; but Myrtaceae were also well represented. Here are comments by a recent ornithologist on the essential ecological relationship between such flora and the hungry honeyeater. He describes the hidden link between the 1820 evidence for flora and fauna in the Sydney area, as brought to Russia by the ever more ambitious Russian Navy:

> Blossoms of trees and shrubs constitute the main feeding place of most honeyeaters. Owing to this fact, they are very efficient pollinators; in fact they form. . . the most important agents in the fertilization of. . . Myrtaceae, Proteaceae, and Epacridaceae. An intimate connection exists between these plants and the honeyeaters.[90]

Simple though it is, the Russian evidence for flora complements the Russian evidence for birds, and vice versa.

On returning to St. Petersburg in 1822, Mikhailov spent one year putting his portfolios and notes in order and preparing a coloured album (aquarelle with a tincture of white lead). That album remains in the State Historical Museum in Moscow. Many of its sheets, including those of the two birds here described and of the Waratah, were lithographed at state expense for publication in the Bellingshausen narrative of the Antarctic and Pacific expedition (*Dvukratnye izyskaniia*. . .; St. P., 1831). The lithographer was Ivan Pavlovich Fridrits (1803–60). In 1824, he was finishing a nine-year stay at the St. Petersburg Academy of Arts under the guidance of Nikolai I. Utkin. Fridrits was of middling ability, and it cannot be denied that the Mikhailov aquarelles lost in the process of lithography. A folder containing 307 of the originals composed during two voyages around the world (1819–22 and 1826–29, as artist of the *Moller,* commanded by Captain-Lieutenant Staniukovich) is now in the care of the State Russian Museum, in Leningrad.[91] Of 30 aquarelles entrusted to Fridrits in 1824, half-a dozen were of Australian provenance, including "A View of the Town of Sydney in Port Jackson," "Boongaree, Matora: The Chief of the Broken Bay Tribe and His Wife," "Natives of New Holland,"[92] "Waratah," and the two bird studies that have been discussed. All duly appeared, together with 19 maps and 15 other views, in the atlas accompanying Bellingshausen's 1831 monograph. Six hundred copies were produced.[93]

A note may usefully be added here on political constraints to the efficient propagation of the results of Russian science in Australia. Bellingshausen's polished narrative was handed to the Russian Naval Ministry in April 1824. The ten component notebooks were examined and approved, and in 1825 the Chief of Naval Staff was asked to gain the tsar's approval of a printing run of 1,200 copies. Nothing came of this approach and the Decembrist insurrection of 14 December 1825 made it improbable that anything would come of it in the future, for among the naval officers arrested for complicity in the activities of secret political societies was K. P. Torson, late lieutenant in *Vostok*.[94] Two years passed. Mikhailov's aquarelles and Fridrits's new lithographs were shelved. Then, at the close of 1827, Bellingshausen personally wrote to the first chairman of the Naval Scientific Committee of the Naval Staff, that Loggin Golenishchev-Kutuzov who in youth had spent much time translating Cook.[95] Golenishchev-Kutuzov was extremely sympathetic and supported Bellingshausen's contention that at least six hundred copies of his narrative, together with its atlas, should be printed—to the honour of the Russian Crown. But there were more delays. And Bellingshausen, now on active service on the Danube fighting the Turks, was not available to press the printers or indeed to check their work. Officious bureaucrats, first Apollon Nikol'skii, then Chizhov, took full advantage of his absence to delay, to rearrange the text itself, to throw out or include certain Pacific illustrations.[96] Eleven years passed between the time Mikhailov made his drawings in Australia and their eventual appearance between covers in the bookshops of St. Petersburg and Moscow. But political considerations muzzled zoology far less than other sciences such as geology.

Like other Europeans, the Russians in Australia took local plants and animals aboard in hopes of bringing them intact, if not alive, to distant ports. In 1814, Lieutenant Lazarev was happy to accept a small collection of indigenous insects and birds from the obliging Phillip Parker King. The younger King seems to have gone out of his way to help the Russians of *Suvorov,* describing his most recent survey work around Australia, showing them his charts, correcting theirs, making useful introductions, and presenting the enthusiastic Lazarev with "birds and insects carefully gathered for himself."[97] The birds remained in Lazarev's possession. King was equally obliging to the people of *Vostok* in 1820. They, however, had a better source of fauna: Boongaree and the Cammeraigal people. "When all preparations on board were complete," writes Bellingshausen, "I had the... birds and animals also... brought on board."[98] Some were for eating, some for science. Vasil'ev and Shishmarev, too, sailed from Sydney with collections of stuffed birds and mounted insects for St. Petersburg. "The list of natural historical and ethnographic collections that entered the museum of the Admiralty Department and later, in 1827–28, were transferred to the Academy of Sciences, of rock samples, sketches of coastlines and islands drawn by the artist E. Korneev, speaks of the *considerable* scientific and collecting work undertaken by that expedition."[99] *Apollon*, too, must be supposed to have delivered items of natural history to the imperial authorities on reaching Kronstadt in mid-October 1824. As we have seen, her people were materially helped by and indebted to the wealthy local natural historian, John Jamison.[100]

Australian zoological specimens transferred to the Academy of Sciences in 1827–28[101] were studied by the ablest zoologist then in St. Petersburg, A. F. Sevast'ianov. An academician since 1810, Sevast'ianov took an active part in the organization of the zoological department. He did his best to provide other museums with materials for study.[102] In the 1830s, the Australian materials provided grist to the mills of scientific popularizers, notably S. S. Kutorga and K. F. Rouillier. Kutorga, of St. Petersburg University, was widely acclaimed as a public lecturer and spoke on zoology, anatomy, and palaeontology. To him, Staff-Surgeon Zaozerskii's find of bones of an extinct giant marsupial [?] not far from Kirribilli Point in 1820 was something to announce with national pride.[103] Rouillier, by contrast, used Australian materials in pioneering works of theoretical zoology: he was by instinct, as by training, an ecologist.[104] Kutorga was a lifelong admirer of the eminent Scottish geologist and palaeontologist Sir Roderick Murchison; and it is noteworthy that he and other competent Russian geologists, for instance G. E. Shchurovskii, were inspired to make a study of the rocks that form the earth by a study of zoology and/or palaeontology in which Australian materials loomed large.[105]

RUSSIAN GEOLOGY: THE CASE OF DR. SHTEIN

Many Russians visiting the Sydney area were struck by the great difference between, in Wentworth's words, "the barren wastes on the coast of Port Jackson" and the "rich loam resting on a substratum of fat red clay" an hour's ride inland.[106] Not a few made passing reference in published works to Sydney's "yellow sandy soil" and the sandstone underneath it.[107] Bellingshausen's observations on the matter, and his distinction between coastal semi-desert, eight-mile-wide band of better soil giving sustenance to "beautiful resinous trees" and first-rate earth seventeen miles from the ocean, are intelligent and even circumstantial.[108] Yet, from the perspective of geology, they have no value whatsoever. Fedor Shtein alone, of all the Russians in the country in the early nineteenth century, was a geologist in any modern sense, and only he made a solid contribution to the science. His Australian geology and mineralogy were complemented five years later by the work in Polynesia (Tuamotu Archipelago) and Micronesia (Ralik-Ratak Chains) of Ernst Karlovich Hoffmann (in Russian, Gofman; 1801–71).[109] Hoffmann was perhaps the only other first-rate Russian mineralogist at work in South Pacific waters in that period. Like Shtein, he was a graduate of Dorpat (modern Tartu) University and a progressive follower of Abraham Gottlob Werner, the German mineralogist and teacher.[110] To appreciate the circle in which Shtein and Hoffmann moved while at Dorpat is to understand the thrust of Shtein's geology in New South Wales.

The University of Dorpat, far the oldest in the Russian Empire, was in the early 1800s the undisputed centre of Russian physics, physical geography, and, thanks to Friedrich Georg Struve and his sons, astronomy.[111] Its able *rektor*, Georg Friedrich Parrot (1767–1852), an experimental physicist and meteorologist, encouraged international contacts for its students and its faculty alike.[112] As a result, some took the well-trod path to Freiburg University to study further under German specialists like A. G. Werner. Others, supported by Parrot, found berths on Russian expeditions round the world: for example, Johann Eschscholtz, Director of the Dorpat Zoological Museum by the early 1820s and a veteran of Kotzebue's voyages;[113] Heinrich Seewald, the anatomist and surgeon (1797–1830); Emil Lenz, the physicist (1804–65), both veterans of *Predpriiatie*'s Pacific expedition (1823–26).[114] Shtein had reason to be confident that Werner's classifying message to geologists would be acceptable to his superiors in Dorpat. Moritz Friedrich Engelhardt (1779–1842), who held the chair of mineralogy, had personally studied under Werner at Freiburg—before travelling with Parrot to the Caucasus to make a study of its rocks.[115]

Werner had published little since his work on the external characters of minerals, *Von den äusserlichen Kennzeichen der Fossilien* (1774), but in twenty years he had turned a provincial mining school into a European scientific centre to which students flocked from Russia, France, and all the German states. It was the linchpin of his teaching that lithology and the chronology of geological formation must be grasped. Inspired by the work of G. C. Fuchsel, Werner argued, first, for a definite and universal geological succession. He contended, second, that the earth's rocks were precipitates of a primeval ocean: even basalt he supposed to be an

aqueous accumulation and not igneous in origin. And so originated one of
the essential controversies of historical geology. Werner's followers were
known as Neptunists; their rivals—who conceded the important part
played in the forming of the earth's crust by subterranean fire—were the
so-called Vulcanists. Wernerians dismissed volcanoes as abnormal hot
phenomena caused by subterranean coalbeds. Much of Werner's theory
was quite erroneous. Nevertheless, geology was deeply in his debt by
1800 for so clearly demonstrating geognostic principles and for inspiring
his pupils with enthusiastic zeal for the science.[116] In Australia, Shtein's
very attitude, that is, the kinds of questions that he asked, reflected
Werner's influence.

On reaching Sydney, as we saw, he sought permission from Macquarie
to investigate a portion of the Great Dividing Range and, with the help of
Lawson, Cunningham, and others, made a trip up onto King's Table
Land, i.e., the fairly level area above the cliffs due south of modern
Wentworth Falls.[117] He spent some time around Prince Regent's Glen,
"now restricted to a small portion of Jamison's Valley,"[118] then in-
corporating most of Cox's Valley.[119] Being at an elevation of approximately 2,730 feet above sea level, Shtein enjoyed wide-ranging views indeed, as well described in Baillière's seminal *Gazetteer* (1866),[120] but,
more crucially from his professional perspective, also views of sandstone
strata, quartz, and schists.

> The mass of sandstone is seamed by ravines, deep in proportion to
> height, until the profound depth of the valleys adjacent to the
> Weatherboard... imparts to the scenery a wild grandeur.... The
> whole mass consists of ferruginous sandstone, composed of angular
> or slightly worn grains of quartz, cemented by oxide of iron.[121]

Elsewhere, Shtein identified intrusions of granitic massifs and, from
reports of coal at Newcastle and examination of that coal, persuasive evidence of Carboniferous as well as Permian activity. He focused on the
great Triassic beds of New South Wales, of which sandstones and shales
formed an element, then took account of the Triassic limestone islands on
the fringes of Australia. He saw a link. As for the Blue Mountains themselves, he came to recognize in them the weathered remnants of an ancient and enormous peneplain. How ancient? Shtein was ignorant of the
"succession" in Australia and made no use of terms like earlier or late
Tertiary period. He was, however, quite correct to see beyond Triassic
sandstone to a time of geological antiquity. Following his steps, later
geologists perceived Devonian activity.[122] The Great Dividing Range was,

in his view, not only very ancient ("having evidently been produced by very early schistose processes"), but also "linked to Asiatic ranges to the north. . . by means of islands that extend between New Holland and the Asian continent."[123] Shtein's view was broad and basically correct.

Albeit cautiously, he also drew attention to the certainty that, eons earlier, dry regions of Australia had been, if not submerged by ancient seas, at least well watered. "The Newcastle coal deposits," he observed, "consist of schists and clays and contain incalculable quantities of plant- and, especially, reed-imprints." And near King's Table Land he found "small quantities of oil." We now know that those coal-seams, laid down in the Upper Carboniferous period, had formed in swampy lowland forests at the foot of mountains built up by Devonian earth movements. Shtein's chief message was, again, that over ages far too numerous for men to count, the continent had sunk and risen, waters had flooded in and drained away, the mountain ranges had grown and shrunk. Almost in passing, he reported finding gold and silver traces. Only three years later (1823), a Colonial Surveyor, J. McBrien, worried Brisbane by reporting such a find in more or less the same locality that Shtein had visited (Fish River, fifteen miles east of Bathurst).[124]

Shtein was among the first well-trained geologists to study and collect samples of ore from the Great Dividing Range. Like the preceding work of Charles Bailly, the mineralogist with Nicolas Baudin's French expedition to Australia, however, his results were viewed askance by his superiors at home and so, unpublished, could not benefit or harm Australians. It was as though such rock collections and dating had been jinxed: not even Flinders's were available for study, having vanished in the ludicrously understaffed British Museum shortly after they arrived in 1811.[125]

Wishing to avert the certain consequences—stress and labour shortages—officials consistently suppressed all news of gold finds in the colony. Thus, Shtein's discovery (supposing that Macquarie had learned of it) would not have caused rejoicing there. All Macquarie's and Brisbane's censorship, however, was as nothing in comparison with that confronting would-be Russian writers in the field of geology:

> Because of its obvious conflict with Church writings, the study of geology did not advance until the second half of the nineteenth century. According to [Vladimir F.] Odoevskii, geology was not taught in Russian schools and "no Russian books on the formation of the earth's crust could be published, while geological works in foreign languages were a source of headaches for perplexed censors." The

official watchdogs were thrown into the unenviable position of being expected to analyze complex geological theories and match them with the biblical account of creation.[126]

Their publication delayed by the political investigations that ensued after the collapse of the Decembrist insurrection, materials like Shtein's from the Vasil'ev-Shishmarev expedition were minutely scrutinized through the new lenses of official nationalism, Christian Orthodoxy, and autocracy.[127] Small wonder, in these circumstances, that the Russian Mineralogical Society, founded in 1817, was a listless and weak organization. (Bound to publish works only in Russian, it managed to issue only two slim volumes of proceedings in the first twenty-five years of its life!) Official nationalism and political constraint went hand in hand, during the sombre reign of Nicholas I with universal censorship.[128] By an 1826 decree, Church authorities not only gained the right to censor all religious matter (as they had in other times) but also exercised an influence over the publishing of monographs on social, political, and even scientific themes by non-religious bodies. The results of this were analyzed in 1906 by the historian A. Shchapov in his *Social-Educational Conditions of the Intellectual Development of Russia*. Certain passages by Shchapov bear directly on the fate of Russian scientific writings of the early nineteenth century, e.g., reports of work performed in New South Wales and reflections on Australia:

In the period of full censorship, a special category of "unpublishable books" was created in the general field of Russian science. . . . In the natural sciences, for example, "unpublishable" were treatments of the physical formation of the earth, geological eras, the origin of species, the antiquity of man, Neanderthal and other human fossils. . . the importance of force and matter in nature. . . and many other topics.[129]

Shtein lived too soon to benefit from Murchison's extensive geological researches in the Ural Mountains and resultant works; nor was he even privileged to read Charles Lyell's *Principles of Geology* (1830–33). That book was formally admitted into Russia in 1861.[130] Few visitors made use of the Australian rock samples he had brought back to St. Petersburg in 1822 and which, since 1828, had been on unfrequented shelves at the Academy of Sciences' *Kunstkammer*.[131] Few today, in either Russia or Australia, are conscious of his work, This summary alone wil underline the need for scholars to be mindful of the wealth of Australasian materials in Soviet state archives and museums.[132]

ASTRONOMY, SURVEYING, AND HYDROGRAPHY IN NEW SOUTH WALES

More even than linguistics or the two life sciences, Russian astronomy, surveying, and hydrography—the basic naval sciences of measurement by land and sea—bore the impression of the Kruzenshtern-Lisianskii expedition in *Nadezhda* and *Neva* (1803–6). Largely at Kruzenshtern's insistence, the most modern instruments were bought for Russian ventures in the North and South Pacific, mostly from famous London makers.[133] Logs and small sounding machines by Massey, telescopes by Tully, Dolland, or the Troughtons, and chronometers by Arnold and Barraud[134]—all joined the Arrowsmith and Purdy maps aboard those Russian vessels bound for Polynesia or Australia. What greater single task confronted Russians in those waters, after all, than the precise establishment of geographical positions, the locations of specific points, and the whereabouts and progress of the ships themselves? It was to this main end that maritime astronomy had always bent its efforts. Conscious of the work done by *Nadezhda* and *Neva,* no Russian captain on a mission round the globe thereafter could neglect to strive for full, accurate reckonings of latitude and longitude, of air and water temperature, barometric pressure, wind and current variations; and, in general, the Russian practice on such voyages may be compared with the British or the French in the same period to Russia's advantage.[135]

Thanks mainly to the industry of leading British makers of the early nineteenth century, chronometers, for instance, had been adequately standardized by 1810; yet they were far from being part of the required equipment of contemporary Royal Navy ships in the Pacific, as they were of Russian-American Company and expeditionary ships. Again, the Russians took the trouble to investigate the market for specific instruments before acquiring, for instance, an achromatic telescope from Dolland or a brand-new transit instrument from Edward Troughton.[136] Their deliberate approach and thoroughness paid handsome dividends in astronomic data and the consequently accurate hydrography, to which the 1826 Kruzenshtern *Atlas of the South Sea* bears a lasting testimony.

Longitude at sea was measured, of course, with the aid of chronometers. Each ship was obliged to carry two, three, or even more of them, since their readings gave significant errors under the influence of constantly varying physical and meteorological effects. The error grew particularly large when in the tropics, where the movement of chronometers had often to be altered. The average of readings from two or three instruments was regarded as the true one. . . . The best method of finding the longitude of a place, in those days, was reduced to determining the angular distance between the moon and certain stars, with a sextant; and besides this, longitude was also reckoned by means of an octant, giving a variation of one or two minutes from the sextant. Such measurings were done in great numbers and the calculations were performed usually on the basis of lunar tables, for which not a little time was needed. . . . As for latitude, it was determined by many meridianal elevations of the sun and stars. Accuracy was impossible because of any heavy swell. Ships' positions offshore were calculated by bearing on a compass from outstanding points which had been fixed precisely on a map. A ship's position was reckoned on the basis of two or three intersecting compass bearings. The difficulties of navigation were in themselves sufficient to render cartographic surveying practically impossible.[137]

As V. V. Nevskii rightly emphasizes, measurements could be only approximate under such circumstances—and obtained with daily toil. In and by Australia, however, Russian officers gladly submitted to that toil in the interests of science, self-respect, and national pride.

Recognizing the importance of astronomy when far from home, high-ranking Russian naval officers had since the 1750s sought the help of the Academy of Sciences in educating captains in essential astronomical technique, improving or inventing instruments, and generally lending expertise.[138] The distinguished Russian physicist, astronomer, and poet Mikhail V. Lomonosov (1711–65) had in 1764 provided valuable help, lessons, and even a "solid hammock" for a forthcoming Pacific-Arctic venture.[139] This awareness in Admiralty College circles of the need for academic input into long-range naval ventures grew immensely in the wake of Cook's last voyage. Finally, in 1787, the Admiralty College simply asked the president of the Academy to organize small classes in astronomy for serving naval officers who were to make long voyages, e.g., to the Pacific. The Academy responded by appointing the astronomer Petr B. Inokhodtsev as liaison officer and special teacher. Inokhodtsev maintained his naval links for twenty years, collaborating with his colleagues M. V. Severgin the mineralogist and A. Sevast'ianov the zoologist in drawing up sailing instructions for the Kruzenshtern-Lisianskii expedition in 1803,[140] and bringing naval officers to the Academy's St. Petersburg Observatory for practical astronomy by night. At that observatory, then second in the empire to Dorpat's, Kruzenshtern and other officers came into contact with the eminent geodesist and propagandist of astronomy Fedor Ivanovich Shubert (1758–1825).[141] A full Academician since 1789, Shubert was especially well placed to help the Navy if he chose. He was the author of a college-level textbook on theoretical astronomy (1798), was well aware of the value of magnetic variation observations and the problems of establishing position in a watery or dry-land wilderness, and had connections. He decided to be helpful:

A large role in the organizing of studies for officers at the Academy accordingly belongs to F. I. Shubert. In 1803, with this in mind, he published a special *Aid to the Astronomical Determination of Latitude and Longitude for Places*. Republished several times in Russian and in German, this book subsequently had great significance for the development of topography and cartography in Russia. F. I. Shubert also perfected astronomical equipment that was designed to lighten work in expeditionary conditions and. . . adapted a reflecting sextant, pocket chronometer, achromatic tube with one-metre focus, all more easily and conveniently used than earlier instruments. . . . Also in 1803, F. I. Shubert published in German his popular and widely-known three-volume *Popular Astronomy*. In it, the scientific explanation of the Creation was clearly and accessibly laid out, on the basis of the most recent findings of astronomy.[142]

Shubert's dealings with the Navy soon bore fruit in other ways. He extended his teaching to cover meteorology, encouraging assistants (he was named the head of the observatory in 1804) to study it. He helped found naval astronomical observatories at Kronstadt and at Nikolaev on the Black Sea coast. Later, in 1813, he began publishing annually *Morskoi mesiatsoslov* (*Maritime Calendar*), to which naval officers subscribed with the encouragement of their superiors. Inokhodtsev made the daily meteorological readings until 1806, then V. V. Petrov, and finally, from 1812 until his posting on secondment to *Otkrytie*, Pavel V. Tarkhanov. Tarkhanov was a protégé of Shubert, who considered him one of his ablest pupils. Till *Otkrytie* returned him from Australia and Arctic climes, the meteorology was undertaken by the eagle-eyed W. K. Wisniewski.[143] Tarkhanov determined the exact geographical position of Kirribilli Point in Port Jackson, of spots in Rio de Janeiro and Honolulu and a dozen other places, during the expedition of 1819–22. Certain of his materials were published by the Academy of Sciences.[144] In thoroughness and scope, his astronomical and meteorological data surpassed those supplied by the *Nadezhda*'s people.[145] As was seen, both Bellingshausen's and Vasil'ev's squadrons made their shore base on the North Shore, probably at Macquarie's own suggestion, and had their temporary observatories fully functioning within a day of their arrival.[146]

Tarkhanov's counterpart aboard *Vostok* in 1820 was Ivan Mikhailovich Simonov (1794–1855), a friend and colleague of the great mathematician

N. I. Lobachevskii and, like him, a later *rektor* of Kazan' University.[147] Possessed of an enormous scientific curiosity, *Vostok*'s astronomer was Bellingshausen's principal assistant in Australia in scientific matters. Simonov had shown precocious skill in mathematics at Kazan', where he was fortunate to find distinguished German teachers: Johann Bartels, late of Göttingen, Kaspar Renner, the applied mathematician, Joseph Littrow, the astronomer.[148] Like Lobachevskii, the young genius who was already working on his non-Euclidian ("imaginary") geometry,[149] Simonov drew full advantage from the happy accident that brought such teachers to an infant university so far from Germany. By 1816, he was serving as extraordinary professor in its Faculty of Sciences and lecturing on theory of numbers and astronomy. In 1819 he was summoned to St. Petersburg, embarking on the major intellectual and physical adventure of his life.[150]

Like Vasil'ev, Bellingshausen sailed from the Baltic with detailed instructions relating to astronomy, meteorology, magnetic variation readings, oceanography, and even physics.[151] He and his lieutenants took the matter very seriously, as we see from his reports and published narrative. Besides Simonov, Captain-Lieutenant Zavadovskii, Lieutenants Konstantin P. Torson and Arkadii Leskov, and Midshipman Dmitrii Demidov were required to show overall proficiency in maritime astronomy.

> Apart from Lt. Lazarev, Captain-Lieutenant Zavadovskii, and me, nobody on either sloop had had occasion, before this voyage, to occupy himself with astronomical observation; but while we were in London each man bought himself the best available sextant and we all strove to outdo each other in the use and precise checking of our instruments and in measurement of lunar and solar distances. Even before we reached Rio-de-Janeiro, we had all become good observers.[152]

Torson especially distinguished himself with Troughton's sextants in the South Pacific Ocean. As officer of the watch, he made systematic compass-variation readings and meteorological and astronomical reckonings. Almost all traces of his participation in the voyage (e.g., an island named for him, missions performed by him) were removed from the 1831 text by Bellingshausen's own watchdogs and censors, because of his involvement in conspiracy against the tsar in the Decembrist uprising.[153] Nevertheless, Torson's readings are embedded in the Bellingshausen narrative (*Dvukratnye izyskaniia . . .*) and bear eloquent witness to his competence. The Soviet historian V. M. Pasetskii thus draws attention to the "astronomic duties" well performed by men other than Simonov while *Vostok* was in Australia:

1 Peter the Great, tsar and creator of a modern Russian navy; portrait by Kneller (1698). Peter had a lifelong interest in maritime exploration. Through Dutch contacts he learned about ''New Holland'' (Australia) even in the 1690s.

2 Ships of the Dutch East India Company, such as Peter the Great examined at Amsterdam in 1697 and which skirted ''New Holland'' en route to Batavia. Frontispiece to Etienne Roger's *Recueil des Voyages* (Amsterdam, 1705), vol. 4.

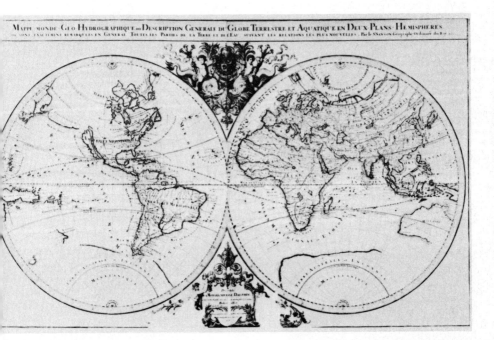

3 Map of the world by the French cartographer Sanson, published in Paris in 1691. Most of "Nouvelle Hollande" is indicated and shown as distinct from La Terre Australe et Inconnue, to its southwest.

4 Captain James Cook, R.N., whose voyage to New South Wales brought Australia into focus for the Russians in 1771–72. Celebrated oil portrait by John Webber.

5 Abel Janszoon Tasman; portrait attrib. Jacob Gerritszoon Cuyp, 1637–38. Tasman's discoveries in Australasia were made known to the Russians by Nicolas Witsen's and F. Valentijn's works.

6 Captain-Lieutenant Iurii Fedorovich Lisianskii (1773–1839). While in India in 1799, he planned to join Matthew Flinders and conduct survey work around Australia's coasts. He was thwarted in that hope, but did cross Oceania aboard the ship *Neva* in 1804.

7 The *Neva* (ex-*Thames*), the 370-ton London-built ship in which a Russian company commanded by Captain-Lieutenant Leontii Adrianovich Gagemeister first visited Australia (1807). From a drawing made by Lisianskii at Kodiak Island early in 1805.

8 Captain-Lieutenant Ivan Fedorovich Kruzenshtern (1770–1846), who led the Russian Navy's first circumnavigation of the globe (1803–6) and, while doing so, made a study of Tasman's movements in Van Diemen's Land of 1642–43.

9 Captain-Lieutenant Leontii Adrianovich Gagemeister (German: Ludwig von Hagemeister), like Kruzenshtern, an influential Baltic German officer with lifelong Pacific interests. He reported on Sydney and New South Wales (1807) to the directors of the Russian-American Company, suggesting that it engage in trade there.

10 View of Sydney from the Rocks, 1807–8; hand-coloured aquatint by the pardoned convict John Eyre. Aboriginals and merchantmen are much in evidence. Published in D. D. Mann's *Present Picture of New South Wales* (London, 1811).

11 Captain William Bligh, R.N., Governor of New South Wales. Engraving by J. Condé after a painting by J. Russell, 1792. Bligh had been sent to bring the New South Wales Corps to heel, but he failed and was overthrown in 1808 in the "Rum Rebellion."

12 Sir Joseph Banks by Sir Joshua Reynolds. Bligh wrote to Banks, whom the Russians had visited in London en route to Oceania during the early 1800s, about *Neva*'s stay at Sydney.

13 Colonel Lachlan Macquarie, fifth Governor of New South Wales, the great builder. He had travelled across Russia in 1807, been very well treated by Russian naval officers, and was hospitable toward Russian companies in 1814 and 1820. Watercolour by Richard Read, 1821–22.

View of Sydney from the North Shore of Port Jackson, by Pavel N. Mikhailov (1820).
tok and *Mirnyi* stand at anchor off Kirribilli Point. Pen, ink, and watercolour.

Another view, also by Mikhailov in 1820, also with botanical and ethnographic em-
es. These aquarelles are held in the State Russian Museum, Leningrad: R 29276/274
9277/275. Fort Macquarie, on the shoreline at left, is not yet complete.

16 Captain-Lieutenant Mikhail Nikolaevich Vasil'-ev, who commanded the first Russian squadron—*Otkrytie* and *Blagonamerennyi*—to call at Sydney in 1820.

17 Captain-Lieutenant Gleb Semeonovich Shis marev, Vasil'ev's second-in-command, had sailed the South Pacific with Kotzebue in 1816. He brous his nephew along, as midshipman in *Blagonamere nyi.*

18 The armed sloop *Mirnyi,* which called at Sydney twice in 1820 under the command of Captain-Lieutenant Mikhail Petrovich Lazarev. From archival documents, by the Soviet artist M. Semenov.

19 Mikhail Petrovich Lazarev, at the height of his career circa 1835: formal portrait by Thompson. The great majority of Russian naval officers who visited Australia later attained high rank within the service of the Russian Crown.

20 Captain-Lieutenant Faddei Faddeevich Bellinsgauzen (Fabian Gottlieb von Bellingshausen); this sketch by *Vostok*'s artist Mikhailov, of 1819–20, is the sole extant portrait of the commander in this period

21 Pavel Nikolaevich Mikhailov (1786–1840), seconded to the Antarctic-Pacific expedition led by Bellingshausen from the Academy of Arts. He produced a magnificent portrait gallery of aboriginal Australians of the North Shore's Cammeraigal tribe, as well as fine *paysages*.

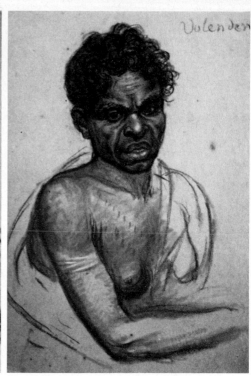

22 Studies of two members of the Cammeraigal tribe of Port Jackson's North Shore, by Mikhailov: Toubi and Volenden. The Russians often met Chief Boongaree and such aboriginals as these in 1820: from State Russian Museum, Leningrad R 29206/204 & 29203/201.

23 Ivan Mikhailovich Simonov (1794–1855), astronomer aboard the *Vostok*. A versatile young scientist from Kazan' University, of which he became rector in 1846. Oil portrait, early 1840s.

24 The governor's residence at Parramatta, where Bellingshausen, Simonov, and Mikhailov stayed as Governor Macquarie's guests in 1820. The portico had been designed recently by Francis Greenway. From drawing by Marchais engraved by Schroeder for Louis de Freycinet's *Voyage autour du Monde* (Paris, 1825), p. 95.

25 Parramatta Anglican Church, 1819, where the Russians saw aboriginal and half-caste girls from the nearby Female Orphan School singing hymns. Taken from Freycinet, *Voyage* (1825), p. 96.

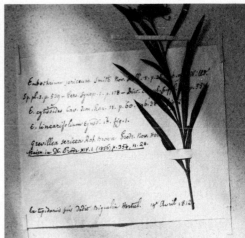

26 A specimen of Australian holly, from the herbarium of Karl-Heinrich Mertens. Bellingshausen collected an exactly similar specimen in Sydney, bringing a total of 77 dried plants to Russia from Australia. From the V. Komarov Institute of Botany, Academy of Sciences of USSR.

27 Allan Cunningham, botanist and explorer, circa 1835. Artist unknown. Cunningham, like Macquarie, had had friendly dealings with Russians in the past. He volunteered to escort the geologist Fedor Shtein and the artist Emel'ian M. Korneev, of the ship *Otkrytie,* into the Blue Mountains in 1820.

28 King's Tableland in the Blue Mountains, by Augustus Earle. Shtein, Korneev, and Cunningham hiked here in March 1820. Shtein collected rock samples, plants, and insects, while Korneev drew landscapes. Taken from the Rex Kivell Collection, National Library of Australia.

29 Birds of the Sydney area, caught, stuffed, and drawn by the Russians in 1820. The preserved specimens are in the Zoological Institute of the Academy of Sciences, Leningrad (ZIAN), Division of Ornithology.

30 Detail of the original label attached to one of these birds, *Meliphaga Lewinii* ssp. Note "Admiralty Dept.," and the several hands that annotated this label, like most others at ZIAN and BIN, in the 1800s.

On 9 September [1820], the sloop entered Port Jackson; and here the expedition passed 50 days, preparing for the second and culminating stage of the mission in the region of Antarctica. From Bellingshausen's book, we know that while in Australia Torson greatly occupied himself with astronomical readings. Among other things, he made 390 measurements of the moon's distance from the sun, on the basis of which he determined the exact longitude of "Russian Cape" on the North Shore of Port Jackson. He found it to be 151°21'S.[154]

Sydney marked the zenith of Torson's industry as an astronomer: even at Rio de Janeiro, he made a mere 316 reckonings of lunar distance.[155] What is to be emphasized, however, is that several of the *Vostok*'s and *Mirnyi*'s officers were aiding Simonov professionally in his task of fixing geographical positions and/or anchorages in the South. Here, to emphasize the point, is Bellingshausen on *Vostok*'s approach to Pigeon House Hill on the shore of New South Wales. This time, it was a question of six officers all taking compass bearings, side by side:

At noon on 29 March we were in Lat. 35°57' 42''S., Long. 150°47' 51''E; the height on the coast of New Holland called the "Pigeon House" [by the Clyde River's head] then bore S. 87°30'W, and a projection of the shore, the headland "Perpendicular Cape," bore N. 7°46'E.; thereby the position of the above-mentioned height works out at 4' farther south and the Perpendicular Cape 4' 30'' farther west than in Flinders' *Atlas*.[156]

Not only were *Vostok* and *Mirnyi* carrying copies of the charts printed officially (1814) on the basis of Flinders's surveys in *Investigator* (1798–1803); their officers stood ready to emend them.

Necessarily, however, Simonov himself bore the main burden of work at "Russian Point" and, rightly conscious of pressing time and the need to build on J. Lacaille's "southern work" of a half-century before, he left the reckoning of latitude and longitude to Zavadovskii, Bellingshausen, and a navigating officer, Il'in.[157] Their work appeared in summary in 1831:

LATITUDE AND LONGITUDE OF THE OBSERVATORY

Average of 5 observations taken about midday	33°51'12''S
Average of a number of meridian altitudes	33°51'08''S
Zavadovskii on 12 observations at the Observatory	33°51'24''S
Longitude fixed by me from 125 lunar distances	151°16'58''E
By Mr Zavadovskii on 125 lunar distances	151°23'28''E
By Navigating Officer Il'in on 120 lunar distances	151°16'54''E

VARIATION OF COMPASSES

On the *Vostok*   8°03'00''
On the *Mirnyi*   8°28'08''

H. W. F. and C. 9 hours 2 minutes

The highest range of tide was 4 feet 5 inches on 17 April and 15 May, at noon.

The large Arnold chronometer No.518 was in advance of mean time by 2 hours 17 minutes 16.79 sec. In 24 hours it gained 5 min. 10 sec. The Barraud chronometer No.922 was in advance of mean time 1 hour 13 min. 20.79 sec. In 24 hours it lost 10 mins. 31 sec. The small Arnold chronometer was in advance of mean time by 2 hours 20 min. 53.79 sec. In 24 hours it gained 6 min. 8 secs.

NB The result of the observations by the Spanish expedition under Malaspina in 1793 was as follows: Lat. 33°51'28''S., Long. 151°18'08''E. It is not at all certain however that they used the same observation station, though they were on the same headland.[158]

Simonov's own data were reserved for other uses. Returning from Antarctica with half-a-dozen journals crammed with many kinds of first-hand information, he published in both popular and, later, more strictly scientific form. "Even during the voyage, he had been submitting papers to Kazan' University on the various regions where the expedition paused, and these appeared in the University's own periodicals."[159] His first popular offering, "A Word of the Success of the Voyage of the Sloops *Vostok* and *Mirnyi*," was a reprint of a public lecture that he gave his alma mater on 7 July 1822.[160] It was an easy piece of travel literature, with the properly exotic references to Australia, and it was well received. Even in 1822, however, Simonov had started to disseminate his Australasian data in traditional academic fashion, starting or in some cases resuming correspondence with a range of other scientists in Russia and abroad. Among the foreigners were the astronomers connected with the Kruzenshtern or Bellingshausen ventures' origins and sailing orders: Johann Caspar Hörner,[161] Baron Franz Xaver von Zach (1754–1832),[162] Shubert, Tarkhanov, and the Dorpat Observatory staff. Baron von Zach, the former director of the Seeberg Observatory at Gotha, shared Simonov's interests in geodesic problems, e.g., needle variation, and had published on the subject.[163] He was also the chief editor of influential learned journals of the day, notably *Correspondence astronomique...* (Genoa, 1818–26). Simonov, who was rewarded with a permanent position at the understaffed and infant university to which, unasked, he brought a precious ethnographical collection,[164] had enough to do in 1821–22. Meeting Lobachevskii in St. Petersburg, for instance, he arranged for crates of books and scientific instruments as well as articles and papers from *Vostok* to be despatched by heavy wagon to Kazan'.[165] Though founded only in 1804 and starved of all resources for a while,

Kazan's new library was even then expanding rapidly into a very major one, replete with scientific works and naval *Voyages* that bore directly on the South Pacific Ocean. In Kazan', indeed, were perhaps more books on that ocean and Australia by 1830 than in Moscow.[166] Overly busy though he was, nevertheless, Simonov sent materials to Zach, notably "letters" that related to his time in Australasia. These appeared in the *Correspondence astronomique . . .* , having been fused into a running narrative by Zach himself or by his assistant. Two years later (1824), we find Simonov re-editing his "letters" and submitting them for printing in a slightly altered form to the *Journal des Voyages, ou archives géographiques du XIXe siècle* (Paris). Once again, certain Australian material appeared.[167] It was promptly retranslated into Russian.[168] It was at this time (1825) that Simonov, urged on by Zach, Friedrich Bronner, now professor of physics at Kazan', and by the recent published work of Heinrich Lenz, who was at this time hard at work in Polynesia,[169] published the results of the *Vostok*'s and *Mirnyi*'s astronomy and oceanography in the Pacific. This paper, "Concerning Temperature Differentials in the Northern and Southern Hemispheres" (1825), was followed by another, "On the Determination of the Geographical Positions of Anchorages of the Sloops *Vostok* and *Mirnyi*" (1828).[170] For the latter, he was made a corresponding member of St. Petersburg's Academy of Sciences. Materials acquired in Australia were incidentally incorporated in these works.

Principal observers aboard *Apollon* at Sydney in 1822 were Lieutenants Pavel Baranov and Mikhail K. Kiukhel'beker the Decembrist. The latter was officer of the watch and, as such, responsible for entering meteorological data in the log, of which a fair copy happily survives in Leningrad. More than one quarter of all entries in that log, one sees, were made by Kiukhel'beker, who took special note of wind strength and direction, barometric variation, and needle fluctuation. Temperature is recorded to a quarter-degree Reaumur, barometric pressure to one-hundredth of an inch, the time of rainfall to the minute, day or night. Regarded as exemplary, the data were presented to the public, together with the frigate *Kreiser*'s log of 1822–25 (which likewise boasted its Australian component, since the ship had called at Hobart Town in 1823).[171] By then, however, Kiukhel'beker had been dead for thirty years.[172]

Like Bellingshausen, Mikhail P. Lazarev came to Australia in 1820 and again in 1823 as commander of the *Kreiser* perfectly conscious of the need to rectify even the best of maps, if readings warranted that step. Both *Kreiser* and her escort, *Ladoga* (ex *Mirnyi*) in fact arrived at Hobart Town on 17/29 May 1823 with more and better charts and atlases, perhaps, than any of their Russian predecessors had. Among the charts were even copies of preliminary printers' sheets for Kruzenshtern's great *Atlas of the South Sea*, "lest changes should be needful so that it may see the light quite accurate."[173] Alterations were, in fact, made to the sheet showing Van Diemen's Land. The fact was not surprising, as at least two highly qualified astronomer-geographers were with the frigate *Kreiser*: Fedor G. Vishnevskii and Dmitrii I. Zavalishin.[174] Despite his youth, the latter had in 1821 been teaching astronomy at the Naval Cadet Corps he had only lately left. Vishnevskii's elegant and detailed meteorological and astronomic data on the period spent in Australia, as in all other parts of the Pacific, appeared as a booklet in October 1882.[175] Of the irascible and prickly Zavalishin's almost equally belated article, "The Voyage Round the World of the Frigate *Kreiser*" (1877),[176] suffice it to note, within this scientific context, that although it is tendentiously composed in such a way as to belittle Lazarev, it does provide a cameo of shipboard astronomical and other reckonings as *Kreiser* came east towards Tasmania.

As on their slow approaches from the south, so also in Port Jackson Russian captains did what survey work they could. Among those most experienced in shallow-water coastal work, thanks to his service in the Marshall Islands and at Kotzebue Sound as first lieutenant of the *Riurik*, was Gleb Semenovich Shishmarev.[177] Port Jackson lacked the deadly coral reefs of Micronesia, to be sure, and had no icepack of the sort he had encountered in the Arctic three years earlier. Nevertheless, Shishmarev looked upon it as a stretch of water still not fully charted and, as such, an invitation to his own *Blagonamerennyi*. Boats set out from Kirribilli Point, commanded by the captain's nephew Nikolai, Lieutenant I. Ignat'ev, or another veteran of *Riurik*, Navigator V. Petrov, "to survey newly discovered spots and unknown shores."[178] These rowing-boats carried a hundred signals for use in making contact in emergencies.

All such work and all related charts, drafts, and corrections to existing charts of New South Wales were submitted to the Russian Naval Ministry at the conclusion of a given expedition. Should publication be envisaged, the Ministry in turn would hand the chart to the imperial Map Depot (*Depo kart*), organized in 1797 as a first step in establishing a Topographic Section in the General Staff. "The functions of the Depot included preparing and compiling maps for both military and general use and serving as the State Archive for maps. Accordingly, the Depot was entitled to demand the originals of all new maps as well as any other information it deemed necessary."[179] Since 1798, a special engraving section had been functioning within the Depot: it was the staff of that small office, numbering twenty-five by 1818 thanks to pressures from the massive preparations for a map of the entire Russian Empire and not from servants of the Navy, who engraved Pacific charts produced by officers of the *Kamchatka*,[180] *Vostok* and *Mirnyi, Predpriiatie, Miüller* and *Seniavin,* all in 1817–27.[181] Australian materials accordingly remained in a specifically non-academic, military section of the large General Staff. Indeed, the Geographical Department of St. Petersburg's Academy of Sciences having in 1800 been incorporated in the new Map Depot, the Academy had lost its role as the centre of cartography in Russia.[182] From the standpoint of Australia, the fact must be regretted: "for inasmuch as the Geographical Department had been annexed by the Military-Topographic Depot, Russian cartography developed, in the first half of the nineteenth century, exclusively under the military jurisdiction and according to its practices."[183] And this in turn has placed materials of interest to the Australian cartographer, if not quite out of reach, then almost so.[184]

As in Port Jackson proper, so also ashore the Russians gathered cartographic data when they could. In this regard, the Reverend Henry Fulton's and Surveyor Hawkley's contacts with the 1820 visitors bear mention. Henry Fulton (1761–1840), chaplain resident at Castlereagh when Fedor Shtein and Allan Cunningham came by,[185] was a particularly scholarly and well-read Irish gentleman of Bishop William Knox's time.[186] Involved tangentially in the rebellion of Tipperary (1798), he had prospered in Australia as a supporter first of Bligh, then of Macquarie. His private school at Castlereagh (established in July 1814), backed by a first-rate mathematics library, was viewed highly by Jamison and Cunningham. Shtein was well received by Fulton, who provided him with solid information and colonial statistics. Hawkley, for his part, gave Simonov the sets of barometric readings he had taken in the Blue Mountains en route to Bathurst plains, as well as data on the freshwater Lakes Bathurst and George that Bigge, Macquarie, and his staff were visiting in 1820. ("The Governor had made plans to settle about 1,000 people near one lake, and to establish a native village near the other.")[187] Furnished with Hawkley's barometric readings, Simonov worked out the heights of certain points by using "Mr Biota's tables based on the Laplace formula."[188] Simonov reckoned the watershed of the mountain range to lie 4,061 feet above sea level, Blackheath at 3,554 feet, and the Fish River at 2,694 feet. Other reckonings, printed with Bellingshausen's narrative in 1831, were: Cox's River—2,187 feet; Campbell's River—2,330 feet; Bathurst—2,190 feet; and Lake George—2,319 feet. By contemporary standards, these estimates were excellent. Not satisfied with all the lunar distances already taken on the North Shore that year, Bellingshausen took an extra 455 during the second visit of *Vostok*. This time, the average longitude of Kirribilli Point worked out at 151°09′753″E. This too was excellent by nineteenth-century, and even modern, standards of precision.[189]

Welcome as they were, the Russians had ample opportunity to listen to the colony's best-educated, best-informed officials. Captain Freycinet and his lieutenants had been less indulged, during their recent Sydney stay, than were the "1820''7 Russian visitors.[190] But then, the latter's industry and neatness impressed the British more. A glimpse of this and of the time freely devoted to the Russians by colonial officialdom at leisure may be had from the unpublished journal kept by Midshipman Nikolai D. Shishmarev of the sloop *Blagonamerennyi*.[191] Four of the 264 pages of that journal, kept consistently from 9 May 1819 to 1 August 1822, were devoted to Port Jackson and the Russians' busy visit. Here are extracts:

> 20 February/4 March 1820. At 9 a.m., *Otkrytie* saluted the local fort with 21 guns, the fort responding with an equal number; and at noon the Governor, with quite a sizeable suite, came out to visit our sloop flying a rear-admiral's flag on his launch. He was pleased with our craft, particularly with their neatness, for we had been preceded here by the French corvette *L'Uranie*, of which our hosts said that great uncleanliness prevailed. A 12-gun salute was fired, on the Governor's leaving us.

> 21 February/5 March 1820. On this day, given a favourable wind, we slipped our mooring and moved closer to shore, whither we sent our tents, instruments, and chronometers. At 5 p.m., all our officers were invited to dine at the Governor's. We found more than forty people at table, and efforts to entertain us were made by one and all, in particular by the Governor's own wife, a woman no longer young and in poor health. The Governor's warm feelings for her were evident. We drank the health of the Prince Regent and then of our Sovereign, before eating. It was past midnight before we returned to the ship.[192]

Macquarie gave a regular ball for Vasil'ev's and Shishmarev's people on 12/24 March, attended by crowds of local dignitaries, some of whom were men of learning. ("A portrait of Tsar Alexander in full length hung beside the entrance to the room, with the Prince Regent on the right wall and Lord Wellington on the left.") Again, the Russians added business to their pleasure, "passing over nothing new, or curious, or useful... and not only with regard to things relating to the naval sciences but also, in the broader sense, to matters that might widen *any field of human knowledge.*"[193]

6

ABORIGINALS, TASMANIANS, AND RUNAWAYS

Contact with the British was inevitable for the visitor to New South Wales in the early 1800s. First-hand contact with the Aboriginals outside the town of Sydney, on the other hand, was a matter of free choice. Russians from half-a-dozen ships, notably Navigator Aleksei Rossiiskii of the *Suvorov* (1814), Bellingshausen and Simonov of the *Vostok*, M. N. Vasil'ev of the *Otkrytie*, Midshipman Pavel Novosil'skii[1] of *Mirnyi*, Aleksei P. Lazarev of *Blagonamerennyi* (all visiting in 1820), and Akhilles Pavlovich Shabel'skii of the *Apollon* (1822), freely elected to make contact with the Aboriginals outside the town. The groups in question were the Cammeraigal of the North Shore of Port Jackson and the "Sydney-speakers" to its south.[2] Besides narratives by the seven men just named, we have, as evidence of Aboriginal material and social culture and adjustment to the European presence, several important drawings by *Vostok*'s artist Mikhailov, "A View of the Town of Sydney in Port Jackson," "Natives of New Holland," and "Boongaree, Matora: The Chief of the Broken Bay Horde and his Wife,"[3] and the Leningrad "pre-1828 collection" from Port Jackson. That collection, held in the Peter-the-Great Museum of Ethnography of the N. N. Miklukho-Maklai Institute of Anthropology and Ethnography, Academy of Sciences of the USSR, consists of nine artefacts from the Port Jackson area and includes a boomerang, a club, a shield, two spear-shafts, three spears, and the only known specimen from Sydney of the First Fleet writers' "fizz-gig," or trident fish-spear.[4] It is among the most important such collections in the world, and was described in full in 1981.[5]

ROSSIISKII, ALEKSEI LAZAREV, AND SIMONOV ON ABORIGINAL SOCIETY

Aleksei Rossiiskii, a graduate of the St. Petersburg Commercial Institute and not a navy man by training, was witness to a "battle" fought by sixty or so Aboriginals on 20 August 1814 with the foreknowledge and approval of the British. There are certain similarities between the incident and that seen five years later by Jacques Arago of *L'Uranie*. Rossiiskii, however, heard no singing or preliminary taunts, nor does he indicate that the combatants were drunk.[6] The English watched with interest as warriors first flung their eight- and ten-foot spears at opponents, then moved in with heavy bludgeons. The longer spears were "of three joined parts, two being of ordinary wood, the third of ironwood, the tip sharpened and with little jags." Bludgeons were three feet long or more and produced severe head injuries despite opponents' skilful use of "shields made of the bark of the ironwood tree, oval and slightly convex... an inch or so thick, and daubed with various red and white figures."[7] One man lost an eye. Next day, Rossiiskii and another navigator in *Suvorov*, Joseph de Silvier, had an encounter with a group of five Aboriginals by Benelong's Point. The Aboriginals were curious and friendly, and were entertained by Russian sextants and an "artificial horizon" (a little wooden box containing mercury). To prevent their damaging a good chronometer, Rossiiskii offered them his watch, which they duly broke. *Suvorov* sailed from Port Jackson with artefacts acquired in exchange for rum, in contravention of Governor Macquarie's regulations on that matter, and with shells, plant seeds, and petrified plants. Rossiiskii found the Aboriginals tall and lean, and rather hideous:

> They paint their face with white lines and other figures, and paint the nose red, which gives them a fearful appearance. Some of them have in their nose a little stick, about four inches long.... The old men have gloomy faces and seem to be sad. The women... carry their infants on their shoulders, bound to them by a wide lashing made of grass and... decorate their faces and breasts with red, yellow, and white colouring. The little craft of these people are made of the bark of a tree called by the English beefwood [i.e., *Casuarina stricta*] which does indeed resemble meat in its colour. They paddle in them with their hands.... Sleeping in the open air, they feed themselves on mussels and seaplants.[8]

It was late summer, not late winter, when *Otkrytie* and her escort *Blagonamerennyi* arrived to find the "local" Aboriginals quite otherwise engaged. Part of the value of the Russian evidence of food gathering and other doings by the natives, one need hardly labour, lies precisely in the fact that first-hand evidence was gathered round the year. Vasil'ev and Lazarev recorded their impressions in the month of March, Simonov and Novosil'skii in April-May, Shabel'skii in June, Rossiiskii in August, Bellingshausen in April-May and September-November. It is thus only midsummer (December-February) for which Russian evidence is wanting. The significance of Russian data is again enhanced by the informants' own awareness of a distinction in the food-gathering patterns of the "coastal" and the "woods" or inland tribes of New South Wales. Here is Vasil'ev:

> The Governor's efforts to educate the natives and attach them to the Europeans have been in vain. They wander with their families, the men completely naked, the women covered with something like a blanket, nourishing themselves on fish and shellfish. They pass the nights in the woods, by a fire prepared by themselves. In Parramatta, however, we saw several children of natives in a school. There, they occupy themselves with the growing of kitchen vegetables and with agriculture, as well as with their studies. . . . [9]

Macquarie himself provided Vasil'ev with statistics for Aboriginals and settlers. The total population was by 1820 reckoned to be 31,570, including 7,000 in Tasmania. Aboriginals were thought to account for half the total (15,000 persons) but, in both New South Wales and Tasmania, to be declining. Aboriginals observed along the North Shore by Aleksei P. Lazarev of *Blagonamerennyi* struck him as "extremely lean, black in colour, and ugly." So far as he could tell in a limited time, they had "neither dwellings nor even huts," but did not suffer for the lack of them. A regular daily routine brought them to hunt, forage for mussels on the shore, then at night retreat to the bush.

Midshipman Pavel Mikhailovich Novosil'skii of the *Mirnyi* typified the younger officers chosen by M. P. Lazarev for the Pacific enterprise, by his abilities and by his breadth of interests. A graduate of the Imperial Naval Cadet Corps at Kronstadt, he returned to it in 1822 as an instructor in astronomy and higher mathematics. In 1825 he was transferred at his request into the Ministry of Public Education. He pursued a not uncomfortable dry-land career, keeping up an interest in polar and Pacific exploration. By late April 1820, Novosil'skii was making quite extensive hikes with I. M. Simonov of the *Vostok* due north from Kirribilli Point, round Neutral Bay, and in the general direction of today's Cremorne and Mosman. Thanks to rum and other European products that had more than once been given to Boongaree and his people since the Russians had arrived, such hikes seemed safe; and so they were. Boongaree himself, replete with heavy copper chain and plate, and his "repulsive" wife Matora, "smeared with fish-oil" and wanting to be kissed, might be encountered in the course of them. Novosil'skii left precise descriptions of the native body ornament and diet of the Cammeraigal ("Burra Burra") people:

> Sometimes they ornament their head with bird bones or fish bones, the tail of a dog, or kangaroo teeth; and sometimes they plait their hair, smearing it with the gummy sap of a plant so that it looks like rope ends. They stain their face and body with red earth. . . . When a youth reaches man's estate, two of his front teeth are knocked out. As for the girls, in early youth they have two joints of the little finger on the left hand cut off: the joints are supposed to hamper them in the winding of fish lines. . . . The New Holland natives. . . have no huts but simply make a semicircular brushwood fence on the side from which the wind blows. They lay a fire within the fencing. The diet of the coastal natives is chiefly fish; they pass the better part of the day in their little craft, fishing. Having caught a fish, they immediately throw it onto burning coals which are kept in the boat itself, and then they consume it, insides and all. Those natives who inhabit the woods nourish themselves on fern-roots, ants' eggs, and certain insects.[11]

Keenly aware of the number of snakes around him, Novosil'skii was impressed by the Aboriginals' scorn of them, noting that they commonly walked head down and killed a snake as soon as they spotted it. Poison from a snakebite was immediately and effectively sucked out by mouth.

Both in April-May and in October 1820, Simonov attached himself for hours at a stretch to Cammeraigal gatherings. "They would often," he records, "be drunk, but I never experienced the least insult or hostile action on their part."[12] Like Novosil'skii, he saw Aboriginals returning from Sydney, where, as usual, they had exchanged fresh fish for wine. Meeting the Russians, Aboriginals would frequently shake hands in British fashion, even bowing. Drunkenness, however, was apparently a regular state of affairs. One perceptive individual, whom Simonov perhaps mistakenly supposed was known as Burra Burra, brought his family and friends on a return visit to Kirribilli Point. There, the Russians entertained him and Mikhailov rapidly sketched him and his party of seven. Lithographed by Ivan P. Fridrits of the St. Petersburg Academy of Arts and published in Bellingshausen's narrative of 1831,[13] Mikhailov's illustration "Natives of New Holland" shows a half-caste girl, a stick-grass shelter, weapons, implements, a roasting fish, and ancient conical coiffure on initiated men of a variety depicted in rock engravings.[14] (Cords of bark or other vegetable material were tied around the stiff, greased hair fourteen to sixteen times to make a solid, "rope-ends" cone.) After a while, the women left the Russians' tent encampment and began to fish, but the four men stayed behind. Simonov examined the "small iron axes with which they fashioned various fishing implements, smoothing them down with glass," the "ancient and threadbare clothing" that the English had provided, and the heavy woollen blankets that the females were wearing "like a mantle or a toga." There was other, more arresting evidence of the extent to which the European culture had impinged upon but not yet shattered ancient ways and predilections:

> One other native would quite often come up to our tents. This individual spoke English better than the others, for he had been in London with Captain Flinders and had lived there for some time. In London, he told me, he had seen the Russian Emperor, the Austrian Emperor, the King of Prussia, King Blücher, and King Platov.
> "Did you talk to them too?" I asked him.
> "I talked to King Biukher."
> "What did he say to you?"
> "He said, 'Are you an American?' And I said, 'Yes, I am'."
> "And why didn't you stay there?" I said. "After all, it's a lot better there than here."
> "Oh, incomprable better! But I started to miss my people and came back to see them."
> "So will you go back to London?"
> "They wanted to take me there, and I was all ready; but just before the ship sailed, I ran into the bush. I suddenly wanted to stay around here some more."

The "kings" encountered by this Aboriginal, during a London interlude (6–20 June 1814) of the Congress of Vienna, were Matvei Ivanovich Platov, Hetman of the Don Cossacks (1757–1818) and Marshal Gebhard von Blücher (1742–1819).[15] Flinders's narrative does not allow us to identify the native whom, as Simonov remarks, London society had dressed and treated "like a doll." Among the other Aboriginals who knew some English and were met by Simonov in 1820 was a certain "Captain Bellau" whom Boongaree brought out to the *Vostok*. Initially demanding one pound sterling for a fish or two, Bellau was content with one small coin worth thirty kopeks. Like his captain, Bellingshausen, Simonov left quite a detailed description of Boongaree and an account of his relations with colonial officialdom since Governor Macquarie had arrived. Boongaree, who seemed a man of fifty-five, "wearing a shabby yellow jacket of the English convict's type and a pair of sailor's trousers, torn," carried himself with a dignity fully in keeping with his chiefly rank. That he had not fulfilled Macquarie's hopes of him, nevertheless, was very plain to Simonov and other Russians:

> The English have settled in the best parts of the country. The natives wandering in their vicinity soon became used to them and now commit no hostile acts against them. But for all that, they have shown no readiness whatever—and the colony has been in existence for more than 30 years—to adapt themselves to the European way of life. . . . The local authorities made Boongaree a present of a garden. It was specially laid out for him by Europeans. Agricultural implements and suitable clothes were issued, and convicts instructed the natives in the work. . . . The tools were sold, the cattle were eaten; and today, as before, the New Hollanders roam the bush and catch fish. . . . Boongaree sells the fruit that grows there so well; but he leaves his garden quite untended.[16]

Once at least, Simonov passed a night in a Cammeraigal encampment and witnessed a nighttime corroboree. The ballroom floor, as he records, was "a fresh, velvety meadow"; the ceiling was "the starry sky." Refreshments took the form of fish or mussels on a flaming pile of switches. His arrival was accepted and his presence tolerated by the group, now much bedaubed with reddish ochre.

> Music consisted of the sound of two small sticks, which the single musician beat time with, and of his loud voice as he sang a dissonant song. The dancers stood before him in a single line. They jumped at each blow of his sticks, and hummed: *prrs, prrs, prrs.*[17]

This was a play corroboree: women were present. Another night, the young astronomer found Boongaree's compatriots less pleasantly engaged. Noisily drunk, they brandished burning logs and, not entirely in jest, threw them at one another's heads. Again, the spirits had been brought from Sydney, plainly visible from Simonov's own tent at Kirribilli. Simonov himself saw Aboriginals returning to the North Shore of an evening, rum in hand. "It seemed," he noted sadly, that "the mouth of the little Parramatta River separated two quite distant planets."

In Simonov's view, the North Shore Aboriginals were unimpressed by British clothing but would dress to boost their chances of a useful barter session in the town. As for the Aboriginals who were effectively employed by Europeans, cleaning glasses with their long, sensitive fingers, for example, it was Simonov's opinion that they, too, were prepared to undergo much inconvenience—for alcohol. Like other Russian visitors of 1820, Simonov was shown the Parramatta school for native girls and left with very mixed emotions. "Clean white dresses," "moral teaching," and "harmonious singing of hymns" were well enough, and highly laudable in principle. Yet it was sad to see the shame with which the children viewed their relatives' "wild customs," and apparent that, in general, the Aboriginals were loath to leave their children at the school. Unlike Rossiiskii, the 1820 visitors were not regaled with a regular mock battle (grim enough though the results of *that* could be), and had no chance to see the Cammeraigal spears, "bent wood sabres," oval shields, and wooden bludgeons being used. To make amends for this, however, they had ample opportunity to study local Aboriginal responses to colonial instruction. What, asked Simonov, would happen to an Aboriginal after he died? "If I live well," came the reply, "all will go well with me; if I live badly, it will go badly with me." Such were the fruits of Christian teaching over twenty-five or thirty years. We learn from Simonov that, though Macquarie had succeeded in preventing corpse burning at least in the locality of Sydney, Aboriginals were still in 1820 very piously "laying away remains of the deceased and keeping graves with reverence." Nor had colonial officialdom produced the least modification to traditional and brutal courtship, nuptial, and marriage customs. ("For abduction, with a battle or without, here comprises the complete nuptial ceremony.") While the Russians watched them, native boys aged eight or nine were seizing girls and dragging them across the ground in playful practice of procedures that would later be in earnest.

Simonov spoke briefly of his dealings with the Aboriginals in an invited lecture at his alma mater, Kazan' University, on 7 July 1822. The lecture was immediately printed as a pamphlet. Further data were presented to the public in a set of polished "letters," sent originally to the eminent director of the Seeberg Observatory at Gotha, Baron Franz Xaver von Zach, for publication in his periodical *Correspondance astronomique . . .* (Genoa, 1823). These were re-edited and printed for a wider readership in *Journal des Voyages, ou archives géographiques du XIXe siècle* (Paris, 1824).[18] But still Simonov's journal of 1819–22 remained unpublished; and, of course, it was the principal repository of all that he had seen and learned about Australia. A decade passed. He was elected to the (then as now conservative) Academy of Sciences, a full professor, a distinguished scientist. He hesitated to present his early comments to the public, but agreed to offer lectures on the subject of Pacific and polar exploration.[19] Once at least, in 1848, he was considering potential publishers for his Australian and other reminiscences,[20] but he collapsed and died before completing his revision of the manuscript, now MS 4533 at the Kazan' State University Main Library, which rested squarely on his 1820 journal.[21] It was ultimately published, in Australia, only in 1981. Because Vasil'ev and Aleksei P. Lazarev both failed to publish their accounts of their experiences in Australia (the expedition of *Otkrytie* and *Blagonamerennyi* was not officially perceived as a success and was—quite rightly— overshadowed by the Bellingshausen-Lazarev Antarctic expedition),[22] and because the Novosil'skii narrative did not appear until 1853, it fell to Bellingshausen, not to his astronomer, to paint a picture for the Russians of beleaguered Aboriginal society and life.[23]

BELLINGSHAUSEN AND THE CAMMERAIGAL PEOPLE, 1820

Immediately upon his arrival at Sydney, Bellingshausen met both Governor Macquarie and Chief Boongaree. Both addressed him in English, both were welcoming and offered him their services. Although repulsed by "Queen Matora's" tousled hair studded with teeth and somewhat saddened by her husband's tattered trousers and grimacing,[24] Bellingshausen promptly offered them not only grog, butter, and sugar, but also tobacco, coins, and European clothing. In return, he was assured that his ship would be supplied with fish, live birds, and such marsupials as Aboriginals could catch. Boongaree's promises were kept in full, though at his countrymen's expense and not his own.

Over the next three weeks (12 April to 2 May 1820), numerous officers, including Bellingshausen, made the walk to Burra Burra's and his people's bush encampment. Not surprisingly, in view of the extent and comprehensiveness of his official narrative, *Dvukratnye izyskaniia v iuzhnom ledovitom okeane . . .* , Bellingshausen left a record of the windbreak, with its smoking fire, fish and crayfish, silent women in their blankets, troughs of sweet *Banksia*-blossom-infused water. Bringing the blossoms home in plaited fibre bags, the Russians saw, the women either simply sucked them or, more usually, put them in fresh water for a soaking and a squeezing. The brush itself was later thrown away. But, understandably, it was the water, not the bush, that Bellingshausen and his officers kept principally in view. As naval officers, they had a natural and proper interest in navigation and associated skills. Thus, they examined the boat that Boongaree had been presented with by the authorities in Sydney, and reflected on its use:

New Hollanders are given these craft by inhabitants of Sydney on the condition that they surrender to them part of the daily catch of fish.

They put out in these boats every day, fish at the mouth of the bay, then hasten back to the town to surrender the due portion of the catch; the remainder they exchange for drink or tobacco. . . . They also get themselves fish from rocks by the shore, holding in their hand a long spear made of the stem of a tree called the gummy-plant. The tip is like a fork; and to the prongs of this fork are attached small, sharply serrated bones. . . . From bark fibre. . . they also plait ropes with which to tie up their little craft. . . . Having stripped from a tree a piece of bark 11 or 12 feet long or even more, and 3 or 3 1/2 feet wide, they bend it flat. They then place stretchers a little distance from the ends of the bark, and tie up the ends themselves with pieces of the aforementioned rope. In such wretched craft do they go about the coves—and always with a fire aboard.[25]

Bellingshausen's description of Aboriginal diet, body ornament, physique, fishing techniques, and attitudes towards the British hardly differs in essentials from the Simonov account. In part, perhaps, because his narrative was an official one, approved and published by the state, he did present the "native schools" at Parramatta in a generally softer light. ("All the girls wore modest white dresses. An English upbringing had transformed their morality and way of thinking. Only their black faces remained as proof of their origin.") Not even Bellingshausen, though, denied that, like the Southern Russian Gypsies, Aboriginals did not elect to live "a settled, quiet existence."

The backwardness and lack of manufacturing skills of the New Hollanders [in Bellingshausen's view] in some measure derived from the vast extent of the country they inhabit, the shortage of sufficiently numerous (!) societies, rare contact with neighbours, and a sufficiency of food—which they obtain without mental exertion, great effort, or interference on the part of nature or men.[26]

From such a classic European nineteenth-century position, Bellingshausen marches on to his "Short Notice on the Colony of New South Wales." It, too, offers observations on the Cammeraigal people, Aboriginal society in general, and Anglo-native stress. Here, to indicate the scope and tenor of the article (which was included in the narrative of 1831), is a short extract:

All natives live in communities of 25, 50, 60 or even more, each with its own name. In one, called Burra Burra, there were last year [1819] reckoned to be as many as 120 persons. Until the coming of the

English, their government was patriarchal; each community was ruled by a senior man. But various English Governors have thought fit to select the chiefs themselves. . . . Such arrangements have been brought in to accustom the natives to submission and, through them, to learn of escaped convicts. In this respect they are extremely useful, for they act as guides to military units or the police. For the most part they live in open areas. . . and, because they live constantly in the open air, they can predict the state and change of the weather.[27]

Bellingshausen here enlarges on the social and sexual arrangements and the many languages of Aboriginals; on skills taught to the native young; on simmering hostility towards the British; and on illnesses and cures (shamanism, herbs for chewing, coughs and snakebites). Finally, sword-bearing officer that he was, he turns once more to "native warlike operations":

They usually employ spears made of the wood or, more accurately, the stem of the gummy-plant. This unusual tree is. . . distinguished by long straight stems, between 7 and 10 feet long, which rise straight from the centre of a low black stump. . . . When the stem is too short to form a spear, another and similar stem is fitted to it by means of a splice; the joint is then strengthened by a binding of bark fibre from a tree called Stric Wood [sic] by the English. . . . The natives also make use of a smooth piece of wood about 3 feet long and 2 1/2 inches broad, bent like a sickle. This they cast skilfully and accurately: it ricochets on striking the ground. They also have clubs 3 feet long, and for body protection they use wooden shields ornamented with a dry, white colouring substance over which they paint red stripes. Conflicts among them chiefly result from the abduction of their womenfolk. Then all, even the women, go onto the battlefield. . . . In general, husbands treat their wives like slaves.[28]

Making use of data just provided by Macquarie and his officers, and padding cautiously from other printed sources, Bellingshausen next moves on to other topics: Aboriginal employment in the Sydney taverns, native suffering from smallpox and venereal disease brought by the British, Aboriginal contempt for British clothing and sartorial example. All in all, it is as thorough and correct a ten-page survey as a foreigner with little time to spare and an obvious dependency on local British sources and assistance could have written. One would wish to end by commenting that Bellingshausen's final judgement of the North Shore Aboriginals was kindly; but unfortunately it was not. Quite to the contrary: it was with minimal regret that he departed from an ugly, noisy, lying, thieving people whom, fastidiously, he commended to the mercies of the "English" (London) Missionary Society. Enlightened seamen though they were by any standards, Bellingshausen, Lazarev, and Simonov were in the last analysis too Eurocentric to appreciate the skills, knowledge, or beauty of New Hollanders at home. They were in first-rate company in that regard: so too were Cook and La Pérouse.

AKHILLES PAVLOVICH SHABEL'SKII AND THE ABORIGINALS, 1822

Akhilles Pavlovich Shabel'skii, interpreter aboard the *Apollon* (Captain Irinarkh Tulub'ev), had received a fine liberal education at the Tsarskoe Selo *lycée* where the distinguished poet A. S. Pushkin also passed his adolescence. The two were well acquainted. Shabel'skii seized a chance to see the distant Russian outposts in America and, on his way, called at Port Jackson on 8 June 1822. He was a traveller by choice and avocation. Three years later, he was named the Second Secretary at the Russian Mission in the United States. There too it was his business to observe and to interpret for his seniors. While in America, as in Australia, he took an educated interest in prison management and in relations between governments and prisoners. He published on the subject.[29] He was treated in a friendly way at Sydney by the botanist Charles Frazer and particularly by Sir John Jamison, whom he admired. Travelling a little distance out of Sydney, Shabel'skii came upon groups of Aboriginals and learned about them what he could. Here are passages from his account, *Voyage aux colonies russes de l'Amérique...* , which appeared in St. Petersburg in 1826. The narrative is not to be confused with the contemporaneous but slightly different Russian-language text offered as "Prebyvanie g. Shabel'skago v Novoi Gollandii" in *Severnyi arkhiv* (*The Northern Archive*) that same year.[30]

The hollow of a large tree serves these people as a house, and in it they have only their own body heat as protection against the cold of the night. In summertime, they feed on meat and thereby contract a kind of scurvy or skin disease of which they cure themselves as soon as they begin to eat plants instead. Those of the natives who settled in proximity to the English became infected with smallpox. They died in thousands, whole generations vanishing. The survivors of that dreadful time now give themselves over to drunkenness which, in conjunction with the swift temperature fluctuations typical of Cumberland County, makes consumption quite common among them. . . .

Various kinds of gum-tree, acacia, and ironwood reach gigantic proportions in Cumberland County, and this is assuredly a great boon for
the natives there. . . . Wherever trees have been chopped down or
only half-burned stumps remain, new acacias of the non-coniferous
variety spring up. Several times, I pulled up new acacia shoots to try
to discover the cause of this strange propagation, for I wondered if
the acacia roots were connected with the stumps. I found that they
grew independently, and also found, among the roots themselves, the
large whitish worms that are a delicacy of the local natives.[31]

Sir John Jamison explained the role of "pigeons" in the propagation of
acacia trees; Shabel'skii himself worked out the benefits of burning trees
to Aboriginal society. Another day, he made the usual foreigner's tour of
Macquarie's Parramatta institutions. He was not overly impressed:

The Parramatta institution for the instruction of native children is
more an experiment than an actual school; nor does it serve to show
any obvious goodwill towards the natives on the Government's part.
There are no more than 13 children in it. They speak English pretty
well, but. . . the fact of the matter is that most of them are half-
castes, the offspring of English fathers and native mothers. . . . For
these people, an independent life is the most important thing on earth.
Take them into town, provide them with all the delights of civilized
society, and they will become wretched and sad and flee into the bush
at the first good opportunity.[32]

Like Simonov, Shabel'skii was frustrated by the language barrier and all
too conscious of dependence on the British for the information that he had
about these "sad" and "wretched" people. All he managed to discover
about Aboriginal religion was that all believed that "there exist a good
and evil genius, which must exert a certain influence on men." Like
Novosil'skii, he made a note of finger cutting, ritual eye tooth removal,
and skin incision, among other ancient practices still being followed in
the early 1820s.[33]

RUSSIAN EVIDENCE OF DIET, HUNTING, AND FISHING BY THE
COASTAL TRIBES

Russian evidence suggests that the accessibility of European foods
hardly altered the diet of the coastal Aboriginals near Sydney. They had

"soon wearied" of horticulture and grain growing, and "sold off their implements" (Bellingshausen). Boongaree's people ate the sugar and the butter that the Russians gave them, gratis, on 11 April 1820, but were far more grateful for the liquor and tobacco. Other Aboriginals in the locality were said by the British to have broken into free settlers' fields to steal millet and fruit, at the risk of heavy punishment. Such actions, though, were rare. As in pre-contact times, the coastal Aboriginals ate fish, sea plants, and mussels all year round, and crayfish and other crustaceans when they could. Being accustomed to spend their nights away from water, they were also expert woodsmen, eating "animals of all kinds, birds, snakes, and other reptiles" (Bellingshausen). In April, Boongaree's people found it easy to provide their Russian visitors with "fish, live birds, a kangaroo, and other animals," and to do so at short notice with a view to further barter. In May, we learn from Novosil'skii, coastal tribes found it appropriate to move into the woods or scrubland, foraging successfully for roots and insects, among others, and drinking the diluted "sweet matter" of flowering and "brush-like" *Banksia*. The Russians saw them doing so.

Without exception, those Russians who give physical descriptions of the Aboriginals encountered by them speak of lean or bony limbs. There are differences of opinion as to height: taking a Russian male contemporary as his standard, Rossiiskii finds the Sydney Aboriginals quite "tall and lean" in early manhood. Novosil'skii considers them "of less than medium height." All agree, however, that the diet of the coastal Aboriginals was adequate, though lack of foresight and technology obliged such tribes to pass the best part of their lives in hunting, gathering, preparing, or consuming food. One saw no "very old, or very fat, New Hollanders" (Simonov), "no hunchbacks or cripples among them" (Novosil'skii); and many of the adults were, by middle age, "practically toothless" (Rossiiskii).

Mikhailov's illustrations show Boongaree and Matora both wearing headbands made of netting in the knotted technique. The Russians make no mention of materials woven from vegetable fibres, so most probably the headbands were of possum fur twine. Possums were common in the area: the Cammeraigal roasted "various animals" in stick fires, driving possums from the trees by the traditional smoking technique mentioned by Simonov in passing. ("In several places, we observed trees that had been fired on the inside.") Kangaroos were also to be had along the North Shore of Port Jackson. "Right before my eyes," writes Simonov elsewhere, "our officers shot one in the nearby woods. The meat tastes like venison." The animal was "the size of a borzoi hound." Women of the

Cammeraigal tribe used kangaroo teeth as ornaments.

The Russians found the local Aboriginals fishing from rocks around Port Jackson's coves and from craft, native and otherwise. Since the arrival of the Europeans, boat-fishing had seemingly become more usual and more intensive; for the colonists had led the natives, to whom they offered "skiffs" or "longboats" on condition that they fish and then share the haul, to trade in fish. Both ends and means had thus been altered by the British. True, the Aboriginals were using glass and iron in the fashioning of fishing gear; but the ancient fishing skills remained intact in 1820. Leningrad now has a four-pronged fishing-spear of the sort then being used.[34] And Mikhailov depicts another spear (in "A View of the Town of Sydney") that had evidently furnished lunch in the shape of bream. "Natives of New Holland" shows a bearded man cooking a snapper (with a hump on its head), while other bream await their turn.

Native craft were commonly eleven feet in length or slightly more and formed out of a single strip of bark. The ends were well sewn up with stringy-bark. Such craft, in the unanimous opinion of the Russians, were exceedingly precarious, but even paddling by hand in them, i.e., without a barkstrip paddle, Aboriginals moved rapidly. Women as well as men spent long hours afloat, fishing with lines as well as trident spears. Every prong on such a spear would be "armed with small, sharply serrated bones" or "pieces of bone." Prongs and shaft were both of gummy-plant stem, the shaft being of two spliced parts. Mothers taught their daughters how to harpoon fish, which, like the mud oysters and mussels that abounded, were invariably broiled as in Captain Hunter's day.[35] The Aboriginals, in sum, had mostly limited their borrowing of alien technology to European boats, fish-hooks, and lines. In 1820, they were still using traditional stone axes to construct their own bark craft (although they sometimes filched steel axes from the colonists), and used traditional fishing equipment with conspicuous success. Even the seine had not been commonly adopted.

Fish and shellfish, snakes and other reptiles, birds, and even animals as large as kangaroo were "tossed onto the embers" and "consumed, insides and all" (Bellingshausen). There was no other mode of cooking. Women gathered firewood, and they were not barred from making fire. Fuel gathering was viewed as women's work, as was collecting "bottle-brushes" to be put into "large bags made out of plaited woody fibre." Mikhailov depicts two such containers of the same basic design—one small and delicate and fitted with a handle (left-hand lower corner of "Natives of New Holland"), the other coarsely made and twice as deep (on the head of the third figure in "A View of the Town of Sydney in Port Jackson").

RUSSIAN EVIDENCE OF ABORIGINAL CLOTHING AND ORNAMENTATION

Russian evidence confirms that Aboriginals wore British-style clothing to win favour on occasions when they sought personal contact with the colonists. "They have been told they will receive no help or work unless they cease to go completely naked" in Sydney itself. Nonetheless, one saw completely naked Aboriginals in town in 1820. Like the British, Russian visitors gave clothing to the Cammeraigal—in exchange for fish and animals at first, later as gifts—only to realize that they were fundamentally uninterested in the clothes as such. In 1814, the Aboriginals who visited *Suvorov* even "handed the clothing back and asked for another bottle" (Rossiiskii). Cammeraigal men were often literally naked. Russian evidence suggests that in the Sydney region, native girls also went naked, i.e., did not make use of loincloths or "aprons," as did certain other East Coast tribes. When belts were worn, they were of possum fur twine in many coils.

British blankets had apparently found favour with the North Shore Aboriginals. But their acceptance of an article which colonists did not view as a garment, strictly speaking, neatly symbolized non-contact on the vital plane of culture. Simonov correctly emphasizes that the blankets had been readily adapted to the natives' needs: worn as a mantle and tied with cords around the neck, they left the hands free for the chores of daily life. Rossiiskii suggests another adaptation of the British woollen blanket in the Sydney area. By 1814, some Aboriginals with infants "wrapped them up and bore them on their back," that is, used blankets in place of "lashings made of grass."

Whether for utilitarian or social purposes, the Cammeraigal made much use of headbands. Russian evidence suggests that they were worn by men rather than women, however (though Matora is depicted wearing one). The Cammeraigal were familiar both with the netted band of possum twine in the knotted technique and with the split-rush band worn by one woman in "A View of the Town of Sydney." Boongaree's headband was "decorated with red ochre" (Simonov). Not only for corroborees and rituals but also in daily life, males in Boongaree's tribe tied up their hair "on top of the head, in a high and conical coiffure."[36] Women wore neckerchiefs obtained from Europeans and a necklace of strung dried tubular reed sections.

Rossiiskii saw men with "long straight hair" and implies that this was the norm. Simonov, Bellingshausen, and others describe curly-haired Aboriginals. Shabel'skii alone calls the Aboriginals' black hair remarkably soft. All Russians agree, however, that the hair of members of the Cammeraigal group was "tousled" and smeared with vegetable substances. Whether or not it was so smeared, it hung over the forehead "in rings, à la Titus" (Simonov). The Russians specify that "gummy sap" was applied to the head. A common ornament, it seems, was kangaroo teeth. These teeth were either stuck directly on the hair, an ornamentation known locally as *Ma-na-ran,*[37] or suspended from it. Fish teeth were occasionally hung in the same way, but Russian evidence suggests that Cammeraigal members made no ornamental use of bird feathers—despite the fact that birds were seen "at every step" along the North Shore (Simonov).

As for the face, it was sometimes stained with red earth for special effects. Both women and men so stained themselves, and white colouring substance, too, was to be seen on women's breasts as well as on men's arms, legs, and torso. Nose-sticks about four inches long were worn by men on some occasions, when they wished to look their best, e.g., for portraits. Twigs and hollow bird bones were employed. Traditional scarification of the upper body was apparent still in 1820, scars being particularly numerous over the upper chest, the upper arms, and the lower shoulders. Parallel and triple lines were prevalent in men, arcs over breasts in women. Once again, Matora was exceptional.

ANGLO-ABORIGINAL RELATIONS: RUSSIAN VIEWS

Overall, the Russian evidence is of a local Aboriginal society in general decline as a direct result of contact with the colony. On all planes, that society was under pressure. "Elders" were selected by the Governors in recognition of those qualities that served the colony's own ends (adaptability, complaisance), not qualities more likely to commend themselves to Aboriginals (fighting ability, experience, good knowledge of the lore). Subsistence patterns had been altered by the Europeans' willingness to barter spirits and tobacco, even certain foods, for fish. When children might have been acquiring traditional knowledge and skills, some were at school in Parramatta, slowly learning how to read, write, draw, and sew. The Russian evidence on all these points is welcome but predictable; more valuable, certainly, is Russian evidence of the development of Anglo-Aboriginal relations, both in general and in particular, as shown by attitude.

Essentially, the Cammeraigal attitude towards the colony was opportunistic. Open opposition to the presence and activities of British subjects had already faded out by 1820. The pragmatic policy was one of friendliness. "These people," says Simonov, "are very peaceful and show no hostility towards the Europeans. . . . The English accordingly leave them in peace, and are good to them insofar as they can be." Bellingshausen likewise stresses the pragmatic conduct of the Boongaree-Matora group: "They come into the town in the morning and attempt to get what they can." Is begging implied here? It seems so, and elsewhere Bellingshausen amplifies his point, giving the phrases to be heard ("Give me a dump," etc.). However, there was also daily barter (fish for drink or tobacco; fish and birds for English playing marbles).

Things were different outside the English settlements. There, the Aboriginals had not accepted their displacement, the Russians were informed. Brusquely deprived of local edible resources that had earlier been "theirs for the taking," Aboriginals occasionally stole exotic foods; and British settlers "avenged themselves as far as they were able." Bellingshausen and his officers had evidently learned of the events along the Hawkesbury in 1815–16, and of James Wallis's attack upon the drought-racked Aboriginals led by Carnanbigal.[38] They had also, one deduces, been informed that Aboriginals had rights under the law and were impressed that Aboriginals not only could but did bring loud complaints, e.g., of "thrashings," to Macquarie. Also valuable is the Russian recognition of the Aboriginal's attachment to the land—land often lost to him. Some individuals, says Bellingshausen, would express a claim to certain areas, "saying that they belonged to their forefathers." Boongaree is plainly represented as believing that the whole North Shore, or most of it at least, belonged to him, though perhaps not in a sense that Europeans recognized. "Pointing at the whole northern shore, he said, 'This is my shore.'" Bellingshausen was a careful writer. It may therefore be supposed that it was more than sympathetic recognition of the fact that Aboriginals could not well "be indifferent to having been expelled from their own favourite areas" that led him to declare that, notwithstanding compensation from the British, "a spark of vengeance smoulders in their hearts."

Nothing is plainer from the Russian evidence than that the colonists of Sydney were contemptuous of local Aboriginals, to whose debauch they were contributing. In certain ways, they used the natives. Now and then, an Aboriginal "fetched water and hewed wood," cleaned glasses, or did other kinds of work. But in the main, use and abuse of native skills and labour were identical. Macquarie's practical official statements on the matter of relations with the Aboriginals, which were invariably tinged with eighteenth-century humanism, were ignored in Sydney town. Where race relations were concerned, official words and daily deeds were much at odds. Perhaps deliberately, Russian naval visitors to Sydney in the early 1800s turned a blind eye to the settlers' debauching of the first Australians, preferring to reflect upon Macquarie's Regulations of 4 May

1816.[39] They were his guests and were in any case accustomed to attend to regulations and official policy. While noting uses to which native skills were put by the colonial authorities, e.g., the tracking and arresting of escaped convicts, the Russians make it plain that most Aboriginal experience and knowledge of the country was of casual or incidental use to Europeans, or was utterly ignored. In March 1820, Captain Vasil'ev of the *Otkrytie* heard Hobart Town and its environs openly praised by Sydney government officials as possessing "better-behaved natives." In his view, Macquarie's long-term efforts to "attach" the local Aboriginals to Europeans and their culture had been "altogether vain."[40]

Embedded in the Russian narratives are useful data on the size of native groups in New South Wales in the early contact period. The data are in part derivative indeed, i.e., of British provenance, but partially firsthand. Taken together, they suggest a shrinking native population in the Sydney area—a gradual decline that was reflected (or refracted) in enrolments at the Shelleys' Parramatta institution for the Aboriginals' own children. In 1822, records Shabel'skii disapprovingly, there were "no more than 13 children" there. He does not specify their sex(es).

Russian visitors were told by Boongaree himself about the bones of smallpox victims in the caves of Broken Bay, and recognized that for the coastal tribes a spell of stormy weather might mean hunger, if not death: for storms prevented fishing and the normal gathering of shellfish, mussels, and the shallow-water plants that were consumed at other times. They also gathered that in many cases, death was caused or "hastened by imagination." On the other hand, the Russians learned that native women "said that their confinements were easy." Twins were rare, births were seldom complicated. Nor did battles lead perforce to high mortality among the Aboriginals involved. Sometimes, "hostilities might last more than a day" but end with combatants no more than cut and bruised. These factors would have balanced those above, resulting in a measure of numerical stability.

ARTEFACTS FROM PORT JACKSON NOW IN LENINGRAD:
GENERAL COMMENTS

The Leningrad pre-1828 collection from Port Jackson is described below, in proper form.[41] General comments will be ventured here, even so, regarding provenance and ethnographic value. The nine-item collection, it must first be said, is of significance in several respects. Its provenance is known almost precisely.[42] Russian narratives enable us to say not only when and where certain artefacts in Leningrad were gathered, but also in exchange for what and in what circumstances. Value is accordingly attributable. Third, the collection is apparently the largest one from adolescent Sydney now surviving in a single institution. Fourth, certain of the artefacts have major scientific value, being rarities. The "fizz-gig" (736–280 in the Leningrad collection) is most probably the one known specimen from Sydney in existence, i.e., is the sole surviving specimen of David Collins's *Cal-larr*.[43] Such spears were being used when the British first caught sight of New South Wales.

Textual evidence makes plain that most or all of the nine objects now in Leningrad were bought for European goods in Sydney, by the people of *Suvorov* (1814), *Mirnyi*, and *Vostok* (1820). During the 1820 visits at least, the Aboriginal barterers may be thought to have been members of the Cammeraigal tribe. In the case of *Suvorov*'s visit, they may very well have been tribesmen from the South Shore of Port Jackson, that is, Arthur Capell's "Sydney-speakers."[44] For the men who on 21 August 1814 brought Rossiiskii a regular collection of their artefacts ("I selected three spears, a shield . . . ," etc.) had that same morning been encountered on the south side of the bay; and it seemed to Rossiiskii that a couple of the men had taken part in the long "battle" of the day before. A South Shore group would have comprised a likely object for the Cammeraigal group hostility. Rossiiskii at no point mentioned Boongaree in connection with the men who brought their weapons out for barter.

On returning to St. Petersburg, the members of the Bellingshausen-Lazarev Antarctic expedition were specifically required to submit all native artefacts in their possession to the government. The matter had been dealt with in the fifteenth section of the third set of instructions sent to Bellingshausen in June 1819. "All collections of objects of every sort . . . shall, at the conclusion of the voyage, be entrusted to the Commander of the Division, who shall present them all without exception to His Majesty the Emperor through the Naval Minister."[45] It is of course quite possible that artefacts were broken or mislaid in 1820–22; and, though the Crown reserved the right to keep all artefacts, as other Crowns did not, it is apparent that at least some articles which had been purchased by the Russians in Australia for private use and pleasure were returned to them without delay. We know that Aleksei P. Lazarev was still, in 1829, in full possession of "a small collection of the birds and insects of that country" which, as we have seen, Lieutenant P. P. King had given him "for friendship's sake."[46]

Because *Suvorov* was a Company-owned vessel whose commander—on secondment from the Navy—took instructions from the Company Main Board,[47] it is not certain that her officers were similarly bound. In this connection, it is striking that Rossiiskii should unashamedly have stated that he wanted to enlarge his *own* collection of Pacific artefacts ("for my own collection of rarities"). Both in the case of the *Suvorov* expedition, however, and in that of Bellingshausen, one arrives at the conclusion that by no means all the artefacts taken from Sydney by the Russians found their way into the right, official hands. We know that artefacts were taken that were never in the Admiralty's museum in St. Petersburg. Others may possibly have been in naval keeping in 1822–28 but did not find their way in 1828 into the *Kunstkammer* of the Academy of Sciences which forms the basis of today's Peter-the-Great Museum of Ethnography.[48] Regrettably, all records of the transfer have been lost. In sum, it seems practically certain that more Aboriginal and other artefacts arrived in Russia in the early 1800s than was formally acknowledged then or later.[49] As discoveries of documents by officers who visited Australia while on Pacific expeditions in that period continue to be made from time to time,[50] so too, conceivably, will a discovery of "curiosities."

THE VOYAGE OF THE "KREISER" AND "LADOGA"
TO HOBART TOWN, 1822–23

Like *Apollon* the year before, the frigate *Kreiser* and the armed sloop *Ladoga* paused in Australia (May-June 1823) en route to Sitka on a composite supplying and strategic mission. Alexander I had been ill-advised to promulgate his edicts of September 1821,[51] attempting boldly to protect the Russian interest in northwestern America. Those edicts had asserted absolute, exclusive rights to "all commerce, whaling, and fishery, and all other industry on all islands, posts, and gulfs, including the whole northwestern coast of America. . . south to latitude 51°N."[52] Little wonder that the British government had protested promptly and in heated terms, and had been emulated by the government in Washington. ("The American government," wrote Nesselrode to Count D. A. Gur'ev on 3 June 1822, "protests against what *it* calls the expansion of our possessions.")[53] Nesselrode, at least, saw the full delicacy of the situation in America. The British and Americans, responding to their trading lobbies and to nationalistic sentiment regarding "freedom on the high seas," were annoyed by the new edicts. It could hardly serve the Russian national interest if either English-speaking government clashed with the tsar over so trifling a matter as fur or otter seals on the far side of the globe. The tsar's objective at the time was to bring "order" to the Balkans as a whole: British neutrality was wanted. On the other hand, the Company for whose specific benefit the edicts had been promulgated was in deep financial straits.[54] And edicts were not to be ignored, in any case, if the imperial authority was to remain unquestioned in the Company possessions as they stood. Measures were needed to lend weight to the imperial authority where, as so often in the past, it lacked both ships and guns. Already, in the late summer of 1822, the twenty-eight-gun sloop the *Apollon* was crossing North Pacific waters, there "to cruise as close as feasible to the dry land, though not beyond the latitude in which the Russian-American Company at present [1822] enjoys all its prerogatives."[55] Another ship or two would help to counter Yankee influence, keeping the ever more importunate American free-traders at a distance. So it was that, on 17/29 August 1822, the *Kreiser* and the *Ladoga,* commanded respectively by Mikhail and Andrei P. Lazarev, left Kronstadt bound for the Pacific settlements.

For Mikhail, the eldest and most brilliant of four Lazarev brothers, it was a third voyage around the world within eight years. As commander of *Suvorov,* he had visited Port Jackson in August 1814; as Bellingshausen's second-in-command, he had in 1820 been received and kindly treated by Macquarie. Now, in 1822, a widely travelled and experienced young captain, he was offered the command that was to seal his professional success. He picked his officers judiciously. Among his junior lieutenants were a pair of future admirals, P. S. Nakhimov and E. V. Putiatin; but the Decembrists D. I. Zavalishin and F. G. Vishnevskii also sailed with the *Kreiser.*[56] Their presence was most probably a factor in his own failure to publish an account of the whole venture in the post-Decembrist years (1826–30).[57] At his instances, particularly able surgeons were appointed to both *Ladoga* and *Kreiser. Ladoga*'s surgeon, Petr Ogievskii, was a natural-born scientist of great ability, of use to Andrei Lazarev, his captain and his longtime friend, as Kovalëv had been of use to the deliberate Vasil'ev aboard *Otkrytie,* as Chamisso had been of use to Kotzebue, and Novitskii to Tulub'ev of the *Apollon.* Surgeons appointed to Pacific expeditions in the early nineteenth century were not expected to be ignorant of botany, zoology, or even mineralogy. As for the surgeon of the *Kreiser,* Dr. Petr Aleman, he followed Mikhail Petrovich Lazarev to Nikolaev in the 1830s, and was ultimately named Chief Surgeon of the Black Sea Fleet. Like both the Lazarevs, he built a brilliant career on the basis of ability and hard Pacific service.[58]

Kreiser and *Ladoga* reached Rio de Janeiro in January 1823, after a hard Atlantic crossing. Unknown flags flew at the harbour mouth. Equal to all occasions, M. P. Lazarev sent an immediate despatch to Admiral A. Moller in St. Petersburg explaining how Dom Pedro had been crowned Emperor of Brazil and enclosing handsome sketches of the new Brazilian flag.[59] Not even well-tried ships and officers, however, guaranteed an easy passage from Brazil to the Pacific. Early setbacks led to subsequent delays, and minor troubles were compounded in the South. As a result, thoughts of a speedy westward passage round Cape Horn were set aside. Not till 2 March 1823 was either *Ladoga* or *Kreiser* fit to sail for Australia. They left Brazil on 7 March with some relief.[60] It proved a slow and stormy voyage, but at last, on 17/29 May, Van Diemen's Land was sighted through the rain and heavy mist. The Lazarevs tacked boldly up the D'Entrecasteaux Channel. Four days later, M. P. Lazarev reported to St. Petersburg from Hobart Town as follows:

Your Honours,

I have the honour to report to you the safe arrival of HIM's frigate *Kreiser* and sloop *Ladoga* in the port of Derwent, which is in Van Diemen's Land, on 17/29 May. At dawn on 17 May the southern cape of Van Diemen's Land was, by our calculations, 31 miles distant, at 34°N. . . . In the gloom, we caught sight of a small, high islet which I had seen during my previous visit to these parts and immediately recognized as Mewstone. . . . The wind grew constantly fresher and a drop of the mercury in the barometer presaged stormy weather, which decided me to enter D'Entrecasteaux Channel and find safe anchorage before nightfall. At 4 p.m., we dropped anchor in one of the bays, fully protected from all winds. . . . All that night and all the next day, the wind blew southerly, very strong with sharp squalls. This notwithstanding, however, I resolved to continue up the Channel, which is safe. So, at 9 a.m., we weighed anchors and by 4 p.m. were moored in the harbour of Derwent opposite Hobart Town. . . . Certain adjustments to the rigging and caulking of the wales should, in my view, detain us no more than two weeks, after which, leaving the port of Derwent, it is my intention to visit Tahiti.[61]

Collating Lazarev's despatch with Andrei Lazarev's published account of the sloop *Ladoga*'s Pacific expedition, which appeared in St. Petersburg in 1821 and had a twenty-four-page "Hobart section,"[62] it is clear that the two ships passed the harsh night of 17 May near the Huon River's mouth, then, pressing north by Bruny Island, made a stop in Hobart Town's Sullivan Cove. So, after eighty-seven days at sea from Rio de Janeiro, the Lazarevs entered the River Derwent. Their arrival was noted in *Bent's Almanac* for 1824, "printed by Andrew Brent, Esq., Government Printer," in the following terse form: "Name: Kreuzer & Ladoga; Commanders: Lazaroff; Arrived: May 30 1823; Whence: Russia; Cargo: Discovery; Departure: June 21 1823; Where Bound: On discovery."

THE LAZAREVS IN HOBART TOWN: OFFICIAL BUSINESS

Not twenty years had passed, when the *Ladoga* and *Kreiser* reached Hobart Town, since David Collins had established his small outpost at Port Phillip. One of the men who had accompanied Collins, the Reverend Robert Knopwood (1763–1838), late of Threxton Hall in Norfolk, was presented to the Russian officers.[62] The colony, in short, was in its infancy. Nevertheless, Colonel William Sorell was its third Lieutenant-Governor and its European population had grown as rapidly, since 1812 and the arrival of the first shipload of convicts out from England in the *Indefatigable*, as the native population had declined. Sorell had proved a competent and fair administrator, and the settlers' lot had visibly improved since his appointment in April 1817. No longer were their cabins and their crops burned by marauding bushrangers, escaped convicts at war with all authority.[63] It was Sorell who had, in 1818, hanged the self-styled "Lord of the Woods," Michael Howe. Troubles persisted intermittently on a small scale, but in the main tranquillity prevailed after that date. Sorell proceeded with the major task of setting up administrative systems for his colony. More colonists arrived, including recently retired naval officers and merchantmen, whom Andrei Lazarev and other Russians met. (It seemed extraordinary to Russians that an Englishman could, as in fact a couple had, simply *set sail* for Van Diemen's Land from England with a better life in view.)[64] By 1821, the island census gave a white population of 7,185, owning 35,000 head of cattle and 170,000 sheep.[65] "To his task of restoring order and encouraging progress in settled social conditions, Sorell allied an unshakeable firmness with skill, tact, and patience. Contemporaries record his 'personal charm' and 'friendly manner,' which made official relations easy between governor and governed."[66]

Sorell was busy when the Russians came. Inland, a band of runaways was causing waves of nervousness; in Hobart Town itself, a barrack and the harbourmaster's house needed repairs. Still, he was genuinely glad to greet his visitors, who had the charm of novelty, brought European news, and posed no problem in themselves. There was nothing forced or cold about the way he did his duty to the Lazarevs ("I shall not fail to show them all the attention and hospitality in my power," etc.).[67] Having formally received the Russian officers and given full assurances that water, wood, provisions, and assistance would be theirs, nonetheless, he was relieved to hear that little would be needed by the squadron. Here is M. P. Lazarev again, in a despatch from San Francisco dated 10 December 1823:

Colonel Sorell, the Governor, received us with great courtesy and expressed his willingness to aid us with whatever we might need, even placing his little dockyard at our disposal. . . . But since we needed nothing, being properly and adequately supplied in all departments, I found myself obliged, to his slight vexation, continually to decline his civil proposals which, it seemed to me, were made purely out of respect for the Russian flag, now flying in these parts for the first time.

The River Derwent, with the adjoining D'Entrecasteaux Bay, is without doubt one of the most spacious and beautiful harbours in the world. Wood may be had most conveniently, and one can water in various places in the bay. It is difficult to water at Hobart Town itself, because of the little distance separating it from the spot where rowing vessels lie. These difficulties however will be overcome from next year on, by means of the iron pipes which the Governor has ordered from England and by which the water will be brought to the very quay. The climate is extremely healthy, and generally the weather is fine. Nowhere do I recall our crews having so improved in health and strength as during the three weeks of their stay at Port Derwent, and that despite their working every day, and hard too.[68]

Kreiser and *Ladoga* moved up the Derwent to the Risdon area. Sorell and other leading figures of the infant colony, notably Dr. Bromley, did their duty on the entertainment front. It was at Bromley's house that the Russians met the Reverend Robert Knopwood, a habitual and eager diner-out.[69] Knopwood's own diary provides a glimpse of the two Lazarevs at supper with the Bromleys, Captain Robinson, and Mr. White on 3 June.[70] Six days afterwards, it was the Daws who threw a little dinner party. Mr. Daw enjoyed the Russian seamen's company—or else he was compulsively hospitable, for on the Thursday of the same week he again gave a small party, which the Lazarevs and Knopwood all attended dutifully. Nor was even this the full extent of Knopwood's socializing with the Russian visitors: *between* the Monday and Thursday trips, he dined with Mr. Loans, Messrs. Frazer, Scott, and Keeling, and "met the Surgeon of the Russian Ship," presumably Ogievskii. And on 10 June, according to the ever-watchful *Hobart Town Gazette,* Sorell returned the Lazarevs' first visit, spending time aboard "the Russian frigate *Creuzer.*"[71] Andrei Lazarev records that, for the grandest ball of all in Russian honour, Hobart residents borrowed a Russian flag and tied it to the ceiling of the room in which the king and tsar were toasted.[72] Toasts ensued to Governor Sir Thomas Brisbane and Sorell, both absent from the feast, and to a host of other dignitaries from the Dukes of York and

Clarence to "Count Waitkenstein," "Admiral Muller," and "The Clergy." Not a little wine was drunk, while *Kreiser*'s band and local trumpeters performed.[73] It was the classic Australasian dinner-dance: trivial, noisy, smug, and long.

Sorell being away from Hobart Town, Lieutenant A. F. Kemp maintained liaison with the Russians while they wooded and refitted on the Derwent. All passed off extremely well. The squadron weighed, to heavy gunfire and cheering, on 21 June. For all the compliments that either of the Lazarevs might pay it then or later, Hobart Town had proved a major disappointment to at least some younger men, who had been hoping for a respite from the rain if not for genuine local excitement. "It's an almost *empty* place," shuddered Nakhimov, "and besides that, we were there in winter-time!"[74] Such disappointments put no shadow on the spectacle of Anglo-Russian harmony, which, by agreement, was maintained by hosts and visitors from first to last.

SURGEON OGIEVSKII'S REPORT

So much for the official aspect of the Russian visit. Let us turn to other aspects, beginning with scientific ones. At Andrei Lazarev's request, *Ladoga*'s surgeon, Petr Ogievskii, spent a week or more preparing a report on the resources, climate, flora, fauna, population, and potential of Van Diemen's Land. Predictably, the surgeon largely focused on the area of Hobart Town itself whence, it would seem, he hiked southwest toward Mount Wellington and Collins' Cap and so, traversing modern-day Neika, towards the area of modern Huonville. Nevertheless, it was a useful piece of work and fully merited inclusion in his captain's 1832 *Voyage Around the World....* [75] Here, first, are extracts from the first section, on flora of the Hobart Town locality:

There are three dominant kinds of tree.... One has narrow leaves and gives dense shade; its fruits resemble the kernels of fir-cones. It belongs to the *Thesium* group. The second tree is far taller and even shadier, the leaves being like a juniper's, the bark thick, and the branches no lower than 10 feet above the roots. Internally, it is blood-coloured, and for that reason it is here called the beefwood. The third tree belongs to the myrtle family and grows on hills, but never attains the height that trees of that sort can reach at the feet of mountains... the bark is white and quite thick, sometimes peeling off by itself and so baring the trunk that it looks stripped. The leaves are long, narrow, and sharp-ended, and have a sharply pleasant aroma something like mint, for which reason the local residents call it peppermint. On the same high hill, known as the Table, also grows the tallest of all trees here, known as American oak. . . . But it is useless for shipbuilding because of its extreme heaviness. I could not determine this, for lack of scales, but it can be stated that a piece of its timber sinks in water like limestone. . . .

In the shade of the aforementioned trees, there also grows in large quantity, the new *Eucalyptus globosus;* and on the hillsides, one sees *Embothrium* and, in lower spots, *Leucospermum.* This is known in Europe as a bush but here stands equal with quite tall trees. There is also *Eucalyptus resinifera,* which gives the very finest reddish resin; and many *Philadelphis,* and *Epacris* of a new sort, and *Banksia integrifolia uksibbosa, Exocarpus, Aster, Oasearia, Ptelea, Richea, Glauca, Polypodium,* the parsley known as *Apium prostratum,* and various sorts of *Ancistrum,* whose fruits are used by the natives as food. . . . The woods simply abound with various sorts of orchid, reeds, fennel, wild sorrel, sword-grass, campanula, tears of Jove, ferns, and specialized mosses.[76]

It is for regional historians and botanists to use such evidence. What is apparent at a glance is that in 1823 the Hobart area was rich in eucalypts. Ogievskii appears to have noted *Eucalyptus obliqua* (stringy-bark) and *E. linearis* (white peppermint), as well as *E. globulus,* or Tasmanian blue gum, and *E. resinifera,* or red gum trees. Alas, the Hobart suburbs of today are hardly as rich in wild flowers as they were in Colonel Sorell's day.

Ogievskii made enquiries as to the trees of the interior. He was informed that Aboriginal Tasmanians asserted that inland other varieties of timber could be found, including "a superior pine" about the River Tomara, that is, Tamar; but that bushes were not plentiful in the interior or elsewhere on the island. On the other hand, he could admire for himself the large and motley kitchen gardens of the European colonists, and apple trees that fruited twice a year. Like the *Vostok* and *Mirnyi* three years earlier, the *Kreiser* left Australia with seeds for the imperial botanical collection in St. Petersburg.

During his walks across the wooded hills southwest of Hobart Town, Ogievskii crossed several "wide valleys" and admired newly founded settlements. Among the animals that he described were kangaroo, whose meat, he noted, was eaten by colonists and native tribes alike, and the opossum (very plentiful). In the interior, he was informed, were many emus and a beautiful black cockatoo. Even in Hobart Town, there was a multitude of birds of all varieties. Among the birds collected by the Russians and presumably delivered to St. Petersburg were three pairs of fine black swans and whitish hawks. The little hawks were stowed alive.[77]

Although so rich in flora and in fauna, the island was reportedly quite poor in minerals. A little lead, iron, and copper had been found, but not a single vein of gold. It was asserted that asbestos had been spotted in the north. In this respect, as in so many others, Van Diemen's Land was to surprise the British colonists, and soon. Ogievskii's report came on the eve of major mineral discoveries.[78]

THE ABORIGINAL TASMANIANS

The Russians had no meetings with indigenous Tasmanians. Ogievskii, Lieutenant Matvei Berens, and others from the *Ladoga* did make enquiries about them, though; and on the basis of the information offered by the Governor and other Englishmen of standing, Andrei Lazarev could offer Russian readers these remarks, at least:

The number of the natives is quite unknown, for they have no intercourse with other peoples, even declining the friendliest of connections. Moving off into the island's interior, they there lead so wild a life that it is a rare settler who manages to see them from afar. As a result, we are still indebted to Captain Cook's last voyage (1777) alone for such data as we have on their way of life and character. This extreme alienation of the natives is ascribed to the rash imprudence of the colony's founder, Captain Bowen, who, encountering a band of islanders, fired on them out of precaution for himself—and so drove them from the seashores. In order to dispose them to a peaceable intercourse, so I heard, some small children were seized and raised in London schools and respectable houses, then taken back to their native land and given complete freedom. It was hoped that, by means of education and gentle treatment, the natives could little by little be familiarized with kindness. However, all measures proved vain, and at the first opportunity the native children in question cast off their clothing and shoes and reverted to their original state. . . .

The most recent natural historians to have visited the island's interior describe its natives thus: men and women alike cover themselves with kangaroo skins. Their hair is like wool. The men let their beard grow long. Their body is not particularly black, but they sometimes powder it with coal. In native children, the upper jaw is appreciably longer than the lower, but this passes on the attainment of maturity. In general, these people are of ordinary height. They nourish themselves on mussels, oysters, large crabs and sea-spiders, which they cook on a fire: the preparation of food devolves on the women. They tolerate no authority over them, each household living in perfect independence from all others. Children are very obedient to their parents, and women to men. The occupations of these people are connected with hunting; of fishing they know nothing and they are even ignorant of the manufacture of craft. To cross over large rivers and lakes, they merely bind trees together with bast. Their weaponry consists of rush spears with hardwood points. On flinging a spear, they simply grasp it at the centre and aim at the prey.[79]

It is hard to reconcile what the visitors were obviously told by men like Kemp, who were themselves parties to conscious and deliberate extermination of the Tasmanians,[80] and what was actually happening in 1823–24. As recent state-supported guidebooks to Tasmania have properly acknowledged, "history can never begin to condone the savagery which was applied to the extermination of the aborigines. There were perhaps 6,000 of them when the first white settlers arrived. By 1876 the race was extinct."[81] But would the Lazarevs have been reciprocating courtesy if they had looked into reports of the abuse of "gins" and "lubras" (native women) by the settlers or, more especially, the bushrangers with whom Sorell was still at war?[82] To glance at Bonwick's classic study *The Lost Tasmanian Race* (1884) is to appreciate how little foreign visitors were told—or wished to know. Such little cameos as Lazarev's say more about his "civilized" informants than about the sad "Black War" or the Tasmanians themselves.

THE INFANT HOBART TOWN

All but a few vessels calling at Hobart Town during its infancy came from one of only three points: Sydney, London, or Mauritius. Russian ships offered the charm of novelty and caused a stir, which the behaviour of the "Muscovites" itself intensified within a day. Not only were two hundred seamen free to wander through the settlement in ordered groups, but "various games and songs, and other entertainments, drove away the melancholy that accompanies the long sea-voyage." Local residents looked on with rising interest. Sorell having proposed suitable wooding sites, some forty versts (twenty-six miles) up the Derwent, and a place to check chronometers, most of these seamen had removed themselves from Hobart by 1 June or earlier. Several officers, however, stayed behind and for the next three weeks found ample opportunity to make a study of the place and its environs. What they observed was, in accordance with instructions, all reported to their captains—who, of course, were keeping journals of their own. Here is Andrei Lazarev on Hobart Town's food-yielding fringe:

> Everywhere in the environs one sees a pleasant variety of hills, whose wooded tops were covered in snow during our stay. . . . The soil is rich and amply repays the labour of the tiller, every acre yielding up to 25 bushels of good-quality wheat or from 40 to 50 bushels of oats. The proprietors do not trouble with haymaking here, as their domestic cattle can graze on fresh and desirable meadowgrass all year round. An average bull weighs in at about 20 *poods* [720 lbs], and an average sheep at 2 1/2 *poods* [90 lbs]. We ourselves paid 7d for a pound of meat, one Spanish Thaler equalling 5/-. For a ton of potatoes, we gave 28 Thalers. Even though there was rather little greenstuffs here, the Governor provided us with a sufficiency of them.[83]

But, of course, the Russian officers were mostly in the town and in their journals mostly focus on the town, its churches, houses, barracks, social life, and residents. They were impressed by universal signs of "English neatness" in the wilderness:

> This "capital" consisted in 1811 merely of a few shacks and cabins, scattered anywhere. Now, it boasts properly laid out streets and numerous respectable stone houses of handsome design, quite like English ones. Among them, there are several two-storeyed structures. One also sees a church, the Governor's Residence with its extensive garden, barracks, a hospital, and a prison surrounded by a stone wall where up to 200 convicts are kept. Together with these, the storehouses and a few water-mills form a quite extensive and attractive town.[84]

From local (Hobart) sources, it is evident that Mikhail and Andrei Lazarev's activities were centred upon Franklin Square, the core of Governor Macquarie's civic plan of 1811, and on the streets adjoining it. We know that on 21 June, the "bunyip baronets" and local gentry, led by Anthony Fenn Kemp, who had in 1808 stood against Bligh in Sydney's infamous "Rum Mutiny" and who was soon to topple Sorell from his post in Hobart Town, hired rooms facing Macquarie Street in the possession of the traders Messrs. Macleod, Champion, and Company.[85] There, the Russians were regaled till four o'clock the next morning. Other buildings that the Russians saw survive: Anglesea Barracks, for example, at least two sandstone structures off Elizabeth and Collins Streets, and the important little church of which a shell still stands today within the grounds of Old St. Andrew's, now the Scots Church. As for the "storehouses" or "magazines" mentioned by Lazarev, they or the buildings that replaced them in the thirties are the warehouses on Salamanca Place.[86]

As military visitors, the Russians were escorted through a number of the new government buildings in the town. More unexpectedly, they had encounters with a number of non-English-speaking convicts in the course of these relaxed official tours. In itself, the fact bears witness to the commonsensical humanity that was the hallmark of W. Sorell's, but not his successor Arthur's, reign. Here is A.P. Lazarev:

> In Hobart, we saw four men who knew Russian, including an elderly White Russian. If we were to credit his words, he had been an officer in our army in the time of the Empress Catherine II, carried off to England by the whims of fickle destiny, and thence, in the year 1804, sent off to Van Diemen's Land together with the convicts. Since 1810 he had enjoyed his freedom, and had a house, wife, and grown children in the town, all of which would not seem to indicate entirely reprehensible conduct. However, the Governor and his officials gave very bad reports of the man, and so we had no confidence in him ourselves. He had only lately, it seemed, been convicted for sheepstealing and put in jail. . . . Before leaving, we sent to this White Russian a copy of the New Testament in Russian. Another copy, in French, we presented to a Frenchman who was still wearing the yellow uniform that prisoners wear in England.[87]

Conditions in the Hobart jail did not seem harsh to Andrei Lazarev. As had the officers of the *Vostok* in Sydney three years earlier, he even marvelled that colonial authority should, at the end of most convicts' terms, offer them plots of land and full citizen's rights, "nor even tax them." It was not the Russian way.

In sum, the visitors were generously treated by the Governor, officials, army officers, and leading Hobart residents. If a distinction can be made between the entertainment offered in Van Diemen's Land in 1823 and that provided by Macquarie three years earlier, it lies precisely in the larger and more energetic part played by civilians, many of whom were not officials of Sorell's administration. But, of course, life was decidedly less comfortable and easy in the bush beside the River Derwent, where Russians were encamped—and working hard—for two full weeks.

Among the midshipmen obliged to spend much time with wooding parties and repair squads, away from social gaieties, was Zavalishin, the incipient Decembrist.

MIDSHIPMAN ZAVALISHIN AND THE MISSING "POLISH" SEAMAN

Dmitrii Irinarkhovich Zavalishin (1804–92), last surviving and perhaps most deeply paranoid of the Decembrist insurrectionaries of 1825–26, was barely eighteen years of age when he was posted to the *Kreiser*.[88] In later years, his own lack of importance in the work of the Decembrist Northern and Southern Societies in 1825 and his inability to influence his fellow exiles in Siberia strengthened a self-aggrandizing and profoundly self-important streak in him. Because his writings that relate to the Pacific mostly date from after 1825, they must be treated gingerly: for Zavalishin always strove to show himself in handsome colours—understanding, indispensable to comrades and superiors, and wise. This must be borne in mind when reading those accounts of *Kreiser*'s visit to the Derwent and to other distant parts, written in exile and of which the following gives an idea:

In Australia, we put in at Van Diemen's Land, where Russian ships had never been before, and stayed by Hobart Town. I shall refrain from giving descriptions of a natural scene unusual for a European... and of the English colonial administration in Australia—a country that then fulfilled for them the function that Siberia has for Russia. However, I must recount one incident which affected me closely and which revealed all my moral significance in the expedition and my influence on the crews.

In every port, a place was generally put aside where we could construct temporary workshops, so as not to block up or dirty the frigate with heavy work of various kinds. Naturally, in those places where firewood and coal could not be purchased we had to furnish them ourselves; and such special areas could not always be right by the anchor hold. . . . In Van Diemen's Land, the suitable spot was not less than 40 versts from the frigate, up the River Derwent. A permanent detachment of 50 men, with two officers, Putiatin and Domashenko, was appointed and sent there. I would go there once every four days or so, to see how work was progressing and to bring up necessary provisions.

But once, at 3 a.m. in the middle of the night, I was woken up and asked to present myself to Lazarev as soon as possible. I arrived to find him half-dressed and striding about his room in high agitation. Some paper or other was lying on the table. He referred me to it, silently. I took it and saw that it was a communication from the Governor of Van Diemen's Land to the effect that our detachment had revolted and that, should they join up with escaped English convicts, the colony could find itself in great danger. He had no more than 60 troops with which to defend it, and so asked the Captain to take the most urgent steps to end the revolt. . . . Lazarev launched into a panegyric of me, speaking of my great energy, presence of mind, good sense and so forth, and concluded by telling me that he trusted me alone to put the affair to rights.[89]

One's suspicions that Zavalishin was, to put it bluntly, lying, are considerable. One suspects that, many years having passed since the events occurred, he was remoulding them and placing facts into acceptable designs of his own making. Such suspicions grow the stronger upon reading the conclusion of the incident of the "revolt." To summarize the miniature drama: the brave, resourceful, steady Zavalishin leads his men upriver in a gig. Aboard the *Kreiser,* the captain trembles in his cabin. Zavalishin finds that for the past two days no work has been performed ashore. Four men are hiding in the bushes near the rest, whom the intrepid youth upbraids. His moral influence being so great, he soon makes the majority repent of all their folly, and the four creep out, disgraced. There was a fifth, Seaman Stankevich, but he has fled "with three Englishmen." The "rebels" are brought back to the frigate. Lazarev is overcome with gratitude, yet much embarrassed since, for fear of forfeiting rewards that have been promised on the safe return to Kronstadt of his company, he cannot mention Zavalishin's latest "feat" in his despatch. But Zavalishin understands and soothes the wretched captain; his only wish is to do his duty, and so forth.

The difficulty is apparent. Because Lazarev could not, for obvious reasons, mention riots in reports to A. V. Moller at the Naval Staff, we cannot positively know that Zavalishin's story was fictitious. This is also true of the "revolt" which, Zavalishin claimed, broke out at Sitka when the *Kreiser* arrived. What, then, is to be made of the alleged "revolt"? Three things are clear: first, Zavalishin rarely missed an opportunity to show himself as a superior individual. His exploits must be treated with reserve. Secondly, although Zavalishin often fabricated his tales, improving upon fact (a tendency that deeply irritated such Decembrists as Baron Andrei E. Rozen, Pavel N. Svistunov, and A. Frolov in the 1870s),[90] he generally based his tales upon known, recorded incidents. Therefore, one may suppose that the detachment sent upriver from Hobart Town on or about 1 June was indeed restive and disinclined to work after a while, which is plainly the extent of Zavalishin's claim that it "rebelled." Thirdly, there was in fact sporadic and increasing trouble in the colony during the southern winter and ensuing spring of 1823—although it was nothing compared to what was soon to come in the persons of Mosquito and Black Jack.[91]

Zavalishin's accounts of his achievements while a midshipman in *Kreiser* are hardly to be taken at face value. As Anatole Mazour justly observed, he was "conceited to the point of obsession."[92] Yet the fact remains that bushrangers were certainly about as Russian seamen felled their trees. "Some starved to death in the wild country, some turned cannibal, and some were captured. Many others survived. . . to threaten the colony's existence."[93] Minor wars raged by the early part of 1824, replete with rapes, emasculations, and peculiar atrocities by runaways, Tasmanians, and settlers alike.[94] Hardly surprisingly, Sorell's reports do not contain allusions to rebellions by Russian crews, the possibility of contact between mutineers and convicts, or anything half as dramatic. If a danger had existed and had been removed, why should he dwell on it to London? Very possibly the Governor did hear of trouble in the Russian shore encampment. That a member of the *Kreiser*'s crew, Stankevich, met "three Englishmen" and slipped into the bush under the circumstances drawn by Zavalishin is exceedingly improbable. We know because on 24 July 1823, Lazarev sent a despatch to his superior in which the incident involving Stankevich was touched upon, as follows:

> I think it my duty to report that several days before we weighed anchors and left the port of Derwent, Leading Seaman Stanislav Stankevich went missing. He was of Polish antecedents and was in a party sent to chop wood each day. Finally, when the frigate was ready to sail, he hid in the bush and refused to present himself with the other men. The Governor was promptly informed of this incident and, while taking the strictest measures to search the man out (which proved unsuccessful), expressed the view that the seaman, lost in the bush, had perished—perhaps of starvation. . . . In the eventuality of the man being discovered after our departure, the Governor proposed to send him to Port Jackson as the place most often visited by Russian warships, where he would be held until the arrival of the first such ship.[95]

Stankevich, or Stankiewicz, was never found.

PREPARATIONS FOR DEPARTURE FROM VAN DIEMEN'S LAND

The Russian officers and seamen remained busy for as long as they remained at Hobart Town. Material was gathered, for example, on colonial administration, on the island's "Buckingham and Cornwall Districts," on the purchasing of property and land.[96] And day by day the ships' logs were maintained and filled with regulation data on the atmospheric pressure, wind, needle-variation, time of sunset, height of tides, and greatest temperature levels in air and water.[97] These materials were published in St. Petersburg in 1882.[98] *Kreiser*'s log, which had been held in the Imperial (more latterly the Central State) Naval Archive since the middle 1820s, caught the notice of a Soviet historical geographer, Vasilii M. Pasetskii, in 1975. Two years later, in a little book on the Decembrists as geographers, Dr. Pasetskii drew attention to the competent meteorology performed by Lieutenant Fedor Gavrilovich Vishnevskii at Hobart Town during the visit of the *Ladoga* and *Kreiser*:

The expedition had been furnished with works of geography including the *Voyages* of I. F. Kruzenshtern, G. A. Sarychev, Iu. F. Lisianskii, and J. Cook. And besides this, each ship had been issued with two proof impressions of the charts for the *Atlas of the South Sea* then being prepared for press. The object was to check the charts' accuracy during the voyage and to collect data "necessary for their emendation, that so this *Atlas* may appear in reliable form." Fedor Vishnevskii's own geographical works did not come down to us. . . [but] we know that he kept watch on *Kreiser* six hours in every 24, measured the air temperature and pressure and, besides, made geomagnetic and astronomical observations. These were noted down in the ship's journals and continue to serve science to this day.[99]

To Surgeon Ogievskii's herbarium and seed collection were added, on the last days of the visit, a menagerie of local animals, including swine, fowl, and ducks (for galley use), black swans, small cockatoos, and even tortoises and monkeys.

Had Kemp arranged the playing of the air "There's Nae Luck About the House" when, at the dinner for the Russians on 16 June, Sorell's health had been drunk in his absence? If he had, it was appropriate. Within a year, Kemp had succeeded in enlisting the assistance of Lord Bathurst and the old Bishop of London in ousting Governor Sorell (only to see his own fair prospects in the colony obscured by the coming of the rigid Colonel Arthur).[100] All in all, indeed, the notabilities present at dinner on 16 June did not fare well in the future. Sorell never again found full employment with the British government. Reverend Knopwood was retired in August 1823 on a meagre pension of £100 per annum, and knew penury. And Dr. Edward Bromley was arraigned for the embezzlement of £7,096 of colony funds. He is remembered in Tasmania today "chiefly for a spectacular misappropriation of funds... the evidence at the enquiry revealing a well-nigh incredible laxness and inefficiency."[101] The Lazarevs, Putiatin, and Nakhimov, on the other hand, ended their lives in glory. And by 1843, when M. P. Lazarev, hero of Navarino, was made Admiral, Russian America no longer needed to be visited, provisioned, and protected from the far side of the globe. Commercially declining, it was entering the lengthy final phase that was a prelude to the sale of Alaska to the United States on 18 April 1867. There was no longer any cause for Russian warships to revictual at Hobart or at any other place in Australasia.[102]

Minus Stankevich but replete with fresh supplies and noisy animals, the squadron sailed from the Derwent on 21 June. Crossing Storm Bay and entering the D'Entrecasteaux Channel, it encountered sudden squalls and was severely buffeted within a day of its departure. On the *Ladoga*, a gig was smashed and gun-ports and the stern-shutters were damaged: not the happiest of starts for the long passage north to Sitka.[103] But the Lazarevs pressed on towards the settlements where, alas, they met a cool, restrained reception.[104] For an 1820 ban on trade with foreigners, e.g., New Englanders, had by the early part of 1823 reduced those settlements to desperation. New arrivals placed a new, unwanted burden on the local food supply. For Navy Captain Matvei Murav'ev, the local governor, there was no choice but to request that they be gone: they were a hindrance, not a help, as he attempted to hold Russian North America together in the face of isolation, cold, and want.[105] Such was the sorry culmination of the Navy's hollow victory over the Company in 1821, and of a naval thrust to represent the Crown in the Pacific that removed men of merchant antecedents from positions of control.

7

THE RUSSIAN VISITORS OF 1825–35

The voyages of supply from Kronstadt during the first half of the 1820s were disastrous. In 1821 the *Elizaveta*, which had cost 30,000 roubles to buy and 70,000 roubles to outfit, got no further than the Cape of Good Hope because of disrepair. . . . Owing to the resultant depletion of capital, the Company decided against sending a ship in 1822 . . . but virtually empty Company ships continued to sail from New Archangel to Okhotsk. . . . Although it was clear by the beginning of 1823 that the continuation of the new system of supply would quickly lead the Company to ruin, it was decided to dispatch a ship from Kronstadt in 1823 with 361 tons of State (non-Company) rye for Okhotsk and Petropavlovsk.[1]

The auguries were bad for the selected ship, *Elena*, from the start. While she was readying at Kronstadt, the American and British governments continued to protest against imperial pretensions by the tsar along the Northwest Coast. Pressure was mounting on the North Pacific settlements themselves: Governor Murav'ev had painted an unpleasant picture of distress in two despatches that had reached the capital via Irkutsk. From Petropavlovsk and Okhotsk to Iakutat and Sitka, hunter-traders were in need of all the foodstuffs which "Bostonians" had formerly provided.[2] The *Elizaveta*'s failure to alleviate that pressure meant that grain should have been forwarded by sea two years before. Now, it was needed in considerable quantity despite the major risk of spoilage on the way. Already, servants of the Company were eating carrion, as they had done before in other times of crisis and neglect.[3]

At least the detailed mechanics of the manning, preparation, and despatching of a ship to the Pacific had been mastered long before, and there were many able officers and seamen in the Baltic Fleet who could be sent. The situation had been different in 1812, when naval officers had been required by the Company for what became *Suvorov*'s mission;[4] nor, as recently as 1817, had men of promise been on hand for Golovnin and the *Kamchatka* as they were for the *Elena* and her captain, Pavel E. Chistiakov. By 1823, it was apparent to the Baltic Fleet at large that the elite Pacific branch of naval service could accelerate an officer's promotion wonderfully. Few of the officers whom Sydney had already seen had not returned to Kronstadt roads with much-enhanced career prospects.

Captain-Lieutenant Chistiakov, the future Governor of Russian North America, had sailed to the North Pacific settlements before, as second lieutenant of the Company ship *Borodino* under Captain-Lieutenant Ponafidin. He had left the Northwest Coast only in February 1821.[5] Having experienced a fever-haunted voyage through the tropics, he appreciated similar experience of circumnavigation in his junior lieutenants and, accordingly, invited Nikolai D. Shishmarev, late of *Blagonamerennyi*, to join him. Zakhar Balk was named *Elena*'s first lieutenant. Others, too, joined the *Elena* who were veterans of other voyages to the Pacific: for example, Navigator Dmitrii Iakovlev, late of *Kutuzov* (under Captain Pavel A. Dokhturov) on her 1821 voyage to the Northwest Coast.[6] Though not a graduate of the imperial *kadetskii korpus* that produced the bulk of Russian naval officers, Iakovlev at length made captain's rank. And there were other men of genuine distinction in *Elena*, soon to visit New South Wales and remain no less than seven weeks: Lieutenant Aleksandr A. Stadol'skii, for example, and Surgeon Ivan Sakharov.[7] Proficient officers, however, proved no antidote to hesitation and confusion at the Company Main Office. Months went by before *Elena* could be laden with her rye; and when at last she did make sail, on 12 August 1824, it was with several half-empty holds! As for the holds that *had* been filled, they had been crammed so that the likelihood of spoilage was increased by human hand. Because a loan had been required to finance the expedition, total costs were to amount to half a million silver roubles. In itself, this was a signal that the age of frequent visits to Australia by Russian ships was ending.[8]

Chistiakov was unavoidably delayed at Portsmouth, England, and at Rio de Janeiro, whence he departed for Australia, exhausted, on 17 January 1825. Nor even then did things go easily. But following *Diana*'s route of 1808 and crossing the meridian of Cape Town in latitude 43°S,[9] *Elena* came in sight of Mewstone Rock and South East Cape, Van Diemen's Land, on 25 March. Port Jackson was eventually reached nine days there-

after, Neutral Cove on Saturday, 4 April 1825. Salutes were fired.
Chistiakov called on the Governor, Sir Thomas Brisbane, and was civilly
received. Prominent citizens and government officials offered kindly hospitality: it was a pattern long established in the town where Russian vessels were concerned.[10] Again, the news from "the Brazils" and Northern
Europe soon appeared in the colony's *Gazette*. (All was controlled and
calm at Rio de Janeiro; Elizabeth Macquarie was reported to have died.
The latter claim was soon refuted.) Necessarily, the visitors responded to
the hospitality that they received. It was (predictably) a "splendid Ball
and Supper" that they gave, which was (predictably) attended by "the
Rank and Fashion of Australia."[11] Only the scientific element, traditional
in Russian naval visits to the colony, was less pronounced than usual.
For, able seamen though they were, Shishmarev and Balk had no pretensions to distinction as savants in Chamisso's or Bellingshausen's manner.
The *Elena* was at Sydney first and foremost to revictual, refit, and give
her company a rest before the long Pacific crossing. Not intending to arrive in Sitka Sound until the height of northern summer, Chistiakov enjoyed the climate and facilities of Sydney and was left in peace to do so.
Russians' presence in the colony was calmly viewed, the few allusions to
Elena in the *Sydney Gazette* having to do with social life, not naval
strategy.[12]

Elena sailed from Sydney on 24 May, after a stay of nearly fifty days.
Checking chronometers at Norfolk Island, Chistiakov crossed the Equator
on 23 June (long. 171°40′E), reaching Novo-Arkhangel'sk in mid-July.[13]
Because her voyage proved so free of incident, because no islands were
discovered, and because her captain, Chistiakov, remained at Sitka as the
Governor of Russian North America,[14] his predecessor Murav'ev return-
ing in her to the Baltic, no account of it was published in St. Petersburg.
The post-Decembrist capital of Nicholas I was ill-disposed, in any case,
to fresh reports of naval enterprise in the Pacific; and indeed to think of
Torson, Zavalishin, M. K. Kiukhel-beker of the *Apollon,* V. P.
Romanov of *Otkrytie,* and K. F. Ryleev, poet-insurrectionary in the
Company's employ, is to be conscious of a Company-Decembrist-Navy
nexus.[15] Understandably, the presence of these antiautocratic "ne'er-do-
wells" and "vagabonds" in Russian vessels in the North and South Pacific in the last years of the reign of Alexander prejudiced his younger
brother and successor, Nicholas I, against the naval enterprise in the Pacific and against the Company at large.[16] It had not escaped imperial attention that that enterprise was, *sui generis,* a nursery of Liberals, and that
the influence on younger naval officers of visits to Great Britain and her
colonies had, from the autocratic standpoint, been disastrous.[17]

THE DAWN OF AUSTRALASIAN RUSSOPHOBIA:
"ELENA" AND "KROTKII" IN PORT JACKSON

Russophobic sentiments had been expressed in Sydney now and then throughout the 1820s. Army officers especially had certain reservations about Russia's growing military strength, as well as chauvinistic scorn for Russian "backwardness." But these were isolated voices until 1829 when, in response both to swelling anti-Russian feelings in Great Britain, which themselves sprang from the tsar's Near Eastern policies and European realpolitik,[18] and to the Russians' own return to New South Wales, they combined and grew in strength.[19] By 1830, when news of Russia's quashing of the Polish insurrection had created its impression on the colony, those once-neglected voices formed an influential chorus. Russophobia had come of age in New South Wales, with a boost from W. C. Wentworth's independent-minded paper *The Australian*, and was to reach a ripe old age. It lives today. Nevertheless, the Russian visits (March-April 1829) both passed off easily on the official level; nor were officers and seamen of the *Krotkii* or *Elena*, now returning on her second visit, ill-treated.

Elena had left Kronstadt with supplies and stores for Sitka on 16 August 1828 and had been followed out by *Krotkii* five weeks later.[20] This time, *Elena* was commanded by V. S. Khromchenko, once navigator in the *Riurik* with Kotzebue (1815–18). *Krotkii*'s captain was the patient Hagemeister who had visited Australia with the *Neva* in 1807. *Krotkii* too carried supplies and naval stores, though for Kamchatka and not the Northwest Coast itself.[21] The two ships took the same general route to Portsmouth, Hagemeister then proceeding south to Cape Town by the Cape Verde Islands, Khromchenko preferring the traditional and pleasant stop at Rio de Janeiro. Both ships crossed the South Indian Ocean in February 1829 under high westerly winds. Though it was southern summer, huge icebergs were sighted and avoided in latitude 43°S, longitude 149°39'7E, that is, close to Van Diemen's Land. Some were reckoned to be thirty fathoms high. Cape Pillar, Van Diemen's Land, was sighted from the *Krotkii* on 25 March.[22] By taking shorter routes and by skilful sailing, Hagemeister had already gained a month on the *Elena*; but the unacknowledged race to Neutral Cove was won already. *Elena* preceded *Krotkii* there by just nine days (26 March).[23] The two ships sailed for the North Pacific settlements within a day of each other (30 April and 1 May).

The presence in port of two such vessels, independently arriving from the Baltic Sea, produced considerably greater public interest than had

Elena's call of 1825.[24] It was in general a friendly interest: there were receptions by the Governor and on the *Krotkii*'s deck, parties and promenades ashore, salutes, and even published verses in the Russians' honour ("So shall Russ and Briton vie/ In friendly strife along the deep/ Where pagan isles unnumbered lie,/ And the vast South Seas billows sweep").[25] Nor were the colonists unconscious of the economic fillip that a hundred foreign visitors had given them ("it cannot fail to throw into circulation a considerable influx of money. . . . Now's the time for farmers to bring produce to a profitable market").[26] Hagemeister was remembered by a handful of his hosts from 1807, and the colonists had nothing to object to in the manners of his officers and men. Among the visitors there were, as usual in Russian ships in Australasia, future admirals (Midshipman Evgenii Berens of the *Krotkii*, Captain Pavel Kuzmishchev taking passage in *Elena*) and a scattering of Baltic German nobles.[27] Yet, the mood was not the same as it had been in 1820. All was pleasant, to be sure, but Hagemeister had himself brought out from England the disturbing news that Royal Navy vessels and a Russian squadron had "collided' in the Dardanelles. There were, as the *Gazette* frankly admitted on 9 April 1829, fears of war.[28]

Two manifestations of this new and far less sanguine undercurrent in the colonists' reaction to the Russians will be mentioned. First, the earliest appearances in Wentworth's *Australian* of Sydney's Russian bogey; second, local willingness to magnify the implications of the news, brought by *Elena,* that another Russian vessel (not the *Krotkii*) was about to visit Sydney. Here are extracts from a forward-looking article in *The Australian* of Wednesday, 8 April 1829, the first two paragraphs of which concern the prospects for "provision-trade" between the colony and Petropavlovsk-in-Kamchatka:

> No doubt, should hostilities at no distant day happen to ensue between Russia and Great Britain, the former Power could not fail to take advantage of the unprotected state of Port Jackson; which with that gingerbread work Macquarie Fort, and all the pop-guns at Dawes' Battery, could not for one hour oppose an armed force.[29]

The matter of potential trade and commerce with Kamchatka did not spark enthusiasm in the colony in 1829–31, although a few years later coalers did, in fact, go up from New South Wales; but the matter of colonial defencelessness and hypothetical attack by Russian raiders was soon to flourish like the green bay tree, as Australian historians have shown.[30] It is a mystery to which "third vessel" Khromchenko alluded on arriving with *Elena,* if in fact he did refer to such a vessel as being expected in the next few days,[31] as Wentworth's newspaper asserted. Very probably, he had in mind a ship that was to carry Chistiakov back to St. Petersburg or bring out his replacement. Still, intelligent and educated colonists were speaking of "a Russian Seventy-Four," a powerful new warship "of a type unknown to Sydney."[32] Embryonic though the vessel was, here—already—was the phantom "Russian cruiser," ever threatening attack but never seen, that was to trouble the Australians as late as 1893. Even today, there are Australian folk memories of the repeated Russian scares of the later nineteenth century. From Adelaide to Queensland, heavy guns on ancient platforms are reminders of those times and are symbolic of continuing Australian concerns. By contrast, few modern Australians recall that in the early nineteenth century relations between colonists and Russians were extremely friendly. Even fewer know that there were Russians in Port Jackson at the time of Captain Bligh.

THE SOUNDS OF DISTANT WAR

Britain had been at peace with Russia, as with other powers capable of striking at her distant outposts, when the First Fleet had departed; but a war against some European enemy had then, as later in the 1790s, seemed distinctly possible. When Captain Arthur Phillip saw Port Jackson for the first time, he immediately viewed it as an anchorage for countless warships. Soon after his landing, he despatched Lieutenant William Dawes to build a small and rudimentary redoubt along the eastern end of Sydney Cove to offer shelter for his guns and personnel in case of need. It was not long before the officer commanding his marines, the nationalistic Major Ross, pictured foreign men-of-war with cannon blazing and urged Phillip to construct some better stronghold "to retire to in case of an alarm or a surprise."[33] Phillip had balked at that, but when the *Sirius* left in search of foodstuffs, she left eight guns behind in Sydney Cove for what was promptly called "Dawes Point."

News of a Paris Revolution that had started in July 1789 travelled eleven months before it reached the settlement, and news of Britain's declaration of hostilities against the French (1793) took almost ten to reach Port Jackson. Such a time lapse left imaginations free to gallop wild till the next ship came to calm them. Still, colonial officialdom rightly judged, by the mid-nineties, that the Russians were exceedingly unlikely to assist the French First Consul in his war against Great Britain. And, as we have seen, the fact of Anglo-Russian military entente against Napoleon weighed very heavily in Hagemeister's favour when at length he brought *Neva* to Sydney Cove. For the colonial authorities in New South

Wales, France was *the* essential enemy throughout the early 1800s. Next, in 1812, came the United States. Not until 1829–31 did Russia figure, as a late and distant third, in the colonial authorities' unpublished lists of likely raiders and aggressors in the East and the Pacific.

Russian officers at Sydney in the early 1800s sympathized with Army men, many of whom were most hospitable toward them, who had suffered from the "tyranny of distance" with regard to the Napoleonic Wars. They could appreciate the need Edward Macarthur had experienced to join the colours on the far side of the world in 1808 if he was not to miss the struggle altogether. Russian officers had likewise travelled from remote parts of an empire to join a regiment or squadron at St. Petersburg or Kronstadt. It was also plain to well-connected visitors like Mikhail Petrovich Lazarev and, slightly later, Bellingshausen and Vasil'ev, that authorities at Sydney had been justified in viewing French military strength and naval presence in the East with some concern since 1800. Though the names of French exploring and investigative vessels like *Le Géographe* and *Le Naturaliste* might state their peaceable intentions, had not the military governor at French Mauritius, General Charles de Caen, been told during the Peace of Amiens in 1803—and by a Frenchman who had lately seen Port Jackson—that the settlement should be destroyed as soon as European politics and regional logistics would allow? And had Napoleon not told de Caen, in the spring of 1810, to take the place? Few Russian officers at Sydney with *Suvorov,* which had brought the welcome tidings of Napoleon's defeat and of the allies' occupation of his capital (see Chapter Three), so sealing Anglo-Russian friendship in the colony, had taken note of the defences that Macquarie had constructed or enlarged and for a moment thought them heavy or too numerous.[34] Nor were the 1820 visitors of that opinion, bearing in mind the growing wealth of New South Wales and the proven disposition of the French and the Americans to strike at Britain in a cost-effective way.[35] To the contrary, it was their feeling (and that of Russian naval officers in other parts of the Pacific in the nineteenth century) that British ports were strangely empty, as it were, awaiting regular defences and defenders.[36] Bellingshausen differed basically from Thomas Bigge, special commissioner in New South Wales at the time of his arrival, in assessment of Macquarie's competence as a strategic engineer. In his opinion, the Governor's defence-works and priorities in funding military and non-military projects, in the light of recent wars with the United States and France, were sound enough.[37] Like other Russians, he would personally have increased the strength of the existing Dawes Point Battery and put up heavier and larger fortresses where Fort Macquarie and Fort Phillip had already taken shape, before proceeding to construct a major battery, as

Bigge envisaged, on the South Head overlooking the Pacific and the Port Jackson approaches.

Russian narratives, unpublished journals, and especially the "Sydney" aquarelles of Pavel Nikolaevich Mikhailov in fact throw useful light on the development of Sydney's coast defences.[38] Those materials, in turn, are complemented by Macquarie's own rebuttal of Commissioner John Thomas Bigge's remarks on the inadequacy of his programme for constructing public works across the colony. The Governor's rebuttal was made available, at state expense and in the *Parliamentary Papers of Great Britain*,[39] to his countrymen of all persuasions and to us; it offered numerous statistics and specific observations on the batteries and forts seen and described well by the Russians. Appendix A, "Schedule of Public Buildings and Works erected. . . From 1st January 1810 to 30th November 1821," of Macquarie's *Report on New South Wales* of 1822, lists 67 public works at Sydney, 28 at Newcastle, 25 at Hobart Town, and 20 at Parramatta. One half of those at Sydney were of military designation. Of the structures illustrated by *Vostok*'s competent artist and/or dealt with in at least one Russian narrative, suffice it to mention (No. 40) "a square, stone-built Fort, with four circular bastions and a bomb-proof powder magazine, mounting 15 guns, on Bennelong's Point. . . ," and (No. 41) "a large stone-built bomb-proof Powder Magazine at Fort Phillip, inclosed with a high Stone Wall."[40] Both are plainly visible in Mikhailov's "View of the Town of Sydney in Port Jackson."

Bellingshausen's interest in British New South Wales was, like I. M. Simonov's in Aboriginal society along its fringe, a comprehensive one.[41] He saw the forts; he saw the evidence of an expanding British settlement; and so he sought a link between the Governor's concern about potential foreign threats to New South Wales and the pattern of expanding settlement. He came to see that in Macquarie's colony, the service of the penal system invariably came first, but that commercial and strategic factors also lent encouragement to the accelerating spread of British outposts.[42] Which strategic factors in particular? The French resurgence in the East and, more immediately, Oceania, as represented by de Freycinet, and the increasing consciousness of the New Englanders that Oceania was now open to all. Macquarie's comments to the Russians merely echoed his official policy: as he expressed it in a long despatch to Henry Goulburn in September 1817, "no European Nation" should in future be allowed to form a settlement "in any part" of the entire continent.[43] It seemed unnecessary and discourteous to mention Russia as a colonizing Power to his Baltic German guest.

Governor Darling, too, was frank in his misgivings about France-in-the-Pacific, as embodied (1826–27) by the navigator Dumont d'Urville and *Astrolabe*. Peaceful though the French mission claimed to be, Darling was glad that British warships stood at anchor in the colony, and was undisposed to give his visitors much cheer.[44] The *Elena* had, by contrast, been received with public warmth not long before. Public perception of the Russians and the French had changed but little in the colony since 1810. Few, by extension, gave much thought to the activities or plans of any foreigners outside Australia. There was sufficient occupation, opportunity, and want within the colonies themselves to focus most minds on immediate realities: controlling the environment and getting food, water, and wealth.[45]

Local officialdom apart, it was the infant Sydney press that most concerned itself in 1825–35 with European feint and shadow and reflected on the place of New South Wales in the *realpolitik* of changing times. Two Sydney newspapers especially, the young *Australian* and Robert Howe's *Sydney Gazette,* found space occasionally for a transcript from the London press or an editorial on the emotive theme of foreign occupation of Pacific Islands. In particular, Tahiti and New Zealand caught the eye of Howe, who was a patriot and Sydney-born.[46] His apprehensions did not reach to New South Wales, nor did phantom Russian frigates off its coast disturb his slumber as they would Australians of coming generations.[47] As for Howe's principal journalistic adversary, *The Australian,* it took an even cooler attitude in 1826–29 towards the distant sound of European warfare and the prospects of colonial involvement in a South Pacific clash between the Powers. Would it not indeed, suggested *The Australian* outrageously in 1826, be beneficial to the colonists at large if, say, the Russians or the French established settlements not far away? It would unquestionably "be a little galling to England to see French or Russian Colonies spring up within reasonable distance [of Australia]," but it would probably "be no cause of regret" to the majority in New South Wales.[48] Thus jolted, the imperial authorities might treat that colony on economically more favourable terms and even grant a constitution. This was classic journalistic provocation, and a few indignant patriots rose to the bait. That such remarks did not produce a stir suggests, however, that again few men were seriously thinking of the Russians (or indeed the French), as threats to New South Wales and adjacent British outposts. If the Russians were alluded to at all in such a context and in 1826–27, it was less in fear than in pleasantry. By 1829, we sense a subtle change of tone in *The Australian,* bringing it closer into line—where the matter of non-British colonizing in the region is concerned—with both *The Monitor* and Howe's *Sydney Gazette.* As we have seen, the catalysts of change were deeply negative reactions, first in London, then in Sydney, to the tsar's Balkan and Near Eastern policies, and the arrival within days of each other of *Elena* and the well-armed transport *Krotkii*.[49] It was not, indeed, that verses were not printed in their honour, or that articles were published which suggested that "Russ and Briton" could not "vie in *friendly* strife" in the Pacific. Still, *The Australian* found it appropriate to cast aspersions on the "gingerbread" and "pop-guns" which, it reckoned, would be virtually useless in the face of armed attack by, say, the Russians.[50] This was something very new and realistic. Thus, by 1829, had Wentworth, Howe, and their supporters done as much as the colonial authorities, with Darling and Bourke well in command, to set the stage for 1830 and the birth of Australasian Russophobia.

ANTI-RUSSIAN SENTIMENT AND ECONOMIC INTEREST:
AUSTRALIAN CONNECTIONS

Between November 1830 and November 1831, at least a dozen more or less alarmist articles appeared in the newspapers of Hobart Town and Sydney, to the general effect that if Great Britain did not speedily annex New Zealand, one or another of the "leading foreign Powers" would unquestionably do so. Of those powers, it was readily conceded, one was Russia. Week by week, alleged the *Hobart Town Courier* on 26 March 1831, the Russians, French, and Dutch were "looking out" for "a convenient Spot" on which to plant a southern colony that would both rival and eventually hamper the prosperity of New South Wales and Van Diemen's Land (Tasmania) alike. New Zealand, with its many bays and fertile land, was such a spot. The information that the Russians, among others, had their eyes upon New Zealand had, the *Courier* remarked, been furnished by a group of gentlemen who had connections with the "Fisheries" and South Seas whaling industry.[51]

It was in fact, as the subscribers to the *Courier* might well have guessed, frustration on the part of those same whaling interests over successive British Cabinets' refusal to annex New Zealand formally that had produced the public "warning."[52] Hobart merchants had been striving to establish solid bases in New Zealand's Bay of Islands since the early 1800s; and a few, exploiting rich sealing and whaling resources in surrounding seas and even stimulating exports of New Zealand products (timber, meat, *Phormium tenax* or New Zealand flax), had earned a valuable portion of a commerce worth, by 1831, £65,000 excluding revenue from "Fisheries."[53] Several influential Sydney merchants, too, were well entrenched. It is a commonplace of Australasian history that these, with the support of sympathizers in Great Britain, used whatever argument might come to hand to keep the question of imperial colonization of New

Zealand and the South Pacific Islands in the government's unwilling eye.[54]
One useful argument was that the Russians, lacking bases in the South
Pacific Ocean and constrained to use the ports of friendly powers on the
sea-routes to Kamchatka and Alaska, would be seeking out the right spot
for a colony in—or at least not far from—Australasia more determinedly
as time went by. Thus local anti-Russian sentiment in Hobart Town and
Sydney, largely stemming from a wave of indignation in Great Britain at
the tsar's emphatic quashing of the 1830 Polish insurrection rather than
from anything attempted by the Russians in the East or the Pacific, had by
1831 become expediently fused with very different commercial and colonial considerations.[55] Many colonists, officials, army officers, and others
then in New South Wales or Van Diemen's Land no doubt felt genuine
disgust with Russian trampling on Polish cultural and national aspirations. What is worthy of some emphasis, nevertheless, is the alacrity with
which the "Polish" sins of Russia were applied to an inapplicable South
Pacific setting. Economic factors certainly, as well as feeling on the matters of New Zealand or the Polish liberties, induced the Sydney press to
echo Hobart's warning and its reference to Russia as a colonizing power
to be watched.[56] Much is evident from the position that was taken on that
issue by the least alarmist, least jingoistic of the Sydney newspapers of
1832, the *Sydney Herald*. "We," observed the *Herald* on 9 August, in
connection with alarmist correspondence stimulated by the visit of
Amerika eight weeks before, "can find no fault in the Emperor of Russia's strenuous exertions to find an island of large size in the Pacific."
What was worrying was that Great Britain, whose discoveries had led her
subjects to Australia and other parts of the immense Pacific Ocean, where
their rightful trading interests were fast expanding, might unfortunately
"lose the benefit of her numerous expeditions in the South Seas." Was it
tolerable that the apathy of Crown officials, or administrative sloth, or
penny pinching, or the coming of the Russian Navy should prevent "our
merchants" from pursuing "lucrative trade" in Australia, New Zealand,
and the Islands as a whole? Even the missionary was "the merchant's pioneer."[57]

Did Robert Howe or his successor as the editor of the *Gazette*, Ralph
Mansfield, or the rich Simeon Lord, or any other local sounder of the
anti-Russian siren in this period, honestly fear that the Russians might attempt to found a colony in Australasia, and that Russia's flag might fly
over New Zealand?[58] Hardly so. It would be foolish to dismiss the deep
antipathy they felt toward the Russian state in the abstract as a false or
shallow feeling. To examine published articles or private letters of the
early 1830s is to recognize that it was deep. Russia was mentioned in the
Australasian context, even so, as a particularly serviceable bogey—one

with ships in the Pacific, plain imperial ambitions, and the worst of public images in London and the colonies, at least by 1831–32.[59] Already roles were being cast that would be played till the last years of the century.[60] Already Russia was a lever, ever present as an instrument of argument, ever invisible. Distinct though Russia and the Russian individuals who came to Sydney in the 1830s were (as representatives of governments or systems are distinct from those same systems), such perceptions of "the Muscovite" or "Russian Bear" inevitably influenced the way Russians were treated in Australia. The first to sense a cooler Sydney welcome were the officers and men of the *Amerika,* the first of whose two Sydney calls took place in May-June 1832.

It is not hard to overdramatize that streak of jingoism or that vein of xenophobia that undeniably existed in official and mercantile circles in the colonies by 1832. And it is salutary, in this regard, to see from private letters, public and official correspondence, and the newspapers of Hobart Town and Sydney how exceedingly parochial most people's concerns were.[61] That said, however, we must recognize a new spirit abroad in New South Wales in the thirties where Pacific aspirations of the European Powers were concerned.[62] It was a spirit soon to grow into Australian imperial ambition.[63]

THE ARMED TRANSPORT "AMERIKA" AT SYDNEY: COOLER WELCOMES

Now on his third voyage around the world, and so in company with Kotzebue, Mikhail P. Lazarev, and Hagemeister, Captain-Lieutenant Khromchenko returned to Sydney as commander of the armed transport *Amerika* in 1832.[64] He had a mixed cargo of Company and Crown supplies and stores for Petropavlovsk and the Coast and, having left the Baltic late and then been quarantined in Denmark as a likely carrier of cholera (then raging in St. Petersburg), had found it prudent to avoid Cape Horn. Great rollers and alarming storms inflicted damage on *Amerika* as the meridian of Cape Town was passed in early March. There were other misadventures in the South Indian Ocean, but Van Diemen's Land was sighted on the 31st.[65] She entered Neutral Bay on 9 May 1832.[66]

Governor Darling had set the tone for the official attitude toward his visitors by his behaviour while *Krotkii* had been present three years earlier. It was an attitude of watchful courtesy. In 1829, as we have seen, the Russians had been civilly received by the authorities; but Darling had been watching "their proceedings," finding "nothing. . . to excite suspicion that they have any view to colonisation in New Holland."[67] Much had passed since then to heighten colonists' and government officials' readiness to keep an eye on Khromchenko. As the *Gazette* had put it, three months earlier, the British nation felt the shadow of "the mournful news of the overthrow of Poland," and could see "the iron Sceptre" of the tsar.[68] Almost at once there was a squabble in the town about salutes fired from Fort Macquarie and *Amerika*.[69] The point is not whether colonial or Russian gunnery was competent or whether international etiquette had been observed, but that the squabble was itself a sign of tension. Few contended, like the Fort Macquarie gunner, Mr. Brown, that the colonial defences were in excellent repair, ably manned, and strong enough. Many agreed with Wentworth that the fort was an anomaly, a "gingerbread" construction that could not subdue *Amerika* or any other ship that mounted cannon "for one hour." Such a fort was an embarrassment to Sydney.[70]

Khromchenko remained a month but he was not, it seems, as often or as generously entertained by "Rank and Fashion" (army officers, important pastoralists, wealthy traders and their wives) as even Hagemeister's officers had been. Like Talleyrand (whose bon mot the *Gazette* appropriated), men of influence in Sydney felt their health and readiness to entertain the Russians "much affected by the *Keen Winds* from the North."[71] Significantly, the most sparkling party mentioned by the press was held, not in a set of hired rooms, but on *Amerika* herself, the Russian officers being the hosts. Seventy-two sat down to dinner under awnings on her main deck, while the 39th Regiment's band played martial tunes. Governor Richard Bourke did not attend. His wife Elizabeth had died on 7 May and he felt the blow intensely. Her death had shrunk his willingness to entertain beyond what duty and propriety required.[72] The *Amerika* departed on 10 June without her cooper, who had bolted with a view to better pay on whaling ships. The visit ended on a cool but proper note.

By 1835, when the *Amerika* returned, this time commanded by Ivan Ivanovich von Schants (in Russian, Fonshants),[73] the tide of sentiment had turned and the relaxed and warm exchanges of Macquarie's time had gone forever.[74] The aftermath of the Polish insurrection, local rumours of a formidable warship off the coast of New South Wales, and the Russians' major diplomatic victory over the Turks at Unkiar-Skelessi in 1833 were but three of many incidents that soured Anglo-Russian amity and fostered local Russophobia. *Elena*'s call had been the last by any passing Russian ship that had not marginally or subliminally worried Sydney residents. Their rising apprehension found expression in alarmist propaganda and, in due course, in the gathering of guns at harbour-heads.

Captain-Lieutenant (later Admiral) von Schants was on a routine mission of provisionment in 1835, had left the Baltic Sea the previous August, and had called at Copenhagen, Portsmouth, and Brazil en route to

Sydney. Much is known about the voyage out because, besides Company records that relate to it, we have a narrative by the *Amerika*'s second lieutenant, future Admiral Vasilii Zavoiko, that describes it stage by stage. *Impressions of a Seaman During Two Round-the-World Voyages* (*Vpechatleniia moriaka*... : St. Petersburg, 1840), the first section of which relates to 1834–36 and the *Amerika,* gives useful data on the ship herself ("a three-masted transport... 130 feet long, with a 17-foot draught"), on routes selected, on her officers (the first lieutenant, Berens, had already been to Sydney with the *Krotkii*), and above all on the major ports of call: Rio and Sydney, Taloo Bay in Mo'orea, Honolulu.[75]

The *Amerika* anchored at Sydney on 20 March 1835. A bluff but subtle man, Captain von Schants tested the wind. Governor Bourke received him civilly enough, and it was obvious that "shopkeepers" in town were not so ardently pro-Polish as to spurn the Russians' business.[76] Still, the atmosphere was cool. Correct and businesslike himself, von Schants made haste to make repairs and be gone.

Appendix A

EARLIER RUSSIAN SCIENCE IN AUSTRALIA: SOME CONTRIBUTIONS

HYDROGRAPHY

Kruzenshtern was the pre-eminent Russian hydrographer and map collator of the nineteenth century. Although he personally never paid a visit to Australia, he made a major contribution to contemporary European knowledge of its coasts. First, as a maritime historian with special interest in South Pacific waters, he investigated Tasman's till-then neglected work of 1642 around Van Diemen's Land's "Frederick Henry Bay." The Dutch discoveries, he justly noted in a published work of 1806,[1] could only reasonably be collated with the subsequent Furneaux, D'Entrecasteaux, and other data on the basis of the primary materials; and this, in turn, implied that scholars should pay heed to Tasman's journal and to notes by his associate Franchoijs Jacobszoon Visscher as reported, not by Alexander Dalrymple or Charles de Brosses in their more recent compilations of Pacific Voyages, but in Francois Valentijn's *Oud en Nieuw Oost-Indien* of 1726.[2] Kruzenshtern, in short, held it essential to examine the original materials, not subsequent and often modified accounts, and duly practised what he preached. A far more practical example of the way in which the Russians could themselves contribute largely to the scientific study of the coastlines of Australia, however, was provided to the Baltic Fleet by Kruzenshtern as the commander of *Nadezhda* and as leader of a Russian expedition round the globe that was of major scientific value.[3] Though *Nadezhda* and *Neva* did not look in at New South Wales, they established precedents for later visitors to Sydney where hydrography and coast surveying were concerned.

Kruzenshtern wanted and was given first-rate instruments, equipment, and supplies of every sort in 1803.[4] It was his object to establish an esprit de corps by handsome pay, good food, and lofty expectations of particularly able personnel.[5] With this in view, he turned at once to the St. Petersburg Academy of Sciences, of which he was himself a corresponding member, for assistance in the area of science. It was Kruzenshtern's achievement at the outset of the Russian Navy's South Pacific enterprise to turn a multipurpose voyage, which had earlier been mercantile in its scope, into a venture of importance to the academic world—and to hydrography especially. Using the data he had gathered (1803–6) and reports by many other Russian captains in the coming twenty years, he prepared one of the finest nineteenth-century Pacific atlases: *Atlas Iuzhnogo Moria* (*Atlas of the South Sea*: St. P., 1823–26).[6]

As for his choice of scientific-naval instruments of measurement for use aboard *Nadezhda* and *Neva*, it was deeply influenced by his experience in British warships as a Russian Volunteer (1793–98).[7] While serving in the frigate *Thetis*, for example, he had grown familiar with certain timepieces, reflecting-circles, sextants, telescopes, and heavy quadrants.[8] That familiarity was a contributory factor in the use in Australia, until at least the 1820s, of very comparable instruments by London makers by the people of *Neva*, *Suvorov*, *Vostok*, *Otkrytie*, *Amerika*, and *Kreiser*. Specifically, the Russian government in 1802–3 purchased chronometers by John Arnold (1736–99), an eighteen-inch quadrant by George Adams the younger (1750–95), and an entire set of instruments (reflecting circle, two small sextants, two azimuth compasses, an artificial magnet, false horizons) by the celebrated maker Edward Troughton (1753–1835).[9]

As a Volunteer serving under Rear-Admiral George Murray on the North Atlantic station, Kruzenshtern had read the works of George Adams the younger, who was then (1794–96) instrument manufacturer to George III.[10] His deep respect for Adams's astronomic quadrants was shared by the astronomer appointed to *Nadezhda*, Johann Caspar Hörner, so an Adams quadrant capable of either vertical or horizontal use was duly taken round the world.[11] The four chronometers purchased from Arnold and also carried by *Nadezhda* and *Neva* to the Pacific had been specially designed for use in East India Company ships, for the determining of longitude at sea. All had refinements like the new expansion balance and detached escapement. Such chronometers were in use aboard the Indiamen *Royalist* and *Bombay Castle,* in which Kruzenshtern and Iurii Lisianskii had voyaged in 1799–1801.[12] The timepieces were checked upon arrival in St. Petersburg by Kruzenshtern's older associate in the Academy of Sciences, the German-born geodesist-astronomer Friedrich (in Russian, Fedor Ivanovich) Shubert (1758–1825).[13] He had practical suggestions for their use by naval officers at sea. Kruzenshtern had amicable meetings with Troughton, whom he recognized as a distinguished craftsman, the inventer of the new reflecting circle (1796) and perfecter of the maritime barometer, theodolite, and transit-circle.[14] Made aware of the Russian government's full satisfaction with the theodolites with which *Nadezhda* and, a decade later, *Riurik* had been supplied, the British government itself selected comparable instruments for use in the American Coast Surveys (1815–16) and in other distant geodesic work. Kruzenshtern's praises of "the justly celebrated" Edward Troughton[15] led to further Russian orders from that maker; and in August 1819 he had a visit from the captain of the *Mirnyi*, Mikhail Petrovich Lazarev, then on a tour of the London premises or showrooms of such men as Arnold, Dolland, and Barraud.[16] Among the several young officers and midshipmen accompanying Lazarev was Pavel Novosil'skii, who in old age left this cameo of Edward Troughton:

> We called on the deaf Mr Troughton for sextants and artificial horizons. The old man constantly brought a hearing-trumpet to his ear, but even then he could hear

precious little. On the other hand, his instruments, and especially the sextants with ten-second divisions, were excellent indeed.[17]

Troughton's sextants and Dolland's telescopes were in almost constant use as, in March and early April 1820, *Mirnyi* made her first approach to New South Wales from the west.[18]

The Soviet historian Vladimir Nevskii thus sums up the maritime astronomy required of *Neva* and other vessels bound on "Oceanic missions" in this period:

> Longitude at sea was already established, now, with the aid of chronometers. Each ship usually had two, three, or even more chronometers, since the constantly fluctuating physical and meteorological conditions produced significant errors in readings. The mean of the readings from two or three instruments was generally taken as true, but these readings had also constantly to be emended on the basis of precise astronomical observations. But the very best way of reckoning the longitude of a place in those times was by establishing the angle between the moon and particular stars by sextant. In addition, it could be measured by octant, which gave a reading differing from the sextant's by one or two minutes. Such measurings were undertaken in great numbers and calculations were usually made on the basis of lunar tables, for which much time was required.[19]

Like Kruzenshtern and Lisianskii in 1803–6, Hagemeister in 1807 and Lazarev in 1814 made use of the lunar tables by Bürg, "which had gained the First Consul's double prize at the National Institute" in Paris,[20] as they approached Australia. All four reckoned their latitude when out of sight of land by estimating the meridional height of either the sun or certain stars. Among other physical and professional equipment brought to Sydney by the Russians in the early 1800s were marine barometers and aerometers, dipping-needles, Six-thermometers, camera lucida, and log-sounding machines.[21]

As on her first Pacific voyage, so again in 1806–8 *Neva* carried a good assortment of Pacific charts and atlases, many of British provenance. Among these were the works of Aaron Arrowsmith (1750–1823), notably supplements to the complete *Map of the World* (1794) on globular projection and, inevitably, charts from Cook's three *Voyages*. *Neva* sailed too early to be issued with *Directions for Sailing to and from the East Indies, China, New Holland . . .* (London, 1809–11), compiled by the hydrographer James Horsburgh (1762–1836); but the Directions were issued to the wardroom of *Suvorov*. On returning to Australia in 1820 as commander of the *Mirnyi*, M. P. Lazarev had also *Tables of Positions, or of Latitudes and Longitudes of Places* (London, 1816), by the hydrographer John Purdy (1773–1843).[22]

Russian captains had, as seen, clear instructions from their Naval Ministry to draw the maximal advantage from Pacific voyages, in terms of charting and related "naval sciences."[23] They did so conscientiously on their passages to Sydney. Soundings were taken in close proximity to land, and coastal currents, winds, and air and water temperatures were continuously measured as *Vostok* and *Mirnyi, Otkrytie* and *Blagonamerennyi, Kreiser* and *Ladoga* approached Australia.[24] Here, to typify captains' reports that found their way into the Hydrographic Depot in St. Petersburg (and were surveyed by Kruzenshtern for any data to be noted in the *Atlas of the South Sea* he was working on in 1820), is a small section from M. P. Lazarev's, bearing immediately on the *Mirnyi*'s approach to New South Wales and Port Jackson:

> At dawn on 2 April 1820, we caught sight of the coast of New Holland, bearing N 55°W. I deduced that the land visible must be Cape St George, near Jervis Bay. Our supposition was confirmed at 8 a.m., when we found ourselves within 14 miles of it, by the oddly conspicuous cape called Cape Perpendicular, then visible and bearing N 51°W from us.... Capes St George and Perpendicular were standing in line, S 35°W, and we were a mere 6 miles off the latter. We reckoned our position as latitude 35°00′21″S, longitude 151°03′30″E. . . . By night, we were off Red Bluff, so named by Captain Cook on his first voyage [modern-day Bellambi Point].
>
> 3 April. The variation on an average of many azimuths was 9°20′S, rising amplitude of 9°06′E, in lat. 34°27:S, long. 151°13′E. A depth sounding gave 70 *sazhen,* white sandy bottom. The southern headland at the entrance to Port Jackson became visible at noon, 20.5 miles distant in bearing 21°NW. We tacked in under a gentle NE wind. Depth being 35 *sazhen,* we turned on another tack, Cape Bluff and Cape Banks being in line S 25°W.[25]

The complementary observations of Bellingshausen, who had reached Cape Perpendicular four days before, read thus:

> 29 March 1820. By noon we were in lat. 35°57′42″S. long. 150°57′51″E. The elevation on the New Holland coast known as "the Pigeon House" now bore S. 87°30W., and a coastal projection, the headland called "Cape Perpendicular," bore N. 6°46′E. Thus, the positions of the aforementioned height of land, "Pigeon House," and of "Cape Perpendicular," work out to be 4′ southward and 4′30′ westward of those given in Captain Flinders' *Atlas.*[26]

It is evident that *Vostok,* at least, carried a copy of the *Atlas* published officially in London in 1814 from surveys made by Matthew Flinders in the *Investigator* from 1798 to 1803.[27] Cape Perpendicular is the steep-cliffed northern point of the entrance to Jervis Bay. Such emendations to existing British charts of Australian shores were duly noted by Kruzenshtern.

Kirribilli Point, on the North Shore of Port Jackson, was the spot on which several Russian companies erected shore observatories and workshops.[28] Astronomical readings were made there by trained astronomers like Pavel Tarkhanov of *Otkrytie* and Ivan M. Simonov of the *Vostok,*[29] ship's navigators like Vladimir Petrov of *Blagonamerennyi* and Dmitrii Iakovlev of *Krotkii* (1829), and midshipmen like Aleksei Rossiiskii of the *Suvorov,*[30] Nikolai D. Shishmarev of *Blagonamerennyi,*[31] and Pavel Gagarin of *Amerika* (1835). Besides these, certain captains also worked with telescope, sextant, and chronometers at Kirribilli Point, notably Bellingshausen of *Vostok,* Khromchenko of *Elena* (1829), and Hagemeister of the *Krotkii.*[32] All three officers were mathematically inclined.[33] "While at Port Jackson," reads the official Navy report on *Elena*'s voyage, which was printed in St. Petersburg in 1832, "Captain-Lt. Khromchenko made readings from a spot a half a mile north of the so-called Dower's [Dawes] Battery, and fixed the position as lat. 33°52'46''S., long. 151°13'38''E."[34] Among the naval companies who called at Sydney, there were disproportionate numbers of youths whose proven competence in maritime astronomy or coastal survey work led to careers in the Hydrographic Depot at St. Petersburg in later life. One thinks of Hagemeister's second mate in 1807, Efim Klochkov, later officer in charge of instruments within that Depot; Grigorii A. Nikiforov of the *Apollon*; and Pavel A. Gagarin of the *Amerika*.[35] Rossiiskii was one of several young men who checked chronometers and occupied themselves for lengthy periods with "tedious astronomical observations" with a view to correcting longitudinal error, at the same time taking pleasure in "a spot which by its situation might be called romantic."[36]

It was reckoning of longitude, especially, that taxed the visitors of 1820, who were soon to be at work in high and unfrequented latitudes to North and South, and very possibly in sight of unmapped land: it was desirable to get precision where they could and in conditions of considerable comfort. For *Vostok,* lunar distances were taken by the hundred, over periods of weeks. Of 455 distances taken by Navigator Iakov Poriadin, Captain-Lieutenant Ivan Zavadovskii, and her captain, Bellingshausen, the average gave longitude 151°09'53''E. Third Lieutenant Arkadii Leskov took 40 lunar distances to reach an average of 151°00'22'', Lieutenant Konstantin Torson, the incipient Decembrist, 380 lunar readings, for an estimated longitude of 151°21'36''E. For *Mirnyi,* Midshipman Ivan Kupreianov took 126 distances, for an average of 151°11'7'', while Lazarev himself found time for 228 separate readings, making 151°11'07''E.[37] Both ship's chronometers were checked both in April–May and in September 1820. In April–May, *Vostok*'s chronometers made by John Arnold were discovered to have gained, respectively, 5 minutes 10 seconds and 6 minutes 8 seconds in 24 hours. A Barraud chronometer performed a little worse, losing 10 minutes 31 seconds in the standard period. On 27 October, those same instruments were found to have gained and lost, respectively, 19, 12, and 15 minutes odd per 24 hours.[38] By contemporary British standards, these were tolerable margins. Even so, they went some way towards producing a 23-minute spread in the longitudinal reckonings for Kirribilli Point by Russian officers in 1820. Here are tabulated reckonings of longitude:

Modern gazetteers give the geographical centre of Sydney harbour as 151°15'E, the city core as 151°12'E.[39] The Russian reckonings were accurate, on average, to within two minutes. Bellingshausen's readings were as accurate as any and appreciably better than his second-in-command's, given the fact that he took less than half as many distances (125 to Lazarev's 228). Such were the benefits of early hydrographic missions on the Black Sea station—Bellingshausen's own equivalent of Cook's Newfoundland survey work in early life.[40]

As for the latitude of Kirribilli Point, it was reckoned at 33°51'–52'S by all eight officers above. Contemporary gazetteers all approve.

Port Jackson had yet to be fully surveyed in 1820, and accordingly those Russian officers of hydrographic bent and with the necessary time set out to chart its arms and coves. *Blagonamerennyi*'s boats set out, well armed, within two days of her arrival, on 1 March.[41] Among the officers of her companion ship, *Otkrytie*, who likewise occupied themselves with local survey work was Aleksandr P. Avinov, a hydrographer by training, who concluded his career as an admiral and an honoured member of the Admiralty College.[42] Few results of Russian charting in Australia were ever published by imperial or Soviet authority. We know, however, that the work of naval draughtsmen (charts and plans) went with reports from certain captains who had visited that country to the Russian Naval Ministry in 1822–35.[43] Russian cartography, which had a patriotic character and was essentially for Russian use and national benefit,[44] did not illuminate Australia for foreign eyes. Unpublished charts of both Port Jackson and the River Derwent and adjacent Hobart in Tasmania must be supposed to lie on dusty shelves in Leningrad.[45]

To turn next to Kruzenshtern's own knowledge of and deep respect for Tasman's voyages of southern exploration: as observed, it was an academic interest though one with practical and modern application (had the *Kreiser* and *Ladoga* not been dependent on reliable and tested charts of the approach to Hobart Town?), at least by 1823. Like his companion Lisianskii, who had thought of joining Flinders on a coastal survey voyage round Australia in 1799 because in India he had appreciated fully the significance of Australasian exploration and of limpet British colonies around New Holland,[46] Kruzenshtern thought more seriously about southern exploration, trade, and commerce as a consequence of time spent in the Indies (1797–98).[47] More specifically, he thought of Tasman and the Dutch because, en route from British India (Calcutta) to Canton aboard Lisianskii's former ship, H.M.S. *L'Oiseau*, he had spent a period at Pulo Penang.[48] It was an outpost overshadowed by the nearby Dutch East Indies. Kruzenshtern then passed the long and fever-racked Straits of Malacca, well in sight of Dutch possessions on Sumatra, before entering the South China Sea.[49] Experience of South Pacific sailing with *Nadezhda* (1804) not only reconfirmed this earlier belief that it was time to look at primary materials describing Dutch Pacific-Australasian voyages, but also led him to present without delay his own reflections on that subject in the *Technological Journal* (*Tekhnologicheskii Zhurnal*), then run and edited at the Academy of Sciences. His paper, "Tasman's Discoveries, with an Appended Work on the Position of Ontong Java . . . ," was published in the third issue for 1806.[50] Textual evidence makes clear that the paper had been written while *Nadezhda* was at sea, that is to say, that Kruzenshtern found time to write a learned article amidst the bustle and innumerable duties of his post and situation. It is evidence of fine powers of concentration and persistence.

When [demands Kruzenshtern by way of preface] did the Dutch undertake their great voyages of discovery, and when was their State most powerful and most important? When did they have the most celebrated scholars? We can only answer all such question by saying, the 17th century. It was hardly a single, chance thought that led Peter the Great to choose Holland as the exemplar and source of knowledge: the degree of respect then enjoyed by Holland justified the tsar's opinion, and his desire to inspect the Dutch canals and waterways merely resulted from it.

To them alone are we indebted for the discovery of New Holland, whose yet unmeasured shores were mostly explored by them also. Their discovery was not less important than was that of America, for an entire continent was found—which will in time compose what America does now.[51]

Before him in his cabin in *Nadezhda,* Kruzenshtern had Francois Valentijn's illustrated account of Tasman's 1642–43 voyage in the third volume of his *Oud en Nieuw Oost-Indien* (Amsterdam, 1726); Charles de Brosses's *Histoire des Navigations aux Terres Australes* (Paris, 1756); Alexander Dalrymple's *Historical Collection of the Several Voyages and Discoveries in the South Pacific Ocean* (London, 1770–71); and a translation of Dirck van Nierop's brief summary derived from Tasman's journal and first printed (1674) as *Eenige Oefeningen,* as done by Pierre de Hondt. The relationships between these works, and the great importance of the Nierop account as the principal source of information about Tasman and Tasmania for Continental readers, have been laid forth by the Eminent New Zealand scholar Andrew Sharp.[52] Suffice it here to note that, in the later eighteenth century, the Russians had depended on de Brosses, on A. F. Prévost d'Exiles's *Histoire générale des Voyages* (Paris, 1753), and on M. de Freville's free rendition of the 1771 Dalrymple borrowing, as published in his *Voyages dans la Mer du Sud* (Paris, 1774). It was immediately plain to Kruzenshtern that inconsistency and unattributed or doubtful borrowings were rampant, and that even Francois Valentijn was merely claiming to have sighted and transcribed from Tasman's journal or, elsewhere in his *Oud en Nieuw Oost-Indien,* from an authentic copy of it.[53] These were questions that the Tasman scholar J. E. Heeres was to address, at last, in 1898.[54] Being a seaman, Kruzenshtern was very naturally troubled by the way data on latitude and longitude were simply cut out of supposedly "complete, authentic" accounts of the Tasman voyages. As he expressed it:

> Inclusion of these data of course facilitates description of his course [in *Zeehaen* and *Heemskerck*]. Besides this, Tasman always made notes on compass variations as soon as weather conditions permitted. Nowhere are observations of compass needle inclination so needed today as between the coasts of Africa and New Holland. For it is in those waters that it is subject to the greatest irregularities. Tasman may be said to have made so small an error in his reckoning of the true longitude of Van Diemen's Land because of the great frequency of his reckonings.[55]

The closer Kruzenshtern examined Tasman's reckonings of longitude, the more he recognized their accuracy by the standards of another century, and even of the early 1800s. Tasman's greatest error was apparently of 3° after a two-month passage from the Friendly Islands to New Guinea. By comparison, the Spanish made an error twice as great in half the time, while going from Chile to Tahiti in 1772.[56]

The history of Tasman's important voyage [of 1642–43] has been written in many languages; but the most circumstantial account, Valentijn's *Omstending verhaal van de Gesehiedenissen* etc., has not been translated into any other tongue—though indeed there are numerous brief accounts of Tasman's voyage, in English as in French. It is supposed that Valentijn, who married a daughter of the Secretary at Batavia, obtained the original journal from the archive there by that circumstance. Certainly, the maps in the Valentijn edition are not to be found in any of the many other editions.[57]

Kruzenshtern then proceeded to examine Tasman's seamanship and navigation as they bore on the discovery of Frederik Hendrik (modern Blackman) Bay at the beginning of December 1642. This was the bay, in latitude 41°50'S, longitude 168°50'E by Isaac Gilseman's map of that time,[58] where Visscher led a landing party of eighteen on 2 December, picked up much-needed greenstuffs, found a stream of good sweet water, noted "Timber in abundance," heard the distant "sound of People" and a horn or little gong, and on the following unlikely basis thought the area inhabited by giants:

> The pilot-Major. . . reported. . . that they have seen 2 trees about 2 to 2½ fathom thick 60 to 65 feet high under the Boughs, in which trees gashed with flints and the bark was peeled off (thereby to climb up and gather the birdsnests) in shape of Steps Each being measured fully 5 feet from one another So that they presumed, here to be Very tall people.[59]

Taken in apposition to the subsequent charting of Tobias Furneaux and of Admiral d'Entrecasteaux, both of whom visited this place of so-called giants, Tasman's data posed an interesting cartographic problem. Kruzenshtern rose to the challenge of collating Dutch and subsequent material: it was a single, small preparatory exercise for the more sweeping undertaking that resulted in his *Atlas of the South Sea*. But, of all the many bays that Tasman visited and charted, why did Kruzenshtern choose this one to consider at considerable length? Because, it seems, the basic cartographic task was complemented by a need for theoretical ethnography, and interests that he had recently developed in the Washington-Marquesas Islands, in Kamchatka, and Japan, where he had met and made a study of non-European peoples, had some relevance.[60] Here, to focus on the cartographic aspect, are two extracts from his article of 1806:

> This bay must surely be the same as that lying to the north of Furneaux Bay, called Adventure Bay now. It has two capes, Cape Frederik Hendrik lying to the west and Cornwallis Point or, more correctly, Cape Basalt (as Flinders calls it) to the east. . . . They are about eleven English miles apart. I see that this was also the opinion of Captain Flinders: see his Observations on the Coasts of Van Diemen's Land and Bass's Strait, etc. . . .
>
> I place the true latitude of Prince Frederik Hendrik Bay at 43°4'S., that is, one German mile SE of the small inlet that Tasman's seamen examined on his orders and which is joined by d'Entrecasteaux Channel to Storm Bay—also discovered

by Tasman, as is clear from those detailed charts by Flinders which appear in Arrowsmith's *South Sea Pilot*. . . . According to Cook's reckoning of 1777, Adventure Bay lies in longitude 147°29'E., consequently Prince Frederik Hendrik Bay must be 147°39'E. of Greenwich. D'Entrecasteaux's reckonings give the same result to within one minute. . . . Tasman himself fixed that bay in longitude 146°36', and so his error was 1°3', a very insignificant one when we bear in mind the preceding, difficult and storm-wracked, passage. . . . Was Tasman helped or hindered by the currents? Cook and d'Entrecasteaux have little to say on that matter, except that currents were easterly to the west of New Holland. (At the entrance to Bass Strait, though, they are westerly.) One instance of a powerful oceanic current known to me has been adduced by Captain Bushler, concerning an English mariner on his way to China in 1797. He left the Cape of Good Hope on 21 September, reached Mewstone Rock at the southern tip of Van Diemen's Land on 31 October, and there found that he had been borne 7°12' eastward by the current. . . .

If, on my return to Europe, I succeed in getting hold of the original journal of Tasman's voyage, that fact alone will give me reason to publish a complete translation of it.[61]

Kruzenshtern did not succeed in gaining sight of any 1642–43 journals or logs, but did examine copies of assorted mid-seventeenth-century Dutch maps (by Joan Blaeu and associates, Janssonius, or F. de Wit), between approximately 1812 and 1820.[62] Bringing Tasman and his "South-Land" to the notice of his countrymen, Kruzenshtern also drew attention to the need to study currents and especially magnetic variation in the seas between Mauritius and Australia traversed by *Zeehaen* and *Heemskerck* in 1642 and by the Russian ships *Diana* and *Neva* in 1807–9.[63] Thus were professional and academic interests combined in Kruzenshtern's entire view of naval service. Thanks essentially to *his* great influence within the Admiralty, by the twenties, many Russians left with orders to investigate such geodesic and/or physical phenomena in the Pacific and the South Indian Ocean. These included Kotzebue and the celebrated physicist Emilii (or Emil) Lenz, of *Predpriiatie*;[64] M. N. Staniukóvich and F. P. Lütke (in Russian, Litke), of the *Moller* and *Seniavin* (1826–29);[65] Khromchenko, of the *Elena* (1828–30). Khromchenko crossed the South Indian Ocean (February–March 1829) on his way to New South Wales with the following by Kruzenshtern in mind:

The sudden change in compass magnetic inclination near New Holland, of which Tasman writes in his journal and which depends entirely on changing longitude, not on latitude, has been observed again in recent times. Captains Cook in 1777, Bligh in 1788, and Vancouver in 1791, as well as Admiral d'Entrecasteaux in 1792, all noted precisely the same phenomenon. In latitude 48°22'S., longitude 80°22'E., Cook observed a westward inclination of 30°47'; but in latitude 47°19'S. and longitude 115°28'E., it was only 14°37' to westward. And in 43°27'S., longitude 141°5'E., Cook found his compass inclination to be 1°24' eastward.[66]

The problem had preoccupied more recent Russian visitors to the Pacific and the South Indian Oceans, too, notably Bellingshausen and his versatile astronomer, Ivan M. Simonov. Indeed, the latter had embarked upon a full study of needle variations in the Northern and Southern Hemispheres, having pondered on the work *L'Attraction des montagnes et ses effets sur les fils à plomb* (Avignon, 1814) by Baron Franz Xaver von Zach.[67] The result had been a paper, "On Determining the Geographical Positions of the Anchorages of the Sloops *Vostok* and *Mirnyi*," published in 1828, barely three months before *Elena* left from Kronstadt.[68] Such an officer as Khromchenko, with hydrographic interests, was duty-bound to read the paper. Simonov had, after all, tackled the geodesic question in the South, where he was bound with orders echoing *Vostok*'s of 1820 ("With regard to geodesic, physical, and astronomical investigations, every opportunity will be embraced to study noteworthy phenomena").[69] And Simonov had kept abreast of an important, even fashionable, scientific problem, corresponding on that subject both with Zach, who as director of the Seeberg Observatory at Gotha had in 1802 commended J. C. Hörner as astronomer to Kruzenshtern, and with the admiral himself.[70] Finally, Khromchenko was quite familiar (as Bellingshausen had not been in 1820) with the seminal "magnetic atlas" of the eminent Norwegian physicist Professor Christoph Hansteen (1784–1873). Hansteen's *Magnetischer Atlas gehörig zum Magnetismus der Erde* (Christiania, 1819) had appeared just too late to be of use to Bellingshausen but had made a deep impression on such scientists as J. C. Hörner, F. I. Shubert, M. V. Severgin, and V. Vishnevskii,[71] all of whom had good relations with the Navy, and on Simonov himself when the *Vostok* finally returned to Kronstadt (August 1822). Nor was it long before the need to draw up isomagnetic charts was being studied at the University of Dorpat by the youthful physicists still, in this period, directed by Professor I. Parrot: Emil K. Lenz (1804–65) and Ernst K. Hoffmann (in Russian, Gofman, 1801–71) were in 1823–26 to make their scientific mark in the Pacific, as, respectively, the physicist and mineralogist of *Predpriiatie*.[72] Their work has been well summarized by H. R. Friis in *The Pacific Basin* (1967), and by Daniel Tumarkin in the 1981 Moscow edition of the Kotzebue narrative of 1830, *Neue Reise um die Welt* (in Russian now, *Novoe puteshestvie vokrug sveta v 1823–26 godakh*). In short, *Elena*'s officers were under orders, as the men in *Predpriiatie* had been and as the officers with Captain Lütke in *Seniavin* had remained even in 1829,[73] to check the earth's magnetic force by means of needle variation as they moved towards Australia and the Pacific from the west. Resultant data were not published in "The Voyage of the ship *Elena*... in the Year 1829," printed in *Papers of the Scientific Committee of the Naval Staff* (*ZUKMS*) in 1832,[74] but were collated with materials from other officers, including Admiral d'Entrecasteaux, who had followed broadly comparable routes across the South Indian Ocean. The result was a learned paper, "The Magnetic Strength of the Terrestrial Globe: Professor Hansteen in Christiania," also published in the *Papers* in 1832.[75] It made the following appeal for research:

> In the Southern Hemisphere, there is still very little precision in our measurement. It is plain, however, that in latitude 50°S. and a little west of South Amer-

ica there is great magnetic force. . . which rises towards New Holland. From the Cape of Good Hope to Van Diemen's Land, as is well known, the compass inclination is westerly, whereas between New Holland and New Zealand it is the opposite. Sequential readings taken from the Southwest coast of New Holland right to the Persian Gulf would now merit particular attention by scientists. (pp. 118–20)

On her passage to the coast of New South Wales from Brazil, *Elena* was carried "almost 1,200 miles to the NE" by ocean currents.[76] In the view of Akhilles P. Shabel'skii of *Apollon,* which had preceded her along the same easterly route in 1822,[77] "the Polar current in the Southern Hemisphere between the meridian of the Cape of Good Hope and Van Diemen's Land might be supposed, on the basis of observations, to be running at a rate of 14 nautical miles per diem."[78] Neither estimate was at essential variance with the conclusions drawn by Navigators Mikhail Rydalev of *Otkrytie* and Iakov Poriadin of *Vostok* in 1820. As observed by Bellingshausen, on the other hand, no ship approaching Sydney from the south and west could fail to be borne southwest (away from port) unless the winds were *very* helpful:

The current that sets N and NE near the coasts of New Holland eventually takes an almost completely opposite direction. We ourselves were carried 33 miles S 19°W in 24 hours [on 1–2 April 1820], and observations made the next day at noon indicated that we had been borne 37 miles due S in that 24-hour period.[79]

On their passages from Sydney to Kamchatka or the Russian Northwest Coast of North America, several Russian captains tried experimental routes in hopes of saving time. A common tendency during the twenties was to press due east between the 25th and 30th degrees of southern latitude with the intention of eventually passing (north by east) between the Friendly (Tonga) Islands and the Cooks, and so proceeding with the southeast trade wind through the Marshalls to the north of Micronesia. These experiments were largely unsuccessful. Though "the backing of the wind from little islets" in the Fijis or the Ellises or Gilberts might be thus escaped and "the expanses of the Great South Sea" attained, the southeast trade wind was itself a fickle helper; nor were currents east of Tonga very helpful for the northbound Russian vessel.[80] Such experiments, however, brought the Russians into view of Lord Howe Island, Ball's Pyramid, and Norfolk Island—those localities through which *Vostok* and *Mirnyi* passed in 1820 on their passage back to Sydney from the Lau Group (Fiji).[81] No Russian vessel passed such pinpoints in the sea without determining their latitude and longitude and looking out for any sign of human life. Among those that deliberately passed in sight of Norfolk Island were *Elena* under Captain-Lieutenant P. E. Chistiakov (June 1825) and under Khromchenko (28 April 1829).[82] Lord Howe Island was observed by M. P. Lazarev in the *Suvorov* (September 1814) and again (5 September 1820) in the *Mirnyi.*[83] *Vostok*'s lookout observed it that same morning, under clouds of wheeling gannets. It was reckoned to be centred in latitude 31°46'S, but Bellingshausen, more concerned with longitudinal precision, did not trouble to confirm Governor King's or Captain Hunter's early fixes on the place. By his Barraud and two Arnold chronometers, he fixed its longitude at 159°08′54″E, corroborating Hunter's estimate.[84] Today, it is officially considered to lie 2′30″ westward of the Bellingshausen fix.[85]

All charts, drafts, and corrections to existing maps that were made during a given naval venture were submitted to the Russian Naval Ministry at its conclusion. Copies went to the Imperial Map Depot (*Depo kart*), which was legally entitled to demand any original "as well as any other information" that the military branches of the government might hold,[86] and to the Navy's own small Cartographic Office. Since 1798, a well-endowed engraving section had been functioning within the Depot. In the first years of the century, eight craftsmen each received 3,000 roubles for supplies and salaries, and worked on plates for the most massive of contemporary cartographic projects: an official map of the entire Russian Empire.[87] By 1818, there were twenty-five engravers, some of whom, notably G. Meshkóv, K. Ushakóv, and I. Makárov, were occasionally set to work on naval maps.[88] Materials submitted by the officers of ships like *Apollon*, *Vostok*, *Krotkii*, and *Kreiser*, who had been active in Australia, therefore remained in a non-academic, military section of the large General Staff and in the Navy's own small Cartographic Office.[89] The latter was, as common sense dictated, closely linked for most administrative purposes with the Admiralty Hydrographic Depot and Department. The Department and the Office grew together from the 1820s onward, both depositing materials in what is now TsGAVMF (Central Naval Archive) in Leningrad. From the Australian perspective, it is helpful that, by long tradition, the authority at TsGAVMF kept its map and chart depository separate from naval archives proper. Now officially known as the Archive of the Central Cartographic Production of the Navy (Arkhiv Tsentral'nogo Kartograficheskogo Proizvodstva Voenno-Morskogo Flota, or ATKP-VMF), it is housed in the same archive building as TsGAVMF, at Leningrad D-65, Ulitsa Khalturina 36, and offers accredited scholars a wide variety of manuscript maps and navigational charts.[90]

It is typical of the splintering imperial organization of Central State Archives that the Archive of the Hydrographic Department of the Naval Ministry, which likewise contains much of interest to Australian geographical studies, should also have been kept separate, although placed in the same building.[91] One is grateful at least that alone of the pre-Revolutionary Russian ministerial archives, that of the Navy was placed in its own separate building (1886) and that the essential ordering of *fonds* and files has remained largely the same since 1840. An official catalogue of ATKP-VMF's holdings of maps and atlases, compiled by V. V. Kolgushkin, appeared in 1958 under the title *Opisanie starinnykh atlasov, kart i planov XVI, XVII, XVIII, i poloviny XIX vekov, khraniashchikhsia v arkhive Tsentral'nogo kartograficheskogo Proizvodstva VMF* (Leningrad; 270 pp.). For the logs of ships in the Pacific from which materials were taken for the published atlases of Kruzenshtern and Bellingshausen among others, we have an elderly but essential guide: *Opis' shkanechnykh zhurnalov s 1719 po 1853 god...* (St. P., 1856) with its supplement (n.d.), *Dopolnenie k opisi shkanechnykh zhurnalov, 1736-1832 godov*. This is now a bibliographical rarity. One copy is held by the M. E. Saltykov-Shchedrin Public Library (GPB), formerly the Imperial Public Library of St. Petersburg, in Leningrad.

ZOOLOGY

Russian interest in Australasian fauna began, like the associated scientific interest in Australasian flora, in the mid-1770s, in connection with accounts of Cook's first visit to Australia in the *Endeavour*.[1] More specifically, it was sparked by Cook's own narrative as first "improved upon" by Hawkesworth then translated into French,[2] and by *A Journal of a Voyage to the South Seas* (London, 1773, 1784) by Sydney Parkinson, *Endeavour*'s best-remembered artist.[3] Publication of translations of Cook's subsequent Pacific *Voyages* into Russian (see Chapter One) strengthened interest, among a handful of St. Petersburg savants, in Australasian animals of every sort. So too, at least by 1779, did the activities and international correspondence of Dr. Johann Reinhold Forster and his son George (Johann George Adam), both of whom, as we have seen, had Russian academic contacts.[4] By the mid-1780s, Johann Reinhold was in private correspondence over zoological and/or botanical questions with at least three members of St. Petersburg's Academy of Sciences, and had concluded sales of Pacific "curiosities," dried plants, and other articles collected by himself and other men in *Resolution* (1772–75).[5] He was not averse to turning a considerable profit from his own earlier enterprise, at the expense of large museums and academies abroad.[6] It was to George Forster, however, that the Russian government in June 1787 sent a formal invitation to participate as naturalist in the voyage round the world then on the point of leaving Europe under Captain G. Mulovskii's command.[7] Admiral Loggin Golenishchev-Kutuzov gave these details in 1840, in a booklet on Mulovskii's North Pacific expedition, which, regrettably for Australasian studies, was aborted at the last moment by Catherine II:

> The celebrated Professor Forster, who had sailed with Captain Cook on his Second Voyage, was invited to undertake physical and meteorological observations and also to undertake natural science on this mission; and he was granted 5,400 roubles to cover travelling expenses to St Petersburg from Vilno, where he then was. His salary was set at 3,000 roubles per annum, and he was promised, in addition, an annual pension of 1,500 roubles, payable on his return and to his wife following his death.[8]

Golenishchev-Kutuzov himself had, while translating James Cook's *Voyage* of 1772–75 into Russian,[9] shown considerable interest in those small parts of it, notably passages in Furneaux's report on Van Diemen's Land, that touched on native animals.[10] As well became a President of the Scientific Committee of the Russian Naval Staff, he was an officer of wide-ranging and catholic pursuits and even something of an amateur zoologist.[11] Here are extracts from his generally competent translation of the 1773 Furneaux report as it was given by Jean-Baptiste-Antoine Suard in his version of the English text, *Voyage dans l'Hémisphère australe . . .* (Paris, 1778):

> 11 March. . . . As for quadrupeds, we saw only one opossum, but we noted the tracks of many quadrupeds and it was my conclusion that they had been made by

a variety of wild goat. There were few fish in the bay, but we did catch some so-called sea-gluttons, some sharks, and fish unknown to us which our seamen called "nurses." They were very like sharks but were covered by small white patches. . . . 19 March. No part of the terrestrial globe so merits investigation by mariners as the large continent called New Holland. . . . In size, it equals Europe and it is within the Tropics. For these reasons, and in light of the quantity of different animals that have been collected on the shores of that vast land on Captain Cook's first Voyage, one must conclude that the interior holds a treasure of natural history.[12]

The "bay" in question was, of course, Adventure Bay, a little south of modern Hobart, where Furneaux's men had landed and discovered, *inter alia,* several "Huts or Wigwams" made of branches and containing bags and nets, Blue-gums and stringy-bark, and assorted ducks and teals. Collation of Furneaux's narrative (given in J. C. Beaglehole, ed., *The Journals of Captain James Cook: The Voyage of the Resolution and Adventure, 1772–1775,* Hakluyt Society Extra Series Vol. 35 [Cambridge, 1961], p. 734) with that produced by Golenishchev-Kutuzov (pt. 1, ch. 7, p. 243— offers a case study in blurring through the prisms of translation. (Furneaux's deerlike animals emerge as goats, dogfish became "sea-gluttons," and lagoons are shrunk to ponds.)[13] What is important here, however, is the Russian annotation to the rendering of Suard's paraphrase. Here, for instance, is the foot note placed by Admiral Kutuzov in his translation of Cook's second *Voyage* to explain his asterisk beside "opossum":

The opossum is a quadruped known to natural scientists by various names, including, in French, *oppossum, sarigue, didelphe,* and *philander.* In size and in appearance, the creature resembles a large rat with greyish brown wool and small back spots, black and white.[14]

By 1800, Russian readers could refer to many works of travel literature for allusions to the kangaroo, the platypus, and other creatures never seen in Russian towns, alive or dead. Nor was there a lack of illustrations to provoke a slowly growing public interest in such exotica.[15] It was inevitable that savants should, by the early 1800s, be attempting to obtain for proper study in St. Petersburg, if not live animals, at least the skeletons of mammals from Australia and circumstantial data on such marsupials and other creatures as had recently been brought to Europe by the British or the French. Of those savants, none showed more energetic interest in Australasian fauna than did Aleksandr Fedorovich Sevast'ianov (1771–1824). A geographer, zoologist, and writer all at once, Sevast'ianov was a regular contributor to two of Russia's leading scientific journals of the early 1800s: *Novye Ezhemesiachnye Sochineniia* (*New Monthly Compositions*) and the Academy of Sciences' own organ, *Tekhnologicheskii Zhurnal* (*Technological Journal*). In 1804–5, he placed in the latter two reports entitled, respectively, "Concerning Live Animals Brought to France Aboard the Ship 'Le Géographe' in April 1804" and "Information Regarding Certain Newly Discovered Mammals."[16] Both contained information printed in Paris, only months before, about the zoological results of the French naval expedition to Southwestern Australia and to Van Diemen's Land of *Le Géographe* and *Le Naturaliste*, commanded by Captain Nicolas Baudin (1750–1803). Both rested largely on the collecting of François Péron, but both appeared in St. Petersburg some time before the first volume of Péron's own *Voyage de Découvertes aux Terres Australes* (Paris, 1807–16) was printed. Those reports were the beginning of significant Russian zoology where Australasia is concerned.

In "Concerning Live Animals," Sevast'ianov drew the attention of his countrymen to the wealth of zoological specimens that had been landed in France by *Le Géographe* on 23 April 1804. As he observed, that vessel had carried from Australia "all the fruits of the expedition" formerly led by Baudin and, since his death on Isle de France in 1803, by Captain Milius:

> They actually brought back 72 live creatures, and four times that number of creatures frozen entire, as well as 80 boxes of natural products, of which 5 contained minerals, 8 seeds, roots and dried grasses, and no less than 67—items from the animal kingdom.[17]

There followed an annotated list of the Australian animals in Paris. Naturally, these included kangaroos and other large marsupials. One king kangaroo, "so named by M. Péron, as he had caught the creature on King's Island at the entrance to Bass Strait," was "as yet undescribed" in 1804; another, which had "failed to withstand the long voyage and had died," was reported to be in the hands of Dr. Georges-Leopold Cuvier (1769–1832), the leading palaeontologist of that day. ("Cuvier is at present engaged in a study of the animal's internal structure.") Cuvier's conclusions found their way into his seminal work of comparative anatomy and systematic zoology, *Le Règne animal, distribué d'après son organisation* (Paris, 1816), copies of which went to St. Petersburg at least by 1817. Also on Sevast'ianov's annotated list were (No. 16) "Two casuaras, live birds, without head growths, from New Holland, discovered by Commodore Phillip" and (No. 21) "Five parrots from New Holland."

In the paper "Information Regarding Certain Newly Discovered Mammals," published in 1805, the spotlight moves from kangaroos to wombats:

> The Paris Museum of Natural History recently acquired two live mammals brought by the ship *Le Naturaliste* from New Holland. These animals, previously unknown to our naturalists, live in the western parts of New Holland. The pelt may prove very useful and the meat, according to Captain Hamelin and his companions on the voyage, is a very tasty food. The body structure of this creature is no less worthy of naturalists' attention. The head and number and arrangement of the teeth resemble *Arctomys marmotta,* or the marmot; and the front legs, with which it digs underground holes, are also marmot-like. But by her pouch under the belly and near the genital parts, the female of this creature is very like the marsupial *Didelphis opossum.* It further resembles the opossum in rear leg structure and in having a large toe separate from the others and nail-less. Alive, these animals now in Paris are a shade larger than a rabbit.[18]

The creatures, apparently *Vombatus ursinus* of the sort first brought from Bass Strait to Sydney in 1798, had according to Sevast'ianov been entrusted to the zoologist St.-Hilaire Geoffroy (1772–1844); the latter, so Russians were informed, had named it *Fascolonus* and tentatively placed it "between the species of marmot and marsupial." Sevast'ianov's colleagues were referred to Pfaff's and Friedlander's *Die neuesten Entdeckungen französischen Gelehrten* for 1803 (pp. 96, 153).

Among Sevast'ianov's associates with Australasian interests in 1805–10 were two whose approach to François Péron's new collection was by way of taxidermy, then a science in its infancy but one that obviously bore on such exotic creatures as the kangaroo and wombat. These were the Abbé Denis Joseph Manesse (1743–1820) and the Russian naturalist Timofei Bornovolókov. Manesse was the author of perhaps the first serious work on taxidermy, *Traité sur la Manière d'empailler et de conserver les Animaux* (Paris, 1787). Since the French Revolution, he had been living partly in Northern Germany, partly in Russia. The *Traité* was translated into Russian by Sevast'ianov, so giving occasion for his friend Bornovolókov's long discussion of the methods that the abbé had proposed. Bornovolókov's paper, "Regarding Preservation of Stuffed Birds and of Insects," appeared in 1809.[19]

Sevast'ianov himself kept abreast of Australian discovery and zoological news from abroad: his "Report on Lately Published Books" of 1809 (*Tekhnologicheskii zhurnal* 6: pt. 3, pp. 144–51) was only one of several such pieces, but bore immediately on Pacific and Australian zoology. In it, Sevast'ianov surveyed British and French works of zoology published since 1798. One work considered worthy of the Russians' close attention was George Shaw's monthly compilation, *The Naturalist's Miscellany*. It was enlivened by the intermittent Australasian item—an exotic bird, perhaps, or unknown fish, or new marsupial.[20]

In its Russian guise, *Rassuzhdeniia o sposobe nabivki...*, Manesse's guide to taxidermy played a large role in the early Russian effort to preserve at least a portion of the animal collections brought from Sydney in the Russian Fleet's own ships. At least one *Sericulus chrysocephalus,* or Prince Regent bird, and one *Philemon corniculatus,* or noisy friarbird, brought back to Russia from Sydney in *Vostok* in August 1822 were well treated at the Academy of Sciences' laboratory and remain, even today, in good condition (see Plate X). Other specimens of early but efficient taxidermy almost certainly remain among the Australasian drawers of the Ornithological Division of ZIAN (the Zoological Institute of the Soviet Academy of Sciences) in Leningrad.[21]

It will be useful at this juncture to survey the growth of Russia's academic zoological collection in relation to Australian and South Pacific items. The collection had been started, in the first instance, because in 1698 Peter I had bought a motley zoological assemblage from the Dutch during his own Great Embassy; on his second trip to Holland (1716), he topped it up with "an excellent collection of quadrupeds, birds, fish, snakes, and so forth... from the West and East Indies.[22] The seller was a surgeon, Dr. Albert Seva. The following year, another Dutchman, the anatomist Ruish, provided Peter with more insects from the Dutch East Indies—and with grisly anatomical and bottled specimens. Work began on a special building to hold such novelties, the *Kunstkammer,* in 1719. Only months before his death, however, did the tsar order his "Project" for imperial establishment of regular academies of science and of arts (22 January 1724). The building, designed by Domenico Trezzini and replete with library and hall for naturalia, was officially opened on 27 October 1727. Within fifteen years, it held specimens of 479 fish, more than 500 insects, and 1,034 birds. Most were lost in a disastrous fire in 1747.[23]

Deliberate acquisition of Australian specimens began in the late 1770s. From the first these were kept with, and completely overshadowed by, items from Oceania.[24] First-hand Russian collecting in the South Pacific began in 1804 with the arrival of *Nadezhda* and *Neva*. Aboard *Nadezhda* were Georg Heinrich Langsdorf and Wilhelm Gottlieb Tilesius von Tilenau, both efficient natural historians.[25] The latter's diary of 1803–6, now held at the Academy of Sciences' own archive,[26] contains numerous fine drawings of Pacific fauna; Langsdorf brought or sent back to St. Petersburg, in 1805–7, what was certainly the richest zoological collection to have reached it from the mid- and North Pacific until then. Of more importance from the standpoint of Australian zoology, however, was the energetic Langsdorf's recognition of the urgency of building up a programme of exchanges such as Russian botanists had been developing for the past half-century. By exchange with foreign scientists and institutions, he remitted duplicates from the Academy's own stores and so acquired, *inter alia*, 6,000 insects. Both Australian and Indonesian insects were among them, though Pacific specimens were almost lost among the thousands from Brazil, where he himself was Russian consul-general from 1813 to 1829.[27]

The first large zoological collection to reach Russia directly from Sydney in a Russian ship was that brought in *Vostok*. Among the items presented to the Naval Ministry in 1822, we know, were preserved mammals and birds, corals, and shells. Space was already wanting in the Admiralty's own museum so, in 1828–29 or slightly earlier, these items were transferred to the Academy. But the *Kunstkammer*, too, was filling up: many zoological specimens were put in boxes squeezed between display cabinets. By 1830, the need for a new building was being discussed at the official, formal meeting (*konferentsiia*) of the Academy. The necessary moves were made and funds voted in 1832. That year, on the recommendation of Alexander von Humboldt, a youthful professor at Berlin University named F. F. Brandt was named director of the future Zoological Museum.[28]

Fedor Fedorovich Brandt (1802–79), by baptism Johann Friedrich, was a palaeontologist of distinction. Insofar as he interested himself in the Australian fauna in St. Petersburg in the 1840s, it was within that context or that of zoogeography. While he studied the skeletons of small marsupials, two other German specialists lately arrived in Russia, E. Schäder and E. P. Menetrier, worked at the *Kunstkammer* and (after 1832) in the newly built Zoological Museum as "preservers" (taxidermists). Schäder was in 1836 named first curator of that same museum and, with Brandt's encouragement, taught taxidermy to half-a-dozen Russian-born apprentices. These in turn took their skills to Moscow and Dorpat (Tartu) Universities in 1841–44.

Even by 1832, when Brandt left Germany, there was an adequate collection of Australian marsupials, insects, and birds for zoological research within St. Petersburg. Besides the Regent bowerbird and friarbird mentioned already, there were certainly, from Bellingshausen's 1820 Sydney visits, parrots, lories, and assorted other birds.[29] Bellingshausen himself alludes to emus, black and white cockatoos, "New Holland pheasant," "different kinds of kingfishers," "quails, pigeons, sparrows, and many other species."[30] Captain Zavadovskii of *Vostok* shot birds for science as well as for the galley in various parts of the Pacific, New South Wales included. It is clear that among the parrots that reached St. Petersburg alive, in August 1822, were crimson rosellas (*Platycercus elegans* Gmelin). When collected, these had green plumage with a few thin red feathers underneath, that is, they were immature; but in 1822–23, they moulted and grew bright red feathers.[31] As noted, both Pavel Mikhailov and his fellow artist of the ship *Otkrytie*, Emel'ian Korneev, drew several birds whilst in New South Wales. These included "blackbirds of New Holland," ostriches, tufted cockatoos, and a "Van Diemen's goose."[32] It is reasonable to suppose that some, at least, were painted *post mortem*.

By contrast, Mikhailov's rough sketches of kangaroos of 1820 (there are half-a-dozen in the original portfolio now held in the Russian Museum, Leningrad), were certainly of live animals. Some are sitting, others leaping.[33] And certainly the Russians attempted to bring live kangaroos to St. Petersburg in 1820 and on several subsequent occasions. They proved to be awkward passengers: some died of unknown causes, and at least one or two leapt overboard into the waves. (One creature, taken from Sydney by the *Krotkii* in May 1829, caused general grief by *falling* overboard north of the Marshall Islands on 15 June; "it had been a very tranquil and tame animal and entertained us all.")[34]

We know from the diaries of Akhilles Shabel'skii of the *Apollon* and Evgenii Berens of *Krotkii* that animals were deliberately acquired in New South Wales with a view to taking them alive to the authorities in Russia. One creature that demanded to be taken, yet seems not to have reached the Russian capital alive until the sixties, was the duck-billed platypus (*Ornithorhynchus paradoxus*). Both in 1820 and 1822, the Russian visitors were shown the platypus in the vicinity of Sydney, whither colonists had brought them for display. The quadrupeds, wrote Bellingshausen honestly, "have flattened horny snouts which closely resemble a duck's bill, and their fur is rather soft, like a beaver's, whitish underneath."[35] Eighteen months later, Shabel'skii procured no less than four, meaning to carry them to Russia. "Only one of them had spurs, which led me to suppose that, like fowl, the females of the species lack them; but this has yet to be demonstrated."[36] On examination, Shabel'skii found the fur covering his animals' "beaver-like tails" to be rougher than over other parts of their bodies. His reflections on the oddness of the creature and the prevalence of marsupials in Australia point to the general direction of zoological enquiry in Russia in that period:

At present, we know only of the kangaroo, opossum, different sorts of rat, and the native dingo. The females of all these save the last, which might be regarded as having come from some past shipwreck, show a striking degree of conformity in their body organism, all possessing pouches. This lack of variety among the Australian animals, and the very conformity of their organisms, might lead us to suppose that insufficient time has yet passed for the species in question to have become more varied in form.[37]

Shabel'skii was no zoologist, but he did have an eye for scientifically suggestive information and was civilly received by the pastoralist-scientist Sir John Jamison, who told him interesting things about the emu. ("The emu's movements are said to indicate the state of the atmosphere, the bird growing more active and nervous as wind begins to rise and a storm is thus heralded.") Emu bones were in St. Petersburg by 1825.

Many early Russian visitors to New South Wales were impressed by the brilliantly hued and unfamiliar (to them) species of fish in coastal waters. Both Korneev and Mikhailov painted such fish while at Sydney. The former's major study was of an almost circular porcupine fish, a pelagic creature of the family Molidae. Mikhailov appears to have painted five fish caught in Port Jackson. The original watercolour study is on sheet 29047/47 of the Leningrad portfolio, where it is headed "Exocet volant." The upper half is light blue, the lower half golden, the tail tip is red, and the "wing" end is almost black. The second Sydney fish, also on 29047/47, is a yellow-finned leatherjacket (*Cantherines trachylepsis*). It has likewise been published, and was described by the artist as "Leatherjacket fish from Port Jackson." It has the expected brown body with blue dots around the edges, and corn-coloured fins and gills. The original measures 16 × 5 cm (a 4-cm-long sword being suggestive of a tiny pike).

Unpublished studies of fish by Mikhailov include a large grey "skate" or ray (No. 29046/46), 37 cm broad, shown from top and below; a "Corifeno," light blue in colour, with spiky back (obverse of the same sheet); and, below it, "*Osphronemus*: fish shown in life-size, Port Jackson, Sydney Town." This last is deep blue, 28 cm long, 2–3 cm across, and with a 5-cm sword. Mikhailov's "Corifeno" is a member of the family Coryphaenidaie, (*Coryphaena hippurus* Linn.): identification may be attempted, very cautiously, on the basis of published works by Cuvier and Valenciennes (*Histoire naturelle des Poissons*, vol. 9, 1833) and, in the first instance, by Allan R. McCulloch (*Check-List of the Fishes Recorded from Australia* [Sydney, 1929–30], pp. 194–95).

The Russian material has value in the context of the study of fish population movement and ecology. It is viewed in that light by Soviet ichthyologists, notably the research unit at the Academy of Sciences' Institute of Oceanography (23 Krasikova, Moscow) headed by Professor N. V. Parin.[38]

With regard to provenance, the Russian narratives offer no data, but the internal ordering of Mikhailov's original portfolio is reassuring. The fish illustrations immediately follow sheet No. 29045/45, which is explicitly headed "The Entrance to Port Jackson, 30 March 1820, from Five Italian Miles." That drawing, which has yet to be published, measures 37 cm by 11 cm and clearly shows Macquarie's Lighthouse on the South Head. It would seem to follow that the ray, *Coryphaena*, and perhaps other fish also were painted during *Vostok*'s first visit to Sydney, that is, in southern autumn.

BOTANY

Russian botanists led other scientists by ten or fifteen years in their knowledge of those products of Australia that fell within their field of interest: seeds, leaves, dried plants intended for herbaria, and living plants brought from Australia in British ships. That Russian science should have been alert and welcoming to such botanical arrivals from the island-continent that Cook found is best explained in terms of Russian continental exploration of the eighteenth century. For fifty years, when members of St. Petersburg's Academy of Sciences woke to the possibility and value of obtaining dried plant samples from Australia by barter with associates abroad if not by outright purchase, Russian botany had been developing under the impetus of expeditions to the Urals and beyond, into Siberia. It is, as Soviets are wont to say, "no accident" that most distinguished botany in eighteenth-century and fast-expanding Russia was the work of travellers who saw the flora of Siberia and other distant fringes of the empire *in situ*: Stepan P. Krashennikov (1711–55), explorer of Kamchatka and author of the seminal *Description of the Land of Kamchatka* (1751) and *Flora of Ingria* (1761); Johann Georg Gmelin (1709–55), who passed almost a decade in Southern Siberia with Captain Vitus Bering's second Kamchatka Expedition (1733–42) and published *The Flora of Siberia* (1747–69; 4 vols.); Peter Simon Pallas (1741–1811), leader of the Academy's own Siberian Expedition of 1768–74, collector, and author of *The Flora of Russia* (1784–88). Such men had special reason to appreciate the massive contribution made to global botany by Linnaeus, the Swedish classifier, and to praise the plant classification undertaken in more recent years by his followers—Lamarck, the Jussieu brothers, Adanson. For them as pioneer botanists in the remote Northeast and East, in the Altai, and on the borders of Mongolia, discoveries of unknown plants were almost commonplace. And from the first, their basic classifying efforts were accompanied by simple plant morphology and anatomy. Perhaps cytology still lay on the horizon, for want of instruments to study plant cell structure; nor was embryology attemptable, certainly not by individuals whom expeditionary living taxed and worried half to death hundreds of miles from the nearest Russian town.[1] What is pertinent, however, is that field work in areas whose flora was unknown at least to European botany disposed the Russians—and the Germans in their midst, whose foreign links proved highly serviceable in obtaining wanted specimens from Germany or France—to concentrate on plant morphology and classifying problems. Parallel with this ran an awareness of general questions of botany. Thus, in his *Theory of Generation* (1759), the Russian naturalist K. F. Vol'f described the process of development of organs in plants and their occasional transformation into others. Such ideas, which again predisposed their holders to consider whatever Australian plants came to hand by the 1770s and 80s, deeply interested the poet Goethe, whose book *The Metamorphosis of Plants* appeared in 1790. In sum, the preceding conditions and development of Russian botany made it likely that, in the 1780s, Australian flora would be studied with much seriousness by men anxious to "place" them. The German antecedents and professional connections of such men as Gmelin, Pallas, and Karl Friedrich Ledebur, director of the Dorpat Botanical Garden by 1805, paled in scientific importance by comparison with those of the two botanical Fischers in Russia in the early 1800s—Ferdinand or Fedor Bogdanovich (1780–1854), director of Count Razumóvskii's botanical gardens at Górenki till 1823, when he moved to St. Petersburg, and Aleksandr Grigor'evich Fisher, or Fischer von Waldheim (1803–84), his counterpart in Moscow.[2] Fedor Bogdanovich, especially, was to be instrumental in the Russians' acquisition of a first-rate representative collection of Australian flowers and plants by 1830. His Australian collection was indeed, with that of Karl Friedrich von Ledebur, to form the basis of today's collection at the Institute of Botany (Higher Plants Division) of the Soviet Academy of Sciences in Leningrad. Once more, the Russians were the major beneficiaries of Russo-German academic links, of which exchange-and-barter, steady correspondence, and connected scientific publications were but three of many facets in the period from 1775 to 1860.[3]

The first significant botanical garden in Russia was the so-called Apothecary's or Pharmaceutical Garden, laid out in St. Petersburg in 1714 on the orders of Peter the Great. Its significance, however, was relative merely to the preceding botanical darkness and ignorance.[4] As late as 1819, it held only 1,500 living plants and was allocated the inadequate annual budget of 12,000 roubles. Dramatic changes occurred in 1823, the year of the establishment of the Imperial Botanical Garden in St. Petersburg. Suddenly, huge sums of money became available. Plant collections were purchased from private and other sources. And Ferdinand Ernst Ludwig Fischer was enticed from Górenki as first director.[5]

Born at Halberstadt in Prussia, Fischer had studied at Halle before coming to Russia and so had come into contact with the Forsters and Pacific botany. Even before becoming adjunct professor of botany at Moscow University in 1812, a time of national stress and European crisis, he had bound himself to Russian and, indeed, Pacific science by collaborating fruitfully with Georg Heinrich Langsdorf, lately naturalist in *Nadezhda*.[6] His important contributions to the latter's *Plantes receuillies pendant le Voyage des Russes autour du Monde* (Tübingen, 1810) not only brought his name before a wider European readership but, more importantly within the Australasian context, turned his thoughts towards the South Pacific Ocean.[7]

Expansion of the Imperial Botanical Garden in 1823–25 was complemented by a parallel and necessary growth of the St. Petersburg herbarium. The adequate description of all flora being grounded in herbaria, renewed efforts were made at the same time to fill in gaps in such assemblages of dried flowers from Australasia as had earlier been purchased for St. Petersburg.[8] And this, in turn, led to more systematic storage of collections and to the use of duplicates in barter programmes. By the later 1820s there were regular botanical exchanges (for herbaria) between St. Petersburg and all the major institutes, societies, and gardens of Great Britain, France, and Germany.

Until 1856, unfortunately, no adequately precise records were kept of the accessions of various new collections to the St Petersburg herbarium. It is therefore impossible to say exactly how, when, or in what quantities of specimens or plant species those collections arrived. . . . A manuscript does survive however with the title, "Bestand des Herbariums des Kaiserlichen Botanischen Gartens in St-Petersburg am Ersten September 1856." And by its title-page, one can see that at that time the herbarium consisted of four basic subcollections: those of Fischer himself, Mertens, Schräder, and Schumacher. These in turn had been built up from a greater number of smaller component collections.[9]

Fischer's own collection, we know, was of some 60,000 specimens. It was deposited with the government shortly after his death in 1854 and remains in BIN (Botaniches-kii Institut, or the V. L. Komarov Botanical Institute of the Academy of Sciences of the USSR), which also holds the original and a subsequent catalogue, *Index Herbarii Proprii Fischer, 1806–1826*. Like Mertens's, it contains several hundred Australian dried flowers. A number were examined in Sydney and re-identified in 1978 by D. J. McGillivray of the National Herbarium of New South Wales.[11] The richest of the four base collections for Pacific botany at large, however, is unquestionably that bequeathed by Dr. Karl-Heinrich Mertens (1796–1830).

Mertens had already travelled widely in the cause of botany when he received an invitation from the Russian Admiralty to accompany Captain-Lieutenant Bellingshausen to the South Pacific Ocean and Antarctica aboard the sloop *Vostok* (1819).[12] His father, Pastor Franz-Karl Mertens, and particularly Johann Reinhold Forster, who had both studied and taught at Halle, where the younger Mertens also went in 1817, had made it natural for students of that university to look abroad for new botanical horizons. Karl-Heinrich went first to England. From the University of Halle, which, as we have seen, was also Fischer's alma mater, he applied to be included in a Russian expedition to the North and South Pacific.[13] His request was granted but, retrettably for Australasian studies generally, he missed the boat: detained inland in June 1819, he could not keep his rendezvous with Bellingshausen and *Vostok* at Copenhagen, as had had been arranged with the imperial authorities. Not until 1821 did he finally arrive in the Pacific with another major scientific venture, that of Captain Ferdinand Petrovich Lütke in the Russian sloop *Seviavin*.[14] Lütke's work was in the North and chiefly focused on the Eastern Carolines. That fact is echoed in the final composition of the Mertens (and associated Lütke-linked) herbaria. Nevertheless, Australian and other Southern plants are represented in the large Mertens collection, for, like Fischer, he bartered and exchanged plant specimens throughout his academic life.

What, then, *can* be determined of the earlier accessions of Australian ("New Holland") specimens in the Imperial collection? In effect, all that is needed by the history of science, thanks essentially to the survival in the modern BIN collection of the labels (*etiketki*) that accompany all specimens within a given "species folder." Happily, all nineteenth-century descriptions of specific specimens, that is, all labels, have been kept. Many have once or twice been annotated, giving details of provenance, for instance, or of nomenclature change. All have been pasted by the Soviet authorities on large, stiff cardboard sheets.

Here are details of the 77 specimens of plant that reached St. Petersburg from Sydney in the sloop *Vostok* in 1822. Brief comments on the families or species represented in that naval offering to Russian botanists are also made here. Suffice it to observethat the herbarium was promptly handed over to the specialists at hand: Ferdinand Fischer and the Vilno-based zoologist and botanist Eduard Ivanovich

Eikhval'd (1795–1876).[15] In the course of a visit to BIN in 1985, the present writer established the modern folder numbers corresponding to 31 of the 77 Australian plant specimens obtained by Bellingshausen's people in 1820. They follow below. The second figure is the 1830 enumeration, as given in Bellingshausen's *Voyage*.

1	1	*Banksia serrata* (honeysuckle)	2068
2	2	*Hakea gibbosa* (wooden cherry)	2047
3	3	*Pimelea rosea* (rice-flower)	5467
4	6	*Tetratheca ericifolia*	4272
5	8	*Casuarina torulosa* (she-oak)	1855
6	10	*Acacia verticillata*	3446
7	11	*Boronia serrulata* (native rose)	4017
8	12	*Grevillea sericea* (silky oak)	2045
9	14	*Platylobium formosum* (flat pea)	3648
10	15	*Kennedya monophylla* (beanflower)	3868
11	19	*Lomatia silaifolia* (holly)	2063
12	22	*Dillignia pungens* (Dillenia)	5106
13	23	*Boronia rubioides*	4013
14	24	*Banksia oblongifolia* (honeysuckle)	2068
15	26	*Correa speciosa* (Austr. fuchsia)	4031
16	28	*Pultenea* (wallflower)	3636
17	53	*Conosperma conferta*	2040
18	54	*Acacia linifolia* (sally)	3446
19	55	*Lysinema pungens*	6258
20	56	*Styphelia tubiflora* (five-corners)	6262
21	60	*Dodonea latifolia* (native hop)	4831
22	61	*Buddleya carpodetus* (cabbage-tree)	6473
23	63	*Leptospermum ambiguum* (myrtle)	5599
24	64	*Melaleuca ericifolia* (swamp teatree)	5603
25	65	*Viminaria denudata* (rush-broom)	3632
26	66	*Aster tomentosus*	8900
27	69	*Gompholobium grandiflorum*	3628
28	70	*Billardiera longiflora* (appleberry)	3258
29	71	*Eucalyptus resinifera* (red gum)	5598
30	72	*Hypericum* (St. John's wort)	5168
31	73	*Gnaphalium repens*	8992

We know from Bellingshausen's comment in the *Voyage* (11:349, by the 1945 Debenham edition) that Nos. 21–30 inclusive of the above collection were taken, with Lachlan Macquarie's and his able gardener's permission, from the Governor's own garden, Parramatta. Bellingshausen also observed in passing that many or all specimens were stored in duplicate ("I kept some of each species"). This seems to apply to the entire collection of 77.

Examination of the aforementioned "species folders," now held in dark, room-height cupboards at the V. L. Komarov Botanical Institute's Division of Higher

Plants (Herbarium) Floor 2, revealed the anticipated labels. Beneath *one* specimen in each of the 31 folders in question (a folder may hold more than 20 specimens of a given flower type), was glued a label of the sort illustrated: Plate 30. It typically reads (as for Folder 2063: *Lomatia silaifolia* Robt. Brown): "From New Holland, Captain Commander F. F. Bellingshausen. 1823. N. V. Timianskii." Thus, the specimen of Australian holly was in the Imperial Botanical Garden's herbarium by 1823, having briefly been held by the Naval Ministry, to which Bellingshausen had presented it on his return to Kronstadt; was at once identified on the basis of *Prodromus Florae Novae Hollandiae* (London, 1810) by the eminent botanist and traveller Robert Brown (1773–1858), a man much respected by Fischer; and was subsequently in the possession of the private collector and botanist from Kazan', Nikolai V. Timianskii. The latter's name appears on all plants seen by the present writer which reached Russia aboard *Vostok* in 1822. From this circumstance, it appears to follow that Timianskii, a friend of the better-known botanist Karl Fuchs,[16] obtained much or all of Bellingshausen's Sydney collection from Fischer and that, on his death, the specimens reverted to the Imperial Botanical Garden's herbarium.[17] It was certainly common enough, in that period, for officials in state employ and especially for scientists at the Academy of Sciences to sell material for personal advantage. And, as seen, Fischer's collection remained—in his own sight and in that of his subordinates—distinct from that of the Imperial herbarium and yet a crucial element therein throughout his life. Another possibility is that, on Fischer's death, part of his huge herbarium was purchased by Timianskii, whose own death followed thirty-two years later, thereby signalling the fortunate return of the Sydney flora. It is plain, at all events, that many specimens collected by the visitors of 1820 were beyond official reach for many years. In his listing of accessions to St. Petersburg's herbarium from 1823 to 1908, V. Lipskii writes, in enigmatic vein: "Bellingshausen, Australia one packet received, in 1886."[18]

More important for the history of botany in Russia than the full elucidation of such minor mysteries is what such labels *also* tell, about the provenance of plants *like* those that Bellingshausen brought. In this respect, indeed, the 1820–30 listing is a valuable one, pointing to species from Australia that had perhaps been represented in St. Petersburg still earlier. Folder 2045 (*Grevillea sericea*) may serve to illustrate that usefulness to the historian of science and the modern plant ecologist alike.

Folder 2045 is, in fact, a file containing five folders, all full of specimens of silky oak. The specimens are not arranged in order of chronological accession. Nonetheless, it is a simple task to find material that antedates the 1820 "Bellingshausen" specimen, and so identify the sources by the labels. One specimen, for instance, was presented to the Russians by one Biquelin in 1812; the label reads, in part, "*Embothrium sericeum* Smith Nov. Holl, I: p. 25, tab. 9 . . . *Ex tepidariis suis dedit Biquelin Horticul.* 14 Avril 1812." An earlier specimen, described by the same hand (and apparently therefore after 1856) as *Embothrium sericeum* var. Willd., had been sent in 1801 from the garden of D. Koenig, a botanist then based in Halle. Even by the later eighteenth century, many Australian (and other Southern) plants were being grown by British, French, and German botanists. Koenig was one.[19] In this instance, however, he had not, despite the reference to "garden" on the label that survives, grown it himself. The sample had originated in the better-known herbarium of Johann Friedrich Pott (1738–1805).[20] Another specimen of silky oak is even more evocative of that immense network of scientific contacts of the early 1800s that brought Fischer and St. Petersburg directly into focus for the likes of Biquelin and Dr. Pott. It is, according to the label, *"Ex Coll.* Robt. Brown, *Iter. Austr.,* 1802–1805,"* and originated in the herbarium of the Royal Botanic Garden, Edinburgh. Brown, whose botanizing from Flinders's *Investigator* and *Porpoise* in 1802–5 had brought him European fame, was known to Fischer and indeed to Russian botany in two capacities: as author of *Prodromus* (1810) and as clerk and chief librarian first at the Linnaean Society (1805–10), then for Sir Joseph Banks (1810–20).[21] He was a much respected Scot. Fischer had personally taken interest in Brown's support for Antoine Jussieu's "natural system" of plant classification as against Linnaeus's rigid practice. It was certainly the case that that support had brought a welcome breath of life and controversy to the whole science of botany in 1810–12. As for Brown's splendid appendix to Flinders's own *Voyage to Terra Australis* (1814), "General Remarks, Geographical and Systematical, on the Botany of Terra Australis," it was recognized in Russia as the basis of the discipline of plant geography. Thus, plant geography had been connected from the first, in Russian scientific circles, with Australia.[22]

Of the many other specimens of *Grevillea sericea* held in Folder 2045 at BIN, suffice it to mention five: those sent by Karl Friedrich von Ledebur (1785–1851; professor of botany at the University of Dorpat from 1811 to 1836), by the explorer and colonial botanist Allan Cunningham, by the Frenchman Verreaux in 1844, and by Mossman of Sydney in 1850; and that grown in the Imperial Botanical Garden's own grounds in 1835–36. Ledebur's contribution had been obtained from the herbarium of the Musée de Paris. Cunningham's perhaps reached St. Petersburg direct, but possibly through a third party: he had, like his patron, Governor Lachlan Macquarie, long-term and generally pleasant connections with Russian and Russified Germans. En route to Sydney as a younger man, he had spent two years in South America and greatly benefitted from the hospitality and aid of Georg Heinrich Langsdorf, then the Russian consul-general. Bearing this in mind, he willingly assisted Dr. Fedor Shtein of the *Otkrytie* in 1820, accompanying him and the artist Emel'ian Korneev on a hike into the Blue Mountains (King's Table Land) from Sydney.[23] As was seen (Chapter Four), that hike of March 1820 yielded botanical as well as zoological and geological material for the St. Petersburg Academy of Sciences. If necessary, Cunningham even told Sir Joseph Banks, he would defray the costs of the entire outing from his own pocket. The Russians had a right to his assistance.[24] It is reasonable to assume that when the latter called on him on 6 March, Shtein took a good look at the 410 or so plant specimens that he had lately brought, at great cost to his health and strength, from Admiralty Gulf.[25] (When Shtein showed up, he was preparing a report and specimens for Kew.) Perhaps the Russians were not given specimens as gifts on that occasion, but it is apparent from the BIN records themselves that Cunningham did send flowers to Russia and that other specimens arrived circuitously. Cunningham's compatriot and fellow colonial botanist Charles M. Frazer (1788–1831), we may note in this connection, did provide visiting Russians with Australian plant specimens in 1822 and very probably in 1820 also. Akhilles P. Shabel'skii of the armed sloop *Apollon*, visiting Sydney in the cool winter of 1822, spent hours in Frazer's company at Farm Cove and did not leave empty-handed.[26] V. I. Lipskii's history of the St. Petersburg herbarium throws light on certain subsequent accessions of Australian and South American material, originally sent by Cunningham to Kew Gardens in London, which were evidently purchased by the Russians. In 1872, for instance, 105 packets of *Hakea gibbosa* (wooden cherry shrub), "collected by Cunningham in South America," went from Kew to the Russian herbarium. Very likely, most Cunningham specimens from Australia arrived there after his death in 1839. Some had been in Fischer's own collection in the later 1840s when, as labels now in BIN's Folder 2047 indicate, additional specimens of wooden cherry leaves and seeds arrived from M. Verreaux of Paris. As was usual throughout the nineteenth century, some went to the St. Petersburg herbarium itself, others to the Academy of Sciences' Botanical Museum. It is to the merging in 1931 of those two institutions that BIN owes the immense richness and scope of its herbarium today.

Examination of other herbarium folders containing, *inter alia,* Australian specimens "from New Holland: Captain-Commander F. F. Bellingshausen. N. V. Timianskii," quickly reveals other facets of international botanical exchange during the Napoleonic period. Folder 2063, for instance, holding *Lomatia silaifolia* (Australian holly), has a specimen from Robert Brown of 1805; another from the Jardin de la Malmaison of 1808 (acquired by Mertens and referred to by him as *Protea anemonefolia*); a third from Ledebur; and a fourth from Samuel Mossman, "gathered on the Botany marshes." Others again arrived from "Mr. Schomburg of Adelaide" and from the Imperial Botanical Garden itself (having prospered there in 1865–67). Among the specimens of honeysuckle (*Banksia serata*) in Folder 2068 are one from Bellingshausen, three or four from Fischer, and another from the Paris botanist, Jacques Etienne Gay (1786–1864). The label is suggestive: "Herb. J. Gay, *ex tedipariis celsianis attulit Hardy,* Octobre 1816." The year 1817 saw the acquisition of *Eucalyptus resinifera* specimens (Folder 5598) "from the Governor's Garden" (Parramatta). They joined others from Sydney "sent in Sept. 1809." Next year, 1818, Mertens provided, *inter alia,* specimens of *Billardiera longiflora* (Folder 3258). Few years passed thereafter without the arrival, generally from some European source, of at least one further packet of Australian material.

Thanks partly to Fischer's and Mertens's efforts, but more fundamentally to the scope and efficiency of international scholarly exchanges of botanical material by 1810, St. Petersburg was well abreast of new developments in the study of Australian and other Southern flora. It remains merely to emphasize the quantity of specimens from New South Wales and Van Diemen's Land especially that were available to Russian botanists yet earlier, as a result of such exchanges. Johann Friedrich Pott and Daniel Koenig have been mentioned as suppliers of Australian material in 1801; but other men are equally deserving of attention by the student of Australian, botanical, and European science. Australian flora reached St. Petersburg in 1801 or earlier from Dietrich(?) Bierbaum (specimens of *Kennedya monophylla*, then known as *Glycine binaculata* Don.); (Johann) George (Adam) Forster (1754–94); Anders Sparrmann (1748–1820), Captain Cook's Swedish savant of the Second Voyage; and Jacques

Julien de Labillardière (1755–1834), who had visited Australia with d'Entrecasteaux in 1791–93. The Tasmanian material obtained by St. Petersburg from Labillardière was in all probability in the herbarium that was forwarded to Joseph Banks in London while the collector himself was a prisoner of the Dutch in Java (1793–95) and which Banks thereafter released to him. Australian botanical specimens from eighteenth-century (and later) collectors were acquired in considerable number in the early 1800s by the botanist Christian Steven (1781–1863). Steven encouraged large-scale exchanges with foreign institutions, and he himself exchanged specimens, including Australian ones, with the Forsters, Daniel Solander (of Cook's *Endeavour*), Robert Brown, and Fedor Fischer of St. Petersburg.[27]

Appendix B

NOTES ON SOVIET AND OTHER ARCHIVAL SOURCES

A NOTE ON SOVIET ARCHIVAL SOURCES AND RESEARCH RELATING
TO THE EARLY RUSSIAN PRESENCE IN AUSTRALIA

Bibliographies and adequate descriptions of the holdings of the main Soviet archives are the indispensable foundations for research by Soviet or foreign scholars in any area of nineteenth-century Pacific history. Soviet historians have long been competently served in this regard. Since Stalin's death in 1953, several hundred such descriptive works and papers have appeared. Many are referred to by P. Kennedy Grimsted in her survey of 1972 (see Bibliography). Those items listed here are particularly useful in the context of research into New Holland and the early Russian circumnavigation of the globe that led to Anglo-Russian dealings in Port Jackson.

Conscious of Western interest in Soviet archival holdings, G. A. Belov, then Director of the Main Archival Administration of the Council of Ministers of the USSR (Glavnoe Arkhivnoe Upravlenie), in 1964 published an English-language survey of their organization as it stood in 1960. His paper, "The Organization of the Archive System in the USSR," appeared in *Archives,* 7 (October 1964): 211–22. An Italian variant also appeared, as "L'Organizzazione degli Archivi nell'URSS," in *Rassegna degli Archivi di Stato,* 24 (1964): no. 1, pp. 23–42. Soviet scholars themselves, however, already had a far more detailed coverage of the subject, and a comprehensive bibliography of Soviet books and articles on the topic, in *Katalog arkhivovedcheskoi literatury, 1917–1959 (A Catalogue of Literature in Archive Studies, 1917–1959)* (M., 1959). The first of several supplements had also appeared, in 1963. Dr. Belov and his successors at Glavnoe Arkhivnoe Upravlenie were as willing to assist foreign scholars to locate materials in particular State Archives, and to place requests for copies thereof, as political conditions would allow. (Requests from abroad were addressed to: The Director, *Direction Générale des Archives d'Etat de l'URSS,* 17 Bol'skaia Pirogovskaia, Moscow 119435. And so they are today.) But already Soviet researchers enjoyed a great advantage over non-Soviet workers, who depended on such sound but general handbooks as Belov's and A. I. Loginova's

Gosudarstvennye arkhivy Soiuza SSR: kratkii spravochnik (The State Archives of the USSR: A Brief Guide) (M., 1956), and were far from the materials themselves.

Even in the late Stalinist period, politically innocuous work in "All-Union" archives resulted in articles that were of incidental value to Pacific naval history. The Georgian scholar V. Z. Dzhincharadze, for example, in 1950 published his "Obzor fonda Vorontsovykh, khraniashchegosia v TsGADA" ("Survey of the Vorontsovs' Collection Held at TsGADA") in *Istoricheskie zapiski,* 32: 242–68. Among the 14,800 items in that huge family *fond* (No. 1261) were several bearing on Semen R. Vorontsov's activities in London where, in 1797, he assisted Kruzenshtern and Lisianskii on their way to the East Indies, and others bearing on the work of his brother Aleksandr (1741–1805) as minister of commerce with Pacific interests. The year 1950 also saw the publication by TsGAVMF of A. I. Solov'ev's edition of Aleksei P. Lazarev's *Zapiski,* pp. 148–54 of which dealt with the 1820 visit to Port Jackson of *Blagonamerennyi.* Others too, including A. I. Andreev and V. Sementovskii (see Bibliography), found it safe enough to publish in the late Stalinist period, making much use of Navy manuscript material that bore directly on New Zealand and Australia. It will be recognized, nevertheless, that the "first" and "second thaws" (1953–57 and 1961–64) changed the positions and perspectives of such men. Scholars like the military historian L. G. Beskrovnyi published different material and, more importantly, with less immediate regard to Party dictates. Chauvinism also lessened in intensity. Of works published during the "first thaw" that aided students of Pacific naval questions and were grounded in archival documents, suffice it to mention two: Beskrovnyi's *Ocherki po istochnikovedeniiu voennoi istorii Rossii (Essays in the Study of Sources for Russia's Military History)* (M., 1957), and the first-ever description of the holdings of VIMAIV, A. P. Lebedianskaia and E. V. Rozenbetskaia's *Putevoditel' po istoricheskomu arkhivu muzeia* (L., Artilleriiskii Muzei, 1957). Beskrovnyi, the pre-eminent Soviet student of pre-Revolutionary naval sources, made mention of dozens of documents at TsGADA never used in scholarly works. The guide to the youthful Military History Museum of Artillery revealed the presence in Leningrad of Bellingshausen MSS, of which there are so few extant and catalogued. Other Soviet scholars publishing in these post-Stalinist years on Russian enterprise in the Pacific and Antarctic were L. S. Berg, N. Ia. Bolotnikov, B. N. Vishnevskii, and V. A. Divin. Nineteenth-century Pacific history had, in the dark Stalinist context, been a relatively safe and peaceful haven for professional historians and bibliographers. So much is evident from a consideration of the works by S. B. Okun', L. S. Berg, A. D. Dobrovol'skii, O. A. Evteev, V. F. Gnucheva, V. V. Nevskii, B. G. Ostrovskii, V. S. Lupach, and others, all using archival material, that were published between 1948 and 1953 (see Bibliography). That very fact, together with the growth of archive-grounded publication on Pacific naval matters in the period immediately following, put younger Soviet researchers in an excellent position by the early 1960s and invigorated old "Pacific hands" like Ia. M. Svet, a Cook authority who had survived in Stalin's kitchen, and the "Northern Sea Route" writer, M. I. Belov.

Major bibliographies and guides to primary materials of use to students of the early Russian voyages around the world came during the "second thaw," though preparations had perhaps begun by 1960. One was a two-volume directory to personal or family papers held in State Repositories: *Lichnye archivnye fondy v Gosudarstven-nykh khranilishchakh SSSR: ukazatel'* (*Personal Archival Collections in the State Repositories of the USSR: A Guide*), compiled by E. V. Kolosova, A. A. Khodak, *et al*. (M., 1962–63). Another was the essential guide to the literary *fonds* of TsGALI, N. B. Volkov's and R. D. Voliak's *Tsentral'nyi gosudarstvennyi arkhiv Literatury i Iskusstva SSSR: putevoditel': literatura* (M., 1963). In the former were specific ref-erences to MSS of half-a-dozen early Russian visitors to Australasia, including Hagemeister, Unkovskii, I. P. Butenev, and I. M. Simonov. In the latter were allu-sions to TsGALI's fair copy of the Lisianskii journal (1793–1800), which, as seen, dealt with that officer's Pacific and Australian awareness and, in a broader sense, with Anglo-Russian maritime entente. A third volume of *Lichnye . . . fondy* appeared in 1977, likewise listing *fonds* alphabetically according to family names of former owners and referring to a score of minor archives. All three volumes have retained their usefulness up to the present. A typical entry, "The Vorontsovs," covering ma-terials by Semen and Aleksandr Romanovich among other family members, leads the researcher to four institutions: TsGADA, ORGPB, the State Historical Museum in Moscow (GIM), and the Leningrad Division of the Institute of History of the Acad-emy of Science (LOII). In conjunction with the 1963 and 1967 supplements to *Katalog arkhivovedcheskoi literatury, 1917–59* and earlier reference works, such books fired the interest of many Soviet researchers (1963–68).

These researchers had interests in areas that brought them into contact with materi-als on Russian visits to Australia: ethnography in the Pacific; South American history and ethnohistory; traditional earlier post-contact Hawaii; and the history of illustra-tive art. It is important to appreciate that none was focusing on Australasia. As Patricia Polansky's bibliography of *Russian Writings on the South Pacific* (Honolulu, 1974; pp. 35–60) plainly shows, numerous articles and monographs were being pub-lished in the sixties (as before) on the economy, the socio-political shortcomings, the toponymy, communications systems, foreign policy, and agriculture of Australia. And Soviet ethnologists, including Nikolai A. Butinov and his wife Mariia Sergeevna, Vladimir R. Kabo, and Iulia M. Likhtenberg, were writing frequently on Aboriginal material and social culture. What is curious, in retrospect, is the fact that even anthropologists paid little, if any, heed to the data that their countrymen had gathered on the spot. Preoccupied with theory and classifying problems, even Likhtenberg—who had been trained before the 1917 Bolshevik coup—and the Butinovs took a look at the Australian collections then at MAE, but overlooked im-portant manuscript materials. In short, those primary materials relating to Australia which, taken from the main Soviet archives, *were* presented to the public in the six-ties, were presented incidentally and in a quite different academic context. Insofar as leading Soviet historians (or even anthropologists) were interested in the South Pa-cific Ocean and Australia at all, it was in modern rather than in earlier colonial Aus-tralia. Still, as we have observed, naval historians, ethnologists, and others who had access to the archives and research tools mentioned above did periodically, in passing or in footnotes, draw attention to materials relating to the early Russian presence in that country.

Boris G. Ostrovskii was one of many scholars involved, in 1948–51, in the preparation of works devoted to the Bellingshausen-Lazarev Antarctic Expedition of 1819–21, in which the USSR had just acquired a heightened political interest. Others caught up in the same process, which had to do with Antarctic territorial claims and with an international conference of 1949, were A. I. Andreev and V. N. Sementovskii, editors of primary materials on Bellingshausen's venture (see Bibliography). Moscow's concerns ever affecting the provincial centres, I. N. Aleksandrov of Kazan's Pedagogical Institute was one of many hundred persons also working in the area in 1949. His paper on Kazan's own representative in Bellingshausen's expedition, I. M. Simonov, appeared in the spring of 1950 (see Bibliography). TsGAVMF provided research facilities and assistants for Andreev's and Sementovskii's projects. Ostrovskii made excellent use of these. He was in any case, like Andreev, well acquainted with the outline of the Bellingshausen-Lazarev Antarctic expedition. As A. I. Solov'ev put it in 1950, introducing A. P. Lazarev's *Zapiski* (p. 5), Bellingshausen's triumphant voyage—well described in several accounts—eclipsed the Vasil'ev-Shishmarev venture, certainly; but even of that expedition, there were "brief reports... in a series of articles in *Severnyi arkhiv* from 1822 onward, in *Otechestvennye zapiski* for 1822, in V. N. Berkh's book, *Chronological History of all Journeys to the Arctic Lands,* 1823, Pt. 1, in *Syn Otechestva* for 1830 and 1850, in *Moskvitianin,* and in the journal of the Ministry of Public Education." Like the groups working with Solov'ev, Sementovskii, and Andreev, all in contact with TsGAVMF's working staff, led by A. A. Samarov (who was himself by 1951 collecting primary material for his edition of *Russkie flotovodtsy: M. P. Lazarev*), Ostrovskii also recognized the likelihood that fresh materials relating to the double polar venture would be found. Aleksei P. Lazarev's account, with its important "Sydney section," had not actually been *discovered* in the forties, it was true: Solov'ev, its editor, was one of many scholars who had read D. I. Abramovich's *Katalog sobraniia rukopisei Professora I. V. Pomialovskago (A Catalogue to the Manuscript Collection of Professor I. V. Pomialovskii...)* (St. P., 1914), with its allusions to the Lazarev materials in ORGPB (as that great library was called by 1920). But some genuine discoveries were being made in Leningrad and in the provinces. In Suzdal', a manuscript had come to light that proved to be a journal kept, in 1819–22, by Leading Seaman Egor' Kiselev of the *Vostok*. It had its little "Sydney section" and appeared, in regrettably "improved" and poorly edited condition, in the travel journal *Round the World* (*Vokrug Sveta*) (1941: no. 4, pp. 40–43. Aware that the manuscript deserved more careful treatment, the authorities at GAU entrusted it to A. I. Andreev. It was included in Andreev's compilation *Plavanie shliupov "Vostok" i "Mirnyi" v Antarktiku* (*Voyage of the Sloops "Vostok" and "Mirnyi" to Antarctica...*) (M., 199). Ostrovskii's researches, like Andreev's own, centred on Leningrad. In 1949, he published a provocative short paper, "O pozabytykh istochnikakh..." ("On Forgotten Sources for, and Participants in, the Bellingshausen-Lazarev Antarctic Expedition"), *IVGO*, vol. 81, pt. 2.

The works and articles of Ostrovskii, Andreev, Sementovskii, Samarov, Okun', Solov'ev, and their associates in 1949–53 stirred interest not only in the Bellingshausen venture in Antarctica but also in the riches still unmined in Central State (and other) Archives of the USSR. And once again, ethnohistorians, ethnologists, and polar specialists turned up materials, both manuscript and printed, that related incidentally and partially to New South Wales. After all, the naval journal, log, or letterbook connected with a voyage round the world or with the scientific-polar enterprises of Vasil'ev's and Bellingshausen's ships (1819–22) was of as much potential value to Australian or Polynesian studies as Alaskan ones. Perforce, the student of the early Russian presence in the South Pacific Ocean takes an interest in Soviet research into the Company's and Navy's Northern (Arctic and American) involvements of the early 1800s, into problems of provisionment and international trade, and into Bellingshausen's routes and observations round the fringes of Antarctica. Typical of papers by ethnologists and cultural historians of post-Stalinist years who could build on the research of older scholars, synthesizing and advancing on the basis of materials at TsGAVM, TsGADA, ORGPB, and elsewhere, were Vladimir A. Lipshits and Leonid A. Shur. As early as 1956, Lipshits was surveying "The Ethnographic Research on Russian Round-the-World Expeditions" ("Etnograficheskie issledovaniia...") in *Ocherki istorii russkoi etnografii, fol'kloristiki, i antropologii* (*Essays in the History of Russian Ethnography, Folklore Studies, and Anthropology*) (M., vol. 1). Attention was paid to Australia in passing (pp. 299–300, 320–21). Shur, a younger man with interests in Latin American (chiefly Peruvian and Chilean) history and early Russian contacts with those countries, wrote a number of solid papers in the sixties, drawing general attention to materials in TsGAVMF and other central archives of significance to South Pacific studies. A good example, in terms of scope and reference, is his essay on "Materials of the Russian Voyages of the Eighteenth and Nineteenth Centuries as Sources for the Geography, History, and Ethnography of Latin American Countries," *IVGO* (1968): no. 3. While remaining Latinocentric, Shur had broadened his Pacific naval interests by 1970. That year, he contributed another competent survey, "Diaries and Memoirs of Russian Voyagers as a Source for the History and Ethnography of Countries of the Pacific Ocean: First Half of the 19th Century" ("Dnevniki i zapiski russkikh puteshestvennikov...") to the Soviet compilation entitled *Avstraliia i Okeaniia* (*Australia and Oceania*) (M., pp. 210–12). Unfortunately from the Australian perspective, Shur's monograph of 1971, *K beregam Novogo Sveta* (*To the Shores of the New World*) presented archival materials by F. P. Lütke, F. F. Matiushkin, and others connected with the 1817–19 Pacific voyage of the *Kamchatka,* which had relevance to Chilean but not Australian studies. There were compensating articles and academic thrusts. By 1960, for example, controversy over whether Bellingshausen and his officers had truly recognized Antarctica (which they had obviously sighted) as a land-based continent, was growing heated. There were international aspects to the issue, and the Soviet historians of polar exploration were themselves not in complete accord. Among resultant articles that drew attention to the primary materials of 1820 (Bellingshausen's, M. P. Lazarev's, and others' notes and letters) were two by V. L. Lebedev that were of interest to Australasian studies (see Bibliography). Both appeared in issues of Antarctic Commission reports (1961–63), more recent relatives of which have also, now and then, made passing reference to Bellingshausen's pioneering voyage.

As Lebedev had built on articles about that voyage by an older generation of historians, including Iurii A. Shokal'skii, who had commemorated "the centennial of the departure" of *Vostok* and *Mirnyi* (*IVGO*, 60: pt. 2, pp. 175–212), so did V. V. Kuznetsova build on "searches" undertaken almost twenty years before by older visitors to TsGAVMF. Kuznetsova, a descendant of lieutenants in the Pacific naval service, was in 1966–68 involved in the preparation of a new collection of archival materials relating to the double polar venture and was working at ORGPB and TsGAVMF. She did her homework well, reading the published literature on her subject, which included many articles, seldom consulted in her day, that had appeared in official periodicals in 1822–35 (*ZADMM, ZGDMM,* and *ZUKMS*) or in more popular contemporary journals. Even so, pieces of information known to the preceding generation of historians in Leningrad had been misplaced, so Kuznetsova, unfamiliar with D. Abramovich's catalogue to ORGPB's "Pomialovskii Collection" (which admittedly had first appeared in the *Otchot Imperat. Publichnoi biblioteki* for 1907), could speak of "finding" A. P. Lazarev's *Blagonamerennyi*-based journal at ORGPB. This she did in her important article "Novye dokumenty o russkoi ekspeditsii k Severnomu Poliusu" ("New Documents Concerning the Russian Expedition Toward the North Pole"), which appeared in *IVGO* in 1968 (no. 3, pp. 237–45).

Kuznetsova chose her *fonds* with care. She was looking for journals of Lieutenant A. P. Lazarev's companions aboard *Blagonamerennyi*, all formally submitted to the Naval Ministry in 1822. There were sound reasons for believing that such journals could be found. The former captain of that ship, Gleb S. Shishmarev (1781–1835), had a politically acceptable career link with Kotzebue through the *Riurik,* achieved flag rank, and had his own sizable file. His nephew, Nikolai D. Shishmarev, who served in *Blagonamerennyi* as a midshipman and who returned to New South Wales with *Elena* in 1825, retired a commodore. The papers of the Shishmarevs had not been previously sought and so should have lain over the decades undisturbed. Kuznetsova came upon Nikolai's *putevoi zhurnal* for 1819–22 in TsGAVMF's *fond* 203, op. 1.

From the Australian perspective, it was disappointing that, as Kuznetsova wrote, "whereas [Aleksei P.] Lazarev describes the scene in southern lands in some detail... Shishmarev pays more attention to Russian America" (p. 240). Nevertheless, it was encouraging that such a find should have been made; and Kuznetsova's notes referred to other naval *fonds* of "southern promise." *Fond* 215, it was stated (p. 244, n. 36), contained data on ethnographic materials brought back from the Pacific and perhaps Australia by the Vasil'ev-Shishmarev expedition, which by 1827 were in the care of the Academy of Sciences. Again, *fond* 213, op. 1, *delo* 99, bore on Korneev's coastal sketches and on specimens of rocks from the Pacific brought to St. Petersburg in 1822. Kuznetsova's work was energetically and competently followed up, in 1969–73, by a historian of illustrative art, Miss N. N. Goncharova, and by Daniel D. Tumarkin, a prolific specialist in Polynesian and especially Hawaiian history with long-term interests in early Russian voyaging and central naval *fonds.*

N. N. Goncharova collated materials in TsGAVMF's *fonds* 166 and 213, referred to by Samarov, Solov'ev, and Kuznetsova, with others held at TsGIA (*fond* 789, containing materials of the St. Petersburg Academy of Arts). The result was a detailed study of Emel'ian E. Korneev as expeditionary artist in the Pacific and Arctic in 1819–21 ("Khudozhnik krugosvetnoi ekspeditsii 1819–1822 gg. E. Korneeva," in *IVGO*, 105 [1973]: no. 1; pp. 67–72). Goncharova was the first Soviet scholar to make heavy use of the wealth of documentation in TsGIA's *fond* 789 that illuminated the conditions of service of artists, like Korneev and P. N. Mikhailov of the *Vostok,* who worked extensively in Polynesia and Australia in 1820. Placing Korneev's Pacific work in wider context by allusions to his service in Siberia, the Volga region, and the Caucasus (1802–4), and stressing the involvement of the president of the Academy of Arts, A. N. Olenin, in the virtual secondment of such artists to the Navy, Goncharova saved that able but eventually wretched artist from oblivion. Of interest to Australasian specialists were the instructions, reproduced by Goncharova (p. 69), that Korneev and Mikhailov were to follow whilst "ashore in distant parts." In a second paper, "Vidopisets E. Korneev" ("The *Paysagiste* E. Korneev"), published in the journal *Iskusstvo* (*Art*) (1972): no. 6, pp. 60–64, Goncharova placed historians still further in her debt by reproducing several fine aquarelles and India ink drawings by Korneev from *Les Peuples de la Russie* (Paris, 1812–13), now a bibliographical rarity. Finally, Goncharova summarized what TsGIA records showed about the fate of Korneev's portfolios from the Pacific and Australia (pp. 70–72), the whereabouts and even the survival of those drawings being then, as now, uncertain. Her articles provoked fresh interest in the "Mikhailov collections" from Australia and Polynesia on the part of a historian of art based at the State Historical Museum (GIM) on Red Square, Moscow, V. M. Rastiapin. In 1978–79, Rastiapin was able to provide the present writer with remarks on the techniques used by Mikhailov while in Australia and in St. Petersburg in 1822–23, on the lithography to which his "New South Wales drawings" were subjected by Ivan P. Fridrits, and on other aquarelles now held at GRM (the State Russian Museum), Leningrad. This last museum has its own sizeable Manuscripts Division, is accessible to Western visitors, and corresponds with parties interested in its holdings (address: Leningrad D-11, Inzhenernaia Ulitsa 4). GIM offers more than the Mikhailov aquarelles to any student of the early Russian presence in Australia. In *fond* 60 of its Manuscripts Division, for example, are 220 documents relating to Count Semon R. Vorontsov who, as ambassador in London, aided Kruzenshtern (1797), or to Mikhail Semenovich, his son.

Daniel D. Tumarkin, now the pre-eminent Soviet authority on early Russian dealings in Hawaii, has been writing on Hawaiian ethnological and ethnographic themes for thirty years. (For typical examples of his early work, one may consult *Sovetskaia etnografiia* [1954]: no. 4, pp. 106–16 and [1958]: no. 6, pp. 38–53). Since 1959, he has been gathering materials in TsGAVMF and other main Soviet archives that relate to early European dealings in Hawaii (ibid., [1960]: no. 2, pp. 158–60), concentrating on American and British "colonizers" and "usurpers" in the "Land of Endless Spring" and on the Russian naval visits to Oahu or the Kona Coast of 1804–25 (see Bibliography). In 1978–79, Tumarkin published detailed surveys of the primary archival sources for, and ethnographical results of, the *Nadezhda*'s and *Neva*'s Hawaiian visit in 1804. One of these, entitled "Materialy pervoi russkoi krugosvetnoi ekspeditsii kak istochnik po istorii i etnografii Gavaiskikh ostrovov" ("Materials of the First Russian Expedition Round the World as Sources for the History and Ethnography of the Hawaiian Islands'') in *Sovetskaia etnografiia* (1978): no. 5, pp. 68–84, served as a model for Tumarkin's later paper on the similar significance of documents from the Vasil'ev-Shishmarev Arctic venture (1819–22). Here, of course, he moved to areas of interest to students of the early Russian presence in Australia; and all such students must consult Tumarkin's article of 1983 (see Bibliography).

Among materials referred to that have interest in the Australian connection are reports, in TsGAVMF *fond* 205, giving reasons why M. N. Vasil'ev was not prepared in 1822–26 to write a large-scale, official narrative (even supposing such a volume would be welcomed by the Naval Ministry: p. 48); and documents in *fond* 162 illuminating K. K. Gillesem's attempts to have his narrative, based on the journal he had kept as a young midshipman in *Blagonamerennyi*, approved and published by the Ministry itself (p. 49). Major Karl von Gillesem (as he was by 1828) retained the keenest memories of his experiences on the far side of the world and, like his comrade Aleksei P. Lazarev, was disappointed but elated by Vasil'ev's decision not to offer an account of the *Otkrytie-Blagonamerennyi* Pacific expedition. He immediately wrote his own. In Chapter Four he dealt with Sydney and its hinterland. On weighing Gillesem's completed manuscript, Tumarkin found in 1983, the Scientific Committee of the Russian Naval Staff found it wanting—or at least did not press hard for publication. Gillesem finally published an account of certain portions of his voyage in a journal well disposed to travel literature, *Otechestvennye zapiski* (*Notes of the Fatherland*), only in 1849. It was a shadow of the journal of his youth, which he had properly submitted to imperial authority in 1822. The "Sydney section" was omitted. Both Vasil'ev and Shishmarev were dead; the cause and marginal successes of their mission were forgotten.

Soviet research is of increasing value to Pacific and Australian historians. Not only does it spare much time and energy on working visits to the USSR, suggesting leads, opening doors; it also doubles the potential usefulness of such collections of original Russian materials as may be found in North America. (On the United States National Archives as a source for Russian dealings in Australia to 1829, see below.) Enquiries to the Elmer E. Rasmuson Library at the University of Alaska, Fairbanks, on the basis on Tumarkin's and Goncharova's recent works show that that library's lately-acquired Shur Collection holds material from TsGIA, touched upon by Goncharova and relating both to Korneev's and Mikhailov's numerous drawings from Australia and to the Gillesem account. Among the papers microfilmed (Shur Collection, reel 98) are letters of 1830 to Prince Aleksandr Menshikov, then Chief of Naval Staff, regarding Gillesem's ambitions (TsGAVMF, *fond* 162, op. 1, *delo* 44: No. 98/3737, etc.). And appended is a copy of the outline of the work that Gillesem, living in Riga in retirement, wrote out in German. Of the resumé of Chapter Four, "The Voyage from Rio-de-Janeiro... and Continuation of the Voyage to Port Jackson in New South Wales," suffice it to offer this extract: "Friendly reception by the Governor and residents of Sydney Town; Trip to Parramatta, Windsor, and the Blue Mountains; Remarks on Convicts; Colonial Regulations; the Native People; Beasts and Plants."

A NOTE ON LENINGRAD AND MOSCOW ARCHIVES HOLDING DOCUMENTS
RELATING TO THE RUSSIAN NAVAL PRESENCE IN AUSTRALIA, 1807–25

It would be wrong for Western students of the Russian Navy's earlier activities in
New South Wales or Van Diemen's Land to think that TsGAVMF (Tsentral'nyi
Gosudarstvennyi Arkhiv Voenno-Morskogo Flota SSSR, or the Central State Naval
Archive of the USSR) is the only source of relevant material and hence the key to all
their chances. In reality, a wealth of relevant original material, basically of three
kinds—articles, letters, and despatches or reports—may be examined in a number of
the main Soviet archives. Because it seems that access to at least *some* central Soviet
repositories of original material is growing easier than was the case in 1980–84, it is
appropriate to end this survey with remarks that may spare others needed time and effort. These remarks concern the larger Leningrad and Moscow archives only, touching incidentally on bibliographies to serve as starting points and on research facilities. All contemplating working visits to the institutions mentioned are advised first
to acquaint themselves with P. Kennedy Grimsted's first-rate guide, *Archives and
Manuscript Repositories in the USSR: Leningrad and Moscow* (Princeton, 1972).

Tsentral'nyi Gosudarstvennyi Arkhiv Voenno-Morskogo Flota SSSR (TsGAVMF)

Among the best-organized ministerial archives of the nineteenth century, and a direct
descendant of the Admiralty College formed in 1718, TsGAVMF remains officially
closed to foreign scholars. However, the administration of this archive is at times
prepared, if foreign visitors have ample time and excellent credentials, to make documents from earlier historical collections (*fonds*) available to them in the main
reading-room of the Tsentral'nyi Gosudarstvennyi Istoricheskii Arkhiv SSSR,
known as TsGIAL. Armed with a reader's ticket, the researcher has his own archival
worker, or *sotrudnik,* help him place specific orders for materials, which are in due
course sent out to the reading-room of TsGIAL, (where materials from other local archives are consulted by the foreigner). Because the visitor must know *a priori* what
he requires, the potential benefits of serendipity are lost; but this is no less true of
work in Western libraries in which card catalogues have been replaced by the com-
puter, not just complemented by it.

   Of especial value to the student of colonial Australia are those of the 3,000 *fonds*
of TsGAVMF that hold the chancellery papers of the naval chiefs-of-staff and of the
Admiralty College (ministry from 1802). Still more important are the *fonds* (e.g.,
166, 212, 213, 1152) of naval officers who played a major role in the Pacific enterprise and/or who visited New Holland (Bellingshausen, Mikhail P. Lazarev), or who
hoped to do so (Grigorii I. Mulovskii, *fond* 172). Accredited Soviet researchers are,
quite reasonably, given preference over the foreigner where access to historical materials and other information is concerned. Always assuming that no Soviet researcher
is at work on them when the request is made, hundreds of documents relating in-
directly or directly to the Russian naval presence in colonial Australia may be accessible to the accepted foreigner in TsGIAL. Other *fonds* of interest, within the context
of Australia and early Russian visitors to Sydney, are: 203 (Voennaia po flotu kant-

seliariia); 432 (Morskoi Kadetskii Korpus; officers of distinction with Naval Cadet Corps Links, who visited Port Jackson); and 1166 (Mikhail F. Reineke). While waiting for the delivery of materials, the visitor may avail himself of TsGAVMF's own library of 16,000 volumes.

Major inconveniences for the would-be user of documents held at TsGAVMF are the unavailability (to him) of detailed *opisi* of various constituent collections and the non-existence of a modern and comprehensive published description of the archive's total holdings. The secrecy with which the *opisi* are still surrounded must be taken fatalistically. There is, however, something to lessen the inherent inconvenience of having no contemporary guide at hand: one can consult, before departure, *Arkhivy SSSR: Leningradskoe otdelenie Tsentral'nogo Istoricheskogo Arkhiva: putevoditel' po fondam* (*Archives of the USSR: The Leningrad Section of the Central Historical Archive: A Guide to the Collections*) (Leningrad, 1933). Compiled by M. Akhun, V. Lukomskii and others, and edited by A. K. Drezen, this guide covered the archive in question as it was then constituted. Almost a fifth of its holdings were naval (described on pp. 197–248). Although shortly afterwards transferred to TsGAVMF, these essentially naval holdings were not described elsewhere; nor has another, more global list yet been published—though work is said to be progressing on one—to make the 1933 guide obsolete for the purposes of naval research. One or two of the ten volumes of *Opisaniia del arkhiva Morskago Ministerstva za vremia s poloviny XVII do nachala XIX stoletiia* (St. P., 1877–1906) have similarly retained their usefulness. The archive housing naval materials that bear on Australia has indeed had several minor name changes since 1918, but the ordering of naval *fonds* has been maintained over the generations to a noteworthy extent. Materials are very rarely "shuffled."

A number of *fonds* may hold materials relating to a single Russian visit to Australia: for instance, *fonds* 203, 213, 166, and 1153 all bear on *Otkrytie* and *Blagonamerennyi* and, by extension, on their 1820 Sydney call. Again, the value of the Akhun and Lukomskii guide is self-apparent. Of the many *fonds* that bear tangentially on Russian naval dealings in Australia to 1835, suffice it here to mention three: those of Admiral Ivan F. Kruzenshtern (14); of the history of the Russian Fleet (223); and of the Admiralty College (Gosudarstvennaia Admiralteistv-Kollegiia, 1717–1827). This last contains many documents relating to the service with the British (on secondment) of young Russian officers like Kruzenshtern and L. A. Hagemeister, who arrived in Oceania in 1804–8.

Tsentral'nyi Gosudarstvennyi Arkhiv Drevnikh Aktov (TsGADA)

For students of the Russian naval enterprise in the Pacific and Australia, the documents of greatest value that are kept in TsGADA, or the Central State Archive of Ancient Acts, are of later eighteenth-century origin. (In theory, pre-Revolutionary papers that postdate 1801 are kept at TsGIA, but in fact some nineteenth-century materials are to be found at TsGADA, and among them are documents such as those in *fond* 30, which most strikingly suggest conditions under which a Russian officer served as a Volunteer with the Dutch and British navies.) Of special interest to all naval historians are papers in the subdivision known as Gosarkhiv, that is, the State Archive of the Russian Empire, founded in 1834, that have to do with naval progress, and materials in *fond* 796 from the head office of the Russian-American Company. Other collections also bear on Company voyages to the Pacific settlements, the problems of provisionment along the Northwest Coast, securing Russian interests against New Englanders in 1786–96, and other matters touching incidentally on South Pacific crossings to Kamchatka and the Northwest Coast. There are, for instance, those of A. R. Vorontsov and M. M. Buldakov (183), chairman of the Company Main Board when the *Neva* sailed from Kronstadt. The former bear on the Pacific plans and orders of Captain Joseph Billings, Lieutenant James Trevenen, and Captain-Lieutenant Grigorii I. Mulovskii (1785–87), in short, on Russian naval hopes of circumnavigation and control. The latter cast a useful light on Kruzenshtern's and Iurii F. Lisianskii's sailing orders of 1802–3 and, by extension, on contemporary Russian knowledge of—and attitudes towards—the South Pacific, which was largely known to the St. Petersburg authorities through Cook's and other foreign seamen's *Voyages*. Also held at TsGADA is the *fond* of the Imperial Senate, with records (September 1732, etc.) and other papers dealing with Nikolai F. Golovin's and Vice-Admiral Thomas Saunders's plan to send a squadron from the Baltic to Okhotsk or Petropavlovsk-in-Kamchatka. Gosarkhiv contains documents relating to the equipping and manning of Mulovskii's squadron (1787), also bound for Petropavlovsk round the world, and to projected routes and tasks in the Pacific.

   A good starting-point is Mikhail Putsillo's *Ukazatel' delam i rukopisiam, otnosiashchimsia do Sibiri i prinadlezhashchim Moskovskomu Glavnomu Arkhivu Ministerstva Inostrannykh Del* (*A Guide to the Collections and Manuscripts Relating to Siberia and Belonging to the Moscow Main Archive of the Ministry of Foreign Affairs*) (Moscow, 1879). Records of the Ministry of Foreign Affairs also formed part of the post-Revolutionary TsGADA, though those postdating 1719 were later moved to the Arkhiv Vneshnei Politiki Rossii. Although ancient in its own right, the Putsillo guide retains some value since, again, the documents referred to have retained their order for a century and more. The same applies to the now venerable *Opisanie dokumentov i bumag, khraniashchikhsia v Moskovskom arkhive Ministerstva Iustitsii* (*Description of Documents and Papers Held in the Moscow Archive of the Ministry of Justice*) (St P.-M., 1869–1921; 21 vols.), still used by the archival assistants at TsGADA. Though the current *fond* numbers were allocated to materials comparatively recently, the nineteenth-century enumeration system has been kept for their contents (files).

Tsentral'nyi Gosudarstvennyi Istoricheskii Arkhiv SSSR (Leningrad) (TsGIAL)

Here, as in TsGAVMF, the foreigner is much hampered by the lack of recent comprehensive guides to holdings and is thoroughly dependent on the efforts of *sotrudniki* who do have access to such typed partial inventories as are at hand. He can, however, make good use of *Arkhivy SSSR: Leningradskoe otdelenie Tsentral'nogo Istoricheskogo Arkhiva . . .* , ed. A. K. Drezen (Leningrad, 1933), pages 197-248 of

which list naval items which were then in TsGIAL. Among the former ministerial records now preserved at TsGIAL which bear on naval and Pacific issues are those of
the nineteenth-century Ministries of Commerce, Trade, and Justice (branches outside
Moscow), as well as of the Imperial Chancery. In the *fond* of this last and massive
chancery's First Section, for example, is Nikolai P. Rezanov's correspondence from
the North Pacific of 1805–7, bearing on Company Chief Manager Baranov and Russian hopes of Upper California and the Hawaiian Islands. A starting point is S. Valk
and V. V. Bedin, *Tsentral'nyi Gosudarstvennyi Istoricheskii Arkhiv SSSR v
Leningrade: putevoditel'* (*The Central State Historical Archive of the USSR in
Leningrad: A Guide*) (Leningrad, 1956).

TsGIAL holds many records of the relationships between the Russian-American
Company and its servants and naval officers who served on Company-owned ships in
the Pacific. *Fond* 853 is that of Mikhail M. Buldakov, long the chairman of the Company's embattled board, and illuminates preparations for the Kruzenshtern-Lisianskii
expedition, *inter alia*. *Fond* 15 contains papers relating to the readying of the
Suvorov in 1813 and throws light on the selection of naval officers who visited Australia next year. It also contains documents bearing on the Kruzenshtern-Lisianskii
expedition, its scientific and other results, the rewards of participants, and so forth,
spanning the period 1802–9. Of even greater importance from the Australian perspective is *fond* 789 (St. Petersburg Academy of Arts), with its materials on the participation of the Artists Pavel N. Mikhailov and Emel'ian M. Korneev in the round-
the-world voyages of *Vostok* and *Otkrytie* (1819–22). Documents in four *opisi* (1, 2,
3, 20) and more than two dozen *dela* (files) relate to those artists' training, secondment to the Navy, orders, portfolios from 1819–22, rewards, and attempts to see
their work in print thereafter. These materials formed the basis of N. N. Goncharova's articles on Korneev of 1972 and 1973 (see Bibliography), and are available
in microfilm at the Elmer E. Rasmuson Library of the University of Alaska at Fairbanks (Shur Collection, reel 85).

Also at TsGIAL and of incidental relevance to Australian studies are the holdings
of the former Department of Manufacture and Domestic Commerce, under whose
jurisdiction the Company Main Board was placed in 1811 and remained for many
years (see Okun', *Russian-American Company*, pp. 97–98). One thus finds materials relating to the 1816–17 "Company-and-Navy crisis" in which Mikhail P.
Lazarev was deeply involved, and more specifically, materials on the charges laid
against Lazarev, as captain of *Suvorov*, by Herman Molvo, supercargo. Molvo's assertion that Lazarev knowingly traded in spirits in Sydney, thereby infringing on
Macquarie's "Port Regulations," was touched on earlier, in Chapter Three.

Materials in TsGIAL and TsGAVMF are often complementary where Russian
scientific and naval activities in the Pacific basin are concerned. TsGIAL's *fond* 789,
for instance, is enhanced by TsGAVMF's *fond* 166 as a source on Pavel N. Mikhailov's activity (e.g., in New South Wales, 1820) as expeditionary artist; and
TsGIAL's *fond* 15, with its materials on preparations for Pacific voyages, is complemented by the naval *fonds* 203 and 205 (*Blagonamerennyi* and *Otkrytie* in the Pacific;
notes and journals, publication of results).

Arkhiv Vneshnei Politiki Rossii (AVPR)

Like all other major navies, Russia's had repeated and at times important dealings, in the early 1800s, with the representatives of other powers. In Australia, for instance, naval officers were all, perforce, apologists for Russian policies; and ship commanders were accorded many meetings with lieutenant-governors which protocol alone, as well as real need or interest, required. It is no exaggeration to assert that, broadly speaking, Russian maritime and diplomatic interests and objects in the Australasian colonies of Britain were so interwoven in the age of sail as to be almost inextricable. AVPR contains the diplomatic record of the Russian Crown and empire from Petrine times to 1917. From the Australian perspective, its most significant holdings are those of the chancery of the Ministry of Foreign Affairs (Ministerstva Vneshnikh Del) which until 1923 had been retained in the old archive of the ministry itself in Petrograd. These chancery papers are now arranged by year, with subdivisions for outgoing and incoming correspondence and for embassies and missions overseas. Under such years as 1817–1822, a wealth of information may be found about the Navy's changing role in the Pacific: papers for 1822 relate, among other things, to *Apollon*'s "cruising and surveillance" mission off the Northwest Coast and give details of her route and slim accomplishments. Her visit to Australia is touched upon. Among the AVPR files for 1802–3 are documents indicative of Count N. P. Rumiántsev's and A. R. Vorontsov's increasing readiness to back a major naval effort in the North Pacific basin. Mention should also be made of *razriad* (section) II of the Ministry of Foreign Affairs' Main Archive, holding voluminous records of relations with the governments of Asia and North and South America. These occasionally complement documents bearing more directly on Russian requirements in British colonies and outposts (e.g., Cape Colony, New South Wales), which are held in AVPR's "London Mission *fond*" (*fond Londonskoi missii Kollegii Inostrannykh Del*) and/or the *fond Administrativnykh Del*. The "London Mission *fond*" offers Semen R. Vorontsov's official correspondence with St. Petersburg and the British authorities in regard to Kruzenshtern's voyage to Bengal and Canton in 1797–99 and the possible arrival of *Nadezhda* and *Neva* at Sydney in 1804.

Two further collections bear incidentally on Russian vessels and their Pacific ports of call: *fond Rossiisko-Amerikanskoi Kompanii,* and *Glavnyi Arkhiv Ministerstva Vneshnikh Del v Sankt-Peterburge* (or Glavarkhiv). The former contains a wealth of data on Company activity in the Pacific—fur sales, shipping movements, personnel problems, stock values, international contacts; the latter's Section II-3 contains Company instructions to commanders of Company ships bound for the Pacific settlements, e.g., Hagemeister of *Neva* in 1807, as well as correspondence between the Company Main Board, Count Nikolai P. Rumiántsev, and Alexander I.

Arkhiv Geograficheskogo Obshchestva Akademii Nauk SSSR (AGO)

The holdings of the Archive of the (All-Union) Geographical Society, one of whose founders was Admiral Ferdinand P. Lütke (Litke) of Pacific fame, were described in a comparatively recent guide, *Russkie geografy i puteshestvenniki: fondy arkhiva*

Geograficheskogo Obshchestva, compiled by T. P. Matveeva *et al.* (L., 1971). Among the materials of interest to students of the Russian naval presence in the South Pacific Ocean are the F. F. Veselago Collection and AGO's vital *razriad* 99 (Russian-American Company papers). *Razriad* 99 holds information about the officers and crews of ships that called at Sydney; the logs of certain such ships; reports by their commanders, e.g., Klochkov of the *Riurik,* 1821–22; and many works by and about the Company servant and historian Kiril T. Khlebnikov, e.g., his reflections on the Russians' place in Upper California and on likely trade, provisionment, and shipping patterns in the Pacific basin (*dela* 18, 112, 142–43).

Tsentral'nyi Gosudarstvennyi Arkhiv Literatury i Iskusstva SSSR (TsGALI)

The Central State Archive of Literature and Art, situated in a suburb of Moscow, was founded in 1941 but assumed its present name in 1954. In its short life, it has grown to become a repository for 25,000 *fonds* with some 660,000 storage units, most acquired from older specialized literary museums concentrating on one major author. One of TsGALI's two major divisions covers Russian literature in all its aspects from the sixteenth century to the present; and within that division, the largest sections contain personal *fonds* built around a single important literary figure. Iurii F. Lisianskii qualifies as such, as the author of a classic *Voyage Round the World,* as his own translator into English, as well as as a diarist of (in the official view) literary merit. TsGALI's *fond* 612 thus contains a typed copy of Lisianskii's personal journal for 1793–1800, kept whilst a Russian Volunteer with the Royal Navy, and related materials. The final pages of this 177-page copy (for a discussion of its provenance, see N. N. Bashkina *et al., Rossiia i SShA,* pp. 202–3) reflect Lisianskii's keen interest in the Pacific, the China trade, and British exploration around Australia in 1794–99. An editor's copy of the same journal is held in TsGALI's *fond* 1337, comprising a collection of diaries and memoirs of all kinds.

The holograph of Lisianskii's journal is held in the Central Naval Museum (TsVMM) in the old Stock Exchange building in Leningrad until recent times, under reference No. 9170/1938. TsVMM retains various items by Lisianskii to this day, including his *Neva* journal of 1803–6 (No. 9170–8/1938) and a 185-page journal kept in the years 1813–14, when he was preoccupied with the English-language edition of his *Voyage* (details in Nevskii, *Pervoe puteshestvie Rossiian,* pp. 193–94 and n. 2.) But the original of the 1793–1800 journal is missing. The Soviet historian N. V. Novikov asserts (*Rossiia i SShA,* p. 202, n. 1) that a fair copy of it was made—with publication in view—in 1913, but that the original went missing in the Civil War period (1918–19), World War I having prevented publication of the text, which finally appeared, in extract, in 1980. Novikov himself was instrumental in providing the director of the State Literary Museum (later absorbed in TsGALI) with a copy of the 1913 typed copy. This was in 1935.

Kruzenshtern liked to comment, *les marins ecrivent mal, mais avec assez de candeur* (see his *Voyage,* 1). In fact, a number of Russian naval officers or others seconded to the Navy for Pacific expeditions are represented in TsGALI or other literary institutions. The poet Pushkin's friend Fedor F. Matiushkin, for example, who sailed with Golovnin in *Kamchatka* in 1817–19, is represented at the Academy of Sciences' Institute of Russian Literature ("Pushkinskii Dom") in Leningrad.

Of all Soviet central state archives, TsGALI holdings are best covered by comprehensive published guides. *Tsentral'nyi Gosudarstvennyi Arkhiv Literatury i Iskusstva SSSR: putevoditel': literatura*, compiled by N. B. Volkova *et al.* (M., 1963), is an 810-page guide to literary *fonds*, replete with useful descriptions, details of MSS, and a personal name index. A supplementary volume, covering acquisitions of 1962–66 and compiled by I. I. Abroskina *et al.*, appeared in 1968. The clearest survey of TsGALI's holdings, though, remains N. B. Volkova's article "Sokrovishchnitsa sovetskoi kul'tury" ("The Treasury of Soviet Culture"), printed in *Sovetskie Arkhivy* (1966): no. 2, pp. 34–40.

Gosudarstvennaia Publichnaia Biblioteka imeni Saltykova-Shchedrina: Otdel Rukopisei (ORGPB)

The Manuscripts Department of the Saltykov-Shchedrin Public (formerly the Imperial St. Petersburg) Library contains sections of two variants of the slightly polished text of the *Zapiski . . . (Notes on the Voyage of the Armed Sloop Blagonamerennyi . . . in the Years 1819 to 1822)* written by that ship's Second Lieutenant Aleksei P. Lazarev on the basis of his original journal of 1819–22. One, held under reference F. XVII.106.11, is part of a clerk's copy of the original MS, covering the six-month period July–November 1820. The other, which now forms part of the I. V. Pomialovskii Collection (item no. 72), is well described by the Soviet historian Daniel D. Tumarkin (see his "Materialy ekspeditsii M. N. Vasil'eva," p. 51) as "part of an intermedial variant of the Notes . . . heavily corrected." It covers the slightly overlapping period from October 1820 to May 1822, and is 140 pages in length. Thus, both variants deal with *Blagonamerennyi*'s Pacific voyage in the period following her Sydney visit. From the Australian perspective, their principal significance lies in their demonstrating the process whereby Lazarev's original journal or diary was worked up for the publication which, for reasons discussed by A. I. Solov'ev in his introduction to the *Zapiski . . .* (pp. 5–6, etc.), failed to occur in 1830 and finally came about in 1950. Nautical details were omitted, general reflections and some additional factual data were inserted, and numerous stylistic changes were made, between 1820 and 1829. By inference, naval or nautical material in the original MS was omitted from the "Sydney section" (pp. 148–55) of the 1950 edition, but its general sequence was followed. The editing process of Lazarev's MS, first discussed by Solov'ev in 1950 (op. cit., p. 6), interested several of his research associates. The text he published had been found in the 1940s, not in St. Petersburg or Moscow but in the provincial archive of Smolensk (Smolenskii Gosudarst. Oblastnyi Arkhiv); and as the actual finder, T. G. Timokhina, observed to Solov'ev, it showed many minor variants from the manuscript acquired by the nineteenth-century bibliophile Pomialovskii. The text on which the 1950 edition itself was based, edited and annotated with the aid of A. A. Samarov and his colleagues at TsGAVMF, was presented to TsGAVMF and remains there today (reference: *fond* 1153, *delo* 1). In 1968, V. V. Kuznetsova again surveyed the matter ("Novye dokumenty," pp.

237–38), drawing scholarly attention to other original materials of the *Blagonamerennyi-Otkrytie* expedition which complemented, and were complemented by, the Lazarev account. Kuznetsova herself had uncovered at TsGAVMF the 1819–22 journal of Midshipman Nikolai D. Shishmarev, Lazarev's comrade. That manuscript, too, bore on the 1820 visit to Australia. It is self-evident that all materials relating to that naval expedition *may* have relevance to Sydney: hence the interest, within the South Pacific context, of Tumarkin's recent work relating chiefly to the early Russian presence in Hawaii (see Bibliography, under Tumarkin, D. D.).

THE NATIONAL ARCHIVES AND RECORDS SERVICE (GENERAL SERVICES ADMINISTRATION), WASHINGTON, DC (USNA)

Second only to the Mitchell Library and Archives Office of New South Wales in its importance and potential for students of the early Russian presence in Australia is the Collection of Records of the Russian-American Company acquired by the United States in 1867 and now held at the United States National Archives in Washington, DC. Those records include 25 volumes of "Communications from the Main Office in St. Petersburg to Governors General in America," many of which contain items relating directly to Company-sponsored voyages around the world. Several of the voyages in question, e.g., by *Suvorov* (1813–16), *Riurik* (1821–23), and *Elena* (1824–26 and 1828–30), brought Russian companies to New South Wales. Materials of relevance to Australia in the Records, which fill 92 volumes in all and are conveniently available on 77 rolls of microfilm (*Records of Former Russian Agencies: Record Group 261: Russian-American Company—Correspondence of Governors General . . .*), include Company instructions to captains (E. Klochkov, V. S. Khromchenko) who called at Sydney to revictual; contracts for officers in those vessels; reports submitted, and cited in extract, at the conclusion of voyages from Kronstadt to Novo-Arkhangel'sk; documents regarding the Company's efforts to sustain round-the-world provisionment, regulations for its servants that reflect the earlier or, usually, subsequent careers of officers who called at Sydney. Also useful are allusions to cargoes and supplies brought round the world; to Company-Navy tensions; and to the imperial authorities' expectations of the Company in non-commercial areas (e.g., diplomacy, natural sciences) in the Pacific.

Despite the fact that certain captains had instructions to call at Sydney (for example, Khromchenko in 1828), Company dealings with the British in Australia were, in their essence, incidental and peripheral. More than three-quarters of the Records have to do, as one might properly expect, with Northern matters: trade, administration, and jurisdiction on the Russian Northwest Coast of North America and on the East Coast of Siberia, the hunt for furs, market conditions, ever strained lines of communication and supply, the Aleuts and the Tlingit Indians, New Englanders encroaching on the North Pacific fur trade. Of the Records that do *not* directly focus on the North itself, most echo Company activities or aspirations in Hawaii or in Upper California, both likely sources of essential foodstuffs and as such of major interest to Russians on the grain-starved Northwest Coast. In short, there is no section of the

Records headed, usefully, "Australia." To find materials of relevance to it and to the early Russian presence, one must sort through many volumes. This in turn lends great importance to the microfilm publications, the complete titles of which are: *Correspondence of Governors General: Communications Received,* and *Correspondence of Governors General: Communications Sent,* and places all Pacific scholars in the debt of Raymond H. Fisher, editor of the National Archives Microfilm Publications pamphlet describing "M 11," *Records of the Russian-American Company, 1802, 1817–1867* (Washington, 1971). Making use of Wladimir Poliakow, then a student at UCLA, and of other competent translators, Dr. Fisher personally sponsored the preparation in the early 1960s of a "calendar or descriptive list" of at least some of the voluminous records acquired by his country at the time of the purchase of Alaska (30 March 1867: *Convention . . .* Art. II, 15th Stat. 541). The 1971 pamphlet covers only six volumes of the twenty-five in *Communications Received,* it is true; but the quarter of the whole that *is* revealed makes apparent what the student might expect from the remaining volumes. It alerts him to communication (file) numbers which, because they are referred to in that pamphlet, might be sought out in the microfilmed *Communications Sent* with expectations of discovering material relating to, for instance, New South Wales or Hawaii. After all, it is the function of "received" and "sent" letter and file numbers to facilitate such searching. We are thus the beneficiaries of Company punctilio in all such bureaucratic matters.

The most serious gap in the Company Records acquired by the United States in 1867 is correspondence sent and received by Chief Manager Aleksandr A. Baranov between 1799 and 1817. These were hard years, during which the Company was being set on its feet despite all manner of adversities. One must regret the absence of complete communications on the voyages of the *Neva* and *Suvorov* in that period. There were, however, other "absentee materials" in 1867, some of which would have illuminated Russian visits to Australia (logbooks of the Company's round-the-world ships and all related maps and charts). R. H. Fisher surmises that those papers, among other things, went to St. Petersburg in 1858–60 and were used by the historian Petr A. Tikhmenev in his monumental study of the Company, published in 1861–63 (*Records of the Russian-American Company,* p. 4.) Such gaps are certainly regrettable today, whether or not Fisher is right about their cause. The fact remains, nevertheless, that Washington possesses the largest known collection of materials remaining from the Company. Assuredly, the records of the Company Main Office in St. Petersburg were more voluminous by far; but they had vanished by the time Alphonse Pinart, who was employed as a researcher and transcriber by Hubert H. Bancroft, came to look for them in 1875. Frank A. Golder also sought them in vain on the eve of World War I; and so have many recent Soviet historians. Company records that survive in the USSR, at AGO, TsGADA, ORGPB, and elsewhere, are not indeed devoid of value from the standpoint of the South Pacific Ocean and Australia; quite to the contrary. Still, the destruction or at least the loss of Company Main Office records from St. Petersburg does further heighten the significance of Washington's collection.

Company records bearing incidentally on round-the-world voyages and the officers involved in them appeared in V. A. Bilbasov, ed., *Arkhiv grafov*

Mordvinovykh (St. P., 1902), 6: 577–690, and have appeared in several Soviet works by Semen B. Okun' (see Bibliography), A. I. Blinov (*K istorii Rossiisko-Amerikanskoi Kompanii: sbornik dokumental'nykh materialov* [Krasnoiarsk, 1957]), and Daniel D. Tumarkin (see Bibliography). The very fact that Fisher can mention half-a-dozen Soviet articles *about* the lost and surviving Company records, however, (op. cit., p. 182), suggests a certain preoccupation with their fate in the USSR—and a corresponding consciousness of the importance of the documents now in the United States.

Those materials cited below are from the period of most frequent Russian visits to Australia, 1817–29, and come from Volumes 1–6 of *Correspondence of Governors General: Communications Received* (Rolls 1–6 inclusive in USNA microfilm series M 11). Roll numbers for the corresponding volumes of *Communications Sent*, covering the years 1818–29, are 26–31.

THE MITCHELL LIBRARY, SYDNEY

The Mitchell Library remains the supreme source of documentary materials relating to colonial Australia. A component of the State Library of New South Wales, it functions independently, has its own wing of that library's large building on Macquarie Street, and is accustomed to assisting visitors. David Scott Mitchell, founding father of the Mitchell Library, was early in the field of Australiana, and certain of the papers he acquired bear, directly, or tangentially, on Russian dealings in Port Jackson. But the Library continues to obtain primary documents and first editions, some of which are also pertinent to Russian visits to Australia. Materials in the Mitchell Library are sometimes complemented by others in the adjacent Dixson Collection (for example, the Dixson's George Johnson Papers, MS Q22), or in the Archives Office of New South Wales. AONSW holds the original journal kept by the botanist and traveller Allan Cunningham at the time of *Otkrytie*'s and *Blagonamerennyi*'s visit (March 1820), for example, of which the Mitchell Library has a copy as well as many associated notes, letters, and a slightly earlier journal. It is most convenient that these sister institutions should share a single building at the core of Sydney.

First in importance among materials at the Mitchell Library that illuminate aspects of the early Russian visits to Australia are papers by individuals who met Russians and helped them. Among these persons were Lachlan Macquarie, Phillip Parker King, William Lawson, and Cunningham. Either the papers in question make direct reference to Russian ships and officers or they at least elucidate their authors' attitudes towards their visitors by explaining circumstances which, most naturally, Russian sources fail to mention (deaths, the recent loss of money, hopes of profit, profits unrealized). A second category of papers includes those left by individuals who received letters from others who had lately dealt with Russians in the colony and/or had heard about them. Here one may mention Joseph Banks, William Bradley, and Edward Riley. Third, there are more recent papers left by individuals with personal or academic interests in Russian dealings in Australia. Most significant of these, perhaps are the Australian writer Ida Marriott's letters and notebooks (1898–1931). Ida

Marriott (to use her nom de plume) had a keen interest in early Australian and Antarctic exploration. Having been alerted to the Antarctic part of the Bellings-hausen-Lazarev expedition (1819–22) by those sections of the 1831 narrative that appeared in English in Robert McNab's publications of 1907–8 (*Murihiku* and *Historical Records of New Zealand*), she made notes on Bellingshausen. This led, in turn, to a greater awareness of Fedor Shtein, or Stein, who in 1820 had trekked up to King's Table Land with Allan Cunningham. Mrs. Marriott transcribed Cunning-ham's letters to Banks and William Aiton of Kew Gardens (1817–21) from originals held at the British Museum in London. These letters made occasional reference to Shtein and his associate, *Otkrytie*'s artist Emel'ian Korneev, to his own pleasant memories of Russians in Brazil, and to his willingness—should Governor Macquarie prove intransigent over the matter of the transport and associated costs of Shtein's excursion—to defray those costs himself. Mrs. Marriott went one stage further, an-notating the Cunningham journal and letters of that period. Her notebooks that bear on the 1820 Russian visits are classified ML MSS 75/26-28 and 337/A & B.

In general, the Mitchell Library offers far more on the 1820 and subsequent Rus-sian visits than on earlier ones (1807, 1814). This applies equally to papers directly alluding to Russian ships and dealings, and to contemporaneous materials of a "scene-setting" variety. Mention may be made, in the 1820 connection, of the Bon-wick Transcripts containing papers of Commissioner John Thomas Bigge, whose ob-servations often complement Bellingshausen's and his peoples', and of private letters in the Mitchell Library's "Miscellaneous Files." Russian comments (and Mr. Bigge's comments also) on the Female Orphan Asylum at Parramatta, as it stood in April-May 1820, are well balanced by those of William H. Jewell, an intelligent con-vict servant ("Miscellaneous: DOC 1042"). Lachlan Macquarie's diary (ML A774), covering 1820 up to 28 February, offers disappointingly little on the first Russian visit of the year. The Governor was not an expansive writer. On the other hand, his private journal for 1807 (ML CY A771) contains a graphic description of his un-avoidable journey home from India by way of Persia, the Southern Russian Prov-inces, St. Petersburg, and Kronstadt (pp. 166–226). The description places Mac-quarie firmly in the context of the Anglo-Russian entente of the Napoleonic period. For official correspondence dealing with Russian visits to Port Jackson, *inter alia*, one turns to the published *Historical Records of Australia: Series 1* (Sydney, 1913–19), and to the extensive microfilmed collection of papers in the Public Re-cord Office, London, now also in Sydney. In *HRA: Series 1*, see 4: 306–7; 5: 92–93; 6: 159; 8: 588; 10: 369, etc.

Last but not least, in the list of Mitchell Library holdings relevant to Russian visits of the early 1800s, are Australian newspaper files. On microfilm or in original edi-tions, issues of two Sydney papers, the *Sydney Gazette and New South Wales Ad-vertiser* (1803–42) and the *Australian,* and of the *Hobart Town Gazette and South-ern Reporter* (1816–27), are essential to the study in hand. The *Sydney Gazette* ap-peared weekly until 1825, and the Russian visits of 1807, 1814, 1820, and 1822 were reflected both in shipping news and in social columns, as well as in government notices. In response to the political news brought by *Suvorov,* a *Sydney Gazette Ex-traordinary* was printed by "Happy George" Howe (a West Indian creole of much talent) on Thursday, 25 August 1814 (no. 558). The issue echoed an earlier *Gazette Extraordinary* which, by coincidence, had also appeared on 25 August in 1811 and had gladly reported Wellington's victory in Portugal over Masséna. Then, too, the news had been brought out in a foreign vessel (the trader *Sally,* of Boston). After 1827, the *Sydney Gazette* appeared three times weekly. There were, accordingly, more frequent allusions in the press to the 1829 visits than to the preceding ones. For 1830s visits, we have W. C. Wentworth's embryonic nationalist and neo-British paper the *Australian,* the *Sydney Gazette,* and the antiautocratic *Sydney Herald.* Issues of 31 March to 30 April 1829, 9 May to 7 June 1832, and 21 March to 16 April 1835 contain numerous allusions to and reflections on the Sydney visits of *Elena, Krotkii,* and *Amerika.* The frequency of editions by 1827 goes some way towards compensating for the absence of a guide like J. S. Cumpston's *Shipping Arrivals and Departures: Sydney, 1788–1825* (Canberra, 1964), for the period 1825–1840. Because they are precisely dated, newspaper pieces often permit us to follow Russian activities in New South Wales as despatches to St. Petersburg and Russian memoirs do not. Furthermore, they eliminate confusion arising from discrepancies between the Julian, or Old Style, calendar used by the Russians everywhere in the nineteenth century and the Gregorian, or New Style, calendar in use at Sydney.

By 1800, the Gregorian was twelve days ahead of that employed by Russians in their logs and journals in the South Pacific Ocean as well as at home. Thus, the *Riurik* reached Sydney on 15/27 July 1821, *Amerika* on 8/20 March 1835. Discrepancies between Australian and Russian sources are, with few exceptions, reconcilable with due regard to calendars and to the fact that naval logs began at noon, not midnight, in their dating. Even so, it is a very useful function of the newspaper to focus the chronology of Russian actions (visits, movements) while ashore.

PUBLIC RECORD OFFICE, LONDON

Some eighty miles of shelving in the Public Record Office, London, contain millions of documents . . . the surviving archives of central government in England.

Public Record Office: Catalogue of Microfilm (1977)

Materials bearing on Russian naval contacts with the British colonies are held in numerous collections. The largest and richest of these are Colonial Office and Admiralty Records. In-letters, from captains and commanders-in-chief on distant stations, form Adm. 1 files; and among them are many that allude to Russian Volunteers (Lisianskii, Hagemeister, Unkovskii) who subsequently visited New South Wales and, incidentally, maintained professionally useful connections with the British. Mention is made in this study of communications to London (Adm. 1/498, cap. 370; Adm. 1/1516, cap. 404; Adm. 1/1927, cap. 10, etc.) that reflect the movements—in the Atlantic and Caribbean, in South Africa and the East Indies—of all three officers named above, as well as Kruzenshtern and V. M. Golovnin. These communications, which by and large place the Russian Volunteers in an excellent light, underline just why the latter made strong friendships with their British counterparts in the Napoleonic Wars: they fought the French together, sharing dangers and considerable hardship on the North Atlantic station (1793–1806). Lisianskii saw action in H.M.S. *L'Oiseau* (Captain Robert Murray), Kruzenshtern in H.M.S. *Thetis* (Rear-Admiral George Murray), both in 1793–94; Golovnin in the frigates *Plantagenet* and *Ville de Paris,* in 1802–5; Hagemeister in H.M.S. *Argo* (Captain B. Hallowell) in 1802–5. All four spent periods in other ships besides those named above, which saw close actions (all successfully concluded) with the French; all four had ample opportunity to study British naval practice and manoeuvres, spending time in Nova Scotia, Bermuda and Barbados, Surinam, Jamaica, or the smaller British Caribbean Islands. All took note of local commerce and administrative customs. These despatches are supported by the memoirs of the Volunteers themselves and, in the case of Kruzenshtern, by manuscripts now held at AGO in Leningrad. AGO's *razriad* 119, *delo* 361, for example, comprises an essay by Kruzenshtern, written later on the basis of his 1796–97 journal, entitled "O ekspeditsii frantsuzov v Irlandiiu v 1796 godu" ("Concerning the French Expedition to Ireland of 1796: A Description of an Action Fought by Ships of England and Republican France"). It appears to date from 1841.

Reaching Bengal aboard H.M.S. *Sceptre* (Captain Edwards) in mid-January 1799, Lisianskii made those contacts which, as we have seen, gave him the notion of assisting Matthew Flinders on his coastal survey work around Australia. Unkovskii too went to Bengal in 1804, and like his predecessors there, grew profoundly conscious of the value to Great Britain of her outposts in the East— and to the South. An impressionable midshipman aged barely seventeen, he could no more avoid the intellectual shadow of the captain of the frigate he was serving in, Captain the Honourable Charles Fleming of *L'Egyptienne,* than ten years earlier Lisianskii could have shaken that of Murray. Of the shadow thrown by Fleming while in India, suffice it to say that it was deeply nationalistic and imperialist. Vice-Admiral Sir Charles Elphinstone Fleming was Commander-In-Chief, Portsmouth, by 1839. Unkovskii was abroad till 1807. Six years later, he was anxious to proceed to the Pacific with *Suvorov,* M. P. Lazarev having been given the position of commander by default. (On Admiral Spafar'ev's first choice of Lieutenant A. Makarov, on that officer's attempt to "milk" the Company directors, and on Lazarev's appointment: TsGAVMF, *fond* 15, op. 1, *delo* 12.)

PRO C.O. 201/95/609 serves to illustrate the British press's relevance to foreign visitors to New South Wales. The French, unlike the Russians, it is plain from Phillip Parker King's November 1819 comments to Goulburn, had been kept under continual surveillance and, though Freycinet himself had been hospitably received, that proper watchfulness would be maintained until the last Frenchman had gone. No such surveillance was considered necessary for *Vostok* or her companions four months later.

Much official correspondence between the Home authorities and successive Governors of New South Wales was edited by the Australian scholar Frederick

Watson on the eve of World War I, appearing in the indispensable *Historical Records of Australia* (Sydney, Library Committee of the Commonwealth Parliament, 1914–25). In Series 1, containing despatches, Secretaries of State and Governors, allusions to expected or occurring Russian visits may be found in Vol. 4: 306 (Hobart to P. P. King, 27 June 1803); 6: 159 (Bligh to Secretary of State, 31 October 1807); 7: 608 (Macquarie to Lord Liverpool, 17 November 1812); 10: 369 (Macquarie to Secretary of State, June 1820). The Lazarevs' hospitable reception by Sorell at Hobart Town in 1823 was secured by an order from Macquarie to Lieutenant-Governor Davey of 28 June 1813, also given in *HRA: Series 1, 7* ("Port Regulations").

The 629 volumes of the Colonial Office's original correspondence with New South Wales (1784–1900) and Tasmania (1803–25), held under reference C.O. 201, are complemented by the New South Wales Entry Books (1786–1873: C.O. 202) and by Miscellanea files (1803-1925: C.O. 206). Microfilms of these, and of small runs from F.O. 65: "Russia, General Correspondence, 1781–1905," are held by the Archives Office of New South Wales.

Appendix C

BELLINGSHAUSEN'S LIST
OF PLANT SPECIMENS

Bellingshausen's list is supplemented here by indications of a) plant family or species, and b) Australian common name, if any. Here, C = Coniferae, Co = Compositae, E = Epacridaceae, L = Leguminosae, Li = Liliaceae, Lo = Loganiaceae, M = Myrtaceae, R = Rutaceae, S = Sapindaceae, U = Umbelliferae, P = Proteaceae, Ch = Chenopodiaceae, D = Dilleniaceae, D = Dematiaceae, Eu = Euphorbiaceae, Cu = Cucurbitariaceae, H = Hypericaceae, Ma = Malvaceae, P = Pittosporaceae, Ra = Ranunculae, Ro = Rosaceae, Th = Thymelaceae, Tr = Tremandraceae, Ur = Urticaceae.

1	*Banksia serrata*	P	Honeysuckle
2	*Hakea gibbosa*	P	Wooden cherry tree
3	*Pimelea rosea*	Th	Rice-flower
4	*Epacris grandiflora*	E	Australian heath
5	*Crawea saligna*	—	
6	*Tetratheca ericifolia*	Tr	
7	*Bassutha filiformis*	Ma	Broom, hemp
8	*Casuarina torulosa*	—	She-oak
9	*Trevillea buxifolia*	P	
10	*Acacia verticillata*	Ac	
11	*Boronia serrulata*	R	Native rose
12	*Grevillea sericea*	P	Silky oak
13	*Banera rubioides*	—	
14	*Platylobium formosum*	L	Flat pea
15	*Kennedya monophylla*	L	Beanflower
16	*Stentanthera pinifolia*	—	
17	*Tulpea (Telopea) speciossima (Telop)*		Waratah
18	*Labertia formosa*		
19	*Lomatia silaifolia*	P	Holly

20	*Lomatia ulnaefolia rigida*	P	
21	*Calythrix tetragona*	M	Haircup flower
22	*Dillignia (Dillenia) pungens*	D	
23	*Boronia rubioides*	R	
24	*Banksia oblongifolia*	P	Honeysuckle
25	*Acacia discolor*	Ac	
26	*Correa speciosa*	R	Australian fuchsia
27	*Dillignia (Dillenia) grandis*	D	
28	*Pultenea*	L	Wallflower
29	*Dillopnea*	—	
30	*Gibberdia linearis (Gibbera)*	Cu	
31	*Diuris elongata*	Orc	Orchid
32	*Acacia suaveolens*	Ac	
33	*Ricinicarpus linifolia*	Eu	Native jasmine
34	*Pultenea speciosa*	L	Wallflower
35	*Lycopodium*		Club moss
36	*Conospermum (Coniosporium) taxifolium*	P	
37	*Conospermum confertum*	P	
38	*Fabricia laevigata*	Ur	
39	*Smilax latifolia*	Li	Sarsaparilla
40	*Isopogon anemonifolius*	P	
41	*Leucopogon microphyllum*	—	
42	*Cupressus*	Co	Cypress
43	*Conospermum erectum*	P	
44	*Burckardia umbellata*	Ch	
45	*Epacris pulchella*	E	Australian heath
46	*Azorella linifolia*	U	Balsam gum
47	*Uter*		
48	*Gnaphalium ericaefolium*	Co	Cottonweed
49	*Pultenea villosa*	L	Wallflower
50	*Clematis aristata*	Ra	Supple Jack
51	*Gnaphalium diosmifolium*	Co	
52	*Mirbelia reticulata*	Ro	
53	*Conosperma conferta*	P	
54	*Acacia linifolia*	Ac	Sally
55	*Lysinema pungens*		
56	*Styphelia tubiflora*	E	Five-corners
57	*Pultenea stipularis*	L	
58	*Styphelia longifolia*	E	
59	*Pultenea pyriformis*	L	

"Collected from the Governor's garden" at Parramatta:

| 60 | *Dodonea latifolia* | S | Native hop |
| 61 | *Buddleya carpodetus* | Lo | Cabbage-tree |

62	*Matrosideros lanceolata*		
63	*Leptospermum ambiguum*	M	Myrtle
64	*Melaleuca ericifolia*	M	Swamp tea-tree
65	*Viminaria donadata (denudata)*	L	Rush-broom
66	*Aster tomentosus*	Co	
67	*Eriokelia major*		
68	*Leptospermum florescens*	M	Flowering tea-tree
69	*Gompholobium grandiflorum*	L	
70	*Billardiera longiflora*	P	Appleberry
71	*Eucalyptus resinifera*	M	Red gum tree
72	*Hypericum*	H	St. John's wort
73	*Gnaphalium repens*	Co	
74	*Boronia*	R	Native rose
75	*Melaleuca capitala*	M	Tea-tree
76	*Obtusifolia*		
77	*Helichrysum*	Co	Everlasting

Notes

ABBREVIATIONS

ACLS	American Council of Learned Societies
ADB	*Australian Dictionary of Biography: 1788–1850* (Melbourne, 1966)
AE	*Australian Encyclopaedia* (1958)
AGO	Arkhiv Geograficheskogo Obshchestva SSSR (Leningrad)
AONSW	Archives Office of New South Wales (Sydney)
AVPR	Arkhiv Vneshnei Politiki Rossii SSSR (Moscow)
CHSQ	*California Historical Society Quarterly*
DAB	*Dictionary of American Biography* (New York, 1928–36)
DNB	*Dictionary of National Biography* (London, 1885–1901)
EB	*Encyclopaedia Britannica*, 11th ed. (Cambridge, U.K., 1911)
ES	Entsiklopedicheskii slovar' (St. Petersburg, 1890–1907)
GBPP	Great Britain: Parliamentary Papers
GIM	Gosudarstvennyi Istoricheskii Muzei
Granat-Ist	*Istoriia Rossii v XIX veka* (St. Petersburg, Granat, n.d.)
HRA	*Historical Records of Australia*: Series 1 (Sydney)
HRNSW	*Historical Records of New South Wales*
HRNZ	*Historical Records of New Zealand*, ed. R. McNab (Wellington, 1908–14)
IVGO	*Izvestiia Vsesoiuznogo Geograficheskogo Obshchestva*
JRAHS	*Journal of the Royal Australian Historical Society*
L.	Leningrad
LOAAN	Leningrad Division, Archive of the Academy of Sciences of the USSR
M.	Moscow
MM	*Mariner's Mirror*
MSb	*Morskoi sbornik*
NMM	National Maritime Museum (Greenwich)
NZSJ	*New Zealand Slavonic Journal* (Wellington)
ORGPB	Otdel rukopisei Gosudarstvennoi Publichnoi Biblioteki, i.e., Saltykov-Shchedrin Public Library, Leningrad
PHR	*Pacific Historical Review*

PSZRI	*Polnoe Sobranie Zakonov Rossiiskoi Imperii*
SEER	*Slavonic and East European Review* (London)
SMAE	Sbornik Muzeia Antropologii i Etnografii (Leningrad)
St. P.	St. Petersburg
TIIE	*Trudy Instituta Istorii Estestvoznaniia i Tekhniki*
TsGIAL	*Central State Historical Archive* (in Leningrad)
TsGADA	Central State Archive of Ancient Acts (Moscow)
TsGALI	Central State Archive of Literature and Art (Leningrad)
TsGAVMF	Central State Archive of the Navy of the USSR (Leningrad)
TsGIAE	Central State Historical Archive of the Estonian SSR (Tartu)
TUAK	Tartu Ulikooli Ajaloo Küsimusi (Tartu)
USNA	United States National Archives (General Services Administration)
ZADMM	*Zapiski Admiralteiskogo Departamenta Morskogo Ministerstva*
ZGDMM	*Zapiski Gidrograficheskogo Departamenta Morskogo Ministerstva*
ZUKMS	*Zapiski Uchenogo Komiteta Morskogo Shtaba* (St. Petersburg)

NOTES TO CHAPTER ONE

1. John Perry, *The State of Russia under the Present Czar, in Relation to the Several Great and Remarkable Things He Has Done*, etc. (London, 1716), pp. 60ff.; S. M. Solov'ev, *Istoriia Rossii s drevneishikh vremen*, 2d ed. (St. P., n.d.), 4: 641.

2. K. Trusevich, *Posol'skie i torgovye otnosheniia Rossii s Kitaem* (M., 1892), pp. 155–88.

3. V. N. Berkh, *Pervoe morskoe puteshestvie Rossiian, predpriniatoe dlia resheniia geograficheskoi zadachi—soediniaetsia li Aziia s Amerikoi* (St. P., 1823), pp. 3ff.; *PSZRI* (1830–1916): 8, doc. 4649; A. V. Efimov, *Izistorii russkikh ekspeditsii na Tikhom okeane: pervaia polovina XVIII veka* (M., 1948), pp. 28–30.

4. V. Guerrier (Ger'e), *Leibnitz in seinem Beziehungen zu Russland und Peter dem Grossen: eine geschichtliche Darstellung* (St.P. and Leipzig, 1873), pp. 185ff.

5. M. M. Bogoslovskii, *Petr I: materialy dlia biografii* (M., 1941), 2: 113–58; N. A. Ustrialov, *Istoriia tsarstvovaniia Petra Velikogo* (St.P., 1858), 6: 26–28; A. V. Efimov, *Iz istorii velikikh russkikh geograficheskikh otkrytii v severnom ledovitom i Tikhom okeane* (M., 1950), pp. 288–89

6. Saint-Simon, *Mémoires*, ed. A. de Boislisle (Paris, 1920), 31: 374–88; O. Roy, *Leibnitz et la Chine* (Paris, 1972), pp. 66ff.

7. Sven Waxell (Vaksel), *Vtoraia Kamchatskaia ekspeditsiia Vitusa Beringa* (M.-L., 1940), pp. 22–23; D. M. Lebedev, *Geografiia v Rossii petrovskogo vremeni* (M.-L., 1950), pp. 19–29.

8. Guerrier, *Leibnitz in seinem Beziehungen*, p. 187.

9. G. R. Barratt, *Russia in Pacific Waters, 1715–1825* (Vancouver and London, 1981), pp. 12–15.

10. John Perry, *The State of Russia*, p. 61; G. A. Lensen, *Russia's Push Toward Japan: Russo-Japanese Relations, 1697–1875* (Princeton, 1959), ch. 1.

11. C. R. Boxer, *The Dutch Seaborne Empire, 1600–1800* (New York, 1965).

12. Ustrialov, *Istoriia tsarstvovaniia*, 2: 125–28 and 3: 91; I. Grey, *Peter the Great* (London, 1960), p. 108.

13. Efimov, *Iz istorii russkikh ekspeditsii*, pp. 58–60; Bogoslovskii, *Petr I*, 2: 136ff.; I. I. Golikov, *Deianiia Petra Velikago, mudrogo preobrazitelia Rossii*, 2d ed. (M., 1837), 1: 120–23.

14. Grey, *Peter the Great*, p. 108.

15. *Pis'ma i bumagi Imperatora Petra Velikogo* (St. P.-L., 1887–1952), 1: doc. 71.

16. I. P. Kozlovskii, *A. Vinius, sotrudnik Petra Velikogo* (St. P., 1911).
17. Bogoslovskii, *Petr I*, 2: 153ff.; Golikov, *Deianiia*, pp. 120–25.
18. For the chronology of European maps showing Japan and parts of New Holland, see R. V. Tooley, *Maps and Map-Makers*, 4th ed. (London, 1970), pp. 107–9, 118–24.
19. Reproduced by F. G. Kramp in *Remarkable Maps of the XV, XVI, and XVII Centuries* (Amsterdam, 1897), 4: plate 1. See also G. Cahen, *Les Cartes de la Sibérie au XVIIIe siècle* (Paris, 1911), p. 57.
20. B. P. Polevoi, "Zabytyi nakaz A. A. Viniusa," *Priroda* (M., 1965): no. 5, pp. 4–12.
21. Bogoslovskii, *Petr I*, 2: 218.
22. A. Sharp, *The Voyages of Abel Janszoon Tasman* (Oxford, 1968), pp. 341–45.
23. Ibid., p. 341.
24. J. E. Heeres, "Abel Janszoon Tasman: His Life and Labours," in *Abel Janszoon Tasman's Journal* (Amsterdam, 1898), pp. 77–78. For a reproduction of the floor admired by the Russians, see D. Danckerts, *Afbeelding van 't Stadt huys van Amsterdam* (Amsterdam, 1661).
25. R. P. Meyjes, ed., *De Reizen van Abel Janszoon Tasman en Franchoys Jacobszoon Visscher in 1642–3 en 1644* (Amsterdam, 1919), pp. 264–68; also C. H. Coote, ed., *Remarkable Maps of the XV, XVI, and XVII Centuries*, pt. 3, no. 1.
26. See Sharp, *Voyages* p. 346. On works held in the St. Petersburg Academy library and other Russian libraries in the early 1700s, see Schumacher's *Bibliothecae Imperialis Petropolitanae* (St. P., 1742–44) and *Verzeichniss allerhand... Hollandischer und Teutscher Bücher* (1731–34); also, N. V. Zdobnov, ed., *Istoriia russkoi bibliografii do nachala XX veka* (M., 1951), pp. 49ff.
27. Cited in Sharp, *Voyages*, p. 332.
28. Ibid., pp. 313ff.
29. Ibid., p. 332.
30. Tooley, *Maps and Map-Makers*, p. 121.
31. *Materialy dlia istorii Imperatorskoi Akademii Nauk* (St. P., 1885–88), 1: 233ff; K. Weber, "Zapiski," *Russkii arkhiv*, 7 (St. P., 1883): 8 1419–20 (richness of the Academy library).
32. Captain James Cook refers in his journal, 23 August 1770, to "that barren and Miserable Country that Dampier and others have discribed": see Sharp, *The Discovery of Australia* (Oxford, 1963), p. 177.
33. Barratt, *Russia in Pacific Waters*, ch. 2.
34. Lebedev, *Geografiia v Rossii*, pp. 133–35.
35. Lebedev, *Geografiia v Rossii*, pp. 157ff.; V. A. Divin, "O pervykh proektakh russkikh krugosvetnykh plavanii," *Trudy Instituta Istorii Estestvoznaniia i Tekhniki*, 32 (L., 1961).
36. See n. 26; also V. F. Gnucheva, *Geograficheskii departament Akademii Nauk XVIII veka* (M.-L., 1946).
37. Barratt, *Russia in Pacific Waters*, pp. 24–25; G. Williams, *The British Search for the Northwest Passage in the Eighteenth Century* (London, 1962), passim.
38. Tooley, *Maps and Map-Makers*, p. 122.
39. Barratt, *Russia in Pacific Waters*, pp. 40 and 52.
40. An active Russian agent was George Tate the elder, who emigrated to Falmouth, Maine, however, in 1754. See R. C. Anderson, "British and American Officers in the Russian Navy," *MM*, 33 (1947): 26; also V. Aleksandrenko, *Russkie diplomaticheskie agenty v Londone v XVIII veke* (Warsaw, 1897).
41. W. L. Cook, *Flood Tide of Empire: Spain and the Pacific Northwest, 1543–1819* (London and New Haven, 1973), pp. 4–8.
42. Barratt, *Russia in Pacific Waters*, pp. 55 and 26–28 (the Golovin-Saunders proposal of 1732, saving of time and training value of Kronstadt-Kamchatka voyages, etc.).
43. V. F. Gnucheva, "Lomonosov i Geograficheskii departament Akademii Nauk," in *Lomonosov: sbornik statei i materialov* (M.-L., 1940), and N. E. Dik, *Deiatel'nost' i trudy M. V. Lomonosova v oblasti geografii* (M., 1961).

44. Dik, *Deiatel'nost'*, chs. 2–4.
45. See Tooley, *Maps and Map-Makers*, p. 122.
46. Further on this, see I. Wynd and J. Ward, *A Map History of Australia* (Melbourne, 1963).
47. M. S. Anderson, *Britain's Discovery of Russia, 1553–1815* (London, 1958), pp. 9, 71–72; M. S. Anderson, "Great Britain and the Growth of the Russian Navy in the Eighteenth Century," *MM*, 42 (1956): no. 1, pp. 132–46.
48. F. F. Veselago, *Admiral Ivan Fedorovich Kruzenshtern* (St. P., 1869), pp. 3ff.
49. R. C. Anderson, "British and American Officers," pp. 17–27; A. G. Cross, "Samuel Greig, Catherine the Great's Scottish Admiral," *MM*, 60 (1974): no. 3, pp. 251–65.
50. Details in A. G. Cross, *By the Banks of the Neva: Russians in Eighteenth-Century Britain* (Newtonville, MA, 1980), pp. 165–71.
51. M. S. Anderson, "Great Britain and the Growth of the Russian Navy," pp. 138–44; also, by the same author, "Great Britain and the Russian Fleet, 1769–70," *Slavonic and East European Review*, 21 (1952): 148–64; Barratt, *Russia in Pacific Waters*, pp. 70–72.
52. P. H. Clendenning, "Admiral Sir Charles Knowles and Russia, 1771–74," *MM*, 61 (1974): 42–46; and n. 49 above.
53. Survey in C. M. Hotimsky, "A Bibliography of Captain James Cook in Russian— 1772–1810," *Biblionews and Australian Notes and Queries*, 5 (1971): no. 2, pp. 3–12.
54. *Kalendar' ili mesiatsoslov geograficheskoi na 1773 god* (St. P., 1772), pp. 29–73 offered extracts from Joseph Banks's *Voyage Round the World*, published in London anonymously in 1771, as well as his letter to the *Académie* in Paris and an engraved map by N. Zubkov showing Cook's discoveries in Australia. On Hawkesworth, see J. C. Beaglehole, ed., *The Journals of Captain James Cook: Volume I, the Voyage of the Endeavour, 1768–1771* (Cambridge, 1955), pp. ccxliii–ccliii.
55. See R. V. Tooley, *One Hundred Foreign Maps of Australia, 1773–1887* (London, 1964).
56. E. V. Tarle, *Chesmenskii boi i pervaia russkaia ekspeditsiia v Arkhipelag* (M., 1945); Cross, "Samuel Greig," pp. 253–54.
57. Survey in Barratt, *Russia in Pacific Waters*, pp. 26–28.
58. S. R. Tompkins and M. L. Moorehead, "Russia's Approach to America: From Spanish Sources, 1761–75," *British Columbia Historical Quarterly*, 13 (1949): 246ff.; Cook, *Flood Tide of Empire*, pp. 69ff.; Barratt, *Russia in Pacific Waters*, pp. 66–69.
59. C. E. Chapman, *The Founding of Spanish California: The Northwestward Expansion of New Spain, 1687–1773* (New York, 1916), pp. 221–27.
60. Cook, *Flood Tide of Empire*, p. 53.
61. Chapman, *Founding of Spanish California*, pp. 221–23.
62. Barratt, *Russia in Pacific Waters*, pp. 67–69; also H. R. Wagner, ed. and trans., "The Memorial of Pedro Calderon y Henriquez Recommending Monterey as a Port. . . With a View to Preventing Russian Encroachment in California," *CHSQ*, 23 (1944): 219–25.
63. Archivo General de Indias, Catalogue 2901 (Bancroft Library copy, Berkeley, CA).
64. I. Andreevskii and K. Arsen'ev, eds., *Entsiklopedicheskii slovar'* (St. P., 1890–1904), 79: 199–202.
65. V. I. Smirnov, ed., *Leonard Eiler: perepiska: annotirovannyi ukazatel'* (L., 1967). On Gmelin and Steller in the Pacific connection, see F. A. Golder, *Bering's Voyages: An Account of the Efforts of the Russians to Determine the Relation of Asia and America*, 2 vols. (New York, 1922–25).
66. Williams, *British Search for the Northwest Passage*, p. 141; M. S. Anderson, *Britain's Discovery of Russia*, pp. 86–87; H. T. Fry, *Alexander Dalrymple and the Expansion of British Trade* (Toronto, 1970), pp. 100–28.
67. V. A. Divin, *Russkie moreplavaniia na Tikhom okeane v XVIII veke* (M., 1971), pp. 164–65; A. S. Sgibnev, "Okhotskii port s 1649 po 1852 god," *Morskoi sbornik*, 105 (St. P., 1869): no. 11, pp. 1–92.
68. A. Savin, "Okhotski *ZGDMM*," (St. P., 1851): pp. 148–61; A. I. Alekseev, *Okhotsk—*

kolybel' russkogo tikhookeanskogo flota (Khabarovsk, 1959), ch. 2.
69. Barratt, *Russia in Pacific Waters*, pp. 43–45; Sgibnev, "Okhotskii port," no. 11, pp. 36ff.
70. Martin Sauer, *An Account of a Geographical and Astronomical Expedition to the Northern Parts of Russia, Performed in the Years 1785 to 1794 . . .* (London, 1802), pp. 41–42; also pp. 275–76 (Okhotsk galiots).
71. Sgibnev, "Okhotskii port," no. 11, pp. 36ff.; Divin, *Russkie moreplavaniia*, pp. 200–14; Barratt, *Russia in Pacific Waters*, pp. 44–46, 61.
72. Sauer, *An Account*, p. 296
73. Ibid., pp. 297–98; Barratt, *Russia in Pacific Waters*, pp. 64–66, 75.
74. A. P. Sokolov, "Ekspeditsii k Aleutskim ostrovam kapitanov Krenitsyna i Levasheva, 1764–1769 godov," *ZGDMM*, 10 (1850): 97 ff.; Barratt, *Russia in Pacific Waters*, p. 65.
75. Nevskii, *Pervoe puteshestvie Rossiian*, pp. 15–16.
76. V. N. Berkh, *Khronologicheskaia istoriia otkrytiia Aleutskikh ostrovov* (St. P., 1823), pp. 70–72 (medals for enterprising fur merchants, etc.).
77. Barratt, *Russia in Pacific Waters*, p. 65.
78. Williams, *British Search for the Northwest Passage*, pp. 169–72; Cook, *Flood Tide of Empire*, ch. 4.
79. Cook, *Flood Tide of Empire*, pp. 69–84; Tompkins and Moorehead, "Russia's Approach to America," pp. 248–50.
80. Chapman, *Founding of Spanish California*, pp. 221–26.
81. See J. C. Beaglehole, ed., *The Journals of Captain James Cook: The Voyage of the Resolution and Discovery, 1776–1780* (Cambridge, 1967), 3: pt. 1, pp. 649–66; pt. 2, pp. 1240, etc.
82. Ia. M. Svet, "Cook and the Russians," trans. P. Putz; in Beaglehole, *The Journals of Captain James Cook*, 3: pt. 2, appendix; W. Lenz, ed. *Deutsch-Baltisches Biographisches Lexikon, 1710–1960* (Köln—Wien, 1970), p. 37.
83. Beaglehole, *The Journals of Captain James Cook*, 3: pt. 1, pp. 650–51.
84. Svet, "Cook and the Russians," pp. 5–6.
85. Beaglehole, *The Journals of Captain James Cook*, 3: pt. 1, pp. clxiii–iv.
86. Ibid., pp. 700–1, 703.
87. Ibid., pt. 2, appendix, pp. 7–8; A. S. Sgibnev, "Istoricheskii ocherk glavneishikh sobytii v Kamchatke, 1650–1856 godov," *MSb*, 105 (1869): no. 7, pp. 23–25.
88. Beaglehole, *The Journals of Captain James Cook*, 3: pt. 1, p. clxiv.
89. Described by L. G. Rozina, "Kollektsiia Dzhemsa Kuka v sobraniiakh Muzeia Antropologii i Etnografii," *Sbornik Museia Antropologii i Etnografii*, 23 (L., 1966).
90. 38 items remain.
91. Beaglehole, *The Journals of Captain James Cook*, 3: pt. 2, appendix, pp. 6–7.
92. Ibid., pt. 2, p. 1553.
93. I thank Mr. A. Ignat'ev, of the Library of TsGAVMF, Leningrad, for this information.
94. Barratt, *Russia in Pacific Waters*, pp. 76–77.
95. Beaglehole, *The Journals of Captain James Cook*, 3: pt. 2, p. 1550.
96. Ibid., pt. 1, p. 714; Williams, *British Search for the Northwest Passage*, pp. 210–11.
97. *Vneshniaia politika Rossii XIX i nachala XX veka* (M., 1961–75), 2: 297–98; P. Tikhmenev, *Supplement of Some Historical Documents to the Historical Review of the Formation of the Russian-American Company*, trans. D. Krenov (Seattle, 1938), pp. 206–7.
98. Peter Dobell, *Travels in Kamtschatka and Siberia* (London, 1830), 1: 297–98, 2: 24–25; A. I. Andreev, *Russkie otkrytiia v Tikhom okeane i Severnoi Amerike v XVIII–XIX vekakh* (M., 1948), pp. 365–67.
99. *Vneshniaia politika*, 2: 298; L. Dermigny, *La Chine et l'Occident: le Commerce à Canton au XVIIIe siècle* (Paris, 1964), 3: 1240ff.; Barratt, *Russia in Pacific Waters*, pp. 100, 110.

100. P. A. Tikhmenev, *Istoricheskoe obozrenie obrazovaniia Rossiisko-Amerikanskoi Kompanii* (St. P., 1861–63), 1: 210ff.; A. P. Sokolov, "Prigotovlenie krugosvetnoi ekspeditsii 1787 goda pod nachal'stvom kapitana Mulovskogo," *ZGDMM*, 6 (1848): 143–50; E. P. Silin, *Kiakhta v XVIII veke* (Irkutsk, 1947), chs. 3–4.

101. TsGAVMF, *fond* 1214, *delo* 1; *Mesiatsoslov na 1779 god* (St. P., 1778), pp. 21–83 (extracts from Cook's *Voyage* of 1772–75, chiefly relating to health measures, with comments on the need for further translation); Hotimsky, "Bibliography of Captain James Cook in Russian," pp. 4–5.

102. V. N. Berkh, "Izvestie o mekhovoi torgovle, proizvodimoi Rossiianami pri ostrovakh Kurilskikh, Aleutskikh, i severozapadnom beregu Ameriki," *Syn Otechestva* (St. P., 1823): pt. 88, pp. 97–98; F. W. Howay, *A List of Trading Vessels in the Maritime Fur Trade, 1785–1825*, ed. R. A. Pierce (Kingston, Ont., 1973), pp. 16ff.; H. H. Bancroft, *A History of Alaska, 1730–1885* (San Francisco, 1886), pp. 242–44.

103. M. B. Grenader, "Istoricheskaia obuslovlennost' vozniknoveniia Severovostochnoi ekspeditsii 1785–1795 godov," *Uchonnye Zapiski Petropavlovskogo Gosudarstvennogo Pedagogicheskogo Instituta* (Petropavlovsk, 1957): bk. 2, pp. 22–35; J. F. G. de La Pérouse, *Voyage autour du monde*, 4 vols. (Paris, 1797), 1: 2–4.

104. TsGADA, *fond* Vorontsova, *delo* 754, passim; S. B. Okun', *The Russian-American Company*, trans. C. Ginsburg (Cambridge, MA, 1951), p. 11; Sokolov, "Prigotovlenie krugosvetnoi ekspeditsii," pp. 143–48.

105. See Hotimsky, "Bibliography of Captain James Cook in Russian," pp. 4–11, on manifestations of this urgency: Peter Simon Pallas's bibliographic work; a Russian translation of Antoine François Prévost d'Exiles' *Histoire générale des Voyages* (Paris, 1780–86) as edited by La Harpe (Russian v. 21, 1787, on Cook); a Russian account of Cook's last voyage by Heinrich Zimmermann (St. P., 1786).

106. Full details in M. K. Beddie, ed., *Bibliography of Captain James Cook*, 2d ed. (Sydney, 1970).

107. Beaglehole, *The Journals of Captain James Cook*, 2: 149–53 and 732–36.

108. L. I. Golenishchev-Kutuzov, *Predpriiatiia Imperatritsy Ekateriny II dlia puteshestviia vokrug sveta v 1786 godu* (St. P., 1840), pp. 7–9; M. E. Hoare, *The Tactless Philosopher: Johann Reinhold Forster, 1729–98* (Melbourne, 1976), ch. 8.

109. See R. V. Tooley, ed., *Early Maps of Australia: Dutch Period* (London, 1965), and Sharp, *Voyages*, pp. 344–47 (M. de Freville's *Voyages dans la Mer du Sud* of 1774, giving Dalrymple's version of F. Valentijn's Australian data from *Oud en Nieuw Oost-Indien*, 1726); also P. Stolpianskii, "Kniga v Starom Peterburge: magaziny inostrannykh knig," *Russkoe proshloe*, 4 (Petrograd, 1923): 123–34.

110. Beaglehole, *The Journals of Captain James Cook*, 3: pt. 1, pp. 49–58.

111. Surveys in F. W. Howay, *Zimmermann's Captain Cook: An Account of the Third Voyage ... 1776–1780, by Henry Zimmermann, of Wissloch in the Palatine* (Toronto, 1930), pp. 7–9, and in Beaglehole, *The Journals of Captain James Cook*, 3: pt. 1, pp. ccv–ccvii; pt. 2, pp. 1473–74.

112. Howay, *Zimmermann's Captain Cook*, pp. 7–8; also by Howay, "An Anonymous Journal ... ," *Washington Historical Quarterly*, 12 (1921): 51–54.

113. Hoare, *The Tactless Philosopher*, pp. 26–36; G. Beratz, *Die deutschen Kolonien an der unteren Wolga in ihrer Entstehung und ersten Entwicklung*, 2d ed. (Berlin, 1923), pp. 111–25.

114. Hoare, *The Tactless Philosopher*, chs. 9–10.

115. Ibid., pp. 32–3.

116. Ibid., pp. 264–66; Golenishchev-Kutuzov, *Predpriiatiia Imperatritsy Ekateriny*, pp. 8–10; V. V. Nevskii, *Pervoe puteshestvie Rossiian vokrug sveta* (L., 1951), pp. 18–19.

117. Howay, *Zimmermann's Captain Cook*, p. 8.

118. I. P. Kondakov et al., eds., *Svodnyi katalog russkoi knigi XVIII veka: 1725–1800* (M., 1963–68), 3: 351; Hotimsky, "Bibliography of Captain James Cook in Russian," pp. 10–11.

119. St. P., tipografiia Vil'kovskago i Galchenkova, 1786: 265 + 10 pp.

120. See Howay, *Zimmermann's Captain Cook*, p. 3.
121. Ibid., pp. 10–11.
122. Details in V. Sopikov, *Opyt rossiiskoi bibliografii*, ed. Rogozhin (reprinted London, Holland House, 1962), no. 9208; see also Barratt, *Russia in Pacific Waters*, pp. 77, 90, 92.
123. On whom, see Kondakov, *Svodnyi katalog*, 1: 112–13.
124. Pt. 7, pp. 255–72, 363–83, 528–43; pt. 8, pp. 646–76, etc.
125. Captain Tobias Furneaux had done the same, though Zimmermann would not, of course, have had sight of his captain's journal: see Beaglehole, *The Journals of Captain James Cook*, 2: 733ff.
126. Ibid., 3: pt. 1 for details.
127. Ibid., 1: cclxxxiii; S. Ryden, *The Banks Collection: An Episode in Eighteenth-Century Anglo-Swedish Relations* (Gothenburg, 1963), pp. 67–68.
128. Discussed fully in G. R. Barratt, *The Russians at Port Jackson, 1814–1822* (Canberra, 1981).
129. Sopikov, *Opyt rossiiskoi bibliografii*, nos. 9206–9207; Gennadi, *Slovar' russkikh pisatelei* (Berlin, 1876), 1: 233.
130. *Puteshestvie v Iuzhnoi polovine zemnago shara, i vokrug onago, uchinennoe v prodolzhenie 1772, 1773, 1774 i 1775 godov... kapitana Iakova Kuka*, 6 pts. (St. P., 1796–1800); T. Armstrong, "Cook's Reputation in Russia," in *Captain James Cook and His Times*, ed. R. Fisher and H. Johnston (Vancouver, 1979), pp. 5–6.
131. Sopikov, *Opyt rossiiskoi bibliografii*, no. 5802.
132. Kondakov, *Svodnyi katalog*, p. 155; see also pp. 311 and 415 on other translations by Novikov (of works on commercial practices).
133. Gennadi, *Spravochnyi slovar'*, 1: 232.
134. See my paper, "Russian Verse Translation... A Note on Changing Conventions," *Canadian Contributions to the Seventh International Congress of Slavists* (The Hague, 1973): pp. 41–46.
135. Sopikov, *Opyt rossiiskoi bibliografii*, no. 9206.
136. See Beaglehole, *The Journals of Captain James Cook*, 2: 149–53 (on Van Diemen's Land's southern coast, etc.); also P. Larousse, ed., *Grand Dictionnaire Universel du XIXe siècle* (Geneva and Paris, Slatkine Reprint, 1982), 14: 1164 (Suard's career). On William Hodges (1744–97), see Beaglehole, *The Journals of Captain James Cook*, 2: xli–ii and *DNB*, 27: 61.
137. *DNB*, 48: 425–30. *History of America* (2 vols., 1777), translated by Suard within nine mcnths, was, like Robertson's earlier *History of Charles V*, admired by Catherine II of Russia.
138. See n. 134.
139. Volume 6 contained maps and drawings, e.g., of Dusky Sound, New Zealand, made by Hodges in 1773: see n. 136.
140. On Demeunier, see *Grand Dictionnaire Universel*, 6: 397.
141. Hotimsky, "Bibliography of Captain James Cook in Russian," p. 9; Gennadi, *Spravochnyi slovar'*, 1: 233. This translation, entitled *Puteshestvi v Severnyi Tikhii okean, po poveleniiu korolia Georgiia III, ... v prodolzhenie 1776, 1777, 1778, 1779 i 1780 godov* (St. P., Tipografiia I. Glazunova, 1805–10; 2 pts.), ended with the entry for 17 January 1779. Thus, the account of Cook's death was omitted and nothing was said of the 1779 British visits to Kamchatka.
142. J. F. G. de La Pérouse, *A Voyage Round the World, performed in the years 1785, 1786, 1787 and 1788, by the Boussole and Astrolabe...* (London, 1799), 2: 179–80 (La Pérouse's entries for 23–27 January 1788). Sopikov, *Opyt rossiiskoi bibliografii*, no. 9208.
143. As in the English *Voyage* of three years earlier (1799): see vol. 2, p. 505 (La Pérouse to Minister Fleurieu, Botany Bay, 7 February 1788).
145. Barratt, *Russians at Port Jackson*, pp. 5–6.
144. Howay, *Zimmermann's Captain Cook*, pp. 7–9 (Ellis and Rickman).

146. The *Voyage* made by Antoine Raymond d'Entrecasteaux (1793–94), in a vain attempt to find traces of the vanished La Pérouse, appeared only in 1808: survey by M. de Brossard, *La Pérouse: des combats à la Découverte* (Paris, 1978), pp. 568–71. As for Alessandro Malaspina, *his* South Pacific movements of 1793–94 in *Descubierta* remained unknown to European readers until the 1930s.

147. V. M. Vladimirov, *Dzhems Kuk* (M., 1933), chs. 7–8; Ia. M. Svet, introduction to the 1971 Soviet ed. of Cook's third *Voyage;* Armstrong, "Cook's Reputation in Russia," pp. 2–6.

148. A. J. von Krusenstern (Kruzenshtern), *Voyage Round the World in the Years 1803, 1804, 1805 and 1806...*, trans. R. B. Hoppner (London, 1813), 1: 190 and 216; 2: 203 and 222; Otto von Kotzebue, *A Voyage of Discovery into the South Sea and Beering's straits... in the Years 1815–1818* (London, 1821), 1: 155 and 156.

149. M. I. Ratmanov, "Vyderzhki iz dnevnika...," cited by E. E. Shvede, ed., in his introduction to F. F. Bellinsgauzen (Bellingshausen), *Dvukratnye izyskaniia v iuzhnom ledovitom okeane* (M., 1949), p. 30; Armstrong, "Cook's Reputation in Russia," pp. 5–7 and notes.

150. This questioning perhaps began with Iu. F. Lisianskii, puzzled by Cook's coordinates for Easter Island in April 1804: see his *Voyage Round the World in the Years 1803, 4, 5 & 6, Performed in the Ship "Neva"* (London, 1814), p. 59.

151. Ibid., p. 109; also Barratt, *Russia in Pacific Waters*, p. 123 (Lisianskii retracing Cook's steps at Kealakekua-Kaawaloa, on Hawaii Island, 1804).

152. On this, see R. Wilson, "The Literary Travelogue: A Comparative Study," *Canadian Slavonic Papers*, 17 (1975): no. 3, pp. 550–62.

153. Kondakov, *Svodnyi katalog*, 1: 112–13; S. A. Vengerov, *Istochniki slovaria russkikh pisatelei* (Petrograd, 1917), 1: 282.

154. Larousse, *Grand Dictionnaire Universel*, 10: 268; Vengerov, *Istochniki*, 4: 393.

155. *DNB*, 31: 195–97.

156. Kondakov, *Svodnyi katalog*, 1: 35 and 110; Sopikov, *Opyt rossiiskoi bibliografii*, no. 7685.

157. Bibliog. details in Hotimsky, "Bibliography of Captain James Cook," p. 9.

158. Larousse, *Grand Dictionnaire Universel*, 10: 75; and 13: 134–35.

159. Vengerov, *Istochniki*, 1: 547–48; Kondakov, *Svodnyi katalog*, 5: 147.

160. Hotimsky, "Bibliography of Captain James Cook," pp. 9–10.

161. Beddie, *Bibliography*, nos. 657 and 722; Beaglehole, *The Journals of Captain James Cook*, 1: cclxvii–cclxix.

162. Hotimsky, op. cit., pp. 6–7.

NOTES TO CHAPTER TWO

1. Ia. M. Svet, "Cook and the Russians," trans. P. Putz; in Beaglehole, *The Journals of Captain James Cook*, 3: pt. 2, appendix; also pt. 1, p. 654 and pt. 2, pp. 1242, 1338–39.

2. Beaglehole, *The Journals of Captain James Cook*, 3: pt. 1, p. 714; pt. 2: p. 1550.

3. C. Vinicombe Penrose, *A Memoir of James Trevenen, 1760–1790*, ed. C. Lloyd and R. C. Anderson (London, 1959), pp. 88ff.

4. Beaglehole, *The Journals of Captain James Cook*, 3: pt. 1, p. 714; Williams, *The British Search for the Northwest Passage*, pp. 210–11.

5. S. D. Watrous, ed., *John Ledyard: Journey through Russia and Siberia, 1787–88* (Madison, 1966), intro.; *Gentleman's Magazine*, 55 (1785): pt. 2, pp. 570–71.

6. Beaglehole, op. cit., 3: pt. 2, p. 1550.

7. Sauer, *Account of a Geographical Expedition*, intro.; G. A. Sarychev, *Puteshestvie kapitana Billingsa cherez Chukotskuiu zemliu ot Beringogo proliva...* (St. P., 1811), pp. 3–13.

8. Cook, *Flood Tide of Empire*, p. 115; Grenader, "Istoricheskaia obuslovlennost'," pp. 22–35.

9. TsGAVMF, *fond* 1214, *delo* 1 (Billings's orders in relation to foreign activities off Kamchatka); TsGADA, *fond* Vorontsova, *delo* 754, passim (Commerce College and British threats to the Russian fur trade by 1785); Tikhmenev, *Istoricheskoe obozrenie*, 1: 210ff.

10. On this, see Barratt, *Russia in Pacific Waters*, pp. 77–88.

11. TsGAVMF, *fond* 172, *delo* 367, pp. 260–64.

12. Barratt, *Russia in Pacific Waters*, pp. 88–89.

13. Beaglehole, op. cit., 3: pt. 2, p. 1474; Watrous, *John Ledyard*, pp. 12–23.

14. Who, as *Reise durch verschiedene Provinzen des russischen Reiches* (St. P., 1776) had demonstrated, was an observant traveller and a naturalist with adeep interest in Siberia. Biographical sketch in C. Urness, ed., *A Naturalist in Russia: Letters from Peter Simon Pallas to Thomas Pennant* (Minneapolis, 1967). Pallas had been appointed historiographer ofthe Russian Imperial Navy in 1787, so took an official interest in Ledyard.

15. Andreev, *Russkie otkrytiia v Tikhom okeane*, pp. 202ff.; Sokolov, "Prigotovlenie krugosvetnoi ekspeditsii," pp. 143ff.; Grenader, "Istoricheskaia obuslovlennost'," pp. 18–20.

16. Watrous, *John Ledyard*, p. 12

17. Ibid., p. 13; Beaglehole, op. cit., 3: pt. 1, p. ccviii; Howay, *Zimmermann's Captain Cook*, pp. 8–9.

18. Watrous, *John Ledyard*, pp. 52, 123–24.

19. Letter to M. Pictet, given in Penrose, *Memoir of James Trevenen*, p. 89.

20. Barratt, *Russia in Pacific Waters*, pp. 108–9.

21. Penrose, *Memoir of James Trevenen*, p. 90.

22. Aleksandrenko, *Russkie diplomaticheskie agenty*, 1: 230ff.; Krusenstern, *Voyage*, 1: xxiv–v; also Cross, *By the Banks of the Thames*, pp. 23–28, etc.

23. Survey in Andreev, *Russkie otkrytiia v Tikhom okeane*, pp. 202–4; on Shemelin's subsequent activities in the South Pacific (1804), see his *Zhurnal pervago puteshestviia Rossiian vokrug zemnago shara* (St. P., 1816), pt. 1.

24. Berkh, "Izvestie o mekhovoi torgovle," pp. 97–98; Howay, *List of Trading Vessels*, pp. 3–5; Bancroft, *History of Alaska*, pp. 242–44.

25. See Okun', *Russian-American Company*, pp. 16–17.

26. Barratt, *Russia in Pacific Waters*, pp. 95–96.

27. Cited by Okun', op. cit., p. 17.

28. Penrose, *Memoir of James Trevenen*, p. 90.

29. Ibid., pp. 91–94. The estimate of optimal size for ships obviously reflected Trevenen's experience with Cook.

30. Nevskii, *Pervoe puteshestvie Rossiian*, pp. 3–4,247; Krusenstern, *Voyage*, 2: 404.

31. Penrose, *Memoir of James Trevenen*, p. 96.

32. Ibid., p. 90.

33. On sailing times from Kronstadt to Kamchatka in the age of sailing ships, see my paper, "Russian Warships in Van Diemen's Land: The *Kreyser* and *Ladoga* by Hobart Town, 1823," *Slavonic and East European Review*, 53 (1975): no. 133, pp. 566–78; V. Fitzhardinge, "Russian Ships in Australian Waters, 1807–1835," *JRAHS*, 51 (1965): pt. 2, pp. 113–15.

34. Report cited in "Nachalo nashikh krugosvetnykh plavanii," *ZGDMM* 7 (1849): pp. 501–2.

35. TsGAVMF, *fond* 172, *delo* 367, pp. 1–13; Sokolov, "Prigotovlenie krugosvetnoi ekspeditsii," pp. 168–87.

36. Sokolov, op. cit., pp. 143–48.

37. Okun', *Russian-American Company*, p. 17; Tikhmenev, *Istoricheskoe obozrenie*, 1: 210ff.

38. TsGAVMF, *fond* I. G. Chernysheva, *delo* 376, pp. 20ff.

39. Ibid., p. 322; Sokolov, op. cit., pp. 148–52.

40. Hoare, *The Tactless Philosopher*, pp. 248–49, 264–65; Golenishchev-Kutuzov, *Predpriiatiia imperatritsy Ekateriny*, pp. 12–15.

41. Divin, *Russkie moreplavaniia*, p. 289.

42. Barratt, *Russia in Pacific Waters*, pp. 29–30; Iu. K. Efrenov, "P. S. Pallas," *Otechest-vennye fiziko-geografy i puteshestvenniki* (M., 1959): pp. 132–45.
43. TsGAVMF, *fond* 172, *delo* 376, pp. 262–63 (V. P. Fondenzin's collation of maps indicating foreign voyages and discoveries in the Pacific Ocean); Divin, *Russkie moreplavaniia*, pp. 291–92 (use of water-purifying stills and other new apparatus); Lensen, *the Russian Push*, p. 71 and S. I. Novakovskii, *Iaponiia i Rossiia* (Tokyo, 1918), pp. 45ff. (the need to disregard Japanese claims to Kurile Islands including Uruppu, etc.); Sokolov, "Prigotovlenie krugosvetnoi ekspeditsii," pp. 172–76 and *PSZRI*, 22: doc. 16,530 (orders for Mulovskii to annex the Northwest Coast to Russia, leaving iron crests or plates in certain places north of 55°N, etc.).
44. J. R. to Geo. Forster, Halle, 25 August 1787, cited by Hoare, *The Tactless Philosopher*, p. 265.
45. Sokolov, op. cit., pp. 151ff.; Nevskii, *Pervoe puteshestvie Rossiian*, pp. 19–20.
46. TsGAVMF, *fond* I. G. Chernysheva (1788), *delo* 376, pp. 285ff. (Mulovskii's sailing orders, routes to Japan and the Northwest Coast, etc.).
47. M. V. Lomonosov, "Petr Velikii" (1760): Canto 1, lines 165–73; Barratt, *Russia in Pacific Waters*, pp. 27, 53–54.
48. Nevskii, *Pervoe puteshestvie Rossiian*, pp. 19–20; N. Frolov, *Sobranie novykh i starykh puteshestvii* (M., 1855), 4: 529–41.
49. D. M. Lebedev, *Plavanie A. I. Chirikova na paketbote "Sv Pavel" k poberezh'iam Ameriki* (M., 1951), pp. 204–8; A. Pokrovskii, ed., *Ekspeditsii Beringa: sbornik dokumentov* (M., 1941), pp. 276–78; Bancroft, *History of Alaska*, pp. 75–98.
50. *PSZRI*, 22: doc. 16530; Sokolov, "Prigotovlenie krugosvetnoi ekspeditsii," pp. 172ff.
51. On this, see H. R. Wagner, "The Creation of Rights of Sovereignty through Symbolic Acts," *PHR*, 7 (1938): 297–326.
52. Edict of 28 October 1787, reserving Mulovskii's whole force for use in the Mediterranean Sea: TsGAVMF, *fond* I. G. Chernysheva, *delo* 376, pp. 411–12; Sokolov, "Prigotovlenie krugosvetnoi ekspeditsii," pp. 189–90.
53. TsGADA, *fond* Gosarkhiva, *razriad* 10, op. 3, *delo* 16, pp. 132–33.
54. Okun', *Russian-American Company*, p. 17.
55. Fitzhardinge, "Russian Ships in Australian Waters," p. 115.
56. Penrose, *Memoir of James Trevenen*, pp. 98–99; F. F. Veselago, *Kratkaia istoriia russkogo flota* (M., 1939), p. 136; S. Elagin, ed., *Materialy dlia istorii russkogo flota* (St. P., 1867), pt. 12, pp. 551–52.
57. *Zhurnal dlia chteniia vospitannikov voenno-uchebnykh zavedenii*, 55 (St. P., 1847): no. 257; F. F. Veselago, *Admiral Ivan Fedorovich Kruzenshtern* (St. P., 1869), ch. 1.; Barratt, *Russia in Pacific Waters*, pp. 107–8; Nevskii, *Pervoe puteshestvie Rossiian*, pp. 21–25.
58. For biographies, W. Lenz, *Deutsch-Baltisches Biographisches Lexikon*, p. 421; I. Andreevskii and K. Arsen'ev, eds., *Entsiklopedicheskii slovar'* (St. P., 1890–1904), 16: 849; Veselago, *Admiral Kruzenshtern*, pp. 1–3.
59. See my study, *The Rebel on the Bridge: A Life of the Decembrist Baron Andrey Rozen, 1800–84* (London, 1975), pp. 17, 27–32.
60. Veselago, *Admiral Kruzenshtern*, p. 3.
61. Golenishchev-Kutuzov, *Predpriiatiia imperatritsy Ekateriny*, p. 364.
62. P. V. Chichagov, "Zapiski," *Russkaia starina* (St. P., October 1886): pp. 35–53; Barratt, *Russia in Pacific Waters*, pp. 54–55.
63. E. L. Shteinberg, *Zhizneopisanie russkogo moreplavatelia Iuriia Lisianskogo* (M., 1948); N. V. Dumitrashko, "Iu. F. Lisianskii i krugosvetnye plavaniia," in *Lisianskii: puteshestvie vokrug sveta na korable "Neva" v 1803–1806 godakh* (M., 1947); Nevskii, *Pervoe puteshestvie Rossiian*, pp. 32–34, 193–94; G. R. Barratt, *The Russian Discovery of Hawaii* (Honolulu, 1988), part I.
64. PRO Adm. 1/498, cap. 370; Nevskii, op. cit., pp. 33–35.
65. TsGALI, *fond XVIII veka*, no. 5196: "Zapiski leitenanta Iuriia Lisianskago,vedennye im

vo vremia sluzhby ego volonterom," pp. 10ff.; *DNB*, 11: 342 (Murray in India).
66. Lisiansky, *Voyage*, p. xviii; J. Ralfe, *Naval Biography* (London, 1828), 3: 212 and 4: 98–99; Krusenstern, *Voyage*, 1: 32–33; N. N. Bolkhovitinov, *Stanovlenie otnoshenii, 1765–1815: Rossiia i SShA* (M., 1980), pp. 196–203; Nevskii, *Pervoe puteshestvie Rossiian*, pp. 25, 33.
67. AGO, *razriad* 119, *delo* 361: "Zapiski Leitenanta I. F. Kruzenshterna o Ekspeditsii frantsuzov v Irlandiiu v 1796 godu"; Nevskii, *Pervoe puteshestvie Rossiian*, pp. 25–26; Lisiansky, *Voyage*, p. xviii.
68. Krusenstern, *Voyage*, 1: xxiv–v.
69. PRO Adm. 1/1516, cap. 404 (Boyles to Nepean, 16 March 1797); see also Cross, *By the Banks of the Thames*, pp. 169–71.
70. Lisianskii's journal (1793–1800) has yet to be published in full: the best test is held at TsVMM, as MS 41821. Copy in TsGALI, *fond* 1337, op. 1, *delo* 135. See V. V. Pertsmakher, "Iu. F. Lisianskii v Indii, 1799," in *Strany i Narody Vostoka*, 12 (1972): 248–52, for details of Lisianskii MSS held in TsVMM, Leningrad, and of his activities in and around Bombay in 1799. Also, N. N. Bolkhovitinov, op. cit., pp. 202–3 for details of transcription and archival holdings; also Krusenstern, *Voyage*, 1: xxv; and W. James, *Naval History of Great Britain from the Declaration of War by France* (London, 1822–26), 1: 495 (Russians in engagements, 1794–97).
71. TsGALI, *fond XVIII veka*, no. 5196, p. 41. On the civil and political situation at Cape Town in 1797, see E. A. Walker, *History of Southern Africa*, 3d ed. (London, 1962), pp. 124–27. On the naval position, W. Laird Clowes, *History of the Royal Navy* (London, 1899–1904), 4: 279–83, 296–97, etc.
72. Nevskii, *Pervoe puteshestvie Rossiian*, pp. 26–27; Cross, *By the Banks of the Thames*, pp. 170–71.
73. Veselago, *Admiral Kruzenshtern*, ch. 4; Nevskii, op. cit., pp. 26–27.
74. L. Dermigny, *La Chine et l'Occident: le commerce à Canton au XVIIIe siècle* (Paris, 1964), 3: 1240–42; Barratt, *Russia in Pacific Waters*, p. 110.
75. Sauer, *Account of a Geographical and Astronomical Expedition*, p. 287; Howay, *List of Vessels in the Maritime Fur Trade*, p. 16; Bancroft, *History of Alaska*, p. 296.
76. Krusenstern, *Voyage*, 2: 289; Tikhmenev, *Supplement*, pp. 206–7; Nevskii, *Pervoe puteshestvie Rossiian*, pp. 241–42.
77. Laird-Clowes, *History of the Royal Navy*, 4: 296–97, 408, 411–12; TsGAVMF, *fond 7*, op. 1, *delo* 2, pp. 240–43 ("Zapisnaia knizhka" with details of Lt. Vasilii M. Golovnin's work as liaison officer during the Anglo-Russian blockade); Ralfe, *Naval Biography*, 1: 322–23; Veselago, *Kratkaia istoriia russkogo flota*, pp. 176–77.
78. TsGALI, *fond* 1337, op.1, *delo* 135, pp. 82ff.; C. N. Parkinson, *War in the Eastern Seas*, pp. 86–90.
79. *DNB*, 2: 667 and 5: 205; *Gentleman's Magazine*, 72 (1802): 35–36.
80. R. Rea, "John Blankett and the Russian Navy in 1774," *mm*, 41 (1955): 245–49; Barratt, *Russia in Pacific Waters*, pp. 70–71.
81. *DNB*, 5: 205 (1790 visit).
82. J. Barrow, *Some Account of the Public Life of Earl Macartney* (London, 1807), p. 1; *DNB*, 34: 404–6.
83. Nevskii, *Pervoe puteshestvie Rossiian*, p. 34.
84. TsGIAL, *fond* 1337, op. 1, *delo* 135, p. 86.
85. A. F. Calvert, *The Exploration of Australia* (London, 1901), 1: 21–22 (origins of the *Investigator* venture, 1799–1801); *DNB*, 19: 325–28; NMM ms 60/1 = 017: Fli/1: Flinders's contacts with Paddy Smith, 1700–1800.
86. TsVMM, MS 41821 ("Zhurnal... Lisianskago s 1793 po 1800 god," p. 60). MS 41820/2, kept with this journal, is Lisianskii's *vakhtennyi zhurnal* ("watch journal") kept aboard H.M.S. *Sceptre* and other ships in 1797–1800, and contains long extracts from the writings of Erasmus Gower (1742–1814), master's mate in H.M.S. *Dolphin*, in the Pacific with Commodore Byron in 1764–66. Sharp, *Discovery of Australia*, pp. 20–20 (*Norfolk*'s surveying of 1798–99); J. S. Cumpston, *Shipping Arrivals and*

Departures: Sydney, 1798–1825 (Canberra, 1964), pp. 33ff.; Lisiansky, *Voyage,* pp. xviii–xx.
87. TsGAVMF, *fond* 198, op. 1, *delo* 36; *fond* 406, op. 7, *delo* 62; also Nevskii, *Pervoe puteshestvie Rossiian,* p. 34.
88. M. Greenberg, *British Trade and the Opening of China, 1800–42* (Cambridge, 1951), pp. 24–25 (Beale and J. H. Cox); H. B. Morse, *Chronicles of the East India Company Trading to China, 1635–1834* (Oxford, 1926–29), 2: 206, 285, 295, 322; Dermigny, *La Chine et l'Occident,* 3: 1240–42.
89. Details in Howay, *List of Trading Vessels,* pp. 33–35.
90. Krusenstern, *Voyages* 1: xxv–vi.
91. See Nevskii, *Pervoe puteshestvie Rossiian,* pp. 247–48.
92. *Fond* 1414 contains 482 items relating to Kruzenshtern, his sons, career, etc., and is complemented by the holdings of the Estonian State Museum of History in Tallin.
93. Krusenstern, *Voyage,* 2: 288–90, 293; C. M. Foust, *Muscovite and Mandarin: Russia's Trade with China and Its Setting, 1727–1805* (Chapel Hill, N.C. 1969), pp. 319–20; Dermigny, op. cit., 3: 1269, 1334 (James Drummond's business).
94. *Sbornik Russkogo Istoricheskago Obshchestva,* 10 (St. P., 1872): 384–86; 27 (1880): 430–32; Okun', *Russian-American Compan;y,* pp. 50–52.
95. Peter Dobell, *Travels in Kamtschatka and Siberia* (London, 1830), 1: 297–98; Andreev, *Russkie otkrytiia,* pp. 365–67.
96. Dobell, *Travels,* 2: 24–25; Berkh, *Khronologicheskaia istoriia,* passim; Sauer, *An Account of a Geographical Expedition,* pp. 275–76.
97. Krusenstern, *Voyage,* 1: xxvi–xxix; *Vneshniaia politika Rossii XIX i nachala XX veka* (M., 1962), 2: 297–98; Okun', *Russian-American Company,* pp. 51–52.
98. Nevskii, *Pervoe puteshestvie Rossiian,* p. 28.
99. Greenberg, *British Trade and China,* pp. 25–27, 222–23; Morse, *Chronicles of the East India Company,* 2: passim; *Jardine, Matheson & Co.: An Outline of the History of a China House for a Hundred Years, 1832–1932* (Hong Kong, 1934), ch. 1; see also, on Kruzenshtern's maritime acquaintances aboard *Bombay Castle* (and Lisianskii's in *Royalist*) in 1799, E. Cotton and C. Fawcett, *East Indiamen: The East India Company's Maritime Service* (London, 1949), and C. Hardy, *Register of the Ships of the East India Company from 1760 to 1812* (London, 1820).
100. Dermigny, *La Chine et l'Occident,* p. 1093: my translation.
101. Morse, *Chronicles of the East India Company,* 2: 389; C. Bateson, *The Convict Ships, 1787–1868* (Glasgow, 1959), pp. 129–30.
102. N. V. Dumitrashko, intro. to *Iu. F. Lisianskii: puteshestvie vokrug sveta na korable 'Neva' v 1803–1806 godakh* (M., 1947), pp. 15–17; Foust, *Muscovite and Mandarin,* pp. 319–20; Barratt, *Russia in Pacific Waters,* p. 110.
103. Vol. 2, p. 328.
104. Nevskii, *Pervoe puteshestvie Rossiian,* p. 27; Krusenstern, *Voyage,* 1: xxx.
105. N. I. Turgenev, *Rossiia i russkie,* 3d ed. (M., 1915), pp. 90–92; S. Ikonnikov, *Graf Nikolai Sergeevich Mordvinov* (St. P., 1873), chs. 3–4; Cross, *By the Banks of the Thames,* pp. 160ff.
106. *Arkhiv grafov Mordvinovykh,* ed. Bilbasov (St. P., 1988–1902), 3: 311–12; Nevskii, *Pervoe puteshestvie Rossiian,* pp. 28–29; Foust, *Muscovite and Mandarin,* p. 320.
107. Further on this, see Barratt, *Russia in Pacific Waters,* pp. 112ff.
108. Okun', *Russian-American Company,* pp. 9ff.
109. Barratt, *Russia in Pacific Waters,* pp. 88–89 (Billings and G. I. Shelikhov).
110. Tikhmenev, *Historical Review,* 1: 121–23; K. Voenskii, "Russkoe posol'stvo v Iaponiiu v nachale XIX veka," *Russkaia starina,* 84 (St. P., 1895): bk. 7, pp. 125–28; V. G. Sirotkin, "Dokumenty o politike Rossii na Dal'nem Vostoke v nachale XIX veka," *Istoricheskie zapiski* (M., November 1962): pp. 87–88.
111. Nevskii, *Pervoe puteshestvie Rossiian,* pp. 52–53.
112. Barratt, *Russia in Pacific Waters,* pp. 104–5, 114–15; Okun', *Russian-American Company,* pp. 32ff.; M. I. Ratmanov, "Vyderzhki iz dnevnika krugosvetnogo puteshestviia

na korable 'Neva'," *Iakhta*, 22 (St. P., 1876): 30–35; G. Atherton, "Nikolai Petrovich Rezanov," *North American Review* (1909): no. 189, pp. 651–61.

113. Foust, *Muscovite and Mandarin*, p. 320; see also M. E. Wheeler, "The Origins of the Russian-American Company;" *Jahrbucher für Geschichte Osteuropas* (1966): pp. 485–94; A. G. Mazour, "The Russian-American Company, Private or Government Enterprise?" *PHR*,13 (1944): 168–73; Tikhmenev, *Supplement*, pp. 309–14.

114. Krusenstern, *Voyage*, 1: 2.

115. Veselago, *Kratkaia istoriia*, pp. 178–90 (naval operations of 1798–1800); Lenz, *Deutsch-Baltisches Lexikon*, index under Bellingshausen, F. G., Berg, V. N.; Nevskii, *Pervoe puteshestvie Rossiian*, pp. 58–59.

116. Novakovskii, *Iaponiia i Rossiia*, pp. 77–78; Tikhmenev, *Historical Review*, 1: 123; Barratt, *Russia in Pacific Waters*, p. 114; *Russkaia starina*, 84 (1895): bk. 7, pp. 125–27.

117. Barratt, *Russia in Pacific Waters*, p. 197 (V. M. Golovnin on the ship purchases).

118. Tikhmenev, *Historical Review*, 1: 123.

120. 1802, No. 137: my translation.

121. Ibid.: this item, headed "Concerning the Russians' Voyage Round the Globe," was extracted by the poet-historian N. M. Karamzin and appeared in his periodical, *Vestnik Evropy*, shortly after (1802, no. 5, pp. 146–47).

122. On Rumiántsev, see A. D. Ivanovskii, *Gosudarstvennyi kantsler graf Nikolai Petrovich Rumiantsev: biograficheskii ocherk* (St. P., 1871); Foust, *Muscovite and Mandarin*, pp. 330–44 and bibliography.

123. Cited by Nevskii, op. cit., p. 35.

124. Ratmanov, "Vyderzhki iz zhurnala," pp. 31ff.; Lensen, *The Russian Push*, pp. 126–27.

125. *Historical Records of Australia: Series I* (Sydney, 1921), 4: 307.

126. J. R. Gibson, *Imperial Russia in Frontier America: The Changing Geography of Supply of Russian America, 1784–1867* (New York, 1976), pp. 76–77.

127. For career details of officers who visited Australia, see the Russian Navy List, *Obshchii morskoi spisok*, 14 vols. (St. P., 1885–1907); also *Russkii biograficheskii slovar'*, 25 vols., ed. Polovtsov and Modzalevskii (St. P., 1896–1918); F. F. Veselago, comp., *Materialy dlia istorii russkogo flota* (St. P., 1880–1904); Lenz, *Deutsch-Baltisches Biographisches Lexikon*.

128. Nevskii, *Pervoe puteshestvie Rossiian*, pp. 57–58; Krusenstern, *Voyage*, 1: 2ff.

129. J. G. Kohl, *Russia and the Russians in 1842* (London, 1843), 2: 200–2; G. R. Barratt, *Rebel on the Bridge*, pp. 17–37.

130. Lenz, *Deutsch-Baltisches Biographisches Lexikon*, pp. 40–41, 52, 468.

131. Ibid., p. 410; Krusenstern, *Voyage*, 1: 11.

132. Lisiansky, *Voyage*, pp. 318–19. On Lisianskii's subsequent career successes and premature retirement, see E. L. Shteinberg, *Zhizneopisanie russkogo moreplavatelia Iuriia Lisianskogo* (M., 1948); Barratt, *The Russian Disocvery of Hawaii, 1804*, pt. 2; Nevskii, *Pervoe puteshestvie Rossiian*, pp. 192–94.

133. Lensen, *The Russian Push*, pp. 142–56.

134. Barratt, *Russia in Pacific Waters*, pp. 121–22, 129–30.

135. Nevskii, op. cit., pp. 269–71 (the expedition members' publications).

136. Beaglehole, *The Journals of Captain James Cook*, 1: cclxxxiii.

137. Full description in Rozina, "Kollektsiia Dzhemsa Kuka" (1966).

138. Ryden, *The Banks Collection*, p. 68; Barratt, *The Russian Discovery of Hawaii, 1804*, pt. 3.

139. G. H. Langsdorf, *Voyages and Travels in Various Parts of the World, during the Years 1803–1807* (London, 1813–14), 1: 100–6; Lisiansky, *Voyage*, pp. 87–105; N. I. Korobitsyn, "Journal," in Andreev, *Russian Discoveries*, pp. 213–15; Krusenstern, *Voyage*, 1: 75ff.

140. TsGIAL, *fond* 853 (M. M. Buldakova), *delo* 1: no. 74 ("Zhurnal prikazov kapitana Kruzenshterna komande sudov...."). Further on this, see N. A. Gvozdetskii, "Pervoe morskoe puteshestvie Rossiian vokrug sveta," *Priroda* (M., 1947): no. 1, pp. 85–88.

141. F. I. Shemelin, *Zhurnal pervogo puteshestviia Rossiian vokrug zemnago shara* (St. P.,

1816–18), 1: 121–22; Andreev, *Russian Discoveries*, pp. 213–14; Lisiansky, *Voyage*, pp. 88–90; G. M. Dening, ed., *The Marquesan Journals of Edward Robarts, 1797–1824* (Canberra, 1974), intro.

142. D. D. Tumarkin, *Vtorzhenie kolonizatorov v "Krai vechnoi vesny": Gavaiskii narod v bor'be protiv chuzhezemnykh zakhvatchikov* (M., 1964), and "Iz istorii gavaitsev v kontse XVIII-nachale XIX veka," *Sovetskaia etnografiia* (1958): no. 6, pp. 38–53. But see also *Zapiski Uchonogo Komiteta Morskago Shtaba* (St. P., 1828), 1: 144–49, on the death of Russians at Nukuhiva on 16 April 1826.

143. Tilesius von Tilenau, "Izvestie o estestvennom i politicheskom sostoianii zhitelei ostrova Nukugivy," *Tekhnologicheskii zhurnal* (St. P., 1806), pt. 4; Iu. F. Lisianskii, *Sobranie kart i risunkov, prinadlezhashchikh k puteshestviiu... na korable "Neva"* (St. P., 1812), pl. 1; L. F. Rudovits, "Pervoe russkoe krugosvetnoe plavanie, 1803–06: obzor nauchnykh rabot," *Trudy Gos. Okeanograficheskogo Instituta*, 27 (L., 1954): 3–12.

144. On Russian contact with the Cammeraigal people of Port Jackson's North Shore (1820 and subsequently), see above, pp. 253–80.

NOTES TO CHAPTER THREE

1. See Hotimsky, "Bibliography of Captain James Cook in Russian," pp. 6–12.

2. Ibid., pp. 6–7, 10; Beddie, *Bibliography*, nos. 10, 722.

3. Survey in A. G. Cross, *Nikolai M. Karamzin: A Study of His LIterary Career* (Carbondale, IL, 1971), pp. 193–217. See *Vestnik Evropy* (1802): no. 5, p. 146, for an extract from the Hamburg press on the Kruzenshtern-Lisianskii expedition.

4. See Vol. 1 for Governor Phillips, Vol. 9 for White and Bligh, and Vols. 21–22 for Hunter. Details also in Ferguson, *Bibliography of Australia*, 1: 56, etc.

5. Ferguson lists several works reflecting an "exotica" penchant, e.g., Southey's "Botany Bay Eclogues" (1799) and George Bond's *Brief Account of the Colony of Port Jackson* (1803). Further on this large subject, see B. Smith, *European Vision and the South Pacific, 1768–1850* (Oxford, 1960).

6. Beddie, *Bibliography*, no. 1570; Sopikov, *Opyt rossiiskoi bibliografii*, no. 9203; Kondakov, *Svodnyi katalog*, no. 5613.

7. This poem by Helen Maria Williams (1762–1827), on whom see *DNB*, 61: 404–5, appeared in the first edition of the *Life of Captain Cook* by Kippis, a family friend of Miss Williams and the main source of her literary interest in Polynesia.

8. Sopikov, *Opyt rossiiskoi bibliografii*, no. 9205; A. Smirdin, *Rospis' rossiiskim knigam dlia chteniia* (St. P., 1828), no. 3100. Another Zubkov (a relation?) in 1772 engraved the coloured map of the Southern Hemisphere which embellished the Russian version of Joseph Banks's *Voyage* of 1771 and letter to the *Académie* in Paris: see Hotimsky, "Bibliography of Captain James Cook in Russian," p. 6.

9. Sopikov, op. cit., no. 9164, no. 10,990.

10. *DNB*, 3: 288–89.

11. Vengerov, *Istochniki*, 2: 10; Kondakov, *Svodnyi katalog*, index under Golitsyn, Aleksei P.

12. See Chapter 5 here.

13. Nevskii, *Pervoe puteshestvie Rossiian*, p. 35–37; Barratt, *Russia in Pacific Waters*, p. 112.

14. Sopikov, *Opyt rossiiskoi bibliografii*, no. 5802.

15. Kondakov, *Svodnyi katalog*, nos. 941, 5314, 4666.

16. Ibid., 5: 147; also Vengerov, *Istochniki*, 1: 547–48 (Verevkin) and 4: 393 (Mozhaiskii).

17. A. Rossiiskii, "Zhurnal shturmana Alekseia Rossiiskago, puteshestvuiushchego na korable 'Suvorov'...," *Sorevnovatel' prosveshcheniia i blagodeianiia* (St. P., 1820): no. 11, pp. 125–46; no. 12, pp. 246–56.

18. AVPR, *fond* Glavarkhiva, II-3 (1806–10), op. 34, *dela* 3–5 (orders for Hagemeister from Company Head Office, etc.); N. A. Ivashintsev, *Russian Round-the-World Voy-*

ages, 1803–1849, trans. G. R. Barratt (Kingston, Ont., 1980), pp. 14, 137.
19. Hotimsky, "Bibliography of Captain James Cook in Russian," p. 9.
20. Ivashintsev, *Russian Round-the-World Voyages*, pp. 13–14; Tikhmenev, *Historical Review of the Formation*, 1: 407–8.
21. Lenz, *Deutsch-Baltisches Biographisches Lexikon*, pp. 284–85; *Zapiski Uchonogo Komiteta Morskago Shtaba* (St. P., 1835), 2: 355–57.
22. Barratt, *Rebel on the Bridge*, pp. 12–14.
23. Laird-Clowes, *History of the Royal Navy*, 4: 279, 378; James, *Naval History of Great Britain*, 2: 181.
24. PRO, Adm. 1/1927, cap. 9–10 (Captain Hallowell from St. Thomas); H. H. Breen, *St. Lucia, Historical, Statistical, and Descriptive* (London, 1844), pp. 110–12 (actions of June 1803, etc.).
25. See Sir N. Nicolas, *The Despatches and Letters of Vice-Admiral Lord Nelson* (London, 1844), 5: 448–49, 6: 42–43; also C. Oman, *Nelson* (London, 1948), p. 108 (thoughts of Russian service). On Hagemeister's family and connections, *Genealogisches Handbuch des deutschen Adels* (Glucksburg, 1951–58), 3: 174–79. See p. 178 on the Alexander Hagemeister, lineal descendant, who settled in Adelaide, S.A., in the 1930s.
26. AVPR, *fond* Glavarkhiva, II-3 (1806–10), op. 34, *delo* 4.
27. Ivashintsev, *Russian Round-the-World Voyages*, p. 137.
28. See Barratt, *Russia in Pacific Waters*, chs. 6 and 9, on the growth of these tensions.
29. V. Fitzhardinge, "Russian Ships in Australian Waters, 1807–1835," pp. 114–15; E. F. McCartan, "The Long Voyages—Early Russian Circumnavigation," *Russian Review* (1963): pp. 30–37; Gibson, *Imperial Russia in Frontier America*, pp. 76–77.
30. Ivashintsev, op. cit., p. 14.
31. G. Blainey, *The Tyranny of Distance* (Melbourne, 1966), pp. 38–39.
32. Lenz, *Deutsch-Baltisches Biographisches Lexikon*, p. 52.
33. Ivashintsev, op. cit., pp. 137–38; R. G. Liapunova and S. G. Federova, comps. and eds., *Russkaia Amerika v neopublikovannykh zapiskakh K. T. Khlebnikova* (L., 1979), pp. 164, 271.
34. Survey in Bancroft, *History of Alaska*, pp. 510–27; see also Gibson, *Imperial Russia in Frontier America*, passim; K. T. Khlebnikov, *Baranov*, trans. C. Bearne (Kingston, Ont., 1973), pp. 96–97, and Barratt, *Russia in Pacific Waters*, pp. 189–91. Thumbnail sketch by R. A. Pierce, "Two Russian Governors: Hagemeister and Yanovskii," *Alaska Journal*, 1 (1971): no. 2, pp. 49–51.
35. In the nineteenth centruy, the Russian calendar lagged twelve days behind the New Style or Gregorian calendar; thus, *Neva* arrived at Sydney on 3/15 June 1807.
36. Mitchell Library, Sydney: *Banks Papers*, 22–26; also *Historical Records of Australia: Series 1* (Sydney, 1913–19), 6: 159 (*Neva*'s arrival and the official reaction).
37. Perm' District State Archive, Perm': *fond* 445 (Kiril T. Khlebnikov), op. 1, *delo* 58: Hagemeister despatches to Company Main Board, Sydney, 24 June 1807. On Campbell's earlier career and appointment at Sydney, see Bach, *Maritime History*, pp. 27, 50, 71–72; on Bligh's conflict with Macarthur and Johnston of the New South Wales Corps, M. H. Ellis, *John Macarthur* (Sydney, 1955), and H. V. Evatt, *Rum Rebellion: A Study of the Overthrow of Governor Bligh* (Sydney, 1938).
38. Blainey, *Tyranny of Distance*, pp. 40–50; O. H. K. Spate, *Australia* (New York, 1968), pp. 34–36.
39. Perm' District State Archive, *fond* 445, op. 1, *delo* 58: fol. 4; see Bach, *Maritime History*, pp. 71–72 on the exporting of sealskins and oil by Robert Campbell; and Blainey, op. cit., pp. 48–49, on grain prices.
40. Blainey, op. cit., p. 65; also Bach, op. cit., pp. 46–47, and T. Dunbabin, "New Light on the Earliest American Voyages to Australia," *American Neptune*, 10 (1950): no. 1, pp. 52ff. (New England vessels met by the Russians), and B. Little, "Sealing and Whaling in Australia before 1850," *Australian Historical Review*, 9 (1969): no. 2 (mechanics of the sealing witnessed by Hagemeister).
41. Ellis, *John Macarthur*, Bk. 4; Evatt, *Rum Rebellion*, passim.

42. HRA, 6: 159.
43. Mitchell Library, *Banks Papers*, 22: 266; ADB (1788–1850), 2: 22 (George Johnston, Jr. and early beef production).
44. Beaglehole, *Journals of Captain James Cook*, 3: pt. 2, pp. 449–58.
45. Items from 21 and 28 June.
46. For details of ships met by Russian vessels at Sydney, see J. S. Cumpston, *Shipping Arrivals and Departures: Sydney, 1788–1825* (Canberra, 1964), p. 61 for *Hannah* and *Sally;* see also n. 40 above.
47. Perm' District State Archive, *fond* 445, op. 1, *delo* 58: fol. 5.
49. Surveys in R. A. Pierce, *Russia's Hawaiian Adventure, 1815–1817* (Berkeley, 1965), pp. 37–39; Khlebnikov, *Baranov*, p. 74; Barratt, *Russia in Pacific Waters*, pp. 154–56.
50. Further on this, see A. Campbell, *A Voyage Round the World from 1806 to 1812, in which Japan, Kamchatka, the Aleutian Islands, and the Sandwich Islands were Visited*, 2d ed. (New York, 1819), pp. 80–81, and K. Mehnert, *The Russians in Hawaii, 1804–1819* (Honolulu, 1939).
48. Ivashintsev, *Russian Round-the-World Voyages*, p. 14.
51. Pierce, "Two Russian Governors," p. 50.
52. Khlebnikov, *Baranov*, pp. 86–87; Gibson, *Imperial Russia*, pp. 161–62; Howay, *List of Trading Vessels*, pp. 32ff.
53. *Zapiski Uchonogo Komiteta Morskago Shtaba* (St. P., 1835), 2: 355–37.
54. V. M. Golovnin, *Puteshestvie na shliupe "Diana" iz Kronshtadta v Kamchatku v 1807–1811 godakh*, 4th ed. (M., 1964), ch. 1; N. I. Nozikov, *Russian Voyages Round the World*, trans. Lesser (London, n.d.), pp. 76–80.
55. TsGAVMF, *fond* 7, op. 1, *delo* 2: pp. 256ff.; Ivashintsev, *Russian Round-the-World Voyages*, pp. 15–16; Golovnin, *Puteshestvie*, intro.
56. TsGAVMF, *fond* 7, op. 1, *delo* 2 ("Zapisnaia knizhka"): p. 256.
57. Ibid., pp. 240–43 and 251–52.
58. Port of Spain: see Laird-Clowes, *History of the Royal Navy*, 4: 395 and nn. 23–24 above (Russian Volunteers in the West Indies).
59. Golovnin, *Puteshestvie*, pp. 74–147; Ivashintsev, *Russian Round-the-World Voyages*, pp. 16–18.
60. Golovnin, *Puteshestvie*, p. 126.
61. Ibid., pp. 146–48; Barratt, *Russia in Pacific Waters*, pp. 160–61.
62. V. M. Golovnin, "Ostrov Tana: iz zapisok flota-leitenanta V. M. Golovnina," *Syn otechestva* (St. P., 1816): pt. 31, no. 31, pp. 177–200; no. 32, pp. 217–33.
63. V. M. Golovnin, "Zamechaniia, uchinennye... v 1808 godu, na puti ot Mysa Dobroi Nadezhdy do ostrova Tany...," *ZADMM* (St. P., 1815): pt. 3, pp. 212–38; Ivashintsev, *Russian Round-the-World Voyages*, p. 18.
64. Golovnin's *Memoirs* of captivity by the Japanese in 1811–13 were translated into English (London, 1818). See P. Polansky, *Russian Writings on the South Pacific*, University of Hawaii Work Papers, PIP, no. 5 (Honolulu, 1974), pp. 20–22, for Golovnin and the South Pacific.
65. Krusenstern, *Voyage*, vol. 1, chs. 3–4.
66. Ivashintsev, *Russian Round-the-World Voyages*, pp. 14, 18; see also Blainey, *Tyranny of Distance*, pp. 38–40, and S. Ia. Unkovskii, "Istinnye zapiski moiei zhizni," in A. A. Samarov, ed., *Russkie flotovodtsy: M. P. Lazarev* (M., 1952), 1: 24–26.
67. Ivashintsev, op. cit., pp. 20–21, 50–51, 64–65, 104, and 110.
68. Gibson, *Imperial Russia*, pp. 156–62; Barratt, *Russia in Pacific Waters*, pp. 173–74.
69. Dobell, *Travels*, 1: 197–98, 2: 24–26; F. P. Vrangel' (Wrangel), *Statistische und ethnographische Nachrichten über die russischen Besitzungen an der Nordwestküste von Amerika* (St. P., 1839), pp. 20–21; Andreev, *Russkie otkrytiia*, pp. 365–67.
70. Gibson, *Imperial Russia*, pp. 76, 83–87.
71. Khlebnikov, *Baranov*, pp. 86–87; Gibson, op. cit., pp. 156–61; M. E. Wheeler, "Empires in Conflict and Co-operation: The Bostonians and the Russian-American Company," *PHR*, 40 (1971): 419–41.

72. See Gibson, *Imperial Russia*, pp. 161ff.
73. Samarov, *Russkie flotovodtsy*, 1, 11ff.; Aleksei P. Lazarev, *Zapiski o plavanii voennogo shliupa Blagonamerennogo v Beringov proliv... v 1819, 1820, 1821, i 1822 godakh* (M., 1950), pp. 28–32; Barratt, *Russia in Pacific Waters*, pp. 174–75.
74. Ivashintsev, *Russian Round-the-World Voyages*, pp. 20 and 138; TsGAVMF, *fond* 1152, op. 1, *dela* 1–2: "Putevoi zhurnal leitenanta Semena Ia. Unkovskogo... 1813–1816 godov," typewritten copy, pp. 2–4 (copy entitled "Istinnye zapiski moiei zhizni").
75. Unkovskii, "Putevoi zhurnal," p. 1.
76. Ivashintsev, *Russian Round-the-World Voyages*, p. 20; Fitzhardinge, "Russian Ships in Australian Waters," pp. 119–20.
77. Summaries in Pierce, *Russia's Hawaiian Adventure*, ch. 1, and Gibson, *Imperial Russia*, pp. 143–49.
78. Samarov, *Russkie flotovodtsy*, 1: 17.
79. Ivashintsev, op. cit., p. 22.
80. HRA, 8: 588–89.
81. "Vypiska iz zhurnala shturmana Alekseia Rossiiskago," *Sorevnovatel' prosveshcheniia i blagodeianiia* (St. P., 1820): no. 11, pp. 134–35 (12–13 August, Old Style).
82. M. Barnard Eldershaw, *Life and Times of Captain John Piper* (Sydney, 1939); ADB, 2: 334–35; also Bach, *Maritime History*, pp. 26 and 29, on Middle Head, "Sow and Pigs," and other navigational hazards in Port Jackson.
83. TsGAVMF, *fond* 1152, op. 1, *delo* 2: p. 32; on the hospital (western side of Sydney Cove) and Hospital Wharf at which the Russians landed in 1807 and 1814, see Bach, op. cit., pp. 26–27, and J. T. Bigge, *Report on Agriculture and Trade in New South Wales* (London, 1823), 3: 61.
84. TsGAVMF, *fond* 1152, op. 1, *delo* 2: p. 32; also, on Richard Brooks, Rossiiskii, "Vypiska iz zhurnala," p. 136. On pilotage and pilots encountered by the Russians in these years, *Port of Sydney Journal*, 2 (1948): no. 1, p. 10; (1970–71), nos. 3–4.
85. *Sydney Gazette Extraordinary*, 25 August 1814: no. 558. See also Ruth Park, *Companion Guide to Sydney* (Sydney, 1973), p. 52.
86. TsGAVMF, *fond* 1152, op. 1, *delo* 2: p. 2–4; Veselago, *Kratkaia istoriia russkogo flota*, pp. 246–47.
87. Samarov, *Russkie flotovodtsy*, p. 48; Barratt, *The Russians at Port Jackson, 1814–1822* (Canberra, 1981), pp. 11, 14, 23–26.
88. Mitchell Library, Lachlan Macquarie Journals: CY A771, p. 178; see also M. H. Ellis, *Lachlan Macquarie: His Life, Adventures, and Times* (Sydney, 1947), pp. 166–67.
89. Macquarie Journals: CY A771, p. 198.
90. Ibid., pp. 215–17. See Cross, *By the Banks of the Thames*, pp. 158 and 166 on Admiral P. I. Khanykov (1743–1813) and his English links.
91. Colonel George Molle (1773–1823), lieutenant-governor of New South Wales, commanding in Macquarie's absence: ADB, 2: 243.
92. ADB, 2: 22. In 1814, Johnston was 24, Unkovskii 25.
93. Samarov, *Russkie flotovodtsy*, 1: 23–24.
94. Ibid., p. 24. On Marsden, ADB, 2: 207–13; on the Parramatta road taken by the Russians, D. G. Dowd, *Macquarie Country: A History of the Hawkesbury* (Melbourne, 1969), pp. 56–57; also *Sydney Gazette*, 27 November 1813. The Maoris seen by the Russians included the chiefs Hongi Hika and Ruatara, recently arrived in the *Active* from the Bay of Islands, New Zealand: J. R. Elder, ed., *Samuel Marsden's Letters and Journals* (Dunedin, 1932), p. 79; J. Binney, *The Legacy of Guilt* (Auckland, 1968), pp. 23–25.
95. See Peter Cunningham, *Two Years in New South Wales* (London, 1827), 1: 95.
96. See my paper, "Russia and New Zealand: The Beginnings," *New Zealand Slavonic Journal* (1979): no. 2, pp. 33–34.
97. Rossiiskii, "Vypiska iz zhurnala," p. 136.
98. TsGAVMF, *fond* 1152, op. 1, *delo* 2: pp. 32; on chandlery and the 1811 port regulations by which *Suvorov* was bound, see A. Birch and D. S. Macmillan, *The Sydney Scene,*

1788–1960 (Melbourne, 1962), pp. 44–45, etc.; also D. R. Hainsworth, *The Sydney Traders* (Melbourne, 1972), chs. 2–3.

99. Rossiiski, "Vypiska iz zhurnala," pp. 136–37.
100. Samarov, *Russkie flotovodtsy*, 1: 48.
101. no. 11, pp. 125–46; no. 12, pp. 246–56.
102. Barrat, *Russians at Port Jackson*, pp. 24–25.
103. HRA, 8: 588 ("Report of Ships and Vessels Entered Inward... 1st July to 30th September 1814"); on *Suvorov*'s crew, Ivashintsev, *Russian Round-the-World Voyages*, pp. 137–38.
104. TsGAVMF, *fond* 212, *delo* 3735, pp. 151–52.
105. On these matters, see Okun', *Russian-American Company*, p. 10; Gibson, *Imperial Russia*, p. 65; Barratt, *Russia in Pacific Waters*, pp. 175, 185; Pierce, *Russia's Hawaiian Adventure*, p. 57 (Molvo's tippling).
106. Bach, *Maritime History*, p. 46.
107. Rossiiskii, "Vypiska iz zhurnala," no. 12, pp. 250–51; Samarov, *Russkie flotovodtsy*, 1: 25–26.
108. Rossiiskii, "Vypiska iz zhurnala," no. 12, p. 252. *Suvorov* reached Peru in December 1815, staying nearly three months: Ivashintsev, op. cit., p. 23.
109. Cumpston, *Shipping Arrivals and Departures: Sydney*, p. 93; also Cunningham, *Two Years in New South Wales*, 1: 56.
110. TsGAVMF, *fond* 1152, op. 1, *delo* 2: p. 39; a different version was prepared for printing by the author and is given in Samarov, *Russkie flotovodtsy*, 1: 25–26. (Barnes's delight on meeting Russians is increased, his familiarity with Archangel noted, etc.) On New England whalers, Little, "Sealing and Whaling before 1850," no. 2; Dunbabin, "New Light on the Earliest American Voyages," passim; Blainey, *Tyranny of Distance*, pp. 99–103. On Captain Thomas Raine, whom *Suvorov*'s officers met socially at Sydney, R. H. Goddard, "Captain T. Raine of the *Surry*," JRAHS, 26 (1940): pt. 4.
111. TsGAVMF, *fond* 1152, op. 1, *delo* 2: p. 39. David Porter, U.S.N., *Journal of a Cruise made to the Pacific Ocean in the United States Frigate Essex in the Years 1812–1814*, (New York 1815), on the capture of the British whaler *Seringapatam;* Porter's raids surveyed in *DAB*, 15: 84–85.
112. TsGAVMF, *fond* 1152, op. 1, *delo* 2: p. 40.; ADB, 2: 22.
113. Samarov, *Russkie flotovodtsy*, 1: 26.
114. TsGAVMF, *fond* 1152, op. 1, *delo* 2: p. 40.
115. See Barratt, *Russia in Pacific Waters*, p. 175.
116. TsGAVMF, *fond* 212, *delo* 3735, p. 152.
117. Barratt, *Russia in Pacific Waters*, chs. 6 and 9 (Navy-Company stress).
118. Unkovskii, "Istinnye zapiski moiei zhizni," TsGAVMF, *fond* 1152, op. 1, *delo* 2: p. 40.
119. A. D. Ivanovskii, *Gosudarstvennyi kantsler graf Nikolai Petrovich Rumiantsev: biograficheskii ocherk* (St. P., 1871), pp. 69ff.; Krusenstern, *Voyage*, 1: xxx–xxxi; Otto von Kotzebue, *A Voyage of Discovery into the South Sea and Beering's Straits* (London, 1821), 1: 6–8.
120. Barratt, *Russia in Pacific Waters*, pp. 177–78; F. F. Veselago, *Kratkaia istoriia russkogo flota* (M., 1939), pp. 290–91.
121. A. D. Dobrovol'skii, *Otto fon Kotsebue: russkie moreplavateli* (M., 1953), chs. 2–4; A. C. Mahr, *The Visit of the "Rurik", to San Francisco in 1816* (Stanford, 1832), pp. 11–14; Friis, *The Pacific Basin*, pp. 191–93; Barratt, *Russia in Pacific Waters*, p. 176.
122. Kotzebue, *Voyage of Discovery*, 1: 8–10; A. von Chamisso, *Werke* (Berlin, 1856), 2: 14–18; Mahr, *Visit of the "Rurik,"* pp. 12–18; L. Choris, *Voyage pittoresque autour du monde* (Paris, 1822), pp. 2–8.
123. Dobrovol'skii, *Otto fon Kotsebue*, chs. 4–5.
124. Kotzebue, *Voyage of Discovery*, 1: 29–30; see also D. D. Tumarkin, intro. to *O. Kotzebu: novoe puteshestvie vokrug sveta v 1823–1826 godakh* (M., 1981), pp. 5–8.
125. Ivashintsev, *Russian Round-the-World Voyages*, p. 24; Aleksei P. Lazarev, *Zapiski o plavanii voennogo shliupa Blagonamerennogo v Beringov proliv... v 1819–1822*

godakh (M., 1950), pp. 29–30, and V. V. Kuznetsova, "Novye dokumenty o russkoi ekspeditsii k severnomu poliusu," *IVGO* (1968): no. 3, pp. 237ff. (on Shishmarev).
126. R. A. Pierce, *Russia's Hawaiian Adventure, 1815–1817* (Berkeley, 1965); H. W. Bradley, *The American Frontier in Hawaii: The Pioneers, 1789–1843*, 2d ed. (Gloucester, MA, 1968), pp. 46–49; Gibson, *Imperial Russia*, pp. 143–49.
127. G. Barratt, *The Russian View of Honolulu, 1809–1826* (Ottawa, 1988), ch. 1.
128. Details in Bradley, *The American Frontier*, pp. 46–49.
129. HRA, 8: despatch no. 47, encl. 1.
130. *Sydney Gazette*, 17 April 1819, p. 2.
131. HRA, 7: 475–76; Pierce, *Russia's Hawaiian Adventure*, pp. 190–91.
132. See Bradley, *The American Frontier*, pp. 48–49.
133. Kotzebue, *Voyage of Discovery*, 1: 325.
134. Ibid., 3: 241. Further on Anglo-Russian contacts of this time involving Port Jackson, see Howay, *A List of Trading Vessels*, pp. 21, 28, 31, 112; L. A. Shur, *K beregam novogo sveta* (M., 1971), p. 127; and Pierce, *Russia's Hawaiian Adventure*, pp.157–58.
135. Kotzebue, *Voyage of Discovery*, 2: 359; 3: 77, 399.
136. Ibid., 1: 33, 37–39; also p. 6, for praise of Flinders, etc. The "English expedition" referred to byKruzenshtern was P. P. King's in *Mermaid*.

NOTES TO CHAPTER FOUR

1. B. M. Gough, *To the Pacific and Arctic with Beechey* (Cambridge, 1973), p. 4. See also A. Day, *The Admiralty Hydrographic Service, 1795–1919* (London, 1967), pp. 27–38.
2. Lt. A. M'Konochie, *Considerations on the Propriety of Establishing a Colony on One of the Sandwich Islands* (London, 1816); Bradley, *The American Frontier*, pp. 48–49, 103; Barratt, *Russia in Pacific Waters*, ch. 10.
3. HRA, 6: 159; 8: 588–89.
4. Gibson, *Imperial Russia*, passim; S. B. Okun', "Tsarskaia Rossiia i Gavaiskie Ostrova," *Krasnyi arkhiv* (M., 1936): no. 6; Peter Corney, *Voyages in the Northern Pacific* (Honolulu, 1896), pp. 87–88.
5. Bradley, *The American Frontier*, pp. 48, 103.
6. Cited by Day, *Admiralty Hydrographic Service*, pp. 27–28; see also L. P. Kirwan, *History of Polar Exploration* (New York, 1960), p. 77.
7. Day, op. cit., pp. 28ff.; Laird-Clowes, *History of the Royal Navy*, 6: 507–11.
8. Details in E. E. Shvede, ed., *F. F. Bellingsgauzen: dvukratnye izyskaniia v Iuzhnom ledovitom okeane i plavanie vokrug sveta v prodolzhenie 1819, 1820, i 1821 godov* (M., 1960), pp. 9–12.
9. Aleksei P. Lazarev, *Zapiski o plavanii voennogo shliupa Blagonamerennogo v Beringov proliv v 1819–1822 godakh* (M., 1950), pp. 22–23.
10. Ibid., pp. 24–25; V. N. Sementovskii, ed., *Russkie otkrytiia v Antarktike v 1819–1821 godakh* (M., 1951), pp. 21–22; V. V. Kuznetsova, "Novye documenty o russkoi ekspeditsii k severnomu poliusu," *IVGO*, 100 (1968): no. 3, pp. 237–45.
11. Lazarev, *Zapiski*, pp. 27–29.
12. Ibid., pp. 29–30; O. E. Kotzebue, *Puteshestvie v Iuzhnyi okean i v Beringov Prorliv . . . v 1815, 1816, 1817 i 1818 godakh* (St. P., 1821), 1: 20ff.; S. G. Fedorova, *The Russian Population in Alaska and California: Late Eighteenth Century–1867*, trans. R. A. Pierce and A. S. Donnelly (Kingston, Ont., 1973), pp. 257–59.
13. TsGAVMF, *fond* 213, *delo* 45; Lazarev, *Zapiski*, p. 87; Ivashintsev, *Russian Round-the-World Voyages*, pp. 42, 50, 140–41.
14. See Bibliography under Lazarev, Andrei, Aleksei, Mikhail Petrovich.
15. G. Barratt, "Russian Warships in Van Diemen's Land: The *Kreyser* and the *Ladoga* by Hobart Town, 1823," *SEER*, 53 (1975): no. 133, pp. 566 ff.
16. Kuznetsova, "Novye dokumenty," pp. 237–40; TsGAVMF, *fond* 203, op. 1, *delo* 730 (N. D. Shishmarev's 1819–22 journal, of 264 pp.); K. Gillesem, "Puteshestvie na

shliupe 'Blagonamerennyi' dlia issledovaniia beregov Azii i Ameriki. . . c 1819 po 1822 god," *Otechestvennye zapiski,* 66 (St. P., 1849): nos. 9–10; 67: nos. 11–12; Lazarev, *Zapiski,* p. 5.

17. Lazarev, op. cit., p. 25 (Ukaz Admiralteisk-Kollegii, 13 March 1819); see also Sementovskii, *Russkie otkrytiia,* pp. 21–22, and Ivashintsev, *Russian Round-the-World Voyages,* pp. 140–41.
18. Lenz, *Duetsch-Baltisches Biographisches Lexikon,* pp. 40–41; Shvede, *F. F. Bellinsgauzen,* pp. 20–21.
19. See Barratt, *Bellingshausen: A Visit to New Zealand, 1820* (Palmerston North, N.Z., 1979), p. 17, and *Voices in Exile: The Decembrist Memoirs* (Montreal and London, 1974), passim, on Torson's later life.
20. On Simonov, see Barratt, *Bellingshausen,* pp. 14–15, 18–22, 169–70; on Mikhailov, pp. 24–25.
21. Ibid., pp. 15–16, 22–24.
22. Nevskii, *Pervoe puteshestvie Rossiian,* pp. 261–66; Barratt, *Russia in Pacific Waters,* pp. 140–41; Ivashintsev, *Russian Round-the-World Voyages,* pp. 140–41.
23. Lazarev, *Zapiski,* p. 25.
24. Ivashintsev, *Russian Round-the-World Voyages,* pp. 50–51.
25. Kuznetsova, "Novye dokumenty," p. 237; N. N. Zubov, *Otechestvennye moreplavateli—issledovateli morei i okeanov* (M., 1954); I. P. Magidovich, *Ocherki po istorii geograficheskikh otkrytii* (M., 1957).
26. For reasonable assessments, see V. A. Esakov *et al., Russkie okeanicheskie i morskie issledovaniia, XIX-nachala XX vekov* (M., 1964), pp. 69–72, and Fedorova, *Russian Population,* pp. 257–58.
27. On this, see Barratt, "Russian Naval Sources for the History of Colonial Australia to 1825," *JRAHS,* 67 (1981): pt. 2, pp. 169–74.
28. Portfolios described in TsGIAL, *fond* 789 (Akademii Khudozhestv), op. 20, *dela* 28, 30, 36; copies held at Elmer E. Rasmuson Library, University of Alaska at Fairbanks: Shur Collection, reel 85.
29. Gough, *To the Pacific and Arctic with Beechey,* intro. (orders of 10 February 1825 suggesting use of Kotzebue Sound, etc.); Fedorova, *Russian Population,* p. 259.
30. E. W. Hunter Christie, *The Antarctic Problem: An Historical and Political Study* (London, 1951), p. 109. The 1831 edition of Bellingshausen's account of his expedition has appeared in two Soviet editions, of 1949 and 1960, and was translated by Frank Debenham as *The Voyage of Captain Bellingshausen to the Antarctic Seas, 1819–21,* 2 vols. (London, 1945).
31. Shvede, *F. F. Bellinsgauzen,* pp. 25 ff, 66; Barratt, *Russians at Port Jackson,* pp. 8–10.
32. Via Lord Cathcart, British ambassador at St. Petersburg, and the Foreign Office: TsGAVMF, *fond* 213, *delo* 9: p. 1; HRA, 10: 369.
33. Ivashintsev, *Russian Round-the-World Voyages,* pp. 42–43; Shvede, *F. F. Bellinsgauzen,* ch. 1.
34. V. L. Lebedev, "Geograficheskie nabliudeniia v Antarktike," *Antarktika: doklady kommissii, 1960* (M., 1961); "Donesenie kapitana Bellinsgauzena iz porta Zhaksona o svoem plavanii," *ZADMM,* 5 (St. P., 1823); Friis, *The Pacific Basin,* pp. 195–96.
35. Shvede, *F. F. Bellinsgauzen,* pp. 190–93; P. M. Novosil'skii, *Iuzhnyi polius: iz zapisok byvshego morskago ofitsera* (St. P., 1953), ch. 3.
36. Mitchell Library: Macquarie Journal, CY A774, p. 124; Ivashintsev, *Russian Round-the-World Voyages,* p. 46; Bellingshausen, *Voyage,* 1: 156–58.
37. Lazarev, *Zapiski,* pp. 154–55.
38. Ivashintsev, op. cit., p. 50.
39. A. I. Andreev's intro. to *Zapiski o plavanii voennogo shliupa Blagonamerennogo v Beringov proliv i vokrug sveta dlia otkrytii v 1819, 1820, 1821 i 1822 godakh* (M., 1950), pp. 6–8; on the discovery of the MS in Smolensk District Archive ca. 1948, its editing, and its present location: TsGAVMF, *fond* 1153, *delo* 1.
40. Andreev, op. cit., pp. 31–33.
41. TsGIAL, *fond* 789, op. 20: Report, No. 351, 23 December 1830 (A. Olenin to A. S.

Menshikov); Saltykov-Shchedrin Public Library, Leningrad: *Rukopisnyi otdel*, F. 17, 106.11.
42. Lazarev, *Zapiski*, pp. 149–50.
43. Ibid., p. 151; Bellingshausen, *Voyage*, 1: 39, 159; 2: 320.
44. Iu. M. Shokal'skii, *Okeanografiia* (Petrograd, 1917), pp. 2–10; Friis, *The Pacific Basin*, pp. 186–97.
45. Lazarev, *Zapiski*, p. 150; HRA, 10: 284.
46. A. von Chimisso, *Werke*, 3: 18; see also Mahr, *Visit of the "Rurik,"* p. 12.
47. Biographical sketch in Lazarev, *Zapiski*, pp. 29–30; see also Kotzebue, *Voyage of Discovery into the South Sea*, 1: 22, 87, and Kuznetsova, "Novye dokumenty," pp. 239–41.
48. Lazarev, *Zapiski*, p. 150. On King's situation when these Russians met him, and the likeliest subjects of discussion, see W. G. McMinn, *Allan Cunningham, Botanist and Explorer* (Melbourne, 1970), pp. 41–2.
49. Compiler of Hawaiian and Chukchi word lists in 1820–21: TsGAVMF, *fond* 213, op. 1, *delo* 43; Ivashintsev, *Russian Round-the-World Voyages*, p. 140.
50. Lazarev, *Zapiski*, p. 150.
51. Nevskii, *Pervoe puteshestvie Rossiian*, p. 34; for evidence of Gleb Shishmarev's own ethnographic interests, see his "Svedeniia o Chukchakh," ZGDMM, 11 (St. P., 1852).
52. Sailing orders from Admiralty Department to Commanders of polar-bound divisions, 3d set, 1819: see my *Bellingshausen*, p. 16. Related papers in TsGAVMF, *fond* 213, *delo* 45ff. (G. A. Sarychev and Kotzebue on the need for wide-ranging observations and data, etc.).
53. Ivashintsev, *Russian Round-the-World Voyages*, p. 140; Lazarev, *Zapiski*, pp. 35–36; Fedorova, *Russian Population*, pp. 37, 72–75.
54. Lazarev, *Zapiski*, p. 27, 87.
55. I. N. Aleksandrov, "Professor Ivan M. Simonov, uchastnik antarkticheskoi ekspeditsii F. F. Bellinsgauzena," *Uchonnye zapiski Kazanskogo Pedagogicheskogo Instituta* (Kazan', 1950): no. 9; Shvede, *F. F. Bellinsgauzen*, p. 28; V. R. Kabo and N. M. Bondarev, "Okeaniiskaia kollektsiia I. M. Simonva," SMAE, 30 (L., 1974): 101–3; Barratt, *Bellingshausen*, pp. 14–15, 18–22.
56. Lazarev, *Zapiski*, p. 151; HRA, 10: 369.
57. TsGAVMF, *fond* 215, op. 1, *delo* 1203; Lazarev, *Zapiski*, p. 153; F. Russov, "Beiträge zur Geschichte der etnographischen und anthropologischen Sammlungen...," *Sbornik Muzeia po Antropologii i Etnografii pri Imperatorskoi Akademii Nauk* (St. P., 1900): no. 1 (earlier development of the *Kunstkammer*, etc.).
58. TsGAVMF, *fond* 213, op. 1, *delo* 52; Kuznetsova, "Novye dokumenty," pp. 244–45; Barratt, *Russians at Port Jackson*, pp. 82–83.
59. Lazarev, *Zapiski*, p. 154.
60. Shvede, *F. F. Bellinsgauzen*, p. 68; Barratt, *Bellingshausen*, pp. 101–6.
61. Lazarev, *Zapiski*, p. 151.
62. Ibid., p. 150. Further on "Macquarie Tower," which the Russians saw emitting its rotary light for 25 seconds every 108 seconds, and thought a handsome structure, see Bellingshausen, *Voyage*, 2: 318 and 348.
63. Lazarev, op. cit., p. 152.
64. Mitchell Library: Riley Papers, vol. 1, p. 91, etc.; C. M. Hotimsky, "A Russian Account of New South Wales in 1822," *Melbourne Slavonic Studies*, 1 (1967): 86; ADB, 2: 11–12.
65. TsGAVMF, *fond* 1153, op. 1, *delo* 1: p. 44; M. N. Vasil'ev, "Zamechaniia... o Novoi Iuzhnoi Valisskoi zemle," ZADMM (St. P., 1823): pt. 5.
66. D. S. Macmillan, *Scotland and Australia, 1788–1850* (Oxford, 1967), p. 106; ADB, 2: 243 on Erskine's immediate predecessor as lieutenant-governor, whom Russians had met in 1814. See also, on other Scots encountered by the Russians at Sydney (e.g., John Piper, George Johnston, Charles Frazer, Sir Thomas Brisbane), M. D. Prentis, *The Scots in Australia* (Sydney, 1983), pp. 34–38, etc.
67. See n. 64.

68. Mitchell Library: Macquarie Diary, CY A774, p. 117; also ADB, 2: 12.
69. Lazarev, *Zapiski*, p. 86 (crew list, with trades and grades).
70. Ibid., p. 151. Soundings and measurements made from these boats were presented to the Naval Ministry in 1822 by Vasil'ev: TsGAVMF, *fond* 166, *delo* 660, p.t 2. See n. 44 above on Russian hydrography and coastal surveying.
71. Lazarev, *Zapiski*, pp. 150–51. The French vessel was Captain Audibert's *Trois Frères*, from Isle de France.
72. TsGAVMF, *fond* 162, op. 1, *delo* 44: A. S. Menshikov to President of Scientific Committee, Naval Staff, 6 November 1830, No. 3737, with K. Gillesem's proposed book: ch. 4 describing his trips towards the Blue Mountains; Lazarev, *Zapiski*, p. 152; on Lieutenant Lawson (1774–1850) and his house, W. A. Steel, "The First Land Grant beyond the Blue Mountains," *JRAHS*, 24 (1938).
73. *Sydney Gazette*, 27 November 1813; Dowd, *Macquarie Country*, pp. 56–57.
74. *Sydney Gazette*, 20 November 1813; Dowd, op. cit., p. 42.
75. TsGAVMF, *fond* 166, *delo* 660, pt. 2: p. 207; *Sydney Gazette*, 29 March, 1817; Parish Register (1820), St. Matthew's Anglican Church, Windsor, NSW.
76. *Sydney Gazette*, 30 March and 6 April 1806; *HRNSW*, 6: 826 (Rev. Saml. Marsden to Governor King).
77. Lazarev, *Zapiski*, pp. 152–53.
78. Bellingshausen, *Voyage*, 2: 346 and 350; Lazarev, *Zapiski*, p. 371; Mitchell Library: Bigge Appendix, Bonwick Transcripts, box 2, p. 725 (1817 wharf).
79. *Sydney Gazette*, 29 July 1815; W. C. Wentworth, *Statistical, Historical, and Political Description of the Colony of New South Wales. . .* (London, 1819), pp. 22–23; Mitchell Library: Bigge Appendix, Bonwick Transcripts, box 1, pp. 344–45, and box 12, page 318; Dowd, *Macquarie Country*, pp. 42–43, 67–68, 145.
80. TsGAVMF, *fond* 166, *delo* 660, pt. 2: p. 205.
81. See Ellis, *Lachlan Macquarie, His Life*, pp. 548–49, 568–71.
82. Lazarev, *Zapiski*, p. 152; Prentis, *The Scots in Australia*, p. 36; ADB, 2: 187ff.
83. Dixson Library: George Johnston MSS, No. Q22: doc. 443; *Sydney Gazette*, 18 March 1820, p. 2.
84. TsGAVMF, *fond* 166, *delo* 660, pt. 2: p. 206. Like Bellingshausen (*Voyage*, 1: 184), Vasil'ev received a far more favourable impression of the factory and native school than did Commissioner John T. Bigge: see the latter's *Report. . . on the State. . . of New South Wales* (London, 1823), pp. 69–71.
85. Lazarev, *Zapiski*, pp. 369–71 (App. 14).
86. Kuznetsova, "Novye dokumenty," p. 237.
87. English translation by Debenham, in Bellingshausen's *Voyage*, 2: 321–39.
88. Lazarev, *Zapiski*, pp. 370–71. These statistics were apparently provided by Macquarie, or at his behest. Bigge's *Reports* give close, but not identical, figures.
89. TsGAVMF, *fond* 166, *delo* 660, pt. 2: p. 207. On the spread of settlement across the Cumberland Plain witnessed by the Russians, T. M. Perry, *Australia's First Frontier: The Spread of Settlement in New South Wales, 1788–1829* (Melbourne, 1963); compare 1821 livestock data (p. 132) with Vasil'ev's for 1820.
90. Lazarev, *Zapiski*, p. 27; TsGAVMF, *fond* 213, *delo* 45 (Kotzebue on natural science on Oceania).
91. Bellingshausen, *Voyage*, 1: 328; Perry, *Australia's First Frontier*, pp. 26–33.
92. Chamisso, *Werke* (Leipzig, 1836), 1 Band ("Reise um die Welt"), pp. 345–47; TsGAVMF *fond* 213, op. 1, *delo* 52.
93. Lazarev, *Zapiski*, pp. 392ff.; Fedorova, *Russian Population*, pp. 72–73.
94. See n. 72 and H. Selkirk, "The Discovery of Mudgee," *JRAHS*, 8 (1922); also, on Lawson's searches for pasturage and (1819) appointment, Perry, *Australia's First Frontier*, pp. 29, 83–84. Lawson's own papers, now in the Mitchell Library (A1952, unpaged), contain only fleeting references to the Russians.
95. Hotimsky, "A Russian Account," pp. 90–91; ADB, 1: 416; John Oxley, *Journals of Two Expeditions into the Interior of New South Wales* (London, 1820); Perry, *Australia's First Frontier*, pp. 82–83; McMinn, *Allan Cunningham*, ch. 2; ADB, 1: 265–69.

96. McMinn, *Allan Cunningham*, p. 42.
97. Mitchell Library: Kew MSS Transcripts, Cunningham to Banks, 1 May 1820; L. A. Shur, "Russian Travellers of the 18th and 19th Centuries: Source Materials on the Geography... of Latin America," *Ibero-Amerikanisches Archiv*, 1 (Berlin, 1976): no. 45, pp. 395–401.
98. TsGIAL, *fond* 789, op. 20, *dela* 17, 19, 28, 30 (appointment in 1819; service, promotion, and pension notice, 1 July 1823; Golitsyn-Olenin memoranda, etc.).
99. TsGIAL, *fond* 789, op. 20, *delo* 36.
100. Survey in J. H. Wuorinen, *History of Finland* (New York, 1965), pp. 104–6.
101. TsGAVMF, *fond* 166, *delo* 660, pt. 2: p. 208. The Russians were in eucalypt woodland (cf. Perry, *Australia's First Frontier*, pp. 12–13) of the park like sort admired by their predecessors as by Peter Cunningham: see *Two Years in New South Wales...*, 2d ed. (London, 1827), 1: 118.
102. AONSW: Allan Cunningham Journal, microfilm reel 47: 8–9 March 1820; Wentworth, *Description of the Colony*, p. 60; Perry, op. cit., pp. 18–19 (local geology and soils).
103. TsGAVMF, *fond* 166, *delo* 660, pt. 2: pp. 210–11 ("Iz mineralogicheskikh zamechanii, uchinennykh naturalistom Shteinom...").
104. Ibid., p. 21. Shtein's detection of gold preceded that of colonial surveyor J. McBrien, slightly further west on the Fish River, by eighteen months.
105. AONSW: Allan Cunningham Journal, reel 47: 9 March 1820. The party was encamped west of Bullaburra and 2–3 miles south of (modern) Wentworth Falls, Great Western Highway.
106. Also "acidic iron springs" near "King's Table Land": see n. 103.
107. G. Blaxland, *A Journal of a Tour of Discovery across the Blue Mountains in the Year 1813* (London, 1823); HRA, 8: 149, 165–77; Perry, *Australia's First Frontier*, p. 30.
108. Perry, op. cit., pp. 80–82.
109. HRA, 8: 165–77 ("Assistant Surveyor Evans' Journal, 1813–14").
110. From a point south of Mount Blaxland.
111. Lazarev, *Zapiski*, pp. 371–72; A. H. Chisholm, ed., *Australian Encyclopaedia* (Sydney, 1958), 2: 37–40, 5: 128–29 (early knowledge of caves in Silurian limestone, nomenclature).
112. AONSW: Allan Cunningham Journal, reel 47: 12–16 March 1820; ADB, 1: 421–22. Korneev sketched Castlereagh hamlet.
113. TsGIAL, *fond* 789 (Adakemii Khudozhestv), op. 20, *dela* 7, 9, 17, 21, 28, 30, 36, 48, 74. Microfilm copies (reel 85) at Elmer E. Rasmuson Library, University of Alaska at Fairbanks (Shur Collection). The same collection, acquired in 1983, contains complementary papers from TsGAVMF, e.g., *fond* 162, op. 1, *delo* 44 and *fond* 205, op. 1, *delo* 644 (reel 98).
114. TsGIAL, *fond* 789 op. 20: L. Golenishchev-Kutuzov to A. S. Menshikov, 23 December 1830 (No. 351); *delo* 30: A. Olenin's files, 2 July 1823. Five of these extra drawings were added to 26 of the 101 in the two main portfolios (65 + 36), to make the 31 illustrations proposed for Vasil'ev's (ultimately unprinted) *Voyage;* and four of these were Australian in content: "View of Sydney Town and Port Jackson"; "A Night Dance of the New Hollanders, Called the Dog Dance"; "Bat and Butterflies of New Holland"; and "Van Diemen's Goose, New Holland Ostrich, and Kangaroo."
115. TsGAVMF, *fond* 162, op. 1, *delo* 44: Menshikov to Golenishchev-Kutuzov, 6 November 1830, No. 3737; Lazarev, *Zapiski*, pp. 5–9; Saltykov-Shchedrin Public Library, Leningrad: *Rudopisnyi otdel*, F 17, 106": pp. 1–3 (Lazarev's publication efforts of 1830).
116. "Puteshestvie na shliupe 'Blagonamerennyi' dlia issledovanii...," *Otechestvennye zapiski*, 66 (St. P., 1849): nos. 9–10; 67: nos. 11–12; Ivashintsev, *Russian Round-the-World Voyages*, p. 141.
117. TsGAVMF, *fond* 162, op. 1, *delo* 44: No. 3737 (Governor-General Paulucci to forward the (German-language MS) from Riga to the Scientific Committee of the Naval Staff, before censoring, etc.).
118. Gillesem, "Puteshestvie," 66: sect. 8, p. 213.

119. Lazarev, *Zapiski*, pp. 154–55; HRA, 10: 369.
120. Wentworth, *Description of the Colony*, pp. 34–35; the brand new fort on Benelong's Point (see Bellingshausen, *Voyage*, 1: 161 and Wentworth, op. cit., p. 36) was not operational.
121. Lazarev, *Zipiski*, p. 155. The adjutant was Lt. Hector Macquarie, the "cape" Benelong's Point, the time 9:00 AM, 28 March 1820.
122. Bellingshausen, *Voyage*, 1: 158.
123. Ibid., 1: 136.
124. See my *Bellingshausen*, pp. 14–15, 18–22.
125. Bellingshausen, *Voyage*, 1: 159.
126. Iu. M. Shokal'skii, "Stoletie so vremeni otpravleniia russkoi antarkticheskoi ekspeditsii," *IVGO*, 60 (1928): bk. 2, pp. 55–71; Aleksandrov, "Professor Ivan Mikhailovich Simonov," passim; V. R. Kabo and N. M. Bondarev, "Okeaniiskaia kollektsiia I. M. Simonova," *SMAE*, 30 (1974): 101–11; N. I. Vorob'ev, "Etnograficheskie nabliudeniia I. M. Simonova na ostravakh Tikhogo okeana," *IVGO*, 81 (1949): bk. 5, pp. 497–504.
127. Bellingshausen, *Voyage*, 1: 159.
128. Ibid., 1: 160.
129. Mitchell Library: Macquarie journals, CY A774, p. 124; also PRO C.O. 201/95/609 (P. P. King to Goulburn, 9 November 1819, etc.), for indications that the Sydney authorities had had orders to keep Freycinet's people—but not Russians—under close surveillance.
130. HRA, 10: 283.
131. Lazarev, *Zapiski*, p. 370; Bach, *Maritime History of Australia*, p. 27; ADB, 1: 204.
132. E.g., "British Extracts," 9 September 1820.
133. Bellingshausen, *Voyage*, 1: 40.
134. Ibid., 1: 164; for details of crews in Australia, V. N. Sementovskii, ed., *Russkie otkrytiia v Antarktike v 1819–1921 godakh* (M., 1951), p. 285; further on activities at Kirribilli Point in these days, P. M. Novosil'skii, *Iuzhnyi polius: iz zapisok byvshego morskago ofitsera* (St. P., 1853), ch. 4.
135. See my *Russians at Port Jackson*, passim; Bellingshausen, *Voyage*, 1: 163.
136. Bellingshausen, *Voyage*, 1: 165.
137. Letter to A. A. Shestakov of October 1821, cited by Sementovskii, *Russkie otkrytiia v Antarktike*, p. 24.
138. Perry, *Australia's First Frontier*, p. 19.
139. Bellingshausen, *Voyage*, 1: 183; Wentworth, *Description of the Colony*, p. 434 (local shipwright and dockyard staff).
140. Bach, *Maritime History of Australia*, pp. 46–53; Blainey, *Tyranny of Distance*, pp. 47–49, 61–62.
141. Bellingshausen, *Voyage*, 2: 327–29; Fitzhardinge, "Russian Ships in Australian Waters," p. 133. Russians in Sydney in 1822 also took an interest in the system and in penal arrangements made ashore: see A. P. Shabel'skii, "Pis'mo kniaziu A. B. Kurakinu," *Severnaia pchela* (St. P., 1827): no. 58.
142. See Cumpston, *Shipping Arrivals and Departures: Sydney*, p. 121.
143. Bellingshausen, *Voyage*, 1: 40.
144. Ibid., 1: xxi–ii; Fitzhardinge, "Russian Ships in Australian Waters," pp. 129ff.; V. A. Lipshits, "Etnograficheskie issledovaniia v russkikh krugosvetnykh ekspeditsiiakh," *Ocherki istorii russkoi etnografii, fol'kloristiki i antropologii*, 1 (M., 1956): 299–300, 320–21; L. A. Shur, "Dnevniki i zapiski... kak istochnik po istorii i etnografii stran Tikhogo okeana," *Avstraliia i Okeaniia* (M., 1970): 201–12.
145. Bibliographical data in my *Bellinghausen*, pp. 22, 169–70.
146. Bellingshausen, *Voyage*, 1: xxi.
147. Mitchell Library, CY A774; Fitzhardinge, op. cit., p. 129 (trip to Watson's Bay, etc.).
148. Bellingshausen, *Voyage*, 1: 193.
149. Ibid., 1: 183–84; see also Wentworth, *Description of the Colony*, pp. 15–19 (Parramatta

in 1819); Bigge, *Report on the State of... New South Wales*, pp. 69–70; M. H. Clark, comp. and ed., *Select Documents in Australian History, 1788–1850* (Sydney, 1950), pp. 114–17.

150. Bellingshausen, *Voyage*, 1: 26 (First Set of Instructions, para. 12).
151. Ibid., 1: 184; Ellis, *Lachlan Macquarie*, chs. 12–13.
152. Further on these matters, J. Dennis, "Bigge versus Macquarie," *JRAHS*, 22 (1937), and M. H. Ellis, "Some Aspects of the Bigge Commission of Inquiry," *JRAHS*, 27 (1942).
153. Mitchell Library, Bonwick Transcripts: Bigge Appendix, box 2, pp. 706–7; also *Windsor Advertiser*, 1 September 1860.
154. Bellingshausen, *Voyage*, 1: 185.
155. Ibid., 1: 186; Barratt, *Russians at Port Jackson*, pp. 35, 54; Wentworth, *Description of the Colony*, pp. 20–22 (native institution).
156. Bellingshausen, *Voyage*, 1: 226ff.; Ivashintsev, *Russian Round-the-World Voyages*, pp. 44–46; A. Sharp, *The Discovery of the Pacific Islands* (Oxford, 1960), pp. 196–98.
157. Sementovskii, *Russkie otkrytiiv Antarktike*, p. 168. On Piper's "cottage" and increasing affluence, ADB, 2: 334–35.
158. Bellingshausen, *Voyage*, 2: 320.
159. Ibid., 2: 337–38.
160. AE, 3: 150–51.
161. Fitzhardinge, "Russian Ships in Australian Waters," p. 133; also Bellingshausen, *Voyage*, 2: 342–44.
162. Ibid., 1: xxii.
163. Bellingshausen, *Voyage*, 2: 344.
164. Further on this, see my *Russians at Port Jackson*, pp. 13–16, 94–96.
165. Mitchell Library: CY A774, p. 171.
166. Sementovskii, *Russkie otkrytiia v Antarktike*, p. 168.
167. HRA, 10: 369.

NOTES TO CHAPTER FIVE

1. The essential biography remains K. T. Khlebnikov's: trans. C. Bearne as *Baranov* (Kingston, Ont., 1973).
2. Barratt, *Russia in Pacific Waters*, pp. 190–99.
3. U.K. Government, *The Alaska Boundary Tribunal: Appendix to the Case of Great Britain* (London, 1903), pp. 6–7 (text of ukases); Gibson, *Imperial Russia*, pp. 162–63; Okun', *Russian-American Company*, pp. 82, 128–29, 224–26.
4. Ivashintsev, *Russian Round-the-World Voyages*, pp. 65–66.
5. Ibid., p. 142; also S. P. Khrushchev, "Plavanie shliupa Apollona v 1821–1824 godakh," *ZADMM*, 10 (St. P., 1826): 200ff.
6. C. M. Hotimsky, "A Russian Account," p. 86; B. L. Modzalevskii, *Pushkin i ego sovremenniki* (St. P., 1910), and V. Veresaev, *Sputniki Pushkina* (M., 1937), on Shabel'skii's early years.
7. Ivashintsev, *Russian Round-the-World Voyages*, p. 66.
8. Ibid., p. 67 and Khrushchev, "Plavania shliupa," pp. 210–13; A. P. Shabel'skii, *Voyage aux colonies russes de l'Amérique, fait au bord du sloop de guerre 'l'Apollon' pendant les années 1821, 1822, et 1823* (St. P., 1826), ch. 1.
9. Barratt, *Russia in Pacific Waters*, pp. 219–20, 230–32.
10. M. N. Pokrovskii, ed., *Vosstanie dekabristov: materialy po istorii vosstaniia*, 11 vols. (M., 1925–39): index under Kiukhel'beker, M.; also my study, *Voices in Exile: The Decembrist Memoirs*, on Kiukhel'beker and other Decembrists who had visited Australia in 1822–24, K. P. Torson of *Vostok* and D. I. Zavalishin of *Kreiser*.
11. Pt. 23, nos. 17–18, pp. 43–61: "Prebyvanie g. Shabel'skago v Novoi Gollandii."
12. The publisher was Nikolai I. Grech: bibliographical details given by B. L. Modzalevskii in *Pushkin i ego sovremenniki*, bk. 9 (1910), pp. 330–31.

13. L. A. Chereiskii, *Pushkin i ego okruzhenie* (L., 1975), p. 466; also *Pushkin— issledovaniia i materialy* (M.-L., 1956–69), 1: 250–51.
14. Hotimsky, "A Russian Account," p. 86.
15. General survey by N. N. Bolkhovitinov, *Russko-Amerikanskie otnosheniia, 1815–1832* (M., 1975), ch. 5.
16. *Severnaia pchela* (St. P., 1827), no. 58.
17. Barratt, *Russians at Port Jackson*, p. 29.
18. *Sydney Gazette*, 28 June 1822.
19. Hotimsky, "A Russian Account," pp. 92, 94.
20. Ibid., p. 95; Perry, *Australia's First Frontier*, p. 25.
21. ADB, 1: 151–55 and 338 (on James Dunlop the astronomer, brought to Sydney by Brisbane to compile a catalogue of stars); also D. S. Macmillan, *Scotland and Australia, 1788–1850* (Oxford, 1967), p. 42.
22. Ivashintsev, *Russian Round-the-World Voyages*, p. 66.
23. Tikhmenev, *Istoricheskoe obozrenie*, 1: 336; Gibson, *Imperial Russia*, p. 164; Barratt, *Russia in Pacific Waters*, p. 223.
24. Kotzebue, *Voyage of Discovery*, 1: intro. (by Kruzenshtern); *Severnyi arkhiv*, 24 (St. P., 1826); Ivashintsev, op. cit., pp. 24, 61–62.
25. Ivashintsev, *Russian Round-the-World Voyages*, p. 142.
26. See Fedorova, *Russian Population*, pp. 35, 38, 253–54.
27. Ibid., p. 348; Tikhmenev, *Istoricheskoe obozrenie*, 1: 281ff.; B. N. Vishnevskii, "Puteshestvie po rekam i ozeram v Amerike...," *IVGO*, 94 (1962): no. 6, pp. 507–10.
28. Gibson, *Imperial Russia*, p. 164.
29. Ivashintsev, *Russian Round-the-World Voyages*, p. 64; L. S. Berg, *Ocherki po istorii russkikh geograficheskikh otkrytii* (M., 1939), p. 165.
30. *Atlas iuzhnogo moria* (St. P., 1823–26).
31. Arkhiv Geograficheskogo Obshchestva SSSR, Leningrad; *razriad* 99 (Russian-American Company materials), *delo* 139: "Donesenie E. A. Klochkova pravleniiu RAK...," July 1822. Entry for 15 July, Sydney.
32. Copy at Elmer E. Rasmuson Library, University of Alaska at Fairbanks: Shur Collection, reel 74.
33. ADB, 1: 153–54, 338.
34. Ibid., 1: 416; Hotimsky, "A Russian Account," pp. 90–91.
35. *Sydney Gazette*, 9 and 10 August 1822.
36. R. G. Liapunova and S. G. Fedorova, *Russkaia Amerika v neopublikovannykh zapiskakh K. T. Khlebnikova* (L., 1979), p. 271; Ivashintsev, *Russian Round-the-World Voyages*, p. 137.
37. S. Ryden, *The Banks Collection: An Episode in Eighteenth-Century Anglo-Swedish Relations* (Gothenburg, 1963), p. 68.
38. Nevskii, *Pervoe Puteshestvie Rossiian*, pp. 57, 270–71.
39. Ibid., p. 58; G. H. Langsdorf, *Voyages and Travels in Various Parts of the World...* (London, 1813–14), 1: ch. 1; Barratt, *Russia in Pacific Waters*, pp. 114–18.
40. Unpublished diaries at the Archive of the Academy of Sciences, Leningrad: *razriad* 4, vol. 1, No. 800.
41. *Allgemeine Deutsche Biographie* (Leipzig, 1885), 17: 401–2; 21: 470; Barratt, *Bellingshausen*, p. 10.
42. Shvede, *Bellinsgauzen*, p. 28; Kabo and Bondarev, "Okeaniiskaia kollektsiia I. M. Simonova," pp. 103–4; Aleksandrov, "Professor I. M. Simonov," bk. 9; Barratt, *Bellingshausen*, pp. 19–20.
43. See G. H. Langsdorf and F. B. Fischer, *Plantes recueillies pendant le Voyage des Russes autour du monde* (Tübingen, 1810–18); Tilesius von Tilenau, *Naturhistorische Früchte der ersten... Erdumseglung* (St. P., 1813); A. Chamisso, "Nabliudeniia i zamechaniia...," in Otto von Kotzebue's *Puteshestvie v Iuzhnyi okean i Beringov proliv* (St. P., 1823), p. 3; D. D. Tumarkin, trans. and ed., *O. Kotsebu: novoe puteshestvie vokrug sveta v 1823–1826 godakh* (M., 1981), p. 317 etc. (on Johann Friedrich Es-

chscholtz); on Baron Kittlitz, Karl Mertens, and botany from the Russian sloop-of-war *Seniavin* in 1826–29, see Kittlitz's *Denkwürdigkeiten einer Reise um die Welt...* (Gotha, 1858), pts. 1–2, and F. P. Litke (Lütke), *Puteshestvie vokrug sveta... v 1826–1829 godakh* (St. P., 1835–36): *Atlas*.

44. A. Vucinich, *Science in Russian Culture: A History to 1860* (Stanford, 1963), pp. 241–42, and G. D. Komkov *et al.*, *Akademiia nauk SSSR: kratkii istoricheskii ocherk* (M., 1977), 1: 188–89 (on physician-botanists and pharmacology); Ivashintsev, *Russian Round-the-World Voyages*, pp. 140–42; also Barratt, *Bellingshausen*, pp. 15, 23, 69 (Dr. Galkin in Australasia).

45. Perm' District State Archive, *fond* 445, op. 1, *delo* 58: Navy Lt. Hagemeister to Directors, RAK, May 1807.

46. A. Rossiiskii, "Vypiska iz zhurnala shturmana Alekseia Rossiiskago," *Sorevnovatel' prosveshcheniia* (St. P., 1820): no. 11, pp. 136–37.

47. TsGAVMF, *fond* 1152, op. 1, *delo* 2: S. Ia. Unkovskii, "Istinnye zapiski moiei zhizni," typed copy, p. 35.

48. Bellingshausen, *Voyage*, 1: 183.

49. Cunningham, *Two Years in New South Wales*, 1: 118 ("nobleman's park," etc.).

50. Shvede, *Bellinsgauzen*, pp. 96, 160, 208, 240 (Mikhailov's work); see also my *Russians at Port Jackson*, pp. 13–14, 77 (the "Sydney" aquarelles, their lithographing by I. P. Fridrits, etc.).

51. Barratt, *Russians at Port Jackson*, pp. 23 and 26.

52. Bellingshausen, *Voyage*, 2: 320.

53. Ibid., 2: 319.

54. See his "View of the Town of Sydney in Port Jackson"; Barratt, *Russians at Port Jackson*, p. 31.

55. Wentworth, *Description of the Colony*, pp. 45–46.

56. Kazan' State University Main Library, Kazan': MS 4533: I. M. Simonov, "Shliupy 'Vostok' i 'Mirnyi', ili plavanie Rossiian v iuzhnom ledovitom okeane i okolo sveta," 10 April 1820.

57. Barratt, *Russians at Port Jackson*, p. 55.

58. Mitchell Library: Transcripts of Kew MSS: Cunningham to Banks, 1 May 1820; McMinn, *Allan Cunningham, Botanist*, p. 42.

59. TsGAVMF, *fond* 166, *delo* 660, pt. 2: p. 205.

60. TsGAVMF, *fond* 215, op. 1, *delo* 1203.

61. See Ivashintsev, *Russian Round-the-World Voyages*, pp. 52–56.

62. I. Andreevskii and K. Arsen'ev, eds., *Entsiklopedicheskii slovar'*, (St. P., 1895), 8: 492.

63. See B. D. Levin, *Ocherki istorii organizatsii nauki v Leningrade, 1703–1977* (L., 1980), pp. 40–41.

64. Komkov, *Akademiia nauk SSSR*, pp. 188–89. Data on "Southern" plants already in St. Petersburg by 1810 in Smelovskii's *Sistematicheskoe ischislenie rastenii, nakhodiashchikhsia v sadu Akademii Nauk* (St. P., 1811).

65. See n. 62 and *Entsiklopedicheskii slovar'*, 71: 77.

66. Trautfetter, "Zhizneopisanie," *Bulletin de la Société Impériale des Naturalistes de Moscou* (1865): pp. 585ff.

67. Bellingshausen, *Voyage*, 2: 345.

68. Ibid., 2: 349.

69. See my *Russians at Port Jackson*, pp. 76–77.

70. Shvede, *Bellinsgauzen*, pp. 77–78.

71. 1822 portfolio no. 2, p. 65. The tree in question is *Ficus rubiginosa*.

72. Bellingshausen, *Voyage*, 1: 185; AE, 9: 220.

73. Bellingshausen, *Voyage*, pl. 16.

74. ADB, 2: 10.

75. R. Therry, *Reminiscences of Thirty Years' Residence in New South Wales and Victoria*, 2d ed. (London, 1863).

76. Shabel'skii, "Prebyvanie g. Shabel'skago v Novoi Gollandii," p. 56.

77. Ibid., p. 58; also AE, 2: 56.
78. I.e., that dedicated by Macquarie in 1816.
79. J. H. Maiden, *Forest Flora of New South Wales* (Sydney, 1922), p. 7.
80. On Tilesius von Tilenau, see Nevskii, *Pervoe puteshestvie Rossiian*, pp. 57ff., 271; on Eschscholtz, see I. Heidemaa, "Zooloogia Kateedri ja Zooloogiamuuseumi Ajaloost," *Tartu Ulikooli Ajaloo Küsimusi*, 2 (Tartu, 1975): 164–66; Tumarkin, *O. Kotsebu: novoe puteshestvie*, p. 317; *Biologicheskii slovar' professorov... byvshego Derptskogo Universiteta, 1802–1902* (Iur'ev, 1902). Langsdorf is the subject of a recent biography by B. N. Komissarov, *Grigorii Ivanovich Langsdorf* (L., 1975), replete with archival references.
81. But see *Materialy dlia istorii nauchnoi i prikladnoi deiatel'nosti v Rossii po zoologii* (M., 1889), and Lenz, *Deutsch-Baltisches Biographisches Lexikon*, pp. 199–200.
82. For a useful list of such publications, see *Katalog izdanii Imp. Akademii Nauk: chast' 1: periodicheskie izdaniia, sborniki... c 1726 po 1912 god* (St. P., 1912) and the corresponding *Katalog* for monographs (St. P., 1902). Materials of relevance to the history of science in Australia may be found in three series of *Mémoires de l'Académie Impériale des Sciences...*: the 11-volume 5th series (St. P., 1809–30), the 8-volume "Sciences Naturelles" set of the 6th series (St. P., 1835–59); and the contemporaneous series entitled merely *Mémoires présentés à l'Académie des Sciences... et lus dans ses Assenblées*, 9 vols. (St. P., 1831–59). Also pertinent is S. I. Vavilov *et al.*, *Voprosy istorii otechestvennoi nauki: obshchee sobranie Akademii Nauk SSSR... 5–11 ianvaria 1949 goda* (M.-L., 1949).
83. Bellingshausen, *Voyage*, 1: 185. Such allusions are too vague to allow precise identifications of subspecies, but gain interest in the light of data on habitat and diet in, for instance, J. Gould's *Birds of Australia*, 8 vols. (London, 1840–69) and G. M. Mathews's later classic work of the same title (12 vols.; 1910–25).
84. Bellingshausen, *Voyage*, 1: 190.
85. Barratt, *Russians at Port Jackson*, p. 47.
87. See n. 82. Korneev may have drawn a sixth Australian bird, a bunting: but the term used, *podorozhnik*, also describes certain plants (plantain, buckthorn, etc.). The drawing has long been lost. The "ostrich" was of course an emu. The sunfish, or porcupine fish, a pelagic fish of the Family Molidae, doubtless caught Korneev's eye because of its bizarre, almost round form: see AE, 8: 356–57.
88. A. G. Campbell, "Australian Magpies of the genus *Gymnorhina*," *Emu*, 28 (1929): 165–76; D. Amadon, "Family *Cracticidae*," in E. Mayr and J.C. Greenway, eds., *Check-list of Birds of the World*, 15 vols. (Cambridge, MA, 1962); A. Landsborough Thomson, *New Dictionary of Birds* (London, 1964).
89. K. A. Hindwood, "Honeyeaters of the Sydney District (County of Cumberland, N.S.W.)," *Australian Zoologist*, 10 (1944): 231–51.
90. Landsborough Thomson, op. cit., p. 376.
91. Archive ref.: R-29001-29308. I thank Dr. V. M. Rastiapin, curator at the State Historical Museum (Gosundarstvennyi Istoricheskii Muzei) on Red Square, Moscow, for the information offered here. On the lithographing, see also Shvede, *Bellinsgauzen*, p. 7.
92. See Barratt, *Russians at Port Jackson*, pp. 31, 37, 45.
93. Shvede, *Bellinsgauzen*, pp. 5–6.
94. Barratt, *Voices in Exile*, pp. 42, 82–3, 282, etc.; M. V. Nechkina, ed., *Materialy po istorii vosstaniia dekabristov... dokumenty* (L., 1976), 14: 195–213 (Torson's case before the Commission of Enquiry of 1826).
95. On Torson's Pacific service in *Vostok* (astronomy and meterology), see V. M. Pasetskii, *Geograficheskie issledovaniia dekabristov* (M., 1977), pp. 34–40.
96. Shvede, *Bellinsgauzen*, pp. 5–7; Pasetskii, op. cit., pp. 39–40.
97. Lazarev, *Zapiski*, p. 154.
98. Bellingshausen, *Voyage*, 1: 190.
99. Kuznetsova, "Novye dokumenty," pp. 244–45.
100. Hotimsky, "A Russian Account," pp. 94–96

101. TsGAVMF, *fond* 215, op. 1, *delo* 1203; N. A. Butinov and L. G. Rozina, "Nekotorye cherty samobytnoi kul'tury Maori," *SMAE*, 21 (L., 1963): 85, and Barratt, *Bellingshausen*, pp. 130–31 (the 1828 transfers).
102. Komkov, *Akademiia Nauk SSSR*, pp. 189–90. On the subsequent treatment of Australian zoological specimens, *inter alia*, see A. Brandt, *Putevoditel' po Zoologicheskomu Muzeiu Imperatorskoi Akademii Nauk* (St. P., 1868; 2d ed., 1872), and *Zoologicheskii muzei, osnovan v 1832 godu* (L., 1925).
103. TsGAVMF, *fond* 166, op. 1, *delo* 660, pt. 2: "Iz Mineralogicheskikh Zamechanii uchinennykh Naturalistom Shteinom..." (palaeology of the North Shore of Port Jackson); Komkov, *Akademiia Nauk SSSR*, pp. 188–89; A. Vucinich, *Science in Russian Culture: A History to 1860* (Stanford, 1963), pp. 345–46.
104. Vucinich, op. cit., pp. 331 and 335.
105. G. P. Gel'mersen, "Sir Roderick Impei Murchison," *Zapiski Imp. Akademii Nauk*, 20 (St. P., 1872): 183–84; D. N. Anuchin, *O liudiakh russkoi nauki i kul'tury* (M., 1950), pp. 172–74; Vucinich, *Science in Russian Culture*, p. 344–46.
106. Wentworth, *Description of the Colony*, pp. 47, 61.
107. Lazarev, *Zapiski*, p. 152; Bellingshausen, *Voyage*, 1: 187.
108. Bellingshausen, *Voyage*, 2: 345.
109. *Geognostische Beobachtungen auf einer Reise um die Welt in den Jahren 1823–1826* (Berlin, 1829); biographical data in A. M. Prokhorov, ed., *Great Soviet Encyclopaedia*, 7: 240.
110. Tumarkin, *O. Kotsebu: novoe puteshestvie*, p. 318; S. G. Frisch, *Lebensbescheibung G. G. Werners* (Leipzig, 1825), ch. 7; *Mineralogicheskii muzei, osnovan v 1716 godu* (L., 1925).
111. Kh. Tankler, "Vospitanniki Tartuskogo Universiteta na sluzhbe v Pulkovskoi Observatorii," *TUAK*, 11 (1981): 72–77; Vucinich, *Science in Russian Culture*, pp. 207, 300–1.
112. E. F. Varep, "O prepodavanii fizicheskoi geografii v Tartuskom Universitete v 1802–1917 godakh," *TUAK*, 11 (1981): pp. 61–66; Vucinich, op. cit., pp. 212 and 260; G. V. Levitskii, ed., *Biograficheskii slovar' professorov... Derptskogo universiteta* (Iur'ev, 1902–3); J. Eilart, "G. F. Parrot looduse uurimise arendajana," in *Parrot'i 200-ndale sünni-aastapäevale pühendatud materjale* (Tartu, 1967), pp. 126–29.
113. Heidamaa, "Zoologia kateedri," pp. 164–66; by the same author, "Zoologiamuuseumi Fondidest," *TUAK*, 11 (1981): 87–88; Lenz, *Deutsch-Baltisches Biographisches Lexikon*, pp. 199–200; A. Marksoo, "Admiral A. J. Krusensternist ja tema sidemetest Eestiga," *Teaduse Ajaloo lehekülgi Eestist* (Tartu, 1968): pp. 177–86.
114. Tumarkin, *O Kotsebu: novoe puteshestvie*, pp. 317–18; Vucinich, *Science in Russian Culture*, pp. 242, 301–5; Friis, *The Pacific Basin*, pp. 191–93.
115. M. Engelhardt and F. G. Parrot, *Eine Reise in die Krym un den Kaukasus* (Berlin, 1815); also Varep, "O prepodavanii fizicheskoi geografii," pp. 63–64 and Lenz, *Deutsch Baltisches Biographisches Lexikon*, p. 192.
116. See Sir A. Geikie, *Founders of Geology* (London, 1897) and Frisch, *Lebensbeschreibung*, passim.
117. W. H. Wells, *A Geographical Dictionary or Gazetteer of the Australian Colonies, 1848*, facsimile ed. (Sydney, 1970), p. 225; AE, 2: 39.
118. J. R. Richards, ed., *Blaxland, Lawson, Wentworth, 1813* (Sandy Bay, 1979), p. 131.
119. Compare early maps of N.S.W. (e.g., T. L. Mitchell 1834 and Robert Dixon 1837) with modern tourist maps, e.g., *Blue Mountains Holiday Map* (Sydney, 1981).
120. R. P. Whitworth, comp., *Baillière's New South Wales Gazetteer and Road Guide...* (Sydney, 1866); together with Allan Cunningham's diary for 7–10 March 1820 (AONSW, micro. reel No. 47) and contemporary letters to Macquarie (Mitchell Library, A 1749), one may profitably consult Macquarie's *Journals of His Tours, The Early History of New South Wales: Two Old Journals, Being the Diaries of Major H. C. Antill... in 1815* (Sydney, 1914), pp. 41–42, and J. F. Campbell's "Notes on our Great Western Highway: Springwood to Leura," *JRAHS*, 22 (1937): 291–94, to estab-

lish Shein's and Korneev's route with some precision.

121. Whitworth, *Bailliere's New South Wales Gazetteer*, p. 302.
122. *Encyclopaedia Britannica*, 11th ed. 2: 943–45, for survey.
123. TsGAVMF, *fond* 166, *delo* 660, pt. 2: p. 210 ("Iz Mineralogicheskikh zamechanii uchinennykh naturalistom Shteinom vo vremia 12-dnevnogo puteshestviia ot Sidneia k Sinim goram v Novom Iuzhnom Valisse").
124. AE, 4: 313.
125. Ibid., 6:95.
126. Vucinich, *Science in Russian Culture*, p. 343.
127. S. V. Rozhdestvenskii, *Istoricheskii obzor deiatel'nosti Ministerstva narodnogo prosveshcheniia, 1802–1902* (St. P., 1902), pp. 333–37; V. S. Ikonnikov, "Russkie universitety v sviazi s khodom obshchestvennogo obrazovaniia," *Vestnik Evropy* (1876): no. 11, pp. 94ff.
128. "Iz bumag kniazia V. F. Odoevskogo," *Russkii arkhiv* (1874): no. 7, pp. 11–54; Rozhdestvenskii, *Istoricheskii obzor*, pp. 334ff.
129. A. P. Shchapov, *Sochineniia* (St. P., 1906–8), 3: 187.
130. On these matters, see Vucinich, *Science in Russian Culture*, pp. 343–44.
131. See *Mineralogicheskii muzei, osnovan v 1716 godu* (L., 1925) on the history of that central museum.
132. I touch on this in "Russian Naval Sources for the History of Colonial Australia to 1825," *JRAHS*, 67 (1982): pt. 2, pp. 159–75; see also Bibliography here.
133. Iu. F. Lisianskii, *Puteshestvie vokrug sveta...* (St. P., 1812), p. 1, pp. 14–15; Nevskii, *Pervoe puteshestvie Rossiian*, pp. 55–56; Kotzebue, *Voyage of Discovery*, 1: 15–16; Barratt, *Russia in Pacific Waters*, pp. 161 and 179; K. Gorner (Hörner), "Instruktsiia, dannaia flota-leitenantu Kotsebu ob astronomicheskikh i fizicheskikh nabliudeniiakh...," in Kotzebue, *Puteshestvie v Iuzhnyi okean i beringov proliv...* (St. P., 1821), pt. 1, pp. 169–72; Iu. M. Shokal'skii, *Okeanografiia* (L., 1917), pp. 33–34.
134. Kotzebue, *Voyage of Discovery*, 1: 16; Bellingshausen, *Voyage*, 1: 39; on the exportable craftsmanship of John Arnold, George Dolland, and Edward Troughton, see *DNB*, 2: 109–10; 15: 195–96; 57: 259–60.
135. For a survey of navigational practice in this period, see *EB*, 19: 290–96; on Russian advances, N. A. Bestuzhev, *Opyt istorii rossiiskago flota* (St. P., 1825) and Shokal'skii, *Okeanografiia*, chs. 6–7; on particular experiments performed in the South Pacific on board Russian vessels, D. F. Rudovits, "Pervoe russkoe krugosvetnoe plavanie 1803–1806 godov," *Trudy Gos. Okeanografich. Instituta*, 27 (L., 1954): 5ff.; Kruzenshtern, *Puteshestvie*, 3: 228–59, 331–41 (water temperatures, barometric fluctuation, etc.); see also, for an overview of Russian navigational emphases, N. N. Zubov's somewhat chauvinistic *Otechestvennye moreplavateli-issledovateli morei i okeanov* (M., 1954) and, for a survey of Russian exploration in Oceania, Friis, *The Pacific Basin*, pp. 185–97.
136. See F. Debenham's notes to Bellingshausen, *Voyage*, 1: 39 and, on the transit-instrument in question, *Monthly Notices of the Royal Astronomical Society*, 3 (London, 1827): 149–54 and *EB*, 27: 311.
137. Nevskii, *Pervoe puteshestvie Rossiian*, pp. 39–40.
138. On this large subject, see V. A. Divin, *Russkie moreplavaniia na Tikhom okeane v XVIII veke* (M., 1971); V. I. Grekov, *Ocherki iz istorii russkikh geograficheskikh issledovanii v 1725–1765 godakh* (M., 1960); A. I. Andreev, "Rol' russkogo voenno-morskogo flota v geograficheskikh otkrytiiakh XVIII veka," *Morskoi sbornik* (1947): no. 4; also, on the eminent Russian hydrographer A. I. Nagaev, V. N. Berkh, *Zhizneopisanie admirala A. I. Nagaeva* (St. P., 1831).
139. V. Zakharov, "M. V. Lomonosov i russkoe nauchnoe moreplavanie," *Morskoi flot* (L., 1948): nos. 7–8, pp. 66–81; also my *Russia in Pacific Waters*, pp. 54–55, 65.
140. TsGADA, *fond* 183 (Buldakova), *delo* 89: "Ob otpravlenii... morem na Vostochnyi okean...''; M. V. Severgin, "Instruktsiia dlia puteshestvii... po chasti mineralogii," *Severnyi vestnik* (St. P., 1804): nos. 2–3; Nevskii, *Pervoe puteshestvie Rossiian*, pp.

37–38; Komkov, *Akademiia Nauk SSSR*, pp. 183–84.

141. On Shubert, see V. Vorontsov-Vel'iaminov, *Ocherki istorii astronomii* (M., 1956); *Istoriia Akademii Nauk SSSR* (M. L., 1958–64), 2: 84–86.

142. Komkov, *Akademiia Nauk SSSR*, pp. 183–84. *Populare Astronomii* appeared in St. P. (1803–10; 3 pts.) under the name F. Schübert.

143. Iu. G. Perel', "Vikentii Karlovich Vishnevskii,"*Istoriko-astronomicheskie issledovaniia*, 1 (M., 1955): 133–48; R. Grant, *History of Physical Astronomy from the Earliest Ages* (London, 1852), p. 504; Vucinich, *Science in Rusian Culture*, p. 205.

144. Komkov, *Akademiia Nauk SSSR*, p. 205.

145. See Nevskii, *Pervoe puteshestvie Rossiian*, pp. 248–50, and Friis, *The Pacific Basin*, pp. 187–88 and notes.

146. See Belllingshausen, *Voyage*, 1: 163–64 and 2: 319.

147. See Barratt, *Bellingshausen*, pp. 14–15; also, on Simonov, Lobachevskii, and material from Oceania and Australasia, A. G. Karimullin and B. Laptev, *Chto chital N. I. Lobachevskii: zapisi knig i zhurnalov, vydannykh N. I. Lobachevskomu iz biblioteki Kazanskogo Universiteta* (Kazan', 1979), pp. 12, n. 9, 26, 111–12; reviewed by G. J. Tee in *Mathematical Reviews* (1984), Item e01o67. On Lobachevskii and his circle at Kazan' in 1810–20, see Vucinich, *Science in Russian Culture*, pp. 219–20, 317–20.

148. B. G. Kuznetsov, *Ocherki istorii russkoi nauki* (M.-L.., 1940), pp. 42–43; L. A. Tarasevich, "Nauchnoe dvizhenie v Rossii v pervoi polovine XIX veka: estestvoznanie i meditsina," *Granat-Ist*, 6 (St. P., n.d.): 289–90; Vucinich, op. cit., pp. 219, 317.

149. Vucinich, *Science in Russian Culture*, pp. 318–25.

150. Simonov's own account of this happy development and of his later scientific activities, e.g., in New South Wales, remains unpublished: the MS, "Shliupy Vostok i Mirnyi, ili plavanie Rossiian v Iuzhnom ledovitom okeane i okolo sveta," is No. 4533 at Kazan' State University Library. The "Australian section," Chapter 5, is headed, "Plavanie k Port-Zhaksonu i prebyvanie v Novoi Gollandii," and covers some 30 pp. Bibliographical details and extracts in my *Russians at Port Jackson*, pp. 18–19, 47–53. See also, on Simonov's orders and expectations, Iu. M. Shokal'skii, "Stoletie so vremeni otpravleniia russkoi antarticheskoi ekspeditsii . . . ," *IVGO*, 60 (L., 1928): bk. 2, pp. 58ff. and Shvede, *Bellinsgauzen*, p. 28.

151. Shvede, *Bellinsgauzen*, pp. 65–66, 77–78; Friis, *The Pacific Basin*, pp. 195–97.

152. Bellinsgauzen, *Dvukratnye izyskaniia*, p. 76.

153. Because he was a Decembrist, Torson's contribution to the 1819–22 Antarctic expedition has drawn the attention of several Soviet commentators, notably S. Ia. Shtraikh, *Moriaki-dekabristy* (M., 1946); A. B. Sheshin, "Dekabrist-moreplavatel' K. P. Torson i ego nenaidennye zapiski ob otkrytii Antarktidy," *IVGO*, 108 (1976): bk. 1; and V. M. Pasetskii, *Geograficheskie issledovaniia dekabristov* (M., 1977), pp. 36–51.

154. Pasetskii, op. cit., p. 45.

155. Bellinsgauzen, *Dvukratnye izyskaniia*, p. 335.

156. Bellingshausen, *Voyage*, 1: 159.

157. Ivashintsev, *Russian Round-the-World Voyages*, p. 140; Larousse, *Grand dictionnaire universel*, 10: 21–22; Bellingshausen, *Voyage*, 2: 191.

158. J. Espinosa y Tello, *Memorias sobre las observaciones* (Madrid, 1809).

159. V. R. Kabo and N. M. Bondarev, "Okeaniiskaia kollektsiia I. M. Simonova," *SMAE*, 30 (L., 1974): 103–4.

160. Given in V. N. Sementovskii, ed., *Russkie otkrytiia v Antarktike v 1819–1821 godakh* (M., 1951), pp. 31–47.

161. See Nevskii, *Pervoe puteshestvie Rossiian*, pp. 269–70; Krusenstern, *Voyage*, 1: 5–6, 8–9. See also pp. 8–9 on Baron von Zach.

162. *Meyers Enzyklopädisches Lexikon*, 25: 583.

163. E.g., *L'Attraction des montagnes et ses effets sur les fils à plomb* (Avignon, 1814).

164. See n. 159 and my *Bellingshausen*, pp. 103–13, 118–19.

165. Karimullin and Laptev, *Chto chital N. I. Lobachevskii*, pp. 111–12.

166. Ibid., p. 13; Vucinich, *Science in Russian Culture*, pp. 221–22, 320.

167. 69e cahier (juillet 1824), pp. 5–26.
168. "Izvestie o puteshestvii kapitana Bellinsgauzena v 1819, 1820, i 1821 godakh," *Severnyi arkhiv*, 8 (St. P., 1827).
169. Tumarkin, *O. Kotsebu: novoe puteshestvie*, pp. 24, 318; Vucinich, *Science in Russian Culture*, pp. 242, 301–2; Friis, *The Pacific Basin*, p. 193.
170. "Opredelenie geograficheskogo polozheniia mest iakornogo stoianiia shliup 'Vostok' i 'Mirnyi'," *Zapiski Ministerstva Narodnogo Prosveshcheniia*, 22 (St. P., 1828): 44–68.
171. Survey by G. R. Barratt, "Russian Warships in Van Diemen's Land," *SEER*, 53 (1975): 566–78; on Kiukhel'beker's work in Oceania and elsewhere, see Pasetskii, *Geograficheskie issledovaniia dekabristov*, pp. 70–73.
172. *Meterologicheskie nabliudeniia, proizvodivshiesia vo vremia krugosvetnogo plavaniia shliupa "Apollon"* (St. P., 1882).
173. TsGAVMF, *fond* 166, op. 1, *delo* 666: pp. 314–15.
174. TsGAVMF, *fond* 870, op. 1, *delo* 3599a and b; Pasetskii, *Geograficheskie issledovaniia*, pp. 74–79; Andreevskii, *Entsiklopedicheskii slovar'*, 12: 96; Barratt, *Voices in Exile: The Decembrist Memoirs*, passim; Zavalishin, "Krugosvetnoe plavanie fregata 'Kreiser'," *Drevniaia i novaia Rossiia* (St. P., 1877): no. 5, pp. 55ff.
175. *Meteorologicheskie nabliudeniia, proizvodivshiesia vo vremia krugosvetnogo plavaniia fregata "Kreiser" v 1822, 23 i 24 godakh* (St. P., 1882).
176. See n. 174. Zavalishin touched again on his Australian sojourn in his memoirs, *Zapiski dekabrista* (München, 1904), 1: 117–20. See also Chapter 7 here.
177. Lazarev, *Zapiski*, pp. 29–30; A. von Chamisso, ed. Bartels, *Werke*, 3: 18; Mahr, *Visit of the "Rurik" to San Francisco*, pp. 12 and 20.
178. Lazarev, *Zapiski*, p. 153.
179. L. Bagrow, *History of Russian Cartography to 1800*, ed. H. W. Castner (Wolfe Island, Ont., 1975), p. 238.
180. On Midshipman V. Tabulevich's 1818 chart of Honolulu harbour, see my study, *The Russian View of Honolulu, 1809–1826*, ch. 4.
181. Bagrow, *History of Russian Cartography*, pp. 203ff.
182. "Svedeniia. . . ," *Zapiski Voenno-Topograficheskogo Depo*, pt. 1 (St. P., 1837).
183. V. F. Krempol'skii, *Istoriia razvitiia kartoizdaniia v Rossii i v SSSR* (M., 1959), p. 16.
184. On this and related matters of access, see P. Kennedy Grimsted, *Archives and Manuscript Repositories in the USSR: Leningrad and Moscow* (Princeton, 1972).
185. See Chapter 4 above.
186. ADB, 1: 421–22.
187. Bellingshausen, *Voyage*, 2: 347.
188. Ibid., 2: 346; *EB*, 11th ed., 3: 956 (Jean-Baptiste Biot.)
189. Sydney centre is today reckoned in lat. 33°51'S, long. 151°16'E.
190. A summary, convenient for comparative purposes, is given by W. and O. Havard, eds. and trans., "A Frenchman Sees Sydney in 1819: Translated from the Letters of Jacques Arago," *JRAHS*, 24 (1938): 17–42. See also AE, 4: 216–17, on Freycinet's 1819 visit.
191. Now held at TsGAVMF, *fond* 203, op. 1, *delo* 7306. Complementary materials, at TsGAVMF, *fond* 213, op. 1, *delo* 52 (correspondence re diaries and travel notes of ex-crew members of *Blagonamerennyi* and *Otkrytie*); 101–2 (notes by M. N. Vasil'ev on the outfitting and manning of his squadron, etc.). See Kuznetsova, "Novye dokumenty," pp. 237–40.
192. "Putevoi zhurnal. . . ," TsGAVMF, *fond* 203, op. 1, *delo* 7306: pp. 44–45. Further on archival materials from this expediton relating to colonial Sydney, see Bibliography here.
193. Shvede, *Bellinsgauzen*, p. 26.

NOTES TO CHAPTER SIX

1. Biographical data in Barratt, *Bellingshausen*, pp. 15 and 22.
2. A. Capell, "Aboriginal Languages in the South Central Coast, New South Wales: Fresh

Discoveries," *Oceania*, 41 (1970): no. 1, pp. 20–21; Barratt, *Russians at Port Jackson*, p. 83.

3. Folder containing 28 original aquarelles at the State Historical Museum, Red Square, Moscow; a large set is held by the State Russian Museum in Leningrad, under ref. R-29001-29038.

4. David Collins, *An Account of the English Colony in New South Wales...* (London, 1798), 1: 612; J. V. S. Megaw, "Archaeology, Art, and Aborigines: A Survey of Historical Sources," *JRAHS*, 53 (1967): 286–87; D. J. Mulvaney, *The Prehistory of Australia* (London, 1969), p. 260; Barratt, *Russians at Port Jackson*, pp. 90–91.

5. By Nikolai A. Butinov, Head of the Oceania Section, Institute of Anthropology and Ethnography of the Academy of Sciences of the USSR, Leningrad: in Barratt, *Russians at Port Jackson*, pp. 84–85.

6. A. Rossiiskii, "Zhurnal shturmana Alekseia Rossiiskago...," *Sorevnovatel' prosvesh-cheniia i blagodeianiia* (St. P., 1820): no. 11, pp. 125–46; W. and O. Havard, "A Frenchman Sees Sydney in 1819," pp. 17–42.

7. Barratt, *Russians at Port Jackson*, p. 23.

8. Ibid., pp. 25–26.

9. "Zamechaniia kapitana-leitenanta M. N. Vasil'eva o Novoi Iuzhnoi Valisskoi Zemle," originally in *ZADMM* (St. P., 1823; Pt. 5), reprinted in Lazarev, *Zapiski*, pp. 369–71. Vasil'ev's original 1819–22 journal remains at TsGAVMF, under reference: *fond* 166, *delo* 660, and has yet to be published.

10. P. M. Novosil'skii, *Iuzhnyi polius: iz zapisok byvshego morskago ofitsera* (St. P., 1853), ch. 4 ("Port-Dzhakson").

11. See n. 1.

12. Kazan' State University, MS 4533, "Shliupy *Vostok* i *Mirnyi*", p. 142.

13. Discussion in my *Russians at Port Jackson*, pp. 76–77.

14. See W. D. Campbell, "Aboriginal Carvings of Port Jackson and Broken Bay," in *Geological Survey of New South Wales: Ethnological Series, no. 1* (Sydney, 1899), pl. 19, fig. 11; pl. 23, fig. 1.

15. I. M. Simonov, "Plavanie k Port-Zhaksonu i Prebyvanie v Novoi Gollandii," Part 5 of the MS entitled, "Shliupy *Vostok* i *Mirnyi*, ili Plavanie Rossiian v Iuzhnom ledovitom okeane i okolo Sveta," MS 4533, Kazan' State University: p. 146/obv. On the London interlude of June 1814, see H. Nicholson, *The Congress of Vienna* (London, 1946), pp. 115–16.

16. MS 4533, "Shliupy *Vostok* i *Mirnyi*," p. 144.

17. Ibid., p. 152/obv. "This account reveals far more about the writer than it does about the Aborigines. The sound 'prrs' could be no more than a conventional sound accompanying the clapping sticks" (R. M. Berndt in letter to the author, 1979).

18. 69e cahier, pp. 5–26 (Sydney section on pp. 9–11). This "Précis du Voyage de découvertes..." was itself translated back into Russian, appearing in the journal *Severnyi arkhiv* (St. P., 1827, vol. 7) as "Izvestie o puteshestvii kapitana Bellingsgauzena v 1819–1822 godakh." The "Sydney section" thus reached yet another audience.

19. His "Brief Historical Review of the Voyages of the Most Celebrated Mariners...," based on lectures and polished, appeared in *Zhurnal Ministerstva Narodnogo Prosvesh-cheniia* (St. P., 1844): pt. 42, pp. 92–115.

20. N. P. Barsukov, *Zhizn' i trudy M. P. Pogodina* (St. P., 1896), 10: 389.

21. See Barratt, *Russians at Port Jackson*, pp. 18–19.

22. Kuznetsova, "Novye dokumenty," pp. 237–38; Lazarev, *Zapiski*, pp. 3–6.

23. Shvede, *Bellingsgauzen*, p. 77 (instructions of 1819); Fitzhardinge, "Russian Ships in Australian Waters, 1807–1835," pp. 124–33.

24. Bellingshausen, *Voyage*, 1: 162.

25. Ibid., 1: 187–89.

26. Ibid., 1: 190.

27. See my *Russians at Port Jackson*, pp. 38–39. PRO C.O. 201/95/609 (Phillip Parker

King to Goulburn, 9 November 1819, and related papers) indicates that Freycinet was kept under close surveillance in New South Wales. See HRA 10: 283 for Macquarie's position.

28. Barratt, *Russians at Port Jackson*, pp. 41–42.
29. *Severnaia pchela*, no. 58 (St. P., 1827): letter to Prince A. Kurakin. On Shabel'skii, see C. M. Hotimsky, "A Russian Account of New South Wales in 1822," p. 86; V. Veresaev, *Sputniki Pushkina* (M., 1937); on *Apollon*'s voyage, S. P. Khrushchev, "Plavanie shliupa Apollona v 1821–1824 godakh," *ZADMM* (St. P., 1826): pt. 10, pp. 200–72; Ivashintsev, *Russian Round-the-World Voyages*, pp. 65–67.
30. *Severnyi arkhiv* (1826): pt. 23, nos. 17–18, pp. 43–61. Though recognized by Rear-Admiral Ivashintsev, apparently on the basis of a report by Klochkov, this sighting must be regarded as highly questionable. It is not mentioned in the account of *Riurik*'s voyage, "Puteshestvie vokrug sveta...," that apeared in the journal *Severnyi arkhiv* in 1826 (24: 214–16). Yet that account gives circumstantial details of the sightings of Swilly ("Sevilla"), Ediston Rock, the so-called "Pedro Bank," etc.
31. Ibid., p. 57.
32. Ibid., p. 55.
33. See above, pp. 000–00, on *Apollon*'s visit.
34. Barratt, *Russians at Port Jackson*, pp. 90–91, 62–63.
35. John Hunter, *An Historical Journal of the Transactions at Port Jackson...* (London, 1793), p. 44.
36. See n. 14.
37. Hunter, *Historical Journal*, ch. 15 (Port Jackson vocabulary).
38. Details in R. H. W. Reece, *Aborigines and Colonists: Aborigines and Colonial Society in New South Wales in the 1830s and 1840s* (Sydney, 1974), p. 109ff.
39. HRA, 9: 141–45.
40. "Zamechaniia... o Novoi Iuzhnoi Valisskoi Zemle," in Lazarev, *Zapiski*, p. 370.
41. See pp. 000.
42. On the ethnographic significance of this, see I. McBryde, "Ethnographic Collections of Governor La Trobe now in the Musée d'Ethnographie de Neuchâtel, Switzerland," *Artefact*, 2 (1971): no. 2, pp. 46–47.
43. Collins, *Account of the English Colony*, 1: 612.
44. See n. 2.
45. Lazarev, *Zapiski*, p. 154.
46. Relevant papers in TsGIAL, *fond* 15, op. 1, *delo* 12 (conditions of secondment, outfitting costs, etc.); and TsGAVMF, *fond* 1152, op. 1. *Delo* 1 in the latter, S. Ia. Unkovskii's journal, formed the basis of the text of "Istinnye zapiski moei zhizni" which appeared in A. A. Samarov's edition of *Russkie flotovodtsy: M. P. Lazarev* (M., 1952), 1: 11–26.
48. Russov, "Beiträge zur Geschichte der Sammlungen," passim.
49. See my *Bellingshausen*, pp. 103–7, for a discussion of this problem in the Maori connection.
50. Kuznetsova, "Novye dokumenty," p. 237; see also D. D. Tumarkin, "Materialy ekspeditsii M. N. Vasil'eva —tsennyi istochnik po istorii i etnografii Gavaiskikh ostrovov," *Sovetskaia etnografiia* (1983): no. 6, pp. 48–61, on primary sources that bear on the 1820 visits to Port Jackson as well as Hawaii; also Bibliography under Lipshits, Ostrovskii, Shur.
51. Barratt, *Russia in Pacific Waters*, pp. 216–18; Huculak, *When Russia was in America*, chs. 1–2.
52. *The Alaska Boundary Tribunal: Appendix to the Case of Great Britain*, p. 7.
53. AVPR, *fond* Kantseliarii Ministerstva Vneshnikh Del: 1822, *delo* 3645: pp. 31–32.
54. Okun', *Russian-American Company*, pp. 224–26; A. G. Mazour, "The Russian-American Company: Private or Government Enterprise?" *PHR*, 13 (1944): 168–73.
55. AVPR, *fond* K.M.V.D.: 1822, *delo* 3645: p. 33.
56. TsGAVMF, *fond* 166, *delo* 666: pp. 362–70 (readying for departure, etc.); TsGAVMF, *fond* 870, op. 1, *delo* 3599a and b (Vishnevskii's scientific-service work of 1823–24); Pasetskii, *Geograficheskie issledovaniia*, pp. 72–78; Ivashintsev, *Russian Round-the-*

World Voyages, pp. 70 and 143; Shtraikh, *Moriaki-dekabristy*, ch. 3.

57. On this, see Lazaerv, *Zapiski*, pp. 6–9, 34 (Aleksei Lazarev's vain efforts to publish in 1826–30); Samarov, *Russkie flotovodtsy*, 1: intro.; Barratt, *Russia in Pacific Waters*, pp. 231–32 and notes.
58. Ivashintsev, op. cit., p. 143.
59. TsGAVMF, *fond* 166, *delo* 666: pp. 383–85.
60. Andrei P. Lazarev, *Plavanie vokrug sveta na shliupe "Ladoga" v 1822, 1823, i 1824 godakh* (St. P., 1832), pp. 49ff.; Ivashintsev, *Russian Round-the-World Voyages*, p. 70.
61. TsGAVMF, *fond* 212, *delo* 4093: pp. 119–20.
62. Pp. 54–81. Also pertinent, but to be used cautiously, is D. I. Zavalishin's essay, "Krugosvetnoe plavanie fregata Kreiser," in *Drevniaia i novaia Rossiia* (St. P., 1877): nos. 5–7, pp. 9–11; no. 9 on Van Diemen's Land.
63. R. Travers, *The Tasmanians* (Melbourne, (1968), pp. 101–11; J. Bonwick, *The Bushrangers* (Melbourne, 1856), passim; H. Melville, *History of the Island of Van Diemen's Land, 1824–1835* (London, 1835), pp. 3–16; on Rev. Knopwood, ADB, 2: 67.
64. Andrei Lazarev, *Plavanie*, p. 59.
65. *Van Diemen's Land Almanack for the Year 1832* (Hobart Town, 1832), p. 112. Compared with W. C. Wentworth's *Statistical, Historical, and Political Description . . .*, the Russian figures of 1823 show rapid growth in pasturing and agriculture.
66. "William Sorell," in ADB, 2: 461.
67. HRA, Series 3, 4: 73; see also *Hobart Town Gazette*, 31 May 1823, p. 3 (arrival of "Discovery-ships" and the brothers "Lazaroff").
68. TsGAVMF, *fond* 203, *delo* 1123: pp. 3–8; also Zavalishin, "Krugosvetnoe plavanie," no. 9, pp. 44–47.
69. ADB, 2: 67.
70. *The Diary of the Rev. Robert Knopwood, 1805–1808* was prepared for the Royal Society of Tasmania's *Proceedings* in 1946 by W. H. Hudspeth and S. Angel; and Hudspeth's later *Introduction to the Diaries of the Rev. Robert Knopwood* (Hobart, 1955) does cover the period of 1823–24. Nevertheless, the complete text of the diaries has yet to be published.
71. *Hobart Town Gazette*, 10 June 1823, p. 7.
72. Andrei Lazarev, *Plavanie*, p. 67.
73. *Hobart Town Courier*, 21 June 1823 (notice by Knopwood).
74. TsGAVMF, *fond* 315, *delo* 1404: p. 3 (P. S. Nakhimov to M. F. Reineke, San Francisco, 4 January 1824).
75. In the first (1832) ed., it appeared as pp. 68–78.
76. Ibid., pp. 68–71.
77. Ibid., p. 73.
78. F. S. Greenop, ed., *Tasmania, Australia* (Sydney, 1968), pp. 49–63.
79. Andrei Lazarev, *Plavanie*, pp. 60–62. On the natives "seized," see Travers, *The Tasmanians*, pp. 138–39.
80. Travers, op. cit., pp. 140–44 and 237 (bibliography).
81. Greenop, *Tasmania, Australia*, p. 30.
82. See Zavalishin, "Krugosvetnoe plavanie," no. 9, pp. 45–47.
83. Andrei Lazarev, *Plavanie*, pp. 64–65.
84. Ibid. Compare Wentworth, *Description of the Colony*, p. 120. Again, progress since 1819 is evident (stone houses replacing weatherboard cottages, etc.); also AE, 4: 509.
85. *Hobart Town Courier*, 21 June 1823.
86. AE, 4: 506.
87. Andrei Lazarev, *Plavanie*, pp. 65–66.
88. Zavalishin, "Krugosvetnoe plavanie," no. 5, pp. 55–56; official MSS at TsGAVMF, *fond* 166, *delo* 666: pp. 313–15; on Zavalishin, *ES.*, 12: 96; A. G. Mazour, "Dimitry Zavalishin . . . ," *PHR*, 5 (1936): 26–34; Pasetskii, *Geograficheskie issledovaniia*, pp. 73ff.
89. D. I. Zavalishin, *Zapiski dekabrista* (Munich, 1904), 1: 117–20. Midshipman Aleksei

Domashenko died heroically, trying to save a drowning sailor, in September 1827: *ZUKMS*, 1 (1827): 149–52.

90. A. E. Rozen, *Zapiski dekabrista* (St. P., 1907); "Vospominaniia A. F. Frolova," *Russkaia starina*, 5 (St. P., 1882): 465–82.
91. Melville, *History of the Island*, pp. 30–35.
92. A. G. Mazour, *The First Russian Revolution, 1825* (Berkeley, 1937), p. 250; see also Barratt, *Russia in Pacific Waters*, pp. 226–28.
93. Greenop, *Tasmania, Australia*, p. 29.
94. Great Britain, Commons, *Copies of All Correspondence between Lt.-Governor Arthur and H.M. Secretary of State for the Colonies on... Military Operations... of Van Diemen's Land* (London, 1831); J. Bonwick, *The Last of the Tasmanians* (London, 1870); Wentworth, *Description of the Colony*, pp. 132–46; Travers, *The Tasmanians*, pp. 101–11.
95. TsGAVMF, *fond* 212, *delo* 4093: pp. 126–27 (M. P. Lazarev to A. V. Moller).
96. Andrei Lazarev, *Plavanie*, p. 63.
97. TsGAVMF, *fond* 870, op. 1, *delo* 3599; N. D. Medvedev, "Vekovye varianty magnitnogo skloneniia i dreif iuzhnogo magnitnogo poliusa," *Biulleten Sovetskoi Antarkticheskoi Ekspeditsii* (1970): no. 77, pp. 99–100.
98. *Metereologicheskie nabliudeniia, proizvodivshiesia vo vremia krugosvetnogo plavaniia fregata "Kreiser" v 1822, 23 i 24 godakh* (St. P., 1882).
99. Pasetskii, *Geograficheskie issledovaniia*, p. 74.
100. ADB, 2: 461; Travers, *The Tasmanians*, pp. 139–40.
101. ADB, 1: 155.
102. Survey in Okun', *Russian-American Company*, pp. 218–24.
103. Andrei Lazarev, *Plavanie*, p. 81.
104. TsGAVMF, *fond* 1166, *delo* 9: pp. 4–5 (P. S. Nakhimov to M. F. Reineke re *Kreiser*'s arrival, the Sitka situation, etc.); USNA, "Records of the Russian-American Company," 4: 6.
105. Tikhmenev, *Istoricheskoe obozrenie*, 1: 335–50; Okun', *Russian-American Company*, pp. 68–72; Barratt, *Russia in Pacific Waters*, pp. 223–24.

NOTES TO CHAPTER SEVEN

1. Gibson, *Imperial Russia*, p. 164.
2. Ibid., pp. 168–70; Bancroft, *History of Alaska*, pp. 508ff.
3. Barratt, *Russia in Pacific Waters*, pp. 143–49; TsGAVMF, *fond* 212, *delo* 4093; pp. 126–27 (M. P. Lazarev to A. V. Moller re Governor Murav'ev's problems, the "superfluity of all patroling," etc.).
4. TsGIAL, *fond* 15, op. 1, *delo* 12 (O. P. Kozodavlev-Traversay corresp. re lieutenants for Company service).
5. Ivashintsev, *Russian Round-the-World Voyages*, pp. 58, 141.
6. Ibid., pp. 60–61.
7. Ibid., p. 144; Kuznetsova, "Novye dokumenty," pp. 237–38, on N. D. Shishmarev and his 1819–22 journal; Tumarkin, "Materialy ekspeditsii M. N. Vasil'eva," pp. 50–51 (N. D. Shishmarev); Tikhmenev, *Istoricheskoe obozrenie*, 1: 339–40 (despatching of *Elena*); Gibson, *Imperial Russia*, pp. 164–65 and notes; R. A. Pierce, "Alaska's Russian Governors...," *Alaska Journal*, 1 (1971): no. 4, pp. 38–42.
8. Okun', *Russian-American Company*, pp. 71–72.
9. Ivashintsev, *Russian Round-the-World Voyages*, p. 80; V. M. Golovnin, *Puteshestvie na shliupe "Diana" iz Kronshtadta v Kamchatku* (M., 1961), ch. 1.
10. *Sydney Gazette*, 11 and 14 April 1825.
11. Ibid., 28 April 1825.
12. See Fitzhardinge, "Russian Ships in Australian Waters," p. 140.
13. Ivashintsev, *Russian Round-the-World Voyages*, p. 80.

14. See n. 8 and Barratt, *Russia in Pacific Waters*, pp. 224 and 230.
15. Shtraikh, *Moriaki-dekabristy*, passim; Sheshin, "Dekabrist-moreplavatel' K. P. Torson," passim; Pasetskii, *Geograficheskie issledovaniia*, pp. 36–51 (Torson), 70–81 (Kiukhel'beker and Zavalishin); G. R. Barratt, "The Russian Interest in Arctic North America: The Kruzenshtern-Romanov Projects, 1819–1823," *SEER*, 53 (1975): 38–40.
16. Okun', *Russian-American Company*, pp. 109–12; M. K. Azadovskii, "14 dekabria v pis'makh A. E. Izmailova," *Pamiati dekabristov*, 1 (L., 1926): 242.
17. Okun', op. cit., pp. 107ff.; Barratt, *Russia in Pacific Waters*, pp. 231–32; Shtraikh, *Moriaki-dekabristy*, passim.
18. The classic study remains J. Gleason's *The Genesis of Russophobia in Great Britain* (Cambridge, MA, 1950).
19. *Sydney Gazette*, 8 April 1829 (Russian warship expected); 9 April (war rumours from London); see also L. Paszkowski, *Polacy w Australii i Oceanii, 1790–1840* (London, 1962), pp. 5–12, and my *Russophobia in New Zealand, 1838–1908* (Palmerston North, N.Z., 1981), pp. 13–14.
20. Ivashintsev, *Russian Round-the-World Voyages*, pp. 101, 103.
21. On Hagemeister, see above, pp. 105–17 and R. A. Pierce, "Two Russian Governors: Hagemeister and Yanovskii," *Alaska Journal* (1971): pp. 49–51; *ZUKMS* (1833): pt. 2, pp. 355–56; Lenz, *Deutsch-Baltisches Biographisches Lexikon*, pp. 284–85; Barratt, *Russia in Pacific Waters*, pp. 154–57. The Elmer E. Rasmuson Library of the University of Alaska at Fairbanks (Shur Collection) has microfilms of K. T. Khlebnikov's unpublished biographical sketch of Hagemeister (Reel 6: holograph in Perm' District State Archive, Perm', USSR: *fond* 445, op. 1, *delo* 43).
22. *Australian* (Sydney), 27 March 1829 (*Elena*'s voyage, danger from icebergs); Ivashintsev, op. cit., pp. 101, 104. On Vasilii S. Khromchenko, see Kotzebue, *Voyage of Discovery*, 1: 328–29, etc.
23. *Sydney Gazette*, 9 April 1829; on *Krotkii* herself, see F. P. Vrangel' (Wrangel), "Otryvok iz rukopisi, pod zaglaviem: Dnevnye Zapiski o plavanii voennogo transporta *Krotkago* v 1825–1827 godakh," *Severnyi arkhiv* (St. P., 1828): no. 36, pp. 49–51. Wrangel's service notes on *Krotkii* of 1825 form part of the Wrangel' Archive, *fond* 2057, op. 1, *dela* 310–12, held at TsGIAE in Tartu.
24. *Australian*, 31 March 1829 and 28 April 1829; *ZUKMS* (1832): pt. 9, pp. 304–12 (V. S. Khromchenko's survey of *Elena*'s voyage).
25. Cited by Fitzhardinge, "Russian Ships in Australian Waters," p. 142.
26. *Australian*, 31 March 1829.
27. Ivashintsev, *Russian Round-the-World Voyages*, p. 146.
28. Fitzhardinge, op. cit., p. 142.
29. On the Sydney defences, see Wentworth, *Description of the Colony*, pp. 34–36; A. B. Shaw, "Fort Denison, Sydney Harbour," *JRAHS*, 23 (1937); AE, 4: 165–66; Inglis, *Australian Colonists*, p. 300.
30. See D. MacCallum, "The Alleged Russian Plans for the Invasion of Australia, 1864," *JRAHS*, 44 (1959): 301–22; V. Fitzhardinge, "Russian Naval Visitors to Australia, 1862–1888," *JRAHS*, 52 (1966): 129–58.
31. *Australian*, 27 March 1829. Further glimpses of *Elena* and her captain appear in R. G. Liapunova, ed., *Russkaia Amerika v neopublikovannykh zapiskakh K. T. Khlebnikova* (L., 1979), pp. 221–27, 276, and B. Dmytryshyn and E. A. Crownhart-Vaughan, eds. and trans., *Colonial Russian America: Kyrill T. Khlebnikov's Reports, 1817–1832* (Portland, OR, 1976), pp. 84, 88 (British woollens for Sitka, costs, etc.).
32. *Australian*, 8 April 1829; see also *Hobart Town Courier*, 28 March 1829, for allusions to perhaps the same expected vessel.
33. Austin, "The Early Defences," p. 192 (Ross's request); on Phillip's vision of a naval harbour, see Cobley, *Sydney Cove 1788*, p. 31; Collins, *An Account* (1798), pp. 47, 189.
34. TsGAVMF, *fond* 1152, op. 1, *delo* 2: pp. 35ff. (Unkovskii's description); Samarov, *Russkie flotovodtsy*, 1: 68' (Rossiiskii). On the Macarthurs and the likelihood of non-

involvement in Napoleonic affairs, S. Macarthur-Onslow, ed., *Some Early Records of the Macarthurs of Camden* (Sydney, 1914), p. 46, etc.

35. TsGAVMF, *fond* 166, op. 1, *delo* 660, pt. 2: pp. 6–7; Walsh and Horner, "The Defence of Sydney in 1820," pp. 13–14.
36. See *Morskoi sbornik*, 188 (St. P., 1881): no. 11, pp. 31–32 (Rear-Admiral Aslanbegov at Esquimalt, Vancouver Island, in August 1881: "they say that when soldiers are needed, they will be sent!"). Like those of Russian officers at Melbourne in the later 19th century (bibliographical refs. in Fitzhardinge, "Russian Naval Visitors, 1862–1888"), such comments echoed the colonial misgivings of W. C. Wentworth: see his *Description of the Colony*, pp. 44–48.
37. See Bellingshausen, *Voyage*, 2: 342ff.; HRA, 10: 385 (J. T. Bigge to Macquarie, 2 October 1820); *GBPP*, 1823, X ("Report of the Commissioner of Inquiry on the State of Agriculture and Trade in New South Wales, 3rd Report,") 136, pp. 60 and 102.
38. Mikhailov's best-known view of Sydney (given in Bellingshausen, *Voyage*, 1: pl. 13), for instance, demands close comparison with the view, also from the vicinity of Milson's Point, printed in Joseph Lycell's *Views in Australia* (London 1824) and reproduced in Walsh and Horner, "The Defence of Sydney in 1820," p. 17. Both show the new fort on Benelong's Point (extreme left), Fort Phillip to the right, and Dawes Point Battery below it; but there are also intriguing differences, enhanced in Mikhailov's other (preliminary) studies of Sydney town and harbour from the North Shore. These remain in his portfolio at the State Russian Museum, Drawings Division, Leningrad: ref. R29277/275 and 29276/274. Both measure 26 cm by 37 cm. The former is headed "View of the Northern Side of Sydney Town" and shows two ships at centre. The town silhouette would change within nine months, in 1820.
39. *GBPP*, 1828, XXI, 477, pp. 531–600 (Report of July 1822 and extract from Macquarie's letter of October 1823 responding to part of Bigge's Report (*GBPP*, 1823, X, 136). For military assessments of the Sydney area's defensive capability by Majors James Taylor and Thomas Bell (1820), used by Bigge to criticize Macquarie's defence works, see PRO C.O.201/132, Bigge Appendix, roll 119. Copies at ML, Bonwick Transcripts, Bigge Appendix, boxes 21 and 24.
40. *GBPP*, 1828, XXI, 477, pp. 534ff., 565.
41. Bellingshausen, *Voyage*, 2: 321–54; Barratt, *Russians at Port Jackson*, pp. 47–53; Vorob'ev, "Etnograficheskie nabliudeniia," pp. 497–99.
42. Bellingshausen, *Voyage*, 2: 343ff.; C. M. H. Clark, *History of Australia* (Melbourne, 1962), pp. 296–98.
43. HRA, 9: 488; see also 9: 207 (Bathurst to Macquarie, 8 February 1817).
44. HRA, 12: 699–703 (Darling to Bathurst, 24 November 1826) and 12: 729 (Darling to Hay, 4 December 1826).
45. See Blainey, *Tyranny of Distance*, pp. 118–31.
46. *Sydney Gazette*, 9 January, 10 August, 1827 (D'Urville's true aims, the Royal Navy and Pacific Islands, etc.); 24 August 1827 (the undesirability of foreign-dominated islands near Australia); also R. C. Thompson, *Australian Imperialism in the Pacific* (Carlton, N.S.W., 1980), pp. 8–12.
47. Fitzhardinge, "Russian Naval Visitors," passim; MacCallum, "The Alleged Russian Plans for the Invasion," pp. 301–14.
48. *Australian*, 6 December 1826; see also issues for 28 October, 8 November 1826.
49. Gleason, *Genesis of Russophobia*, ch. 5. Ivashintsev, *Russian Round-the-World Voyages*, pp. 101 and 104.
50. *Australian*, 8 April 1829. Governor Gipps echoed W. C. Wentworth's criticisms of Sydney's ordnance in despatches to the Home authorities: see HRA, 20: 305–6; and the theme was again taken up in the early forties: see *Sydney Herald*, 12 February 1841, 1 *Sydney Gazette*, 30 December 1841, and *Sydney Morning Herald*, 22 September 1843 (bombardment fears and demands for larger and more guns. Wentworth's points were also underlined by Commodore Charles Wilkes, U.S.N., who sailed into Port Jackson by night on 29–30 November 1839, quite undetected: see his *Narrative of the United States*

Exploring Expedition, 2: 168–69. Colonial Office rebukes to Gipps in connection with Sydney's defences in HRA, 21: 51–53; 22: 327–29.

51. R. McNab, ed., *Historical Records of New Zealand* (Wellington, 1908–14), 1: 663–66, 707–8.
52. See A. H. McLintock, *Crown Colony Government in New Zealand* (Wellington, 1958), pp. 12–17.
53. PRO C.O.209/1 (Governor Bourke to Goderich, 23 December 1831 and Enclosure A); *Sydney Gazette,* 16 September 1830; H. M. Wright, *New Zealand, 1769–1840: Early Years of Western Contact* (Cambridge, MA, 1959), ch. 2; Thompson, *Australian Imperialism,* p. 11–12.
54. See W. P. Morrell, *British Colonial Policy,* ch. 1; C. C. Eldridge, *Victorian Imperialism,* pt. 2 (London, 1978); J. M. .R. Young, ed., *Australia's Pacific Frontier: Economic and Cultural Expansion into the Pacific, 1795–1885* (Melbourne, 1967); Hainsworth, *The Sydney Traders,* chs. 1–2; HRNZ, 1: 598–605, 681–83 (proposals for Crown support of colonizing in New Zealand, etc.).
55. See *Sydney Gazette,* 24 September 1831; Gleason, *Genesis of Russophobia,* pp. 113–30 (London sources of anti-Russian animus); L. Paszkowski, *Polacy w Australii i Oceanii, 1790–1840* (London, 1962), pp. 5–12 (beginnings of pro-Polish sentiment in New South Wales).
56. *Sydney Gazette,* 21 April 1831; also *GBPP,* 1838, 680, p. 11 (evidence of J. L. Nicholas).
57. *Sydney Herald,* 9 August 1832; also *Sydney Gazette,* 24 September 1829 (links between missionary work and commercial expansion from Sydney).
58. See my study, *Russophobia in New Zealand,* pp. 13–14 and P. W. T. Adams, *Fatal Necessity: British Intervention in New Zealand, 1830–1847* (Auckland, 1977), chs. 1–2.
59. Gleason, *Genesis of Russophobia,* ch. 5.
60. Barratt, *Russophobia in New Zealand,* passim, and "The Enemy that Never Was," *New Zealand Slavonic Journal* (1976): no. 1.
61. Thompson, *Australian Imperialism,* pp. 11–12.
62. *Hobart Town Courier,* 26 March 1831; E. J. Tapp, *Early New Zealand: A Dependency of New South Wales, 1788–1841* (Melbourne, 1958), pp. 75 ff.
63. Thompson, op. cit., ch. 1.
64. Ivashintsev, *Russian Round-the-World Voyages,* pp. 109–10, 147; Fitzhardinge, "Russian Ships in Australian Waters," p. 144.
65. Ivashintsev, op. cit., p. 110.
66. *Sydney Gazette,* 11 May 1832.
67. C. M. Hotimsky, "Russians in Australia," in AE, 7: 526.
68. *Sydney Gazette,* 14 February 1832.
69. Ibid., 24 May 1832.
70. See n. 29 above. For clear echoes of this view, see *Melbourne Argus,* 11 November 1864 and *The Age,* 16 November 1864.
71. *Sydney Gazette,* 14 February 1832.
72. J. W. Metcalfe, "Governor Richard Bourke or the Lion and the Wolves," *JRAHS,* 30 (1944): pt. 1; AE, 2: 65–66.
73. Ivashintsev, *Russian Round-the-World Voyages,* pp. 113–14, 147.
74. PRO C.O.201/122 (Acting Governor Lindesay to Goderich, 4 November 1831) set the tone adopted at Government House after 1832): permanent occupation of any part of the South Pacific "by any foreign Power" could cause intolerable "injury" to British and colonial interests. See also Fitzhardinge, "Russian Naval Visitors," p. 129; AE, 7: 526–28; and T. B. Millar, "History of the Defence Forces of the Port Phillip District of Victoria, 1836–1900," M.A. thesis, Melbourne, 1957.
75. V. S. Zavoiko, *Vpechatleniia moriaka vo vremia dvukh puteshestvii krugom sveta,* pt. 1 (St. P., 1840), pp. 57–58.
76. Ibid., p. 59; *Sydney Morning Herald,* 16 April 1835.

NOTES TO APPENDIX A

HYDROGRAPHY

1. "Otkrytiia Tasmana, s prilozheniem sochineniia o polozhenii Ontong Iavy i Marochnykh Ostrovov," *Tekhnologicheskii zhurnal*, 3 (St. P., 1806): pt. 3, pp. 134–85. Surveys of Kruzenshtern the hydrographer in Nevskii, *Pervoe puteshestvie Rossiian*, pp. 250–66 and Friis, *The Pacific Basin*, pp. 187–90.
2. Further on these matters, see Sharp, *The Voyages of Tasman*, pp. 345–47, and especially J. E. Heeres, "Abel Janszoon Tasman: His Life and Labours," pp. 59–62, 83–84.
3. Barratt, *Russia in Pacific Waters*, pp. 000.
4. Krusenstern, *Voyage*, 1: 5–6; M. V. Severgin, "Instruktsiia dlia puteshestviia okolo sveta po chasti mineralogii," *Severnyi vestnik*, 2–3 (St. P., 1804); Iu. M. Shokal'skii, *Okeanografiia* (Petrograd, 1917), pp. 32ff.; Nevskii, *Pervoe puteshestvie Rossiian*, pp. 54–58.
5. Kruzenshtern, *Puteshestvie*, 1: 19; Kotzebue, *Voyage of Discovery*, 1: intro.; Barratt, *Russia in Pacific Waters*, pp. 000.
6. F. F. Veselago, *Admiral Ivan Fedorovich Kruzenshtern*, pp. 11–12; A. S. Greig, "Otgzyv ob Atlase Iuzhnago Moria i Gidrograficheskikh Zapiskakh Vitse-Admirala Kruzenshterna," in *Shestoe Prisuzdenie Uchrezhdennykh P. N. Demidovym Nagrad* (St. P., Akademiia Nauk, 1837), pp. 97ff.; Nevskii, *Pervoe puteshestvie Rossiian*, pp. 250–60. Kruzenshtern's *Atlas* was supplemented by several separately published appendices or "memoirs," and materials relevant to Australia appear in *Sobranie sochinenii, sluzhashchikh razborom i iz'iasneniem "Atlasa Iuzhnago Moria"* (St. P., 1823–26).
7. Barratt, *Russia in Pacific Waters*, pp. 108–11.
8. PRO Adm 1/498, cap. 370 (Murray to Stephen, 16 August, 1794); Ralfe, *Naval Biography*, 3: 212 and 4: 98–99. Lisianskii's private diary of 1793–99 is held at the Central Naval Museum (TsVMM) in Leningrad (ref. 9170-1938), together with a 180-page *vakhtennyi zhurnal* that he kept aboard H.M.S. *Raisonnable* and *Sceptre* in 1797–99 (ref. 41820/2). For Kruzenshtern's professional occupations and movements of the same period, see "Puteshestvie ot Mysa Dobroi Nadezhdy k Madrasu," *ZADMM*, 3 (St. P., 1815).
9. Krusenstern, *Voyage*, 1: 7–9; *DNB*, 1: 581–82 and 97; 19: 1186.
10. *DNB*, 1: 97 (*Geometrical and Graphical Essays*..., etc., 1790).
11. Krusenstern, *Voyage*, 1: 8; on Hörner, see *Tekhnologicheskii zhurnal*, 5 (1820): pt. 3.
12. TsGAVMF, *fond* 406, op. 7, *delo* 62: pp. 62–64 (Lisianskii aboard the *Royalist*); V. V. Pertsmakher, "Iu. F. Lisianskii v Indii, 1799," in D. Olderogge, ed., *Strany i narody Vostoka*, bk. 12 (M., 1972), pp. 248–59, esp. 252–53.
13. See V. A. Vorontsov-Vel'iaminov, *Ocherki istorii astronomii v Rossii* (M., 1956), on Shubert's naval links.
14. Kotzebue, *Voyage*, 1: 16; *DNB*, 19: 1187.
15. Kotzebue, *Voyage*, 1: 16; *Monthly Notices of the Royal Astronomical Society*, 3: 149–54; Grant, *History of Astronomy*, pp. 491–92.
16. *DNB*, 1: 581–82 (on John Arnold, 1736–99, the London maker); 19: 1186; and 5: 1100–1 (on George Dolland, 1774–1852). Bellinsgauzen, *Dvukratnye izyskaniia* (1960), p. 88 and relevant notes by F. Debenham in his edition thereof, *Voyage of Captain Bellingshausen*, 1: 39 (London purchases of chronometers, planimeters, achromatic telescopes, etc.); see also materials in Samarov, ed., *Russkie flotovodtsy*.
17. Novosil'skii, *Iuzhny polius*, p. 5. Compare Bellingshausen, *Voyage* (1945), 1: 39. Further on Novosil'skii, see Sementovskii, *Russkie otkrytiia*, p. 285; Bellinsgauzen, *Dvukratnye izyskaniia*, p. 62; Barratt, *Russians at Port Jackson*, pp. 13 and 16.
18. Bellingshausen, *Voyage*, 1: 178–81.
19. Nevskii, *Pervoe puteshestvie*, p. 39.
20. Krusenstern, *Voyage*, 1:9. On Johann-Tobias Bürg (1766–1834), who had won his prizes from the Institut de France in 1800, see Berthelot, *Grande Encyclopédie*, 8: 461 .

21. See Kotzebue, *Voyage of Discovery*, 1: 16 and *New Voyage*, 3 (the range of modern instruments now used in the Pacific).
22. British materials used and often corrected by the Russians in their Pacific expeditions of 1815–22 may be identified by examination of such works as Bellingshausen's *Atlas* (St. P., 1831) and Kruzenshtern's *Popolneniek izdannym v 1826 i 1827 godakh ob' iasneniam osnovanii . . .* (St. P., 1836). It becomes clear that Arrowsmith's semi-official maps of the 1790s were still being used, though with decreasing faith, in the 1820s and even 30s.
23. See Shemelin, *Zhurnal*, pt. 1, pp. 4ff.; Golovnin, *Puteshestvie na shliupe "Diana,"* ch. 1; Kotzebue, *Voyage of Discovery*, 111: passim; Golovnin, *Puteshestvie na shliupe "Kamchatka" v 1817, 1818 i 1819 godakh*, ed. V. A. Divin (M., 1965), pp. 6–7, 15; Bellinsgauzen, *Dvukratnye izyskaniia*, p. 66ff.; Klochkov, "Puteshestvie," No. 21; Friis, *The Pacific Basin*, pp. 191, 194–95, 198.
24. Further on these matters, see above and my study, *The Russian View of Honolulu, 1809–1826*, ch. 11, h ("Meteorology"). Logs of all Russian ships in Australia contain meteorological data, the potential value of which for local climatology has been demonstrated by V. M. Pasetskii in *Geograficheskie issledovaniia*, pp. 73, 76–77. Few such data, however, have been published. Some with relevance to Hobart Town (Russian visit of 1823) appeared in *Meteorologicheskie nabliudeniia, proizvodivshieesia vo vremia krugosvetnogo plavaniia fregata "Kreisera" v 1822, 23 i 24 godakh* (St. P., 1882) and in the companion bulletin on *Ladoga*'s voyage.
25. Bellinsgauzen, *Dvukratnye izyskaniia*, pp. 210–11.
26. Ibid., p. 191. The Pigeon House is a prominent hill near the head of the Clyde River.
27. Flinders's *Voyage to Terra Australis . . . prosecuted in the Years 1801, 1802 and 1803 in His Majesty's Ship the Investigator . . .* (London, 1814), and the accompanying *Atlas* (1814), were among the "necessary information, charts, and publications" issued to Bellingshausen by the Admiralty Department in 1819: see Bellingshausen, *Voyage*, 1: 15, 162, 172 (Russian awareness of Flinders and respect for him); 2: 338 (Boongaree's association with him). Kruzenshtern had publicly expressed shock at the manner of Flinders's death, whilst a prisoner of the French at Mauritius in 1814.
28. Barratt, *Russians at Port Jackson*, p. 35; Lazarev, *Zapiski*, p. 151; Bellingshausen, *Voyage*, 2: 320; Novosil'skii, *Iuzhnyi polius*, p. 36; "Plavanie sudna 'Elena', pod nachal'stvom flota-leitenanta Khromchenko," *ZUKMS*, 9 (1832): 304. *Suvorov*'s shore work was partly done on Benelong's Point (see Rossiiskii, "Vypiska," p. 129), and *Riurik*'s on "the nearest islet" to Sydney Cove—probably Pinchgut (AGO, "Donesenie E. A. Klochkova pravleniiu RAK," *razriad* 99, *delo* 139: 16 July 1821). See also Fitzhardinge, "Russian Ships in Australian Waters," pp. 129, etc.
29. Lazarev, *Zapiski*, p. 87; Aleksandrov, "Professor I. M. Simonov," passim; Barratt, *Bellingshausen*, pp. 14–15. Order relating to astronomy by *Vostok* and the three other ships at Sydney in 1820 are given in Bellingshausen, *Voyage*, 1: 24–28. Tarkhanov and Simonov followed instructions modelled on those drafted by Johann Caspar Hörner of Zurich for the officers of *Riurik* in 1815 (see Kotzebue, *Voyage*, 1: intro.), but had received higher scientific training than Lts. Gleb Shishmarev and Ivan Zakharin of that ship; see ch. 5 above, nn. 143–49.
30. Barratt, *Russians at Port Jackson*, pp. 11, 24.
31. TsGAVMF, *fond* 203, op. 1, *delo* 730b: entries for 23–27 February (O.S.) 1820.
32. See Bellingshausen, *Voyage*, 1: 191 ("longitude fixed by me"); *ZUKMS*, 9 (1832): 304 ("Lt. Khromchenko made observations at a spot half a mile north of the Battery").
33. On Hagemeister's abilities, see K. T. Khlebnikov's biographical sketch: Perm' District Archive, *fond* 445, op. 1, *delo* 43: p. 6 (microfilm copy at Elmer E. Rasmuson Library, University of Alaska at Fairbanks: Shur Collection, reel 6.
34. *ZUKMS*, 9 (1832): 304. The reading was good to within a minute. Compare Tarkhanov's reckoning of Macquarie's South Head Lighthouse of April 1820: lat. 33°51′40″S, long. 151°16′50″E (TsGAVMF, *fond* 166, *delo* 660, pt. 2: p. 205).
35. Ivashintsev, *Russian Round-the-World Voyages*, pp. 137, 147.
36. Rossiiskii, "Vypiska," pp. 136–37.

37. Bellingshausen, *Voyage*, 2: 320. Further on Torson's skills and large contributions to the preparation of Bellingshausen's *Dvukratnye izyskaniia*... in 1822–23, see Pasetskii, *Geograficheskie issledovaniia*, pp. 44–45 and A. B. Sheshin, *Dekabrist Konstantin Petrovich Torson* (Ulan-Ude, 1980), pp. 32–37.
38. Bellingshausen, *Voyage*, 2: 321.ʹ
39. U.S. Department of the Interior, Office of Geography, Board on Geographic Names: *Australia: Gazetteer No. 40* (Washington, DC, 1957).
40. See N. Ia. Bolotnikov, "Faddei Faddeevich Bellinsgauzen...," in *Russkie moreplavteli* (M., 1953); Barratt, *Bellingshausen*, p. 12; K. F. W. Russwurm, *Nachrichten uber die adelige und freiherrliche Familie von Bellingshausen* (Reval, 1870).
41. Lazarev, *Zapiski*, p. 151. Captain-Lt. Gleb Shishmarev acted in accordance with orders issued to his superior, Vasil'ev, in having "mainland or islands not indicated on charts" thus surveyed by boat: see Bellingshausen, *Voyage*, 1: 25 (para. 10).
42. Ivashintsev, *Russian Round-the-World Voyages*, p. 140; Lazarev, *Zapiski*, pp. 35–36.
43. See *Opis' delam Upravleniia general-gidrografa i Gidroграficheskogo Departamenta Morskogo Ministerstva, 1827–1852 godov* (St. P., 1857) and V. V. Kolgushkin, comp., *Opisanie starinnykh atlasov, kart i planov XVI, XVII, XVIII, i poloviny XIX vekov, khraniashchikhsia v arkhive Tsentral'nogo kartograficheskogo proizvodstva Voenno-Morskogo Flota* (L., 1958). Both guides point to Australian materials among the hydrographic papers held at TsGAVMF.
44. F. A. Shibanov, *Ocherki po istorii otechestvennoi kartografii* (L., 1971), p. 5–40 and Gnucheva, *Geograficheskii Departament*, pp. 154–61.
45. For useful leads, see Grimsted, *Archives and Manuscript Repositories*, pp. 138–42 and Shibanov, *Ocherki*, pp. 111–16.
46. TsVMM, No. 9170/1838 ("Zhurnal leitenanta Iuriia Lisianskago s 1793 po 1800 god), p. 60, and No. 41820/2 ("Zhurnal Vakhtennyi"), the latter containing long extracts from observations made by Admiral Erasmus Gower (1742–1814); see also Kruzenshtern, "Puteshestvie ot Mysa Dobroi Nadezhdy...," in *ZADMM*, 3 (St. P., 1815).
47. Krusenstern, *Voyage*, 1: 24–25; Government of India, *Fort William-India House Correspondence and Other Contemporary Papers: Public Series, Volume 13: 1796–1800*, ed. K. D. Bhargava (Delhi, 1959), pp. 310, 355, etc.; Nevskii, *Pervoe puteshestvie Rossiian*, pp. 26–27; V. V. Pertsmakher, "Iu. F. Lisianskii v Indii, 1799," in D. A. Olderogge, ed., *Strany i narody Vostoka*, bk. 12 (M., 1972), pp. 248–59.
48. Then Prince of Wales Island to the British: *Fort William-India House Correspondence*, 13: 296–97, 537.
49. Ibid., 41: 455 and 508 (Dutch loss of possessions through war, opium trade, etc.); Krusenstern, *Voyage*, 1: 25.
50. Pt. 3, pp. 134–85.
51. Pp. 136, 139.
52. Sharp, *Voyages of Tasman*, pp. 345–47.
53. Kruzenshtern, "Otkrytiia Tasmana," p. 148; Sharp, op. cit., pp. 56, 346–47.
54. J. E. Heeres, "Abel Janszoon Tasman: His Life and Labours," in *Abel Janszoon Tasman's Journal* (Amsterdam, 1898).
55. Kruzenshtern, "Otkrytiia Tasmana," pp. 144–45.
56. Ibid.; the reference is to the voyage of the frigate *Aguila* (Captain Domingo de Boenechea): see B. G. Corney, trans., *The Quest and Occupation of Tahiti*, Hakluyt Series 2, vol. 36 (London, 1915).
57. Kruzenshtern, "Otkrytiia Tasmana," p. 150. *Omstandig verhaal* was vol. 3 of J. van Braam's (1724–26) ed. of *Oud en Niew... Oost-Indien*, dealing mostly with the island of Amboina in the Moluccas—a fact suggesting that Kruzenshtern had read it and reflected on Tasman's navigation, in November–December 1805 or very early in 1806, as *Nadezhda* was preparing to leave Macao and make for the Sunda Strait.
58. Reproduced in F. C. Wieder, ed., *Monumenta Cartographica*, vol. 4 (The Hague, 1932), plate 97. See also Heeres, "Abel Janszoon Tasman," 76–77, 106–7.

59. Sharp, *Voyages of Tasman*, p. 110.
60. Barratt, *Russian Discovery of Hawaii, 1804*, passim; Krusenstern, *Voyage*, 1: 151–84, 251–77, etc; K. Voenskii, "Russkoe posol'stvo v Iaponiiu v nachale XIX veka," *Russkaia starina* (July, October 1895).
61. Kruzenshtern, "Otkrytiia Tasmana," pp. 164, 169–70, 148.
62. Relevant papers here are not in TsGAVMF's map depository, i.e., the Archive of the Central Cartographic Production of the Fleet (see n. 43 above for the most recent Soviet guide), but in TsGIAE at Tartu (*fond* 1414) and in TsGAVMF's separate Kruzenshtern collection, *fond* 14. On the Dutch maps in question, see Heeres, "Abel Janszoon Tasman," pp. 76–77 and Coote, *Remarkable Maps*, pt. 3, nos. 1–6.
63. Kruzenshtern, "Otkrytiia Tasmana," p. 160; ch. 3 above on *Neva*'s and *Diana*'s eastward tracks to Australian waters.
64. Kotzebue, *New Voyage*, 1: 2–3; *Novoe puteshestvie vokrug sveta* (1981), pp. 9–10; Friis, *The Pacific Basin*, pp. 192–93.
65. F. P. Litke, *Puteshestvie vokrug sveta, sovershennoe na voennom shliupe "Seniavin" v 1826, 1827, 1828 i 1829 godakh: otdelenie tret'e* (St. P., 1833) and *otdelenie chetvertoe* (St. P., 1836); Ivashintsev, *Russian Round-the-World Voyages*, pp. 85–86, 98.
66. Kruzenshtern, "Otkrytiia Tasmana," p. 160.
67. See Barratt, *Bellingshausen*, pp. 19–20.
68. "Opredei enie geograficheskogo polozhenia...," *Zapiski Ministerstva Narodnogo Prosveshcheniia*, 22 (1828): 44–68.
69. See Bellingshausen, *Voyage*, 1: 27.
70. E. Escher, *Hörner's Leben und Werken* (Zurich, 1834); Berthelot, *Grande Encyclopédie*, 20: 280; and n. 67 above.
71. See Vucinich, *Science in Russian Culture*, pp. 205ff.; Komkov, *Akademiia Nauk SSSR*, pp. 183–84; Iu. G. Perel', "Vikentii Karlovich Vishnevskii," *Istoriko-astronomicheskie issledovaniia*, 1 (M., 1955): 133–48.
72. Kotzebue, *Novoe puteshestvie*, pp. 24, 318.
73. Ivashintsev, *Russian Round-the-World Voyages*, p. 98.
74. *ZUKMS*, 9 (1832): 300ff.
75. "Sila magnitnosti zemnago shara...," *ZUKMS*, 9 (1832): 110–29.
76. Ivashintsev, op. cit., p. 101.
77. Khrushchev, "Plavanie," pp. 203–6.
78. Shabel'skii (Shabelsky), *Voyage aux Colonies*, p. 104.
79. Bellingshausen, *Voyage*, 1: 181.
80. *ZUKMS*, 9 (1832): 304–5. Among the Russian ships that went from Sydney to the SE of the Tonga Islands then northward were *Suvorov* in September 1814 and *Riurik* in August–September 1822 (Ivashintsev, *Russian Round-the-World Voyages*, pp. 22, 65). The more usual route from Sydney to the Russian possessions took ships between the New Hebrides and Fiji archipelagoes. It was taken by *Krotkii* in April–May 1829, by *Amerika* in June 1832 and again in May 1835 (*ibid.*, pp. 104, 110, 114). The pattern of seasonal sailings into Melanesia is plain.
81. Bellingshausen, *Voyage*, 2: 312–16.
82. Ivashintsev, op. cit., p. 80.
83. Bellingshausen, *Voyage*, 2: 316–17.
84. Hunter, *Historical Journal*, pp. 33–35.
85. See Ibid., p. 39.
86. Cited by Bagrow, *History of Russian Cartography*, p. 238.
87. "Svedeniia...," *Zapiski Voenno-Topograficheskogo Depo*, pt. 1 (St. P., 1837); *PSZRI*, 26: no. 19607 (the role in the earlier growth of the *Depo kart* played by Admiral Koshelev, naval minister in 1798–1802); Shibanov, *Ocherki po istorii otech. kartografii*, pp. 106–11.
88. See Shibanov, op. cit., p. 112 and Bagrow, *History of Russian Cartography*, pp. 203ff.
89. V. F. Krempol'skii, *Istoriia razvitiia*, p. 16; *PSZRI*, 32: no. 24971, 33: no. 26256, and 38: no. 28901.

90. Further on these matters, see Grimsted, *Archives and Manuscript Repositories*, pp. 13, 138–39.
91. See also here, "A Note on Soviet Archival Sources," on materials in TsGAVMF relating to New South Wales.

ZOOLOGY

1. See Hotimsky, "Bibliography of Captain James Cook," pp. 5–12.
2. Further on this, ch. 2 above.
3. A. M. Lysaght, "Banks's Artists and his *Endeavour* Collections," in T. C. Mitchell, ed., *Captain Cook and the South Pacific*, British Museum Yearbook 3 (London, 1979), pp. 11–16.
4. For survey, M. E. Hoare, ed., *The Resolution Journal of Johann Reinhold Forster, 1772–1775*, Hakluyt Society Series 2, no. 152 (London, 1982), 1: 14–19.
5. Ibid., 1: 21ff., 118–19, etc.; 2: 288; *Russkii biografich. slovar'*, 21: 201–2.
6. MAE records indicate that at least two pieces of Tahitian *kapa* were received from Forster in 1779–82, and are now in Collection No. 737. Confirmation in LOAAN, *fond* K-IV, op. 1: p. 28.
7. Golenishchev-Kutuzov, *Predpriiatie*, p. 7; Sokolov, "Prigotovlenie," pp. 185–89; TsGAVMF, *fond* Grafa Chernysheva, 1788, *delo* 367. Also invited to accompany Mulovskii was the former astronomer of Cook's *Adventure* in 1772–75, William Bayly.
8. Golenishchev-Kutuzov, *Predpriiatie*, p. 7; also Hoare, *Resolution Journal* 1: 108–9 (Vilno position).
9. Full details in Sopikov, *Opyt Rossiiskoi Bibliografii*, no. 9206.
10. Beaglehole, *Journals of Captain James Cook: Voyage of the Resolution and Adventure* (Cambridge, 1961), pp. 732–35. From BM Add MS 27890, ff. 7–11.
11. *Entsiklopedicheskii slovar'*, 9: 43.
12. Golenishchev-Kutuzov, trans., *Puteshestvie v iuzhnoi polovine zemnago shara . . .*, pt. 1 (St. P., 1796), p. 243.
13. See Beaglehole, *Voyage of the Resolution and Adventure*, p. 734 and nn.
14. The admiral was evidently familiar with Georges-Leopold Cuvier's description of the opossum.
15. See ch. 2 above, for works by S. Zubkov, Barrington, Ivan I. Novikov published in 1802–5.
16. "O zhivykh zhivotnykh, privezennykh vo Frantsiiu . . ." appeared in 1805, pt. 2, pp. 181–86; "Izvestie o nekotorykh novootkrytykh mlekopitaiushchikh" also in pt. 2, pp. 159–61.
17. "O zhivykh zhivotnykh," p. 182.
18. "Izvestie," p. 159.
19. "O sokranenii ptichnykh chuchel i nasekomykh," *Tekhnolog. zhurnal*, 6 (1809): pt. 2, pp. 96–110. For animals taken back to France in *Le Géographe*, we have Péron's *Voyage de Découvertes aux terres australes*, 6 vols. (Paris, 1807–16).
20. Attention was drawn to issue no. 116 of the *Miscellany*, for instance, with its fine plate and description of *Trachicitys australis*, "a new species of fish of the *Thoracici* family."
21. I thank Dr. Vladimir Paevskii, of ZIAN's Ornithological Division, for identifying "1820" specimens of *Sericulus chrysocephalus* Lewin (regent bowerbird) and *Philemon corniculatus* (noisy friarbird) for me in May 1985, during my visit to his Institute.
22. D. V. Naumov, *Zoologicheskii muzei Akademii Nauk SSSR* (L., 1980), p. 6.
23. *Katalog Zoologicheskogo Razdela Muzeia Akademii Nauk* (St. P., 1742) had 755 pages of items; see also *Zoologicheskii muzei Akademii Nauk* (St. P., 1889), ch. 1.
24. LOAAN, *fond* K-IV, op. 1: "Zhurnal postuplenii Otdela fondov," no. 1 (confusion of artefacts and objects of natural history from Oceania at the Academy, etc.); Russov, "Beiträge" (St. P., 1900). Orest Beliaev, *Kabinet Petra Velikogo*, pt. 2 (St. P., 1800), pp. 228–30 (Polynesian and other articles jumbled together).

25. Komissarov, *Langsdorf,* pp. 8–15; Nevskii, *Pervoe puteshestvie Rossiian,* pp. 57–58.
26. LOAAN, *razriad* 4, vol. 1, no. 800.
27. Komissarov, B. N. *Russkie istochniki po istorii Brazilii pervoi chetverti XIX veka* (L., 1977), pp. 26–33; Naumov, *Zoologicheskii muzei Akademii Nauk SSSR,* p. 12.
28. A. Shtraukh, "Akademik Fedor Fedorovich Brandt, osnavetel' i pervyi direktor Zoologicheskogo Muzeia," *Zoologicheskii Muzei Akademii Nauk* (St. P., 1889).
29. Bellingshausen, *Voyage,* 1: 185.
30. Ibid., 2: 354.
31. See J. M. Forshaw, *Australian Parrots,* 2d ed. (Melbourne, 1978), p. 185.
32. TsGIAL, *fond* 789, op. 20, *dela* 28, 30, 36.
33. Two sheets of Mikhailov's 1819–22 portfolio (Nos. 29078 and 29171 by modern enumeration at the Russian Museum, Leningrad, Nos. 75 and 108 by the original schema), offer kangaroo sketches. The former shows two faint, preliminary drawings, the latter, four; the former also has a bird described as "Ezel' Duk." No. 29082 (originally No. 81) shows, among other things, seals and a pair of pencilled cockatoos.
34. E. A. Berens, "Zapiski," *MSb* (1903): no. 3, p. 21.
35. Bellingshausen, *Voyage,* 2: 353.
36. Shabel'skii, *Voyage aux colonies,* p. 24.
37. Ibid., p. 23.
38. I thank Dr. D. F. Hoese, Head of the Vertebrate Zoology Division at the Australian Museum, Sydney, for placing me in contact with Professor Parin, and Michael L. Augee of the Royal Zoological Society of New South Wales at Mosman for venturing ichthyologoical identifications on the basis of 1820 material.

BOTANY

1. Barratt, *Russia in Pacific Waters,* ch. 2; Golder, *Bering's Voyages* (New York, 1925), 2: 242–49, etc.
2. V. I. Lipskii, *Imperatorskii St. Peterburgskii Botanicheskii Sad za 200-letie ego sushchestvovaniia, 1713–1913,* pt. 3 (Petrograd, 1913–15); E. Trautvetter, *Grundriss einer Geschichte der Botanik in Bezug auf Russland* (St. P., 1837) and *Kratkii ocherk istorii Imperatorskogo St. Peterburgskogo Botanicheskogo Sada* (St. P., 1873); H. G Bongard, "Esquisse historique des travaux sur la botanique entrepris en Russie depuis Pierre le Grand jusqu'à nos jours," in *Receuil des Actes de la Séance Publique de l'Académie de Sciences de St Pétersbourg tenue le 29 décembre 1834* (St. P., 1835), pp. 83–108.
3. For German sources on Australian flora, see Karl E. Berg, *Catalogus systematicus bibliothecae Horti Imperialis Botanici Petropolitani* (St. P., 1852; 514 pp.).
4. V. I. Lipskii, *Gerbarii Imp. St. Peterburgskogo Botanicheskogo Sada, 1823–1908,* 2d ed. (Iur'ev, 1909), pp. 5–10.
5. *Voenno-meditsinskii Zhurnal* (St. P., 1854): pt. 64; *Severnaia pchela* (1854): no. 127. Fischer's namesake, the arguably greater botanist Aleksandr Grigor'evich Fisher (Fischer von Waldheim: 1803–84) succeeded his won teacher, Georg Franz Hoffmann (1760–1826) as Director of the Botanical Garden in Moscow, becoming professor of botany there in 1830. He, too, stimulated Russian awareness of Australian flora, through the work of the Moscow Society of Naturalists.
6. Komissarov, *Grigorii Ivanovich Langsdorf,* pp. 50–51; Nevskii, *Pervoe puteshestvie Rossiian,* pp. 58 etc.
7. V. Nekrasova, "O russkikh krugosvetnykh ekspeditsiiakh," *Botanicheskii zhurnal* (1950); *Drug zdraviia* (St. P., 1854): no. 30.
8. Lipskii, *Gerbarii,* pp. 7–10; Trautvetter, *Kratkii ocherk,* ch. 2.
9. Lipskii, *Gerbarii,* p. 33.
10. See n. 4.
11. I thank Dr. Andrei E. Bobrov, of BIN, for this information.
12. *Allgemeine Deutsche Biographie,* 21: 470.

13. Bellingshausen, *Voyage*, 1: 10ff.
14. See Barratt, *Russian Exploration in the Mariana Islands, 1816–28,* Historic Preservation Office, Commonwealth of the Northern Mariana Islands, Micronesian Archaeological Survey Report no. 17 (Saipan, 1984), pp. 11–12; F. H. Kittlitz, *Denkwurdigkeiten einer Reise um die Welt* (Gotha, 1858), passim.
15. *Entsiklopedicheskii Slovar'*, 79: 209–10.
16. *Acta Horti Petropolitani* (St. P., 1880), 7: 88 ("Florae Rossicae Fontes," no. 414); Lipskii, *Gerbarii*, p. 52.
17. See n. 11.
18. Lipskii, *Gerbarii*, p. 52.
19. See Carl Christensen, *Index Filicum, sive Enumeratio omnium generum specierumque Filicum et Hydropteridum, 1753–1905* (Hafniae, 1906), p. 710.
20. I. Kukkonen and K. Viljamaa, *The Herbarium of Christian Steven*, University Botanical Museum, Pamphlet 4 (Helsinki, 1971), p. 81.
21. S. Savage, "Robert Brown as an Official of the Linnaean Society," *Proceedings of the Linnaean Society* (London, 1931–32): pt. 2; N. B. Kinnear, "Robert Brown's Collections on the Investigator," *Proceedings of the Linnaean Society* (London, 1931–32): pt. 2; J. Knight, *On the Cultivation of the Plants belonging to the Natural Order of Proteacae* (London, 1809).
22. A. N. Beketov, *Geografiia rastenii* (St. P., 1896); ADB, 1788–1850, pt. 1, pp. 166–67.
23. TsGAVMF, *fond* 166, *delo* 660; pt. 2: pp. 210–11; AONSW, Allan Cunningham Journal, reel 47: 8–9 March 1820.
24. Mitchell Library: Kew MSS Transcripts, Cunningham to Joseph Banks, 1 May 1820.
25. McMinn, *Allan Cunningham*, p. 42.
26. Hotimsky, "A Russian Account," pp. 90–91; Shabel'skii, *Voyage aux colonies*, pp. 26ff.; ADB, 1: 265–69 and 416.
27. Kukkonen and Viljamaa, *Herbarium of Christian Steven*, pp. 34, 64, 94.

Bibliography

ARCHIVAL MATERIALS

1. Central State Archives of the USSR

(a) Tsentral'nyi Gosudarstvennyi Arkhiv Voenno-Morskogo Flota SSSR (TsGAVMF: Leningrad)

fond 7, op. 1, *delo* 2 (V. M. Golovnin's notebook, 1802–5; service as a Volunteer, early actions); *delo* 5 (his early distinction as signals officer, interpreter).

fond 14 (I. F. Kruzenshterna), op. 1, *dela* 12–13 (Kruzenshtern's earlier service); *delo* 898 (Lisianskii in Brazil with *Neva*, 1803). This *fond* contains 529 items dating from 1787, and many bear on Pacific issues and expeditionary plans.

fond 162, op. 1, *delo* 44 (materials relating to the publication of M. N. Vasil'ev's, A. P. Lazarev's K. Gillesem's accounts of the *Otkrytie-Blagonamerennyi* expedition; A. S. Menshikov-L. I. Golenishchev-Kutuzov corresp., 1823–30; MSS containing descriptions of New South Wales, their editing, etc.).

fond 166, *delo* 660, pt. 2 (Vasil'ev to Naval Staff on hydrography, etc., while in Port Jackson); *delo* 691 (letters re participation of Pavel N. Mikhailov in Bellingshausen's expedition, his terms of service and duties); *delo* 660, pt. 2 (Fedor I. Shtein's "Mineralogical Observations" from New South Wales, as given in resumé by Vasil'ev, etc.); *delo* 666, pp. 314–16 (orders for *Kreiser* and *Ladoga*, 1822, re cartography and possible emendations to Kruzenshtern's *Atlas*, etc.).

fond 172, op. 1, *delo* 376 (administrative preparations for Mulovskii's Pacific expedition, chart collecting); *delo* 589 (would-be members of that expediton, 1786–87).

fond 203, op. 1, *delo* 730b (Nikolai D. Shishmarev's journal, 1819–22; *Blagonamerennyi* at Sydney, March 1820); op. 1, *delo* 1123 (Mikhail P. Lazarev to A. V. Moller, 10 December 1823, etc., re *Kreiser*'s call at Hobart Town and later movements).

fond 205, op. 1, *delo* 644 (possible publication of Vasil'ev's account, lists of available primary materials).

fond 212 (Gosudarstvennoi Admiralteistv-Kollegii), op. 1765, *dela* 25–26 (materials on the origins of Russian naval service with the British, Volunteers' duties, etc.); op. 2, *delo* 3735 (*Suvorov*'s activities at Sydney, 1814; purchases of local supplies and services); *delo* 4093 (M. P. Lazarev to A. V. Moller *et al.*, 1823; *Kreiser* and *Ladoga* at Hobart Town).

fond 213, op. 1, *delo* 52 (correspondence re diaries and journals of former members of the
Vasil'ev-Shishmarev expedition); *delo* 43 (Aleksei P. Lazarev and Pavel
Zelenoi as linguists in the Pacific, 1820–21; Otto von Kotzebue's expectations
of the expedition in natural science and hydrography, etc.); *delo* 9 (information
on Vasil'ev's proposed route, to be forwarded to London and elsewhere); *delo*
102 (outfitting the expedition, 1819; stores and cordage); *delo* 118 (notes on the
expedition by M. N. Vasil'ev; official reaction).

fond 215, op. 1, *delo* 1203 (natural historical and ethnographic materials from Oceania
and Australia, brought wtih *Otkrytie* and *Blagonamerennyi* to St. Petersburg in
1822).

fond 223 (po istorii Russkogo Flota, XVII-XIX vv.), op. 1 (Admiral N. S. Mordvinov's
support of Kruzenshtern in 1802). Complementary documents are held in *fond*
197, the chancery papers of Admiral Grigorii G. Koshelev, Vice-President of
the Admiralty College, for 1799–1803.

fond 315, op. 1, *delo* 1404 (Pavel S. Nakhimov-Mikhail F. Reineke letters, 1824–25, re
Ladoga and *Kreiser* at Hobart and on the Northwest Coast; the emptiness of Van
Diemen's Land, etc.).

fond 870, op. 1, *delo* 3599a and b (log book of *Kreiser* for 1823, containing meteorological and related data in the hands of Fedor Vishnevskii and Dmitrii I. Zavalishin
of that ship).

fond 1166, op. 1, *delo* 9 (Pavel S. Nakhimov on *Kreiser*'s Pacific voyage of 1823).

fond 1152, op. 1, *dela* 1–2 (Semen Ia. Unkovskii's MS on *Suvorov*'s round-the-world
voyage, 1813–16; Sydney trade prospects, harbour, officialdom; also typed
copy of "Istinnye zapiski moei zhizni" based on the *putevoi zhurnal*).

fond 1153, op. 1, *delo* 1 (M. N. Vasil'ev's "Observations... on New South Wales,"
i.e., "Zamechaniia... o Novoi Iuzhnoi Valisskoi Zemle," with connected
papers; a general survey, with statistics).

(b) Tsentral'nyi Gosudarstvennyi Arkhiv Drevnikh Aktov (TsGADA: Moscow)

fond 30, *delo* 67 (Russian Volunteers with foreign navies, 1802–11, including V. M.
Golovnin, M. P. Lazarev, L. A. Hagemeister).

fond 183, *delo* 89 (merchant V. N. Bosnin's paper on the *Nadezhda-Neva* venture and its
readying; Pacific trade prospects, needs).

fond 290, op. 1, *delo* 754 (A. R. Vorontsov and the Commerce College's growing awareness of foreign threats to Russian interests in the North Pacific, the China trade,
etc., 1785–86).

fond 1261 (roda Vorontsovykh), op. 1 (numerous personal and service papers of S. R.
and A. R. Vorontsov touching on the Russian enterprise in the Pacific, Anglo-
Russian naval understanding, the British presence in waters claimed by Russia);
delo 797 (Commerce College *protokol* re the creation of the Russian-American
Company in 1799, the scope of its activities, etc.).

fond Gosarkhiva, *razriad* 10, op. 3, *delo* 16 (qualifications for membership of
Mulovskii's Pacific mission; procedures to the followed in the Pacific); *razriad*
21, *delo* 9 (additional skills required of seamen for the Pacific service). Echoed
in the *ukaz Admiralteistv-Kollegii* of 3 March 1819 (TsGAVMF, *fond* 212) with

regard to ordinary seamen for the Vasil'ev-Shishmarev expedition then being readied.

(c) Tsentral'nyi Gosudarstvennyi Istoricheskii Arkhiv SSSR (TsGIA: Leningrad)

fond 15, op. 1, *dela* 1–2 (correspondence re organization, objectives, routes, crews of *Nadezhda-Neva* expedition; Company offer of advantageous service to naval officers; *Nadezhda*'s log, Kruzenshtern's and others' scientific work in Oceania, etc.); op. 1, *delo* 12 (correspondence re the release of officers and supply of naval stores for the *Suvorov*, 1812–13; Traversay and O. P. Kozodavlev on terms of service; M. P. Lazarev's despatches to Company Main Board re *Suvorov*'s Pacific voyage, Sydney).
fond 13, op. 1, *delo* 187 (Count N. P. Rumiántsev's reports to Alexander I: 12 November 1809—pp. 78–84—re Hagemeister's voyage out in *Neva*, Hawaiian dealings; Baranov's praise of Hagemeister). Also in *delo* 287 (pp. 46–47) are orders to V. M. Golovnin of *Diana*, to proceed to the Northwest Coast, assist *Neva*, keep watch).
fond 789 (Akademii Khudozhestv), op. 1, *dela* 1854, 1949, 2460 (materials on the training and release of the artists P. N. Mikhailov and E. M. Korneev); op. 2, *delo* 28 (the same); op. 20, *dela* 7, 9, 17, 21 (Korneev and the 1819–22 naval expedition, his functions, qualifications); op. 20, *delo* 28b (A. N. Olenin praises Korneev as an expeditionary artist); *delo* 30 (Korneev's obligations in distant parts of the world, his portfolios, their entrusting to M. N. Vasil'ev in 1822); *delo* 36 (Korneev's hopes of seeing his 1819–22 work published; correspondence between A. N. Golitsyn, A. N. Olenin, and A. V. Moller re that subject; Scientific Committee of Naval Staff acquires Korneev's portfolios); op. 1, *delo* 546 (pension granted him, 1826); *delo* 595 (personal crisis, threat of poverty, 1827). Complementary materials on the fate of Korneev's 1820 drawings and aquarelles in 1822–30 are in TsGAVMF, *fond* 166, *po reestru* 202, nos. 595 and 691, and *fond* 213, op. 1, nos. 52 and 99.

(d) Arkhiv Vneshnei Politiki Rossii SSSR (AVPR: Moscow)

fond Sankt-Petersburgskii Glavnyi Arkhiv (Glavarkhiva), II-3, op. 34 (Company orders re vessels bound for the North Pacific, with associated reports and memoranda); *dela* 3–5 (papers on *Neva*, Hagemeister's sailing orders, 1807); *delo* 7 (Company Main Office correspondence with N. P. Rumiántsev and Alexander I, 1811: movements of Hagemeister and *Neva* in 1810).
fond Kantseliarii Ministerstva Inostrannykh (Vneshnikh) Del: 1814, *dela* 7942–44 (N. P. Rumiántsev's letters to tsar re Pacific trade, the need for naval and other measures to counteract British and American commercial energy, etc.); 1822, *delo* 3645 (*Apollon* to patrol the Russian Northwest Coast until relieved); *dela* 3716–17 (Nesselrode's defence of the 1824 delimitation of Russian America to south and east, etc.).
fond Rossiisko-Amerikanskoi Kompanii, *delo* 183 (data on all fur sales theretofore to foreign subjects, Pacific trade patterns); *dela* 284–85 (Golovnin and M. P.

Lazarev influencing Company directors, 1816–17; Company-Navy relations and strains). On the Molvo-Lazarev affair of 1816, concerning alleged Russian sales of spirits at Sydney in 1814, the official hearing of the charge and Lazarev's exoneration, see TsGAVMF, *fond* 212, *delo* 3735: 150–52.

fond Londonskoi Missii (Kollegii Inostrannykh Del), *delo* 547 (Tsar Paul's rescripts to Semen R. Vorontsov in London of 1799, re international trade and ententes).

(e) Arkhiv Vsesoiuznogo Geograficheskogo Obshchestva SSSR (AGO: Leningrad)

razriad 99 (Rossiisko-Amerikanskoi Kompanii), op. 1, *delo* 65 (crew list of the Company ship *Elena*, at Sydney in April 1829); *dela* 111–12 (Kiril T. Khlebnikov's observations on Company outposts in North America, California, and trade prospects; the value of round-the-world provisioning voyages questioned); *delo* 139 (Captain Efim Klochkov's report to Company Main Office from Sydney, July/August 1821: Sir Thomas Brisbane, fast English merchantmen, Anglo-Russian courtesies).

(f) Tsentral'nyi Gosudarstvennyi Arkhiv Literatury i Iskusstva SSSR (TsGALI: Leningrad)

fond 612, op. 1, *delo* 1627 (materials regarding the acquisition of a fair copy of Iurii F. Lisianskii's *Zhurnal . . . vedennyi im vo vremia sluzhby ego volonterom . . . s 1793 po 1800 god,* by the State Literary Museum; together with a typed copy of that work, of 177 pp., covering Lisianskii's activities and plans whilst in Cape Colony and Bengal, 1798–99; interest in Eastern trade, Pacific hydrography, and Mtthew Flinders).

fond 1337 (Kollektsiia dnevnikov i vospominanii), op. 1, *delo* 135 (an editor's copy of the same journal: for details, see N. N. Bashkina *et al., Rossiia i SShA,* pp. 202–03, n. 1 and Nevskii, *Pervoe puteshestvie Rossiian,* p. 33, nn. 1–2, and 271. Nevskii asserted in 1951 that TsVMM possessed a later journal by Lisianskii, as well as rough drafts of letters dated 1803–32).

(g) Gosudarstvennaia Publichnaia Biblioteka imeni Saltykova-Shchedrina: Otdel Rukopisei (ORGPB: Leningrad)

F. XVII.106.11, pp. 213–57 (scribe's copy of Aleksei P. Lazarev's diary, kept aboard the *Blagonamerennyi,* July–November 1820).

fond Ivana T. Pomialovskogo, no. 72, pp. 1–140 (variant of Aleksei P. Lazarev's *Zapiski,* based on the above, with heavy corrections. Details of these and their relationship to the fair copy of the *Zapiski* now at TsGAVMF *fond* 1153, *delo* 1, in Lazarev, *Zapiski,* p. 6; Tumarkin, "Materialy ekspeditsii M. N. Vasil'eva," p. 51; Kuznetsova, "Novye dokumenty," p. 237, n. 3.

fond 1000, op. 2, no. 1146 (Makar I. Ratmanov's journal from *Nadezhda,* 1803–6; Kruzenshtern as commander and antagonist of Nikolai P. Rezanov; shipboard routines in Oceania; nationalism).

(h) Gosudarstvennaia Publichnaia Biblioteka imeni V. I. Lenina (Moscow)

fond 178 (Butenevy), nos. 3–7 (papers of Midshipman, later Captain, Ivan P. Butenev, late of *Kreiser*, in Australia in 1823).

fond 333 (Chichagovy): materials to and from Vice-Admiral Pavel V. Chichagov, naval minister 1807–11; expeditionary plans and connections with Kruzenshtern and Golovnin re readying and financing *Diana*.

fond 178, M.10693a (Tilesius von Tilenau: album of sketches made in 1803–5: natural history of Oceania, especialy Nukuhiva, Marquesas Islands, and Kamchatka; Russian science). The complementary journal of 1803–6 is held at the Leningrad division of the Archive of the Academy of Sciences of the USSR: *razriad* 4, op. 1, *delo* 800a (data on scientific procedures in *Nadezhda* and the beginnings of Russian botany and zoology in the South Pacific Ocean).

fond 261, *karton* 3: 71 (letters dated 1932 re proposed publication of Semen Ia. Unkovskii's *Zapiski*, which had been edited in 1920s); *karton* 19:6 and 20:1 (Unkovskii's *Zapiski*, with annotations).

fond 255 (Rumiantsevy), 15: 30–35 (papers on Company relations with Upper California, naval and maritime connections in the Pacific).

fond 600, *karton* 1 (memoirs of Semen Ia. Unkovskii and drafts of letters, materials on Unkovskii's naval career, etc., 1817–82). Other documents relating to Unkovskii are held at the Central State Archive of the City of Moscow (TsGAGM), in *fond* 1762 (five items).

(i) Voenno-Istoricheskii Muzei Artillerii, Inzhenernykh Voisk, i Voisk Sviazi (Leningrad)

fond 47 (F. F. Bellingshausen): eleven items, from 1814–48, on various aspects of Bellingshausen's naval career.

2. Soviet Archives Outside Leningrad and Moscow

(j) Tsentral'nyi Gosudarstvennyi Istoricheskii Arkhiv Estonskoi SSR (TsGIAE: Tartu)

fond 1414 (Ivan F. Kruzenshtern): 482 items relating to Kruzenshtern, his career successes, family, and correspondence, the earliest from 1793; much material on the 1803–6 expedition, by Johann F. Eschscholtz, E. E. Levenshtern (von Loewenstern), *et al.;* op. 3, *delo* 42 (L. A. Khoris: letters to Kruzenshtern from Paris, 1821–22, re publication of his Pacific illustrations, lithography).

fond 2057 (Ferdinand P. Vrangel', or Wrangel), op. 1, *dela* 310–12 (MS notes from voyages of the *Krotkii,* 1825–27; *Krotkii's* sailing capabilities, etc.); *delo* 381 (diary of Kiril T. Khlebnikov, Company manager at Novo-Arkhangel'sk from 1817–32 and historian, for 1800–32: materials on voyages to the colonies of *Elena,* 1824–25 and 1828–29).

(k) Tsentral'nyi Tallinskii Gosudarstvennyi Arkhiv (Tallin)

fond 775, *dela* 3–7 (Leontii A. Hagemeister): his naval career and major expeditions and
    service in the North Pacific. Twenty-five *dela* relate to the Hagemeister family
    from 1745 to 1920: certain materials were recently transferred from the Central
    State Historical Archive of the Latvian SSR (TsGALatSSR), Riga, where they
    had been filed under *fond* 764.
fond Semeinykh Kollektsii: family papers assembled by the Eesti NSV Riikliik
    Ajaloomuuseum, 17 Pikk, Tallin, relating to several Baltic German families
    with Pacific naval links, including the Bellingshausens of Saaremaa (Oesel).

(l) Gosudarstvennyi Arkhiv Permskoi Oblasti (Perm')

fond 445 (Kirila T. Khlebnikova), op. 1, *delo* 43 (biographical sketch of Hagemeister,
    stressing his value to the Company); *delo* 58 (Hagemeister's reports to Com-
    pany Main Office re voyage out of the *Neva:* report of May 1807 on Sydney
    market prices, commercial prospects, Sydney-Canton link, Governor Bligh,
    George Johnston, Robert Campbell); *delo* 172 (Khlebnikov-Hagemeister corre-
    spondence: proper use of shipping, efficient provisionment).

(m) Nauchnaia Biblioteka Kazanskogo Gosudarstvennogo Universiteta (Kazan')

fond Ivana M. Simonova: seven items: Simonov's connection with Kazan' University,
    1812–55; his scientific interests.

3. Archives in English-Speaking States

(n) United States of America: National Archives, Washington, D.C.

Records Group 261. "Records of the Russian-American Company, 1802–67: Corre-
    spondence of Governors-General."

Vol. 1	Fols. 54–55	No. 189 (Main Office to Chief Manager Baranov re the punishment inflicted by M. P. Lazarev of Krasil'nik, supercargo on *Suvorov,* and the latter's drunkenness at sea). This complements papers in TsGAVMF *fond* 212, *delo* 3735: 150–52, relating to the Molvo-Lazarev affair, alleged rum selling at Sydney, etc.
	Fols. 73–75 (1817)	No. 218 (Baranov reprimanded for awarding Molvo a gold medal; Molvo said to be a troublemaker, etc.).
	Fol. 234 (1819)	No. 205 (Main Office to Hagemeister re proposed purchase of ship in England and of *Riurik* from Count N. P. Rumiántsev, for Pacific service).
Vol. 2	Fols. 66–67 (1820)	No. 230 (Main Office to Governor-General Murav'ev re Company hiring of V. S. Khromchenko, to be employed as port captain at Novo-Arkhangel'sk; his skills).

	Fol. 191 (1821)	No. 179 (Count Rumiántsev wishes Khromchenko to make an Arctic exploration in *Riurik;* appropriateness of ship and commander for such work in secrecy).
	Fols. 196ff. (1820)	No no. (Company Regulations for Servants: obligations while on round-the-world vessels; behaviour at sea and in foreign ports; round-the-world transport and its maintenance; salaries and food allowances, data on medical care and rewards for extraordinary services).
	Fols. 248–49 (1821)	No. 448 (Main Office to Efim Klochkov, commander of *Riurik,* Orders: 17 June 1821, to guide him on the voyage to the Northwest Coast; calls at foreign ports, revictualling, etc.).
Vol. 3	Fol. 290 (1823)	No. 152 (Admiralty Department findings on the matter of Nunivak Island; Vasil'ev, not Khromchenko, found to be the discoverer, but reward for the latter and praise of his hydrographic and professional skill).
Vol. 4	Fols. 118ff. (1824)	No. 499 (Company contracts for the officers of *Elena,* Petr Egorovich Chistiakov and nine others; terms of service, pay and duties, e.g., of Dr. Ivan Sakharov, fols. 149–51, whilst in the Pacific).
	Fols. 188–90 (1824)	No. 512 (Main Office to Lt. Chistiakov of *Elena,* with instructions for the voyage out to the colonies).
	Fol. 223 (1824)	No. 656 (Notification of Khromchenko's promotion to Navy lieutenant, order of 25 September 1824; service in the Pacific and Arctic).
	Fol. 255 (1825)	No. 254 (Murav'ev to offer Khromchenko higher pay, to in- duce him to remain in Company employment; need of officers with experience of Pacific expeditions).
	Fol. 395 (1825)	No. 47 (Imperial Botanical Garden, St. Petersburg, is request- ing that Company servants collect plants in the Pacific for its collections; procedures, etc.).
Vol. 5	Fols. 103–4 (1826)	No. 287 (Company will send ships to colonies once every three years; essential goods should be obtained from foreigners; triennial shipments of furs, etc.).
Vol. 6	Fol. 244 (1827)	No. 266 (Company petitions for rewards for officers of *Elena,* in view of their outstanding service in 1824–26).
	Fol. 79 (1828)	No. 260 (*Elena* to carry utensils and plateware for new Orthodox church on Aleutian island of Atkha, as well as more books for the library at Novo-Arkhangel'sk).
	Fol. 318 (1828)	No. 281 (Lt. Khromchenko, commander of *Elena,* is to take on woollen goods at Portsmouth, then stop over at Rio and Syd- ney; instructions re revictualling at Port Jackson, schedule to be maintained, etc.).
	Fol. 126 (1829)	No. 351 (Contracts for Khromchenko, Lt. Baron Lavrentii Levendal [von Loewendal], and Company supercargo A. A. Arakelov, an Armenian noble by birth, who are to call at Sydney en route to Sitka; Khromchenko to receive 11,000 roubles

and board per annum, Levendal 6,000, the Armenian commissioner 3,000).

Fol. 334ff.   Nos. 670, etc. (*Krotkii* left Kronstadt very soon after *Elena,* will
(1828)   take eastward route calling at Port Jackson, carrying stores including 926-lb bell for the Okhotsk church; Naval Ministry's request that she return from Pacific quickly, since surveillance off Northwest Coast no longer necessary; Hagemeister's despatches).

Fol. 189   No. 328 (Governor Chistiakov reminded that Imperial Botani-cal
(1828)   Garden appreciates botanizing by Company's employees in various parts of the Pacific).

(o) The Bancroft Library, University of California at Berkeley

P-K 29. Anonymous. "Early Commerce in the North Pacific." (Notes on the Bostonian "Nor'Westers" and early New England-Russian commercial dealings in the Pacific.)

Transcripts from Archivo General de Indias, Spain: Catalogue 2901/3–7 (Conde de Lacy to Grimaldi, dated St. Petersburg, 11 May 1773, re Leonhard Euler's memorial to Catherine II encouraging the despatch of a Russian squadron "around the Cape of Good Hope to Kamchatka," the need for Russian warships to "continue conquests advantageous to the Empire" in the Pacific basin).

P-N 4. The Sheffer Papers: 1874 Alphonse Pinart copies, translated in 1939 by G. V. Lantzeff (details given in Pierce, *Russia's Hawaiian Adventure, 1815–1817,* pp. vi–viii and notes); *Zhurnal doktora Sheffera . . . Journal Kept by Georg Anton Scheffer),* January 1815–March 1818: entries for 10 May 1816, regarding "runaway criminals from New Holland who purchase land" from Kamehameha I but are exploited by him; 10 August 1816, on news brought from Sydney by the Boston merchantman *Atala,* etc; and 3 December 1816, on the arrival at Kauai of the *Traveller,* Captain James S. Wilcocks, the latter's service to Lachlan Macquarie of carrying letters from London and a British dress uniform to Kamehameha I, and the king's pleasure on learning that Macquarie was supervising the construction at Port Jackson of "a vessel of some 40 tons." On this vessel, the *Prince Regent,* and Russians' reactions to her being built in New South Wales, and T. G. Thrum, "Hawaiian Maritime History," *Hawaiian Almanac* (1890): 66–79.

(p) The Mitchell Library (State Library of New South Wales)

Banks Papers, vol. 22, pp. 266–67 (Governor Bligh to Sir Joseph Banks re *Neva*'s visit to Sydney: letter of early November 1807; the Russians' appreciation of fresh-killed meat after voyage from Brazil).

ML A 3631. *William Bradley Journal,* pp. 68–69, etc. (dinners given in March–April 1820 and attended by Russian officers, etc.).

ML A 5326. *Edward Riley Papers* (1-86B). Riley was a merchant and prominent resident of Woolloomooloo. Miscellaneous letters touch mostly on business matters, but Russians are once or twice mentioned.

ML A 774. *Lachlan Macquarie: Diary,* 9 July 1818 to 28 February 1820: p. 117 (John Jamison's residence in Sydney, where Vasil'ev and his officers dined, etc.); p. 124 (*Vostok*'s arrival and fifteen-gun salute, Bellingshausen's first visit to Government House: entry of 11 April 1820); p. 171 (*Vostok*'s and *Mirnyi*'s second departure from Sydney, entry for 12 November 1820: "Royal Salute from Ships and Batteries," courtesies).

CY A 771. *Lachlan Macquarie: Journals,* pp. 166–226 (1807 journey through Russia—Astrakhan, Moscow, St. Petersburg, Kronstadt: pp. 198–212 on St. Petersburg as a city, contacts, affairs; pp. 215–17 on Kronstadt harbour, Admiral Khanykov and Captain Bunin, boarding H.M.S. *Calypso,* Anglo-Russian amity).

ML *Miscellaneous Documents,* DOC 1042 (5-28B). Letter of William Jewell, convict and assigned servant, to his brother, May 1820 (Parramatta River and township, Female Orphan Asylum).

ML B 1475 *Lt. William Lawson Papers:* letters of 1820 to John Sloper of London (re Lawson's business affairs, wool sales, hopes of prosperity, etc., while *Otkrytie* was at Sydney). ML holds other papers of Lawson, who materially assisted Korneev and Shtein on their trip to King's Table Land of March 1820, under A 1952.

ML *Bonwick Transcripts: Bigge Appendix,* Box 1: pp. 344–45; Box 12: p. 318, etc. (Windsor Military Barracks, the "Macquarie Arms," and other structures visited by Russians in 1820); Box 2: p. 725, etc. (George Howe's wharf at Windsor, also visited).

ML Micro FM 4/2094. Phillip Parker King: "Log of the Proceedings of H.M. Cutter *Mermaid*... 19th Sept. 1819–23rd May 1820" (King's daily activities during Russian visit: under catalogue as 4-99B). See also King Family Papers, 1820.

ML Micro FM 4/3104. *Allan Cunningham: Journal,* May 1819 to September 1822. This is a copy of the holograph held in the adjacent AONSW, which has its own microfilm reel of it (Reel 47). Entries for 7–15 March 1820: 7–8 March describe the initial encounter with Shtein and "Karneyeff," Lawson's involvement, Shtein's examinations of river and creek beds, the arrival at King's Table Land, Russian drawing of Prince Regent's Glen, encampment, the return journey via Castlereagh and Rev. Fulton's house, etc.

ML *Kew Transcripts.* Allan Cunningham to Sir Joseph Banks, 1 May 1820 (further on his assistance of Shtein and their mineralogical and botanizing outing of March).

ML A 1749. *Allan Cunningham Letterbooks:* Cunningham to Governor Macquarie, 7 March 1820 (Macquarie's granting Russians permission to travel across Blue Mountains; his own willingness to escort them, aid in scientific aims, etc.).

ML MSS 75/26–28. *Ida Marriott Notebooks, 1898–1922,* Volume D (copies of Allan Cunningham's letters to Banks and William Aiton of Kew Gardens; London, 1817–21). Catalogue 4-130B.

ML MSS337/A and B. *I. Marriott Notebooks, 1919–31:* A (notes on Russian and other Antarctic explorations from 1819 onward); B (extracts from Allan Cunningham's journals, with copious related notes: Cunningham and the Russians). Catalogue 2-130B.

(q) Public Record Office, London

Adm. 1 (In-letters)/498, cap. 370 (George Murray to Stephen, 16 August 1794:
Kruzenshtern leaving for North America aboard H.M.S. *Thetis;* H.M.S.
L'Oiseau accompanying, with Russian Volunteers also aboard). On Russian
service with the Royal Navy in 1794–96, see Ralfe, *Naval Biography,* 3: 212
and 4: 98–99; James, *Naval History,* 1: 495; Lisianskii, *Voyage,* p. xviii. Adm.
1/1516, cap. 404 (Charles Boyles to Nepean, 16 March 1797: Lisianskii leaving for Cape Colony aboard H.M.S. *Raisonnable,* etc.). Russian viewpoint in
Krusenstern, *Voyage,* 1: xxiv–xxv. On Anglo-Russian collaboration of
1795–96 and Royal Navy readiness to carry Russian officers to the East Indies
station, see Laird-Clowes, *History of the Royal Navy,* 4: 279, 283, 296–97,
408–12. Adm. 1/1927, caps. 9–10 (Capt. Benjamin Hallowell to Admiralty
from St. Thomas, West Indies, July 1803: H.M.S. *Argo* in action at storming of
St. Lucia, shore and amphibious operations). Hagemeister distinguished himself in this operation against the French, and was commended by the future Admiral Hallowell. See H. H. Breen, *St. Lucia: Historical, Statistical, and Descriptive* (London, 1844), pp. 110–12, and Adm. 1/2127, caps. 1–5 (various
despatches touching on movements of Russian Volunteers, complemented by
such published works as the *Despatches and Letters of Nelson,* ed. Nicolas
(London, 1844), 5: 448–49; 6: 42–43). In general, secondment to the British
active fleet predisposed young Russian officers to avail themselves of the facilities and amenities of British and British colonial ports.

Adm. 36, Series 1. Ships' Musters and Descriptive Books, 1688–1808. Muster Books for
*L'Oiseau, Thetis, Argo, Plantagenet, Ville de Paris, Prince of Wales, Sceptre,
Cleopatra,* 1794–1806.

Colonial Office 201: New South Wales, Original Correspondence, 1784–1900.
201/95/609 (King to Goulburn, November 1819, regarding the behaviour and
objectives in Australia of Freycinet's ships, the need to keep them under surveillance, etc.). 206: New South Wales, Miscellanea, 1803–1925 (copies of newspapers and statistical lists for New South Wales).

(r) National Maritime Museum, Greenwich

60/017: Fli/1 (MSS of Matthew Flinders and Paddy Smith, 1799–1800: Flinders's
Bengal contacts, news of his explorations).

SELECT ARCHIVAL, BIOGRAPHICAL, AND BIBLIOGRAPHIC AIDS

Akhun, M., Lukomskii, V., *et al., comps. Arkhivy SSSR: Leningradskoe otdelenie
Tsentral'nogo Istoricheskogo Arkhiva: putevoditel' po fondam.* Ed. A. K.
Drezen. L., 1933.
Allgemeine Deutsche Biographie. Leipzig, 1885.
Australian Dictionary of Biography. (Series 1: 1788–1850). 2 vols. Ed. D. Pike, Mel-
bourne, 1966.
Belov, G. A., Loginova, A. I., *et al., eds. Gosudarstvennye arkhivy Soiuza SSR: kratkii
spravochnik.* M., GAU, 1956.

————. "The Organization of the Archive System in the USSR." *Archives,* 7 (October 1964): 211–22.

Beskrovnyi, L. G. *Ocherki po istochnikovedeniiu voennoi istorii Rossii.* M., ANSSSR, 1957.

Biologicheskii slovar' professorov . . . byvshego Derptskogo Universiteta, s 1802 po 1902 god. Iur'ev, 1902.

Bobynin, V. V. *Russkaia fiziko-matematicheskaia Bibliografiia.* 2 vols. M., 1886–92.

Brokgaus, F. A., and Efron, I. A., eds. *Entsiklopedicheskii slovar'.* 4 vols. St. P., 1894–1904.

Bogatkina, N. S., comp. "Literatura ob ekspeditsii Bellinsgauzena-Lazareva." In *Bellingshausen,* 1960, pp. 354–57.

Chentsov, N. M. *Vosstanie dekabristov: bibliografiia.* M., 1929.

Dictionary of National Biography. 66 vols. Ed. L. Stephen. London, 1885–1901.

Dzhincharadze, V. Z., "Obzor fonda Vorontsovykh, khraniashchegosia v TsGADA." *Istoricheskie zapiski,* 32 (M., 1950): 242–68.

Entsiklopedicheskii slovar'. Ed. I. Andreevskii and Arsen'ev. St. P., 1895.

Entsiklopediia voennikh i morskikh nauk. St. P., 1893.

Ferguson, J. A. *Bibliography of Australia.* Sydney, 1941–55.

Frolov, N. *Sobranie novykh i starykh puteshestvii.* M., 1855.

Genealogisches Handbuch des deutschen Adels. Glucksburg, 1951–58.

Gennadi, G. *Slovar' russkikh pisatelei i uchenykh.* 2 vols. Berlin, 1876–80.

Granat, I. *Entsiklopedicheskii slovar'.* 7th ed. 53 vols. M., 1937.

Great Soviet Encyclopaedia. 32 vols. Ed. A. M. Prokhorov. Moscow and New York 1973–80. Translation of *Bol'shaia Sovetskaia. Entsiklopediia,* 3d ed.

Grimsted, P. K. *Archives and Manuscript Repositories in the USSR: Leningrad and Moscow.* Princeton, 1972.

————. *Archives and Manuscript Repositories in the USSR: Estonia, Latvia, Belorussia.* New York, 1981.

Hotimsky, C. M. "A Bibliography of Captain James Cook in Russian, 1772–1810." *Biblionews and Australian Notes and Queries,* 5 (1971): no. 2, pp. 3–12.

Karimullin, A. G., and Laptev, B. *Chto chital N. I. Lobachevskii: zapisi knig i zhurnalov, vydannykh N. I. Lobachevskomu iz biblioteki Kazanskogo Universiteta.* Kazan', 1979.

Kolosova, E. V., Khodiak, A. A., *et al.,* comps. *Lichnye arkhivnye fondy v Gosudarstvennykh khranilishchakh SSSR: ukazetel'.* 3 vols. Ed. Iu. I. Gerasimova. M., 1962–70.

Kondakov, I. P., *et al.,* eds. *Svodnyi katalog russkoi knigi XVIII-veka: 1725–1800.* M., 1963–68.

Larousse, J. *Grand Dictionnaire Universel du XIXe siècle.* Geneva and Paris, Slatkine et Cie reprint, 1982.

Lebedianskaia, A. P., *et al.,* comps. *Putevoditel' po istoricheskomu arkhivu Muzeia.* Ed. I. P. Ermoshin. L., Artilleriiskii Istor. Muzei, 1957.

Lenz, W., ed. *Deutsch-Baltisches Biographisches Lexikon, 1710–1960.* Köln-Wien, 1970.

Marksoo, A. "Admiral A. J. Krusensternist ja tema sidemetest Eestiga." In *Teaduse Ajalooleheku' lgi Eestist.* Tartu, 1968.

Matveeva, T. P., *et al.*, comps. *Russkie geografy i puteshestvenniki: fondy arkhiva Geograficheskogo Obshchestva*. L., 1971.

Meyers Enzyklopäedisches Lexikon. 25 vols. Mannheim, 1971.

Modzalevskii, B. L. *Spisok chlenov Imperatorskoi Akademii Nauk, 1725–1907*. St. P., 1908.

Obshchii morskoi spisok. 14 vols. St. P., 1885–1907.

Pokrovskii, M. N., ed. *Vosstanie dekabristov: materialy po istorii.* . . . M.-L., 1925–39.

Polansky, P. *Russian Writings on the South Pacific*. University of Hawaii, PIP, Miscellaneous Work Papers No. 5. Honolulu, 1974.

Putsillo, M., ed. *Ukazatel' delam i rukopisiam, otnosiashchimsia do Sibiri i prinadlezhashchim Moskovskomu Glavnomu arkhivu Ministerstva Inostrannykh Del*. M., 1879.

Pypin, A. N. *Istoriia russkoi etnografii*. 4 vols. St. P., 1890–92.

Ralfe, J. *Naval Biography*. 5 vols. London, 1828.

Rudovits, L. F. "Pervoe russkoe krugosvetnoe plavanie, 1803–1806: obzor nauchnykh rabot." *Trudy Gosudarstvennogo Okeanograficheskogo Instituta*, 27 (L., 1954): 3–12.

Russkii biograficheskii slovar'. 25 vols. Ed. A. A. Polovtsov, and B. L. Modzalevskii. St. P., 1896–1913.

Shepelev, L. E. *Arkhivnye razyskaniia i issledovaniia*. M., "Vysshaia Shkola," 1971.

Sopikov, V. *Opyt Rossiiskoi Bibliografii*. Ed. V. Rogozhin. St. P., 1813; reprint by Holland House, London, 1962.

Valk, S., and Bedin, V. V. *Tsentral'nyi Gosudarstvennyi Istoricheskii Arkhiv SSSR v Leningrade: putevoditel'*. L., 1956.

Valkina, I. V., *et al.,* comps. *Putevoditel' po arkhivu Leningradskogo Otdeleniia Instituta Istorii Akademii Nauk SSSR*. Ed. A. I. Andreev *et al*. M.-L., 1958.

Vengerov, S. A. *Istochniki slovaria russkikh pisatelei*. 2 vols. St. P., 1900–17.

Volkova, N. B., Voliak, R. D., *et al.,* comps. *Tsentral'nyi Gosudarstv. arkhiv literatury i Iskusstva SSSR: putevoditel': Literatura*. Ed. N. F. Bel'chikov. M., GAU, 1963.

Vorontsov-Vel'iaminov, V. *Ocherki istorii astronomii v Rossii*. M., 1956.

PACIFIC AND AUSTRALIAN MARITIME HISTORY: SELECTED REFERENCE WORKS

Akademiia Nauk SSSR. *Tikhii Okean: russkie nauchnye issledovaniia*. Ed. A. Fersman. L., 1926.

Andreev, A. I. *Russkie otkrytiia v Tikhom okeane i Severnoi Amerike v XVII–XIX vekakh: sbornik materialov*. M.-L., 1944. Trans. Carl Ginsburg as *Russian Discoveries in the Pacific and in North America in the Eighteenth and Nineteenth Centuries*. Ann Arbor, 1952.

Bach, J. P. S. *A Maritime History of Australia*. Melbourne, 1967.

Barratt, G. R. *Russia in Pacific Waters, 1715–1825: A Survey of the Origins of Russia's Naval Presence in the North and South Pacific*. Vancouver and London, 1981.

———. "The Russian Navy and New Holland." *JRAHS*, 64 (1979): pt. 4, pp. 217–34.

Bateson, C. *The Convict Ships, 1787–1868*. Glasgow, 1959.

Berg, L. S. *Ocherki po istorii russkikh geograficheskikh otkrytii*. 2d ed. M.-L., 1949.

———. *Velikie russkie puteshestvenniki*. M., 1950.

Blainey, G. *The Tyranny of Distance: How Distance Shaped Australia's History*. Melbourne, 1966.

Cotton, E., and Fawcett, C. *East Indiamen: The East India Company's Maritime Service*. London, 1949.

Cumpston, J. S. *Shipping Arrivals and Departures: Sydney, 1788–1825*. Canberra, 1964.

Dumont D'Urville, J. *Histoire universelle des Voyages*. Paris, 1860.

Davydov, Iu. V. *V moriakh i stranstviiakh*. M., 1956.

Esakov, V. A. *Russkie okeanicheskie i morskie issledovaniia v XIX–nachale XX vv*. M., 1964.

Hardy, C. *Register of the Ships of the East India Company from 1760 to 1812*. London, 1820.

Ivashintsev, N. A. *Russkie krugosvetnye puteshestviia, S 1803 po 1849 god*. St. P., 1872. English translation by Glynn Barratt as *Russian Round-the-World Voyages, 1803–1849*. Kingston, Ont., 1980.

James, W. *Naval History of Great Britain from the Declaration of War by France*. London, 1822–26.

Laird-Clowes, W. *A History of the Royal Navy*. London, 1899–1904.

Magidovich, I. P., ed. *Ocherki po istorii geograficheskikh otkrytii*. M., 1957.

McCartan, E. F. "The Long Voyages—Early Russian Circumnavigation." *Russian Review*, 1 (1963): 30–37.

Nozikov, N. *Russian Voyages Round the World*. Trans. E. and M. Lesser. London, 1944.

Mitchell, D. W. *A History of Russian and Soviet Seapower*. London, 1974.

Morison, S. E. *The Maritime History of Massachusetts, 1783–1860*. Boston, 1941.

Otechestvennye fiziko-geografy i puteshestvenniki. Ed. N. N. Baranskii. M., 1959.

Sharp, A. *The Discovery of Australia*. Oxford, 1963.

———. *The Voyages of Abel Janszoon Tasman*. Oxford, 1968.

Shokal'skii, Iu. M. *Okeanografiia*. L., 1959.

Veselago, F. F. *Materialy dlia istorii russkogo flota*. St. P., 1880–1904.

Zubov, N. N., ed. *Otechestvennye moreplavateli-issledovateli morei i okeanov*. M., 1954.

PRIMARY PRINTED MATERIAL

Arago, J. E. V. *Promenade autour du monde, pendant les années 1817, 1818, 1819 et 1820, sur les corvettes du Roi l'Uranie et la Physicienne*. Paris, 1822.

———. "A Frenchman Sees Sydney in 1819: Translated from the Letters of Jacques Arago." Trans. W. and O. Havard. *JRAHS*, 24 (1938): 17–42.

Antill, H. C. *Early History of New South Wales: Two Old Journals, being the Diaries of Major H. C. Antill on a Trip across the Blue Mountains in 1815*. Sydney, 1914.

Baillière, J. *Bailliere's New South Wales Gazetteer and Road Guide*. Comp. R. P.

Whitworth. Sydney, 1866.

Barrington, G. *A Sequel to Barrington's Voyage to New South Wales, comprising an interesting Narrative of the Transactions and Behaviour of the Convicts.* . . . London, 1801.

————. *The History of New South Wales, including Botany Bay, Port Jackson, Parramatta, Sydney, and all its dependencies, from the Original Discovery of the Island; with the Customs and Manners of the Natives.* . . . London, 1810.

Beaglehole, J. C., ed. *The Journals of Captain James Cook.* Cambridge, 1955–67.

Bellingshausen (Bellinsgauzen), F. F. *Dvukratnye izyskaniia v iuzhnom ledovitom okeane i plavanie vokrug sveta, svershennye na shliupakh Vostoke i Mirnom v 1819, 1820, i 1821 godakh.* St. P., 1831; 2d ed., 1949, ed. A. I. Andreev; 3d ed., 1960, ed. E. E. Shvede. Large parts of the 1831 text were translated into English by Frank Debenham as *The Voyage of Captain Bellingshausen to the Antarctic Seas, 1819–1821.* 2 vols. Cambridge, 1945.

————. "Donesenie kapitana Bellinsgauzena iz Porta Zhaksona o svoem plavanii." *ZADMM,* (St. P., 1823): pt. 5, pp. 201–19.

Bent, A. *Bent's Almanac for 1824.* Hobart Town, 1824.

Bering, V. *Ekspeditsii Beringa: sbornik dokumentov.* Ed. A. Pokrovskii. M., 1941.

Berkh, V. N. "Izvestie o mekhovoi torgovle, proizvodimoi Rossiianami pri ostrovakh Kuril'skikh, Aleutskikh, i severozapadnom beregu Ameriki." *Syn otechestva,* (St. P., 1823): pt. 88, pp. 243–64; pt. 89, pp. 97–106.

————. *Pervoe morskoe puteshestvie Rossiian, predpriniatoe dlia resheniia geograficheskoi zadachi—soediniaetsia li Aziia s Amerikoi.* St. P., 1823.

————. *Khronologicheskaia istoriia otkrytiia Aleutskikh ostrovov.* St. P., 1823.

————. *Zhizneopisanie admirale A. I. Nagaeva.* St. P., 1831.

Bestuzhev, N. A. *Opyt istorii rossiiskago flota.* St. P., 1825.

Bigge, J. T. *GBPP:* Reports of the Commissioner of Inquiry: 1822, 20: 539–724; 1823, 10: 515–718. Printed separately also, e.g., *Report on Agriculture and Trade in New South Wales.* London, 1823.

Blaxland, G. *Journal of a Tour of Discovery across the Blue Mountains in the Year 1813.* London, 1823.

————. *Blaxland, Lawson, Wentworth: 1813.* Ed. J. R. Richards. Sandy Bay, NSW, 1979.

Campbell, A. *A Voyage Round the World, from 1806 to 1812, in which Japan, Kamchatka, the Aleutian Islands, and the Sandwich Islands were Visited.* 2d ed. New York, 1819.

Catherine II, Empress. *Sochineniia.* Ed. A. N. Pypin. St. P., 1901–7.

Chamisso, A. von. *Werke.* Pt. 1: *Reise um die Welt mit der Romanzoffischen Entdeckungs-expedition . . . auf der Brigg Rurik.* . . . Ed. J. E. Hitzig. Leipzig, 1836.

Chichagov, P. V. "Zapiski." *Russkaia starina* (St. P., October 1886): 35–53.

————. *Arkhiv admirala P. V. Chichagova.* St. P., 1885.

Choris, L. *Voyage pittoresque autour du monde.* Paris, 1822.

Clark, C. M. H., comp. *Select Documents in Australian History, 1788–1850.* Sydney, 1950.

————. *Sources of Australian History.* London, 1957.

Collins, D. *An Account of the English Colony in New South Wales, with Remarks on the . . . Native Inhabitants of the Country.* 2 vols. London, 1798–1802.

Cook, J., and King, J. *A Voyage to the Pacific Ocean, undertaken by the Command of His Majesty, for Making Discoveries in the Northern Hemisphere. . . .* 3 vols. London, 1784. Trans. L. I. Golenishchev-Kutuzov as *Puteshestvie v Severnyi Tikhii okean, po poveleniiu korolia Georgiia III . . . v prodolzhenie 1776, 1777, 1778, 1779 i 1780 godov.* St. P., 1805–10.

———. *A Voyage to the Southern Hemisphere . . . in the Years 1772, 1773, 1774 and 1775.* London, 1777. Trans. M. Suard as *Voyage dans l'hémisphère australe et autour du monde . . . traduit de l'Anglois par M. Suard.* Paris, 1778. Trans. L. I. Golenishchev-Kutuzov as *Puteshestvie v iuzhnoi polovine zemnago shara. . . .* St. P., 1796–1800.

Corney, P. *Voyages in the Northern Pacific: A Narrative of Several Trading Voyages from 1813 to 1818 . . . with a Description of the Russian Establishments on the Northwest Coast.* Honolulu, 1896.

Cunningham, A. *GBPP:* Report of a Select Committee on Secondary Punishments, NSW: 1831–32, 7: 559–720. Evidence and recommendations to avoid abuses (June 1832).

Cunningham, P. M. *Two Years in New South Wales: A series of Letters, comprising sketches of the actual state of society in that Colony.* 2 vols. London, 1827.

Denison, W. *Varieties of Vice-Regal Life.* London, 1870.

Dobell, P. *Travels in Kamtschatka and Siberia.* London, 1830.

Engelhardt, M., and Parrot, F. G. *Eine Reise in die Krym und den Kaukasus.* Berlin, 1815.

Espinosa y Tello, J. *Memorias sobre las observaciones.* Madrid, 1809.

Euler, L., *Leonard Eiler: perepiska: annotirovannyi ukazatel'.* Ed. V. I. Smirnov. L., 1967.

———. *A Voyage to Terra Australis. . . .* 2 vols. London, 1814.

Galkin, N. "Pis'ma g Galkina o plavanii shlipuov Vostoka i Mirnago v Tikhom okeane." *Syn otechestva* (St. P., 1822): no. 49, pp. 97ff.

Gillesem, K. "Puteshestvie na shliupe Blagonamerennom dlia issledovanii beregov Azii i Ameriki za Beringovym prolivom s 1819 po 1822." *Otechestvennye zapiski,* 66 (St. P., 1849), pt. 8.

Gofman (Hoffman), E. K. *Geognostische Beobachtungen auf einer Reise um die Welt in den Jahren 1823–1826.* Berlin, 1829.

Golikov, I. I. *Deianiia Petra Velikogo.* 10 pts. M., 1788–97.

Golovnin, V. M. "Zamechaniia, uchinennye v 1808 godu, na puti ot Mysa Dobroi nadezhdy do ostrova Tany. . . ." *ZADMM,* 3 (St. P., 1815): 212–38.

———. *Sochineniia i perevody.* St. P., 1864–65.

———. *Puteshestvie na shliupe "Diana" iz Kronshtadta v Kamchatku v 1807–1811 godakh.* M., 1964.

Great Britain, Commons. *Copies of All Correspondence between Lieutenant-Governor Arthur and H. M. Secretary of State for the Colonies on . . . Military Operations . . . of Van Diemen's Land.* London, 1831.

———. *The Alaska Boundary Tribunal: Appendix to the Case of Great Britain.* London, 1903.

Historical Records of Australia: Series 1. Sydney, 1913–19.

Hörner, J. C. "O nekotorykh dostoprimechatel'nykh svoistvakh morskoi vody." *Tekhnologicheskii zhurnal,* 5 (St. P., 1820), pt. 3.

———. "Instruktsiia dannaia. . . ob astronomicheskikh i fizicheskikh nabliudeniiakh." In Kotzebue, *Puteshestvie v iuzhnyi okean* (1821), pt. 1: pp. clxix–xxii.

Hunter, J. *An Historical Journal of the Transactions at Port Jackson and Norfolk Island.* . . . London, 1793.

Ivashintsev, N. A. *Russkie krugosvetnye puteshestviia s 1803 po 1849 god.* St. P., 1872. Trans. G. R. Barratt as *Russian Round-the-World Voyages from 1803 to 1849.* Kingston, Ont., 1980.

Kalendar' ili mesiatsoslov geograficheskoi na 1773 god. St. P., 1773.

Khlebnikov, K. T. *Zhizneopisanie Aleksandra Andreevicha Baranova.* St. P., 1835. Translated in shortened form by C. Bearne as *Baranov.* Kingston, Ont., 1973.

———. "Vzgliad na polveka moei zhizni." *Syn otechestva,* (1836): 299–324, 345–73, 413–28.

———. *Russkaia Amerika v neopublikovannykh zapiskakh K. T. Khlebnikova.* Ed. R. G. Liapunova and S. G. Fedorova. L., 1979.

———. "Russian America in 1833: The Survey of Kirill Khlebnikov." Ed. J. R. Gibson. *Pacific Northwest Quarterly* (January 1972): 1–13.

———. *Colonial Russian America: Kyrill T. Khlebnikov's Reports, 1817–1832.* Ed. B. Dmytryshyn and E. A. Crownhart-Vaughan. Portland, 1976.

Khrushchev, S. P. "Plavanie shliupa Apolona v 1821–1824 godakh." *ZADMM,* 10 (1826): 200–72.

Kiselev, E. "Pamiatnik prinadlezhit matrozu pervoi stati Egoru Kiselevu, nakhodivshemusia v dal'nem voiazhe na shliupe 'Vostok' v 1819–1821 godakh." Ed. Ia. Tarnopol'skii, *Vokrug sveta* Moscow, 1941): no. 4, pp. 40–43. (See also Sementovskii below.)

Klochkov, E. A. "Puteshestvie vokrug sveta v kolonii Rossiisko-Amerikanskoi Kompanii." *Severnyi arkhiv,* 24 (St. P., 1826): 202–19.

Knopwood, R., Rev. *Diary of the Rev. Robert Knopwood, 1805–1808.* Ed. W. H. Hudspeth and S. Angel. Hobart, 1946.

Korobitsyn, N. I. "Zhurnal." In A. I. Andreev, *Russkie otkrytiia.* . . . English translation by C. Ginsburg as *Russian Discoveries in the Pacific and in North America in the Eighteenth and Nineteenth Centuries.* Ann Arbor, 1952.

Kotzebue, Otto von. *Puteshestvie v iuzhnyi okean i v Beringov provli v 1815–1818 godakh.* St. P., 1821. English translation as *Voyage of Discovery into the South Sea and Beering's Straits, undertaken in the Years 1815 to 1818.* 3 vols. London, 1821.

———. *Neue Reise um die Welt in den Jahren 1823, 1824, 1825 und 1826.* . . . Weimar, 1830. Translated as *A New Voyage Round the World.* London, 1830.

Kruzenshtern (Krusenstern), I. F. (A. J. von). *Puteshestvie vokrug sveta v 1803, 4, 5 i 1806 godakh na korabliakh "Nadezhda" i "Neva."* 3 vols. St. P., 1809–12. English translation by R. B. Hoppner as *A Voyage Round the World, in the Years 1803, 4, 5 & 6, by Order of his Imperial Majesty Alexander I, on Board the Ships Nadeshda and Neva.* 2 vols. London, 1814.

———. *Atlas Iuzhnogo Moria I. F. Kruzenshterna.* St. P., 1826.

Langsdorf, G. H. *Bemerkungen auf einer Reise um die Welt in den Jahren 1803 bis 1807.*
2 vols. Frankfurt, 1812. Translated as *Voyages and Travels in Various Parts of the World, during the Years 1803–1807.* London, 1813–14.

————, and Fischer, F. B. *Plantes recueillies pendant le Voyage des Russes autour du monde.* . . . Tübingen, 1810–18.

La Pérouse, J. F. G. de. *Voyage autour du monde.* . . . 4 vols. Paris, 1797. Translated as *A Voyage Round the World, performed* . . . *by the Boussole and Astrolabe.* London, 1799. Translated also by L. I. Golenishchev-Kutuzov as *Puteshestvie La Peruza v iuzhnom i severnom Tikhom okeane.* St. P., 1800.

Lazarev, Aleksei P. *Zapiski o plavanii voennogo shliupa Blagonamrennyi v Beringov proliv i vokrug sveta v 1819, 1820, 1821, i 1822 godakh.* Ed. A. I. Solov'ev. M., 1950.

Lazarev, Andrei P. *Plavanie vokrug sveta na shliupe 'Ladoga' v 1822, 1823, i 1824 godakh.* St. P., 1832.

Lazarev, Mikhail P. "Izvlechenie iz zhurnala puteshestvuiuschogo krugom sveta Rossiiskago leitenant Lazareva." *Syn otechestva* (St. P., 1815): no. 26, pp. 255ff.

————. "Pis'mo A. A. Shestakovu." *MSb* (1918): no. 1, pp. 53–63

————. *Russkie flotovodtsy: M. P. Lazarev.* 2 vols. Ed. A. A. Samarov. M., 1952. Contains numerous despatches and reports.

Ledyard, J. *John Ledyard's Journey Through Russia and Siberia, 1787–88.* Ed. S. Watrous, Madison, 1966.

Lisianskii, Iu. F. *Puteshestvie vokrug sveta v 1803, 1804, 1805, i 1806 godakh, na korable "Neva," pod nachal'stvom Iuriia Lisianskogo.* St. P., 1812. Translated by the author himself as *A Voyage Round the World in the Years 1803, 4, 5 & 6* . . . *in the Ship Neva.* London, 1814.

————. *Sobranie kart i risunkov, prinadlezhashchikh k puteshestviiu Iuriia Lisianskogo na korable "Neva."* St. P., 1812.

————. Extract from "Zhurnal leitenanta Iuriia Lisianskogo, vedennyi im. . . s 1793 po 1800 god." Ed. N. N. Bolkhovitinov. In Bashkina, N. N., Bolkhovitinov, N. N., *et al.*, comps. *Rossiia i SShA: stanovlenie otnoshenii, 1765–1815.* M., 1980, pp. 196–203.

Macquarie, L. *GBPP:* 1828, 21: 531–600. Report on New South Wales (July 1822), listing public works and improvements, 1810–21.

————. *Journals of Tours in New South Wales and Van Diemen's Land, 1810–1822.* Sydney, 1956.

Marsden, S., Rev. *Samuel Marsden's Letters and Journals.* Ed. J. R. Elder. Dunedin, 1932.

Materialy dlia istorii russkikh zaselenii po beregam Vostochnogo okeana. St. P., 1861; supplement to *MSb* (1861): no. 1.

Materialy dlia istorii Imperatorskoi Akademii Nauk. 10 vols. St. P., 1885–1900.

Materialy dlia istorii nauchnoi i prikladnoi deiatel'nosti v Rossii po Zoologii. M., 1889.

Mémoires de l'Académie Impériale des Sciences à St.-Pétersbourg. . . . 5th series. 11 vols. St. P., 1809–30; 6th series–'Sciences naturelles.' 8 vols. 1835–39.

Meteorologicheskie nabliudeniia, proizvodivshiesia vo vremia krugosvetnogo plavaniia shliupa "Apollon." St. P., 1882; similar title for the *Kreiser,* also published in 1882.

M'Konochie, A. *Considerations on the Propriety of Establishing a Colony on One of the Sandwich Islands*. Edinburgh, 1816.

Mordvinov, N. S. *Arkhiv grafov Mordvinovykh*. Ed. V. A. Bilbasov. St. P., 1902. Papers relating to naval matters, 1801–4.

Novosil'skii, P. M. *Iuzhnyi polius: iz zapisok byvshego morskago ofitsera*. St. P., 1853.

Odoevskii, V. F. "Iz bumag kniazia V. F. Odoevskogo." *Russkii arkhiv* (1874): no. 7, pp. 11–54.

Ogievskii, P. Report on Hobart Town and environs incl. in Lazarev, Andrei P. *Plavanie*.... St. P., 1832, pp. 68–78.

Oxley, J. *Journals of Two Expeditions into the Interior of New South Wales*. London, 1820.

Pacific Voyages: Selections from Scots Magazine, 1771–1808. Ed. J. S. Marshall. Portland, OR, 1960.

Pallas, P. S. *A Naturalist in Russia: Letters from Peter Simon Pallas to Thomas Pennant*. Ed. C. Urness. Minneapolis, 1967.

––––––. *Reise durch verschiedene Provinzen des russischen Reiches*. 3 vols. St. P., 1771–76.

Penrose, C. V. *A Memoir of James Trevenen, 1760–1790*. Navy Records Society, Vol. 150. Ed. C. Lloyd and R. C. Anderson. London, 1959.

Perry, J. *The State of Russia under the Present Czar*. London, 1716.

Peter I, Tsar. *Pis'ma i bumagi Imperatora Petra Velikogo*. St. P., 1887–1917; L., 1925–52.

––––––. *Petr I: materialy dlia biografii*. Ed. M. M. Bogoslovskii. M., 1941.

Polnoe sobranie Zakonov Rossiiskoi Imperii s 1649 goda. 240 vols. St. P., 1830–1916.

Porter, D. *Journal of a Cruise made to the Pacific Ocean in the United States Frigate "Essex" in the Years 1812–1814*. New York, 1815.

Ratmanov, M. I. "Vyderzhki iz zhurnala krugosvetnogo plavaniia na korable 'Neva'." *Iakhta* (St. P.,1872): nos. 16, 18, 24.

Riley, Alex. *GBPP:* Report of a Select Committee on Gaols, etc.: 1819, 7: 1–560. 139 pp. of evidence re NSW, with app. giving statistical data.

Rossiiskii, A. "Vypiska iz zhurnala shturmana Alekseia Rossiiskago." *Sorevnovatel' prosveshcheniia i blagodeianiia* (St. P., 1820): no. 11, pp. 125–46; no. 12, pp. 246–56.

Rozen, A. E. *Zapiski dekabrista*, St. P., 1907.

Saint-Simon, Duc de. *Mémoires*. Ed. A. de Boislisle. Paris, 1920.

Samarov, A. A., ed. *Russkie flotovodtsy: M. P. Lazarev*. M., 1952.

Sarychev, G. A. *Puteshestvie kapitana Billingsa cherez Chukotskuiu zemliu ot Beringovo Proliva... v 1791 godu*. St. P., 1811.

Sauer, M. *An Account of a Geographical and Astronomical Expedition to the Northern Parts of Russia, Performed in the Years 1785 to 1794*.... London, 1802.

Schumacher, J. D. *Bibliothecae Imperialis Petropolitanae*. St. P., 1744.

Sementovskii, V. N., ed. *Russkie otkrytiia v Antarktike v 1819–1821 godakh*. M., 1951. Contains extracts from the works of Kiselev and Novosil'skii (cf. hereabove), as well as from I. M. Simonov's "Slovo o uspekhakh plavaniia shliupov 'Vostok' i 'Mirnyi' okolo sveta..." (cf. esp. pp. 36–38) and passages from his longer essay, "Shliupy 'Vostok' i 'Mirnyi', ili plavanie Rossiian v iuzhnom ledovitom okeane i vokrug sveta'' (cf. pp. 168ff).

Severgin, M. V. "Instruktsii dlia puteshestviia okolo sveta po chasti mineralogii i v otnoshenii k teorii zemli." *Severnyi vestnik* (1804): nos. 2–3.

Shabel'skii, A. P. *Voyage aux colonies russes de l'Amérique fait à bord du sloop de guerre l'Apollon, pendant les années 1821, 1822 et 1823.* St. P., 1826.

————. "Prebyvanie g. Shabel'skago v Novoi Gollandii." *Severnyi arkhiv* (St. P., 1826): pt. 23, nos. 17–18, pp. 43–61. Translated in extract by C. M. Hotimsky as "A Russian Account of New South Wales in 1822." *Melbourne Slavonic Studies*, 1 (1967): 82–95.

————. "Pis'mo kniaziu A. B. Kurakinu." *Severnaia pchela* (St. P., 1827): no. 58.

Shemelin, F. I. *Zhurnal pervogo puteshestviia Rossiian vokrug zemnago shara.* 2 vols. St. P., 1816.

————. "Istoricheskoe izvestie o pervom puteshestvii Rosiian vokrug sveta." *Russkii invalid,* 146 (St. P., 1823): nos. 23–28, 31–36, 49.

Shishmarev, G. S. "Svedeniia o Chukchakh." *ZGDMM,* 11 (St. P., 1852).

Shtein (Stein), F. "Iz mineralogicheskikh zamechanii, uchinennykh naturalistom Shteinom vo vremia 12-dnevnogo puteshestviia ot Sidneia k Sinim goram." In Lazarev, Aleksei P., *Zapiski...,* pp. 371–72.

Shvede, E. E., ed. *Dvukratnye izyskaniia v iuzhnom ledovitom okeane i plavanie vokrug sveta... v 1819, 1820, i 1821 godakh.* 3d ed. M., 1960. Faithful to Bellingshausen's text of 1831, usefully annotated.

Simonov, I. M. "Plavanie shliupa Vostoka v iuzhnom ledovitom okeane." *Kazanskii vestnik* (1822): no. 3, pp. 15ff.

————. "Précis du voyage de découvertes, fait par ordre du gouvernement russe, en 1819, 1820 et 1821, par le capitaine Bellingshausen." *Journal des Voyages, ou Archives géographiques du XIXe siècle,* 23 (Paris, 1824): 10–12.

————. "Izvestie o puteshestvii kapitana Bellinsgauzen v 1819–1821 godakh." *Severnyi arkhiv,* 7 (1827): 18–20.

————. "Opredelenie geograficheskogo polozheniia mest iakornogo stoianiia shliupov 'Vostok' i 'Mirnyi'." *ZMNP* (St. P., 1828): pt. 22, pp. 44–68.

Smelovskii, T. *Sistematicheskoe ischislenie rastenii, nakhodiashchikhsia v sadu Akademii Nauk.* St. P., 1811.

Sydney Gazette and New South Wales Advertiser. Issues of 1807, 1814, 1819–22, 1825, 1829–32.

Therry, R. *Reminiscences of Thirty Years' Residence in New South Wales and Victoria.* 2d ed. London, 1863.

Tikhmenev, P. A., comp. *Istoricheskoe obozrenie obrazovaniia Rossiisko-Amerikanskoi Kompanii i deistvii eio do nastoiashchego vremeni.* St. P., 1861–63. Trans. D. Krenov as *The Historical Review of the Formation of the Russian-American Company.* Seattle, 1938. Many primary materials.

Tilesius von Tilenau, W. G. *Naturhistorische Früchte der ersten kaiserlich-russischen... Erdumseglung.* St. P., 1813.

Tompkins, S. R., and Moorehead, M. L., eds. "Russia's Approach to America: From Spanish Sources, 1761–1775." *British Columbia Historical Quarterly,* 13 (1949): 231–55.

Torson, K. P. *Materialy po istorii vosstaniia dekabristov... : dokumenty.* Ed. M. V.

Nechkina. 14 (L., 1976): 195–213.

Turgenev, N. I. *La Russie et les Russes*, 3 vols. Paris, 1848. Russian ed., *Rossiia i Russkie*. M., 1915.

Unkovskii, S. Ia. "Istinnye zapiski moei zhizni." In Samarov, A. A. ed., *Russkie flotovodtsy: M. P. Lazarev* (M., 1952), 1: 11–26.

Van Diemen's Land Almanack for the Year 1832. Hobart Town, 1832.

Valentijn, F. *Oud en niew Oost-Indien vervattende een naaukeurige en uitvoerige verhandelinge van Nederlands Mogentheyd in die Gewesten*. Dordrecht and Amsterdam, 1726.

Vasil'ev, M. N. "Zamechaniia kapitana-leitenanta M. N. Vasil'eva o Novoi Iuzhnoi Valisskoi Zemle." *ZADMM* (St. P., 1823): pt. 5.

Veselago, F. F., comp. *Materialy dlia istorii russkogo flota*. 18 vols. St. P., 1880–1904.

Visscher, F. J. *De Reizen van Abel Janszoon Tasman en Franchoys Jacobszoon Visscher in 1642–3 en 1644*. Ed. R. P. Meyjes. Amsterdam, 1919.

Vneshniaia politika Rossii XIX veka i nachala XX veka: dokumenty Rossiiskago Ministerstva Inostrannykh Del: seriia 1, 1801–1815. Vols. 1–2. M., 1961–75.

Vorontsov, S. R. *Arkhiv kniazia Vorontsova*. 40 vols. Ed. P. Bartenev. M., 1870–95.

Waxell, S. *Vtoraia Kamchatskaia ekspeditsiia Vitusa Beringa*. M.-L., 1940.

Wentworth, W. C. *Statistical, Historical, and Political Description of the Colony of New South Wales....* London, 1819.

Witsen, N. *Noord en Oost Tartarye, ofte gondig ontwerp van eenige dier landen en volken, welke voormaels bekent zijn geweest*. 2d ed. Amsterdam, 1705.

Wrangel, F. P. "Otryvok iz rukopisi, pod zaglaviem: Dnevnye Zapiski o plavanii voennogo transporta *Krotkago* v 1825–1827 godakh." *Severnyi arkhiv* (St. P., 1828): no. 36, pp. 49–106.

————. *Statistische und ethnographische Nachtrichten über die russischen Besitzungen an der Nordwestküste von Amerika*. St. P., 1839.

Zach, F. X. von. *L'Attraction des montagnes et ses effets sur les fils à plomb*. Avignon, 1814.

Zapiski Uchenogo Komiteta Morskago Shtaba. 2: (St. P., 1835): 355–57.

Zavalishin, D. I. "Krugosvetnoe plavanie fregata 'Kreiser' v 1822–25 godakh pod komandoiu Mikhaila Petrovicha Lazareva." *Drevniaia i novaia Rossiia* (St. P., 1877): no. 5, pp. 54–67; no. 6, pp. 115–25; no. 7, pp. 199–214; etc.

————. *Zapiski dekabrista*. München, 1904.

Zavoiko, V. S. *Vpechatleniia moriaka vo vremia dvukh puteshestvii krugom sveta: sochinenie leitenanta V. Zavoiko*. Pt. 1: "Puteshestvie v 1834, 1835 i 1836 godakh." St. P., 1840.

Zimmermann, H. *Zimmermann's Captain Cook: An Account of the Third Voyage...*, *1776–1780, by Henry Zimmermann, of Wissloch in the Palatinate*. Ed. F. W. Howay. Toronto, 1930.

SECONDARY SOURCES

Aleksandrenko, V. *Russkie diplomaticheskie agenty v Londone v XVIII veke*. Warsaw, 1897.

Aleksandrov, I. N. "Professor I. M. Simonov, uchastnik antarkticheskoi ekspeditsii F. F. Bellinsgauzena i M. P. Lazareva," *Uchennye zapiski Kazanskogo Pedagogicheskogo Instituta* (Kazan', 1950): pt. 9.

Alekseev, A. I. *Okhotsk—kolybel' russkogo tikhookeanskogo flota*. Khabarovsk, 1959.

Anderson, M. S. "Great Britain and the Growth of the Russian Navy in the Eighteenth Century." *MM,* 42 (1956): no. 1, pp. 132–46.

———. *Britain's Discovery of Russia, 1553–1815*. London, 1958.

Anderson, R. C. "British and American Officers in the Russian Navy." *MM,* 32 (1947): 17–27. Incomplete, flawed list.

Andreev, A. I., ed. *Russkie otkrytiia v tikhom okeane i severnoi Amerike v XVIII–XIX vekakh*. M., 1944. Modifed ed. in 1948. Trans. C. Ginsburg as *Russian Discoveries in the Pacific and in North America in the Eighteenth and Nineteenth Centuries*. Ann Arbor, 1952.

———. "Rol' russkogo voenno-morskogo flota v geograficheskikh otkrytiiakh XVIII veka." *MSb* (1947): no. 4, pp. 34ff.

Anonymous. "Vzgliad na torgovliu, proizvodimuiu cherez Okhotskii port." *Severnyi arkhiv,* 1 (St. P., 1823): 28–45.

———. *Jardine, Matheson, & Co.: An Outline of the History of a China House for a Hundred Years, 1832–1932*. Hong Kong, 1934.

Anuchin, D. N. *O liudiakh russkoi nauki i kul'tury*. M., 1950.

Armstrong, T. "Cook's Reputation in Russia." In R. Fisher and H. Johnston, eds. *Captain James Cook and His Times*. Vancouver, 1979.

Austin, M. "The Early Defences of Australia." *JRAHS,* 49 (1963): 191ff.

Azadovskii, M. K., ed. "14 dekabria v pis'makh A. E. Izmailova." *Pamiati dekabristov,* 1 (L., 1926): 240–48.

Bagrow, L. *History of Russian Cartography to 1800*. Ed. H. W. Castner. Wolfe Island, Ont., 1975.

Bancroft, H. H. *History of Alaska, 1730–1883*. San Francisco, 1886.

Baranskii, N. N., *et al.,* eds. *Otechestvennye fiziko-geografy i puteshestvenniki*. M., 1859.

Barbashev, N. I. *K istorii morekhodnogo obrazovaniia v Rossii*. M., 1959.

Barratt, G. R., ed. *Voices in Exile: The Decembrist Memoirs*. Montreal and London, 1974.

———. *The Rebel on the Bridge: The Life and Times of Baron Andrey Rozen, 1800–1884*. London, 1975.

———. "Russian Warships in Van Diemen's Land: The *Kreyser* and the *Ladoga* by Hobart Town, 1823." *SEER,* 53 (Londong, 1975): no. 133, pp. 566–78.

———. "The Russian Navy and New Holland: Part 1." *JRAHS,* 64 (1979): pt. 4, pp. 217–34.

———. *Bellingshausen: A Visit to New Zealand, 1820*. Palmerston North, N.Z., 1979.

———. "Russia and New Zealand: The Beginnings." *NZSJ* (1979): no. 2, pp. 25–49.

———. *The Russians at Port Jackson, 1814–1822*. Canberra, 1981.

———. *Russia in Pacific Waters, 1715–1825: A Survey of the Origins of Russia's Naval presence in the North and South Pacific*. Vancouver and London, 1981.

———. *Russophobia in New Zealand, 1838–1908*. Palmerston North, N.Z., 1981.

———. "Russian Naval Sources for the History of Colonial Australia to 1825." *JRAHS,*

67 (1981): pt. 2, pp. 159–75.

——. *The Russian Discovery of Hawaii, 1804*. Honolulu, 1988.

Barrow, J. *Some Account of the Public Life of Earl Macartney*. 2 vols. London, 1807.

Barsukov, N. P. *Zhizn' i trudy M. P. Pogodina*. St. P., 1896.

Bateson, C. *The Convict Ships, 1787–1868*. Glasgow, 1959.

Beddie, M. K., ed. *Bibliography of Captain James Cook*. Sydney, 1970.

Beratz, K. *Die deutschen Kolonien an der unteren Wolga in ihrer Entstehung und ersten Entwicklung*. 2d ed. Berlin, 1923.

Berg, L. S. *Ocherki po istorii russkikh geograficheskikh otkrytii*. M., 1939.

——. "Russian Discoveries in the Pacific." In Fersman, A., ed. *The Pacific: Russian Scientific Investigations*. L., 1926, pp. 1–26.

Binney, J. *The Legacy of Guilt*. Auckland, 1968.

Birch, A., and Macmillan, D. S. *The Sydney Scene, 1788–1960*. Melbourne, 1962.

Blainey, G. *The Tyranny of Distance*. Melbourne, 1966.

Bogoslovskii, M. M. *Petr I: materialy dlia biografii*. L., 1940–48.

Bonwick, J. *The Bushrangers*. Melbourne, 1856.

——. *The Last of the Tasmanians*. London, 1870.

Boxer, C. R. *The Dutch Seaborne Empire, 1600–1800*. New York, 1965.

Bradley, H. W. *The American Frontier in Hawaii: The Pioneers, 1789–1843*. Gloucester, MA, 1968.

Brandt, F. "Das zoologische un vergleichend-anatomische Museum." *Bulletin de l'Académie Imperiale des Sciences*, 7 (1864): suppl. 2, pp. 11–28.

——. *Putevoditel' po zoologicheskomu muzeiu Imperatorskoi Akademii Nauk*. St. P., 1868.

Brossard, M. de, ed. *La Pérouse: des Combats à la Découverte*. Paris, 1978,

Bulich, N. *Iz peruykh let Kazanskogo Universiteta 1805–19*. 2 vols. St. P., 1904.

Butinov, N. A., and Rozina, L. G. "Nekotorye cherty samobytnoi kul'tury Maori." *SMAE*, 21 (1963): 78–109.

Calvert, A. F. *The Exploration of Australia*. 2 vols. London, 1901.

Cameron, H. C. *Sir Joseph Banks*. London, 1952.

Campbell, A. G. "Australian Magpies. . . ." *Emu*, 28 (1929): 165–76.

Campbell, J. F. "Notes on our Great Western Highway: Springwood to Leura." *JRAHS*, 22: 291–94.

Campbell, W. D. "Aboriginal Carvings of Port Jackson and Broken Bay." In *Geological Survey of New South Wales*. Ethnological Series, No. 1. Sydney, 1899.

Capell, A. "Aboriginal Languages in the South Central Coast, New South Wales: Fresh Discoveries." *Oceania*, 41 (1970): no. 1, pp. 20–21.

Chapman, C. E. *The Founding of Spanish California: The Northwestward Expansion of New Spain, 1687–1773*. New York, 1916.

Chereikin, L. A. *Pushkin i ego okruzhenie*. L., 1975.

Chinard, G. *La Voyage de La Pérouse sur les côtes de l'Alaska et de la Californie*. Baltimore, 1937.

Christie, E. W. H. *The Antarctic Problem: An Historical and Politial Study*. London, 1951.

Cook. W. L. *Flood Tide of Empire: Spain and the Pacific Northwest, 1543–1819*. New Haven and London, 1973.

Coote, C. H., ed. *Remarkable Maps of the XV, XVI, and XVII Centuries*. Amsterdam, 1897.

Cross, A. G. "Catherine the Great's Scottish Admiral, Samuel Greig." *MM*, 60 (1974): no. 3, pp. 251–65.

————. *By the Banks of the Thames: Russians in Eighteenth-Century Britain*. Newtonville, MA, 1980.

Day, A. *The Admiralty Hydrographic Service, 1795–1919*. London, 1967.

Dennis, J. "Bigge versus Macquarie." *JRAHS*, 22 (1937): 33ff.

Depman, I. Ia. "M. F. Bartels—uchitel' N. I. Lobachevskogo." In *Istoriko-matematicheskie issledovaniia*, 3 (M., 1950): 474–85.

Dermigny, L. *La Chine et l'Occident: le commerce à Canton au XVIIIe siècle*. Paris, 1964.

Dik, N. E. *Deiatel'nost' i trudy M. V. Lomonosova v oblasti geografii*. M., 1961.

Divin, V. A. "O pervykh proektakh russkikh krugosvetnykh plavanii." *TIIE*, 37 (L., 1961): 330–39.

————. *Russkie moreplavaniia na tikhom okeane v XVIII veke*. M., 1971.

Dobrovol'skii, A. D. *Otto fon Kotsebu: russkie moreplavateli*. M., 1953.

Dowd, D. G. *Macquarie Country: A History of the Hawkesbury*. Melbourne, 1969.

Dumitrashko, N. V. "Iurii F. Lisianskii i krugosvetnoe plavanie." In *Iu. F. Lisianskii: puteshestvie vokrug sveta na korable "Neva" v 1803–1806 godakh*. M., 1947.

Dumont d'Urville, J. S. C. *Voyage pittoresque autour du monde: résumé générale des voyages de découverte de Magellan... à Bellingshausen*. 2 vols. Paris, 1835.

Dunbabin, T. "New Light on the Earliest American Voyages to Australia." *American Neptune*, 10 (1950): no. 1, pp. 52ff.

Eddy, J. J. *Britain and the Australian Colonies, 1818–1831: The Technique of Government*. Oxford, 1969.

Efrenov, Iu. K. "P. S. Pallas." In *Otechestvennye fiziko-geografy i puteshestvenniki*. M., 1959.

Efimov, A. V. *Iz istorii russkikh ekspeditsii na Tikhom okeane: pervaia polovina XVIII veka*. M., 1948.

————. *Iz istorii velikikh russkikh geograficheskikh otkrytii v severnom ledovitom okeane i Tikhom Okeane*. M., 1950.

Eilart, J. "G. F. Parrot looduse uurimise arendajana." In *Parrot'i 200-ndale sünniaastapäevale pühendatud materjale*. Tartu, 1967, pp. 126–29.

Eldershaw, M. B. *The Life and Times of Captain John Piper*. Sydney, 1939.

Ellis, M. H. *Lachlan Macquarie: His Life, Adventures, and Times*. Sydney, 1947.

————. *John Macarthur*. Sydney, 1955.

————. "Some Aspects of the Bigge Commission of Inquiry." *JRAHS*, 27 (1942).

Engelhardt, R. von. *Die deutsche Universität Dorpat in ihrer geistes-geschichtlichen Bedeutung*. München, 1933.

Erdos, R. *The Sydney Gazette: Australia's First Paper*. Melbourne, 1961.

Esakov, V. A., et al. *Russkie okeanicheskie i morskie issledovaniia, XIX-nachala XX vekov*. M., 1964.

Evatt, H. V. *Rum Rebellion: A Study of the Overthrow of Governor Bligh*. Sydney, 1938.

Evteev, O. A. *Pervye russkie geodezisty na tikhom okeane*. M., 1950.

Fedorov-Davydov, A. A. "Russkii peizazh XVIII-nachala XIX veka." In *Iskusstvo*. M.,

1953.

Fedorova, S. F. *Russkoe naselenie Aliaski i Kalifornii*. M., 1971. Trans. R. A. Pierce and A. S. Donnelly as *The Russian Population in Alaska and California: Late Eighteenth Century—1867*. Kingston, Ont., 1973.

Fersman, A., ed. *The Pacific: Russian Scientific Investigations*. L., 1926.

Fitzhardinge, V. "Russian Ships in Australian Waters, 1807–1835." *JRAHS*, 51 (1965): pt. 2, pp. 113–47.

———. "Russian Naval Visitors to Australia, 1862–1888." *JRAHS*, 52 (1966): pt. 2, pp. 129–58.

Frisch, S. G. *Lebensbeschreibung A. G. Werners*. Leipzig, 1825.

Friis, H. R., ed. *The Pacific Basin: A History of Its Geographical Exploration*. New York, 1967.

Fry, H. T. *Alexander Dalrymple and the Expansion of British Trade*. Toronto, 1970.

Geikie, A. *Founders of Geology*. London, 1897.

Gel'mersen, G. P. "Sir Roderik Impei Murchison." *Zapiski Imperatorskoi Akademii Nauk*, 20 (1872): 176–90.

Ger'e (Guerrier), V. *Leibnitz in seinem Beziehungen zu Russland und Peter dem Grossen: eine geschichtliche Darstellung*. Leipzig, 1873.

Gibson, J. R. *Feeding the Russian Fur Trade: Provisionment of the Okhotsk Seaboard and the Kamchatka Peninsula, 1639–1856*. Madison, 1969.

———. "Russian America in 1833: The Survey of Kirill Khlebnikov." *Pacific Northwest Quarterly*. (January 1972): 1–13.

———. *Imperial Russia in Frontier America: The Changing Geography of Supply of Russian America, 1784–1867*. New York, 1976.

Gleason, J. *The Genesis of Russophobia in Great Britain*. Cambridge, MA, 1950.

Gnucheva, V. F. "Lomonosov i Geograficheskii departament Akademii Nauk." In *Lomonosov: sbornik statei i materialov*. M.-L., 1940.

———. *Geograficheskii departament Akademii Nauk XVIII veka*. M.-L., 1946.

Goddard, R. H. "Captain T. Raine of the *Surry*." *JRAHS*, 26 (1940): pt. 4.

Golder, F. A. *Russian Expansion on the Pacific, 1641–1850: An Account of the Earliest and Later Expeditions. . . .* Cleveland, 1914.

———. *Bering's Voyages: An account of the Efforts of the Russians to Determine the Relation of Asia and America*. 2 vols. New York, 1922–25.

Goncharova, N. N. "Vidopisets E. Korneev." *Iskusstvo* (1972): no. 6, pp. 60–64.

———. "Khudozhnik krugosvetnoi ekspeditsii 1819–1822 godov E. Korneev." *IVGO*, 105 (1973): no. 1, pp. 67–72.

Golenishchev-Kutuzov, L. I. *Predpriiatie Imperatritsy Ekateriny II dlia puteshestviia vokrug sveta v 1786 godu*. St. P., 1840.

Gough, B. M., ed. *To the Pacific and Arctic with Beechey*. Cambridge, 1973.

Gould, J. K. *Birds of Australia*. 8 vols. London, 1840–69.

Grant, R. *A History of Physical Astronomy from the Earliest Ages*. London, 1852.

Greenberg, M. *British Trade and the Opening of China, 1800–1842*. Cambridge, 1951.

Greenop, F. S., ed. *Tasmania, Australia*. Sydney, 1968.

Grenader, M. B. "Istoricheskaia obuslovlennost' vozniknoveniia severovostochnoi geograficheskoi ekspeditsii, 1785–1795gg." *Uchennye zapiski Petropav-*

lovskogo Gosudarstvennogo Pedagogicheskogo Instituta (1957): bk. 2, pp. 55–72.

Gvozdetskii, N. A. "Pervoe morskoe puteshestvie Rossiian vokrug sveta." *Priroda* (M., 1947): no. 1, pp. 85–88.

Hainsworth, D. R. *The Sydney Traders: Simeon Lord and His Contemporaries.* Sydney, 1972.

Heeres, J. E. "Abel Janszoon Tasman: His Life and Labours." In *Abel Janszoon Tasman's Journal.* Amsterdam, 1898.

Heidemaa, I. "Zooloogia kateedri ja zooloogiamuuseumi ajaloost. *TUAK,* 2 (1975): 164–74.

———. "Zooloogiamuuseumi Fondidest. *TUAK,* 11 (1981): 87–92.

Hindwood, K. A. "Honeyeaters of the Sydney District. . . ." *Australian Zoologist,* 10 (1944): 231–51.

Hoare, M. E., ed. *The Tactless Philosopher: Johann Reinhold Forster, 1729–98.* Melbourne, 1976.

Healy, J. J. "Dimension and Grandeur." *Hemisphere,* 21 (1977): no. 6; pp. 15–20.

Hooker, J. D., ed. *The Journal of the Right Honourable Sir Joseph Banks during Captain Cook's First Voyage in HMS Endeavour.* London, 1896.

Hotimsky, C. M. "Russians in Australia." *AE,* 7: 526–28.

———. "A Russian Account of New South Wales in 1822." *Melbourne Slavonic Studies,* 1 (1967): 82–95.

———. "A Bibliography of Captain James Cook in Russian—1772–1810." *Biblionews and Australian Notes and Queries,* 5 (1971): no. 2, pp. 3–12.

Howay, F. W. *A List of Trading Vessels in the Maritime Fur Trade, 1785–1825.* Edited and introduced by R. A. Pierce. Kingston, Ont., 1973.

———. "An Outline Sketch of the Maritime Fur Trade." *Annual Report of the Canadian Historical Association* (1932): 5–14.

———, ed. *Zimmermann's Captain Cook: An Account of the Third Voyage . . . 1776–1780, by Henry Zimmermann, of Wissloch in the Palatinate.* Toronto, 1930.

Huculak, M. *When Russia Was in America: The Alaska Boundary Treaty Negotiations, 1824–25, and the Role of Pierre de Poletica.* Vancouver, Mitchell, 1971. Ukrainian nationalist stress, but contains useful data.

Hudspeth, W. H., ed. *Introduction to the Diaries of the Rev. Robert Knopwood.* Hobart, 1955.

Ikonnikov, V. S. "Russkie universitety v sviazi s khodom obshchestvennogo obrazovaniia." *Vestnik Evropy* (1876): no. 9, pp. 161–206; no. 10, pp. 492–550; no. 11, pp. 73–132.

———. *Graf N. S. Mordvinov: istoricheskaia monografiia.* St. P., 1873.

Inglis, K. S. *The Australian Colonists: An Exploration of Social History, 1788–1870.* Melbourne, 1974.

Ivanovskii, A. D. *Gosudarstvennyi kantsler graf Nikolai Petrovich Rumiantsev: biograficheskii ocherk.* St. P., 1871.

Kabo, V. R., and Bondarev, N. M. "Okeaniiskaia Kollektsiia I. M. Simonova." *SMAE,* 30 (L., 1974): 101–11.

Kirwan, L. P. *The White Road: A Survey of Polar Exploration.* London, 1960.

Kohl, J. G. *Russia and the Russians in 1842.* 2 vols. London, 1843.

Komissarov, B. N. *Grigorii Ivanovich Langsdorf.* L., 1975.

Komkov, G. D., et al. *Akademiia Nauk SSSR: kratkii istoricheskii ocherk.* M., 1977.

Kozlovskii, I. P. A. *Vinius, sotrudnik Petra Velikogo.* St. P., 1911.

Kramp, F. G., comp. *Remarkable Maps of the XV, XVI, and XVII Centuries.* Amsterdam, 1897.

Krempol'skii, V. F. *Istoriia razvitiia kartoizdaniia v Rossii i v SSSR.* M., 1959.

Kuznetsov, B. G. *Ocherki istorii russkoi nauki.* M.-L., 1940.

Kuznetsov, I. V., ed. *Liudi russkoi nauki: ocherki o vydaiushchikhsia deiateliakh estestvoznaniia i tekhniki....* 2 vols. M., 1961–62.

Kuznetsova, V. V. "Novye dokumenty o russkoi ekspeditsii k severnomu poliusu." *IVGO* (1968): no. 3, pp. 237–45.

Lebedev, D. M. *Geografiia v Rossii petrovskogo vremeni.* M.-L., 1950.

Lebedev, V. L. "Geograficheskie nabliudeniia v Antarktike...." In *Antarktika: doklady kommissii, 1960 god.* M., 1961.

———. "Reshenie spornykh voprosov antarkticheskoi istorii na novoi osnove." In *Antarktika: doklady kommissii, 1962 god.* M., 1963.

Lensen, G. A. *The Russian Push toward Japan: Russo-Japanese Relations, 1697–1875.* Princeton, 1959.

Levin, M. G. *Ocherki po istorii antropologii v Rossii.* M., 1960.

Lipshits, V. A. "Etnograficheskie issledovaniia v russkikh krugosvetnykh ekspeditsiiakh." *Ocherki istorii russkoi etnografii, fol'kloristiki, i antropologii,* 1 (M., 1956): 298–321.

Little, B. "Sealing and Whaling in Australia before 1850." *Australian Historical Review,* 9 (1969): no. 2.

MacCallum, D. "The Early 'Volunteer' Associations in New South Wales." *JRAHS,* 47 (1961).

———. "The Alleged Russian Plans for the Invasion of Australia, 1864." *JRAHS,* 44 (1959): 301–22.

Macmillan, D. S. *Scotland and Australia, 1788–1850.* Oxford, 1967.

Magidovich, I. P. *Ocherki po istorii geograficheskikh otkrytii.* M., 1957.

Mahr, A. C. *The Visit of the 'Rurik' to San Francisco in 1816.* Stanford University Publications in History, Economics, and Political Science, Vol. 2. Palo Alto, 1932.

Maiden, J. H. *Forest Flora of New South Wales.* Sydney, 1922.

Mazour, A. G. "The Russian-American Company: Private or Government Enterprise?" *PHR,* 13 (1944): 168–73.

———. *The First Russian Revolution, 1825: The Decembrist Movement.* Berkeley, 1937.

McBryde, I. "The Ethnographic Collections of Governor La Trobe now in the Musée d'Ethnographie de Neuchâtel, Switzerland." *Artefact,* 2 (1971): no. 2, pp. 45–61.

McMinn, W. G. *Allan Cunningham, Botanist and Explorer.* Melbourne, 1970.

Medvedev, N. D. "Vekovye varianty magnitnogo skloneniia i dreif iuzhnogo magnitnogo poliusa." *Biulleten Sovetskoi antarkticheskoi ekspeditsii* (M., 1970): no. 77.

Megaw, J. V. S. "Archaeology, Art, and Aborigines: A Survey of Historical Sources." *JRAHS,* 53 (1967): 277–94.

Mehnert, K. *The Russians in Hawaii, 1804–1819.* Honolulu, 1939.

Melville, H. *History of the Island of Van Diemen's Land.* London, 1835.

Meyjes, R. P., ed. *De Reizen van Abel Janszoon Tasman en Franchoys Jacobszoon Visscher in 1642–3 en 1644.* Amsterdam, 1919.

Millar, T. B. "History of the Defence Forces of the Port Phillip District of Victoria, 1836–1900." M.A. thesis. Melbourne, 1957.

———. *Australia's Foreign Policy.* Sydney, 1968.

———. *Australia in Peace and War: External Relations, 1788–1977.* Canberra, 1978.

Modzalevskii, B. L. *Pushkin i ego sovremenniki.* St. P., 1910.

Morrell, W. P. *British Colonial Policy in the Age of Peel and Russell.* Reprint. London, 1966.

Mulvaney, D. J. *The Prehistory of Australia.* London, 1969.

Nevskii, V. V. *Pervoe puteshestvie Rossiian vokrug sveta.* M., 1951.

Nicolas. N. *The Despatches and Letters of Vice-Admiral Lord Nelson.* 8 vols. London, 1844.

Nicholson, H. *The Congress of Vienna.* London, 1946.

Novakovskii, S. I. *Iaponiia i Rossiia.* Tokyo, 1918.

Novikov, P. A. "Zoologicheskie issledovaniia A. Shamisso i Eshchol'tsa vo vremia krugosvetnoi ekspeditsii O. E. Kotsebu na 'Riurike' (1815–1818)." *TIIE,* 40 (1962): 248–82.

Nozikov, N. I. *Russian Voyages Round the World.* Trans. E. Lesser. London, 1944.

Okun', S. B. "Tsarskaia Rossiia i Gavaiskie ostrova." *Krasnyi arkhiv* (M., 1936): nos. 5–6, pp. 161–86.

———. *Rossiisko-amerikanskaia Kompaniia.* M., 1939. Trans. C. Ginsburg as *The Russian-American Company.* Cambridge, MA, 1951.

Park, R. *Companion Guide to Sydney.* Sydney, 1973.

Parkinson, C. N. *War in the Eastern Seas, 1793–1815.* London, 1954.

Parsons, T. G. "The Social Composition of the Men of the New South Wales Corps." *JRAHS,* 50 (1964): 297–305.

Pasetskii, V. M. *Geograficheskie issledovaniia dekabristov.* M., 1977.

Paszkowski, L. *Polacy w Australii i Oceanii, 1790–1840.* London, 1962.

Perel', Iu. G. "Vikentii Karlovich Vishnevskii." *Istoriko-astronomicheskie issledovaniia,* 1 (1955): 133–48.

Perry, T. M. *Australia's First Frontier: The Spread of Settlement in New South Wales, 1788–1829.* Melbourne, 1963.

Pierce, R. A. *Russia's Hawaiian Adventure, 1815–1817.* Berkeley, 1965.

———. "Two Russian Governors: Hagemeister and Yanovskii." *Alaska Journal,* 1 (1971): no. 2, pp. 49–51.

———. "Alaska's Russian Governors. . . ." *Ibid.:* no. 4, pp. 38–42. Popular in tone, but useful sketches.

Polevoi, B. P. "Zabytyi nakaz A. A. viniusa." *Priroda* (M., 1965): no. 5, pp. 4–12.

Prentis, M. D. *The Scots in Australia.* Sydney, 1983.

Pypin, A. N. *Istoriia russkoi etnografii.* 4 vols. St. P., 1890–92.

————. *Obshchestvennoe dvizhenie v Rossii pri Aleksandre I*. St. P., 1900.

Rea, R. "John Blankett and the Russian Navy, 1774." *MM*, 41 (1955): 245–49.

Reece, R. H. W. "Feasts and Blankets: The History of Some Early Attempts to Establish Relations with the Aborigines of New South Wales, 1814–1846." *Archaeology and Physical Anthropology in Oceania*, 2 (1967): no. 3, pp.190–206.

————. *Aborigines and Colonists: Aborigines and Colonial Society in New South Wales in the 1830s and 1840s*. Sydney, 1974.

Robinson, K. W. "Population and Land Use in the Sydney District, 1788–1820." *New Zealand Geographer*, 9 (1953): 144–60.

Rowley, C. D. *The Destruction of Aboriginal Society*. Canberra, 1970.

Russell, H. C. "On the Periodicity of Good and Bad Seasons." *Journal of the Royal Society of New South Wales*, 30 (Sydney, 1896): 70–115.

Rozhdestvenskii, S. V. *Ocherki po istorii sistem narodnogo prosveshcheniia v Rossii v XVIII–XIX vekakh*. Vol. 1. St. P., 1912.

————. *Istoricheskii obzor deiatel'nosti Ministerstva narodnogo prosveshcheniia, 1802–1902*. St. P., 1902.

Rozina, L. G. "Kollektsiia Dzhemsa Kuka v sobraniiakh Muzeia Antropologii i Etnografii." *SMAE*, 23 (1966).

Ruprecht, J. F. "Das botanische Museum." *Bulletin de l'Académie Imper. des Sciences de St. Petersbourg*, 7 (1864): suppl. 2.

Rusden, G. W. *A History of Australia*. Melbourne, 1897.

Russov, F. "Beiträge zur Geschichte der ethnographischen und anthropologischen Sammlungen." *Sbornik Muzeia po Antropologii i Etnografii pri Imperatorskoi Akademii Nauk*, 1 (St. P., 1900).

Ryden, S. *The Banks Collection: An Episode in Eighteenth-century Anglo-Swedish Relations*. Gothenburg, 1963.

Savin, A. S. "Okhotsk." *ZGDMM*, 9 (1851): 148–61.

Scott, E. *The Life of Captain Matthew Flinders, R.N.* Sydney, 1914.

————. *Terre Napoléon: A History of French Explorations and Projects in Australia*. London, 1910.

Selkirk, H. "The Discovery of Mudgee." *JRAHS*, 8 (1922).

Sgibnev, A. S. "Okhotskii port s 1649 po 1852 god." *MSb*, 105 (1869): no. 11, pp. 1–92; no. 12, pp. 1–63.

Shchapov, A. P. *Sochineniia*. 3 vols. St. P., 1906–8.

Sharp, A. *The Discovery of Australia*. Oxford, 1963.

————. *The Discovery of the Pacific Islands*. Oxford, 1960.

————. *The Voyages of Abel Janszoon Tasman*. Oxford, 1968.

Shaw, A. W. "Fort Denison, Sydney Harbour." *JRAHS*, 23 (1937).

Shaw, A. G. L. *The Story of Australia*. London, 1955.

Sheshin, A. B. "Dekabrist-moreplavatel' K. P. Torson i ego nenaidennye zapiski ob otkrytii Antarktidy." *IVGO*, 108 (1976): no. 1.

Shokal'skii, Iu. A. "Stoletie so vremeni otpravleniia russkoi antarkticheskoi ekspeditsii pod komandoiu F. Bellinsgauzena i M. Lazareva." *IVGO*, 60 (1928): no. 2, pp. 175–212.

Shteinberg, E. L. *Zhizneopisanie russkogo moreplavatelia Iuriia Lisianskogo*. M., 1948.

Shur, L. A. "Dnevniki i zapiski russkikh puteshestvennikov kak istochnik po istorii i etnografii stran Tikhogo okeana (pervaia polovina XIX veka)." *Avstraliia i Okeaniia* (M., 1970): 201–12. For English variant of this, see "Russian Travellers...." *Ibero-Amerikanisches Archiv*, 1 (Berlin, 1976): no. 45, pp. 395–401.

―――. *K beregam novogo Sveta*. M., 1971.

Sirotkin, V. G. "Dokumenty o politike Rossii na Dal'nem Vostoke v nachale XIX veka." *Istoricheskie zapiski* (November 1962): 87ff.

Smith, B. *European Vision and the South Pacific, 1768–1850*. Oxford, 1960.

Sokol, A. E. "Russian Expansion and Exploration in the Pacific." *SEER*, 11 (1952): 85–105.

Sokolov, A. P. "Prigotovlenie krugosvetnoi ekspeditsii 1787 goda pod nachal'stvom kapitana Mulovskogo." *ZGDMM*, 6 (1848): 168–87.

Solov'ev, S. M. *Istoriia Rossii s drevneishikh vremen*. St. P., n.d.

Spate, O. H. K. *Australia*. New York, 1968.

Stanner, W. E. H. "The History of Indifference Thus Begins." *Aboriginal History*, 1 (1977): no. 1, pp. 3–26.

Steel, W. A. "The First Land Grant beyond the Blue Mountains." *JRAHS*, 24 (1938).

Steven, M. *Merchant Campbell: A Study in Colonial Trade*. Melbourne, 1964.

Stolpianskii, P. "Kniga v starom Peterburge: magaziny inostrannykh knig." *Russkoe proshloe*, 4 (Petrograd, 1923): 123–34.

Svet, Ia. M. "Cook and the Russians." Transl. P. Putz. In Beaglehole, J. C., ed., *The Journals of Captain James Cook....* Vol. 3, pt. 2. Cambridge, 1967.

―――. *Tret'e plavanie kapitana Dzhemsa Kuka: plavanie v Tikhom okeane v 1776–1780 godakh*. M., 1971.

Tankler, Kh. I. "Vospitanniki Tartuskogo Universiteta na sluzhbe v Pulkovskoi Observatorii." *TUAK*, 11 (Tartu, 1981): 72–77.

Tarasevich, L. A. "Nauchnoe dvizhenie v Rossii v pervoi polovine XIX veka: estestvoznanie i meditsina." Ed. I. Granat, *Istoriia Rossii v XIX veke*, 6 (St. P., n.d.): 285–327.

Thompson, R. C. *Australian Imperialism in the Pacific: The Expansionist Era, 1820–1920*. Melbourne, 1980.

Tooley, R. V., ed. *Early Maps of Australia: The Dutch Period*. London, 1965.

―――. *Maps and Map-makers*. London, 1970.

―――, ed. *One Hundred Foreign Maps of Australia, 1773–1887*. London, 1964.

Trautfetter, G. "Zhizneopisanie Fedora Bogdanovicha Fishera." *Bull. de la Société Imp. des Naturalistes de Moscou*. (1865): 585–603.

Travers, R. *The Tasmanians*. Melbourne, 1968.

Trusevich, K. *Posol'skie i torgovye otnosheniia Rossii s Kitaem*. M., 1892.

Tumarkin, D. D. *Vtorzhenie kolonizatorov v Krai vechnoi vesny': Gavaiskii narod v bor'be protiv chuzhezemnykh zakhvatchikov*. M., 1964.

―――. "Materialy pervoi russkoi krugosvetnoi ekspeditsii kak istochnik po istorii i etnografii Gavaiskikh ostrovov." *Sovetskaia etnografiia* (1978): no. 5, pp. 68–84.

―――. "Materialy ekspeditsii M. N. Vasil'eva—tsennyi istochnik po istorii i etnografii Gavaiskikh ostrovov." Ibid. (1983): no. 6, pp. 48–61. Good surveys, with archival references.

Ustrialov, N. *Istoriia tsarstvovaniia Petra Velikogo*. St. P., 1858.

Varep, E. F. "O prepodavanii fizicheskoi geografii v Tartuskom Universitete v 1802–1917 godakh." *TUAK*, 11 (1981): 61–66.

Vavilov, S. I., *et al. Voprosy istorii otechestvennoi nauki: obshchee sobranie Akademii Nauk SSSR . . . 5–11 ianvaria 1949 goda*. M.-L., 1949.

Veresaev, V. *Sputniki Pushkina*. M., 1937.

Veselago, F. F. *Admiral Ivan Fedorovich Kruzenshtern*. St. P., 1869.

———. *Kratkaia istoriia russkogo flota*. M., 1939.

Vishnevskii, B. N. *Puteshestvennik Kirill Khlebnikov*. Perm', 1957.

Vladimirov, V. M. *Dzhems Kuk*. M., 1933.

Vorob'ev, N. I. "Etnograficheskie nabliudeniia I. M. Simonova na ostrovakh Tikhogo okeana." *IVGO*, 81 (1949): bk. 5, pp. 497–504.

Vucinich, A. *Science in Russian Culture: A History to 1860*. Stanford, 1963.

Wagner, H. R., ed. and trans. "The Memorial of Pedro Calderon y Henriquez . . . with a View to Preventing Russian Encroachment in California," *CHSQ*, 23 (1944): 219–25.

———. "The Creation of Rights of Sovereignty through Symbolic Acts." *PHR*, 7 (1938): 297–326.

Walker, R. B. *The Newspaper Press in New South Wales, 1803–1920*. Sydney, 1976.

Walsh, G. P., and Horner, D. M. "The Defence of Sydney in 1820." *Army Journal* (Canberra, May 1969).

Wells, W. H. *A Geographical Dictionary or Gazetteer of the Australian Colonies, 1848*. Facsimile ed. Sydney, 1970.

Wheeler, M. E. "The Origins of the Russian-American Company." *Jahrbucher für Geschichte Osteuropas* (1966): 485–94.

———. "Empires in Conflict and Co-operation: The Bostonians and the Russian-American Company." *PHR*, 40 (1971): 419–41.

Williams, G. *The British Search for the Northwest Passage in the Eighteenth Century*. London, 1962.

Winter, O. F. *Repertorium der diplomatischen Vertreter aller Länder, 1764–1815*. Graz, 1965.

Wynd, I., and Ward, J. *A Map History of Australia*. Melbourne, 1963.

Young, J. M., ed. *Australia's Pacific Frontier: Economic and Cultural Expansion into the Pacific, 1795–1885*. Melbourne, 1967.

Zagoskin, N. P. *Istoriia Imperatorskogo Kazanskogo Universiteta za pervye sto let ego sushchestvovaniia, 1804–1904*. 4 vols. Kazan', 1902–6.

Zakharov, V. A. "M. V. Lomonosov i russkoe nauchnoe moreplavanie." *Morskoi flot* (L., 1948): nos. 7–8, pp. 66–81.

Zdobnov, N. V. *Istoriia russkoi bibliografii*. M., 1951.

Zubov, N. N., ed. *Otechestvennye moreplavateli-issledovateli morei i okeanov*. M., 1954.

Name Index

Ship Index